A HISTORY OF AUSTRALIA

VOLUME VI

BY THE SAME AUTHOR

Select Documents in Australian History, 1788–1850

Settlers and Convicts: or recollections of sixteen years' labour in the Australian backwoods by An Emigrant Mechanic (ed.)

Select Documents in Australian History, 1851–1900

Sources of Australian History

Meeting Soviet Man

A History of Australia I: from the earliest times to the age of Macquarie

A History of Australia II: New South Wales and Van Diemen's Land 1822–1838

A Short History of Australia

A Short History of Australia, 2nd revised edition, New York

Disquiet and Other Stories

A History of Australia III: the beginning of an Australian civilization 1824–1851

In Search of Henry Lawson

A History of Australia IV: the earth abideth for ever 1851–1888

A History of Australia V: the people make laws 1888–1915

Collected Short Stories

TWO BOYS FROM THE AUSTRALIAN BUSH
WHO WENT DOWN TO
THE GREAT CITY OF MELBOURNE

John Joseph Ambrose Curtin

Robert Gordon Menzies

Photographs in
National Library, Canberra

C. M. H. CLARK

A HISTORY OF AUSTRALIA

VI

'THE OLD DEAD TREE
AND THE YOUNG TREE GREEN'

1916–1935

WITH AN EPILOGUE

MELBOURNE UNIVERSITY PRESS

First published 1987
Reprinted September 1987, 1988, 1991, 1992
Typeset by
Abb-typesetting Pty Ltd, Collingwood, Victoria
Printed in Australia by
Brown Prior Anderson Pty Ltd, Burwood, Victoria, for
Melbourne University Press, Carlton, Victoria 3053
U.S.A. and Canada: International Specialized Book Services, Inc.,
5602 N.E. Hassalo Street, Portland, Oregon 97213-3640
United Kingdom and Europe: University College London Press,
Gower Street, London WC1E 6BT, UK

National Library of Australia Cataloguing-in-Publication entry

Clark, Manning, 1915–1991.
'The old dead tree and the young tree green', 1916–1935
with an epilogue.

Includes index.
ISBN 0 522 84352 2.
ISBN 0 522 84353 0 (pbk.).
ISBN 0 522 84235 6 (set).
ISBN 0 522 84314 X (pbk. set).

1. Australia—History—1901–1945. I. Title. (Series: Clark, Manning, 1915–1991. History of Australia; 6).

994'.04

To all the encouragers and to all who gave me their love and their faith

Sons of the South, make choice between
(Sons of the South, choose true)
The Land of Morn and the Lane of E'en,
The Old Dead Tree and the Young Tree Green,
The land that belongs to the lord and Queen,
And the Land that belongs to you.

Henry Lawson, 'A Song of the Republic'

The great idea of immortality would have vanished, and they would have to fill its place; and all the wealth of love lavished of old upon Him, who was immortal, would be turned upon the whole of nature, on the world, on men, on every blade of grass . . . everyone would tremble for the life and happiness of each; they would grow tender to one another . . . and would be as caressing as children. Meeting, they would look at one another with deep and thoughtful eyes, and in their eyes would be love and sorrow . . .

F. M. Dostoevsky, *A Raw Youth*

PREFACE

THIS VOLUME tells the story of Australia from the beginning of 1916 to the end of 1935. It concludes with an Epilogue which reflects on the fate of some of the principal characters in the volume, and the revolution in the way of life and values of Australians since the dropping of the atomic bomb in August 1945. Like its predecessors this volume does not pretend to be a general history of the period. It concentrates on those events which have helped to make Australians what they are, and aware of what they might be. It is an attempt to impose an order on the chaos. It is one man's vision of the past, one man's answer to the Hilda Esson question: 'Can't we do anything ourselves as Australians?'

In the Preface to earlier volumes I have attempted to thank the people who helped me. In this Preface I would like to thank the people who gave me the strength and the faith to keep going until the work was finished. They were: Don Baker, Pat Dobrez, Alison Clark, Nicholas Brown, Don Watson, Bill Gammage, Elizabeth Cham, Bruce Grant, Joan Grant, Patrick White, Lyndall Ryan, Helen Garner, Heather Rusden, Judith Egerton, Suzanne Welborn, Bede Nairn, Catherine Santamaria, Bill Tully, Keith Hancock, Ann Moyal, Arthur Boyd, Humphrey McQueen, David Malouf, John Clive, Richard Southern, Christopher Hill, Kathleen Fitzpatrick, Judith Wright, Jill Roe, Mick Williams, Helen Crisp, Heinz Arndt, Ian Fitchett, Ian Hancock, Geoffrey Blainey, John Ritchie, Max Crawford, Brian Beddie, Ken Inglis, Anthony Cahill, David Fitzpatrick and Michael Holquist. Four of the encouragers—David Campbell, Fin Crisp, Macmahon Ball and Geoffrey Fairbairn—died while I was struggling with the problem of how to get down on paper what was, I hoped in vain, in the head. The first encouragers, my mother and R. P. Franklin, died before the whole work began.

For this volume two people played a very special part. Roslyn Russell was the research assistant every writer of history dreams of having. My wife, Dymphna, was in it all at the beginning and at the end. She was more than an excellent editor and a translator. She also had her own way of getting me to write about what really mattered. She gave generously what she had. I can never repay the debt. I can also never repay the people who encouraged me to believe I had something to say. I have always been aware of my inadequate powers to find words to convey 'what the heart doth say' about one of the great passions of my life—the history of Australia.

Manning Clark
3 March 1987

ACKNOWLEDGEMENTS

I WOULD LIKE to acknowledge the help from two theses: Andrew Moore, 'Send Lawyers, Guns and Money!': A Study of Conservative Para-Military Organisations in New South Wales, 1930–1932, Background and Sequel, 1917–1952, and P. Hart, J. A. Lyons: A Political Biography. I would also like to acknowledge help from Andrew Clark's taped interviews with Dame Enid Lyons. My debt to the Mitchell Library and the National Library of Australia is even greater at the end of the work than it was in the beginning. The Petherick Room, the Manuscripts Room, and the Newspaper Room are present in every page of this volume, just as they are present always in my heart. They are the places where the Magellans and Cooks of Australian Historical Enterprises Proprietary Limited make their voyages of discovery. The research for Volume V and part of Volume VI was helped by a grant from the Australian Research Grants Committee. I would like to thank Val Lyon, cartographer in the Department of Geography, Australian National University, for drawing the maps. I would also like to thank the Pictorial Section of the National Library of Australia for help in selecting the illustrations. I would like to thank the Australian Institute of Aboriginal Studies for the photographs of David Unaipon and William Cooper. I am grateful to Alick Jackomos for permission to reproduce the photograph of William Cooper. I was especially pleased that Pat Counihan gave me permission to use the drawing of Henry Lawson by my old friend Noel Counihan.

CONTENTS

ILLUSTRATIONS

PLATES

MAPS

ABBREVIATIONS

A.C.T.U.	Australasian Council of Trade Unions
A.D.B.	*Australian Dictionary of Biography*
A.I.F.	Australian Imperial Force
A.N.U.	Australian National University
A.W.M.	Australian War Memorial
A.W.U.	Australian Workers' Union
C'wealth	Commonwealth
H.R.A.	*Historical Records of Australia*
M.L.	Mitchell Library
MS.	manuscript
M.U.M.	*Melbourne University Magazine*
N.L.A.	National Library of Australia, Canberra
N.S.W.	New South Wales
O.B.U.	One Big Union
P.D.	*Parliamentary Debates*
Qld	Queensland
S.A.	South Australia
S.M.H.	*Sydney Morning Herald*
Tas.	Tasmania
V. & P.	*Votes and Proceedings*
Vic.	Victoria
W.A.	Western Australia

CONVERSIONS

1d (penny)	0.83 cent
1s (shilling)	10 cents
£1 (pound)	$2
£1 1s (guinea)	$2.10
1 inch	2.54 centimetres
1 mile	1.60 kilometres
1 acre	0.40 hectare
1 stone	6.35 kg
1 pint	0.56 litre
100° Fahrenheit	37.8° Celsius

I

TWO AUSTRALIAS

AT THE BEGINNING OF 1916 many people in Australia responded in various ways to the bugles of old England blowing over the sea. At Mildura in Victoria the girls were knitting khaki woollen socks, scarves and gloves in their lunch hour for the Australian troops recuperating in a camp near Cairo from their terrible ordeal at Gallipoli. In Sydney the Labor Prime Minister of Australia, William Morris Hughes, has heard the call. He has decided to travel to Europe to discuss with the British and the French Governments how Australia could contribute to winning the war. Hughes was then fifty-five years old. There was a mighty spirit encased within his tiny frame. He was not a man with a wizened face and no heart. Frugal with food, moderate with alcohol and never a man to go out of his wits for a woman, he was a passionate man, who had the courage, the drive and the iron will with which to gratify the passions of his heart. His deafness might have been a drawback to lesser men, but it was characteristic of Hughes that he exploited his weakness to gratify the great passion of his life—domination and power. A superb wit, he was a brilliant raconteur of stories about human frailty and folly, with a rasping, mocking note in his voice which contemporaries attempted in vain to imitate. But no one ever uncovered the wound in his life which drove him to act and to speak as though he had a perpetual quarrel either with humanity or with God.

In his early years he dedicated his vast talents and energy to the service of the Australian Labor movement. Now he had another all-consuming enthusiasm—a British victory in the war. Never a man of moderation in his references to those who differed from him he began the year by calling those who opposed the war 'foul parasites'. He was always a man to indulge in hyperbole in his public speeches. At the dinner to farewell him in Sydney on 18 January he asked the question: 'Are we to be the well-fed pigs, to be kicked and driven or free men? I say it would be better to die as free men than live as slaves under the intolerant and brutal Prussian'. In his mind this was a war for liberty. He was going to London, as he put it, 'in the determination that victory would be on the side of England and her allies'.

But at the beginning of 1916 victory for either side seemed a long way away. The 'knock-out blows' of 1914 and 1915 have failed. The German army did not enter Paris. British, French and Imperial Forces did not enter

Constantinople. The Russian army did not reach Berlin. The German army did not drive the British Expeditionary Force out of Flanders and the north-east of France. The Kaiser called on his troops to 'exterminate the treacherous English and walk over General French's contemptible little army'. But at Ypres the British army halted the German advance. Fields were laid waste, soldiers were living in a wilderness of their own creation. Cities were flattened to the ground, the cathedral at Ypres became a skeleton, the Cloth Hall and other glories of human endeavour were reduced to rubble. On a line from Antwerp to Ypres, Ypres to the Somme, the Somme to Verdun and Verdun to the Swiss border south-east of Belfort, the German, British and French soldiers dug their trenches. In the winter of 1915–16 they all shivered in those trenches waiting to be killed in the great 'blood-spilling business', while the Australian troops in their camp near Cairo waited for instructions from the 'top brass' in London on where they were to fight.[1]

The Socialists and the Holy Father called for peace. Turning his 'timorous gaze towards the blood-stained battlefields' with 'the anguish of a father who sees his house wrecked and left desolate by a furious hurricane', Pope Benedict XV in July 1915 called on the belligerent nations to 'end this horrible bloodshed which has dishonoured Europe for a year'. Early in 1916 the Socialists in Great Britain, Germany, Italy and Russia declared that the war could not remedy the wrongs under which mankind was groaning. In Melbourne in December 1915 the Trades Hall Council directed all unionists to ignore recruiting cards. In Melbourne the *Labor Call* told its readers that the war meant an increase in misery among the poor, running parallel with the enrichment of the rich. The toiling masses should not die to make it possible for the rich to live in luxury and idleness. Australians were thousands of miles away from all these 'human disturbances'. Australians should not continue to 'travel the old blood-stained way': they should build up 'an ideal civilisation under the Southern Cross'.[2]

The generals on both sides were still confident they could win. Human inventions would make it possible for an army to punch a hole in the lines of their enemies and destroy their capacity to fight. The Germans had their superior machine-gun: the Germans tried poison gas: so did the Allies. Both sides had the aeroplane: both sides had the wireless. The British were working on a secret weapon. Experiments were going on in the British Isles to

[1] C. E. W. Bean, *Anzac to Amiens* (Canberra, 1961), ch. xiii; Les Coate, *Ypres 1914–18* (London, 1985); E. S. Rose Coombs, *Before Endeavours Fade: A Guide to the Battlefields of the First World War* (London, 1976); personal visit to Ypres Museum, 12 April 1985. For the early career of Hughes, see Volume V, pp. 116–21, of this history; Alice Lapthorn, *Mildura Calling* (Melbourne, 1946), p. 34; *Argus*, 19 January 1916; *Labor Call*, 13 April 1916; Lord Stamfordham to R. M. Ferguson, 22 March 1916, Novar Papers, Box 1, N.L.A.

[2] *Labor Call*, 29 April 1915; *Ross's Monthly*, 1 December 1915, pp. 5–9, and 19 August 1916, p. 3.

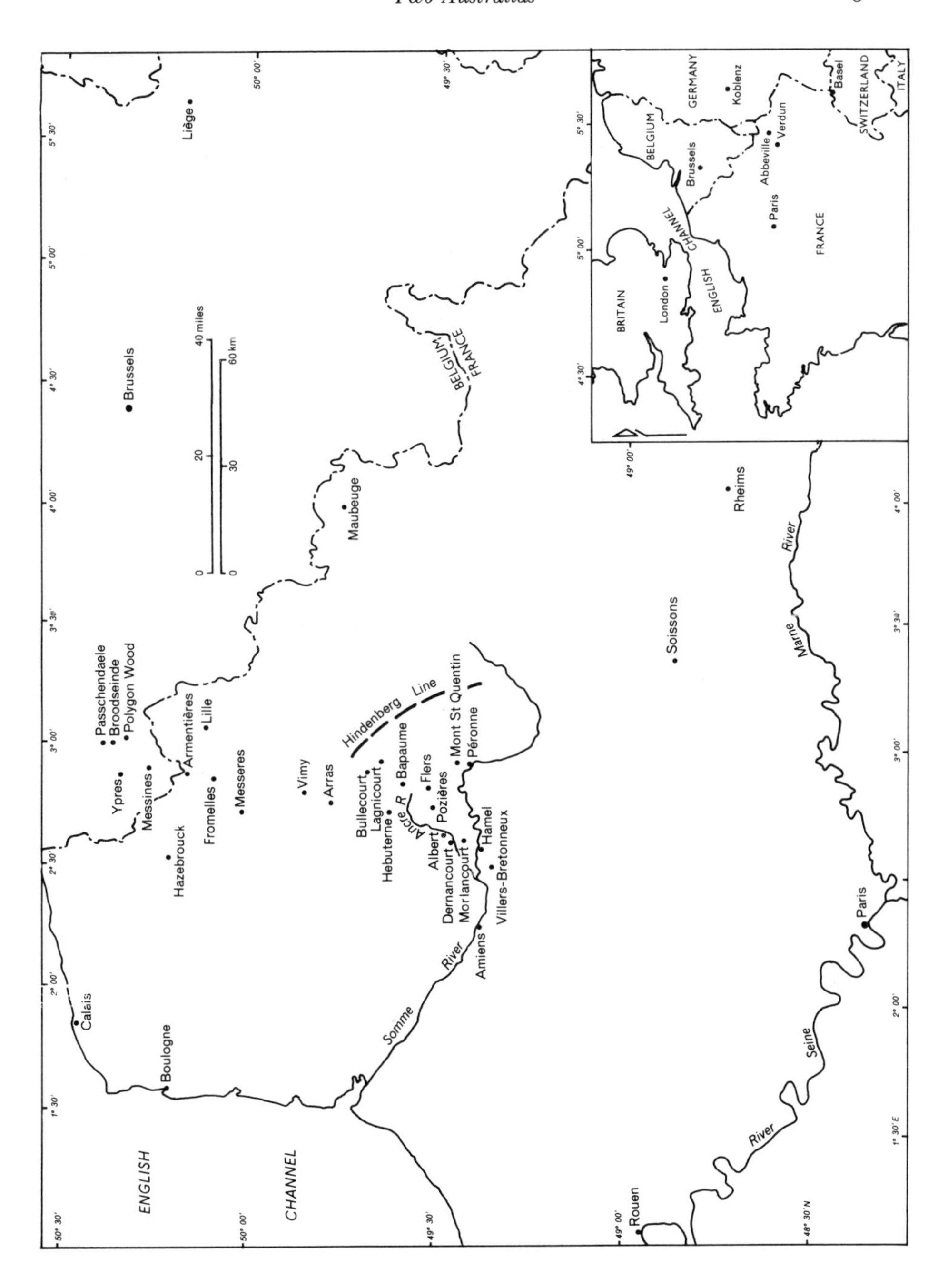

The Western Front

manufacture an armoured car, to be known as the tank. That would achieve what so far no numbers of human beings had achieved: that would breach the German line. British infantry would no longer be slaughtered in the great 'push'.[3]

The German supreme commander on the Western Front, General von Falkenhayn, planned to bleed France to death by an offensive against Verdun. With France crushed, as he put it, 'England's best sword would be struck out of her hand'. England's ability to fight would also be weakened by unrestricted submarine warfare against any ships approaching the British Isles. In February 1916 the German attack began at Verdun. Hundreds of thousands of Germans and French were victims in that 'blood-spilling business'. The madness and the folly have started again. Within a year the French lost 362 000 men and the Germans 336 831. Human beings were like puppets. Human beings were lapsing from civilization into barbarism.

The French commander-in-chief, Marshal J. J. C. Joffre, was not dismayed. He conceived a plan to retaliate with a knock-out blow against the German army on the Western Front. To bring supplies to the German army on the Western Front trains used the railway line from Brussels, Liège, and Koblenz, which all passed through the junction at Maubeuge. Maubeuge was only one hundred kilometres from Maricourt, the junction point of the French and British armies. In October 1915 Marshal Joffre suggested that the British and French should mount an offensive against Maubeuge, setting out from a point half way between Albert and Péronne. The plan for the push was put to the British. They agreed. In December 1915 Sir John French was replaced as commander of the British Expeditionary Force by Douglas Haig.[4]

There was a '*folie de grandeur*' in the losses of human life Haig was prepared to accept as the price of victory. He had in abundance the virtues of the soldier. He was brave, he was unflinching in his loyalty and obedience to the King and the Empire. As a man he was an enigma: no one ever read his mind's construction from his face. He was a tall man with grey hair, a moustache, a delicate fine face, and the manners of a 'gentle and an eager man'. He had the air of authority, the air of a remarkable man. When John Masefield met him in 1916 he was impressed: 'He took my breath away'. The man had a 'pervading power & . . . a height of resolve'. The unkind, and those lacking in charity or pity, said Haig's brilliance ended at the top of his army boots. He spoke French fluently. He enjoyed barrack-room jokes and flippant exchanges. He wept over the dead. Yet this man of a 'very fine

[3] Ronald Clark, *War Winners* (London, 1977), pp. 14–31.

[4] C. E. W. Bean, op. cit., pp. 201, 213–14; Gerard Bacquet, *Les Batailles de la Somme* (Amiens, 1980); Sir James Edmonds, *A Short History of World War I* (London, 1951), p. 159.

delicate gentleness & generosity' was planning to sacrifice millions of human lives for the sake of victory.[5]

'Billy' Hughes arrived in London in March 1916 to tell the English that he had no patience with those armchair visionaries who preached peace. He had begun his public life as a man of the people. But he has already moved away from their world. The one-time Bohemian of Balmain in Sydney has become the sound bourgeois of Kew in Melbourne. He wanted to exchange opinions with the British Government on the prosecution of the war, the relations of the Dominions to the Mother Country, the role of the Dominions at the peace conference, and the eradication of German trade from all parts of the Empire. For Hughes was a punisher. Hughes was a 'heels up' man. Like Jehovah, Hughes thirsted for revenge against his enemies. Hughes was a crusher, a man who took pleasure from visiting on his enemies the fury of his anger. He wanted to raise questions of markets for Australian wool, wheat and meat: he wanted to discuss the policy for German-owned industries within the British Empire. Above all he wanted to discuss the 'stern and bloody business' of war.[6]

Hughes believed he was the representative of a united people. He was there to speak for Australia. He would tell the English what he had already told Australians: that when civilization was tottering to its fall, and was assailed by a relentless and barbaric force, then all British people must be up and doing to defend their freedoms and the liberties they had won. He knew that in the Labor Party there were some doubters. But he rather relished dismissing them with his wrath and his contempt. He believed in rushing to the ramparts and facing the foe. It never occurred to him that he might be stabbed in the back. He had always been fond of calling traitors to the Labor Party 'Judases'. It never occurred to him that a day would come when his colleagues in the Party would denounce him as a Judas. Hughes had admirers. Hughes had acquaintances, but no one with whom he ever shared the secrets of his heart. The comfortable classes were behind him. He was the man of character, the man of sentiment to lead 'the right cause in the right way'. His friends have already praised him as Australia's greatest Prime Minister since the foundation of the Commonwealth of Australia on 1 January 1901. The Church of England synods, the Assemblies of the Presbyterian Church, the Conferences of the Methodist Church have passed

[5] John Masefield to his wife, 21 October 1916. Peter Vansittart (ed.), *John Masefield's Letters from the Front, 1915–17* (London, 1984), pp. 190–1; C. E. W. Bean, *The A. I. F. in France* (Canberra, 1929), pp. 220–37; Lloyd George is quoted in Bertram D. Wolfe, *The Fabulous Life of Diego Rivera* (New York, 1969), p. 420.

[6] J. C. Maxwell to R. M. Ferguson, 21 January 1916; R. M. Ferguson to Bonar Law, 22 December 1915. Items 3578 and 787, Novar Papers, MS. 696, N.L.A., Canberra; W. M. Hughes, 'The Call to Arms', *S.M.H.*, 15 and 16 December 1915; Lord Stamfordham to R. M. Ferguson, 12 March 1916, Novar Papers, Box 1, N.L.A., Canberra.

resolutions in favour of winning the war, and then sung with emotion 'God Save the King'. Clergymen assured their congregations 'the Lord of Hosts is with us'. In a moment of patriotic fervour one clergyman even said that if Christ were to return to earth in Australia He would gladly become a conscript. On Monday morning in the State Schools of Australia the children, placing their right hands on their left breasts, recited after their teachers the oath of loyalty to King and Empire.

In the Protestant non-government schools for boys the pupils gathered that one of the things expected of them was that they would be prepared to lay down their lives on the battlefield for their friends. Death on the battlefield was the way to life everlasting. In February 1915 the Board of the Australian Natives' Association resolved to organize throughout Australia a recruiting campaign to help the Empire and the Allies in the titanic struggle. They repeated the appeal at their meeting in March 1916, adding a recitation of the benefits to Australia of being part of the British Empire.[7]

The poets wrote of the British as crusaders for the righteous against the wicked. On one of his dry spells in Leeton, Henry Lawson told Australian men in his poem 'Conscription' that military service would be good for them. It would make 'men of weeds' in a country where both environment and climate nurtured indolence, where 'Sport is God', where 'fat-fed, narrow workers/And well-paid billet loafers', 'moral cowards and . . . shirkers' paraded the city streets or talked in bars of 'nothing but the races or the strike'; where lying politicians grew fat and lazy and fooled 'our cackling women'; where Christ himself was pounced upon, and 'Greed' dragged the wealth from the country into the city; where hotels were 'palaces of "graft" and infamy', and well-bred girls went 'faster to the sea of ruined girlhood'. Conscription would clear the track to 'perfect nationhood'. Death in war, as Lawson had said in his witty poem, 'Lawson's Dream', would alone work the great miracle: it would clean a man's dirty slate, and leave '. . . the Bill wiped out!' Then all would be understood: all would be forgiven. Henry Lawson would even forgive his wife.

C. J. Dennis put the same message in *The Moods of Ginger Mick*. War was the redeemer of the men corrupted and dirtied by the city. War would do for Ginger Mick what life in the country did for the Bloke: it would be his salvation: it would make him whole:

> So Ginger Mick 'e's mizzled to the war;
> Joy in 'is 'eart, an' wild dreams in 'is brain;

[7] Proceedings of the Annual Conference of the Australian Natives' Association, Warragul, March 1916 (Melbourne, 1916) pp. 22–3.

For Ginger Mick death was the last redeemer: death was swallowed up in victory over a man's past.[8]

Christopher Brennan wrote 'A Chant of Doom', a poem in which he presented the British and the Australians as good men doing

> . . . the last crusaders' work
> on the bastard Teuton-Turk—
> Ring the victory, ring the rout,
> ring the night of evil out—
> Ring deliverance, ring the doom
> (cannon, cannon, cannon, boom)!

The war provided opportunities for men and women to ease the private hells in their hearts. In cartoons in the *Bulletin* Norman Lindsay portrayed the Germans as the monsters inside himself, and then painted naked women to tickle to madness the puritans in Australia. The baiter of the British philistine in peacetime became the propagandist for the militarists of Britain. He loved Brennan's 'A Chant of Doom' when it appeared in the *Lone Hand* on 1 August 1916. 'It is Homeric', he told his brother Lionel in a letter in September, 'A godlike expression of man's just wrath'.[9]

Alfred Deakin, the shell of the man he had once been, wanted Australians to be 'true to Australia and to our great Empire'. So did another young man who believed one day he would wear the mantle of Alfred Deakin. He was Robert Gordon Menzies. His parents gave him the name Gordon in memory of the hero and martyr of Khartoum, not foreseeing a day would come when their illustrious son would say with pride to his fellow Australians: 'I am—like you—dyed in the wool British'. He was himself a country boy, who had been down to the great city of Melbourne where he had fallen among thieves. Born at Jeparit on 20 December 1894, the son of a country storekeeper, by his ability and industry he won his way to Wesley College and the University of Melbourne, where he distinguished himself in Arts and Law, and by his performances as a public speaker. He had his faith. He was saying then what he would say later, and indeed until he died on 15 May 1978 at the age of eighty-three: 'There is a great instinct in all of us for immortality. There is a consciousness in most of us that some day all will come to light and we shall be judged'. He said then what he would say for the rest of his life: Australians were 'unhesitatingly British'. The war worried him. He heard

[8] Henry Lawson, 'Conscription', *Bulletin*, 17 February 1916; Henry Lawson to Ernest Watts ('Benno'), probably April 1916. Colin Roderick (ed.), *Henry Lawson Letters 1890–1922* (Sydney, 1970) pp. 244–5; Henry Lawson, 'Lawson's Dream', *Bulletin*, 26 August 1915; C. J. Dennis, *The Moods of Ginger Mick* (Sydney, 1916) p. 33.

[9] Christopher Brennan, 'A Chant of Doom', *Lone Hand*, 1 August 1916; Norman Lindsay to Lionel Lindsay, *c.* September 1916, R. G. Howarth and A. W. Barker (eds), *Letters of Norman Lindsay* (Sydney, 1979), p. 79.

war's 'wild, barbaric drum'. But for him this war was something more than 'mere insensate slaughter'. To fight for 'King, Country and Empire' was to display 'valour for the right'. It was 'the gleam of truth and righteousness'. He said to all who volunteered to fight for the British cause: 'go with God's glory on your face'.

But there was the rub. He had not volunteered himself. The mockers at the University of Melbourne accused him of hypocrisy and humbuggery. 'The promising military career of Robert Gordon Menzies', one student wrote, 'was cut short by the outbreak of war'. A shadow has fallen across his life—a shadow which will not go away. Nature had played a trick on him. He wanted to be number one, to be first rather than last—in the classroom, the examination room, the Students' Representative Council, the *Melbourne University Magazine*, and in his chosen profession. But chance and circumstance have developed in him a taste for inflicting pain on those with lesser ability. He knew, as was clear from his later diaries, what was in human beings and what was in him. He knew he should stop, but found he could not. For him mocking the weak was like the effect of beer on Henry Lawson: it made him feel as he ought to have felt before his teeming brain coined the wounding words. He wanted his contemporaries to take him seriously: something in his nature over which, to his pain, he seemed to have no control often made him a figure of fun. He wanted to be respected, but nothing he could do could ever stop him being a butt for the mockers of Melbourne. He will pay a terrible price for his veneration of the British and the pleasure he received from his sport of tormenting the mediocre. His life will show that history is different from art. He will be the tragic figure of the Australian-Britons, he will have his moment of glory, he will be the man of overweening pride and arrogance, the man of *hubris*, the man with the fatal flaw, and he will know the fate of all tragic heroes. But with him the fall would not be followed by death, but by the flowering time of a man who has overcome weakness and grown in wisdom and understanding.[10]

By the beginning of 1916 not all Australians believed it was a noble thing to respond to 'the bugles of England' blowing over the sea. Before the slaughters of The Nek and Lone Pine there was enthusiasm, a belief in fighting for a noble cause. As one death notice put it in May 1915:

> He who dies for Britain,
> Does not die in vain.

[10] R. G. M. (Robert G. Menzies), 'Frater Ave Atque Vale', *Melbourne University Magazine*, 1 May 1916; R. G. M. (R. G. Menzies), 'What Are We Fighting For?' *Melbourne University Magazine*, October 1916; R. G. Menzies, *The Forgotten People* (Sydney, 1943), pp. 78–9, 24, 41; R. G. Menzies, Myself At Eighty. Menzies Papers, N.L.A., Canberra; Cameron Hazlehurst, *Menzies Observed* (Sydney, 1979), pp. 11–34; Diary of R. G. Menzies, 1948, Menzies Papers, N.L.A.

In 1915 State School teachers in Victoria wrote the names of patriotic contributors on the blackboard. By 1916 the practice has stopped. A different spirit was abroad. Some men and some women, just as high-minded as Billy Hughes and Bob Menzies, were now doing all they could to persuade Australians not to volunteer for the Australian expeditionary forces. At Sea Lake in Victoria the poet John Shaw Neilson has advised his brother, Frank, not to be carried away by the recruiting sergeants. Tension between supporters and opponents was increasing. For speaking against recruiting in Melbourne Mr Katz of the Federated Clerks' Union was tarred and feathered. Ugly scenes occurred at meetings against recruiting. Opponents accused recruiting sergeants of drunkenness. Soldiers, unsteady on their feet and foul of tongue and gesture, have broken up anti-war meetings. The opponents have called such behaviour an 'outrage . . . not compatible with the spirit of British fair play'. Supporters such as Hughes called the opponents 'foul parasites; leeches on labour, who know no nationality, religion or principle'. They should be cast out of Australia like the devils who were transplanted into the Gadarene swine.[11]

Some Labor men and women, especially the socialists, were suspicious of the war. The war increased misery among the poor and enriched the few. Mr Money Bags, alias Mr Fat, was coining money: he was up to his neck in the 'patriotic grab'. The war was tightening the grip of the 'money lords' of London on the Australian people. The war was enslaving the Australian workers more and more to that villain, the English bond-holder. While the whites were butchering each other in Europe, Asia was 'waiting and grinning'. Millions of Asiatics would invade an Australia weakened by war. The war was endangering White Australia, endangering Labor's belief in an enlightened community based on 'racial purity and the maintenance of a White Australia'. Men and women feared that militarism was fastening a new despotism on Australia. 'The new despotism', wrote the *Labor Call* in March 1916, 'has arrived'. Soldiers were beating up men and women with 'frightful devilry' just for talking about the war in public. The democratic rights and traditions of the Australian people, especially their 'imprescriptible right to public assembly and freedom of speech' were in danger. Australian democracy must not permit the 'abyss to open wide its jaws to drag us [ie., the Australians] down to the deeps of darkest duress'.[12]

The author of those words was John Joseph Ambrose Curtin, a trade union organizer already known in Labor circles for the passion in his speeches. Like Menzies, Curtin was a boy from the bush who moved to the suburbs of Melbourne. But there was a difference. Menzies lived in a middle-class suburb and went to a middle-class school: Curtin lived in a working-

[11] *Wonthaggi Sentinel*, 21 May, 6 August 1915; *Argus*, 8, 19, 22 January 1916.
[12] *Labor Call*, 30 March, 6 April, 13 April 1916.

class suburb and went to a State School. Both barracked for Carlton in football. Menzies learned his politics from the works of Edmund Burke, Alexis de Tocqueville, and the lectures of Professor Harrison Moore and Professor Ernest Scott—both distinguished and eloquent apologists for British civilization in Australia. Menzies, like Deakin, believed the Australian dream could be achieved without any change in the ownership or distribution of wealth. Curtin learned his politics from John Ruskin's *Unto This Last*, Edward Bellamy's *Looking Backward*, the novels of Charles Dickens and the speeches of Tom Mann, talks with Frank Anstey and the articles of Bernard O'Dowd in the *Tocsin*. Menzies dismissed such works as 'twaddle' and food for 'squirts'. Menzies believed in free enterprise. Curtin was a socialist. For him, as he wrote in 1913, Labor was 'a religion both in dogma and conduct'. Belief in Labor was 'something stronger than the love between a man and a woman'. Menzies believed it was his destiny to be Prime Minister of Australia: Curtin also believed it was his destiny to hold that high office. Menzies believed history was on the side of British civilization. Curtin believed history was on the side of Labor. Curtin saw himself as one of 'Labor's sons', a tool of the 'eternal processes', that he and his fellow members of the Labor movement were 'comrades in a holy war'. The Australian working class would shift 'the centre of economic gravity' to its 'final repository in the bosom of the toiling and teeming multitudes'.[13]

Menzies' eye was always single. Curtin has been a desperate pilgrim for the means of salvation. He has tried Catholicism, the Salvation Army (playing the cornet for a brief time at street corners), Rationalism ('giving' it to Jesus being one of his sports at a time when Bob Menzies was 'giving' it to those he despised), and Socialism. He has also tried 'salvation in the muck'. He has been a seeker, but not a finder. He was the man with the sorrowful countenance, the man with the droop at the two extremities of his lips. Menzies was a jolly man, a man who loved a chuckle: Curtin was a sad man. A shadow has fallen across the life of Bob Menzies: there was also a shadow across the life of Jack Curtin. Like Henry Lawson nature endowed him with a temperament which needed some crutch. The crutch on which he has leaned cast the shadow between him and what he wanted to be. Like Henry Lawson he knew he should stop, but found to his dismay he could not stop. He became engaged to Elsie Needham in 1908, but she refused to marry him until he kept his promise never to drink again. He promised her many times that because he loved her so he would give up drinking alcohol. Not even love gave him that strength. That must come from the man within. There were terrible descents into that hell.

The 'strange infirmity' also cast a shadow across his public life. Early in

[13] John Curtin to E. Needham, 6 June 1913, Lloyd Ross Papers, Box 33, N.L.A., Canberra; Lloyd Ross, *John Curtin* (Melbourne, 1977), pp. 1- 37.

1916 he was to be the speaker at the Socialist Sunday School in Melbourne. He was then a hot gospeller of secular salvation, of Socialism performing the marvel that the churches preached God alone could work. But Jack Curtin did not turn up: he was unconscious in a house in Brunswick. He had a time in Lara Hospital. Frank Anstey, who never lost faith in him, told him the 'man who has carried his crucifix and climbed his Calvary is a better man than he who never touched the stony road of suffering . . . Stand upright, proud of yourself, proud of the conquest that you are going to achieve, and the good that you yet will do'. The only redemption would be in finding the strength to stop. That would come, and with it the prize he coveted, the prize he believed destiny has reserved for him—the prize of teaching Australians the dream which had sustained him all through his years of the dark night of the soul. So two men in 1916 entered on their years of suffering in preparation for their tasks as missionaries for two quite different visions of Australia's future.[14]

The young Vance Palmer presented a different plea to Australians—a supplement to John Curtin's political nationalism—a plea for a living culture in Australia. Academic classicism in the universities, he said, had produced the 'Cultured Philistine' who ignored or stifled whatever was alive or creative in their own day. The cultured philistine resisted anything that was new or novel in ideas, art or social refinement. The cultured philistine also believed nothing was important unless it came out of England, Europe, or the Greeks and the Romans. The 'Cultured Philistine' was 'The Old Dead Tree'. Australians needed a living culture that would seek out what was 'vital and creative in our national life and link up with it'. Australians should stop spending their time reading second-rate Elizabethan dramatists, and read Bernard O'Dowd's *The Bush* or Price Warung's *The Ring*.[15]

Hughes was a stranger to that view of Australia. Hughes was a Welshman, an immigrant. Hughes was a supporter of British civilization in Australia. Like his predecessor in office, Andrew Fisher, also an immigrant, Hughes was an 'England "to the last man and the last shilling" ' supporter. Hughes was a King and Empire man. Hughes was a Labor man—or had been. But now, on the eve of his departure for London, in his Call To Arms in December 1915, he sneered at Labor men and women who indulged in 'mere empty vapourings about the future, or dwell in the land of Utopia'. Hughes had always believed in the battlefield as the best training for men. Blood-letting, he believed, opened men's eyes to the meaning of life. Life was a struggle, in which the cunning and the strong survived, and the weak went to the wall. Within the Labor movement eyebrows have been raised. The *Labor*

[14] Lloyd Ross, op. cit., pp. 38–49.
[15] Vance Palmer, 'Towards A Living Culture', *Fellowship*, May 1916.

Call wanted to know whether Billy Hughes was still a Labor man, whether he was loyal to his 'old mates'.[16]

At the same time, near Cairo, the members of the Australian Imperial Force, composed of those evacuated from Gallipoli and recent arrivals, waited for the next move. Their numbers have increased. Reports of the casualties at the Gallipoli landing, at The Nek and Lone Pine, and knowledge that in France things were not going very well, have swollen the numbers of men volunteering for service overseas. In June 1915, 12 505 had volunteered; in July 36 575, in January 1916, 22 101. They drilled, drank their beer, and indulged in the usual 'carry on' and pranks of Australians while the British High Command debated their fate.

It had been intended to use them for the defence of the east bank of the Suez Canal against an expected Turkish offensive. But on 21 February 1916 the Germans attacked the fortress of Verdun. To take the weight off the French, the British must start a push. The ANZACS were needed in France. On 29 February General Murray, the British supreme commander in Egypt, instructed Birdwood to make preparations for the ANZAC Corps (the 1st and 2nd Australian and the New Zealand divisions) to be transported to France. Murray wondered whether this was wise. He feared the Australians might rampage around the sleazy districts of Marseilles as they had roared around the brothels of Cairo. But there was no time for assurances on those questions. The Australians and the New Zealanders must leave. The soldiers promised their officers to 'do their level best'. Birdwood asked that gifted organizer, Cyril Brudenell White, to prepare the departure. On 13 March the first ships bearing members of the Corps sailed from Egypt for Marseilles.[17]

On 19 March 1916 the first transports arrived in Marseilles from Alexandria. The officers were delighted with the behaviour of their men. A band on a troop ship played the 'Marseillaise'. French children begged the Australians for 'souvenours' (*sic*) which one soldier proudly explained to his people back home was the French word for 'baksheesh'. Charlie Bean wrote with relief in his diary: 'The men here in Marseilles are trying their level best. Every officer says that wherever he went he was punctiliously saluted . . . I only saw one man in the least the worse for liquour . . . The place swarms with women—very fascinating ones too'. But this time the men were strong. As one sergeant wrote to his mother: 'The boys are behaving themselves this time, even though beer and wine were only one penny a glass'. They marched to the troop trains commandeered to carry them to the British

[16] W. M. Hughes, The Call To Arms, 15 December 1915, Hughes Papers, Series 21, Folder 4, N.L.A., Canberra; *S.M.H.*, 19 January 1916; W. M. Hughes, *Crusts and Crusades* (Sydney, 1947), p. 88; *Call* (Sydney), 8 August 1906, p. 2.

[17] C. E. W. Bean, *Anzac to Amiens* (Canberra, 1961), pp. 188–93; E. Scott, *Australia during the War* (Sydney, 1936), p. 871.

sector of the front. One private found the French countryside came 'pretty close to Australia' for beauty as his troop train rushed in that early spring past Versailles, and on for the first view of the Somme at Abbéville.

The men were in good spirits. They clowned in the carriages, complaining of the 'frog' narrow seats, far too brief for good Aussie 'bums', threw souvenirs out of the trains for the girls—autographed hard army biscuits with their addresses written on them, hoping perhaps for the miracle of a response from those lovely girls cheering them on their way to the Somme. From the hooded religious shrines Christ looked out at them with the eye of pity, as they learned to sing a new song about a Mademoiselle of Armentières: 'Up the stairs the officer went/Parlez-vous/And when he came down his knees were bent/Inky-pinky parlez-vous'. Kitchener addressed them. 'Well, boys', he said, 'I am very pleased to see you in France. You made your name in Gallipoli'. The legend was still alive. They were the men who never knew defeat, the men forged in the mighty bush of Australia into the finest steel of manhood. They were the descendants of the hardy race of people who had pioneered civilization in Australia, the men and women with 'hearts of lions' who had fought against fire and flood, drought, and the great Australian dryness. Joffre and Haig drank wine, joked with each other, and exchanged views on where the boys from 'down under' could best be used, as though, in the words of Pirandello, human beings could be 'sold like a flock of sheep'.[18]

In London that March Hughes was dismayed by the mood in government circles. To all his suggestions about what must be done Herbert Asquith, the British Prime Minister, replied: 'Not now'. Bonar Law told him, my dear chap, no human affairs were worth taking seriously. In August 1914 there had been fervour and enthusiasm: now there was disenchantment. Cynicism was in the air. Favours could be bought: there was a price, it was said, for the stripes of a corporal, and a price for not being sent into the front line. The red tab on the collars of the army tunics at military headquarters was called 'the Red Badge of Funk'. The military chaplains were despised as hypocrites for telling the soldiers God would reward those who 'scragged the Hun'. The English, he believed, needed gingering up.[19]

Hughes decided to go on a lecturing tour of the country. He delivered his battle cry in England, Scotland and Wales, but stayed away from Ireland. In

[18] H. B. Hutchinson to his mother, 31 March 1916, MS. in A.W.M., Canberra; Diary of K. H. McConnell, 28, 29, 30 March 1916, and Diary of C. Smith, 6 June 1916, A.W.M., Canberra; Gaspare Giudice, *Pirandello* (London, 1975), p. 90; Bernard O'Reilly, *Cullenbenbong* (Brisbane, 1944), pp. 15–16; P. J. C. Wallace, *Playing a Man's Part* (Melbourne, n.d.), p. 1.

[19] C. E. Montague, *Disenchantment* (London, 1922), pp. 3–18, 30–5, 48, 70–1; Piers Brendon, *Eminent Edwardians* (Penguin Books edn, London, 1981), pp. 78, 128; W. M. Hughes, *The Splendid Adventure* (London, 1929), p. 42; L. F. Fitzhardinge, *The Little Digger* (Sydney, 1979), p. 73; *The Times*, 8 March 1916; *Age*, 10 March 1916.

every lecture theatre, public hall, and in the open air he roused his listeners to wild enthusiasm with his message: time was running out, call more men to the colours, manufacture more guns, improve wireless communications, invent better weapons, perfect aerial bombardment, end trade with German firms, render impossible the survival of German trade after the war, make Germany pay for the destruction of little Belgium and France. It was the message of a man who had no doubts about human beings usurping the divine prerogative of revenge. It was the joyless creed he had learnt in his childhood: the enemies of righteousness must be ground into the dust. Victory must be achieved no matter what the cost in men and money. Endurance must be the watchword, even if the war lasted sixty months. 'More men, and still more men', he shouted to his audiences. The audiences whistled and cheered. The war was, he continued, doing great things for the Empire. The war, he shouted, has saved the British people from becoming flabby, saying this as boys from the Australian bush gazed with awe and wonder at aeroplanes in the sky overhead, and felt the ground under them sway with shell fire.[20]

The English, the Scots and the Welsh were delighted. Arthur Balfour, the witty mocker of all enthusiasts, called Hughes 'the apostle of a great cause'. Lloyd George joined in the chorus of praise and thanksgiving. Hughes, he said, was a 'successful leader of democracy', a man who had 'the rarest gift of all', the capacity to 'instruct, persuade and move the multitudes'. The Lord Mayor of Liverpool called him 'a breath of fresh air'. Marie Corelli, the novelist with the numerous reading public, told him in a letter, 'an enormous public in Great Britain wait upon your brave utterances with *unspeakable* relief and gratitude! ... you have said what they feel and long to express'.[21]

Herbert Asquith, the British Prime Minister, did not quite know what to do with him. Hughes asked that Australia be represented at the forthcoming conference in Paris. Asquith wanted the British delegation to be onlookers, like himself, noticing everything but saying nothing. Hughes, he told his colleagues in the Cabinet, could be relied on to note everything, but could not be relied on to say nothing. Hughes turned on one of his tantrums. The King counselled Asquith to let him go. Asquith agreed. It was the great moment in the life of Hughes. London for him was as London had been for

[20] W. M. Hughes, *Crusts and Crusades*, pp. 71–2; Norman Cowper, 'W. M. Hughes', *Australian Quarterly*, December 1952, vol. XXIV, pp. 5–7; *The Times*, 14, 25 March, 19, 20, 28 April 1916; *Age*, 16 March 1916; H. H. Asquith to W. M. Hughes, 20 March 1916, Hughes Papers, Series 22, Item 2, N.L.A.; *Daily Telegraph*, 22 March 1916.

[21] Marie Corelli to W. M. Hughes, 23 March 1916, Hughes Papers, Series 22, Item 3, N.L.A.; *Daily Telegraph* (London), 20 May 1916; H. H. Asquith to W. M. Hughes, 20 March 1916. Hughes Papers, Series 22, Item 2, N.L.A.; *Age*, 12, 24, 27 May 1916; *Daily Telegraph*, 22 March 1916.

Henry Lawson in 1900. It was his 'high tide'. He bantered with the members of his delegation. He told them stories. With eyes lit up, he played with them, and spun one of his yarns, about his days as a stone-breaker on the rail tracks of Queensland, or how he had once run for his life when his opponents in a pre-selection ballot chased him through the streets of Balmain.[22]

While he cracked jokes in London, Haig and Joffre were calculating how many more men the Allies would need for the big push on the Somme. The men of the 1st and 2nd Australian Divisions heard the roar of cannon fire, saw the aeroplanes overhead, and read the trench notices such as: 'Do not stand here. Even if you are not shot, someone else will be'. Laugh on, laugh on, for time is short: a great storm was brewing on the Somme. Back in Australia the *Labor Call* was half amused and half dismayed by the reports that an Australian Labor leader was wearing a 'topper' and a swallow-tailed coat in London. 'William Morris Hughes', they wrote on 13 April 1916, 'Prime Minister of the Commonwealth, formerly "Billy Hughes", is having a royal time in London . . . "joined with nobility . . . burgomasters and great one-eyers" '. They wondered whether Hughes had become a traitor to his class. They would watch closely 'William's progress from Jingoism to Imperialism'.[23]

In Australia a chin-wagging contest was being waged between the cold teaites (total abstainers), and Bung (the liquor interests). To protect the morals and the health of the public the cold teaites wanted governments to introduce six o'clock closing of all bars. But the reports of the horrors of Gallipoli, The Nek, Lone Pine and Ypres have introduced a new sense of division in Australia. People in the Labor movement said the war was a moral disgrace to humanity. The war has transformed the beautiful countryside of France into a 'garbage heap, a cesspool and a charnel house'. The war was not a story of heroism, sacrifice and nobility. It was 'misery and muck'. It was shameful, on 25 April 1916, to 'hold a picnic o'er Australia's dead'. It was shameful for overdressed women and 'precocious flappers' to weep and mourn for the loved and the lost. It was immoral for Australians to come to the aid of the British aristocracy, that 'diseased and degenerate race that has battened on the pension list of Great Britain for generations'. Australians had more important things to do. This was no time for 'flag-flapping, chin-wagging, hideous howling' by bourgeois patriots. Australians should now demand the punishment of those responsible for the 'ghastly, ghoulish "gamble" ' at Gallipoli.[24]

Others saw Gallipoli in quite a different way. On the eve of the first Anzac commemoration on 25 April 1916, the Minister for Defence, Senator G. F.

[22] R. R. Garran, *Prosper the Commonwealth* (Sydney, 1958), pp. 226–8.
[23] Ypres Museum; *Labor Call*, 13 April 1916.
[24] *Truth*, 16, 25, 26 March, 9, 30 April 1916; *Bulletin*, 27 April 1916.

Pearce, told Australians the thunder of the cannon had not been necessary to inspire them with a conception of their duty. What had happened on 25 April 1915 was proof that Australians had regained that spirit of their forebears which had enabled them to overcome 'with indomitable pluck the awful hardships of a pioneering life'. On 25 April in Sydney four thousand soldiers marched through the city to the Domain. The people clapped: they did not cheer: they looked at them with awe. The people, like their leaders, knew this was something significant, something deep, but did not know what it was. Recruiting sergeants moved through the crowd, catching the mood of the moment by calling for volunteers, pointing with veneration to these wounded heroes as though asking the question: is it nothing to you, all ye that pass by? On the Sydney Domain the Anglican Archbishop of Sydney, Dr Wright, called on Australians to do their part until the work was finished. Anzac Day was not only 'a new and glorious page' in Australian history: it had opened a new page in the history of the Empire: '25 April was the date on which Australia suddenly found herself lifted to a place among the peoples'.

Australians now had a faith, but what that faith was no one could say. Leading articles were written in the newspapers; the clergy preached; the politicians and the generals made their speeches; the poets had their shot at putting it into memorable words. Dorothea Mackellar said it was about 'Honour and dreams and courage'. Nettie Palmer said it was about men who had courage and were strong of heart when they drank 'horror from a brimming cup'. Vance Palmer said the men gave their lives not to 'guard/ An empire's glittering pride', but for Australia—to 'keep the house we build/ Secure against the world'. Christopher Brennan saw them as 'our noblest and our best'. Mary Gilmore was overawed in the presence of these mighty men of renown: for her it was a mystery why men of such grandeur of spirit should die: why 'He who was I is dead'. Louisa Lawson saw them as 'Brave heroes!', 'by honour thriven', men who 'fought their way through hell—to heaven'. The poets were using the language of religion to describe a secular experience. Anzac Day was becoming a secular religion.[25]

Billy Hughes developed this theme of tranfiguration in his speech to Australian soldiers in London at the Hotel Cecil on Anzac Day. 'Soldiers', he said, 'your deeds have won you a place in the Temple of the Immortals. The world has hailed you as heroes'. The Anzacs have inspired generations yet unborn with 'pride of race, courage, tenacity of purpose, endurance, and that casting out of fear without which men, though boasting themselves free, are but wretched slaves'. The soldiers have taught Australians that through sacrifice

[25] *S.M.H.*, 25, 26 April 1916; Dorothea Mackellar, 'Men of Anzac', Nettie Palmer, 'Men of Anzac', Vance Palmer, 'The Signal', Mary Gilmore, 'Gallipoli', Chris. Brennan, 'Lines of War', Louisa Lawson, 'Immortal Passage', *Anzac Memorial* (Sydney, 1916), pp. 53, 58, 67, 69, 70, 78.

alone can men or nations be saved. They have shown the sublime heroism of walking into the jaws of death. No one could possibly say that this 'dreadful war [was] wholly an evil'. Into a world saturated with a lust for material things, which had elevated self into a deity, which had made wealth the standard of greatness, had come 'the sweet purifying breath of self-sacrifice'. The Australians, thanks to the Anzacs, have now 'put on the toga of manhood'. Australians now had a religion: they now needed shrines at which to conduct their worship. In the presence of the mighty dead, Australians should dedicate themselves to their nation, their Empire and their liberties.[26]

Back in Australia some Labor men hoped Hughes did not mean one half of what he said. Others wondered whether the top hat, the knee breeches and the buckles were to blame for the guff he was doling out to Londoners. The *Labor Call* assumed the English had degenerated, seeing they took such notice of the 'fulsome slobber' of the Australian Prime Minister. They quoted the German press, saying it was a sign of decadence that the Australian Prime Minister, the 'circus athlete', the 'strong man swinging paper clubs', was being hailed by the English as an 'ideal statesman'. But this mask of spirituality was soon ripped off the face of the British Imperialists. On 30 April, Easter 1916, the leaders of the Irish Volunteers in Dublin called on their fellow Irishmen to overthrow English power in Ireland and establish an Independent Irish Republic. They seized the Post Office in Dublin for their headquarters. Within a week the British army crushed the Easter Rising. They then tried the leaders of the mutiny by military tribunal and sentenced them to death and some of the rank and file to long terms of imprisonment in English gaols. Early in May the leaders were shot. Some of them told their relations in farewell letters to be of good cheer until they all saw each other again 'in a better world'. Friends and relatives should console themselves with the thought that their loved ones were 'going to heaven tomorrow'.[27]

While the court martials in Dublin were showing the world the ugly side of British Imperialism Billy Hughes and his wife were dining at Windsor Castle with the King and Queen of England, Scotland, Ireland and the British Dominions beyond the seas. Billy Hughes had a long conversation with the King over cigars after dinner. The King and Queen graciously showed their guests all the gorgeous apartments in the Castle. They drank orange juice at the dining table because, like the Russian Czar, George V has vowed not to drink again of the fruit of the vine until the Allies won the war. The Labor press in Australia was disgusted when it heard the news of Billy's fraternizing

[26] W. M. Hughes, Notes for a speech delivered at the Hotel Cecil, Anzac Day, April 25, 1916, Hughes Papers, Series 22, Item 6.

[27] Letters in showcases on Easter Rising in Irish National Museum, Dublin. Read in Dublin, 9 April 1985; *Labor Call*, 1 June 1916.

with royalty: 'Ye Gods', wrote the *Labor Call* early in May, 'a Laborite dining with monarchs'.

Events in Ireland would confront Hughes with a terrible dilemma. The savagery of the British government against the Irish national leaders made conscription in Ireland a virtual impossibility, and would probably reduce the number of volunteers for the British army. The Haig–Joffre plans for the big push depended for their success on superiority in numbers. Without Ireland, the British looked to the British Dominions for men. Events in Ireland might affect the attitudes of the Irish and their descendants in Australia. Those events might sour the enthusiasm for the Empire felt in August 1914. Billy Hughes and his faithful lieutenant, Senator George Pearce, must find means to keep up the numbers in France. The *Labor Call* was already sounding a warning to Hughes. Glorious, bloody blood, they wrote early in May, was not the way to salvation for the people of Australia. The war, they told their readers, was primarily a class war, and all this 'blood-letting business' was a means to protect the bowler-hatted population of the British Isles against social revolution. If Hughes tried any tricks such as introducing conscription to curry favour with his imperial masters then he would find he had a war on his hands in Australia—this time a class not an imperialist war.[28]

Hughes went on speaking in London of the moral and spiritual benefits of the war. The war, he said, has saved Australians from physical and moral degeneracy and decay. This angered even more members of the Labor movement. An Australian Labor leader was suggesting that making rivers of blood and plains of dead men, for men to be blown to pieces, their brains scattered, their arms and legs and entrails strewn in every direction, was the way to prevent Australians 'becoming flabby'. An Australian Labor leader was suggesting that blood-spilling was the way to salvation, that war, like the glorious beams of the sun, lit the way to Paradise. A Labor leader was suggesting that the spilling of 'glorious, bloody blood' was the duty of all those who were loyal to the King and the Empire. Well, said the *Labor Call*, if that was what Billy Hughes wanted then Labor should support the demands of the European Socialists for peace by negotiation. But Hughes went on hammering away at his themes: don't rely on 'muddling through': destroy Germany now.[29]

Dr Mannix, the coadjutor Archbishop of Melbourne, added his voice to the debate about the war. He had come to Australia to save Catholics from secular education, to win justice for Catholics in education, and to rescue them from being permanently second-rate citizens. Now he had a new cause: to speak some words in favour of the Irish rebels, and to say the Australians

[28] *Labor Call*, 11 May 1916; *Age*, 4 May 1916, *The Times*, 3 May 1916.
[29] *S.M.H.*, 26 April 1916; *Labor Call*, 11, 18 May 1916; *Labor Call*, 13 July 1916.

had already made enough sacrifices in the war. At Bendigo in July 1916 he told Catholics to have nothing in their minds that would postpone peace or make it impossible. This angered some members of the Protestant ascendancy. The *Argus* said he should shut up in wartime. The Irish question has given the combatants in the old sectarian dog-fight a new life: the Protestants in the Empire corner, and Catholics in the Irish corner, both limbering up for the battle to come. The executions in Ireland have given the anti-conscriptionists a man who had the makings of a people's hero.[30]

The argument in Australia over the war has reached boiling point. On 3 May 1916 the Australian Natives' Association held a meeting in the Melbourne Town Hall in favour of conscription. As soon as the first speaker (A. C. Ostrom, the Chief-President of the Association) started speaking, anti-conscriptionists interjected, shouted, hissed and booed. Soldiers rushed to where they were seated, rough-handled a man, grabbed him by the seat of his trousers and bundled him towards a door. Then the soldiers turned their attention to a man and woman at the press table, and amid cries of 'Put them out' seized them and bundled them towards the door. Police protected the woman. The man jumped on to the stage. The soldiers insisted that he leave the hall. The police persuaded the man to go quietly.

The police department in Sydney prohibited the sale of anti-war papers in the Sydney Domain, on grounds that their distribution promoted disturbances. Tom Barker was fined one hundred pounds or twelve months' gaol for suggesting the capitalist class was gloating over the profits made during the war. People assembling on the Yarra Bank in Melbourne on Sunday afternoons to hear speakers present the case against the war were surrounded by howling and threatening soldiers. Not even women were safe from their strong-arm tactics. The Women's National League expressed great indignation with members of their own set who expressed disloyal sentiments. It took courage to stand up to the soldiers, the strong arm of a mass hysteria. The patriots demanded all German citizens be interned and dismissed from their occupations in Australia. Dissent has become synonymous with treason.[31]

On 5 June 1916 all those who put their faith in the British navy received a shock. On that day the Australian press gave some details of a naval battle between the German and British fleets off the coast of Jutland. On 31 May the British battle cruiser squadron, commanded by Admiral Sir David Beatty, met the main German fleet proceeding north-west from the coast of Jutland, and gave battle. Beatty planned to keep the Germans engaged until

[30] *Advocate*, 13 May 1916; F. Anstey to Harry —— n.d., probably 1916, Lloyd Ross Papers, Box 33.

[31] *Age*, 4 May 1916; *S.M.H.*, 4 May, 3 July 1916; *Worker* (Brisbane), 4 May 1916; *Argus*, 10 May, 3, 10 July 1916.

the British battleships under the command of Admiral Jellicoe arrived. The engagement lasted until daybreak on the following morning, when the survivors in the German fleet returned to ports on the coast of Jutland. The First Lord of the Admiralty, Winston Churchill, claimed there was no great difference between German and British losses, that Britain was still in unquestioned control of the sea, and that the battle had shown that Germany had no 'surprises' in either armament or ships. The King congratulated Sir John Jellicoe on 'the splendid gallantry of the officers and men of your command', and added his regrets the Germans had not stayed to fight. But the report of heavy British losses in ships and men—at least equal to the German losses—filled the British and the Australians at first with dismay and anxiety. A day later Australian confidence recovered as the press printed 'thrilling stories' of British bravery and reports by neutrals that German claims of victory were unwarranted. The British blockade of Germany was still impassable. Perhaps the British were no longer invincible at sea. Admiral Beatty looked sad. He feared the British navy, like British industry, had been outmatched by the Germans—that the British were on the way down. In his private life David Beatty was tormented by a sense of failure, the never-ending pain of knowing he was not loved by his wife. Now he had another source of torment: Britannia no longer ruled the waves.

The following day, 6 June 1916, Lloyd George learned that the *Hampshire*, carrying Field Marshal Lord Kitchener of Khartoum and his party to Russia, had struck a mine off the Orkneys. Kitchener, the architect of British strategy on the Western front, was drowned. Lloyd George was shocked. Kitchener, he believed, had been a man of 'great driving force but no mental powers. Hard eyes—relentless—without a glimmer of human kindness'. A hero of the British Empire was no more. The German submarine campaign was also challenging the British control of the seas. The Empire was in danger.

By the time news of Kitchener's death reached Australia a conference of delegates from State branches of returned servicemen's organizations in Victoria, New South Wales, Queensland and South Australia was being held in Melbourne. The press was excluded. In a statement issued later the delegates declared that they had decided to form the Returned Sailors and Soldiers League of Australia. Later the name was changed to the Returned Services League. History was to know them as the R.S.L. Their aims were: to perpetuate in the civil life of the Nation the principles for which they fought; to protect the interests and forward the welfare of members and their dependants; to promote social intercourse among members; to perpetuate the close and kindly ties of friendship created by mutual service in the Great War; to inculcate loyalty to Australia and the Empire, and preserve the records of those who suffered and died for the nation.

So the men who were prepared to pay the supreme sacrifice to defend Australia as a nation confessed their belief in keeping Australia within the

Empire. They vowed to be non-sectarian and non-partisan in relation to party politics. They vowed, too, to establish in honour of their fallen comrades an annual commemoration of Anzac Day. They had ideas on the form of any such commemoration. A bugler should sound the Last Post. Those present should recite solemnly the Rudyard Kipling words: 'Lest we forget'. One of their members should say reverently the words from Laurence Binyon's poem, 'For the Fallen':

> At the going down of the sun and in the morning
> We will remember them.

This was a man's country. The rites for dead servicemen should be performed by men. There should be no mention of God or Christ. A mystique about Anzac and Australia was taking shape: Australia was acquiring a secular religion. Australia was being chained to the past. To question that religion was an act of impiety against the lore of the tribe.[32]

On 1 June 1916 Hughes arrived in France for talks with Haig and Joffre at British military headquarters at Croix du Bac. The roses were already blooming in Picardy, the skylarks rising in the sky, and the statues of the Virgin in the wayside shrines were covered with the flowers of the late spring and the early summer. The Australians of the 1st and 2nd Army Corps were oiling and cleaning their rifles, sharpening their bayonets to give the Germans the 'pen-knife' treatment, or carousing and taking their 'horizontal refreshment' in brothels behind the lines. The chaplains told them Christ had come so that they might have life and have it more abundantly. Hughes, Haig, Joffre and their advisers were talking of them as though they were the flies that 'wanton boys' killed 'for their sport'. But that was war. Hughes and Haig understood each other. Hughes asked Haig to agree to Australian troops being under the administrative command of General Birdwood. He also asked that Australian troops should be an army under the command of General Birdwood. Haig agreed with the first, but could not put all the Australian forces in France under Birdwood's command, though promising to bear the wishes of the Australian Government in mind. Haig wanted promises from Hughes to send more men. He and Joffre were planning the big push: losses would be heavy: numbers were vital for an Allied victory. Hughes did not say no. Hughes met Joffre and liked him.

Hughes went out into the open air to address Australian troops. He told them, 'We are all proud of you'. 'What a glorious and inspiring sight they were', he said. 'Fit: Magnificent of physique: sublimely confident: and cheer-

[32] *S.M.H.*, 5, 6 June 1916; Peter Rowland, *David Lloyd George* (New York, 1976), p. 340; Report of Conference of Returned Soldiers Association of Vic., N.S.W., Q. and S.A. held in Victoria 6–12 June 1916, typescript in N.L.A.; Loftus Hills, *The Returned Sailors and Soldiers Imperial League of Australia* (Melbourne, 1927), pp. 10–11; *Argus*, 19 July 1916.

ful'. To his delight the troops gave three cheers for Australia. To him that was comforting: that was 'a final answer to those miserable wasters who try every dodge to avoid doing their duty'. He was half dead with fatigue, but the exaltation of the occasion kept him going. He was playing a part, with the British and the French, in the world's salvation. He was the leader of these heroes. He was not bothered by what these men would go through.[33]

There was one doubt. The voluntary system of recruiting in Australia might not supply the men Haig needed. Reports from Australia were not favourable. Despite much drum-whacking, much distribution of free drinks, and much travelling around the countryside, recruiting trains returned from their enterprises almost empty. The anti-war movement was becoming more voluble. Sections of the Labor movement were passing resolutions against conscription for overseas service. Reports of British savagery in Ireland were changing the attitude to the war of many Irish Catholics in Australia. As early as 16 September 1915 the Melbourne Trades Hall Council condemned the proposals of the Universal Service League: Labor was opposed to 'Prussianising democracy' in Australia. John Curtin signed that resolution on behalf of the Timber Workers' Union. The cartoons in the Labor press were becoming more savage about the profits Mr Fat Man was making out of the war. Pearce has warned Hughes in letters that Australia would have difficulty in recruiting by the volunteer method the numbers Haig required, and that there would be even more considerable difficulty with compulsory service. But Hughes was like a man possessed. He raged against the wasters and the shirkers, and went to Paris. There he presented the Australian case with a passion the French politicians and generals found 'formidable'.[34]

In London the British governing classes still enthused over him. *The Times* praised him for 'sweeping the Empire with his eloquence'. The *Daily Mail* said he was 'what's wanted in England'. Lord Fisher's flattery went further. In a private letter to Hughes on 12 June Fisher likened Hughes to God: 'Behold', he wrote, 'God himself is with us as our captain'. Hughes, Fisher repeated nine days later, had read England like an open book. Hughes was 'an apostle of Empire'. *Britannia*, the Official Organ of the Women's Social and Political Union edited by Christobel Pankhurst said the British people wanted Hughes to come back to London and take his place on the War Council to lead the Empire to that complete victory which alone could save it from downfall. Hughes purred. Cities conferred their freedom on him. Uni-

[33] *Age*, 9 June 1916; C. E. W. Bean, *The A.I.F. in France* (Sydney, 1935, first edition 1929), p. 471; L. F. Fitzhardinge, op. cit., pp. 119–21; W. M. Hughes to G. F. Pearce, 3, 4 June 1916, Pearce Papers, A.W.M.; W. M. Hughes to General Birdwood, 19 June 1916, Fisher Papers, N.L.A.

[34] *Age*, 1 May 1916; *Australian Worker*, 23 September 1915; Cablegram of W. M. Hughes to G. F. Pearce, 8 June 1916, Pearce Papers, A.W.M.

versities decorated him with their doctorates. In a state of exaltation Hughes moved from office to office in Whitehall trying to persuade the British to buy Australian products with all the coyness of the lovely Irish girl pleading with people: 'Won't you buy my pretty flowers?' Hughes was on top of the world. But in Australia the *Labor Call* was not impressed. Hughes, they said, was like a circus clown who made jokes when others were gasping at all the horror in France.[35]

Australia was changing. The Broken Hill Proprietary Limited has begun to produce iron and steel in its works at Newcastle. Industrialization, trade and urbanization were ending the era of Australia as a sheep walk, a cattle ranch, a wheat farm, a dairy and a quarry. In the case of *Farey* v. *Burvett* before the High Court in June 1916, in which W. A. Farey, a Glenferrie baker, challenged the power of the Commonwealth Government to control prices, the High Court has ruled that the defence power of the Commonwealth conferred by Section 51, sub-sections vi and xxxix of the Constitution, included a power during the present state of war to fix within the limits of locality the highest price which during the continuance of the war might be charged for bread.[36]

The days of the kangaroo, emu and noble bushman image of Australia were drawing to an end. The President of the Arts and Crafts Society in Melbourne, Professor Baldwin Spencer, has told his members all those emblems must go—the kookaburra, the kangaroo, the emu and the wattle. They belonged to the age of the bowyang and the sliprail. Australia was advancing into a quite different world. Electricity, urbanization and more leisure have provided the setting for the cinema to flourish. Moving pictures were no longer a fill-in at a vaudeville show, or a backyard entertainment. In the cities picture houses have been built which showed exclusively motion pictures. In the country local halls have been hired for that purpose by the distributors and their agents. Huge numbers were crowding the cinemas. By 1916 the average weekly attendance at the cinemas in Melbourne was 426 910. Taking the average charge for admission as sixpence that meant £10 672 15s was spent each week on this form of entertainment. The cinemas had new popular heroes. Charlie Chaplin, with bowler hat, butterfly collar, bow tie, waistcoat, baggy trousers and walking stick was sending audiences into fits of laughter.[37]

At the same time Hughes prepared to return to Australia. On 24 June 1916 he told the Australian troops training on Salisbury Plain: 'I am leaving you, you to do your duty and I mine . . . We shall never hesitate or stop until we

[35] Lord Fisher to W. M. Hughes, 12, 21 June 1916, Hughes Papers, Series 22, Items 20 and 22; *Britannia*, 21 July 1916.

[36] Helen Hughes, *The Australian Iron and Steel Industry* (Melbourne, 1964), pp. 55–70; *C'wealth Law Reports*, 21, 1915–16, pp. 450–6.

[37] *Age*, 28, 29 April 1916.

have seen our cause triumphant on the field of victory, and this Empire and civilization rid of a dreadful menace which has oppressed us for forty years'. He proposed to present this message to his colleagues in the Labor Government and the people when he returned to Australia. He has won the admiration of the King, the dukes, the lords and others in high places in England, Scotland and Wales. Now he must win the admiration of the people of Australia.[38]

He was not to know a terrible storm was brewing there. While he was on the high seas a clergyman in the Sydney Domain told his large audience that if Christ had been there in the Domain he would have preached his gospel of peace and goodwill. A Labor Government would have put Christ in gaol for discouraging recruiting. The *Worker* in Sydney warned readers that the aim of the conscriptionists was 'the smashing of Unionism, the suspension of factory laws, the breaking of strikes by armed violence, the trial of protesting wage-slaves at the drum-head, the unlimited supply of cheap labour; with glistening eyes they see it all before them—if only they can get conscription here'. Hughes was a stranger to fear. He was a man with a mission: the armed might of the British, the French, the Australians and the other British Dominions must be employed to smash Germany which, in his mind, barred the world's road to something better. The choice, he believed, was between freedom and being enslaved by Germany. He chose freedom. And so, he believed, did most of the Australian people, no matter what the cost. Hughes sailed for Australia on the *Euripides* on 29 June.[39]

Two days later on 1 July the British offensive began on the Somme. On that morning the English historian, R. H. Tawney, took communion to strengthen him for the ordeal, believing that a man should meet death 'brimful with Christ'. He heard the beautiful words of the communion service above the rattling of rifle-bolts, the bursts of song and occasional laughter from his comrades. He heard a priest of the Church of England invite all those who intended to lead a new life following the commandments of God to draw near with faith and take this holy sacrament to their comfort, meekly kneeling upon their knees. As he and his comrades climbed out of the trench he suddenly understood a passage in Bunyan's *Pilgrim's Progress*: 'Then I saw that there was a way to Hell'. By the end of the day he was lying face down with a bullet wound in his chest. When they attacked they were 820 strong: at nightfall 370 were left, and two days later 54 were left. Richard Henry Tawney murmured to himself: 'God forgive us all'. Within a week the fields around the Somme were littered with bodies. All the trees had been cut off by shells. Raymond Asquith, the son of the British Prime Minister Herbert Asquith saw 'craters swimming in blood and rotting and swelling bodies

[38] *The Times*, 9, 26 June 1916.

[39] *Australian Worker* (Sydney), 29 June, 6 July 1916.

and rats like shadows fattened for the market moving cunningly and liquourishly among them, limbs and bowels nesting in the hedges and over all the most supernaturally shocking scent of death and corruption that ever breathed o'er Eden'. He thought the horror of it might 'almost be held to prove the existence of God. Who else', he asked, 'could have thought of it?'[40]

Then the Australians moved into the battle. Haig has decided to use the Australian soldiers to capture the village of Pozières to give the 4th British Army a chance to push eastwards and punch a hole in the German line. To prepare the way for the Australians, British artillery softened up the German lines. On the night of 19 July the Australian First Division marched past the part-ruined cathedral at Albert where a golden statue of the Virgin swayed precariously from the steeple. On 23 July two of the Australian divisions began the attack to capture Pozières. Later that day they had captured the village, where they behaved as Australians always did after an ordeal: they smoked cigars, wore German helmets, and carried on as though they were men of the people satirizing their elders and their betters—a situation which always gave Australians great satisfaction. The real agony was about to begin.

By mid-August around Pozières and the British sector of the Somme the road and the trenches were strewn with the dead. The shrapnel left human bodies 'mere lumps of flesh'. A lieutenant cried like a little child. Some struggled and called out for their mothers, while others blabbered sentences no one could make out. The moans of the wounded and the dying were heard above the din of battle. One Australian soldier wrote to his parents: 'Don't forget to pray for me, as it's absolute hell here. Anyhow I have had the honour of being in the biggest battle in history. I expect to get a decoration out of it'. The soldiers had moved into a 'perfect Hell'. The men from the bush were blown into smithereens. Henry Farmer had roamed the bush in east Gippsland shooting wallabies and possums for skins, fossicking for gold, and snigging logs out of the forest. When he volunteered he decided not to let the banks have his money while he was away. He buried his gold sovereigns under a tree, and, cunning old bugger that he was proud to be known to be, he decided to tell no one where it was. He was killed in the capture of Pozières. No one found his sovereigns. William E. Perry, teacher in the school at Combienbar, where Henry Farmer had worked, was much loved despite his frequent use of the strap, especially on days after lights had been seen in the bar at the local hotel. No trace of him remained after Pozières. On his gravestone the words were cut: 'Known Unto God'.

[40] R. H. Tawney, *The Attack and Other Papers* (London, 1953), pp. 11–20; Raymond Asquith to Diana Manners, 23 June 1916, quoted in Jeanne Mackenzie, *The Children of the Souls* (London, 1986), p. 233.

'The men', C. E. W. Bean wrote in his diary,

> are simply turned in there as into some ghastly giant mincing machine. The[y] have to stay there while shell after shell descends with a shriek close beside them—each one an acute mental torture—each shrieking tearing crash bringing a promise to each man—instantaneous—I will tear you into ghastly wounds—I will rend your flesh and pulp an arm or a leg—fling you half a gaping, quivering man like others that you see smashed around you, one by one, to lie there rottening and blackening'.

During several days of heavy bombardment the

> ground rocked and swayed backwards and forwards . . . Like a well-built haystack swaying . . . men were driven stark staring mad & more than one of them rushed out over the trench towards the Germans, any amount of them could be seen crying and sobbing like children their nerves completely gone . . . we were nearly all in a state of silliness & half dazed, but still the Australians refused to give ground'.

Dear, kind Charlie Bean could not understand why a benevolent God would permit such things to happen. But, as he thought later, perhaps it was not for human beings to scan the mind of God: '*Non nobis Domine*'. It was not for us to say.[41]

By the time the Australians were withdrawn from Pozières on 5 September and replaced by the Canadians there were 22 826 Australian casualties. The survivors never forgot the experience. For them the illusions of heroism and sacrifice and all the ideals of warfare were shattered. The 'bloody British top brass' had done it again, just as the same inhuman bastards had done it to their cobbers at The Nek and Lone Pine on the Gallipoli peninsula. After the fighting died down observers walked over the battlefield. The English poet, John Masefield, was one of them. Masefield wanted to believe humanity was moving from the darkness into the light. Impatient with all religious doctrines, he still had a shy faith in what he called 'the Everlasting Mercy'. Masefield was a great lover, a great enlarger of life. For him his wife was his 'dearest heart' and he to her 'your old lover'. He believed the war was working out now luckily for the British after the nightmare of the first German advance on Ypres. He had the 'general feeling', as he put it, 'that Tolstoi was right, in war & peace & that no man can conduct either a war or a battle, but that Providence works through a sort of blind-

[41] *Labor Call*, 1 June 1916; *Bulletin*, 13, 20 July 1916; G. R. Dyce, *Combienbar* (Bairnsdale, 1982), pp. 25–6, 48; *S.M.H.*, 2 August 1916; *West Australian*, 2 August 1916; Diary of C. E. W. Bean, 5 August 1916, A.W.M.; Bill Gammage, *The Broken Years* (Canberra, 1974), pp. 162–9; Diary of J. Bourke, 19, 30 July 1916; W. G. Boys to Father and family, 2 August 1916, and Diary of R. A. McInnis, 19 July 1916, A.W.M., Canberra; Janet Morice, *Six Bob-a-Day Tourist* (Ringwood, 1985), p. 64.

ness and welter to a kind of justice'. But what he saw of what human beings had done to those lovely plains and quaint villages on the Somme and at Pozières and to each other shook him. Later he told his wife men had turned the landscape into 'such a hell of desolation all round as no words can describe'. 'Can you imagine', he asked his 'dear heart', 'a landscape in the moon, made of filth instead of beauty?'[42]

There was also the human filth.

> There was a cat eating a man's brain, & such a wreck of war as I never did see, & the wounded coming by, dripping blood on the track, & one walked on blood or rotten flesh, & saw bags of men being carried to the grave. They were shovelling parts of men into blankets.

He had seen in a hospital the men suffering from burns.

> There were people with the tops of their heads burnt off & stinking like frizzled meat, & the top all red and dripping with pus, & their faces all gone, & their arms just covered with a kind of gauntlet of raw meat, & perhaps their whole bodies, from their knees to their shoulders, without any semblance of skin.

But despite all these horrors the gentle, kind-hearted John Masefield believed the British should continue to fight until victory was attained. Theirs was a righteous cause—they were working with Providence towards 'a kind of justice'.

One man whose soul was not troubled was the G.S.O.1 of the Australian First Division, Thomas Blamey. Before the assault on Pozières Blamey asked God for one thing: 'God grant me', he asked, 'a clear brain to plan and think for it'. Blamey was a Byronic figure nurtured in a Methodist family. He was born at Lake Albert near Wagga on 24 January 1884. He became a pupil teacher and then a professional soldier. During military service at Quetta he shed the habits of the Methodist, and took on the life of a soldier. The martinet of the schoolroom became the martinet of the parade ground. He read widely. Kipling's 'If' was his creed for what a man should be. He had a contempt for those who cracked under pressure, and for those who broke down under attack. Under him he believed were 'the finest fighting men in all the world'. He would train them in 'military virtue'. There must be no weakness. The seven thousand Australians killed at Pozières must not die in vain. Their brothers must fight on. Theirs was a noble cause. This was no time for the men with tender consciences, or those troubled by what human beings had done to each other at Verdun and the Somme. The world belongs to the brave. In politics the men for the times were those with the toughness

[42] John Masefield to Constance Masefield, 16 October 1916. Peter Vansittart (ed.), op. cit., p. 187; John Masefield to Constance Masefield, 6 March 1917, ibid., p. 206.

of a Billy Hughes, and in the army those with the qualities of a Tom Blamey or a John Monash.[43]

Bob Menzies agreed. The British and the Australians, he believed, were displaying 'valour for the right'. While some Australian soldiers sobbed and cried like children in the Pozières blood-bath, Bob Menzies wrote an article for the *Melbourne University Magazine*. His subject was: 'What Are We Fighting For?' With all the certainty he always displayed when answering the big questions in life he told his readers that 'in all the spiritual forces which alone can bring about a lasting peace, Great Britain has been, and is, superior to her enemies'. The British flag was the 'glowing emblem of liberty and hatred of all tyranny and oppression'. The British were the upholders of 'right against might'. He added some months later: 'We are a mighty host fighting beneath the banners of truth and justice and honour, and all that counts for much in the world's future. Their [i.e. of the British, the Australians and the other Dominions] armour is shining and their shields are white'.[44]

That was also the faith of Billy Hughes. On 31 July, as the earth swayed and rocked at Pozières, Hughes spoke to the people at Fremantle, on his return to Australia, of the Empire's great task. He believed in his destiny: he would work a great marvel. The Americans have just called him 'Australia's Abraham Lincoln'. He told the people of Fremantle that the peoples of the British race scattered wide over the earth held essentially the same ideals wherever they were settled. They were 'animated by the same resolute determination to uphold them, come what may'. The crowd cheered. Hughes believed the people were behind him. In France he has sealed an everlasting bond with the diggers: now he was forging a bond with the Australian people. Like 'Birdie' in France he believed in the courage and endurance of Australians, their strength to endure to the end. The Australian people could descend into Hell and rise again. The war was their salvation. The Australian people, he believed, would overcome the storm and stress of this dreadful war. But stories have got back to Australia about what had happened at Pozières. Country people have heard of how their mates were blown to pieces. Men they had known all their lives were no more. Wives and mothers were afraid of a knock on the door from the clergyman or the priest bringing news of the death of their loved ones. Patriots wanted the war to go on. But the number of the doubters has increased. They were not so vocal. They feared being hounded as disloyal. Hughes was returning to a divided Australia.[45]

[43] John Masefield to Constance Masefield, 22 October, 12 October 1916, ibid., pp. 194, 180; John Hetherington, *Blamey: Controversial Soldier* (Canberra, 1973), pp. 39–40.

[44] R.G.M. (R. G. Menzies) 'What Are We Fighting For?' *Melbourne University Magazine*, October 1916, pp. 73–5; R.G.M., 'Jingoes and Junkers', MS. in Esmonde Higgins Papers, M.L.

[45] *S.M.H.*, 1 August 1916; *West Australian*, 1 August 1916; *Western Champion* (Barcaldine), 5 August 1916; Bill Gammage, *Narrandera Shire* (Narrandera, 1986) pp. 199–201.

All the way from Fremantle to the east he received a hero's welcome. Crowds gathered to see him. Men tried to shake his hand: women threw him kisses and hugged him. Billy Hughes was on a crusade to 'destroy the beast let loose by the barbarian' in Europe. In Adelaide he received the warmest of welcomes. He repeated to them that the Empire would fight on 'with all our soul and strength, no matter what the sacrifice or what the cost'. He loved the roars of approval. While he was speaking of not 'sheathing the sword' the bodies of Australians were being thrown into a 'giant mincing machine', and cats were eating men's brains.[46]

In Melbourne he was received at the Town Hall with cheering which lasted for several minutes. He told the overflow audience the war was Australia's war as much as it was France's or Russia's or Britain's. Australians were fighting for their very existence. Remoteness would not save Australia. Again the audience clapped and cheered, and Billy Hughes had that warm glow of the man who was putting into words what Australians wanted to hear. He was the prophet of the Australian people, the new Moses leading Australians out of the deserts of flabbiness and decadence.[47]

The passions of war have tickled the inhabitants of the Australian suburbs at times into a drunken frenzy. The human imagination soon found bizarre justifications for what was going on in Europe. Mr Deakin was unable to 'comprehend the situation'. Life for him was now a 'chatter & mere play upon barren & idle sounds'. Yet like John Masefield and Lev Tolstoi he wanted to believe there was a God who 'rides above the storm'. Henry Lawson hoped the war would enable drunkards to win forgiveness. He wondered whether if his body were blown to pieces in Belgium or France the sacrifice would bring the prize of redemption, and give him what he had found so elusive—'the Bill Wiped Out'.[48]

The war has had a bizarre effect on the Australian political scene. An Australian Labor leader has become the darling of British royalty and the nobility. On his return to Australia the traditional enemies of Labor praised and flattered him. For the first time in the history of the Australian Labor movement the platform of a Labor leader was crowded, not with his political colleagues and his mates in the Labor Party, but with the 'very best', the 'cream of society', leaders in the world of commerce, manufacturing, transportation and finance. The capitalist press lavishly praised the speeches of an Australian Labor leader. Prominent Liberals now threw their arms around a Labor leader and kissed him, hugged him, and told him he was the most lovable man they had ever known. The *Worker* in Sydney and the *Labor Call* in

[46] *S.M.H.*, 7 August 1916.

[47] Ibid., 8 August 1916; *Age*, 9 August 1916; *Argus*, 9 August 1916.

[48] Diary of A. Deakin, 11, 18 December 1916, Deakin Papers, MS. 1540, Deakin Papers, N.L.A.; Henry Lawson, 'Lawson's Dream', *Bulletin*, 26 August 1915.

Melbourne suspected the Liberals were after a coalition government. The Liberals wanted Hughes to commit himself to conscription, and so precipitate a split in the Labor Party. W. H. Irvine, a Victorian conservative, has already said he would love to be one of Billy Hughes's 'most loyal and devoted followers'. The Labor press was doing what the capitalist press traditionally did. They were criticizing a Labor leader. William Morris Hughes, the *Labor Call* said, should 'scratch his head and look serious, and work out for himself why these fat sirens of Boodle were waddling after a Labor Prime Minister'. They wondered whether there was anything left in the old William; whether he realized the Liberals were just playing on his vanity, and that the sirens of capitalism were luring him to his destruction.[49]

Hughes was not dismayed. His mind was made up. Winning the war must take priority over the platform of the Australian Labor Party. The secretary of State for War in England has announced what Great Britain expected Australia to do: Australia must do it. Victory must be won no matter what the price in human suffering. The only question was: could Australia do what the British wanted by the voluntary system or must they introduce conscription, and if so, how? Billy Hughes was about to become the 'greatest prize the capitalist class' had ever drawn out of a political lottery.[50]

The Trades and Labor Council of Victoria passed resolutions against conscription and the Australian Workers' Union condemned it. Those inspired idealists who were the conscience of the Labor movement were already warning Australians Hughes wanted to create a militarist state, complete with a 'clanging sabre'. That was not the ideal of the Australian Labor movement. Labor had a soul. Labor had an ideal. Labor wanted 'to build up an ideal civilisation under the Southern Cross'. That could not be done by war: that could be done only by peace.[51]

Hughes dismissed all that as the 'vapourings' of men with their heads in the clouds. As he saw it, the brave men who had fallen at Pozières must be replaced. The horrors, the desolation and the cost in human lives in the Somme battle have not persuaded Haig and Joffre to abandon the strategy of the 'big push'. They have decided more men were needed. The faithful comrade of Billy Hughes, George Pearce, one of the few who called Hughes 'My dear Will', has told him the voluntary system was not providing the numbers the Empire needed for victory. The number of volunteers has declined from 22 101 in January 1916 to 6170 in July. Hughes has always been an Empire man, an Australian-Briton rather than an Australian. Hughes has always emphasized survival rather than what he called the

[49] *Australian Worker*, 10, 17 August 1916; *Labor Call*, 10, 17 August 1916.
[50] *Labor Call*, 17 August 1916.
[51] Ibid., 10 August 1916; *Ross's Monthly*, 19 August 1916, p. 3.

'empty vapourings' of some persons in the Labor movement. The Labor press wrote of him as though he were a leopard who had changed his spots under the influence of the flattery from the dukes and noble lords of the Old Country. But Hughes has not changed his spots. He was no coward soul. He was not afraid of any terror by day. He knew it had been said of old in the Wisdom of Solomon: '. . . for a sharp judgement shall be to them that be in high places. For mercy will soon pardon the meanest: but mighty men shall be mightily tormented . . . a sore trial shall come upon the mighty'. He was no conscience-stricken Hamlet of the Australian suburbs. He believed in his destiny: he believed the world belonged to the brave.[52]

Cables from the Army Council in London informed him of the numbers required. On 23 August 'Birdie' cabled the Australian Defence Department for reinforcements. On 24 August the Secretary of State for the Colonies, on advice from the Army Council, cabled for reinforcements owing to heavy casualties suffered by the Australian troops in France. The British were putting the pressure on. Hughes met Caucus on 24 August at a welcome home meeting. The following day he met Cabinet and showed them the cable asking for more men. Hughes suggested conscription. A furious argument ensued. Hughes wheedled and cajoled: pleading the desperation of the hour, with the French threatening to pull out, the Russians rocked by internal convulsions, the possibility of social revolution, and the plans of the Industrial Workers of the World, the Sinn Feiners and other traitors exploiting the situation. Cabinet must act. Cabinet would not accept out-and-out conscription. Hughes came up with a compromise: Government would apply compulsion only to fill any deficit in the numbers suggested by the Army Council in London. There would be exemptions. No one under twenty-one would be called up. Cabinet agreed by a majority of one on 26 August. Then it was the turn of Caucus. At 2 a.m. on Tuesday 29 August they accepted the Government's compromise proposal by a majority of one.[53]

Next day on 30 August Hughes announced the Government's proposals to the House of Representatives. The Government, he said, had arrived at the conclusion that the voluntary system could not be relied upon to supply the steady stream of reinforcements necessary to maintain the Australian Expeditionary Forces at their full strength. Believing that the people agreed with the Government that those numbers must be kept up, the Government had formulated a policy to meet the gravity of the circumstances, proposals

[52] *Wisdom of Solomon*, VI, 5–8. *The Books Called Apocrypha* (Oxford University Press edn; L. F. Fitzhardinge, op. cit., pp. 171–85.

[53] L. F. Fitzhardinge, op. cit., pp. 185–7; Cablegram of General Birdwood to Defence Department, 23 August 1916, and cablegram of Secretary of State for Colonies to the Australian Government, 24 August 1916, copy in Hughes Papers, Series 20, Folder 1, Items 31–2; R. M. Ferguson to Bonar Law, 25 July 1916, Novar Papers, MS. 696, Item 878.

compatible with the system of democratic government under which it was their privilege to live. On 28 October the Government would hold a referendum. He still hoped it would not be necessary for the Government to proclaim compulsion. They were passing through the greatest crisis in their history: 'Our national existence, our liberties, are at stake'. He hoped the patriotism of Australian youth would make the proclamation unnecessary. He believed the people were behind him. Willie Watt, the boy from Phillip Island, warned him the Government was precipitating one of the bitterest struggles in the history of Australia. But Hughes only said: 'Well then, so be it'. There was a fatalist in Hughes, a man who believed that Fate rather than human endeavour was the deciding factor in human affairs.[54]

On 13 September Hughes introduced the second reading of the Military Service Referendum Bill to the House of Representatives. This contained the words of the question to be submitted to the electors on 28 October:

> Are you in favour of the Government having, in this grave emergency, the same compulsory powers over citizens in regard to requiring their military service, for the term of this war, outside the Commonwealth as it now has in regard to military service within the Commonwealth?

That day Frank Tudor resigned from the Government. The opponents of the proposal within the Labor Party came into the open. Frank Brennan predicted the Hughes Government would crumble. The Liberals voted with Hughes and some Labor members behind him. The outlines of a regrouping of parties have been drawn. Conscription was showing the shape of things to come.[55]

It was clear there was not going to be a debate on the Government's proposals: there was going to be just over eight weeks of hysteria. On 6 September Dr Alexander Leeper, graduate of Trinity College, Dublin, fine flower of the Protestant ascendancy in Ireland, now warden of Trinity College in the University of Melbourne, moved in the Anglican Synod in Melbourne: 'That this Synod is so convinced that the forces of the Allies are being used by God to vindicate the rights of the weak and to maintain the moral order of the world that it gives its strong support to the principle of universal service . . .' Archdeacon Hindley seconded the motion which was carried without discussion. The National Anthem was then sung.[56]

On 16 September Daniel Mannix replied to Dr Leeper and other Protestant conscriptionists. He said, of course he wanted an honourable peace,

[54] *C'wealth P.D.*, 30 August 1916, vol. LXXIX, pp. 8402–3.

[55] Ibid., 13 September 1916, vol. LXXIX, pp. 8485–90; An Act to submit to a Referendum a question in relation to Military Service Abroad. No. 27 of 1916, *C'wealth Acts*, vol. XIV, pp. 44–9; L. F. Fitzhardinge, op. cit., pp. 190–2; *Stanley Herald*, 13, 20 July, 2 August 1916.

[56] *Age*, 8 September 1916.

but he believed that peace could be secured without conscription in Australia. Conscription was a hateful thing and always brought evil in its train. The crowd sang 'God Save Ireland'. Three days later the Archbishop launched an appeal for the relief of the victims of the Easter Rising in Ireland. Some Protestants accused the Archbishop of treason. The cry went up: deport him, throw the traitor out of the country. The sectarian issue has tickled to madness some sections of the Australian population. Conscription has revived the old hatreds and the old suspicions.

Mannix came to Melbourne in 1912 from the post of President of the Catholic Seminary at Maynooth to take up his position in Melbourne. He was too massive a man to be captured in a simple generalization by a scribbler. Mannix was many things, and he spoke with many voices. He was the mystic who saw in the face of the Irish peasant the image of Christ. He was the Irish patriot nursing a grudge against those guilty of that ancient wrong against the Irish people. He was the priest who believed he had a divine mission to save all souls from damnation in his care. He was the Jansenist who feared that the lusts of the flesh would condemn a human being to Hell for all eternity. Like Christ, he was more at ease with publicans and sinners than with the Pharisees who thanked their God they were not as other men. Many who met him adored him. The man had something more than immense charm. He had the power to move people to bow down and worship him. He said memorable things, using words and phrases which lived on because he spoke about things that mattered, and things that moved the human heart. He said simple things to simple people. For him any reflection on his people, any slur on their honour and their reputation was like the sin against the Holy Ghost—something which would never be forgiven. In Catholic countries legend had it that when a person committed mortal sin a shadow fell across the face of the Virgin. For Daniel Mannix any slur on his faith or on his own people by the eternal enemies of the Irish caused a shadow to pass over his face. He spoke as one possessed: he spoke from the heart: in such moments he was the spell-binder, the speaker who aroused in his audience some of the righteous anger in his own breast. Protestants have goaded a Catholic Archbishop to enter the ring for the conscription fight. 'I notice', he said in this first statement on conscription, 'that certain authorities in the Anglican Church have given their public support to conscription'. The dog-fight was on. A man out of sympathy with the temper of his age, a man who believed God alone could save human beings from all their folly, became for a brief moment an ally of the future of humanity men.[57]

[57] *Argus*, 18, 19 September 1916; B. A. Santamaria, *Daniel Mannix* (Melbourne, 1984), pp. 74–9; Michael Gilchrist, *Daniel Mannix: priest and patriot* (Blackburn, 1982); interview with Dr Mannix, January 1958; *Advocate*, 16 September 1916.

To the members of the circle close to Herbert Brookes, the men in the heartland of 'Yarraside', Mannix was 'the Rasputin of Australia', the man whose treasonable speeches were preparing Australia for social revolution. Hughes agreed. He opened the 'Yes' campaign in the Sydney Town Hall on 18 September by reminding Australians they were only free as long as Australia remained part and parcel of the British Empire and Britain was unconquered. There was loud and prolonged cheering for that. A Labor Prime Minister was preaching to Australians about their duty to the British Empire. He told them this was no time for party strife. The nation was in peril. 'Let us rise like men, gird up our loins, and do that which honour, duty, and self-interest alike dictate'. W. A. Holman, the Labor Premier of New South Wales, suggested a national committee under the Presidency of the Premier (a Labor man) and the leader of the Opposition (a Liberal) should be formed. Hughes and Holman were moving towards what Irvine has been working on behind the scenes: the formation of a national government.[58]

Hughes and Holman were fighting for their political lives. On 15 September the central executive of the Political Labor Leagues of New South Wales carried a motion expelling W. M. Hughes, the Prime Minister, from the Labor movement. They also withdrew the endorsement of W. A. Holman, Premier of New South Wales for the next State election. They reaffirmed the resolution of the 1916 State Conference of the Political Labor Leagues to oppose by all means conscription of human life for military service abroad, to oppose all Labor members who voted for or otherwise supported conscription, to oppose the endorsement of any conscription candidates. They instructed the Leagues and the Federal Executive to oppose at all costs the policy of conscription.[59]

Hughes took up the fight with a fiendish pleasure. He hissed and spat at his opponents like a cat defending its own territory against an intruder. He behaved like a man possessed by a demon. He behaved like a man who believed he had a divine mission to grind his enemies into the dust. He has told the Australian people many times that the war was being waged to preserve their liberties, those liberties they had inherited from the British. Convinced his proposals were essential for victory, his Government has prosecuted men and women for making speeches or publishing material prejudicial to recruiting. The Prime Minister of the 'freest country in the world' suppressed the issues of the *Socialist* which had printed the Manifesto on Conscription by the Interstate Trade Union Congress. His opponents promptly seized on this as evidence for their argument: conscription would endanger the liberties of the people.

[58] *S.M.H.*, 19 September 1916.
[59] Ibid., 16 September 1916.

Hughes also believed he was fighting for the liberties of the people. On the day after the executive of the Political Labor Leagues of New South Wales expelled him from the Labor Party he told the women of Australia this was the 'freest, the best country in the world, a country worth fighting and, if needs be, dying for'. He urged the women of Australia to guard the liberties and privileges which they and their husbands and their fathers enjoyed. He urged them not to vote in the forthcoming referendum for men who shut the mouths of all those who dared to differ from them. He issued a Manifesto to the Women of Australia:

> Women of Australia, mothers, wives, sisters of free men, what is your answer to the boys at the front? Are you going to leave them to die? What is your answer to Britain, to whom we owe so much; to France, to Belgium? Are you going to cover with shame and dishonour the country for which our soldiers are fighting and dying?
> Now is your hour of trial and opportunity. Will you be the proud mothers of a nation of heroes, or stand dishonoured as the mothers of a race of degenerates?
> Prove that you are worthy to be the mothers and wives of free men.[60]

Hughes saw himself as a moral man: Hughes believed conscription was right, and righteousness was on his side. His opponents did not agree. They saw him not as a man who had made an honest mistake, a man with whom they had an honest disagreement, but as a man guilty of a 'great betrayal'. Hughes has become the tool of the plutocracy. Hughes has forced Labor to engage in 'a disheartening struggle . . . against the powerful forces of the Plutocracy'. Hughes was just another 'scurvy politician', a man who seemed to see things others did not. Labor had three reasons against compulsion. First, compulsion was advocated and engineered by the people's enemy, the metropolitan money-press. Second, compulsion was anti-British. Freedom was the breath of a man or woman with British nostrils: without freedom any people born in a British society were 'but slaves and hirelings'. Third, a few thousand Australian conscripts could not possibly affect the situation one iota.[61]

By then the rowdies on both sides changed the terms of the debate before the Australian people. In the country districts Shire Councils have passed resolutions in favour of conscription. Local papers supported conscription. The bush was the cradle of the bush culture, and the virtues of courage, resource, initiative and compassion which conferred a mantle of glory on the

[60] *Socialist*, 4 August 1916; *Labor Call*, 17 August 1916; Lloyd Ross, *John Curtin* (Melbourne, 1977), pp. 50–1; Manifesto From W. M. Hughes, Prime Minister, to the Women of Australia, 15 September 1916, Collection of War Pamphlets and Posters, N.L.A.

[61] *Worker* (Brisbane), 7, 21 September 1916.

Digger. It took courage to stand up to the tyranny of opinion in the country. Opponents of conscription were tarred and feathered. By contrast in Catholic districts such as Koroit in Victoria and Yass in New South Wales boys and girls whose parents supported conscription were tormented by the other schoolchildren. At public meetings soldiers intimidated the anti-conscriptionists. A war of pamphlets and posters broke out. John Curtin, secretary of the Anti-Conscription League, authorized a poster telling the women of Australia a vote for 'Yes' was 'The Blood Vote':

> "Why is your face so white, Mother?
> Why do you choke for breath?"
> "Oh I have dreamt in the night, my son,
> That I doomed a man to death."

The Universal Service League countered with 'A Mother's Lament':

> . . . .
> Should this fair land be blighted,
> Should Australia meet her doom—
> Befouled, outraged, like Belgium
> In the shadow, in the gloom?
> Through all the years before me,
> As in solemn file they go,
> Burnt in my brain will be the stain:
> My God! I voted 'No'.

Within the Protestant community some clergymen besought their flocks not to 'shelter curs' when they strode up to the ballot box. Some clergy were confident that if Christ were to appear in the 'wide brown land' he would favour conscription. Other parsons said Christ would have been 'exceedingly sorrowful' with the 'boosters of bash and blood', these men in clerical garb who were 'dragging unwilling sacrifices to the altar of the Moloch of War'. At Sea Lake the poet Shaw Neilson found he could not forget the hypocrisy of one clergyman. 'I can remember', he wrote later in his *Autobiography*, 'one man, a young clergyman about twenty-five, splendidly-made fellow over six foot high and as sound as a bell. He went round advising every young fellow to go to the war yet he never volunteered himself not even as a chaplain'. Some Protestant ministers warned their fellow Christians that a new religion was being built on the ruins of the Christianity the war was trampling underfoot. This new religion was the religion of the State. Christians should acknowledge the incompatibility between conscription and their religious beliefs by voting 'No'. Within the Catholic Church there was also division. Dr Mannix thought Australians had already done enough, and that conscription was a 'hateful thing' which was 'certain to bring evil in its train'. Archbishop Kelly in Sydney thought conscription would aid the British in their fight for right against might. Families were divided, churches were divided, parties were divided; friends of a lifetime found they were on opposite sides.[62]

On 22 September rumours were current in Fremantle that Hughes had arranged to import one thousand Maltese labourers. Maltese labourers were being permitted to work in Australia in 'decent men's billets' at this period of the Empire's history. The *Worker* in Brisbane asked: 'What's afoot?' The darkest fears of the Labor men were being confirmed. Cheap Maltese labour was replacing conscripts. This was what conscription meant. Here was the proof that Hughes was a tool of Mr Money Bags who was plotting to destroy White Australia as a prelude to lowering the working-class standard of living, and defanging the Australian trade unions. Panic and hysteria swept through sections of the Labor movement. Rallies were held in the Sydney Domain and on the Yarra Bank in Melbourne. The wits of Labor mocked Hughes as William 'Maltese' Hughes. Labor organizations resolved to rid themselves of all traitors. The drive against Hughes was intensified. In the electorate of West Sydney the branches of the Political Labor Leagues endorsed the action of the executive of the New South Wales Political Labor League in expelling Hughes from the Party. On 21 September the Melbourne wharf labourers moved to remove Hughes from the office of President of the Waterside Workers' Federation. On 27 September the Sydney Wharf Laborers' Union expelled Hughes. On 3 October the Trolly and Drayman's Union expelled him. Hughes was stripped of his power in the political and industrial wings of the Labor movement. Labor has treated the Prime Minister of Australia as the diggers on the goldfields ministered justice to offenders against their code. He had been banished into the deserts to feed off locusts and wild honey: the men and women of the Labor movement would know him no more.[63]

The Labor press portrayed the supporters of conscription as moral cripples, men and women who were no longer worthy in the sight of the politically virtuous. The conscriptionist was a traitor, a defiler, and a man who 'scabs on his mates'. By voting for conscription, the Brisbane *Worker* wrote on 28 September:

[62] War Pamphlets and Posters, N.L.A.; *Labor Call*, 2 November 1916; Don Garden, *Hamilton: A Western District History* (Hamilton, 1984), pp. 187–8; personal conversations with Ian Fitchett, a pupil at the Terang School in 1916; *Advocate*, 23 September 1916; *The Autobiography of John Shaw Neilson* (Canberra, 1978), p. 92.

[63] *Worker* (Brisbane), 28 September 1916; *Australian Worker*, 21, 28 September, 26 October 1916.

The mother enslaves her son,
The son betrays his brother.
The wife forsakes her husband.
The father defiles his children.
The politician betrays his trust.
The parson scorns his God.
The unionist scabs on his mate.
The employer robs his country.

The *Mirror* in Sydney portrayed the anti-conscriptionists as purveyors of 'false slanders and gross misrepresentation'. 'Think of the Australians in France', it wrote on 23 September, 'Shall we leave them unsupported whilst shirkers crowd the Racecourses and the Stadium?'[64]

Hughes fed the rumour mongers. In this atmosphere of suspicion and hysteria he issued a proclamation on 29 September calling on all men between the ages of twenty-one and thirty-five to render continuous military service within the limits of the Commonwealth and any Territory forming part of the Commonwealth during the continuance of the present war. Hughes was endangering the liberties, the standard of living, and the lives of Australians. A monster rally was held at the Guild Hall in Melbourne on the following Sunday night. The audience sang the 'Red Flag' with all the fervour with which people once sang 'A safe stronghold our God is still'. Jack Curtin roused audiences in Melbourne to fever pitch with his denunciations of the evils of militarism, speaking like one of the prophets of old denouncing the worshippers of the golden calf. On 1 October in the Gaiety Theatre Frank Anstey accused Hughes of bringing in 'slavery, misery and degradation'. Hughes, he said, was robbing Australia of its white blood and leaving it open to the coloured workers of the world. England wanted to fill Australia with coloured labour: that was why England wanted the white workers in the country on the battlefields of France. England wanted Australia to be for ever the servant of English capitalism.[65]

The trade unions declared 4 October a stop-work day to protest against conscription. Hughes ordered all government servants absent from work on that day to be prosecuted. The anti-conscriptionists repeated that Billy Hughes was plotting to destroy the liberties of the working class. For being absent from work on 4 October a worker in the Melbourne tramways was sacked. Australians must wake up. The fatal grip of militarism was fastening

[64] *Worker* (Brisbane), 28 September 1916.

[65] *C'wealth Gazette*, 29 September 1916; *Argus*, 30 September 1916; *Socialist*, 29 September, 6 October 1916; *Age*; 3 October 1916; *Mirror* (Sydney), 23 September 1916; Michael McKernan, *The Australian People and the Great War* (Melbourne, 1980), pp. 170–2.

on their throats. The people were fighting for their manhood, and their lives. To keep Australia free the answer on 28 October must be 'No'.[66]

Hughes accused the anti-conscriptionists of being the tools of the Sinn Feiners and the Industrial Workers of the World. To prove his point on 10 October twelve members of the I.W.W. organization were charged at the Central Police Court in Sydney with organizing rebellion against the King, conspiring to burn down buildings and shops in Sydney, and attempting to intimidate or overawe Parliament. The press stressed that all of the twelve save one were not Australians, and some were associates of a notorious German who had escaped from an internment camp. One of them, Donald Grant, had said on 2 April that he was a rebel, and knew no King, and sabotage was the only effective weapon by which the workers could combat the master class. The magistrate committed them for trial in the Supreme Court. Dr Mannix has said Australia had done enough. No man could say he had done enough when his wife and children were in danger. The anti-conscriptionists talked of peace, but the only peace Billy Hughes would accept was a peace which destroyed absolutely the military power of Germany and reduced her to impotence. Beware of the I.W.W! They planned to set Sydney alight in preparation for a social revolution. The conscriptionists had a noble ideal: 'Your King and country need you'. The anti-conscriptionists only had the petty cry: 'Your wives, your mothers and your children demand you'.[67]

All through the second half of October the supporters of both sides held their last rallies. Hughes prepared to issue his final appeal. Waverers, previously not prepared to take sides, declared themselves. In Western Australia John Scaddan, the ex-Labor Premier, said he would sign the final appeal by W. M. Hughes. Labor had another 'rat' to treat with 'undying hostility'. On 17 October the Anglican Synod in Sydney carried a resolution saying that inasmuch as the liberty of Australia and of the world was at stake, and without liberty all spiritual progress was gravely imperilled every man was bound in honour to place his services at the disposal of his country. On 20 October Hughes again accused his opponents of working with the I.W.W. who believed in murder for political purposes. He asked the Australian people to prove on 28 October they wanted to be their own masters and not slaves.[68].

On 24 September Adela Pankhurst presented the mission of the Australian people. The time had come, she said, when Australia and other countries must protect themselves against not only Militarism but also Capi-

[66] *Socialist*, 22, 29 September, 6 October 1916.
[67] *Age*, 13 October 1916.
[68] Ibid., 18, 21 October 1916.

talism. Australians must unite with the other peoples of the world to establish a social system in which goods would be produced for use and not for profit. The time had come to form a new political party in Australia which would embody those ideals and secure the people's full and free internal and external development. The people must answer Hughes, the imperial conscriptionist, with a demand for the complete independence and neutrality of Australia. Out of the struggle against conscription an Australian nation would be born. Australia must not remain 'a docile and unquestioning part of a military Empire'. Australia must belong to the Australians. The huge audience rocked and roared. At the final rally held by the anti-conscriptionists at the Guild Hall in Melbourne on the night of 22 October Frank Hyett repeated these sentiments. The overflow audience sang the 'Red Flag' and the 'Internationale'. Socialist hymns were sung. The hymn singing induced in those present the mood of a religious revival. A new vision of Australia was being born during all the sound and fury.[69]

The vote at the referendum on 28 October was to be the beginning of a legend about Australia. By 30 October it was clear there would be a majority against conscription. By 11 December the figures were: Yes: 1 087 332; No: 1 151 881—a 64 549 majority for No. The anti-conscriptionists hailed the results as the beginning of a new era in the history of Australia. On 3 November the *Socialist* wrote of the 'glory of the uprising of the people': 28 October, it said, has shaped Australia for centuries to come: Australian democracy has been saved. Now the people must kick out Hughes. There must be an election, and a people's government must be formed. The *Labor Call* said Hughes had cut himself off from his party: he had slobbered with Cook: he let himself be refrigerated by Irvine: he became the god of the *Argus* and the high-priests of all the tea-cup leagues and women's perversions. Hughes was left 'sans party, sans office, sans credit, sans everything'. Hughes must go. Blathering Billy must be thrown out. The people must form their own government. On 19 November Jack Curtin preached the message of salvation. Men, Rousseau had said, were born free, but everywhere they were in chains. The people of Australia have now loosed their chains. Now they must abolish class rule: they must begin a social revolution to end class domination. One week later, on 26 November, at the Guild Hall Frank Anstey called on Australians to believe no more in loyalty to King and Empire, to stop being the servants of British capitalism. Australians must choose their own flag: Australians must fly a rebel flag, and sing a rebel chorus. The slogan of the people must be: Australia First! Advance Australia![70]

[69] *Socialist*, 22 October 1916.

[70] Ibid., 3, 10 November 1916; *Labor Call*, 2 November 1916; 'The First Conscription Referendum, October 1916', *Round Table*, March 1917, pp. 378–96; *Freeman's Journal*, 2 November 1916.

The conscription debate has shown there were two Australias. There was the Australia of the respectable elements in the community, all those who paid lip-service to '*comme il faut*' behaviour. They came from the leaders of the Protestant churches, all the professors in the universities except for a few Bohemians and mavericks, the editors of the capitalist press, the owners of the means of production, the squatters, and all the members of the 'comfortable classes' in Australia. They had their ethic: they had their slogan—Loyalty to King and Empire. They had their culture—British culture in Australia. They set up as their ideal the way of life and the values of the British middle classes. Australia would achieve nothing so long as her aim was to be an 'outlandish suburb of England or Europe'. There was another Australia, the Australia which now had an opportunity to develop a culture of its own, an Australia for which the victory of 28 October had provided the setting to proclaim their own independence. But no one has put into words what Australia's 'self-evident truths' would be, or what they would put on their flag, or what the words would be in their national anthem. There was a moment of hope.[71]

After the referendum Hughes mooched around the house in Kew, dressed in the clothes he always wore in his moods of despair. His opponents chanted: resign, resign, resign. Hughes believed he had a mission to save Australia from German tyranny and Japanese threats to White Australia. Hughes had one ray of light. In the interests of Australia he would offer the olive branch to his enemies: there would be an emotional reconciliation: they would embrace as brothers: the tears would flow: they would ask him to remain in office. At the Lord Mayor's banquet in Melbourne he flew this kite of reconciliation between all parties for the sake of Australia. Labor said another loud 'No'. Labor was not going to be 'diddled, damned and done for' by the Liberals. Hughes was told he and his clique had no right to remain in charge of Australian affairs. The people must kick Hughes out. The people have sensed their power on 28 October: let them use their power again for a political and social revolution.[72]

On 14 November sixty-four members of the Labor Party held a special meeting in Parliament House in Melbourne. W. F. Finlayson moved that Mr W. M. Hughes no longer possessed the confidence of this Party as leader. J. F. Hannan seconded the motion. After heated debate the meeting adjourned for lunch. When they assembled again Hughes made a statement, after which he left the chair asking those who agreed with him to follow him out of the room. Twenty-four followed him. The meeting then adjourned until 11 a.m. the following day. On that day the remnant elected Frank

[71] F. Sinclaire, 'The Two Australias', *Socialist*, 22 December 1916; and *Socialist*, 17, 14 November, 22 December 1916.

[72] *Socialist*, 17, 24 November 1916; *Labor Call*, 2, 9, 16 November 1916.

Tudor as their leader and Albert Gardiner as his deputy. Hughes was the Australian Coriolanus, the man with the courage to call his erstwhile supporters 'Ye common cry of curs'. Labor has paid an irreparable price for its stiff-necked adherence to principle and virtue. They have lost able men such as W. M. Hughes, J. C. Watson (the first Labor Prime Minister), W. A. Holman, the Labor Premier of New South Wales, W. G. Spence, the founder of the Australian Workers' Union, and G. F. Pearce, the efficient Minister for Defence. Labor has chosen mediocrities to replace a mighty spirit. The juntas of Labor have followed the Roman tradition and 'cut the heads off the tallest poppies'.[73]

The Labor press called on Labor to purify the movement of all its traitors, all backsliders, opportunists and temporizers. Labor must get rid of all those who worshipped 'Mammon in the synagogue of Fatmanry'. Labor must cleanse itself of all the mean-souled people who 'deserved a swipe on the head with a dead cat'. Labor must teach the people about this other Australia. Time was short. On the afternoon of 14 November Hughes had an interview with the Governor-General. On 14 November the Governor-General commissioned him to form a new government. Hughes called his followers the National Labor Party. The Liberals assured him they would sink differences and co-operate cordially. He could now grapple with problems unhampered by Caucus meetings. On 15 November he addressed a meeting in the Melbourne Town Hall. He explained to the people he had decided to retain the office of Prime Minister to win the war and to keep Australia white and British. Loyalty to King and Empire were, he believed, essential for the salvation of Australia. Hughes's political survival was tied more firmly to a British victory in the war. It was all 'froth, bluster, abuse and thunder'. He called the anti-conscriptionists pro-Germans, vipers, cowards, dirty dogs, parasites and other choice names. He preached sectarian hatred: he told lies: he indulged in vituperation against Catholics. Hughes has returned to where he belonged: among the mockers of Botany Bay.[74]

Irvine, Watt and Hume Cook held conversations on what to do. Out of a conversation on 15 November there emerged the idea of a Win the War Party. By the end of November they agreed that there should be a new National Organisation: they also agreed they should try to get Hughes interested. The problem was to get him to their discussions. Herbert Brookes, the son-in-law of Alred Deakin, offered to invite Hughes to a weekend at

[73] *Argus*, 15 November 1916; *Labor Call*, 2, 16 November 1916; Minutes of Special Party Meeting, 14 and 15 November 1916. Patrick Weller (ed.), *Caucus Minutes 1910–1949* (Melbourne, 1975), vol. 1, 1901–1917, pp. 438–40.

[74] *Argus*, 15 November 1916; *Age*, 15, 16 November 1916; *Socialist*, 24 November 1916; E. J. Holloway, *The Australian Victory over Conscription* (Melbourne, 1966); *Labor Call*, 16, 23 November 1916; *C'wealth Gazette*, 15 November 1916; R. Munro Ferguson to A. Bonar Law, 25 November 1916, Novar Papers, Item 841, N.L.A.

his holiday home at Macedon. Hughes agreed. They walked together on the lawn. The patrician from South Yarra had to endure as best he could the Hughes habit of calling every man 'brother': Hughes had to put up with the condescension of the man from 'Yarraside'. Hughes was being asked to work in the interests of the King and Empire with Joseph Cook whom he called a 'Bible basher', with William Watt whom he had dismissed as a 'nonentity', and William Irvine who was, in his own words, an 'iceberg'. Hughes preferred a fiery furnace of a man. Brookes gave him assurances. They should start by saying what they agreed upon:

1. Win the War.
2. Preserve Australian National Life.
3. Maintain Empire Solidarity.

But Hughes played hard to get.[75]

On 6 December Hume Cook met Hughes in the latter's room in Parliament House, Melbourne. Hughes did not want to join with the Liberals. He wanted to form a new National Labor Party. Hume Cook asked him where his power base would be, and where the money would come from. Hughes did not know. Hume Cook said that if he, Hughes, accepted the proposals he had put forward the new organization would have at its disposal as much money as would be required. Hughes would have a majority. 'And last, but not least, you thereby make certain that the Government of Australia will be in the hands of those who are for the Empire and not against it'. Hume Cook then left without another word. Two days later Hughes again told Hume Cook: 'I shall be surer of and happier with a National Labor Party. I do not like combinations'. But, he added, he would see Hume Cook again and talk a little more about it. Hughes was like a woman who winked after she had said 'No'. There would be another time.[76]

Hume Cook had a brainwave. He would ask Alexander Peacock, the Premier of Victoria, to approve of a new Organisation, to be called the National Party. Ryan, the Labor Premier of Queensland, should be excluded. Peacock arranged the meeting for 8 p.m. on 13 December. Peacock, without telling Hume Cook or Irvine, invited Hughes. Hughes was truculent: 'Well, Gentlemen! What have you got to say?' The Premiers told him a fusion of National Labor and the Liberals would mean a victory for 'Winning the War'. Hughes, impatient as ever, said: 'Well! We all seem to be agreed, so there's no use wasting time in discussion'. With that he picked up his hearing

[75] J. Hume Cook, Memoranda, Conscription, the National Federation and other matters, Hume Cook Papers, Series II, Folder 4, N.L.A.; *Bulletin*, 16 November 1916.

[76] J. Hume Cook, New Organisation, Memo of 6 and 8 December 1916, Hume Cook Papers, Series II, Folders 3(a) and 3(b); Notes by Hume Cook of meeting with Hughes, 21 December 1916, Hume Cook Papers, Series II, Folder 3(b), N.L.A.

aid and stalked out of the room. As they walked together down Collins Street Peacock said to Hume Cook: 'But great Scot! What a victory!'[77]

The *Labor Call* ridiculed the idea. A marriage of convenience had occurred, they said, between the Hughes Ministry and Joe Cook's Liberal Party. The Plute Press was the celebrant, and Fat was the Best Man. The rats of Labor, they said, were scampering to save their hides. Hughes has abandoned the workers of Australia at the behest of a clique of Imperialist Empire builders. He has 'wantonly, callously, and cunningly' handed the people of Australia into the hands of the military. William ('Maltese') Hughes was no longer the servant of the Australian people: he was now the servant of the British Army Council. He was leading the Australian people to their Calvary.[78]

On 1 December His Honor Mr Justice Pring delivered the summing up in the hearing of the charges preferred against the twelve members of the I.W.W. Sedition, he told the jurors, was 'anything that tended to stir up strife, disunion, or discontent'. Liberty of speech did not mean licence. It meant that 'every man was entitled to discuss in a fair and temperate way any subject. Liberty of speech must have its reasonable limitations'. The jury found the twelve guilty. On the following day His Honor delivered a homily to the guilty before pronouncing the sentence. 'You are members of an association of criminals', he said, 'of the very worst type and a hotbed of crime'. He condemned them for circulating 'pernicious literature' which fostered 'class hatred'. He hoped the literature would be destroyed, and that the authorities would use their best endeavours to prevent any more of it coming into the country. He agreed with the learned counsel who had told the court that the crime with which they were charged was 'the act of devils'. He then sentenced them to various periods of hard labour in the gaols of New South Wales, some for fifteen years, some for ten years, and one for five years.[79]

Hughes was supremely confident. He would easily accommodate that 'Bible banging Billy', Joseph Cook. A united party of National Laborites and Liberals would get a majority in both Houses in the forthcoming elections. Then Cook might be turned from a 'public calamity into a public benefactor' by offering him a job outside politics. A combination of National Labor and Liberals would support a 'Win the War' policy. National Labor would appeal to forward Liberals. It would make Australia safe for the King and Empire supporters for decades to come. The 'comfortable classes' and 'Yarraside'

[77] Hume Cook Memoranda, 12 and 13 December 1916, Hume Cook Papers, MS. 601, Series II, Folder 3(a), N.L.A.

[78] *Labor Call*, 14 December, 23 November 1916; *Ross's Monthly*, 18 November 1916, pp. 5, 14.

[79] *S.M.H.*, 2 December 1916.

would be safe from revolution. Australia would add its voice to those who wanted to obliterate Germany from the trade of the world, and punish Germany for her crimes against humanity. Australia was tied to the Empire. Australia has followed the English lead. In England David Lloyd George, another Welsh maverick and a man of the people, has formed a win-the-war-at-any-cost coalition government. Months later, Hughes would do the same.[80]

The other Australia has not been silenced. In England Lord Lansdowne proposed that as neither side could win except at a cost in human misery and suffering no civilized man would want to pay there should be a negotiated peace. In Australia in November 1916 John Curtin told a huge audience the war was only a phase in the history of the capitalist system. The class war was more important than the war between nations. The Australian worker must join with the workers in other countries to finish the war, and end the exploitation of man by man. Loyalty to King and Empire belonged to the past. Australia must have a flag of its own to fly under its own 'bonny skies'.[81]

At Merbein on the Murray River the poet John Shaw Neilson had a strange vision when he was weeding in his orange grove. There was 'some enchantment' he wanted to 'drag in' to a poem he was composing in his head about the Orange Tree. He had seen prints of Botticelli's picture, *Spring*. He said he knew nothing about art but 'anything of Botticelli's fills me with emotion'. He began to compose the poem 'The Orange Tree':

> The young girl stood beside me, I
> Saw not what her young eyes could see:
> —A light, she said, not of the sky
> Lives somewhere in the Orange Tree.

On the Western Front the Australian soldiers were ankle deep and sometimes knee deep in mud. Snow was falling. The men suffered from 'trench feet'. Their spirits were revived after the horrors of the Somme and Pozières and Ypres by Tommy Cookers (tins of solidified alcohol) for the drinkers, mugs of coffee and cocoa, a digger newspaper 'The Rising Sun', a small cinema show, and other comforts from the Comforts Fund, all the socks, and gloves and Balaclavas knitted by the girls 'back home'. In England Henry

[80] W. M. Hughes to R. M. Ferguson, 8, 26 December 1916, Items 2553 and 2575, Novar Papers, N.L.A.; *Worker* (Brisbane), 16 November 1916; R. M. Ferguson to W. Long, 14 February 1917, Item 879, Novar Papers; G. F. Pearce to A. Fisher, 21 November 1916, Item 265, Fisher Papers, Series 1, MS. 2919, N.L.A.

[81] *Socialist*, 22 December 1916.

Handel Richardson was prophesying what might happen to those who had succumbed to the 'unholy hunger' and exposed themselves to the revenge of the ancient continent for their 'loveless schemes of robbing and fleeing'. No such fears of retribution crossed the minds of the new political friends of Hughes when they said to each other on that December night in 1916, 'But great Scot! What a victory!'[82]

[82] *The Autobiography of John Shaw Neilson*, pp. 96–7, 106; John Shaw Neilson, *The Orange Tree* (A. R. Chisholm ed.), *The Poems of John Shaw Neilson* (Sydney, 1965), pp. 62–3; C. E. W. Bean, *The A.I.F. in France 1916*, pp. 954–6; Henry Handel Richardson, *The Fortunes of Richard Mahony* (Heinemann edition, London, reprint of 1965), p. 13.

2

VICTORY OF THE COMFORTABLE CLASSES

ON 6 JANUARY 1917 Hughes invited the 'many well-wishers of the National Cause' to attend a meeting in the Melbourne Town Hall on 9 January to consider the steps to be taken to demonstrate 'Australia's inflexible resolve to prosecute the War to a successful issue, to preserve and develop our National Life, and to maintain the solidarity of the Empire'. J. C. Watson, the first Labor Prime Minister, had wanted the words 'desirous of ensuring a progressive National Policy' in the letter of invitation. Hughes refused. On 9 January the foremost citizens from every State in the Commonwealth packed into the Town Hall. J. C. Watson was in the chair. Hughes told them they were there to form a party to co-operate in a resolute determination to prosecute the war to a successful conclusion. He asked them to lay the foundation stone of an organization which might serve not only present needs but those of the immediate future. They agreed. The party would be the National Party, not the National Labor Party, or a Win the War party.[1]

Hughes wanted political stability. His Government lacked a majority in the Senate where the Opposition was holding up Government business. Haig had plans for another attempt at a breakthrough in France. More men would be required from Australia. The voluntary system was not bringing in one-fourth of the numbers 'Birdie' wanted as reinforcements for the Australian divisions. 'Birdie' hoped Australia would send enough men to form a fifth Australian Division. Pearce thought they might manage to train the four to five thousand required each month. Embarkations fell from 12 638 in November 1916 to 8289 in December, and 5049 in January 1917. Attitudes to the war have changed. The talk of August 1914 about honour and glory has disappeared. After 25 April 1915 there was talk of 'naught but the horrors'. After August 1916 the horrors of the Somme and Pozières slowly sank into the consciousness of Australians. Soldiers were irritated by what they read in the papers about 'patriotism and glory'. To some of them that was 'lies, all lies'. The socialists talked of flooding with love and light the

[1] Copy of letter of invitation to inaugurate the new National Party, 6 January, Hume Cook Papers, Series 2, folder 3(b), N.L.A.; *Age*, 10 January 1917; *Argus*, 10 January 1917.

germs of good in every soul, and making Australia the first country in the world to bring about the abolition of war. Others said suffering, such as the war, was part of human life. Suffering was part of God's plan: suffering was the means of fulfilment, the way to wisdom and understanding. Some were gloomy about the future of humanity, foreseeing the day when all human beings acquired the faces of measurers, and even music ceased to comfort, because human beings lost their belief in a better life.[2]

Hughes must act before the dreams of the visionaries or the despair of the pessimists won the battle for the minds and hearts of the people. The time for mooching around the house in Kew without coat, collar, tie or trousers was over. The time of boasting to the gullible Hume Cook of how he could do as much office work in a day as Andrew Fisher could do in a week was also over. He must get down to serious talks with the Liberals. To win the war Hughes must stomach that fool, Joe Cook, or possibly take into his Government that likeable nonentity, Frank Tudor, who was under Caucus control—an irritant he had been relieved to get rid of in the previous November. He must put up with that pompous, vain, provincial fool, John Forrest. Frank Tudor made things easier by saying Labor would not join any coalition. So Hughes would not have to fight again the boss sheriffs and bully boys of Labor. Besides, he knew from Hume Cook that all the Liberals had been praying to God that 'Tudor's people outside' would not let him join in any coalition government. Tudor, thank God, did not have many brains, and was too frightened of the Labor Leagues. Labor refused to work with a 'rat' and a 'scab' and a 'traitor'. Labor wanted what Hughes and the Liberals would not concede—equality of sacrifice. That suited Hughes. That left Hughes's National Labor and Joe Cook's Liberals to sort things out. The Governor-General and 'Birdie' hoped that for the sake of the Empire they would bury the hatchet as Conservatives and Liberals had buried the hatchet in England the preceding December.[3]

All through January and into February the principals pirouetted between agreement and deadlock, dancing a tango in which the two main dancers, Billy Hughes and Joe Cook, took many steps forwards and backwards. Hughes wanted to talk Cook and the Liberals into a coalition, to create a national organization in which members of the Liberal and National Labor

[2] R. M. Ferguson to W. Birdwood, 20 January 1917, Birdwood Papers, A.W.M.; G. F. Pearce to W. M. Hughes, 12 February 1917, Hughes Papers, Series 20, Folder 3, N.L.A.; Embarkations of A.I.F. for Overseas Destinations to 30 September 1917, Hughes Papers, Series 20, Folder 3; diary of sister Lydia Kate Penny, 25 April 1915, A.W.M.; Marilyn Lake, *A Divided Society* (Melbourne, 1975), p. 194; *Ross's Monthly*, October, December 1916.

[3] Notes from meeting with Hughes at his home, Cotham Rd, Kew, 6 January 1917, and Notes from meetings with Hughes, 19, 29 January 1917, Hume Cook Papers, Series 2, folder 3(b), N.L.A.; *Argus*, 18 January 1917; W. Birdwood to R. M. Ferguson, 17 January 1917, Birdwood Papers, A.W.M.

parties could find common ground for the period of the war. He was anxious to preserve the image of himself as a Labor man. Cook and the Liberals wanted a National Government, representing one National Party. The British War Council told Hughes on 1 February it believed there were 350 000 men in Australia fit for military service. The Imperial Army urgently needed additions to its fighting strength for the plans to pierce the German lines. Casualties would be heavy. The Australian divisions must have reinforcements and, if possible, enough men to form a Sixth Division. A decision must be made.[4]

Dr Mannix was again putting into the heads of his people ideas likely to damage drives for more recruits. At the opening of the new Roman Catholic school in Brunswick on 28 January 1917 he dropped another of his memorable remarks about the war: 'They heard a great deal', he said, 'about the cause of the war, that it was a question of the rights of the smaller nations, but, as a matter of fact, it was simply a sordid trade war. Those who were now our enemies before the war had been capturing our trade'. Australians were being 'hustled to their death by the recruiting campaign'. The King and Empire men were shocked. The Governor-General was shocked by 'our stormy Archbishop Mannix'. One man, calling himself a loyal Catholic, asked whether Dr Mannix was a candidate for the place taken recently by Sir Roger Casement, or whether he was just a childish show-off, a seeker after notoriety and publicity. The King and Empire men renewed the cry: deport the traitor, chuck him out of the country. Sir Robert Best rebuked the Archbishop for being sympathetic with rebellion. The war, he said, was 'no sordid trade war, but a war in the interests of humanity'.[5]

By 18 February 1917 bargains were struck, compromises were made in the interests of a wider loyalty than obligations to old political mates and allies. Hughes accepted five portfolios for his group and six for the Liberals. Conservatives had a majority in the Australian Government. Cook accepted Senator Pearce as Minister for Defence, despite the Liberals' ambition to put Defence under one of their own men. Hughes gave up his hope that Joe Cook would be kicked upstairs. Hughes accepted John Forrest, a man he mocked as a politician whose ambition was infinite and capacity limited. On 19 February the Governor-General announced he had commissioned the Right Honourable William Morris Hughes to form a new Government. On the same day the Commonwealth of Australia *Gazette* published the names and portfolios of the members of that Government. Hughes had a windfall. He

[4] Cablegram of Secretary of State for Colonies to Defence Department, 1 February 1917, Hughes Papers, Series 20, Folder 3; Text of telegram of W. M. Hughes to G. F. Pearce, 8 January 1917. G. F. Pearce Papers, Series 5/1, Item 138, N.L.A.

[5] *Argus* 29, 31 January 1917; R. M. Ferguson to W. Long, 2 February 1917, Novar Papers, N.L.A.

had had to accept Forrest as Treasurer, but asked the Governor-General to persuade Forrest to represent Australia at the forthcoming Imperial Conference in London. The Governor-General knew his man. He knew a 'little judicious flattery and social attention' were never wasted on Sir John. He told Sir John a man of his experience and reputation would be greatly welcomed at the Conference. Sir John liked that.[6]

Hughes turned to deal with a hostile Senate. Again luck combined with his own brilliance brought him victory before his opponents woke up to what he was doing. Once again Hughes turned to the Governor-General, Sir Ronald Munro Ferguson, for collaboration. Sir Ronald found Hughes 'a curious combination of candour and secretiveness'. Sir Ronald was the man to whom Hughes 'often pours out his soul'. Sir Ronald knew that Hughes was after a working majority in the Senate. The Senate was refusing obstinately to agree to a postponement of the elections. On 1 March a Tasmanian Senator, R. K. Ready, resigned because of ill health. Hughes drove up to Government House in Melbourne with John Earle, who showed the Governor-General the letter of resignation from the Tasmanian Parliament. The Tasmanian Government, their Parliament not being in session, nominated Earle as a Senator. Sir Ronald thought it all savoured too much of a trick in which he did not wish to be involved. But he signed. As for Hughes, Sir Ronald knew he always liked a dramatic situation and bringing off a '*coup de main*'. Hughes now had a workable majority in both Houses. Labor and the *Bulletin* ridiculed Hughes as the 'recognized blatherskite of the world', Pearce as a 'dull, commonplace bluffer'—a group of men whose vanity was boundless, and whose faith in their parliamentary gag was 'irremovable'. But words could not put their Humpty-Dumpty together again. Hughes has won another struggle for power. The Australian Constitution was an ingenious device for the protection of the privileges of the comfortable classes.[7]

Ignoring the Governor-General's request for a prior notification of an interview, Hughes turned up at Government House in Melbourne and asked for a dissolution of the House of Representatives and of half the Senate to make sure of the Government's control of the Senate. Sir Ronald told his friend, Walter Long: 'I granted his request'. Sir Ronald knew that the British Government, Douglas Haig and William Birdwood believed Hughes was vital for the victory of King and Empire. Sir Ronald was always prepared to do his duty.[8]

At the same time John Curtin, who had spent five days in gaol for failing to

[6] *Age*, 16, 19 February 1917; *C'wealth Gazette*, 19 February 1917; R. M. Ferguson to W. Long, 21 February 1917, Novar Papers.

[7] R. M. Ferguson to W. Long, 2 March 1917, Novar Papers; *Socialist* 9, 23 March 1917.

[8] R. M. Ferguson to W. Long, 5 March 1917, Novar Papers; *Age*, 6 March 1917.

enlist in accordance with the proclamation of September 1916, was starting a new life in Perth. He renewed his promise to Elsie Needham to give up drinking, her condition for marrying him. He had been offered and accepted the position of editor of the *Westralian Worker*. In February 1917 he was farewelled at the Socialist Hall in Melbourne. It was his last speech as a socialist. On 21 April 1917 he married Elsie Needham and went to live at Cottesloe, Perth. There a new man was born. The socialist became a pragmatist, a man who set out to prove that a pragmatist need not become an opportunist or a careerist concerned only with the capture of political power. The man with the brilliant wit, the man who talked nonsense because the world was too painful, the man who used to tell his friends the world was suffering from too much work and should be converted to the glorious gospel of doing nothing, was now to find salvation in work. From that time John Curtin preached the gospel of work. He was never to say again that there could be no satisfactory system of government without social revolution.[9]

A change has also come over Hughes. The undying hositility of his former colleagues in the Labor movement and the defeat in the referendum have unsettled him. He looked for scapegoats on whom to pour his rage and his hurts. He blamed the Germans in Australia and the radicals in the Labor movement for the humiliations of October and November 1916. They must be punished: they must be crushed and rendered harmless. Hughes was already well known for his outbursts of savagery against the Germans in Australia. As Attorney-General in the Fisher Government in July 1915 he had ordered the arrest of Walter Schmidt and Franz Wallach of the *Australische Metallgesellschaft*. The court had set them free. Hughes had changed the order and ordered they be re-arrested. In London from April to June 1916 he had been out at the head of the pack hounding the Germans in England. Under the War Precautions Act of 29 October 1914, and as amended on 30 April 1915, Hughes had interned Germans resident in Australia, and deported others. Under the War Precautions Act German schools had been closed, licences to publish newspapers in the German language revoked, and the use of the German language in churches prohibited. Hughes was exploiting the emotions roused by the casualties in France. There was talk of prohibiting the use of the German language on the telephone.

Hughes also invoked the War Precautions Act to reduce to silence all critics of the wisdom of the war, or of the methods used to wage it. The War

[9] Lloyd Ross, *John Curtin* (Melbourne, 1977), pp. 52–8; *Labor Call*, 30 November 1916, 8 February 1917; *Argus*, 13 December 1916; *Socialist*, 24 November, 22 December 1916, 9 February 1917.

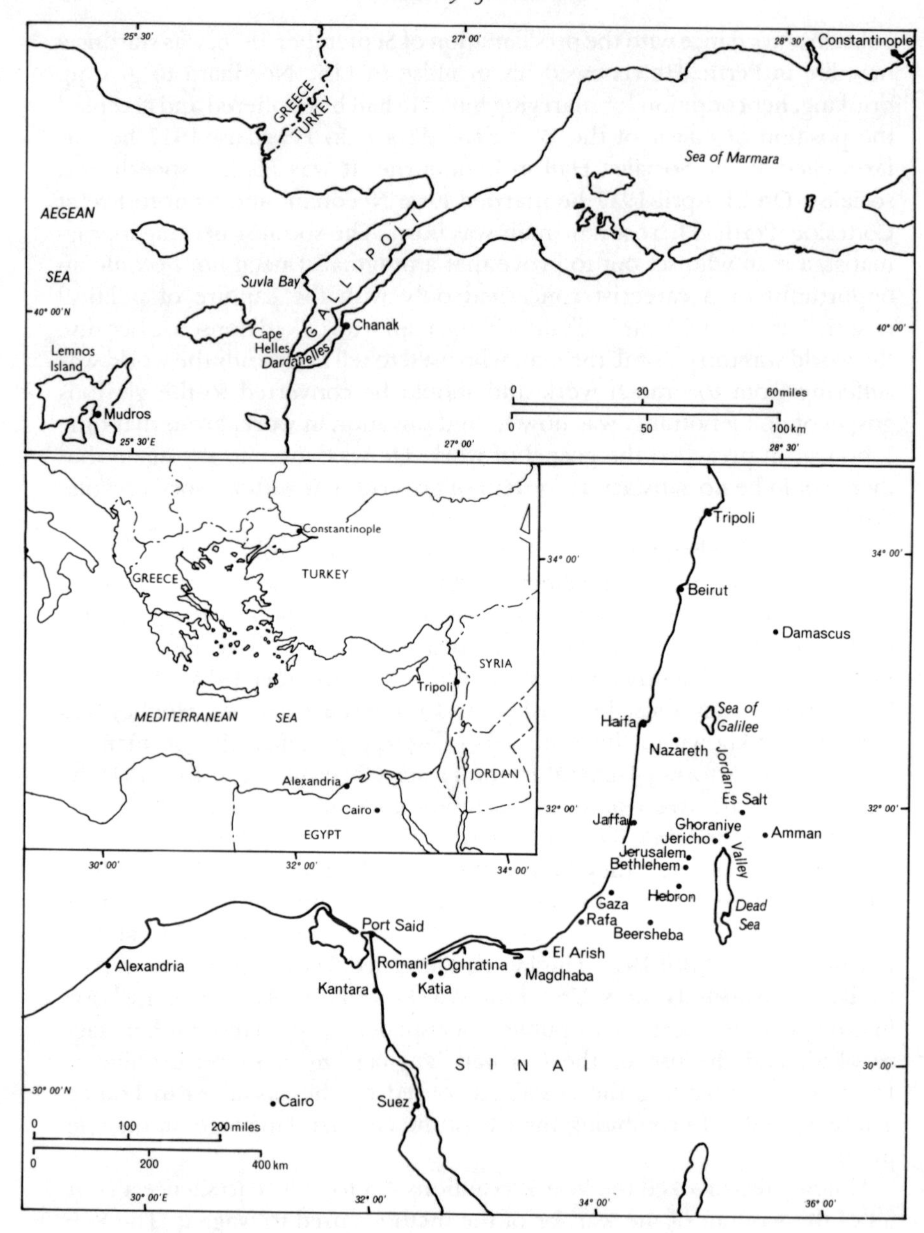

The Middle East

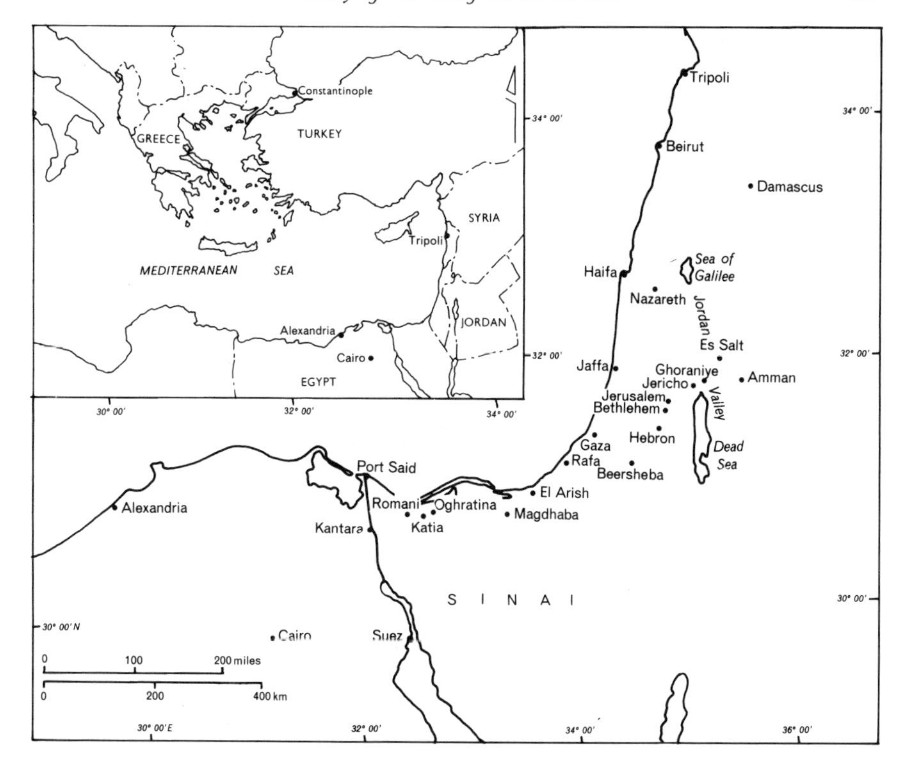

The Eastern Mediterranean

Precautions Act has given the Government wide powers against all opponents of the war. They have been given power to make regulations for securing the public safety and defence of the Commonwealth. In March and April 1917 an avenging Hughes made wide use of those powers. One speaker in Adelaide was fined for using words calculated to cause disaffection amongst the civilian population. In Sydney and Melbourne charges were laid against men making speeches calculated to prejudice recruiting. On 1 March police and military officers broke up an Adela Pankhurst meeting in Perth convened to present the case for the immediate cessation of hostilities. Anyone suspected of being wobbly on loyalty or patriotism was liable to prosecution. In Tasmania the loyal middle-class 'comfortables' persecuted their critics. The revolution in Russia in March has alarmed the comfortable classes in Australia. The Czar has been deposed and a political revolution has occurred. In Australia the comfortable classes feared a revolution might start. Labor might raise a rebel flag, might revive its republican spirit. Labor might try to bring the war to an end. Hughes and his Government were now fighting two wars: the war in Europe and the Middle East, and the class war in Australia.[10]

The Australian Labor Party shied away from the role events had given it the opportunity to play. Their new leaders were cautious men: Frank Tudor was a nice chap. He was good in the ruck at football, and had a correct stance in cricket. He played his life and his cricket with a straight bat. But the times called for something more than correct behaviour: they called for a man of vision. Labor had a commonplace man pushed into prominence by the split of 1916. Tudor was not capable of presenting the case for Labor with the electorally essential 'decorative effects'. Tudor was too timid a man to teach the Australian people that the unscrupulous Imperialism of Hughes and his sycophants would lead Australia to the rocks. He was not the man to inspire Australians to stop grovelling. Men on the fringe of the Labor Party spoke of revolution and building a new world. A member of the Legislative Assembly of New South Wales said on 26 March that the red flag was 'the only flag I'll spill my blood for'. But the Labor leaders dared not speak in that way. The *Argus* summed them up in a sentence that would live on: 'When the Caucus party expelled the most intelligent, most enlightened, and most capable of its members it blew out its brains . . . The weak limbs said to the brains, "We have no need of you." '[11]

On 27 March Hughes presented himself to the electors as the head of a 'Win the War Ministry'. His Government would do whatever was necessary to aid the Empire to win the war. His was a 'War Government'. As proof of his intentions Hughes floated a proposal to restrict the import of luxury goods. Loyal Australians, he said, should vote for the Nationalist candidates on 5 May. Although most members of the Labor Party were loyal, all the disloyalists and pro-Germans supported that party. No Britisher would want to vote for them. A Nationalist victory on 5 May would show the world that Australia's heart was in the right place. He called on Australians to put their country before party, and face the enemy with a united front. Australians believed in the British qualities of heroism, cheerfulness, endurance, and the

[10] *Socialist*, 2, 9, 23, 30 March 1917; *Daily Telegraph*, 2 March 1917; *Worker* (Brisbane), 5 April 1917; *Age*, 10 April 1917; Marilyn Lake, op. cit., p. 195; An Act to enable the Governor-General to make Regulations and Orders for the safety of the Commonwealth during the present state of war (War Precautions Act), 29 October 1914, 30 April 1915, 30 May 1916, *C'Wealth Acts*, vol. XIV, 1916; A. Lodewyckx, *Die Deutschen in Australien* (Stuttgart, 1932), pp. 236–40; Michael McKernan, *The Australian People and the Great War* (Melbourne, 1980), pp. 166–9.

[11] *Bulletin*, 5 April 1917; *Socialist*, 6 April 1917; *Age*, 27 March 1917; Hughes Papers, Series 21, Folder 1; *Argus*, 13 April 1917.

willingness to sacrifice all to benefit humanity. No sacrifice was too great for victory.[12]

God had a prize for those prepared to make the supreme sacrifice for King, Country and Empire. The Anglican Archbishop of Sydney, John Charles Wright, told all Anglicans the war was a reminder of 'the glorious truth of immortality'. Take the prize now before it was too late. The Germans might win. The Germans were threatening to starve the British into surrender. On 31 January 1917 the German Govenment informed neutrals of its intention to wage unrestricted submarine warfare. Morale in the French army has been low ever since the losses and horrors of Verdun. The French have had enough. The Russians were in a parlous condition. The morale of their army was low: Holy Russia was on the eve of revolution. The German generals, M. P. von Hindenburg and E. Ludendorff, were regrouping the German armies on the Western Front. The Allies must strike before the German army was again on the march. Douglas Haig wanted action: punch a hole in the German line before they launch an offensive.[13]

The Fourth Australian Division would attack the German line at Bullecourt. This Division was composed mainly of men from the 'outer' States: those country-bred men, the inheritors of the traditions and values of 'Old Australia', the men of resource, of pluck and courage and a will to endure and endure again until their agony was beaten out into joy. Haig was confident of success. The tank would cut through the barbed-wire entanglements, knock over the concrete machine-gun pillboxes, and prepare the way for the foot-sloggers to advance and finish off what the tanks and the land and air bombardment had softened up. The attack began on 11 April 1917. The British promised at least 75 per cent would reach the trenches of the enemy. The soldiers found Bullecourt a Hell. As one Australian soldier said, the war was 'sapping the best men and all that [was] beautiful in civilized life'. There were ten thousand casualties. The awful horrors were enough to drive men mad. Australians paid a terrible price for fighting under British officers. 'Birdie', who had all along been doubtful about the Haig plan, wept.[14]

'Birdie' sent off letters to the Defence Department in Australia, and to the Governor-General, asking for more volunteers to fill up the thinning ranks.

[12] *Age*, 27, 28 March 1917; *Argus*, 27, 28 March 1917; Twelve Reasons why Loyal Australians should vote for the National Candidates on May 5th, Broadsheet of National Campaign Council, Melbourne; *Daily Mail* (Brisbane), 17 April 1917; R. M. Ferguson to W. M. Hughes, 24 March 1917, G. F. Pearce Papers, Series 5/1, Item 138.

[13] *Ross's Monthly*, 23 June 1917, p. 17; C. E. W. Bean, *Anzac to Amiens* (Canberra, 1961) pp. 314–17.

[14] C. E. W. Bean, *The Australian Imperial Force in France, 1917* (Canberra, 1933, reissued St Lucia, 1982), pp. 280–5; Suzanne Welborn, *Lords of Death* (Fremantle, 1982), pp. 125–7; Bill Gammage, *The Broken Years* (Canberra, 1974) pp. 181–3.

Sir Ronald was not hopeful. The countryside was already drained of men: there were not even enough left to work the land. The towns were full of men who would not enlist and would not be conscripted. Australia was now an urban society composed of 'irresponsible, selfish and self-complacent men'. Conscription, he believed, was the answer, but Hughes has rashly promised the electors his Government would not introduce conscription for overseas service without seeking their approval in a referendum. Hughes was becoming reckless. Hughes was the prime example of the hysteria of the time. He wanted national unity. He spat at members of the Labor 'junta', at the followers of Sinn Fein, at Dr Mannix, and at Germans in Australia. Hughes sooled the British in Australia on to each other, calling on sedate Australians to act like a pack of wild dogs in pursuit of their prey. He despised all those who opposed him, calling them 'irresponsible nobodies'. Hughes was the patriot. The *Labor Call* was disgusted: this patriotism of Billy Hughes, it said, was nothing but a garment under which a scoundrel hid his mean actions. Hughes was a prodigal son who had gone to his father, Mr Fat, and begged him to forgive him and give him a place somewhere in the middle of the stage. The *Socialist* wanted Labor to work for regeneration and salvation: Australia should be a beacon to the world in this new era in the history of humanity. But its voice was drowned in all the madness and the uproar.[15]

The King and Empire men played on the emotions of the people. In Sydney there was the Sportsmen's Recruiting Committee. The rallying cry was 'Be a Sportsman'. No sportsman should remain at home and shelter behind the heroism of his mates. There were Recruiting Football Matches. But the people were not carried away. Crowds counted out the speakers. Barrackers shouted: 'Get on with the bloody game. That's what we've paid to see'. There was the Sportsmen's Thousand, a recruiting campaign to raise one thousand men from the sportsmen's world. In Gippsland, in the Western District, in the Wimmera and the Mallee drums were beaten, trumpets blared, beer flowed, sergeants bellowed: 'Roll up, roll up. Your mates need you'. While the sergeants bellowed mice ran over the wheat fields in the Mallee. Mice ate the mattresses, ran through the hair of people as they sat at the table. They bit children while they were asleep. They ate bags of seed wheat. The 'swells', said the people in the Mallee, should live in the Mallee for a while to see what the men on the land had to put up with.[16]

[15] R. M. Ferguson to W. Birdwood, 14 March 1917, Birdwood Papers, A.W.M.; R. M. Ferguson to W. Birdwood, 20 April 1917, ibid.; Gammage, op. cit., pp. 183–4; *Labor Call*, 26 April 1917; *Argus*, 4 May 1917; W. M. Hughes to R. M. Ferguson, 11 May 1917, Novar Papers; Poster, 'The Man Who Doesn't Like Husks', Collection of Election Posters, N.L.A.; *Socialist*, 27 April, 4, 11 May 1917.

[16] *Argus*, 1, 5 May 1917; McKernan, op. cit., pp. 113–15; *The Autobiography of John Shaw Neilson* (Canberra, 1978), pp. 92–3.

While the mice had their sport with human beings in the Mallee the people of Australia went to the polls on 5 May. By Monday 7 May it was clear the Hughes Government had won a decisive victory. In the House of Representatives the Nationalists (fusion of National Labor and the Liberals) won fifty-three seats and Labor twenty-two. In the half Senate election the Nationalists won eighteen and Labor none. The Nationalists won 54.22 per cent of the valid votes, Labor 43.95 and Independents 1.84. Hughes was greatly cheered: for him, as he told the Governor-General, it was a 'magnificent victory'. The 'junta' and Sinn Fein were down and Australia was 'herself again'. Once again in the history of Australia, despite the talk about mateship, equality and the democratic traditions of the Australian people, Australians had voted conservative—to be chained to their past, rather than take the way forward. Like other immigrant societies such as the United States, Canada and New Zealand, a majority of Australians believed the Australian dream of getting on, of owning a block of land and a house, could be achieved in a capitalist society. Immigrants and their descendants believed in 'getting on', believed in the capitalist incentives. The Australian working class had the same petty bourgeois values as the middle class. Middle-class affluence was another source of the strength of conservatism. Australia was a society of men and women proud of being egalitarians, proud of breaking with Old World ideas of hierarchy and deferment, who voted for the world of the comfortable classes to continue.[17]

The members of the Labor Party were dismayed. The socialists blamed the Labor Party for the defeat. Labor, they wrote in the finger-wagging way of men who knew all the answers to the human situation, has once again been punished for its 'betrayal of principles'. Now was the time for the 'regeneration and salvation' of the Labor movement. A student at the University of Melbourne, Guido Baracchi, declared there was 'only one thing sure about our present social structure—that it cannot last'. In succeeding articles in the *Melbourne University Magazine* he proposed to show how the workers, 'organised in their unions and fired with a revolutionary ideal', might bring salvation to the modern world. Australia would lead the way. In Europe Lenin wrote that democracy was the perfect shell for the capitalists: but no one in the Australian Labor movement had ideas on what institutions should be devised to replace the bourgeois democratic state.[18]

While the Australians were walking to the polling booths on 5 May the troops were gazing at the stumps of what had been the village of Bullecourt. The second battle for Bullecourt began on 3 May 1917. By 7 May this battle,

[17] *Argus*, 7 May 1917; *Age*, 7 May 1917; W. M. Hughes to R. M. Ferguson, 11 May 1917, Novar Papers; Colin A. Hughes and B. D. Graham, *A Handbook of Australian Government and Politics 1890–1964* (Canberra, 1968), pp. 315–16.

[18] *Socialist*, 11 May 1917; Guido Baracchi, 'Australian National Guilds', *M.U.M.*, May 1917, pp 7–8.

which was intended to engage only one Australian division, had already used most of the 1st and 2nd Divisions. Exhausted by the first battle the troops needed a rest. Again casualties were heavy—7482 all told. The horrors, the noise of the barrage, and the desolation again left some men raving mad. Once more the Australian officers and men were angered by the deficiencies of the British command. The officers and the men renewed their demands for the appointment of an Australian as supreme commander of the Australian Expeditionary Forces on the Western Front.[19]

The Australian diggers were conscious of and proud of the differences between themselves and the men in other armies. They were the egalitarians of the New World. Even in adversity and defeat they were never downhearted. They had a cheeky confidence in their own abilities. 'You give me the bloody battalion', one digger said on the Somme, 'I'll take the bloody place right now'. They believed the English had let them down, and said so. They were not afraid to speak their minds, no matter how lofty or 'la-di-da' the person to whom they were speaking. They enjoyed shocking refined Englishmen by asking them whether they would like to learn how to spit. They were proud to smell 'like a rum-vat' when not in the trenches. They were uneasy with all the English ways of expressing respect for those in authority—saluting, addressing officers as 'Sir', or speaking only when spoken to. In March 1917, on the eve of the Bullecourt blood-bath a British staff captain ticked off an Australian soldier for not saluting. The Australian patted him on the shoulder and said, 'Young man, when you go home, you tell your mother that to-day you've seen a real bloody soldier'. They were proud of their reputation for not keeping a civil tongue in their heads. They were egalitarians, dinky-di democrats, not grovellers.[20]

Like their fellow Australians at home, the soldiers were both egalitarian and conservative. They were individualists, who resented commands and condescension; they were men who believed no dinkum Aussie ever called any biped lord or sir, or touched his hat to any man. They would cheerfully push overboard or bully and stand over anyone who offended against their own code or lore, but they had no interest in any move to create a society in which domination ceased to be. The French army was in a state of mutiny for six weeks in the middle of 1917, an event which shook it to its foundations. The Australians were mutinous in their language and casual in their dress, but dismissed mutineers contemptuously as 'f------ no-hopers', 'fellers who ought to have their heads read', 'bloody fools who had gone clean off their rockers'. Their past had not fashioned them into participants in any Boston Tea Party or creators of a Paris Commune. Ignorant of their

[19] C. E. W. Bean, *The A.I.F. in France, 1917*, pp. 481–7, 542.

[20] Peter Vansittart (ed.), *John Masefield's Letters from the Front, 1915–1917* (London, 1984), pp. 207–8, 222, 227, 278.

own history, they were doomed to go on repeating the past. They were rebels against authority, but not revolutionaries.[21]

'Birdie' was pleased Hughes had a working majority in both Houses, 'which we trust means all is well'. His only interest in politics was their effect on maintaining a requisite supply of reinforcements. On that he and Hughes saw eye to eye. The soldiers now had high hopes. America had entered the war on the side of the Allies. The sinking of the *Lusitania* on 7 May 1915 led to President Wilson demanding on 13 May that Germany should not jeopardize the lives of non-belligerents. After the German announcement that indiscriminate submarine warfare would be resumed on 1 March 1916, the American Government announced that it would not allow Germany to violate 'human rights'. On 1 February 1917 Germany again resumed unrestricted submarine warfare. On 3 February the United States broke off diplomatic relations with Germany. On 26 February the British handed the Americans a German note they had intercepted in which Germany offered to return to Mexico the slice of territory lost to America in 1848 as a bait to declare war on the United States. On 6 April Congress passed a joint resolution declaring war on Germany. The Australians were delighted. The men from the New World were coming to the rescue of the Old World. The descendants of the brave men who fought for American independence, and the heroes of both sides in the bloody battles of the Civil War, would ginger up the troops on the Western Front. American numbers and American arms production would provide the western Allies with the means of victory. President Wilson promised on 2 April that America would 'spend her blood and might for the principles that gave her birth . . . God helping her she can do no other'. Americans had the same beliefs as Australians. They believed all men were born equal: they believed all men had a right to life, liberty, and the pursuit of happiness.[22]

Haig had plans for yet another attack on the German lines. He would mount an artillery barrage on Messines: mines would explode. The Allies would start their 'step-by-step' advance towards Germany. John Monash was in the thick of all the preparations for the forthcoming offensive operations at Messines. He was satisfying one of the great passions of his life—he controlled the actions of twenty thousand men under his command. He was organizing their food, their transport, ammunition supply, cutting the enemy's wire, the preliminary bombardment, and the blowing up of the mines—all in preparation for twelve thousand infantrymen 'going over the top' for the attack on Messines. The artillery barrage turned the country into a 'churning dust-cloud'. Exploding mines cut huge craters in the earth: the

[21] *Anzac to Amiens*, p. 346.

[22] W. Birdwood to R. M. Ferguson, 9 May 1917, and G. F. Pearce to W. Birdwood, 7 June 1917, Birdwood Papers, A.W.M.; *Soldier*, 25 May 1917; Robert Birley (ed.), *Speeches and Documents in American History* (4 vols, Oxford, 1942), vol. 4, pp. 20–37.

nerves of the German defenders were unstrung. The Australians lost two thousand men. On 7 June Monash sent a message to his troops: 'I desire to convey my gratitude to all commanders and all troops of the division for the magnificent valour and splendid co-operation . . . in the achievement of this day's great victory'. They had captured many field guns, machine-guns, trench mortars and munitions. He was proud of one other thing: 'I fired', he wrote in a letter, 'from first to last over £1,000,000 worth of ammunition, large and small, in the three days' fighting'.[23]

Monash was pleased he and his men had 'practically blotted out' two Bavarian Divisions. Monash played the piano beautifully; he knew about the 'wonder of a man with a maid', and how a man could lose his wits for a woman. Monash had a job to do, and was pleased he was doing it very well. 'Birdie' had the eye of pity. He wept when he heard the Australians had lost two thousand men in this new move to drive the Germans out of Flanders and France. One Australian soldier told his parents that if he lived he would stand by red hot socialists and peace cranks to stop any further wars, but while he was 'at it' he would fight like only one facing death could fight. He died one month later. Another man was recommended for a medal for doing 'the best work in the whole brigade'. 'Not bad', he told his parents, 'for an old loafer'. He was soon killed in action. In war the world belonged to men like John Monash and Tom Blamey. This was no time for those who, like Shaw Neilson, saw 'a light in the Orange Tree'.[24]

Back in Australia Labor supporters kept alive their vision of a different Australia. The *Labor Call* said the people were 'heartily sick of the whole silly business. Blood has been made to flow like water, and tears like mist but the people must conquer in the end'. They must get at the root of the evil, which was the system under which the people lived. They had high hopes of the conference of socialists in Stockholm then being held. The socialists would teach the workers not to make munitions to kill one another, but rather to unite to destroy their arch-enemy the capitalist. The *Socialist*, too, was full of hope: it believed in the 'upbuilding of life, not the destroying of life'. The Stockholm Conference showed Labor was for 'peace and humanity and against the barbarities of war and poverty'. Vida Goldstein was rescuing women from the streets. Maurice Blackburn was teaching the workers that economic power was more important than political power. Robert Ross was preaching about a day when the vilenesses of human civilization would end and an era of peace, plenty and progress would be ushered in.[25]

[23] John Monash to ——, 19 May, 7 June 1917. F. M. Cutlack (ed.), *War Letters of General Monash* (Sydney, 1934) pp. 177–9; C. E. W. Bean, *The A.I.F. in France, 1917*, pp. 576–93.

[24] Gammage, op. cit., pp. 187–8; F. M. Cutlack (ed.), op. cit., pp. 177– 9.

[25] *Labor Call*, 14 June 1917; *Socialist*; 8 June, 6 July 1917; *Ross's Monthly*, 23 June 1917, p. 16; *Australian Worker*, 14 June 1917.

Labor demanded that those imprisoned during the conscription campaign be released from gaol. Hughes had painted a picture of the Industrial Workers of the World as monsters whose sole purpose was to burn and destroy simply for the sake of it. But Donald Grant was not a monster. Donald Grant was still in gaol. His only offence was his work for fifteen years as an agitator against capitalism. A judge in New South Wales had sentenced him to fifteen years in gaol for saying fifteen words: 'For every day Tom Barker is in gaol it will cost the capitalists ten thousand pounds'. Grant must be released. Grant was not a man to conspire to burn down buildings or to excite sedition.[26]

Over in Western Australia John Curtin was making some 'rattling good speeches': he was proving 'a great acquisition' to the Labor movement in the West. He has almost ceased to believe socialism to be the only way to rescue humanity from the barbarities of war and poverty. He has ceased to be an ideologue and become a pragmatist. He no longer talks of humanity's power to steal fire from heaven, but rather of the mission of Labor to make life more cosy for the working classes. He has stopped talking of the need for social revolution: he now believes in gradualism, in progress through the ballot box. He has stopped talking of a 'great, good time': but attacks all ideologues and doctrinaires. The 'strange infirmity' still cast a shadow across his life. The *Westralian Worker* reported he was having 'a few days' spell'.[27]

At the University of Melbourne Bob Menzies was telling his fellow students the progress of Australia would come from the élite and not from the masses. He enjoyed practising on his fellow students what Charles Dickens called in *Little Dorrit* the 'art of subtraction': he subtracted from any human being any claim he or she might have to distinction, difference or achievement. Bob Menzies enjoyed telling the 'yahoos' that democracy was not pandering to class passions. Politicians were thinkers: they were not dreamers or visionaries. The British and the Australian soldiers, he said, were knights robed in white fighting for right against might. One of his fellow students, who found something odious in this young man from Jeparit extolling the political virtues of the British and the social values of Windsor Castle, composed this verse about the antics of R.G.M.:

> It would soothe me much, I own,
> R.G.M.,
> If you left this theme alone;
> R.G.M.,
> On the Empire pour your gush,

[26] H. E. Boote, *The Case of Grant* (Sydney, 1917), pp. 4–9; *Australian Worker*, 21 June 1917.

[27] *Socialist*, 8 June 1917; Lloyd Ross, op. cit., pp. 63–5.

Throw the Shop [University] a platitude;
Shower on Mister Hughes some mush,
Strike a *loyal* attitude.
Shake your world-redeeming sabre,
Dominate the cowering mob,
But Democracy!—and Labour! . . .
—Chuck it, Bob.

The man who wanted his contemporaries to esteem him as a person of consequence has made himself an object of derision. From that time he began to entertain the hope that there must be a place somewhere where he would be recognized as a man of consequence. He will find that place: the discovery will bring him great joy. He began also to behave like a man who was nursing some private wound. He began speeches with a confession of his weaknesses, and then proceeded to parade his ability and his achievements. He wanted something more than the recognition that he was a most remarkable man: he wanted to love and be loved. That fruitless quest will plant a private Hell in his heart.[28]

In Oxford Charlie Bean was telling the poet John Masefield that the best thing the world could get out of the war was a revolution to end, forever and all, the assumption of the English snobs that no one was to rule 'except us'. At the same time Adela Pankhurst was telling the people in the Melbourne Socialist Hall she wanted Australia to remain a white man's country. Coloured people had different ideas of morality from white people: intermarriage was a social evil: if admitted, coloured people would soon outnumber the white. Australia had been conquered by force: the white man must be prepared to use force to hold what he had taken. Scott Bennett, lecturer for the Rationalists, hoped Christianity would not survive the war.[29]

In July 1916 Pope Benedict XV again appealed for peace, calling on all countries to return to their existing borders. The Germans refused to withdraw from Belgium, the French insisted on retaining Alsace-Lorraine, President Wilson declared there could be no negotiations with the autocratic government of Germany, Hughes still talked of destroying Germany's commercial power. Haig ordered the Australians to participate in a sortie from Ypres, designed to drive the Germans from the coast of Belgium. Those tired troops, who had fought in the first and second battles of Bullecourt and at Messines were again called back into the line. General White demanded that Australia should have on the staff of the commander-in-chief a representative with the unquestioned right to present the Australian view. 'Birdie' passed on the request to Haig's Chief of Staff. Before a decision could be

[28] R.G.M. (R. G. Menzies), 'Of Politics', *M.U.M.*, vol. VI, no. 1, May 1917, and S. C. L. (S. C. Lazarus), 'Of Politics', ibid., August 1917.

[29] Diary of C. E. W. Bean, Oxford, June 1917; *Socialist*, 15 June 1917.

made Haig commanded the Australians to go into action again in the third battle of Ypres. Continuous rain turned the plains of Flanders into a mud-heap, a waterhole. The Haig tactics of 'step by step' were just as costly and demoralizing as the tactics of the 'big push' or the 'knock-out blow'.[30]

Losses meant Australia must send reinforcements. 'Birdie' explained the situation to George Pearce. George Pearce was at a loss to know what to do. The number of volunteers has dwindled each month. Hughes has made that rash promise during the election campaign not to introduce conscription without consulting the Australian electors in a referendum. So he could not use his majority in both Houses to legislate for conscription. Hughes has made his stirring appeals to the workers of Australia. On 6 July 1917 he had reminded them of the privileges they enjoyed: how they worked the shortest hours of any workers in the field, far shorter than their brothers across the sea, those men who had gone out to fight for them. But still the numbers did not increase. On the contrary, the agitation against the war was growing. In England the poet Siegfried Sassoon declared he believed the war was being deliberately prolonged by those who had the power to end it—'I can no longer be a party to prolong these sufferings for ends which I believe to be evil and unjust'. He wanted to help to 'destroy the callous complacence with which a majority of those at home regard the continuance of agonies which they do not share'. In Australia the anti-war supporters accused Hughes of being like a man who was holding the carrot of death before a donkey.[31]

'Many are the spoken words', the Governor-General told General Birdwood in July 1917, 'yet few are the recruits enrolled or deeds done to help the war nowadays in this country'. There were crowds of 'slackers' in every town. It would not be prudent for Birdwood to anticipate large reinforcements from Australia. 'Birdie' did not know what to do. Major-General J. J. T. Hobbs and Brudenell White were pressing him to give the Australians a spell. That was all very well, but who would replace them? Maddened by the increasing support for those opposed to the war Hughes turned, like a wild dog, to savage such men and women for sapping the will of the people to fight on to victory, or accept the price in human lives of such victory.[32]

As though to confirm his deepest suspicion about a Labor conspiracy against the war, on 2 August a strike began in the Randwick State Workshops in Sydney. The workers ceased work to protest against the introduction without due notice of a card system of recording the amount of work done in a given time by each worker. Hughes and Pearce believed this was a plot to

[30] *The A.I.F. in France, 1917*, pp. 683–7, 721–5.

[31] *S.M.H.*, 7 July 1917; S. Sassoon, 'Finished With The War', quoted in Robert Graves, *Goodbye to all That* (revised edn, London, 1957), pp. 230–1.

[32] R. M. Ferguson to W. Birdwood, 19, 24 July 1917, Novar Papers.

sabotage the war. In the words of Pearce the strike was 'the aftermath of the Conscription Referendum and the recent Elections'. By the end of August 95 000 workers in the railways, the tramways and coal mines were out on strike. The *Socialist* wondered whether the strike was the prelude to revolution in Australia. Hughes accused the strikers of preferring social revolution to victory in France. The war must be won quickly before the maggots of revolution ate too deeply into the foundations of capitalist society. On 10 September the men accepted the terms offered to them by the Railway Commissioners.[33]

The crushing of the strike increased the bitterness within the Labor movement against the comfortable classes. To the *Labor Call* the war was a horror enriching one class and destroying another. The civilized world was being called on to participate in slaughter, misery and disease to enrich the 'boodlers, traders, manufacturers and profiteers'. Labor should have nothing to do with a society which produced 'scrofulous kings, and lying priests, and greasy millionaires, and powdered prostitutes, and ferret-faced thieves'. But, like the Labor opinion makers they had no clear idea of any society which would abolish these evils, nor of how that society could be created.[34]

In Flanders the Australian soldiers were still floundering in the mud-heaps and waterholes around Ypres. The mud was so deep that exhausted men who fell face downward into it drowned before they could lift themselves out or be lifted out by their mates. Casualties mounted. 'Birdie' did not believe any recruiting boom could produce the numbers required. He was more convinced than ever that nothing but compulsory service could be effective in producing the numbers the British required from Australia. Men in Australia agreed with him. On 22 October Sir William ('Iceberg') Irvine, speaking at the Nelson Day demonstration in Melbourne told an audience of Empire lovers there was only one way of preserving their liberty and their right to make their own institutions and that was by universal service of all the citizens of the Empire.[35]

Hughes had other things on his mind. He had always made it clear that things would be much better for him if he could get that vain nonentity, John Forrest, out of his Government. Forrest had the effrontery to see himself as the successor to Hughes as Prime Minister. One week before Irvine launched his campaign for conscription a member of the Bonython family, an owner of the *Advertiser* in Adelaide, showed Hughes it was within his power to make John Forrest a very happy man. Forrest, Bonython told Hughes, would love

[33] Labor Council of New South Wales, *Report, Balance Sheet and Statement of Receipts and Disbursements, Railway Strike, 1917* (Sydney, 1917), pp. 1–6; G. F. Pearce to W. Birdwood, 20 September 1917, Birdwood Papers.

[34] *Labor Call*, 9 August 1917; *Socialist*, 5, 12 October 1917.

[35] *Age*, 23 October 1917.

to be a baron. That would be one way of recognizing Forrest's contribution to the building of the East–West railway, and be a source of great joy to him. Bonython also knew Hughes would not be displeased. Hughes made the joke that to get rid of Forrest he would be prepared to make him a duke.[36]

The casualties in France were mounting. In September and October Australian troops were continually at the battle front. On 20 September there was the battle of the Menin Road. On 26 September there was Polygon Wood, on 4 October, Broodseinde. German losses were heavy. General Ludendorff was reported to be wondering whether the German army could sustain such casualties for long. The Anzac Corps again lost heavily; losses must be replaced. Haig had another of his brainwaves: the Germans were tottering, their morale was weakening. Another push and the Germans would be finally routed. Haig had a charisma which led those who met him to believe no enemy could stand against such a man. Once again this man of a very fine delicate gentleness and generosity, of a pervasive power, and a height of resolve, was prepared to send hundreds of thousands of men to their death to capture a ridge overlooking the plains of Flanders.[37]

All through September and October the rain, shell-fire, mine explosions, aerial bombardment and horse-drawn heavy guns turned the green fields around Ypres into mud, water and general desolation. Teams of horses strained in mud and water up to their chests to pull the guns into position. Exhausted men sank in the mud and were drowned. Soldiers were heard to cry out: 'I want to go home to my wife'. The Australians continued to surprise the British with their casual behaviour. They addressed a commanding officer as 'Jack'; they objected to being 'posh' on parade when they were supposed to be resting. The brass instruments in their band were all filthy, yet they played them very well. They pinched some of the rations reserved for British soldiers and thought it a 'good lurk' and a 'good laugh', but were indignant when a British N.C.O. reported them: 'Oh, come on cobber', they said, 'have a heart!' They saw themselves as men with hearts of gold, nice chaps. They spoke of themselves as the finest soldiers in the world.[38]

On 9 October Haig allotted the Australians a role in the final assault on Passchendaele. Charlie Bean was worried: he had seen what had happened at the Somme and Pozières. 'I suspect', he wrote in his diary on 9 October, 'that they are making a great bloody experiment—a huge gamble . . . I think they are playing with the morale of their troops . . . I feel . . . awfully anxious —terribly anxious—about to-morrow!' The Australian soldiers had their cheeky innocence, that resort to comedy on the eve of a descent into Hell.

[36] L. Bonython to W. M. Hughes, 16 October 1917, Hughes Papers, Series 16, Folder 1.

[37] *The A.I.F. in France, 1917*, pp. 761, 813, 830–40, 875; Peter Vansittart (ed.), op. cit., pp. 190–1.

[38] Lyn Macdonald, *They Called It Passchendaele* (London, 1978), pp. 68–9.

When an Australian unit relieved the 2/5th Battalion of the East Lancashire Regiment one of the Australians was actually smoking. After the British lieutenant answered the Australian question: 'What are you?' an Australian said to him amongst other things: '. . . Just fuck off'.

On the following day, 10 November, Charlie Bean saw the Australian survivors of the first assault on the ridge. They were 'pale, white & drawn'. Horses, mules and guns were bogged in the mud. Men slept in wet blankets on sodden straw. Cases of dysentery and influenza were numerous. Bodies of the dead were everywhere. The soldiers became 'broken and demoralised'. *The Times* correspondent reported: 'A distinguished officer said to me this morning that it was like hitting a pudding. There was no resilience in the enemy, no reaction. But wading up to your armpits in pudding is difficult'. The weather, the indescribable condition of the ground, the German shelling and machine-gun fire had created another Hell on earth. British forces, mainly Canadians and New Zealanders, captured what remained of the village of Passchendaele on 10 November.[39]

The British had gained a ridge, but had probably lost 100 000 men. Since July 38 093 Australians had become casualties. That was 60 per cent of the A.I.F. in France. Haig's 'duck march' did not end with the Germans driven from the coast. But the optimism was not diminished. Haig was still cheerful, still in command. The German losses, it was believed, would be decisive. American troops and reinforcements from the Dominions would give the Allies the superiority in numbers they needed. Haig asked Charlie Bean what chance there was of conscription in Australia. Bean replied that because of the opposition of the Irish, the Roman Catholics and the I.W.W. he was doubtful.[40]

'Birdie' still hoped Australia would not let the Empire down. A stubborn man was 'Birdie'. At the height of the blood-bath at Passchendaele 'Birdie' received a letter from the Governor-General written on 25 September warning him there was little likelihood of his receiving any further substantial reinforcements from Australia. He advised 'Birdie' to 'get full advantage from the troops you have'. 'Birdie' did not know what to do: how could the Allies replace the losses inflicted by that futile idea of Haig's to drive the Germans back to the sea? Cables and more cables were sent to Australia. On 18 October the Army Council cabled Hughes, and on 29 October Birdwood cabled Hughes to tell him the British required a minimum number of 6100 per month from Australia. The losses in Flanders and the imminent collapse of Russia meant the British were even more dependent on recruiting in

[39] Diary of C. E. W. Bean, 9, 10 October 1917; Lyn Macdonald, op. cit., pp. 201–2; personal visit to Passchendaele, April 1985.

[40] Gammage, op. cit., p. 190; *The A.I.F. in France, 1917*, pp. 905–7, 939–42; Diary of C. E. W. Bean, 9, 10, 12 October 1917; L. F. Fitzhardinge, *The Little Digger* (Sydney, 1979), p. 279.

Australia. Everyone was marking time until the Prime Minister was fit enough to return to work.[41]

The Labor press was already repeating the chant of October 1916: conscription was the 'king move' of the capitalist class to destroy Labor for generations to come. The supporters of conscription were fighting for the preservation and maintenance of capitalism. The conservatives were speaking with passion about 'duty to the boys at the front', and loyalty to King and Empire. Recruiting was a failure. All the efforts of Ministers of the Crown, all the rhetoric of 'Iceberg' Irvine, ministers of the churches, recruiting sergeants, picture shows and posters have not brought forward the numbers required for victory. The conservatives called on the Government to declare immediately it would not contribute to national humiliation by sticking to the miserable failure of voluntaryism. Australians must show that the sterling blood of their forefathers still flowed in their veins, and that they would have nothing to do with the 'poisonous, insidious doctrine of disloyalty'.[42]

Hughes must make up his mind. But Hughes was not well. His many well-wishers, such as the Governor-General and all those who believed he was essential to win the war, wondered whether his tiny frame could endure another campaign of vituperation, abuse, calumny and excitement. The Conscription Committees in all the States demanded a decision. Each day the news from Europe became more grave. Haig's 'duck's march' had ended, not at the Belgian Channel ports but in the mud and filth of Passchendaele. The news from Russia was just as dark. On 7 November the Bolsheviks stormed the Winter Palace in Petrograd. On that night, in the Smolny Institute, V. I. Lenin announced the birth of a new era in the history of humanity. The masses had a new hero: there was, wrote the Russian poet Vladimir Mayakovsky, 'no one/more alive/than Lenin in the world'.[43]

While Lenin was enthusing over the dawn of a new era in the history of humanity, Hughes was recuperating in the Blue Mountains. Amid all the splendours of early summer in those majestic scenes, no lofty vision of the future of humanity was vouchsafed to him. Lenin spoke of peace, of bread and land, for the people: Hughes spoke of war. On the morning of 8 November just as Lenin was electrifying his followers in the Smolny Institute in Petrograd, the Australian press published the decision of the Government.

[41] R. M. Ferguson to W. Birdwood, 25 September, 5 November 1917, Novar Papers; Memorandum by G. F. Pearce to the Prime Minister, 10 November 1917, Hughes Papers, Series 20, Folder 3; R. M. Ferguson to Walter Long, 25 October 1917, Novar Papers.

[42] *Australian Worker*, 4 October 1917; *Socialist*, 5 October 1917; *S.M.H.*, 26, 31 October, 2 November 1917.

[43] R. M. Ferguson to the King, 4 November 1917, Novar Papers; Vladimir Mayakovsky, *Vladimir Ilych Lenin* (Moscow, 1917); W. Birdwood to R. M. Ferguson, 5 November 1917, Novar Papers.

The voluntary system has proved inadequate to reinforce the Australian armies and the Government has decided to ask the people immediately by referendum for authority to raise by compulsory service the number of troops necessary to maintain the five Australian divisions at effective strength. Hughes undertook to explain the Government's scheme a few days later.[44]

Hughes was beginning to speak like a haunted and a hunted man. The moments of badinage and witty use of whipping boys were becoming fewer and fewer. He was behaving more and more like an animal at bay. He pointed the finger at his opponents, and blackened them as the enemies of the people. He became reckless. He said he was fighting for liberty but curtailed the liberties he claimed he was fighting for. He instructed the men in the intelligence section of his Government to establish the connection between Dr Mannix, the Anti-Conscription Fellowship, the Peace Army, the Sinn Fein and the Socialist Party. To the socialists this was a cruel joke. The rationalists and the socialists knew Mannix was not a people's leader. Mannix was an Irish patriot, a devout Catholic who believed Socialism was one of the idols of corrupt hearts. Hughes also savaged the Germans in Australia. The Germans, he said, would not give a 'patriotic vote' on conscription. He therefore, for the referendum, struck Germans and first-generation German-Australians off the electoral rolls. He estimated that would reduce the 'No' vote by 114 000.[45]

On 10 November the Bolshevik Government in Petrograd issued a proclamation on the war: 'The soldiers are for peace, for bread, for land, and power of the people'. The new Government offered an immediate democratic peace. Hughes was not interested. He found the news 'ominous'. Any government asking for peace was breaking down the last barrier between the madness of anarchy and liberty. The Russians, or the Bolsheviks, or the Bolshies, have joined the Hughes list of villains. The Russians have let down the Allies. The Soviets of Workmen's and Soldiers' deputies were like Sinn Fein, the socialists, Dr Mannix and the I.W.W. They were the enemies of liberty, White Australia and the British Empire.[46]

The Intelligence men supplied him with information which fed his prejudices and filled in the details of the conspiracy of all the 'villains' opposed to the King and the Empire. Within a week of the announcement of the referendum Intelligence showed him a document purporting to represent the aim of Sinn Fein: 'The Germans on top and Ireland free . . . and to hell with the King'. Intelligence also claimed Mannix had said in a speech: 'No

[44] *Argus*, 8, 13 November 1917.

[45] *Argus*, 5 November 1917; Michael McKernan, *The Australian People and the Great War* (Melbourne, 1980), pp. 167–8; A. Lodewyckx, *Die Deutschen in Australien* (Stuttgart, 1932), pp. 234–45.

[46] G. H. Knibbs to W. M. Hughes, 7 November 1917, Hughes Papers, Series 21, Folder 1; *Argus*, 10 November 1917.

Irishman can be true to England and true to Ireland as well . . . the English Government in Ireland is beyond savagery, and a thing that shall never be forgotten . . . The Government of Ireland by England is the most despotic, the most cruel, the most damnable in the world'. These reports jerked Hughes out of the mood of the moocher into the mood of a crusader with a cause.[47]

On 12 November the *Commonwealth Gazette* published the question to be put to the electors: 'Are you in favour of the proposal of the Commonwealth Government for reinforcing the Australian Imperial Force oversea?' 20 December was to be the polling day, and 9 February 1918 the day for the return of the writ. On the same night at Bendigo Hughes announced the proposals of the Government:

1. Voluntary enlistment is to continue.
2. The number of reinforcements required is 7000 per month.
3. Compulsory reinforcements will be called up by ballot to the extent to which voluntary enlistment fails to supply this number.
4. The ballot will be from among single men only, from among the ages of 20 to 44 years (including widowers and divorcees without children dependent upon them).

The physically unfit, judges, ministers of religion, persons employed in industries essential to the war, persons whose religious beliefs did not allow them to bear arms, and persons whose calling up for military service would cause hardship either to themselves or their families, were to be exempted.

On the night of 12 September he told an enthusiastic audience of 3500 in the Lyric Theatre at Bendigo that Australians were engaged in 'a terrific life and death struggle' between two great ideals, might and right, despotism and democratic government. Australians were freemen, sprung from a stock nurtured at the breast of freedom. His Government had given voluntaryism a fair deal, but voluntaryism had failed. Now they must face the tremendous added responsibilities and strain upon the resources of the Empire produced by the Russian betrayal and the Italian débâcle. Australia was in grave danger. In Russia a revolutionary goverment was in control, composed of just that type of men who had tried recently to undermine government in Australia: 'Dreamers, theorists, Anarchists, pro-Germans' and 'enemies of the Empire'. To win the war the Government must have this power to call up compulsory reinforcements. 'It cannot govern the country without it, and will not attempt to do so.' In a moment of great madness he has promised that if the referendum were not carried his Government would resign.

[47] Memorandum re Sinn Fein Movement in Australia, 17 November 1917, and secret report of a speech given by Dr Mannix, n.d. (probably early November 1917) Hughes Papers, Series 21, Folder 1.

Hughes was nourishing the terrible delusion that any human being is ever indispensable.[48]

On 14 November Hughes spoke in the Sydney Town Hall. To wild and enthusiastic applause he accused the I.W.W., Sinn Fein and a 'certain ecclesiastic' of having as their 'foremost idea' a plan to injure England. This man (the 'certain ecclesiastic'), he said, 'and those who follow Sinn Fein, are prepared to offer up Australia on the altar of something attainable only by the destruction of the Empire'. A woman asked Hughes why he did not have the courage to deal with the 'certain ecclesiastic'. Hughes did not answer. He asked those in the audience who agreed with him to stand up. Hundreds stood up. The time for argument was over. The time for men and women to show what they believed was at hand. The audience cheered and waved their hats, stamped their feet, clapped and whistled as Hughes called on Australians to show 'that man' that whether they were English or Irish they put Australia first. The time for differences was over. Hughes screamed: 'I want to warn every man in Australia that if, in the campaign, he lies, he lies at his peril. If anything be said by a speaker which is calculated to mislead the electors unless he proves his words—punishment will be swift and certain'. This was no time for slackers: the whole Anglo-Saxon race must stick together, or they would all find themselves in servitude.[49]

By contrast the leader of the Australian Labor Party, Frank Tudor, spoke with dignity and restraint. Life, he said on 15 November, was sacred, and no government had a right to deal with it. He suggested Australia's role should be to concentrate on providing foodstuffs for Britain instead of conscripting men.

It was not a time for rational argument. Rumours flourished in the atmosphere of panic, multiplying like maggots in diseased flesh. Hughes was planning to take a job in Washington, some said: others spread stories about the low morale in the French army, hoping to convince waverers of the gravity of the situation. The Governor-General asked Hughes to censor speakers repeating such rumours. On Sunday 18 November the socialists gathered in the Sydney Domain and on the Yarra Bank in Melbourne to sing the 'Red Flag'. Speakers talked of the wanton and gross betrayal of the people, of Hughes as the 'rat who broke pledges'. Speakers demanded the end of the war. Like Lenin, they had a vision of a glorious future for humanity:

> For the future in the distance
> And the good that we can do.

Hughes denounced men and women with that vision as 'reckless extremists, peace cranks, disloyalists, pro-Germans, Sinn Feiners who were taking Ger-

[48] *C'wealth Gazette*, 12 November 1917; *S.M.H.*, 13 November 1917.
[49] *Age*, 15 November 1917.

man gold to do Germany's dirty work'. Hughes spoke of duty, of sacrifice, and of loyalty to King, Country and Empire.[50]

The second conscription campaign had many of the features of a comic opera. All the stars of the first campaign sang their arias again. Hughes sang of duty and loyalty and liberty: Dr Mannix also sang of duty—the duty to keep Australia free from military despotism. 'Iceberg' Irvine accused Dr Mannix of leading a pack of rebels against the King and country which protected him. Hughes and his supporters sang of the war as a war for the preservation of civilization and White Australia. Adela Pankhurst sang of how the workers had no interest in winning the capitalists' war: there was only one war, the war of worker versus master, and owner versus non-owner. Dr Mannix sang again his slogan: put Australia first. Dr Wright, the Anglican Archbishop of Sydney, promptly intoned the reply: it was traitorous to suggest that Australia must be first, and the Empire second. Hughes sang again: the soldiers were crying from the trenches: Send us help. You cannot shirk it. Frank Tudor sang in reply: send food to Britain. So it went on.[51]

After rousing to unwonted enthusiasm the inhabitants of Adelaide, Hughes travelled north to confront Tom Ryan, the Labor Premier of Queensland, the one formidable Labor debater (save Frank Anstey). A great comic opera show was being performed in Australia just after hundreds of thousands had fallen in the mud at Ypres, Messines, Polygon Wood and Passchendaele; as 'Birdie' wept again for those golden friends he had lost, and General Monash mused over the 'scope and scale and dynamic splendour of a modern battle', and strove 'to introduce . . . systematic methods and order so that there shall be no muddling, no overlapping, no cross purposes, and everybody has to know exactly what his job is and when and where he has to do it'. On 23 November Ryan argued persuasively in the Queensland Legislative Assembly that ample reinforcements would be forthcoming under voluntaryism to supply the needs of Australian divisions at the front. Ryan also argued that those clamouring for conscription hoped to weaken the power of the unions and pave the way for cheap labour in Australia.[52]

Ryan must be answered. He was a formidable opponent. He was Labor, he was Catholic, he was of Irish descent. He was one of the architects of those government enterprises in Queensland designed to show that Labor could make capitalism more humane without a radical change in the foundations of society. Ryan was one of those Labor pragmatists who had attempted to

[50] *Age*, 16, 17 November 1917; R. M. Ferguson to W. M. Hughes, 10 November 1917, Hughes Papers, Series 16, Folder 1; *Socialist*, 16, 23 November 1917.

[51] *Age*, 17, 21, 22, 24 November 1917; *Socialist*, 16, 23 November 1917.

[52] John Monash to John Gibson, 29 April 1917, F. M. Cutlack (ed.), op. cit., pp. 172–3; 204; *Qld P.D.*, 22 November 1917, vol. 128, p. 3145.

show there was no contradiction between democracy and capitalism, between equality of opportunity and the profit motive. Ryan had his roots deep in the great Australian dream, that there could be equality of opportunity, liberty and fraternity in Australia without raising the rebel flag or singing the rebel chorus. Ryan had himself lived one part of the Australian dream. Born on 1 July 1876 in poverty, the fifth child of an illiterate Irish farmer in western Victoria, by industry, native talent and education he had risen to be a teacher, a journalist and a successful lawyer. In 1912 he was elected leader of the Labor Party in Queensland. He had been Premier of Queensland ever since the Labor victory in the election of May 1915.[53]

Hughes arrived in Brisbane on 27 November. He ordered the Commonwealth censor to forbid the Government Printer to publish in *Hansard* the debate of 22 November in the Legislative Assembly. Ryan protested that this was an 'invasion of the rights of a sovereign State', and an infringement of liberty. Hughes replied that the Commonwealth Government was vested with supreme power to conduct all matters relating to the war: the revolution in Russia and the débâcle in Italy gravely imperilled the cause of the Allies: in this crisis every part of the Empire must do its duty: the safety of Australia and its liberties depended upon an Allied victory: General Birdwood had stated that owing to the lack of reinforcements it was impossible to maintain the five Australian divisions at their full strength.[54]

At the public meeting addressed by Hughes in the Exhibition Building in Brisbane on 27 November there were the same displays of enthusiasm as in other cities. There was prolonged cheering, waving of hats and handkerchiefs. Hughes made the usual charges against Labor and Dr Mannix. The Labor Party had sold itself for the support of the Germans and Sinn Fein. Dr Mannix was the figurehead of the 'No' campaign. That was greeted with loud cries of 'Send him to Germany', 'Deport the traitor'. Ryan replied by accusing Hughes of attempting to stifle discussion on a most vital question. In Melbourne Dr Mannix took up the same point. Hughes was trampling on the liberties of the people. The anti-conscriptionists could not even hire halls for their meetings. Australia, he told his audience at a concert in aid of the Northcote parish, was under the rule of the 'little Czar'. The people did not want such intolerance. Australia has fallen low. 'If these things happened in a green year, what would happen in the dry?' Australians should keep a hold on the freedom they possessed. The following night Dr Mannix roused his audience again in North Brunswick by telling them they did not want any 'little Czars' in Australia. Hughes was trying to silence the Australian people. The people must rally to protect their liberties.[55]

[53] D. J. Murphy, *T. J. Ryan* (St Lucia, 1975), ch. 2.

[54] *S.M.H.*, 28 November 1917.

[55] *Age*, 28, 29 November 1917; *Argus*, 30 November 1917; *Advocate*, 8 December 1917; *Socialist*, 30 November 1917.

With Hughes and Ryan calling each other names in the best tradition of an Australian primary school playground, Hughes travelled by train from Brisbane to Warwick in the Darling Downs. Warwick was one of those country towns where the two traditions flourished: the tradition of the country gentry, of Australia as a new Britannia in another world, and the tradition of the bush as the 'nursery of much that was different from other lands'. Both sides in the conscription debate were on the platform to welcome or taunt Hughes when he arrived. Sandwich men carried placards; banners for and against conscription were hung on the walls; some bands were playing patriotic airs, others played 'The Wearing of the Green'. Neither side had a song or words which were Australian: even in this great convulsion they borrowed the words and sentiments of other people.

As soon as Hughes stepped on to the platform at Warwick on 29 November the supporters and the opponents shouted and yelled. One man threw an egg: it missed. Not to be outdone another man threw a second egg: it knocked the Prime Minister's hat off. A returned soldier pummelled the second egg-thrower. Above the uproar the voice of Hughes, unmistakable in any company, was heard to say: 'Arrest that man, constable'. The policeman, whose name was Senior Sergeant Kenny, said he must obey the laws of Queensland and no other. Above the uproar Hughes adjured them in the name of liberty to cast their votes in favour of the Government's proposals on 20 December. The cheering, the hooting, continued as he returned to his carriage. That night he sent a telegram to Ryan calling on him to suspend the policeman who had connived at the 'disgraceful proceedings'. Hughes also decided to create a Commonwealth Police Force for the protection of officers of the Commonwealth.[56]

On his journey from Warwick through another heartland of King and Empire supporters in the New England district of New South Wales Hughes spoke passionately of loyalty to the Empire as the only way to ensure the safety of Australia. He issued instructions to prosecute Ryan and Theodore. Back in Sydney on 4 December he made an appeal to the women of Australia. 'You are to say', he told them in Her Majesty's Theatre that night,

> whether you will act now as becomes mothers, sisters and wives of free men, or whether you will act in such a fashion as will lead this, our country, down the steep declivity of shame and dishonor. You may listen, as your first mother, to the voice of the serpent in Eden, and fill your minds with the poisonous stories that are circulating . . .

Australia must remain part of the British Empire, or be handed over to traitors. His Intelligence men supplied the information which fed his terrors and his fantasies. They told him in a memorandum that the Queensland

[56] *Age*, 30 November 1917; *Argus*, 30 November 1917.

Police Force was honeycombed with Sinn Feiners. Nellie Melba sent a special message to the women of Australia urging them to do their duty on 20 December. 'I tried to make it strong', she told Hughes, 'because *entre nous* very few Australian women use their brains'. She was prepared to do anything to help Australia in 'this appalling struggle & tragedy'.[57]

On the same day Dr Mannix put the case against conscription with the same appeals to the heart rather than the head which the conscriptionists were exploiting. He accused Hughes of wanting to put the people of Australia under the heel of military domination. He repeated again one of the catch-cries of the anti-conscription campaign. 'I make', he said, 'no apology for putting Australia first and the Empire second'. The time for argument was over. This was a time when music expressed the passions of the human heart. The conscriptionists had their songs. They sang with tears of exaltation in their eyes their 'God Save the King': they beefed out 'Land of Hope and Glory': they sang the great conservative hymn of repentance and resignation, beseeching the Lord of Hosts to be 'with us yet/Lest we forget, lest we forget'. Like the southern gentlemen in the American Civil War who reminded themselves of the high calling of their cause by reciting the beautiful words: 'If I forget thee, O Jerusalem', pro-conscriptionists recited with fervour: 'The King. God bless him'. The antis also had their songs. On the Yarra Bank, Hyde Park, or in the Socialist Hall they looked at each other with hope and faith as they sang:

> Solidarity for ever!
> Solidarity for ever!
> Solidarity for ever!
> For the Union makes us strong.

They had their moments of confident laughter when they sang to each other:

> I met a working man to-day who wore in his lapel
> A photo of a plutocrat, and a Union Jack as well.

They had their faith: there might not be any resurrection of the dead or any life of the world to come, but a new era was about to begin for humanity. The workers were about to put an end to 'Fat's aggression': there would be no more war: socialism would wipe away all tears from their eyes, and there would be no more weeping.[58]

[57] *Age*, 5 December 1917; Memorandum to W. M. Hughes for meeting of Executive Council, December 1917, Hughes Papers, Series 20, Folder 4; Nellie Melba to W. M. Hughes, 4 December 1917, ibid.

[58] *Age*, 5 December 1917; Anti-Conscription Army Songs, Collection in Hughes Papers.

Hughes was like a conjuror who could always pull a new coloured handkerchief out of his pocket. On 6 December he told Australians he had something to tell them of the 'utmost gravity'. Russia had signed an armistice and was preparing to sign a peace treaty with Germany. At one stroke the blockade of Germany was ended: Germany would now have unlimited supplies of fuel and food. On the night of 6 December he repeated his threat to resign if the referendum were not carried. If the people did not do their duty, they would no longer have him to lead them. He repeated his promises: married men would be exempt: farmers would have the labour necessary to carry on their work. He put the situation frankly, he said, because he did not want Australians to live in a fool's paradise.[59]

From that day Hughes dwelt more and more on the consequences of voting 'No': Australia would have to do without him; 'after me the deluge'; their mates in France would be let down; liberty would disappear; White Australia would come to an end. The posters of the Universal Service League also played on the passions and prejudices of the voters in the referendum. There was the poster, 'The Anti's Creed', which read in part:

> I believe the men at the front should be sacrificed.
>
> . . .
>
> I believe that our women should betray the men who
> are fighting for them.
>
> . . .
>
> I believe in murder on the high seas
> I believe in the I.W.W.
> I believe in Sinn Fein
> I believe that Britain should be crushed and humiliated.
>
> . . .
>
> I believe in handing over Australia to Germany
> I believe I'm worm enough to vote No.
> Those who DON'T believe in the above Creed
> will vote YES.[60]

The posters of the Anti-Conscription League also appealed to the heart:

> Forcing other people to risk their lives for me
> is not courage: it is cowardice.
>
> . . .
>
> VOTE NO!!!

The anti-conscriptionists chanted they were the defenders of liberty, the upholders of White Australia. A 'No' vote was a guarantee that the 'hands of Australia's democracy' would never 'lock the chains'. Vote 'No'! Be on the

[59] *Age*, 7 December 1917.
[60] *Age*, 8 December 1917; Collection of War Posters and Pamphlets, N.L.A.

side of those who had faith in a better world, a world in which war and poverty would be no more, and men no longer hurt and destroy each other![61]

On the eve of the referendum, 19 December, the Returned Soldiers Association held their final rally in the Melbourne Town Hall. Captain Stanley Melbourne Bruce, an officer in the 2nd Royal Fusiliers, the winner of a Military Cross and a French War Cross, told them the war was just. Australia had not done enough, Australians should be told what would happen if Germany won the war. Lack of reinforcements would mean that soldiers who needed and had deserved a spell could not come out of the trenches.

Bruce was an Australian who spoke like an Englishman and dressed like an Englishman. Stanley Melbourne Bruce was born in St Kilda, Melbourne, on 15 April 1883. He was educated at Melbourne Grammar School and Trinity Hall, Cambridge. Everything he did was done with great distinction. He played in the first teams and was captain of his school. He then worked in the family firm of Paterson, Laing and Bruce before proceeding to Trinity Hall, Cambridge, in 1902. He was given a rowing blue at Cambridge and coached their crew to victory on the eve of the war. In 1913 he married Ethel Dunlop Anderson, grand-daughter of Thomas Manifold of Purrumbete. It was a union of families in high society in the business world and the world of the country gentry. She was his 'eternal mate'. They became members of the Melbourne world of fashion, the world of bridge, golf, dinner parties and the theatre. But Bruce was more than a handsome playboy of the drawing rooms of Toorak and the putting greens of the Royal Melbourne Golf Club. He enlisted in the British army on the outbreak of war. At Suvla Bay he won the Military Cross for bravery. After being invalided out of the army he won the by-election for the seat of Flinders in April 1917.

So far he had only repeated the parrot cry of the conservatives of the need for business methods in government. But there was more to Bruce than that. Behind the well-groomed face and the elegant clothes there lived a man who did not find it easy to show his view to any human being. Opponents dismissed him as a member of the idle rich. They soon found they were in error. They saw him as a money-changer who wore the clothes and imitated the manners of an English country gentleman. Bruce had the capacity to grow, the precious gift of moving with the great river of life. Bruce was lucky. He liked human beings. Unlike Billy Hughes he was neither a mocker nor a hater. No one whose eyes moistened that night as they all joined in a hopeful rendition of the National Anthem foresaw the role this clean-cut young English army officer would play in the history of Australia. Hughes

[61] War Posters Collection; *Socialist*, 7 December 1917.

welcomed him as an ally in a noble fight. He did not foresee that 'Yarraside' now had one of their own class to lead them in politics.[62]

On 20 December the last appeals were made. Hughes told the people of Australia they were about to decide the destiny of their country. They were about to show the world what manner of men and women they were. They must declare they stood loyally by the Empire and their kinsmen in the trenches or desert those to whom they owed all things. 'Birdie' sent a letter to a brother officer pleading with him to do all in his power to obtain reinforcements for the front. The 'boys' wanted a spell. Alfred Deakin, broken by illness, believing God in his wisdom had decreed that his tongue should be silent, called on what was left of the mighty spirit that used to be Alfred Deakin to write his own appeal to 'keep Australia white and free'. 'My countrymen, be true to yourselves, to Australia, and to our great Empire. Let our voices thunder 'YES', and future generations shall arise and call us blessed. GOD SAVE AUSTRALIA'.[63]

Thousands thronged the city streets as soon as the counting began. They were just as divided as the participants in the long and bitter struggle. The 'Yes' supporters gathered around the banner of the Returned Soldiers in Melbourne, the 'No' supporters around the banners of their opponents with the temperate slogans of the Labor Party and the inflammatory Red Flag of the socialists. By midnight a smile of victory was on the face of Frank Tudor and a look of triumph on the face of Frank Anstey. The morning newspapers on 21 December announced a majority for 'No'. By then the vote was 718 465 for 'No' and 568 670 for 'Yes': Majority for 'No', 149 795. The soldiers' vote, which had not been counted, could not affect the result. When the votes from the front came in, the men who knew the horrors of war were unwilling to force their experiences on their fellow men. 'Birdie' was disappointed with the result. The Governor-General was surprised, his hopes, like those of Hughes, having been so high. The conservatives were depressed. The Victorian conservatives were puzzled that such a loyal State as Victoria did not have a large majority for 'Yes'. Even at Hamilton, the capital of Australia Felix, the district which was expected to remain English for thousands of years, there was a majority for 'No'.[64]

Frank Tudor said the people had declined to swallow the sugar-coated conscription pill which was placed before them by the Government. Fifty thousand people attended a victory rally at Frankston Park to express their gratitude to their great leader, Dr Mannix, for saving Australia from the

[62] *Age*, 20 December 1917; *Table Talk* (Melbourne) 8, 29 December 1921, 15 February 1923; *Stead's Review*, 27 October 1923; C. Edwards, *Bruce of Melbourne* (London, 1965).

[63] *Age*, 21 December 1917.

[64] *Age*, 21 December 1917; Don Garden, *Hamilton: A Western District History* (Hamilton, 1984), p. 187; R. M. Ferguson to W. Birdwood, 7 January 1918, Novar Papers.

'shackles of slavery'. The Archbishop was elated: Mr Hughes's light has gone out, he told them: sectarianism has got a death blow: those who had put Australia first had won a great victory. The *Socialist* was elated. The civilian population had defeated 'the curse of conscription'. The people have defeated the powerful forces arrayed against them: they have defeated the 'dirty daily press, wealth and its influences', those old villains Mr Fat and Mr Money Man, 'Protestantism, five State Governments', most local governments, the recruiting sergeants, and the Commonwealth Government. Now the people must turn their minds and their energies to winning the most important war of all—the class war. Australia must cease 'buttressing Capitalism'. The 'race of Christian bipeds' must not continue to fly at each other with tooth and claw.[65]

Labor and the socialists held victory rallies. Hopes were running high: '... we of this generation', wrote the *Australian Worker* on 10 January 1918, 'shall live to rejoice at the downfall of Capitalism'. There will be 'peace and liberty and happiness for all'. Speakers toasted the beginning of a new era. The people, they said, must proclaim themselves 'masters of the situation and keepers of their own destiny'. Hughes must go. The all-powerful people must not let the 'rat' wriggle out of his promise to resign if the referendum went against him. The people have won one victory. The conscriptionists were still entrenched in power. This was no time for jubilation. This was a time to force the 'rat' and his pitiful political cronies out of political power. The people have stuck a stake in the 'black heart' of Hughes.[66]

In the euphoria of victory men and women spoke of their own hopes for the future. It was the time of the Christ child, the time of 'Peace on earth, goodwill towards men'. Charles Strong of the Australian Church in Melbourne hoped Australia would not go back to the same old Mammon worship. He wanted Australians to breathe into their lives such a 'Christ-spirit' that would 'put a soul into us to work for social reconstruction and re-organisation on lines of goodwill and brotherhood'. The time had come to fulfil the hope of Joseph Furphy: 'to discern through the crudeness of dawn a promise of majestic day'. Charles Strong hoped for a revival of 'spiritual truth and beauty': he appealed for 'spirituality'.[67]

Hughes was busy extricating the country from the political tangle that ensued from his promise to resign if the referendum were not carried. He had promised in a rash moment to resign within twenty-four hours of defeat. Fourteen days later he was still in office. By 3 January 1918 Hughes was ready for the 'horrors of haste'. A party meeting was held. The Nationalist

[65] *Age*, 21 December 1917; *Advocate*, 5 January 1918; *Socialist*, 11 January 1918.
[66] *Socialist*, 11 January 1918; *Australian Worker*, 27 December 1917, 3, 10 January 1918.
[67] *Fellowship*, January 1918, p. 75.

Party by 63 votes to 2 expressed confidence in Hughes, after which they sang 'For he's a jolly good fellow'. Sir John Forrest had let it be known that he was prepared to take over from Hughes. But Hughes had his measure. The party wanted a leader, not a stop-gap. The party has decided that, in the interests of the Empire, Hughes should remain in office. The Empire men still had their supporters. On 6 January 1918, the Sunday after the vote of confidence in Hughes, at St Paul's Cathedral in Melbourne the Anglican Archbishop, Henry Lowther Clarke, put their hopes and faith into words: 'Our Empire stands for certain principles and rights, and these must be maintained or we are lost to honour and bankrupt in reputation'. In Scots Church, Melbourne, the Reverend W. Borland assured the congregation it was God's will that the Empire should continue the struggle for the triumph of right and liberty. 'If God be for us', he asked, 'who can be against us'.[68]

Labor called on Hughes to show he was an honourable man by standing by his promises. Hughes obliged. On 7 January he announced he proposed to wait on the Governor-General and tender his resignation. On the morning of 8 January he did just that. Sir Ronald sent for Frank Tudor and asked him whether he could form a Government. Frank Tudor said no, he could not. Labor militants said that Tudor should have accepted and asked for a dissolution. Others said that would be playing into the hands of Hughes. On 9 January Sir Ronald offered Hughes a commission to form a Ministry. Sir Ronald decided only Hughes could provide the necessary stability. Hughes accepted. The Nationalist Party endorsed his decision. On 10 January the Hughes Ministry was sworn in. On 11 January Tudor moved a vote of no confidence, but he was like a man speaking into a gale of wind. On 12 January the *Commonwealth Gazette* announced the members of the Hughes Government. They were the same as those who handed in their resignations on 9 January. Sir John Forrest has lost his chance. The dreams of the visionaries must wait their turn. In political life in Australia, conservatism was like one of those things from eternity: it did not change. The people won the conscription referendums. The comfortable classes won the struggle for political power.[69]

[68] R. M. Ferguson to King George V, 28 January 1918, Novar Papers; *Australian Worker*, 10 January 1918; *Argus*, 4, 7 January 1918.

[69] *Australian Worker*, 10 January 1918; *Argus*, 8, 9, 10, 11 January 1918; *C'wealth P.D.*, 11 January 1918, vol. 83, pp. 2921–42; *C'wealth Gazette*, 12 January 1918.

3

A DIVIDED AUSTRALIA

WHEN ON 17 October 1917 the news reached Sir John Forrest, the Treasurer of the Commonwealth of Australia, that the last rails necessary to provide a continuous railway line over the 1052 miles between Port Augusta in South Australia and Kalgoorlie in Western Australia had been laid near Ooldea, six hundred miles east of Kalgoorlie, Sir John said it was a great day for Australia and the Empire. Australia has been linked together by bands of steel. The rail link would, he believed, create 'a broader and nobler national life'. There would be a 'wider sympathy with our kinsmen in the "old land" and with the British people throughout the world'. He rejoiced that a great triumph of civilization had come in his day. Iron and steel manufactured in Australia from Australian iron ore, in furnaces fired by local coal, have begun to end industrial backwardness in Australia. Australia would not be a sheep walk for ever, a granary, an orchard and a slaughterhouse supplying raw materials for the advanced people of the world—especially the British.[1]

Australia was ceasing to be a farm. Population was shifting from the country to the cities. Publicists who identified country life with virtue and innocence and city life with corruption and depravity were disturbed. They spoke and wrote of a 'drift to the cities'. Parliaments appointed committees to report on it. They concluded, 'a spirit of restlessness' was abroad: the townward tendency was evident all over Australia. Politicians wanted the 'townward tendency' to be checked. Committees of State Parliaments identified the causes as bad railways, bad roads, bad education and shortage of water in the country districts. The quality of life in the country must be improved. But no palliative could affect the underlying causes: Australia was changing from a primary to a secondary producing country: the cities offered employment: the cities offered the pleasures and the titillations the new age believed essential for human happiness.[2]

Australia was a divided community. Some women were demanding equal-

[1] *Argus*, 18 October 1917.

[2] A. A. Billson, 'A Country Life Policy', *Argus*, 18 May 1918; Report of the Select Committee upon the causes of the Drift of Population from Country Districts to the City, *Vic. P.P.*, 1918, vol. 1.

ity with men—equal pay for equal work, access to the professions, equality of opportunity. At the Empire Theatre in Melbourne, Bella Lavender called on women to revolt against their lot as pack-horses to men in the lower classes or poodles to men in the comfortable classes. At the Women's Convention held under the auspices of the Victorian Branch of the Australian Labor Party in September 1917, Mrs. A. K. Wallace passed a resolution that in the opinion of the Convention the time had arrived when a certain number of seats on the Central Executive of the Party should be reserved for women. Political emancipation of women has been followed quickly by their economic emancipation. Women have won their place amongst wage-earners. But society could not agree on what that place was to be. Some argued for equality with men. Some said a woman ought to be paid what she was worth, or what she could command. Some said woman was a transient in the labour force, and therefore would never have the labour value of a man. The women from the comfortable classes prominent in public life believed the noblest contribution women could make to winning the war was in providing comforts for their menfolk at the front: knitting socks, gloves, scarves, Balaclava helmets, making food parcels, being 'pen pals' to the 'brave boys' in France. Women, they believed, found their fulfilment in ministering to the needs of men. That was the lot God had assigned to them.[3]

Artists and writers were divided. Until the day he died on 20 December 1917 Frederick McCubbin insisted that Australian artists would fulfil their highest destiny only if they remained in their own country. Artists must be in love with the beauty of Australia: they must uncover to Australians the fragile beauty beneath the dryness and the harshness. Artists must not go into exile: all those who lived abroad were in a dream: all those who cultivated 'Englishmanism' walked into the night. As McCubbin lay dying Mary Grant Bruce's huge reading public in Australia was enjoying the story of Jim and Wally at the war. Like Bob Menzies, Mary Grant Bruce was 'dyed in the wool British'. Her two bush boys, Jim and Wally, the inheritors of the bush virtues of pluck, courage, resource and 'decency', were educated in the wilds of Gippsland and at Melbourne Grammar School. They enlisted in the British army, not the Australian Imperial Force. For them the war was being fought so that the world of Melbourne Grammar and 'that sort of thing' might go on for ever. While her reading public was deep in the story of Jim and Wally, the prophet of a different Australia, the one who had called on Australians to give up the 'Old Dead Tree' and to believe in the 'Young Tree Green'—Henry Lawson—was pleading with George Robertson: 'Send

[3] *Argus*, 10, 22 March, 21 November 1917, 23 April 1918; *Labor Call*, 11 October 1917; *Socialist*, 14 June 1918.

down a bob . . . and I'll start on the new books. *You know I never touch it between drinks*'.[4]

In February 1918 it was announced that Sir John Forrest had accepted Mr Hughes's offer to recommend that he be made a peer of the realm in England. The conservatives believed this was a fitting reward for a life of service both as the explorer of the inhospitable deserts and coasts of Western Australia, and as a distinguished servant of Australia and the Empire. The *Australian Worker* thought it might be uncharitable to throw cold water or a brick or a dead cat at the source of Sir John's happiness, but the creation of a titled class did not harmonize with Australian democratic ideals. They did not believe in the creation of a parasitic class which revelled in the philosophy of the snob. They regretted that a man who was so big and splendid in his younger years became 'so small and paltry in his old age'. Billy Hughes told Lady Forrest of the impending honour for her husband. Lady Forrest wept. Billy Hughes told his cronies, 'I wept too—I would have made him a Duke to get rid of him'.[5]

By February there was more to think about or mock at or mourn over than the vanity of Sir John, the man who had conquered the Australian desert but not the ambitions of his heart, or the pitilessness of Billy Hughes. The Russian revolution had created a new situation in the world. The *Argus* at first dismissed the Bolsheviks as a joke. The Bolsheviks had already confirmed the decision of the Kerensky Government to reform the Russian alphabet. That amused the *Argus*: 'It is profoundly interesting', it wrote in its editorial on 8 January, 'to find men who are engaged in regenerating the world teaching their fellow-countrymen how to spell'. Ten days later it reassured its readers:

> Russia is in the hands of quacks. The men who are treating her for various ailments know as much of their business as did the physicians of the Middle Ages who prescribed for various ills such remedies as newts' hearts, lizards' legs and dried spiders, to be swallowed facing the rising moon, and followed with a course of blood-letting.

The Bolsheviks had not achieved liberty and equality. They had only created a 'fanatical fraternity'. The Bolsheviks were not peacemakers: they were the

[4] Frederick McCubbin, 'Some Remarks on Australian Art', quoted in Ann Galbally, *Frederick McCubbin* (Richmond, 1982), p. 140; Mary Grant Bruce, *Jim and Wally* (London, 1916); Henry Lawson, 'A Song of the Republic', *Bulletin*, 1 October 1887; Henry Lawson to George Robertson, n.d., probably November 1917, Colin Roderick (ed.), *Henry Lawson Letters 1890–1922* (Sydney, 1970), p. 364.

[5] *Australian Worker*, 14 February 1918; W. M. Hughes to John Forrest, 18 February 1918, Hughes Papers, Series 16, Folder 2; John Forrest to W. M. Hughes, 21 March 1918, ibid.

instruments of 'wholesale murder', persecutors of all true religion and virtue.[6]

The *Australian Worker* disagreed. The Bolshevik, it said, was 'not the barbarian he is painted by the capitalistic press'. Lenin was not a lunatic as the capitalistic press reported, but one of the most enlightened and educated men of Russia. The working masses in the world would have cause to bless the movement started in Russia. There were two conflicting elements in the world—capitalist rule and social revolution. Between them there was no common ground. The central issue of the day was not the war in Europe, but the irreconcilable class struggle.[7]

Hughes was again in low spirits. Many times he had thought of tossing in the towel, but the knowledge that the Governor-General and others believed in him had kept him going. 'I still wish', he wrote to the Governor-General, 'that Britain may triumph in this great struggle. I'd sooner die a hundred times than that we should be beaten'. But victory must come quickly. The Russian revolution added a new fear to the men and women he led—the fear of social revolution. The Intelligence men have already familiarized him with the aims of Sinn Fein—to drive the 'Protestant Robbers and Beasts in Ireland' into the sea. The Intelligence men have acquainted him with the plans of the I.W.W. for a bloody revolution. They were a joke—a push-over. Now the Intelligence men were telling him of a real threat: Bolsheviks preached world revolution.[8]

The war news from the Middle East was promising. The Australian Light Horse, under the command of Harry Chauvel, were slowly driving the Turkish forces out of Palestine and Syria. The men of the Light Horse were the epitome of the Australian bush legend, men of courage and audacity, with the will to endure, who accepted the idea that men must endure until agony was beaten out into joy. Victories have been won. By 16 December 1917 General Allenby's army reached the outskirts of Jerusalem. Negotiations began for the surrender of the city. The Australians stormed the Mount of Olives against heavy machine-gun fire. When Charlie Bean read in London there had been machine-gun fire on the Mount of Olives he was shocked: 'The Mount—the Mount from which Christ spoke the wonderful sermon of brotherhood & charity & kindliness . . . [was] held by a nest of machine-guns & stormed by a magnificent charge at the point of the bayonet'. He thought the heavens must fall. The victorious Australians saw it in a quite different light. The women of Jerusalem strewed palm leaves in front of them as they

[6] *Argus*, 8, 18 January, 4, 7, 11 February 1918.

[7] *Australian Worker*, 7 February 1918.

[8] W. M. Hughes to R. M. Ferguson, 25 April 1918, Novar Papers; 'The Sinn Fein Oath', copy in Hughes Papers, Series 21, Folder 3.

entered the ancient city. One wit said he was so hungry he could eat Christ's shin-bones. Others wept as the monks sang 'Kyrie Eleison, Christe Eleison' at the midnight Mass to celebrate the birth of Christ.[9]

Before the Australians gave the Turks the 'pen-knife' treatment on the Mount of Olives, Charlie Bean discussed with Douglas Haig the candidates for appointment as the first Australian to be Commander-in-Chief of the Australian Imperial Forces in France and Flanders. Haig argued that the time had come for the Australians to build up a staff of their own. Bean suggested Brudenell White. Haig put forward the name of John Monash: 'now... er... there's General Monash, for example... He has made a great success of everything he has touched—a very solid man'. That was the point: Monash could help to win the war. Charlie Bean did not agree. Monash, he granted, was immensely able, but he was too 'pushy'. Haig wanted a compromise, an appointment which would satisfy the Australian request without conflicting with the interests of the Empire. But that was a winter's subject for the forthcoming spring and summer campaigns.[10]

The era of the iron men has begun. Visionaries must be held up to derision. On 8 January 1918 President Wilson presented to the United States Congress his Fourteen Points. He spoke of justice to all peoples and nationalities, and their right to live on equal terms of liberty and safety with one another whether they be strong or weak. For Wilson this was a 'moral climax' in a 'final war for human liberty'. The world must be made 'fit and safe to live in', and every peace-loving nation must determine its own institutions and be assured of justice and fair dealing. The Fourteen Points were, in his mind, 'the only possible programme' to achieve such a peace. Hughes believed in liberty. But Hughes dismissed all talk of protecting the weak against the strong as 'empty vapourings'. Iron men would win the war: iron men would dictate the peace. The Allies must act quickly. In March those treacherous, godless Bolsheviks agreed to the terms for a peace treaty between Germany and Russia. Conversations were conducted at Brest-Litovsk. On 5 March the Bolshevik Commander-in-Chief ordered the Russians to cease hostilities. The Kaiser was overjoyed: 'The German sword, borne by our great army commanders, has achieved peace with Russia. My feeling of thanks to God, who has been with us, is associated with rejoicing for my army's deeds'. Once again the Allies were confronted with a crisis as grave as when, in September 1914, the advance German troops on the Marne were marching on Paris. The Germans could now move reinforcements to the Western Front. The blockade of Germany could be relieved by German access to the granaries of Russia. Russia might export her revolu-

[9] Diary of C. E. W. Bean, 17 December 1917.
[10] Ibid., 12 October 1917.

tion to Germany and France. Hughes and those who supported him were now fighting not just for the Allies, but for their class.[11]

The behaviour of Hughes during the second conscription campaign had raised doubts about him as a Prime Minister. Sycophants still praised him as the man to hold up the banner of 'Progressive Democracy'. Some conservatives believed an ex-Labor man was an electoral asset. Ex-Labor men helped conservatives to win the vital middle vote at an Australian election. Hughes had one other asset. As an ex-Labor man he had the habit of vibrating 'with sympathy for the downtrodden masses'. Hughes could do this, they said, as no other Australian could. Hughes might also help to win the war quickly, and so save the Empire and Australia from revolution. But some conservatives wondered whether Hughes, their trump card in 1916–17, was now a liability. Hughes was a 'strife-stirrer, sectarian-monger, political schemer and hanger-on-to-office'. Hughes was the 'Great Obstructionist'. The conservatives now needed a conciliator, not a ranter or a raver, or a man with delusions of grandeur. They wanted a man of dignity.[12]

A crisis on the Western Front put an end temporarily to all such speculation. On 21 March 1918 a newspaper boy chalked on his blackboard in London: 'Bombardment on the whole front'. When Charlie Bean read it, his heart raced. The German was really going to do it: the German army was thrusting against the right flank of the British army, hoping to separate it from the French, drive it back to the coast and destroy it as a fighting force, and then turn on the French. General Monash was sunbaking at Mentone on the Riviera when he received the urgent message to return to the front. Panic broke out in the British army. Australians ordered to proceed from Ypres to defend Hébuterne witnessed the rout. The French were alarmed. French civilians spat at the retreating British. The Commander-in-Chief of the French army, Marshal Pétain, lost his nerve. Haig demanded he be replaced. On 26 March the French hastily nominated Marshal M. Foch, a man of iron will, a 'Germany must pay' man, to be their Commander-in-Chief. Foch issued orders: there must be no withdrawal.

Monash arrived at Doullens. The tough men were in command, the men without the eye of pity. On 28 March the Allied withdrawal halted. The Germans began another offensive, this time on 4 April against Villers-Bretonneux. From 4 to 24 April the Germans probed the Allied line. Australian soldiers, who had expected some leave as a reward for enduring the agonies of Passchendaele and the surrounding area, again had to live through all the horrors of bombardment and machine-gun fire and mustard gas. The increasing bitterness of their songs expressed their feelings. 'Dinky

[11] *Argus*, 6 March 1918; Robert Birley (ed.), *Speeches and Documents in American History* (4 vols, Oxford, 1942), vol. 4, pp. 38–42; *Age*, 9, 10, 11 January 1918.

[12] H. Lamond to W. M. Hughes, 10 January 1918, Hughes Papers, Series 2, Folder 5; T. Dunleavy to W. G. Spence, 6, 17 January 1918, ibid.; *Soldier*, 1 March 1918.

Die' spoke eloquently of their anger with the 'bludgers (behind the lines) who dodge all the strafe/By getting soft jobs on the headquarters staff'. There were songs about 'the shambles in France', and of the 'brave men' who were 'dying for loafers like you'.[13]

The Australian Government must persuade more men to volunteer. But age has staled the appeals of the recruiting sergeants. The crisis has not silenced the opponents of the war. Labor speakers renewed their calls to end the 'blood-spilling business'. The Socialists repeated their slogan: there was a war in Europe part of the time, but the class war was everywhere all the time. Despite the air of a patriotic carnival fostered at the recruiting meetings, despite the brass bands, the liberal hospitality, and all the attempts to send country people stark, staring mad with the 'chloroform' dope of the 'superior' classes, the people listened spellbound when Adela Pankhurst and Frank Anstey, Robert Ross and Frederick Sinclaire, presented their appeal for peace.[14]

The Imperial Government addressed an appeal to all the Dominions for help. Hughes did not know what to do. The Chief Justice, Sir Samuel Griffith, has presented the Government with a judicious estimate of the numbers required. The Govenor-General came up with a suggestion to take recruiting out of the political arena. Hughes should free recruiting from the stigma of being identified with the National Party, with the King and Empire men, with Yarraside, Vaucluse, and Englishmanism, by holding a conference in Melbourne, of representatives of all political parties, State premiers, and prominent public men, presided over by the Hon D. Mackinnon, the Director-General of Recruiting. Around the table men of such diverse views as T. J. Ryan and J. H. Scullin on the one side could talk things over with such as men as W. A. Holman and W. M. Hughes and J. C. Watson, the one-time Labor men who had been expelled during the first conscription row. Together they could agree to put their names to recognizing the 'urgent necessity for united effort to secure adequate reinforcements', and consider 'impartially and with all good will' how to appeal to Australians to respond to the Imperial call for help. So it was hoped.[15]

The Labor press warned the workers not to be seduced by the pretence of impartiality fostered by Government House. An outburst of the old sectarian brawl cut across the harmonious atmosphere Hughes and the Governor-General hoped for. On 9 March at St John's College in Sydney Dr Mannix

[13] C. E. W. Bean, *Anzac to Amiens* (Canberra, 1961), pp. 410–31; 'Dinky Die', Collection of War Songs, A.W.M., Canberra.

[14] Report by the Royal Commission as to the Number of Members Fit for Active Service, 4 April 1918; *C'wealth P.P.*, 1917–18–19, vol. 4; *Socialist*, 29 March, 5 April 1918.

[15] Report of the Proceedings of the Conference Convened by His Excellency the Governor-General, Melbourne, April 1918, *C'wealth P.P.* 1917–18–19, vol. 2.

made yet another of his memorable remarks about the war. 'I have been called disloyal', he said, 'because I will not tune my tongue to cant and hypocrisy. If I put Australia and Ireland before the Empire it is not that I love the Empire less, but because I love Australia and Ireland more'. Such sentiments enraged the Protestants. On 9 April forty thousand people gathered at the Exhibition Building in Melbourne to declare their unswerving devotion to His Majesty King George V and to affirm their passionate loyalty to that Empire which had secured Australia in liberty, honour and prosperity. They called for the suppression of all disloyal utterances and swift action against traitors.

On 2 April sixty thousand people filled the grounds of the Melbourne Exhibition Building to express their indignation at the attacks on Dr Mannix by members of the Protestant community. The Catholics in the Labor Party were prominent on the platform. The Chairman, T. G. McGlade, declared to much laughter and applause that the attacks seemed to have been made for the most part by a band of narrow-minded Pharisees who seemed to imagine they possessed all the patriotism and all the loyalty in the community. Speakers dismissed the speeches at the Protestant rally as 'the same old lies, the same old misrepresentations with which people in Melbourne were all too familiar'. Hughes and his 'tawdry following', they said, were 'fomenting intolerance during this desperate hour'.[16]

Three days later Frank Tudor, Tom Ryan and Jimmy Scullin sat down with Billy Hughes, Willie Watt and others to consider with 'all good will' how to increase recruiting in Australia. Labor representatives explained why they were suspicious. The censorship, the War Precautions regulations, the alleged connivance of the Federal Government at profiteering had created ill feeling. Labor still had a real fear that conscription might be introduced. Labor believed that the British had 'bled Australia white'. While Frank Tudor and Jimmy Scullin were trying hard to see whether they could find some common ground with Hughes and the 'win the war' men, other Labor delegates were attending an Inter-State peace conference in Sydney. There the delegates passed a resolution condemning the capitalistic system as provocative of war, calling on women to play a creative role in the coming of peace, and condemning the censorship in Australia.[17]

At the Governor-General's Conference Hughes wanted all the delegates, including the Labor men, to agree on a resolution which would at least tell Australians about this moment of 'imminent peril'. The 'win the war' men wanted something more. They wanted the delegates to agree to resolutions which, as Senator Fairbairn put it, would be 'a tremendous aid to the Old Land, from which our race has sprung'. They were all passing through a

[16] *S.M.H.*, 11 March 1918; *Age*, 13 April 1918; *Argus*, 3 April 1918; *Freeman's Journal*, 11, 18 April 1918; *Advocate*, 13 April 1918.

[17] *S.M.H.*, 12, 23 April 1918.

dreadful time: they ought, therefore, to assist the Empire in every possible way. Labor men could not accept those sentiments. Hughes wanted the delegates to express in their resolution a recognition that this was 'a time of unparalleled emergency', and of 'the necessity for harmony'. Jimmy Scullin would not accept that. For him and Labor the harmony did not exist. On 19 April the Conference resolved that 'at a time of unparalleled emergency' they would make all efforts to avert defeat at the hands of Germany. They urged the people of Australia to join in a whole-hearted effort to secure the necessary reinforcements under the voluntary system.[18]

On 26 April the Victorian Labor Party issued its manifesto to the electors for the by-election in Flinders: 'The Labour Party' [*sic*], the manifesto declared, 'stands for peace by negotiation . . . The Labour Party stands for the immediate cessation of fighting and for the calling of an international conference to settle peace terms'. They added: 'Commonsense bids us say, "We don't want a colonial empire", and if commonsense were silent, humanity would cry, "Let no blood flow to win territory for Australia. She drew the sword for the right, not for reward" '. The opponent of the Labor candidate was Stanley Melbourne Bruce. Hughes was delighted with the electoral victory of Bruce.[19]

Two days after the Governor-General's Conference urged the people of Australia to unite in a whole-hearted effort to secure the necessary reinforcements under the voluntary system, the socialists held a rally in the Melbourne Socialist Hall. To enthusiastic applause John Curtin condemned the Labor Party members for accepting the resolution at the Conference. He accused them of 'intellectual laziness'. Labor's struggle was not against war but against capitalism. Labor should use force not for 'the destruction of our brothers', but for the upheaval which should make for working-class authority in the fields, factories and workshops. The world was clamouring for social change: Labor men should not 'play the game of little children'.[20]

At the same time on the Somme and near Ypres Australian soldiers were living through 'a veritable hell'. A bluish vapour like a pall hung over those fields where once the skylarks sang. The Germans were using mustard gas. Men affected by the gas were stumbling about as though they were drunk. Between 21 March and 7 May fifteen thousand Australians became casualties. At the end of April the first German offensive ended. The Australians then engaged in a type of warfare at which they excelled. One man strolled over to the German trenches in the daylight, yelled at the Germans to come out: selected one and took him back to the Australian line. Despite the years

[18] Governor-General's Conference, op. cit., pp. 160, 164; *Argus*, 19 April 1918.
[19] *Argus*, 27 April 1918.
[20] *Socialist*, 26 April 1918; *Argus*, 27 April 1918.

of military discipline, and the togetherness, the Australians relished running their own show: for Australians being on one's own was the only way.[21]

The Australian soldiers were regaining their confidence. The British stopped referring to Australian 'slack discipline', 'casualness' and irreverence towards officers. The British were beginning to talk of the Australians as the finest troops in the world. There were still patches of snow on the ground. They were anxious, but not 'funky'. They have become 'the best of pals' with the Americans. The Americans were intrigued by the Australian slouch hat: they were also intrigued by Australian slang and odd words. Australian English would, they believed, one day paralyse Broadway—especially that cheeky, confident Australian way of saying 'betcher'.[22]

In May John Monash was appointed to the command of the Australian Army Corps, containing the five Australian divisions. He was to be promoted to the rank of lieutenant-general. He replaced General Birdwood. Charlie Bean was not happy about this. He would have preferred Brudenell White. White did not advertise: Monash did. White was self-effacing: Monash had 'advertising strength'. White held back: Monash insinuated himself into the front rank. White was a server: Monash was proud. He was in command of at least 160 thousand officers and men. Besides, as he said in a letter to Australia, 'owing to the great prestige won by the corps during the last three months', it was 'much the finest corps command in the British Army'. Haig, not the Australian Government, had appointed him. Monash was proud to be selected by General Haig. On 14 May cables were sent to the Australian Government for their approval. Monash was a King and Empire man, interested in the recent 'brilliant success' of the men under his command. He sent back to Australia photographs of two reviews of his troops—photographs which he asked his correspondent to examine with a powerful large-size magnifying glass, because they deserved that 'most minute and careful examination' which he always observed. His victories have made the English sit up and take notice and realize that the Australian Corps was the backbone of the Allied armies. Monash loved the beautiful Alsatian wolf-hound at his headquarters. He patted it. Monash also loved the chestnut trees in full bloom and the glorious copper beeches in the parks of the châteaux in the district.[23]

While John Monash was telling friends how proud he was to be selected by General Sir Douglas Haig, in Melbourne and Sydney socialists celebrated 'Red Week'. They had quite a different vision from that which was driving Monash on to glory. They had a vision of a world where 'thrones have tumbled and kings are dust', of a world where 'the aristocracy of idleness has

[21] Bill Gammage, *The Broken Years* (Canberra, 1974), pp. 197–9.

[22] F. M. Cutlack (ed.), *War Letters of General Monash* (Sydney, 1934), p. 238; *Soldier*, 19 April 1919.

[23] F. M. Cutlack (ed.), op. cit., pp. 239–40; Bean Diary, 17 May 1918.

perished from the earth'. They saw not a new heaven, but a new earth—an earth without a slave, an earth where man at last was free, a world at peace adorned with every work of art, with music, with life lengthening, joy deepening, love covering the earth, and over all there shone the eternal star of human hope. A great, good time was coming for humanity. Working-class outbreaks have occurred in Germany and Austria. Russia was proving that socialism was workable. The people were about to take over the seats of power. The Australian people would challenge the present gang of exploiters, Shylocks and parasites. The soul of humanity was about to burst its bonds. The world must not be crucified on a cross of bayonets in France. The children of this generation would be wiser than their elders. At the Socialist Sunday Schools they would learn not of the life of the world to come but of the life in the here and now.[24]

Dr Mannix told an audience early in May he would never use his pulpit to do the work of a recruiting sergeant, nor would he ever attend any recruiting meetings. On 16 May at a meeting of the New South Wales Labor Council one delegate moved they resolve that careful consideration should be given to whether it was worth while to prolong the war, and to whether the Allied nations were fighting for liberty, justice and peace, or were more concerned with destroying Germany as a competitor in the world markets. The proposed resolution also declared that permanent peace was not possible under capitalism, that the ruling classes of the belligerent powers were placing their class interests above the welfare of suffering humanity. The proposed resolution declared that some of the decisions of the recruiting conference were 'bribes for lives', and that the 'bleeding of the manhood of the white races to death, thereby forcing many millions of women to endure a life of celibacy, was a crime. Hard and uncongenial work, the resolution declared, was a crime against civilization. The populations of the world were war-weary and longed for peace. The greatest service that could be done to the men at the front and their loved ones at home was to stop the war. Labor should therefore call upon the workers to urge their respective Governments 'to immediately secure an armistice on all fronts, and initiate negotiations for peace'. The meeting ended in uproar, without the resolution being put.[25]

Moderates said the proposed resolution only showed that the 'red rag' group was out to take control of the Labor movement. The loyal element in the Trade Union movement must dissociate itself in the most unequivocal manner from the disloyal. The war must be won quickly before the red raggers took over Australia. This was no time for bargaining and bartering: 'Our house can be opened up for the spring cleaning when the wolf has

[24] *Socialist*, 3, 10 May 1918.

[25] R. M. Ferguson to W. Birdwood, 6 May 1918, Novar Papers; *S.M.H.*, 17 May 1918.

passed'. The Labor Party wanted freedom of discussion and public meeting re-established, and all rules and regulations prejudicial to the freedom of Labor organizations repealed. The majority in the Labor Party was too timid to ride the tiger of a people's movement against the war.[26]

The comfortable classes were still in power in Australia. They had their heroes: they had their mythology. At Melbourne Grammar the boys were told they were carrying on to the full the traditions which had made the Public Schools of the Empire such an example of Public Service, by providing leaders to carry on the Empire in war and peace. Scotch College in Melbourne was proud of John Monash as one of their great native sons. Eton School in Nundah, Queensland, was proud of Cyril Brudenell Bingham White, the son of a man who had fought a good fight against the back country in Queensland. Sydney Grammar School was proud of Henry George Chauvel, the commander of the Australian Light Horse in Palestine. They had their world. In June 1918 during a lull in the fighting on the Western Front Lieutenant R. P. Franklin, headmaster of Melbourne Grammar School, heard some good news: Melbourne Grammar had won the boat race.[27]

In the school chapels the boys were exhorted in hushed voices to revere thc honoured dead. At Melbourne Grammar School there was Ronald Guy Larking, killed in France in a motor-cycle accident. He had been a prefect in 1908 and 1909, rowed in the crew in 1910, had run a dead heat with H. Fleming of Wesley in the mile in the Combined Sports of 1908 in a magnificent finish. At Cambridge he had won a half-blue in boxing. Like Stanley Melbourne Bruce, also an Old Melburnian, he had enlisted in the British army. He had been decorated for his bravery at Poziéres. He was the splendid type of young Australian, fearless, dashing, loyal and very popular. Of him, as of many others, the boys in the Melbourne Grammar Chapel said reverently: 'The School Will Not Forget'. The dead were 'Honoured Evermore':

> You, our brother who for all our praying,
> To this dear School of ours, comes back no more.

Man, as the Prayer Book told the boys, 'that is born of a woman hath but a short time to live, and is full of misery. He cometh up, and is cut down, like a flower; he fleeth as it were a shadow'.[28]

Hughes has not wavered in his determination to win the war at any cost. On 25 April 1918 just before he sailed for San Francisco on the *Niagara* he wrote to the Governor-General: 'I wish from the bottom of my heart that

[26] *S.M.H.*, 18 May 1918.
[27] *Melburnian* (Melbourne Grammar School), 1918.
[28] Ibid., 'The Burial of the Dead', *Book of Common Prayer* (Oxford edn), p. 477.

Britain may triumph in this great struggle'. At the Harvard Club in New York on 1 June he made it plain where he stood: he would deprive Germany of its assets in Australia for all time: the Allies should go on fighting until Germany was expelled from France and all the Channel ports, and Germany had to vacate Belgium. 'Having been caught once, we do not propose to be caught again'. Hughes did not want reconciliation: Hughes wanted revenge: Hughes was an 'eye for an eye, and a tooth for a tooth' man. On 29 May he met President Wilson, the man of the 'empty vapourings'. Hughes showed what manner of man he was. Wilson was not impressed. He remained as 'unresponsive as the sphinx in the desert'. Wilson was like 'a stuffed image'. Hughes tottered out into the outside world to take comfort from seeing 'ordinary human beings—going about their lawful occasions'. The roar of the traffic fell upon his ears 'like sweet music'. They would confront each other again.[29]

In London he displayed all the fire of personal conviction and enthusiasm he had shown in May and June of 1916. He called for a Monroe Doctrine for the Pacific. Australia and New Zealand must be given security against the 'predatory power' of Germany. The territorial integrity of Australia could only be secured either by Australian control of the islands to the north or by their being placed in the hands of friendly and trustworthy nations. The situation looked good. At a meeting of the Imperial War Cabinet in London on 20 June the Foreign Secretary reported that Russia had fallen into 'complete anarchy'. The Bolsheviks were mainly Jews—people who did not count. The British had plans to prevent Germany acquiring her food from the Ukraine. Hughes was reassured. Monash was scoring brilliant successes in executing the Haig tactics of 'peaceful penetration' of the German lines. Hughes went to France and was acclaimed again by the soldiers as their 'little Digger'. With the diggers he found a constituency to replace his one-time cronies in the Labor movement. A prophet must have a following. Between him and the diggers there was a bond which only death could break: they would follow him anywhere. With them he has again known a moment of epiphany. The diggers have strengthened his faith. He must not let them down: they were all blood brothers.[30]

Labor had a quite different idea of brotherhood. On 5 June, while Hughes was cracking jokes about winning the war, the Brisbane Industrial Council declared the sole interest of the workers of all countries lay in stopping the war. No Labor man, they said, should appear on a recruiting platform in Australia. There should be an immediate armistice upon all fronts followed by negotiations for peace. Hughes and the Nationalist Party men and

[29] W. M. Hughes to R. M. Ferguson, 25 April 1918, Novar Papers; *New York Times*, 2 June 1918; W. M. Hughes, *Policies and Potentates* (Sydney, 1950), pp. 229–30.

[30] *The Times*, 17 June 1918; Minutes of Imperial War Cabinet, 20, 28 June 1918, Hughes Papers, Series 23, sub-series 3, Folder 8.

women were beating the Imperial drum: Labor was more and more stridently chanting the raucous hymn of Australian nationalism. At the Seventh Commonwealth Conference held in Perth on 17 June speakers asserted the right of Australians to deal with Australian affairs. Some wanted to go further: some asked that the Prime Minister be Australian-born, some that Ministers of State be Australian-born, and others that all candidates for the Federal or State Parliaments should be native born. Wiser councils prevailed. Maurice Blackburn asked whether Labor could be an international movement if it agreed to anything of this sort.[31]

At the Conference in Perth the Labor Party resolved that

> immediate negotiations be initiated for an International Conference, for the purpose of arranging equitable terms of peace, on which conference the working-class organisations shall have adequate representation, and the inclusion of women delegates, and we further urge that the British self-governing Dominions and Ireland shall be granted separate representation thereon.

The people were suffering and dying in millions. Thousands of the ruling and privileged classes were amassing huge fortunes from war profits. The complete victory by the Allies over the Central Powers could be accomplished only by the further sacrifice of human lives and the creation of an intolerable burden of debt, to the further impoverishment of the workers. There must be peace, and it must be now. The Labor Council of New South Wales agreed. In their annual report on 30 June they declared, 'the greatest service we can render the men at the Front, their loved ones at home, and humanity in general is to do all in our power to stop the war'.[32]

Hughes did not agree. He was prepared to pay the price for fighting. The war news was good. In May there had been a scare. The Germans began a push towards Aisne. The British had been routed. Clemenceau had spoken of a 'lamentable rout'. Angry words were exchanged between the British and French generals and politicians. French villagers spat at British troops as they retreated. But the push was contained. Monash again distinguished himself in the campaign of 'peaceful penetration'. The Americans arrived in large numbers—13 000 in January, 17 000 in February, 19 000 in March, 24 000 in April, 33 000 in May, 41 000 in June, giving the Allies that superiority in numbers and quantity of equipment Haig and Foch had always wanted.

Hughes was again in an impish mood. On 10 July he told the Governor-General how well the Australians had fought at Hamel: 'I thought that with a

[31] *Worker* (Brisbane), 6 June 1918; Report of the Seventh Commonwealth Conference of the Australian Labor Party, Perth, 17 June 1918, pp. 15–16.

[32] Ibid., p. 11; *Report and Balance Sheet of Labor Council of New South Wales, 30 June 1918* (Sydney, 1918).

million of such men one could conquer the world': they had 'fought like tigers'. Monash was brilliant. He had conceived the whole thing and had carried it out in a masterly fashion. Monash was purring. 'My car is a magnificent Rolls-Royce . . . my car carries the Australian flag'. The battle has been a 'brilliant success . . . brilliantly, cleanly and perfectly carried through'. The Prime Minister, the Commander-in-Chief and the Army Commander had all congratulated him. Clemenceau came specially from Paris to congratulate the Australians. He made a 'very fine and fiery oration' to them. The Allies wanted nothing less than total victory. Like Hughes, Clemenceau wanted the Germans to pay. The iron men were winning the war: the iron men would draft the terms of peace. Now was the time for revenge.[33]

The optimism was short-lived. On 14 July the Germans began a two-pronged attack on Rheims. Once again the Germans were hoping to occupy Paris. But this time they were like a prize-fighter whose sting has gone out of his punches. Monash put before Haig proposals for a counter-offensive on a large scale. The morale of the troops was high. As one of their balladists put it, they were 'joined with good old John to fight for Freedom of the World'. Back in Australia the recruiting committee was organizing Marches to Freedom in the country districts. Officers in uniform, returned servicemen, and local orators made strong appeals to the young men of the district to 'act as true democrats'. At Cootamundra, of a crowd of two thousand which gathered for the 'show', four men responded but only one was accepted. At the Socialist Hall in Melbourne other sentiments were being expressed. Bella Lavender in a stirring letter told her readers: 'Socialism (good luck to the Red Flag, say I) stands for humanity, and so must stand for woman as well as for man'. Robert Ross was also bringing tears of joy to the eyes of members of such audiences with his prophecy of the day of 'all of us together owning all that we each need'.[34]

In London Hughes had quite different reasons for feeling exuberant. The King and Empire men were about to win a great victory. On 3 August the streets around the Strand were thronged to see the King open Australia House. The King told the audience he had always known that, in any emergency for the Empire, Australia would be ready to play her part for the common cause, and that the loyalty of her sons would never be appealed to in vain. Joseph Cook promised that Australian soldiers would soon smash and punish the enemy for upsetting the world. Hughes spoke of Australia as a loyal son of the Empire. The *Sydney Morning Herald* welcomed the occasion

[33] C. E. W. Bean, *Anzac to Amiens*, pp. 446–51; W. M. Hughes to R. M. Ferguson, 10 July 1918, Novar Papers; F. M. Cutlack (ed.), op. cit., pp. 247–51; W. M. Hughes, *The Splendid Adventure* (London, 1929), pp. 79–80.

[34] F. M. Cutlack (ed.), op. cit., p. 253; 'Sergeant Billabong', *Soldier*, 26 July 1918; *S.M.H.*, 3, 5, 13, 20, 30 July 1918; *Socialist*, 28 June, 5 July 1918.

as a timely reminder, in all the stress and strain of making war, that London was the centre of Australia's commercial and financial world. London was Australia's metropolis, and Sydney a provincial city of the British Empire.[35]

Monash was also having the satisfactions he enjoyed. On 7 August, at Villers Bretonneux where the Australians had made their heroic stand the preceding April, he exhorted the troops under his command to 'inflict blows upon the enemy which will make him stagger, and will bring the end appreciably nearer'. He called on every man to carry on 'to the utmost of his powers until the goal is won: for the sake of Australia, the Empire and our cause'. Germany was breaking up. German spirits were flagging. The German press continued to assure their readers that the Allied armies had not so far achieved a major military success. But the two great German attacks had not ended in victory. Disillusionment was spreading among the people. Morale was falling off: the German mystique has lost its appeal: insubordination, like a mortal disease, was spreading in the army: the authority of the officer class has gone. The Germans were short of men and of ammunition. But still the campaign went on, the dying went on. The iron men wanted revenge: the iron men wanted total destruction. At Villers Bretonneux on 8 August the 1st Australian Division so completely knocked out the 5th Bavarian Division that it seemed unlikely it would be able to recover within two months. The German officers were panic-stricken: if peace did not come soon, there would be revolution. The British and the French ignored the peace feelers.[36]

On 12 August the King paid a visit to the headquarters of General Monash at Bertangles Château. It was a day of brilliant sunshine. A square of carpet was placed in the piazza, and on it a table, a footstool and a drawn sword. The King asked that the name of General Monash be called. Monash knelt on the footstool. Taking the sword in his hand the King dubbed General Monash, and presented him with the insignia of a Knight Commander of the Bath. The King then drove away between the cheering ranks of the Australian troops. Some days later Monash related with pride how his troops were stuffing their pockets with all sorts of interesting relics from the fleeing German troops. The Australians were having their first taste of the spoils of war.[37]

Three days later on 15 August the Imperial War Cabinet debated what to

[35] *S.M.H.*, 5, 6 August 1918.

[36] *S.M.H.*, 9 August 1918; E. Ludendorff, *My War Memories 1914–18* (London, 1919), pp. 679–83; John Monash, *The Australian Victories in France in 1918* (London, 1920), pp. 119–20; Erich Maria Remarque, *All Quiet on the Western Front* (London, 1929), pp. 240–1.

[37] Minutes of Imperial War Cabinet, 13, 14 August 1918, copy in Hughes Papers, Series 23, sub-series 3, Folder 8; F. M. Cutlack (ed.), op. cit., pp. 258–61.

do. Smuts of South Africa and others wanted negotiations with Germany. Lord Curzon did not want the war to end with a 'predominant and unexhausted Germany'. He was convinced it was essential 'to go on hammering till Germany was definitely beaten and brought to a different frame of mind'. Hughes agreed that it was 'essential to bring Germany to a right frame of mind'. He did not want any discussion with that God-botherer, President Wilson, about War Aims: he wanted to bring Germany to her knees. Lloyd George appealed to them to go on until they could dictate terms which would definitely mark 'the view taken by humanity of the heinousness of Germany's offence'.[38]

Hughes and Lloyd George will have their satisfaction. The 'blood-lust' men will have their day. Hughes went on preaching what he called 'the gospel—my gospel'. He said the things the masses wanted to hear. Germany must pay: after the war the raw materials of the British Empire must become a monopoly of the British. He met with a most enthusiastic reception. The British people, he believed, shared the 'blood lust'. They wanted an eye for an eye, and a tooth for a tooth. But the 'blood lust' men must act quickly. Germany must be crushed. The soldiers were becoming restive again. Desertion was becoming a problem in the Australian army. The men wanted home leave. Hughes had to badger the British into providing the ships: Haig had to agree that the time had come for the Australians to have a rest. The recruiting campaigns in Australia have not gone well. The Australian Labor Party was deeply divided in its attitude to recruiting. The Federal Conference of the Party has passed resolutions against recruiting. Some Federal members were unhappy with these resolutions: to abandon voluntary enlistment now, they said, on 2 September, would mean pulling out of the war, and 'leaving those trade unionists who are in the trenches without the help we should give them'. Others within the Labor movement were calling for peace now—an honourable peace, not the Hughes version of revenge and the destruction of Germany.[39]

The weakness of Germany provided the opportunity for Hughes, Curzon, Lloyd George, Haig, Monash and Clemenceau to have their day. But the war was changing the world. Wireless was reducing the isolation of Australia. On 22 September the first messages received direct from England by wireless telegraphy were recorded in Sydney. This was, as the *Sydney Morning Herald* pointed out, 'a signal advance in direct communication between the capital of the Empire and this distant outpost'. Hughes used the occasion to tell

[38] Minutes of Imperial War Cabinet, 15 August 1918, Hughes Papers, Series 23, Sub-series 3, Folder 8.

[39] W. M. Hughes to R. M. Ferguson, 1 September 1918, Novar Papers; R. M. Ferguson to W. Birdwood, 12, 30 September 1918, Novar Papers; 1st Battalion War Diary, June 1918–April 1919, Appendix 20, September 1918, A.W.M.

Australians how proud he was of the Australians on the battlefields. The 'glorious valour and dash' of the Australians have saved Amiens and forced back the legions of the enemy. The German army was on the run on the day when Australia had a victory over isolation. The aeroplane, wireless telegraphy, and secondary industry would change the world Hughes and Monash were fighting to preserve—the world of Australia as part of the Empire.[40]

Monash and Hughes were on top of the world. In the last week of September Monash was planning to break through the Hindenburg Line. Hughes was enjoying himself, trying to persuade the men in black in Whitehall to buy Australian wheat and lead and cotton and butter and tallow and hides and leather. The Whitehall men were not easy: they induced in him a mood he described with glee as 'passionate pessimism'. 'Every day', he wrote to the Governor-General on 28 September

> I bombard the enemy with high explosive with shrapnel and with everything at my disposal. I ask him why he does not buy our beautiful wheat and tallow &c? He says he lives for just that purpose: that he has in fact consecrated his life to the job; He is for the Empire & for our beautiful wheat etc. *But!* Alas he can do nothing unless the Treasury agrees! . . . Well I go & see the Treasury . . . They too want our beautiful wheat'.

And so the comedy went on.[41]

Hughes was in an exuberant mood. 'What great, what wonderful days are these through which we are passing!', he said on 9 October. Every morning brought 'most glorious tidings of some new victory of the Allied forces'. In France great stretches of territory were being regained. In Palestine the Turkish armies have been annihilated. The Australian soldiers were wandering through the bazaars of Jerusalem and Damascus and bathing in the sea of Galilee. Bulgaria has surrendered unconditionally. In Italy the Austrians were on the run: in their time of humiliation they were appealing to Germany for help, but Germany could do nothing. Germany was suing for peace. Hughes warned the British not to be deceived. This was a new trick to avoid the penalty for its awful deeds. Germany wanted peace on the terms of Wilson's Fourteen Points. Hughes mocked at the very idea of justice for the defeated. A few weeks later iron man Hughes repeated his point: 'What we have we hold'. That was the spirit which had built the British Empire: when that spirit died, the Empire died.[42]

Back home in Australia the Nationalist Party was laying plans for future electoral victories. In three-cornered contests a party winning a minority of

[40] *S.M.H.*, 23 September 1918; *Age*, 23 September 1918.
[41] W. M. Hughes to R. M. Ferguson, 28 September 1918, Novar Papers.
[42] *The Times*, 10, 22 October 1918.

the votes might win the seat. Labor might return to power on a minority vote. In Australia, the Nationalists believed, there was a majority for the conservatives. The problem was to find a system of counting the votes which would translate into a majority of seats for the Nationalist Party. In October while Hughes was singing with such gusto the aria 'What we have, we hold', Patrick McMahon Glynn, the Minister for Home and Territories, introduced into the House of Representatives an Electoral Bill which provided, amongst other things, for preferential voting for the House of Representatives. It was designed, he said, 'to secure majority representation in a division under the single seat system'. Labor wanted them to go further and introduce compulsory voting.

Michael Patrick Considine, the Labor member for Barrier in the House of Representatives, a militant in the Labor Party, wanted an electoral system which would be truly democratic. He wanted the people to have an equal and effective voice in deciding the conditions under which they lived: he wanted honourable members to deal with the initiative, the referendum and the right of recall—the intiative to give people outside Parliament the power to initiate Bills for the Legislature; the referendum, to permit electors to signify approval or disapproval of proposed legislation; and the recall, to enable electors to exercise proper and necessary control over their political delegates. Pure democracy would end 'capitalistic production for profit and its consequent camouflaged system of wage slavery'. The ballot box could be the way 'to make and unmake social conditions'. The alternative was revolution.[43]

That was what Ludendorff was saying to the Allies: stop the war now, before revolution begins in Germany, and spreads all over western Europe. But Ludendorff was a spent force. Events have swallowed him. On 26 October the Kaiser dismissed Ludendorff. Hughes would have nothing to do with any negotiations or parleying on a footing of equality. Germany must be humiliated and punished. God might say: 'Vengeance is mine, saith the Lord. I will repay'. That was God's world, not the world of William Morris Hughes. His 'blood lust' was up. Like Clemenceau and Foch he called for surrender.

Hughes was a strange mixture. His passions were not for food or drink, or rich raiment, or any other forms of human display, or manifestations of vanity or pride. He was a microscopic eater, often contenting himself at dinner, as one rather unkind observer put it, 'to peck at the wing of a chicken'. He was moderate with alcohol: he was amused by the foibles of others with women, but not a man himself to 'go out of his wits for a woman'. All his other passions were gargantuan—especially the passions of

[43] *C'wealth P.D.*, 4, 24 October 1918, vol. 86, pp. 6669–82, 7193–201, 7218–20, 7242–9.

hatred and revenge. He was not a hard worker: he thought a lot, and was skilled in the art of turning to his own use the fruits of the reading of others in books, newspapers, and the archives of the past. He had a superb wit, the wit of the mocker and the derider.[44]

It was this childish egotism in Hughes, this irrupting with childish tantrums which found a response in Monash, Haig, Lloyd George, Foch and Clemenceau. It was a time in the affairs of humanity when the men of great passion and great talent became leaders for people who were victims of the wild passions of war. After the four years of agony, horror, loss, sacrifice, suffering and disenchantment, events moved swiftly, like one of those feverish, frantic codas in the fourth movement of a Sibelius symphony. On 28 October Austria asked for an armistice. On 29–30 October some members of the German navy mutinied at Kiel. Anarchy spread behind the German lines. There were flurries among the power men and all the spiritual bullies who wanted to tyrannize over their fellow men. The intriguers had their field day. 'Birdie' was again worried by the machinations of Keith Murdoch, fearing that his influence on Hughes was as great as ever.[45]

It was not a time when the voices of the magnanimous were heeded. It was a time when the madness in men's hearts held sway. It was like a tragedy in a grand opera: the principals have heard the bell of salvation, but have chosen damnation. In Germany clear-thinking men have lost their heads. Ludendorff believed the German army had been demoralized by the corruption of the Jewish traders in eastern Europe and by Bolshevist propaganda. The Jews and the Bolsheviks, not the armies of the Allies, had broken the fighting spirit of the German soldiers. The German press insisted the British and the French had not defeated the German army. Ludendorff again warned the Allies not to plunge Germany into that anarchy which would be fertile soil for the weeds of Bolshevism.[46]

Monash was congratulating himself on his achievements. 'In course of time', he wrote to a friend on 8 October, 'it will dawn upon the Australian nation that the activities of the Australian Corps were by far the biggest factor in the reversal of the fortunes of the Allies in this war'. While the negotiations for peace initiated by the Germans on 7 October were dragging on, he and the Australian Corps rested in a beautiful area in the valley of the Somme. Monash had talks with an active Zionist on the creation of a Jewish State for Palestine. Like God, Monash looked at the world of his creation, and saw that it was good. He did not know that while he was enjoying his

[44] F. W. Eggleston, [Isaac] Isaacs, in F. W. Eggleston, Confidential Notes, typescript in Menzies Library, A.N.U., Canberra.

[45] W. Birdwood to R. M. Ferguson, 28 October 1918, Novar Papers.

[46] E. Ludendorff, *The Nation at War* (trans. A. S. Rappoport, London, 1936), pp. 26–33.

great moment Billy Hughes was talking with Charlie Bean about who should take charge of repatriation in Australia. 'Birdie', Hughes said to Bean,

> He's a man of kindness—a man who thinks of others. Monash is a far more capable man—he has the ability, but he is out for himself all the time . . . showy and so on. Do you think he has the kindliness or the humanity in his nature to deal with men at a time like this? Do you think he is human enough to really be charged with the responsibility of the future of the force and of repatriation?[47]

Between 1 and 4 November the Allies held a Council of War, followed by meetings of the Supreme War Council in Paris. They decided to unite the strategy of all the campaigns against Germany under the control of Marshal Foch. They wrangled over what to say to the Germans. The British wanted the Germans to surrender 16 dreadnoughts, 12 light cruisers, 50 torpedo boats, and 160 submarines. Others said this demand was making it unnecessarily difficult for the Germans to agree to the armistice terms. At a meeting of the War Cabinet in London on 5 November Lloyd George reported on the discussions in Paris. He said the question of the punishment of individuals guilty of crimes would be left to the Peace Conference. Hughes stated he had addressed a letter to the Prime Minister calling his attention to the remarks by the Marquess Okuma in which he had mentioned the Japanese claim to the Marshall and Caroline Islands. Hughes said it would be most unfortunate if such a claim were admitted.[48]

On 3 November Austria-Hungary signed an armistice. On 5 November President Wilson again declared that the Allies should sign an armistice on the basis of the Fourteen Points. Hughes objected, and said so publicly on 7 November. He wanted Germany to pay reparations which would cover the damage done by German aggression. Germany must help Australia to pay in part the cost of the war. 'Let the German people', he said, 'work out their salvation by deeds. Let them pay'. Hughes wanted a reference to the future of the German colonies: he wanted any armistice terms to contain a clause that those islands in the Pacific which had belonged to Germany would be given to the people whose national existence depended on their possessing them.[49]

Again the Labor press in Australia was critical of Hughes. On 8 November the *Socialist* quoted Ramsay Macdonald's picture of Hughes in London. Hughes, Macdonald said, was behaving as usual, 'feasting, gassing, blithering but much boomed and receiving many freedoms of cities'. Hughes was

[47] F. M. Cutlack (ed.), op. cit., pp. 272–5; C. E. W. Bean, Diary, 13 October 1918.
[48] Minutes of the Imperial War Cabinet, 5 November 1918.
[49] *The Times*, 8 November 1918.

being trotted round by the British Empire League, composed of the 'most stiff-necked reactionaries and labor enemies in this country'. How sad, Macdonald added, that a man made by the working class of Australia should now be the tool of such people.[50]

But Hughes was moving with the great tide of the times. Germany was done. The socialists in Germany have said so: 'We want peace, we want it now, and must have it'. The conservatives have said: 'These are fateful times for the German people'. But the German conservatives shrank at the shame of signing the terms laid down by the Allies for an armistice. There was chaos on the home front, impending disaster on the battlefield, and mutiny in the German navy at Kiel. The conservatives feared civil war would break out after the 'foreign war drew to an end'. On 6 November the Social Democrats demanded the abdication of the Kaiser by noon on 9 November. The following day, 10 November, the Kaiser fled to Holland. The new Social Democratic Government indicated it wanted an armistice. The conservatives have accepted the inevitable: 'In these times Germany could only be ruled by a Social Democratic Government'.[51]

Foch suggested that representatives of the new Social Democratic Government should meet representatives of the Allies in a railway carriage in the forest of Compiègne to sign an armistice. The darkness of the forest was a fit setting for the last scene of years of human grandeur and folly. The German delegates still hoped for mercy and magnanimity in their time of agony and humiliation. They wanted bread. Foch offered them a stone. Foch told the German delegation, led by Matthäus Erzberger, Minister of State in the Social Democratic Government in Germany, that the Germans must capitulate or face an Allied invasion of their country. The Germans asked whether the French would make proposals. Foch said he had no conditions. There was to be no bargaining: the iron men had won. The Germans must say whether they accepted the armistice or not. At 2.05 on the morning of 11 November the Germans indicated they were willing to sign. They signed the document at 5.10 a.m. At 11 a.m. on 11 November the cease-fire was sounded on the front. On the following day Foch congratulated the Allied forces on having 'won the greatest battle in human history' and 'saved the most sacred cause, the freedom of the world'. 'Be proud', he said. 'You have adorned your colours with undying glory. Posterity will owe you eternal gratitude.' The criminal pride of the German Empire has been punished by the free people they had aspired to reduce to slavery.[52]

[50] *Socialist*, 8 November 1918.

[51] *Socialist*, 8 November 1918; *Börsen Zeitung Am Mittag*, 8 November 1918.

[52] *The Signing of the Armistice in the Forest Glade of Compiègne* (Compiègne, 1985); *Memoirs of Marshal Foch* (trans. T. Bentley Mott, London, 1931), pp. 549–50; personal visit to forest of Compiègne, 17 April 1985.

General Monash looked forward to being on German soil in command of a considerable slice of Germany. The whole question of his future, he believed, was still open. In Lille, Charlie Bean heard 'an occasional bleating of some child's trumpet'. He guessed what it meant: the armistice must have been signed. At the front the weather was awful. A light drizzle of rain was falling as a bugler sounded 'Attention' at 11 a.m. on 11 November. The men at the front made no demonstration: they stopped firing. There was no cheering, no fraternizing with the enemy: there was an eerie calm. When one private in the Australian army was told it was all over he thought his informants were pulling his leg: 'Garn, yer silly bastards', he said incredulously. Another wanted to know why his dearest pals had fallen and he was still alive.

In London Robert Garran ascended from a basement barber's shop where he had been having his hair cut, and was greeted by the sight of flags fluttering from windows in the Strand. Soon the Strand was packed with a cheering, singing crowd. To celebrate, Robert Garran danced a two-step with a burly Anzac, his kazoo swelling the chorus of the victory songs. At nightfall an overflow audience in St. Paul's Cathedral heard a tenor sing with passion the aria: 'Comfort ye, comfort ye, my people'. Siegfried Sassoon was comfortless: for him the armistice was 'a loathsome ending to the loathsome tragedy'. The singing and the dancing went on for three days and nights in London.[53]

At nightfall in Melbourne on 11 November, at the end of a blousy early summer day when a hot north wind made all human aspirations seem quite out of reach, the magic words 'Armistice signed!' were flashed outside the newspaper offices. Crowds quickly gathered. Cheer after cheer went up into the night. Voices broke out into song. Hundreds of flags were hastily flown, including the Union Jack and some bearing the Australian symbol of the Southern Cross. The words, 'Rule Britannia! Britannia rules the waves. Britons never, never, never shall be slaves' came in a mighty roar. The lore of the tribe has triumphed. Drums rolled: trumpets were sounded: crackers were let off: bells were rung: whistles were blown, sirens hooted. The years of sorrow and agony were over. Crowds of hysterical men and women lifted trams: others commandeered trams and drove them at dangerous speeds. It was long after midnight before the last cracker was heard, and the last cheer went up into that very vast sky. In country towns effigies of the Kaiser were carried in procession and handed over to returned soldiers who burned them to loud cheering. Boys banged tin drums, and let off bungers. Church

[53] F. M. Cutlack (ed.), op. cit., pp. 278–9; C. E. W. Bean, Diary, 11 November 1918; R. R. Garran, *Prosper the Commonwealth* (Sydney, 1958), pp. 248–53; *The Times*, 12 November 1918; Gammage, op. cit., pp. 266–7; Diary of S. Sassoon, 11 November 1918, Rupert Hart-Davis (ed.), *Siegfried Sassoon Diaries 1915–1918* (London, 1983), p. 282.

bells, bullock bells and anything handy were rung to add to the gaiety and the uproar. Men and women danced in the streets.[54]

The people called for revenge. The Government agreed: the Ministers saw no reason to be magnanimous. Willie Watt, the Acting Prime Minister, was stern. 'The nation', he said, 'which hurls civilization over the precipice ought to be made to pay for its awful criminality'. Germany must pay. The following day, 12 November, the celebrators and the men and women calling for revenge flocked to their churches where they went down on their knees and solemnly thanked Almighty God, the Father of all mercies, for delivering them all from a peril so great they shuddered at the thought of it. It was not a time when Australians remembered the Beatitudes. It was not a time for the pure in heart, or the meek, or the peacemakers, let alone those who heeded the divine command to love their enemies.

After the Speaker had read the prayers in the House of Representatives on 13 November William Watt spoke. As a boy he had fished in the deep waters at Pyramid Rock on Phillip Island. He had become the finest orator Australia had produced since Alfred Deakin. The boy from Phillip Island has become a very fine bridge player in the drawing rooms of South Yarra where he startled his partners with his fits of temper and sulks when he was losing. He rose to the majesty of this occasion. He asked Australians to render thanks to God for the triumph of righteousness. The members showed their approval in the traditional way. Willie Watt's voice quivered. For a moment he was unable to proceed. From that time, only those with hearts of stone would remain unmoved, their eyes dry, when a bugler sounded the 'Last Post', or a man said the words 'Lest We Forget', or 'At the going down of the sun, and in the morning/We will remember them'. The horrors of war have left a scar on the national consciousness. Australia now had a historic event which would never be forgotten. Willie Watt recited the reasons for rejoicing and being exceeding glad. Despotism had been 'beheaded in Europe', militarism had been 'burnt at the roots', consequently the world was now, and would be for many generations to come, a safer and happier place to live in. He asked the members to affirm their loyalty to the King and the Empire. No one dissented. Loyalty, too, was part of the lore of the tribe. They stood in their places and sang the National Anthem, followed by 'God save our splendid men'. Willie Watt, like Billy Hughes, was thirsty for revenge. He asked the House to declare that for the future welfare and safety of Australia it was essential that the German possessions in the Pacific should not be restored to Germany. Germany must pay. Australia wanted vengeance. Australia was like Jehovah—a jealous, not a forgiving, God.[55]

[54] *Age*, 12 November 1918; *S.M.H.*, 12 November 1918; Bill Gammage, *Narrandera Shire* (Narrandera, 1986), p. 201.

[55] *Age*, 12, 13, 14 November 1918; F. W. Eggleston, Watt, in F. W. Eggleston, Confidential Notes, typescript in Menzies Library, A.N.U., Canberra; *Labor Call*, 14 November 1918.

John Curtin was relieved the war was over. He had hated Australia sending men to fight on foreign soil. He had his faith. Where a man was from did not matter: what mattered was what he was. Christ was born in a manger: Christ did not wear military boots. Australians must now be Christ-like in a secular age. On 17 November, the first Sunday after the armistice, Dr Mannix preached on the text: 'Unless the Lord keep the city, he watcheth in vain that keepeth it'. He prayed that the Australian Government would be both just and generous at the Peace Conference. The *Australian Worker* said capitalism was doomed. Now the workers must 'level its walls of iniquity' and 'raise upon its ruins a fairer edifice'. The *Socialist* was apocalyptic: 'The Long Night of Darkness' was passing, it said. Production for use would take the place of production for profits. Man would at last be free. Now the people's war would begin, the war for socialism. Under socialism men would be supermen. The horrors of war have removed the blinkers of religion from men and women's eyes. Human beings had a question for God: 'Father, what did You do in the Great War?' God was now on the list of missing persons. Socialism was the new religion of humanity.

At Beagle Bay near Broome in Western Australia German Pallottine Fathers erected a quite different memorial from the worldly prizes coveted by the men in high places or the hopes of the self-appointed improvers of humanity. Restricted in their movements by a Government which treated as potential spies these men who had dedicated their lives to the glory of God and the service of the Aborigines, their letters censored, cut off from their families and their friends, they did not surrender to any temptation to blame their hardships and their suffering on Australians. They decided to bake bricks in their stone kilns for a new church, and to collect enough mother of pearl and other exquisite sea shells to line the walls of the sanctuary. This beautiful building was finished in November 1918, and still stands today. So while the 'heroes of humanity' were conducting their celebrations the Pallottine Fathers were prostrating themselves before the Blessed Sacrament, and rising to their feet to chant with ecstasy and fervour: 'Thine be the glory'. Theirs was a noble task. They were using their talents to prove that with God's help it was possible for a primitive people to adapt themselves to a sophisticated culture. They believed that with God's help they could remove what was bad in the Aborigines without giving them what was bad in white civilization.[56]

At the same time in London Hughes was having a fit of the sulks. He was not consulted on the terms of the armistice. He was afraid the Allies would

[56] Lloyd Ross, *John Curtin* (Melbourne, 1977), pp. 66–7; *Australian Worker*, 14 November 1918; *Socialist*, 22, 29 November 1918; *Advocate*, 23 November 1918; *Labor Call*, 14 November 1918; *Socialist*, 25 April 1919; Mary Durack, *The Rock and the Sand* (Corgi Books, London, 1971), pp. 238–45; personal visit to Beagle Bay, 13 August 1982.

not understand Australia's concern about the former German possessions in the Pacific, the Japanese occupation of the Marshall and Caroline Islands, and the interest of the Japanese in the right to migrate to New Guinea. Lloyd George wrote a conciliatory letter to him on 11 November. The conditions of peace, he said, had not been decided, there being a distinction between an armistice and the terms of peace. Lloyd George recognized that the magnificent efforts by the Dominions and India in the common cause gave them a right to an equal voice with the United Kingdom in the settlement of the terms of peace. The British Government had every intention of associating the Governments of the Dominions and India with itself at every stage in discussing the terms of peace. Lloyd George regretted that the universal joy had been marred by a misunderstanding amongst those who had contributed to the triumph.[57]

The Lloyd George charm worked. Hughes came out of hiding on 14 November to say again in public that Australia's war sacrifices gave her the right to demand the control of the islands formerly occupied by Germany. But by then the armistice euphoria had been lost in the wrangles over the peace terms. The Irish have embarrassed the British by making it clear that if there was to be self-determination they wanted an independent Irish Republic. The socialists and the militants within the Australian Labor movement have embarrassed the Government by saying: well, if the war was a victory for believers in freedom, then prove it by rescinding all the regulations infringing individual liberty under the odious War Precautions Act. Maurice Blackburn, Vida Goldstein and others, all high-minded, virtuous men and women, asked Willie Watt to prove that the power of the people to govern themselves was not an illusion.

Willie Watt was cornered. Willie Watt did not know what to do. For all his brilliant rhetoric about freedom, he was now heart and soul a 'Yarraside' man. The inhabitants of the drawing rooms of 'Yarraside', Vaucluse, *Australia Felix*, Longford, the Derwent Valley, New England, the Riverina, and the Darling Downs were his masters, and Willie Watt was a less erratic servant of his master's voice than Billy Hughes. He ordered the Trades Hall in Melbourne to fly the Australian flag over its building to 'scare away the devils of disloyalty and sedition'. So the brawls on Sunday afternoons on the Yarra Bank and the Sydney Domain between the 'mad jingoes' and the supporters of the Red Flag went on. Willie Watt was not going to let 'Bolshies' and 'red raggers' exploit freedom to bring what he understood by civilization to ruin. The war between the nations has been won. Now 'Yarraside' must win the war between the classes.

'Yarraside' must also continue to be the guardian of the morals of the

[57] D. Lloyd George to W. M Hughes, 11 November 1918, Hughes Papers, Series 23, sub-series 1, Folder 3.

people. Any person of doubtful morals was, they believed, an easy prey to Bolshevist propaganda. When copies of *Married Love* by Marie Stopes arrived from England the Government banned its sale in Australia. Marie Stopes has transgressed the lore of the tribe. She has mentioned the role of the clitoris in the sexual fulfilment of women. In the world of 'Yarraside' that was not done: that was not good form. Marie Stopes must not be read by Australians. 'Yarraside' had decreed that a woman who wanted human beings to have life and have it more abundantly could not be read in sunny Australia. The victory in the war has secured a 'prolongation of the Victorian era in Australia'. Victory has prolonged the life of the 'Old Dead Tree'. The war has given Australians an image abroad. To some they were drunkards, thieves, hooligans, men and women stripped of all the refinements, myths and illusions which human beings have placed between themselves and death. They were the Goths and savages of the New World, who were bringing everything to ruin. To others they were the men and women of pluck, daring and audacity, an innocent people who knew happiness without guilt.[58]

Thomas Carlyle had predicted that a time would come when the new mechanical age produced 'dry souls' who would write of human beings as though they were steam engines. Søren Kierkegaard had predicted spiritual bankruptcy. John Henry Newman had prediced an age of unbelief. Friedrich Nietzsche prophesied an age of nihilism, an age of mediocrity and exhaustion. In 1918 and 1919 some observers of the human scene believed that the age of ruins had arrived. In Munich in 1918 Thomas Mann was asking the question: 'what shall we believe?' In 1918 Oswald Spengler published the first volume of *The Decline of the West.* The following year, in France, Paul Valéry, mindful of the terrible blood-letting in Flanders and Picardy, recorded the 'extraordinary shudder' that had shaken the marrow of Europe. T. S. Eliot was aware, as he put it: 'The rats are underneath the piles'. The war has given religion a severe blow. How could anyone believe a benevolent God would permit the brutalities committed during the war? The war has also delivered a severe blow to the 'dry souls' who accepted the teaching of the Enlightenment: how could any serious person have faith in the capacity of human beings for 'better things', in their ability to build 'heaven on earth' after the slaughters at Verdun, the Somme and Passchendaele? With the gift of a drunkard to sum up the spirit of the times, Henry Lawson wrote to a friend: '. . . it's all over . . . things are rotten all round'.[59]

[58] *The Times*, 15 November 1918; *Australian Worker*, 14 November 1918; *Socialist*, 29 November, 13, 22 December 1918; Marie Stopes, *Married Love* (London, 1918); C. E. W. Bean, *Anzac to Amiens*, pp. 538–9.

[59] Thomas Mann to P. Witkop, 23 May 1918, Richard and Clara Winston (eds), *Letters of Thomas Mann* (Penguin Books, London, 1975), p. 84; T. S. Eliot, 'Burbank with a Baedecker: Bleistein with a Cigar', T. S. Eliot, *Collected Poems 1909–1962* (London, 1963), p. 43; *Labor Call*, 21 August 1919; Henry Lawson to Grace McManus, n.d., probably early 1919, Papers of Henry Lawson, Gundagai.

As a fitting back-drop to that black mood it was another dry year in Australia: grass was as scarce as feathers on a frog. The appearance of some soldiers who had returned from the war strengthened this sombre, melancholy mood. Human beings whose minds had been damaged by what they had seen and suffered were seen in the city streets: men with mutilated faces, limbless men, the lame, the halt and the blind. Henry Lawson, a ghost of the man who had held out the promise of a new world to Australians in the years before he had learned what was in man leading him on to his damnation and destruction, took off his hat when he saw a digger in the street, placed his hat over his left breast and saluted. He knew.[60]

The socialists had no further use for the one who had walked beside the waters of Galilee, and had given humanity a new commandment: that ye love one another. They wanted to rid men's minds of all this filth about depravity and drinking iniquity like water. They were not interested in the God who became man, or the man who became God. They had a cheeky question: did Jesus ever live? They had their own faith. Heaven and hell were priests' inventions: they did not look for the resurrection of the dead, or the life of the world to come. Man was not a 'kneeling animal'. Men should not grovel before a God who was not even there. The bishops preached about the Kingdom of God to keep the masses from rebellion. The socialists had their own Ten Commandments, number ten of which was: 'Look forward to the day when all men will be free citizens of one fatherland, and live together as brothers in peace and righteousness'. They were moral men, too: they were offering humanity not the principle that everything was allowable: they had their law, and they had their prophets. They had their socialist Sunday Schools where children were taught the new law. There trained teachers taught the children socialist culture, science and not superstition. There they learned that priestcraft and Christianity stood in the way of human progress. The socialists stood for the enlightenment and emancipation of humanity.

They had their ceremonies. Babies were baptized, not in the names of the Father, the Son and the Holy Ghost, but in the name of socialism and brotherhood. The baby was marked, not with the sign of the cross, but a symbol of the Red Flag. The Christians sang the hymns of resignation and acceptance; they besought their God: 'Help of the helpless, Lord, abide with me'. For them earth's joys grew dim, its glories passed away. Socialists looked 'straight ahead, forward, upward, and onward, while our ancient, out-of-date mentally bankrupt friends' looked 'ever downwards and backwards'. History was on their side. The death knell of the capitalist system was being tolled. The socialists were setting the world on fire with the

[60] *Socialist*, 1 August 1919; Brian Matthews, *The Receding Wave* (Melbourne, 1972), p. 159.

new gospel of the Brotherhood of Man. They had a noble duty to 'keep the Red Flag flying here'.

> We'll change forthwith the old condition.
> And spurn the dust to win the prize.
> Then comrades come rally
> The last fight let us face;
> The Internationale unites the human race.

They sang of their love for Australia:

> Our Country
> We love our fair Australia,
> The gullies' noonday hush
> The wild things of the ranges,
> The magic of "the bush",
> The spring that breathes of wattle,
> The royal summer's blue —
> We love her, we her children,
> And Freedom, we love you.[61]

But in London Billy Hughes preached 'the gospel of Hughes'. He proposed, he said, to put the 'facts of life' before the delegates in Paris. He had never believed in 'empty vapourings'. He said again in London on 9 January what he had said all his life: the world should not hope for salvation from 'the mists of visions'. He would fight with all his might to ensure that the mighty Australian dead earned a just reward for their sacrifices. While the socialists in Australia were tolling the death knell of capitalist society he was stacking up arguments for his forthcoming encounters with President Wilson. But Billy Hughes has seen the chink in the Presidential armour: Woodrow Wilson, he has decided, was 'the most self-centred of men': he took no interest in anything in which he was not the central figure. Billy Hughes knew how to handle him, and all those 'empty vapourings' about 'Peace based on justice'.[62]

Victory dissipated all the doubts of Hughes about Monash. An iron man helped to win the war: an iron man would help to win the peace. In mid-November Hughes appointed Monash Director-General of Demobilisation and Repatriation. Honours have been showered on him. The French had given him the *Croix de Guerre* in October, the Americans the Distinguished

[61] *Socialist*, 10, 17, 24, 31 January, 7, 14 February 1919; 'The Ten Commandments of Socialism', published in *Socialist Songs* (Melbourne, 1917), p. 33, 'The Red Flag' and the 'Internationale', ibid., Bernard O'Dowd, 'Our Country', ibid.

[62] *The Times*, 10 January 1919; Garran, op. cit., p. 256; W. M. Hughes, *Policies and Potentates*, pp. 232–3.

Service Medal (after promptings from Monash), and George V appointed him a Knight Grand Cross of the Order of St Michael and St George. For his coat of arms Monash chose the Lion of Judah and the compasses of King Solomon. He chose the Latin motto: 'For War and the Arts'. Those two and engineering were the great passions of his life. On 15 November he left London for Melbourne.[63]

Hughes became more and more the victim of his own past and his personality. At the peace talks in Paris he must work with Joseph Cook. The very sight of Cook stirred the madness in the blood of Hughes. Cook, as Hughes said, was 'normally the bane of my life', one of those cheery souls, those Methodists who always had 'a smile for a friend'. Hughes loathed all 'cheery souls'. Cook had a tranquillity of soul to which Hughes was always a stranger and knew something of the peace of God which passed all understanding. Cook knew peace with his family. Hughes only knew uproar and tragedy. Hughes had scores to settle with Cook. There had been the fusion of parties in May 1909; there had been the heated discussions about leadership of the Nationalist Party early in 1917. Hughes despised Cook as a 'bible basher' and a 'political nonentity', who had neither opinions nor ideas. Besides, Hughes always behaved like a Roman centurion: he seldom devolved responsibility on anybody. He was secretive, life having taught him to trust no man, and no woman either. His impatience and autocratic ways made him ill at ease with a pesterer and a botherer like Joe Cook.

Hughes also took with him to Paris John Latham, a lieutenant-commander in the navy. Latham was a Melbourne lawyer, a Rationalist but a conservative, a man who had spent time with John Curtin in Melbourne 'giving it to Jesus'. But there was a difference. Curtin's Rationalism was the Rationalism of a man who had been hurt to find that what mattered most in life could never be, of a man who hoped what he heard in his childhood would be found to be true. Latham's Rationalism was that of a man who saw religious beliefs as evidence of the stupidity of human beings. Latham had a sense of humour, but, as one observer noted, it was humour of the mirthless sort. Latham had the power to dazzle people by his knowledge and his speech. Like others who had climbed to the top in Australia, he had all the features of behaviour of the scholarship boy. He was a snob. He deferred to those in power: he whipped verbally those beneath him, either by not acknowledging their existence, or by using some icy words of dismissal, words to make them aware of their insignificance in the eyes of John Greig Latham. Latham was a cold man, Hughes a fiery furnace of a man.[64]

[63] C. E. W. Bean, Diary, 13 October 1918; Bill Gammage, *The Broken Years*, p. 271; Geoffrey Serle, *John Monash* (Melbourne, 1982), pp. 374–5, 404–5.

[64] C. M. H. Clark, *A History of Australia* (Melbourne, 1981), vol. 5, pp. 115–16; W. M. Hughes, *Policies and Potentates*, p. 134; R. M. Ferguson to W. M. Hughes, 13 January 1919, Novar Papers; Warren G. Osmond, *Frederic Eggleston* (Sydney, 1986), pp. 88–9.

There was Captain H. S. Gullett, a journalist, landowner and littérateur, a man with a great gusto for life, and at the same time a streak of the melancholy which conferred a majesty on the work of his relative, the short story writer, Barbara Baynton. Robert Garran, the Solicitor-General, was in the delegation. A cultivated man this Garran, a son of a former editor of the *Sydney Morning Herald*, a lawyer who wrote poetry and translated Heinrich Heine. Garran was a man of high seriousness, who also liked to relax with other adults like little children. He could give a learned opinion on Section 92 of the Constitution, and then spend the evening throwing flowers at dancers or enjoying a 'sedate waltz' with a woman who was, like himself, a good dancer. He excelled at everything. He could even handle a Hughes tantrum without being hurt, or telling people he had a harpoon in his back, which no one could extract. With Garran, Hughes was at times an Australian Falstaff, and Garran his Prince Hal. Garran heard the confessions of Hughes, that is, as much as Hughes was ever prepared to let anyone know of what went on in his heart. 'Er, Garran my boy, did I ever tell you how I won the pre-selection for West Sydney?' and away he would go on one of his stories, embroidering the facts with his own fantasies, while Garran wore the Mona Lisa smile, and slipped in his Prince Hal comments when Billy paused for breath. Garran enjoyed life: he was not one to let his heart be troubled.

Frederic Eggleston, another member of the delegation, was never quiet. Like Latham and Garran he was a lawyer. Between his conception of what he should be and how others should estimate his ability, and the role or station his contemporaries allotted to him, there was a gap. He was a Methodist who had lost his faith, but not the Methodist morality. He was a Deakinite Liberal with nowhere to go in Australian public life. He was an intellectual in a country where intellectuals often find themselves besieged by hostile people. He loved to belong to groups of special people.

In Melbourne he had been one of the Boobooks, a colonial version of the Cambridge Apostles, men (not women!) who knew what was what, men who believed that what they thought and did was vital to the survival of civilization. He was a member of the Round Table circle in Melbourne, a tiny band of believers in British civilization. He had wanted to flow with the great river of life. By 1919 he was like a man who found he had taken a wrong turning in the river and had ended in a billabong with no chance of moving back into the stream. Eggleston passed the judgements of the disappointed man. He thought of Latham as an 'advertiser and an egotist'. By temperament and upbringing he was not at ease with those 'passions of revenge' which were driving Hughes on. Eggleston was never a 'facts of life man', he having always a shy hope that somewhere in the 'clouds of theory' and 'the mists of visions' he would find an answer. He was a pilgrim who had lost his way. Even before going to Paris he was critical of Hughes, who had already 'faluted about what he was going to do at the Peace Conference in a very silly strain'. Soon he saw Hughes even more unfavourably: 'Of all the criminal lunatics in the world', he wrote to his wife, 'Hughes is the worst. He is unbridled blood lust'.[65]

On 16 January 1919 the Peace Conference held its first session in Paris. The delegates were united in the wish to preserve bourgeois civilization in the world, but divided on how that could be achieved. Clemenceau wanted a Carthaginian peace. Clemenceau had one love, one faith—a love for and a belief in French culture. The rest of the world, those not influenced by French culture, were savages. Clemenceau had one great disillusion: the whole of mankind. He looked very old and tired, a man dry of soul and empty of hope, as he surveyed the scene with a cynical air. The 'Tiger' was in the calm-down years of his life. To Thomas Mann, Clemenceau was as obsolete a piece of furniture as the German Kaiser. Lloyd George was at the height of his powers. He charmed, he mesmerized, he joked. He was a bon viveur, a generous man, magnanimous towards those who despitefully used him, and ill at ease with the Clemenceau call for revenge. But he had seen all those French women in mourning—almost every third woman being dressed in black—and understood why Clemenceau was a never again man, rather than a peacemaker.[66]

President Wilson was an enigma. To mark his distinction as the only Head of State at the Conference, he sat in a chair two or three inches higher than the chairs for the other delegates. To Hughes, a man of long memory who had never forgotten or forgiven Wilson for the freeze-off administered to him in Washington in 1918, Wilson was not the god-like person he was to the man in the street. Hughes detected in Wilson a man much given to 'fulsome and persistent puffing'. To Hughes, Wilson was definitely not a 'facts of life' man. Wilson was great on high principles, 'a former incarnation for that dear little lady, Alice in Wonderland'. Wilson had dreams, Hughes wrote on the day before the Conference began, of officiating as the High Priest in the Ark of the Covenant of the League of Nations. Hughes had a stratagem: 'Give him [Wilson] *a* League of Nations, and he will give *us* all the rest'. Give Wilson his toy—but for heaven's sake recognize that the man was 'indeed incapable of reducing this ideal of his to any shape or applying it to the actual circumstances of mankind.[67]

But Hughes was not a free agent. Australia was part of the British dele-

[65] Personal observation of F. W. Eggleston; personal conversations with Sir Robert Garran, Canberra, 1950; Garran, op. cit., pp. 257–9; John Maynard Keynes, *The Economic Consequences of the Peace* (London, 1920), pp. 1–9, 26–32; Hermann Kesten (ed.), *Thomas Mann Diaries 1913–1939* (New York, 1982), 10 November 1918, p. 21; Osmond, op. cit., pp. 89–91.

[66] W. M. Hughes to R. M. Ferguson, 17 January 1919, Novar Papers; L. F. Fitzhardinge, *The Little Digger* (Sydney, 1979), pp. 372–3.

[67] Garran, op. cit., pp. 257–9.

gation to the Peace Conference. The Australians stayed in the Majestic Hotel, one of the four hotels reserved for members of the British delegation. Like other members of the British delegation, the Australians were served an English breakfast of porridge, eggs and bacon, toast and marmalade washed down with large cups of tea. Hughes and Cook were King and Empire men. Four of their advisers—Gullett, Garran, Latham and Eggleston— were King and Empire men. Like Australia, the delegation was shackled to its colonial and imperial past. They were not advocates for 'the Young Tree Green'. That Australian voice was not heard in Paris. The organization of the Conference also gave them little freedom to manoeuvre. Power rested with the Council of Ten, composed of the Prime Ministers (or their equivalent) and the Foreign Ministers (or their equivalent) of America, France, Great Britain, Italy and Japan, and the 'Big Four'—Woodrow Wilson, Georges Clemenceau, David Lloyd George and Vittorio Orlando.

The sight of all those 'high-brows' gathered together for the 'amiable purpose of settling the peace of the world' brought out the mocker and the cynic in Hughes. 'In this way', he wrote to his friend the Governor-General on 17 January 1919, 'has the world been governed from the beginning'. He had had some preliminary successes. The Dominions had been granted separate representation on the General Assembly—two for Canada, Australia and South Africa, and one for New Zealand. Australia was to be represented on the Imperial Delegation. Lloyd George had asked Hughes to take charge of the Empire case for indemnities. So perhaps he was not 'doomed to ignominious failure'.

On 24 January the test came. Clemenceau invited Lloyd George to 'bring his savages' to the afternoon session of the Council of Ten. After the words of introduction by Lloyd George, Hughes unrolled a map of the South Pacific, and demonstrated to the members that the former German possessions—Nauru, the Solomons and German New Guinea—'encompassed Australia like fortresses'. Australia's dead, he told them, entitled them to guarantees for her security. Wilson, the 'Heaven-born', as Hughes called him behind his back, was not in the best of tempers. Hughes shouted that the trouble with the American delegation was that they had not been near the 'fires of war as the British have, and therefore, being unburned, they have a cold, detached view of the situation'. Wilson again played the role of a man who was 'great on great principles' but, in the eyes of Hughes, weak on 'the facts of life'. Hughes was prepared to let the vanity of Wilson be soothed by having his speeches translated into all languages. He was prepared to let his words be 'the food of men', provided the delegates did not concede the Open Door in New Guinea. Hughes had his way. He strutted on the world stage as the saviour of White Australia. It never seemed to occur to him that, just over twenty-three years after he had performed before the Council of Ten, units of the Japanese army might be advancing towards Port Moresby.

Over the weekend the British delegation agreed on united action. When the Council met again Wilson was still against annexation of former colonies. Lloyd George and Wilson held a private meeting. The British were interested in the former German colonies in Africa. Wilson agreed that the types of mandate might differ, but there must be no annexation. So the debate went on. Hughes wanted to ensure that there could be no menace to Australia from the islands. Wilson wondered whether Hughes was putting an ultimatum to the Conference. Lloyd George proposed a compromise. The Council of Ten agreed. Hughes had got what he wanted. Two afternoons later there was a reception for President Wilson. He spoke with the tongue of an angel: he spoke with malice towards none, and charity towards all. Some in the audience wept. In private Hughes mocked Wilson as a man living in a 'roseate cloud of dreams'. The 'facts of life man' has had his victory.[68]

While Hughes was arguing with the 'Heaven-born', the Government of New South Wales was taking measures to prevent the spread of Spanish influenza. When the troop ship *Sardinia* arrived in Sydney in January 1919 it was announced that eight of its passengers had died from pneumonic influenza. A plague has come to Australia, causing terrible misery, suffering and grief. Doctors predicted it would sweep the country. Governments took precautions. People were warned not to assemble in large numbers. The *Socialist* said capitalism was to blame. Patent medicine advertisements had a new resource: Dr Morse added Spanish influenza to the list of aches, pains and diseases of the body which could be cured by taking Dr Morse's 'Indian Root Pills'. Bovril boasted that their beverage was a more effective preventive than wearing a mask. The comedians exploited the anxiety: 'It may be dangerous, at present, to kiss one's wife', wrote the *Soldier*, 'but it is not half as dangerous as kissing someone else's'. One clergyman explained that the Spanish 'flu (a member of the Spanish royal family being one of the first sufferers) or influenza was God's just punishment for the spread of paganism in Australia. A wicked and adulterous generation should fall on their knees and ask God to forgive them.[69]

On 27 January theatres, picture shows, and places of indoor public resort in New South Wales were closed until further notice. Schools were not to re-

[68] W. M. Hughes to R. M. Ferguson, 17 January 1919, Novar Papers; Fitzhardinge, op. cit., pp. 387–90; Garran, op. cit., pp. 264–5; H. Borden (ed.), *Robert Laird Borden: His Memoirs* (London, 1938), p. 907; P. E. Deane, 'Australia's Rights: The Fight at the Peace Table', pamphlet in National Library of Australia, n.d., pp. 10–12.

[69] *Socialist*, 10, 31 January, 21 February, 25 April 1919; *Daily Telegraph*, 28 January 1919; *S.M.H.*, 26, 28 October, 19, 22, 27 November 1918; Report of Director-General of Public Health . . . in the Influenza Epidemic, 1919, *N.S.W. P.P.*, 1920, vol. 1; *Soldier*, 7, 14 February 1919.

open. Patrols were sent on house-to-house visits distributing advice about the disease. People were advised to wear masks over their faces in public places. Religious services were permitted, provided the clergyman stood at least six feet from members of the congregation. In Adelaide, where no cases had been reported, the chairman of the Central Board of Health recommended people not to 'go talking, coughing and sneezing in each other's faces, or shaking hands, or kissing'. It may be possible, he continued, to 'get each person to say to his neighbour, "Hands off, and don't come within three feet of me" '. In Hobart all vessels from Sydney and Melbourne were to be examined on arrival. In Perth all persons travelling on the Great Western Railway were to be examined at Kalgoorlie. No person was to travel on the main railway line from Sydney to Brisbane beyond Tenterfield, or from Sydney to Melbourne beyond Culcairn. The Commonwealth Government on 27 January proclaimed New South Wales a quarantine area. The *Soldier* bewailed the dull old time governments were enforcing in Australia. 'Seeing', it wrote on 7 February, 'that picture shows and theatres are closed, races off, stadiums shut, bars closed and places of worship unopened, all I can do during my enforced holiday is to stay at home and grow whiskers'.[70]

Australia was in turmoil. The socialists wrote and talked about a new 'democratic consciousness' spreading over the whole world. Returned servicemen enrolled for university courses resented the deference and reverence expected of them towards their professors. In Darwin the workers at the meat-works toasted the beginning of a new order. At Mount Morgan the miners declared that the fruits of the earth belonged to those who had dug them up in the sweat of their brows.[71]

The 'Heaven-born' was still preaching in Paris about a 'new Jerusalem' for the whole world. Hughes mocked at all that as hot air. He was there to 'hold Australia's end up', to get those islands on a satisfactory tenure, to get Australia's share of an indemnity, to get the boys home, to sell Australian wheat, lead, copper and other products and to establish markets for Australian produce in Europe. He believed that if he did all these things he would deserve more than to be hit on the head with an egg as at Warwick in 1917. He remembered the words he had learned in childhood—to be sober, to be vigilant because his adversary the Devil was prowling around seeking whom he may devour. Well, so long as he was alive, the Japanese would not devour Australia. The Japanese delegate, Baron Makino, proposed to insert in the Covenant of the League of Nations a clause recognizing the equality of all the member nations. The 'Heaven-born' was Chairman of the Committee to

[70] *Daily Telegraph*, 28 January 1919; *Soldier*, 1 March 1919; N.S.W. Report on Influenza Epidemic, *N.S.W. P.P.*, 1920, vol. 1.

[71] *Socialist*, 31 January 1919; *Argus*, 11 February 1919.

consider the Japanese proposal. Baron Makino asked to see Hughes on a matter on which his country was gravely concerned. From the manner of the Baron when he entered Hughes's office, 'literally wreathed in smiles, and beslobbering me with genuflexions and obsequious deference' (as Hughes put it later), Hughes 'augured the worst'. The Japanese wanted a recognition of equality. Hughes told the Baron he would do all in his power to defeat the clause in the Covenant Committee, and if defeated there he would take the fight outside and do his best to defeat it. To the surprise of Hughes, this time the 'Heaven-born' was on his side. The Americans had their own immigration problem on their west coast. He ruled that all resolutions affecting the Fourteen Points required a unanimous vote. Thank God, the Racial Equality Clause was dead and buried.[72]

While Billy Hughes was laughing inwardly at the 'genuflexions' of Baron Makino, the Returned Soldiers' and War Workers' Industrial Union held a meeting in the Melbourne Town Hall on 10 March to combat the sinister influences at work in Australia to bring about revolutionary action in the interests of the Bolsheviks and the I.W.W. Pandemonium reigned throughout the whole meeting. One group in the audience kept shouting the slogan, 'Hurrah for Bolshevism', to which another group replied with hoots. The speeches were almost inaudible because women in the gallery screamed out interjections and sang revolutionary songs: another group counted the speakers out: another man in the body of the hall yapped and barked like a dog: interjectors swapped insults—'Traitor', 'Rat', 'Scab': a free fight broke out on the platform, which the police terminated. After two hours of almost continuous uproar the chairman declared the meeting closed. Bourgeois civilization in Australia was under threat, as it was under threat in Europe. Its self-appointed saviours must hurry.[73]

All over Australia the supporters of the Bolsheviks clashed with the supporters of the King and the Empire. In Brisbane on Sunday 23 March 1919 the 'red raggers' held a procession through the streets. Banners were held high, red flags displayed, and revolutionary songs sung. Some onlookers cheered: some expressed their disgust. The following day the supporters of King and Empire replied with a demonstration of loyalty. Seven to eight thousand people gathered at the North Quay to hear returned soldiers call on those present to deal with 'this mob of Russians who let us down on the Eastern front'. To roars of applause one speaker declared: 'We are going to put them right out of Australia, and their sympathisers are going with them'. This display of Bolshevism and of Bolshevik disloyalty by a cowardly

[72] W. M. Hughes to R. M. Ferguson, 15 March 1919, Novar Papers; W. M. Hughes, *Policies and Potentates*, pp. 244–9; E. M. House and Charles Seymour (eds), *What Really Happened at Paris: The Story of the Peace Conference, 1918–19* (London, 1921), pp. 414–16.

[73] *Age*, 11 March 1919.

foreign element, who have come from a country that betrayed the Allies, would not be allowed to continue. The following night between fifteen thousand and twenty thousand people gathered in Edward Street to hear speakers on how to root out the 'monster of Bolshevism'. They marched to the offices of the *Standard.* There they sang the National Anthem. One man did not take off his hat and join in with the others. Two men lifted him on to the roof of a car, as the mob shouted 'Sing it'. The man then sang it.[74]

Turbulence and rioting were also spreading in Europe. The delegates must hurry. Hughes, Clemenceau and others demanded Germany should pay for the cost of the war. Wilson disagreed: Wilson said: 'No indemnities'. Lloyd George and his advisers worked on a British-style compromise. Wilson became like a 'blind and deaf Don Quixote' confronting the Old World's heart of stone. He kept repeating: 'I can do nothing but what is just and right'. Clemenceau, Hughes and others did not want justice or righteousness: they wanted revenge, they wanted punishment. Germany must be bled white. Advisers whispered to Lloyd George that the sums demanded were beyond Germany's capacity to pay. But Lloyd George's hands were tied: he had just won the 'khaki election' on the platform of 'Full reparations and hang the Kaiser'. The blood-lust of Hughes so disgusted Frederic Eggleston that he decided to resign from the Australian delegation and return to Australia. Maynard Keynes warned Lloyd George that they were drafting clauses to punish and impoverish Germany at the risk of revolution. They were proposing that the Saar basin be ceded to France, and Upper Silesia to Poland after a plebiscite, and at the same time demanding German reparation payments of coal to be made to France. One of the German observers, Dr Carl Melchior, invited Keynes to see the conditions in the Saar and the Ruhr. There they looked at each other amid the poverty, the starvation, and the ruins with the eyes possibly of lovers, Melchior with the beautiful melancholic eyes of a man who believed that the hearts of the sons of men were filled with evil, and Keynes with the eyes of one of the *gens superieurs* who feared that once again the passions and follies of humanity were exposing the members of his class and the civilization they had created to destruction by the Goths and barbarians from the East.[75]

In Australia the debate about the future continued. Bob Menzies was making a name for himself as a barrister and a public speaker who was quite heart-warming on questions of loyalty to King and Empire, and the great benefits Australians had received at the hands of the British. John Curtin was teaching members of the Labor Party how Australia could move towards social change. He no longer believed in revolution: he believed in progress

[74] *Brisbane Courier*, 24, 25, 26, 27 March 1919; *S.M.H.*, 25 March 1919; *Soldier*, 28 March 1919.

[75] Garran, op. cit., pp. 268–70; Keynes, op. cit., pp. 74–5; Osmond, op. cit., p. 91.

'YE GODS!'
Billy Hughes in London, 1916
Photograph in National Library, Canberra

'THE LITTLE DIGGER'
Billy Hughes in George Street, Sydney, 20 September 1916
Photograph in National Library, Canberra

'THE NOBLEST AUSTRALIAN BRITON OF THEM ALL'
Stanley Melbourne Bruce
Photograph in National Library, Canberra

THE HAYSEED WHO TOPPLED BILLY HUGHES
Earle Christmas Grafton Page
Photograph in National Library, Canberra

by the ballot box. Australia's past meant that civil war was out of the question. But Labor should warn the conservatives that if they continued to block peaceful progress that might lead to the same result as it had tragically produced in other countries.[76]

Troopships arrived from England, carrying demobilized servicemen. Soldiers saw Australia again for the first time for years. Albert Facey, before the war an itinerant worker in the country districts of Western Australia, was greeted in the streets of Perth by larrikins who sneered at him for going to the war. Being an expert in the 'stoush', he silenced them with a straight left to the chin, and a right below the belt to make sure they would not torment him for a while. He took a job on the trams, married and became a father as Perth and Fremantle were convulsed with the post-war uproar. Martin Boyd, a member of the British Expeditionary Force, and later an officer in the Royal Flying Corps, was called a 'pommy' soon after he disembarked from the *Prinz Hubertus*. He felt he had been repudiated by his own country from the moment of his return. He did not like being in Australia. He was disgusted by a letter published in the *Argus* on whether English soldiers were cowards. He saw this as 'provincial ill-nature'. In Australia, he decided, as a gentleman he was 'the target of the ill-bred'.[77]

Angela Thirkell, who arrived with her husband in Hobart on the troopship *Rudolstadt*, found Australian soldiers and civilians gave people of refinement and culture a 'rotten deal'. Bill Harney, a bushman from north Queensland and the Northern Territory, decided he had had enough of humanity. He chose 'the beaches and the quiet places that surround me'. He went back 'to sit on me beaches out from Darwin. Listen to the sea coming in and get the crabs and the fish and me mates come in and we talk and everybody's happy'. Richard Kirby, a pupil at the King's School, Parramatta, joined his classmates crowding round a war hero, an old boy of the School who had won his school colours in the Rugby XV in 1917. They put questions to the returned soldier. To Kirby's surprise the soldier replied in incoherent whispers. He had been gassed. All over the country young boys and girls saw ex-diggers break down and cry when they met each other, and only manage to say to each other the words of consolation: 'I know, Charl., I know'. Children came suddenly on grown-up men in distress and were told: 'He's . . . crying. Can't stop . . . don't be frightened'.[78]

[76] *Westralian Worker*, 4 April 1919.

[77] A. B. Facey, *A Fortunate Life* (Fremantle, 1981), pp. 86–7; Martin Boyd, *Day of My Delight* (Melbourne, 1965), pp. 109–11.

[78] Angela Thirkell, *Trooper to the Southern Cross* (Sun Books, Melbourne, 1966), pp. 172–4; *Bill Harney's War* (Melbourne, 1983), p. 56; Blanche D'Alpuget, *Mediator: a Biography of Sir Richard Kirby* (Melbourne, 1977), pp. 8–9; personal observation of returned soldiers, 1919–22.

The survivors erected memorials to the dead. Wealthy parents endowed prizes or scholarships at schools and universities in memory of the sons who had lost their lives. The parents of Ronald Guy Larking endowed the Council of Melbourne Grammar School with a fund to award a scholarship which would pay the board and tuition for a boy at the school. The Public Schools erected memorials in their honour—honour rolls in the chapel and stands to carry regimental flags. Charlie Bean persuaded Billy Hughes to provide funds for a war memorial in Canberra, to be a tribute to the mighty dead and a building inside which Australians and others might learn what the war had been all about—'that perfect, simple, solemn exquisite building which for all time will, it is hoped, hold the sacred memories of the A.I.F.'. Charlie Bean entertained the shy hope that the spirits of the dead might hover over the building. But on what the war meant he was not sure: as he put it in his version of the Psalm, it was not for us to say what it was all about—'*Non nobis, Domine*'. When the people chose the words to place on memorials either in a city, a country town, or a sparsely populated district they borrowed words from the Old World. They used Rudyard Kipling's 'Lest We Forget', the words of 'Ecclesiasticus' in the Apocrypha, 'Their Name Liveth For Evermore', the biblical words, 'Greater love hath no man than this', the words from Laurence Binyon's 'For the Fallen'; 'We will remember them', or 'To our glorious dead'. With few exceptions, such as the crucifix on the memorial at Berridale in the Snowy Mountains of New South Wales, there were no religious emblems. God was rarely mentioned, Christ almost never. The past has bequeathed to Australians a long list of unmentionable words.[79]

On most of the memorials the feature which was unmistakably Australian was the statue of the digger, with the left brim of the hat tucked up and pinned to the crown with the medal of the rising sun. Words about Australia were not carved on any monument. There was no profession of love for the country, no reference to their love of 'a sunburnt country', no declaration of attachment to the 'wide brown land', or to the 'vision splendid on the sunlit plains extended'. There was no statement of their values, no reference to 'Kindness in another's trouble/Courage in your own', no profession of hope that Australia was not a 'new demesne for Mammon to infest', but that 'lurks millennial Eden 'neath thy breast', nothing about that country 'down by Kosciusko . . . Where the air is clear as crystal . . . where . . . the rolling plains are wide', nothing about the ones who 'bore the badge of gameness',

[79] K. S. Inglis, *C. E. W. Bean, Australian Historian* (St Lucia, 1970), p. 19; Dudley McCarthy, *Gallipoli to the Somme* (Sydney, 1983), pp. 378–80; C. E. W. Bean, *In Your Hands, Australians* (London, 1918), p. 59; *Daily Telegraph*, 5 April 1919; Ethel Turner, *Brigid and the Cub* (London, 1919).

nothing of what Australians stood for, no mention of mateship or equality, no quotations like

> They call no biped lord or 'sir',
> And touch their hats to no man!

There was nothing of Australia as 'a new Britannia in another world', or a country free from those 'old-world errors and wrongs and lies'. The war has not liberated Australians from their colonial past.[80]

Australia's other voices were still vocal. Hughes propagated the gospel of survival for the bourgeoisie in Paris. The Australian Labor Party decided at its Conference beginning on 24 March 1919 to eliminate from the School Papers (issued by the State Departments of Education) all articles relating to or extolling wars, battles or heroes of past wars. That was on the eve of the fourth Anzac Day. The *Australian Worker* rebuked the bourgeois press and their readers for saying that Australia got a 'world-wide advertisement out of the bloody business'. Capitalism, they continued, considered the 'advertisement' of more importance than the lives of the men who were sacrificed.[81]

The other voice, the voice of 'Yarraside' and all the comfortable classes, wanted Anzac Day to be from that time 'first in the Australian heart'. For them it was a day of honour. In April 1919 the influenza epidemic restrictions robbed it of some of its spectacular side. People were not permitted to see the Anzacs on parade. But bands played patriotic airs in the streets, and wartime tunes such as 'Tipperary', 'Pack Up Your Troubles', and 'Roses are Blooming in Picardy'. Services were held in most of the churches. There was an impressive service in the Randwick Military Hospital where those present joined in singing 'God Of Our Fathers', 'Onward Christian Soldiers' and Kipling's 'Recessional'. There was a service in the Domain. There were pilgrimages to the gravesides of soldiers: honour rolls and monuments were adorned with flowers.[82]

Speakers and writers agreed that on that first sad Anzac morn the deeds of the Anzacs had apotheosized a blunder into an epiphany. They differed on what was the essence of the occasion. To some it was 'an exhibition of sublime heroism': to others it was marked by the deeds of men who

[80] A. B. Paterson, 'The Man From Snowy River', *The Collected Verse of A. B. Paterson* (Sydney, 1941), pp. 3–8; Dorothea Mackellar, 'My Country', *Spectator* (London), 5 September 1908; Bernard O'Dowd 'Australia', *Collected Poems of Bernard O'Dowd* (Melbourne, 1941), p. 35; Henry Lawson, 'The Shearers', *The Children of the Bush* (London, 1902), pp. ix–x; W. C. Wentworth, *Australasia* (London, 1823); Henry Lawson, 'A Song of the Republic', *Bulletin*, 1 October 1887.

[81] *Age*, 25 April 1919; *Australian Worker*, 1 May 1919.

[82] *Age*, 25 April 1919; *S.M.H.*, 26 April 1919.

wanted 'to play a hand in making the world a safer place to live in'. To others again the Anzacs created 'a name and a glory that will never die': to some it was a 'solemn memory', a day of 'great solemnity', a day to commemorate the 'great brotherhood of sacrifice', a day which represented 'what is best in the history of Australia': to some it was a day of reflection on 'the spirit of unselfishness': to others it was a day of inspiration, a day when the brave Anzacs overcame the sharpness of death and opened a kingdom of nobility and achievement to all those who truly believed in them. The soldiers had overcome man's last enemy, death. The survivors could win victories over drought, victories over sloth and incompetence in high places. Anzac Day has become what the poet David McKee Wright called a 'march through the hearts of men'. It has become a solemn occasion which turned the minds of Australians towards the things that mattered in life, an occasion 'not of little gains and little losses', but an occasion to 'hear the trumpet call' to a nobler life. Anzac Day was beginning to be the 'one day of the year', the central event in an Australian secular religion for one section of society.[83]

Labor did not share this vision. For them the class war was the central fact of life. On 22 April 1919 two thousand men gathered on the wharf in Fremantle to prevent 'scab' workers getting on to the *Dimboola*. John Curtin had much to say about the evils of the presence of the police on the wharves, the brazen indifference of the Shipping Ring and the Government of Western Australia, and their wicked attempts to 'govern by starvation'. The workers and the employers were spoiling for a fight. This time, John Curtin believed, capitalism would not win by forcing hunger to 'gnaw at the vitals of the men, women and children'. To ensure victory, to ensure there was no capitulation because of starvation, the Labor movement must make arrangements to feed the wharf lumpers and their families. The time had come for a redistribution of wealth. The wharf lumpers were a vanguard in the movement for social justice. At the moment 59 per cent of the people in this 'happy country' owned less than £200 each and 0.7 per cent owned more than £2000. Something must be done.[84]

Harry (Hal) Colebatch, the Premier of Western Australia, organized a force to achieve by armed might what persuasion and argument failed to achieve. He equipped and trained a squad of police as a military raiding party, complete with rifles, bayonets, ball cartridges, revolvers and other military tools to drive Union workers off the wharves. On Sunday 4 May Colebatch attended in person to help his volunteers erect barricades on the wharves. Enraged by this act of provocation, the lumpers smashed the 'pick-up' bureau and threw the 'scabs' into the Swan River. The Riot Act was read. A crowd of two thousand, composed of men and women armed with pieces of

[83] *Age*, 25, 26 April 1919; *S.M.H.*, 25, 26 April 1919; David McKee Wright, 'April 25', *Bulletin*, 1 May 1919.

[84] *Westralian Worker*, 25 April, 2 May 1919.

coal and stones, surged towards the police. Women, more desperate, it was said, than the men, insisted on being in the front row of the advancing army. The order was given for the police to charge: the mounted men galloped their horses towards the union crowd. One Union man received a bayonet wound in the thigh. The police dispersed the crowd. There were thirty-three casualties. That evening Colebatch declared that the whole point at issue was whether or not law and order and constituted authority were to be maintained. Lawlessness, he said, could not serve the interests of the workers. John Curtin reminded Colebatch that the Czar of Russia had called on law and order to perpetrate a Bloody Sunday, and look what had happened to him.[85]

Public meetings were held in Perth. At some of them resolutions were passed praising Colebatch and his Nationalist colleagues. At others resolutions were passed expressing disgust at the use of armed force. Like other cities Perth was a divided society. The bishops of the Catholic and Anglican Churches heard the point of view of the lumpers and the shipping companies. They wore grave faces: they spoke words of sympathy, but did nothing. Labor was hopeful. There had been solidarity. Labor politicians and unionists who had solemnly resolved: 'We shall not allow a single stone in the temple of Labor to be disturbed' were on the wharves that Sunday. By contrast, not a single Federal Nationalist member had entered the arena of trouble. Some enjoyed the luxury of their well-furnished club in Perth: some, following the example of Pontius Pilate, would have nothing to do with the disturbances. The returned soldiers had rallied to the defence of unionism: blacklegs had been clearly shown they must not return to the waterfront. Negotiations were opened between the Government and the lumpers. An agreement was in sight and peace returned to the waterfront. In Australia riots did not burgeon into revolution. Under that vast sky there would be no storming of any Winter Palace.[86]

Billy Hughes sent messages from Paris. He told his supporters in Brisbane he was delighted with the attitude of the Brisbane returned soldiers towards the Bolsheviks. He was just as enthusiastic about the rough-house tactics of Hal Colebatch—a man who gave the troops the stuff they needed. Hughes was homesick. He told Australian diggers in London he would sooner be in an acre-paddock with an angry bull than with those foreign gentlemen at the Peace conference. He pined for Australia, the place where he was understood. In May he told the Governor-General that though he was 'still chained to the wheel of mocking destiny' there were now 'omens' that his 'battered optimism' would be revived. At long last the 'Greatest Show On Earth' was coming to an end, and he could turn his footsteps homeward.[87]

[85] Ibid., 9 May 1919; *West Australian*, 5 May 1919.
[86] *Westralian Worker*, 9 May 1919.
[87] *Soldier*, 25 April 1919.

He still found the attempts of the 'Heaven-born' to 'carve out the world anew' and make the lion lie down with a lamb a broad farce, especially the mental gymnastics of the President in trying to reconcile those high-sounding phrases he loved to utter with the hard facts. Wilson's Fourteen Points had been a millstone round their necks all through the Conference. Still he had got for Australia much of what he wanted—security in the Pacific, the power to preserve a White Australia, and the omission of any reference to racial equality in the Covenant of the League of Nations. The negotiations for the indemnity had not gone as well as he would have liked. The indemnity awarded to Australia would scarcely pay for the cost of the war and the pensions. It was not a good peace for Australia but a good peace for America. There had been satisfactions. The German delegates were summoned to Versailles for a 'great historic event'. There they learned the terms of the peace. Hughes had relished the moment. He had seen what he had wanted to see for a long time: he had seen a man from the German Junker class humiliated. The war, Hughes said, had taught that Junker nothing: he sat there in the Hall of Mirrors 'arrogant, intolerant, unrepentant'. In Germany men were already asking their gods to curse any hand cowardly enough to sign 'the disgraceful dictation of Versailles'. The iron men have had their satisfaction.[88]

On 28 June the representatives of the Allies sat down again beneath the gilded chandeliers in the Hall of Mirrors. There, where in a previous century poor Marie Antoinette danced on heedless of the warnings of a bloody revolution in retribution for all the follies and crimes of her class, the Allies added their contribution to the long list of human follies. Clemenceau was brusque and bitter. 'Bring the Germans in', he cried in a moment of silence as though the Germans were prisoners on trial for a crime. Escorted by officers, two Germans were led in, looking pale and pitiful. Clemenceau ordered the Germans to sign. A great gasp of relief was heard from the delegates as the two Germans finally laid down the pen.

Woodrow Wilson had an unwonted air of cheerfulness. He looked quite jubilant when he signed the documents. By contrast Lloyd George, who loved to chuckle with men or women, but especially women, looked 'uncommonly serious'. Balfour looked graceful, fine flower that he was of that culture and that society the delegates believed was being given at least a reprieve by the documents they were signing. Hughes looked 'transpontine', as though the day to which he had dedicated his vast talents and energy was at last at hand. The fountains played in those lovely gardens, aeroplanes cavorted overhead, guns boomed as the delegates slipped away. That first night of peace Paris gave itself up to joy completely. It sang, shouted and danced till it seemed that it could sing and dance no more. At 9.30 in the

[88] W. M. Hughes to R. M. Ferguson, 17 May 1919, Novar Papers.

Place de l'Opéra a full orchestra played the 'Marseillaise'. A woman in a flowing white robe unfurled an enormous tricolour, as an almost religious silence fell over the crowd. '*La Patrie*' was no longer '*en danger*'. France had won: France was eternal. '*Vive la France!*'[89]

On 29 June Hughes returned to London where he had an enthusiastic reception from five hundred soldiers at Victoria Station. The soldiers hoisted him on their shoulders. His hat fell off and a soldier jammed his own wide-brimmed Digger hat on to the head of Billy Hughes. The soldiers welcomed him with loud shouts of the words which brought tears to his eyes: 'Good on you, you little Digger', and that other phrase of Australian approval, 'You'll do me'. Before daylight on that same day a militant section of the meat-workers in Townsville raided the railway trucking yards, and dispersed five hundred cattle over the surrounding country. The class war went on, as the war between the nations formally ended.

Two nights later, at a farewell dinner given to him in London, Hughes told those present to do him honour that the Empire was 'a great, a mighty factor, standing for everything that was best in the world's civilization and progress'. Every step forward taken by humanity, every improvement in transport and communication, such as the aeroplane and the wireless telephone, brought the scattered parts of the Empire closer together. In the moment of victory Hughes was a King and Empire man. For him the best assurance of the peace of the world lay not in the Treaty of Versailles but in the triple alliance of Britain, America and France. The celebrations in his honour went on for days. On 4 July the soldiers honoured him as 'Billy Hughes, the Diggers' friend'. He told them the only way they could hold Australia was by the means used by the Australian Imperial Force. He was going back to Australia to another fight, the fight he had fought all his life, the fight against Bolsheviks and wild red-flag socialists. That was the fight, he said, he was better fitted for than anything else in the world. It was his high tide, his moment as the Little Digger, the Diggers' Friend, the Empire statesman.[90]

In Australia on the day when the Treaty of Versailles was signed there were scenes of joy in all the cities. Crackers exploded, drums rolled, trumpets sounded. A week later on Sunday 6 July people flocked to the churches to give thanks to Almighty God for giving them the victory. People sang with fervour 'Land of Hope and Glory'. The God of Hosts has rewarded the loyal sons and daughters of the Empire. So, 'Wider still and wider/May thy bounds to set/God, who made thee mighty/Make thee mightier yet!'. The celebration became an occasion for overweening pride. On 19 July, the day

[89] Sisley Huddlestone, *In My Time* (London, 1938), pp. 172–3; *The Times*, 30 June 1919.

[90] *The Times*, 30 June, 2, 5 July 1919; *Brisbane Courier*, 30 June 1919.

for the peace celebrations, there were processions in the streets. At Kaniva in the Mallee the people thanked the God of battles. Under that vast sky they thanked God they were British. In the enthusiasm of the moment there was little doubt felt at the singing of the words: 'Lest we forget, lest we forget'.[91]

Frank Anstey urged the masses not to be hypnotized by 'patriotic jargon' or 'seduced by mock patriotism and humbug'. Within the Labor movement there was a different vision of the future of Australia. Capitalism was listening with 'quaking soul to the drum-beats of the Armies of Revolution'. The working class would soon completely take possession of and control the destiny of Australia. The women would take a hand. The story of humanity in the future would be the story of women. The old order was dying, giving place to the new. The class war would sound the 'clarion call' to overthrow capitalism, and give the power and restore the lands and the wealth to the whole people. The riots in Melbourne on 20 and 21 July were the prelude to a mighty upheaval. The people were on the march. From Townsville to Wonthaggi groups of people were flying the Red Flag. They were the grain of mustard seed from which a great tree would grow.[92]

The same wild passions were released when Hughes returned in triumph at the end of August 1919. From Perth to Melbourne huge crowds welcomed him with the greatest enthusiasm. In Perth the soldiers hailed him as their man, put the Digger hat on his head, wrapped him in the Australian flag, hoisted him on their shoulders and carried him into halls where huge crowds stamped and cheered. Hughes loved it. The warmer the welcome and the louder the cry of 'Billy Hughes, the little Digger!', the wilder the promises he made to the soldiers of what he would do for them. He spoke of the Australian soldiers as the 'foremost troops in every fight', the saviours of France, the men who had won the war. He told them he would smite all Bolsheviks, shirkers, strikers, One Big Unionists, Wobblies, red-flaggers, socialists, League of Nations dreamers, visionaries. He would teach them all 'the facts of life'.[93]

Labor was sour about all this adulation for a renegade to his Party and a traitor to his class. Hughes, in powder and puff, the *Labor Call* said, had been given 'the cheap claptrap glory of a circus reception' by a small section of hysterics among the returned soldiers. The peace celebrations were a 'profiteer's picnic'—a day to celebrate the enormous profits made out of blood.

[91] *The Times*, 30 June 1919; *Argus*, 30 June, 7 July 1919; *Age*, 30 June, 1 July, 20 July 1919; Bill Gammage, *Narrandera Shire*, pp. 201–4.

[92] R. M. Ferguson to Lord Milner, 1 September 1919, Novar Papers; *Age*, 1 September 1919; Frank Anstey, *Red Europe* (Melbourne, 1919); *Socialist*, 11, 18 July 1919; *Labor Call*, 14 August 1919; *Age*, 21, 22, 23 July 1919.

[93] *Labor Call*, 24 July, 7 August, 4 September 1919.

The people had shivered in the cold while the members of the master class got drunk in their posh clubs. The day would come when the sins of the fathers of Versailles would be visited on the sons of that generation. Clemenceau, the old man with slant eyes, had persuaded the Allies they had a 'blood right to dig the grave of Western culture'. Hughes, Lloyd George and Clemenceau presented themselves as 'heroes of humanity' who would be blessed by generations to come. But prophets were already calling them 'bourgeois imperialists, devotees of power politics and stupid, revengeful devils'.[94]

[94] Thomas Mann to P. Witkop, 12 May 1919, Richard and Clara Winston (eds), *Letters of Thomas Mann* (Penguin Books edn, London, 1975), p. 88; Hermann Kesten (ed.), op. cit., p. 23.

4

THE GOSPEL OF HUGHES OR A NEW ORDER?

HUGHES CAME BACK to Australia in August 1919 to preach 'the gospel of Hughes'. In the Bendigo Town Hall on 1 September he told the people who had gathered to welcome him home: 'Those boys had fought to keep Australia white and free'. He believed in the Australian dream that all men should have justice and few men should not have that which belonged to all. Every man, he told them, should have a fair opportunity. But he must tell them he was a 'facts of life' man. Unfortunately there were some visionaries among them trying to persuade the people that 'there was some short cut to Paradise, or some way by which Australia could be saved if they followed the bloody road along which Lenin and Trotsky had led the people of Russia'. But as long as he was Prime Minister there would be no Bolshevism in Australia. He would give the Bolsheviks all the fighting they wanted. The world belonged to the brave and the strong. He repeated what he had said the day before in Melbourne, that he had become 'ten times more a believer in the glories of our destiny'. In his very soul, he said, as in the soul of the digger, there was a passionate love for Australia and the Australian spirit.[1]

On 10 September 1919 he spoke again of the peace treaty to members of the House of Representatives. Australia, he said, had now 'entered into a family of nations on a footing of equality'. Australia has been born in a blood sacrifice: Australia has been saved by the sword, and could only be kept safe by the sword. The military power of the Allies has left Germany impotent. The treaty of Versailles has made the world safe from further German aggression. There was to be a League of Nations, in which Australia had separate representation. The League consisted of an Assembly to which each nation was entitled to send representatives, and a Council composed of representatives of the five great Powers, and four others elected by the Assembly. There was to be an international tribunal, composed of eminent jurists who would sit for the purpose of trying any disputes brought before them. But, as he saw it, if any nation sought to achieve its aims by the sword then the League would 'collapse like a house of cards'. He was no believer in a new heaven, or any new earth. For the League to work there would have to

[1] *Age*, 1, 2 September 1919.

be a new creation: he had always believed human nature, like the mountains, the sky and the sea was from eternity and would not change.[2]

The question for a 'facts of life' man was: what have we got? The soldiers and the Australian delegates in Paris and Versailles had won what really mattered: they had won 'national safety'. Thanks to the soldiers and the Treaty of Versailles Australia was not threatened by any hostile power in the ring of nations to her north. Australia was not threatened by any 'open door' condition for men and goods in those islands. Australia's national safety was assured. Australia has held securely to 'the great principle of the White Australia', one of the tablets of the law in Australia. Australians were 'more British than the people of Great Britain'. Australians believed in being British, because that gave them their liberties and their White Australia. The soldiers had achieved that victory and, as he put it with pride, 'my colleagues and I have brought that great principle back to you from the Conference'.[3]

He had come back, he told the members of the House of Representatives, to preach again the gospel of work. There was, he said, no salvation save by the gospel of work. Those who endeavoured to set class against class, or to destroy wealth, were counsellors of destruction. There was only one hope for Australia: that was to strive to 'emulate the deeds of those who by their valour and sacrifice have given us liberty and safety, and resolve to be worthy of them and the cause for which they fought'. That was the gospel of Hughes.[4]

But the world was changing. American aviators have already flown an aeroplane across the Atlantic. The isolation of Australia was coming to an end. Australia's defence no longer depended on British naval power. Hughes preached the gospel of work, some other Australians were preaching the gospel of a 'New Order'. That was the subject of Katharine Susannah Prichard's pamphlet, *The New Order*. Born in Fiji on 4 December 1883 during a tropical hurricane, her whole life was lived in that storm centre inhabited by those endowed with great moral passion, and an itch to change things as they are. Her father was a newspaper editor, and she a yarn spinner and a weaver of great dreams from her early days. She wrote well, she spoke well, she danced well. She was an enlarger of life, a woman with a passionate heart and the eyes of a hawk. In Paris before the war she learned from Russian revolutionaries the creed which guided her through life. The revolution of 1917 became the great love of her life.

She believed Australians were standing in one of those periods of history when the old order was changing and yielding to a new one. The tide of

[2] *C'wealth P.D.*, 10 September 1919, vol. 89, pp. 12164–79.
[3] Ibid., pp. 12173–5.
[4] Ibid., p. 12179.

revolution has begun to flow: it could not be stopped. Labor members of Parliament declared that Australians would no longer acquiesce in the 'present abominable social system'; Australian women would not rear more men children for slaughter; Hughes has allowed his body and soul completely to pass under the domination of the governing class—Hughes, in their eyes, was the one-time Labor leader who had sold himself to the mob who were 'decked with starched shirt fronts and furbelows and sparkling diamonds'. Hughes was a 'colossal political failure and fraud'.[5]

The abuse stung Hughes into replying in kind. In September 1919 a slanging match erupted. Hughes ridiculed W. G. Higgs, one of the founders of the Labor Party in New South Wales, as a man with a mind 'like a toad in a cess-pit'. He sneered at Labor members of Parliament as 'worms bred on a dung heap', 'anaemic and flabby' men, and 'dirty dogs'. But time was running out for Hughes. In the first half of the nineteenth century Bishop Broughton had preached the Christian religion as an antidote to the barbarians of the Australian bush. Now the bourgeoisie wanted an antidote to the barbarians of the Australian suburbs. The bourgeoisie were ready for the calm-down years. Material well-being would disarm the potential revolutionary, strip him of his motive for revenge, and settle him for his years in one of the brick veneer or weatherboard bungalows of suburbia. There he could join the 'teaites', quaff his Robur tea, the drink that refreshes but does not inebriate, go to the 'footy' of a Saturday 'arvo' in the winter, and to the beaches or the mountains in the summer.

The bourgeoisie needed a political leader to preside over the New Era. Stanley Melbourne Bruce was already reflecting the temper of the bourgeois mind. He has told the House of Representatives he was aware Hughes had the reputation for 'the hopeless unreasonableness of an unreasonable man' —that Hughes had 'troublesome habits and annoying ways'. Of course Bruce rejected such criticism: like Brutus he was an honourable man. But the idea has been floated. The bourgeoisie had no further need for a needler and a fighter who went into the ring with the gloves off. They wanted one of their kind: a fine flower of 'Yarraside', or one who had been converted to the virtues and values of 'Yarraside'.[6]

The heroes of previous decades were breaking up. J. F. Archibald, the editor of the *Bulletin* in the roaring nineties was groaning to God in St Vincent's Hospital in Sydney, that magnificent institution where the nuns dispensed comfort to all those who were in any way afflicted in mind, body or estate. Archibald died on 10 September 1919. Henry Lawson, who had once

[5] *Argus*, 11 April 1919; Katharine Susannah Prichard, *The New Order* (Perth, 1919), p. 3; *Worker* (Brisbane), 28 August 1919; *Labor Call*, 14 August, 4 September 1919; Ric Throssell, *Wild Weeds and Wind Flowers* (Sydney, 1975), pp. 13–22.

[6] *Labor Call*, 18 September 1919; *C'wealth P.D.*, 19 September 1919, vol. 89, pp. 12603–12.

called on Australians to fly a rebel flag, was now advising them to 'have philosophy or patience'. On 7 October Alfred Deakin died in his home in South Yarra. His sympathies had been broad. He had been the most distinguished apostle of the Australian dream, a man who believed it was possible to achieve the Australian vision of material well-being for all and equality of opportunity without changing the foundations of society. He had been the conscience of the 'comfortable classes' in Australia, ill at ease though he was with their pursuit of 'filthy lucre', their Philistinism and their indifference to 'another and better existence'. To his colleagues in the early history of the Commonwealth he was 'like the effigy of some noble knight of the days of chivalry'. At the memorial service in the Queen's Hall, Parliament House, Melbourne, Willie Watt, Australia's greatest orator, likened his life to 'the track of a brilliant meteor across the dark political sky'. Some thought he had been too delicately constructed for the rough and tumble of Australian political warfare. Yet he proved to be a subtle and successful master in that field. Edmund Barton wondered whether the war had so barbarized humanity that there was no soil left in which to grow the plant of chivalry. Barton wanted to do what all the deprived want to do: he wanted to find words 'which may do thee ease and grace to me'. The myths, illusions, masks and fantasies inherited from the past were being thrown into the dust bin of human history, their utility having ended. A new age was starting.[7]

Class was pitted against class. Bolshevism was being presented as the alternative to the Bible, the Communist Manifesto as the alternative to the Sermon on the Mount. In October Hughes asked the Governor-General to dissolve the House of Representatives so that Australians might show what they wanted to be. The only hope for Australia, he told the Governor-General, was 'in a strong & capable government'. The alternative was chaos and decadence. Troglodytes (he meant the visionaries of the Labor movement) were bleating and whining and howling like the sheep and wolves and dingoes they were. He had his faith: 'God save the King & Australia'. The Governor-General granted his request. The election would be on 13 December 1919.[8]

[7] *Bulletin*, 18 September 1919; *S.M.H.*, 12, 13 September 1919; Sylvia Lawson, *The Archibald Paradox* (Ringwood, 1983), pp. 248–51; Henry Lawson to George Robertson, 5 December 1919, Colin Roderick (ed.), *Henry Lawson Letters 1890–1922* (Sydney, 1970) p. 378; *Soldier*, 10 October 1919; *Age*, 8 October 1919; *Argus*, 8 October 1919; *Herald* (Melbourne), 8, 9 October 1919; *Weekly Times*, 11 October 1919; *The Times*, 8 October 1919; *Christian Science Monitor*, 8 October 1919; *Warwick Daily News*, 9 October 1919; Diary of Catherine Deakin, 5 October 1919, Deakin Papers, Series 23; Edmund Barton to Pattie Deakin, 8 October 1923, ibid.; R. M. Ferguson to W. M. Hughes, 17 October 1919, Hughes Papers, Series 16, Box 1, folder 3; tribute by W. Watt, 8 October 1919, Deakin Papers, Series 23.

[8] *Labor Call*, 21 August 1919; W. M. Hughes to R. M. Ferguson, 11 October 1919, Novar Papers.

For this election there was an unknown card in the pack, a card which its holders hoped would play the role of the joker. On 21 August 1919 the Australian Farmers' Federal Organisation drew up a Federal Political Platform in anticipation of a federal election. They decided to run or support candidates who would represent the interests of farmers. They wanted many things. They wanted ample provision for the future of returned soldiers: they wanted the full encouragement of industries the war had shown to be vital to national interests: they wanted direct representation of producers on all Boards or Commissions dealing with producers' interests: they wanted a vigorous immigration policy, care being taken in the selection of immigrants and preference being given to agriculturalists and farm labourers: they wanted co-operation as against class warfare. They professed their unswerving loyalty to the King and the Empire. They wanted honesty and decency in politics. The bush was the nursery of innocents, the city was the breeding ground of corrupt and decadent men and women. The farmers were the creators of the wealth of Australia, and the city the place where bludgers, street loungers and gas-pipe loafers sponged on the 'hard yakka' of the farmers.[9]

The farmers wanted a larger share of the national cake. A week after the Melbourne conference, on 28 August, Senator Lynch called on the Senate to resolve that the vast number employed in rural industry 'the wheat farmers, the sheep men, the beef and dairy cattle men, the sugar planters, the orchardists &c &c' should not be sweated any longer, that they should not be condemned to a joyless existence of excessive hardships and ill-rewarded toil. The rural community should not be called upon to contribute an undue share to the upkeep of the nation. He asked the Government to ensure a living wage to the wheat cultivators of the Commonwealth, and to cause a permanent and prosperous peasantry to be rooted in the soil.[10]

A confident, truculent Hughes dismissed the threat of a country interest in politics with contempt. Lloyd George won his 'khaki election' with a landslide. He would win his. When he delivered his policy speech to the electors at Bendigo on 30 October 1919 he stuck to the gospel of Hughes—war to the death against Bolshevik and profiteer, preference to returned soldiers, and the defence of White Australia. Country people should recognize that the Nationalists had done all in their power for farmers and graziers. Of course the greatness of Australia depended upon the basis of land settlement. Everyone knew that, and his Government would offer inducements to the men on the land to stay there, and to Australian kinsmen overseas to come and settle here. He was on top of the world—serene, confident,

[9] Federal Platform drafted by the Australian Farmer's Federal Organisation, 21 August 1919, Hughes Papers, Series 16, Box 1, Folder 3; *Land*, 29 August 1919; Ulrich Ellis, Research Notes on Australian Country Party, MS. in N.L.A.

[10] *C'wealth P.D.*, 28 August 1919, vol. 89. pp. 12035–6.

believing the verdict of the electors would be the just deserts for all he had achieved.[11]

Labor spoke with two voices. The leader of the Party, Frank Tudor, was a kind man, a clear-headed man, but his heart was not on fire with any ideal or vision of the future of Australia. He asked the electors not to be deceived by this khaki-style election. Hughes, he said, had only the soldiers left. All the others were forsaking him. T. J. Ryan said the same thing. He was the white hope of Labor, having given up his position as Premier of Queensland to contest the seat of West Sydney (previously held by Hughes) for Labor. But fate was to prove unkind to Ryan. Just as he was making his mark in the House of Representatives by his oratory and his exposure of the political hypocrisy of Hughes's claim that he was protecting Australians against the 'insidious foe within', he was struck down by a mortal illness on 1 August 1921. Labor had not replaced the talents it lost when it blew out its brains in 1916. Labor was no longer a band of inspired idealists but a machine for the capture of political power. Labor must rubbish its opponents and woo the country vote. So Labor derided the candidates of the Australian Farmers' Federal Organisation as the 'profiteers of the countryside', and 'wolves in sheep's clothing'. Labor presented itself as a party for the rural worker, the small farmer, the country shopkeeper, and the people in country towns. In power Labor would cleanse Australian politics of all the filth of corruption, favouritism and cronyism. Labor also spoke with the voice of the visionary: Labor was the party for all those for whom life was 'a difficult and doubtful battle'. Capitalism, gorged with the flesh of men between 1914 and 1918, was already gloating over the prospect of 'another cannibal feast'. The workers alone could save humanity. Labor was the party of the workers.[12]

In the Labor Party vote-catchers and saviours of humanity worked side by side in an uneasy alliance. Labor promised many things. They spoke of a better future for humanity: they solicited crudely for votes by offering to pay a better gratuity to the soldiers than Hughes. Labor promised to lighten the burdens of the poor and to increase old age pensions. The socialists accused the Labor Party of sacrificing principle to expediency. They called on Labor leaders to stop once and for all the tactic of outbidding capitalist leaders for the people's vote. Labor must prove it was not 'the inglorious blundering puppet of the gang of profiteers and exploiters' who owned Australia. Workshop democracy was more important than parliamentary democracy. But the majority in the Labor Party replied that Labor with all its 'pussy-footed poltroonery and pragmatism' was better than a government of

[11] *Age*, 31 October 1919; *S.M.H.*, 31 October 1919.

[12] *Worker* (Brisbane), 6 November 1919; *C'wealth P.D.*, 17 September 1919, vol. 89, p. 12419; *S.M.H.*, 11 November 1919; *Argus*, 5 November 1919; *Australian Worker*, 6, 13 November 1919.

capitalists, militarists and imperialists. A party of ideologues would never win an Australian election: a party of pragmatists did not have to degenerate into a party of demagogues, careerists, faction leaders engaged in unseemly brawls for the loot of power, or corrupt politicians.[13]

Vida Goldstein abandoned Australia in disgust. She decided to live in England. In Australia, she found, women with the broad vision, the cultured mind, and the 'liberal trend' met with but scant recognition or appreciation. Bella Lavender was still keeping up the struggle. All through the election campaign she made stirring speeches in the Socialist Hall in Melbourne. Her theme was simple: the election of a woman to Parliament was not 'a horrible revolutionary idea which would upset creation'. Australians had a chance to prove they were a democracy and not a 'male-ocracy'. Without Vida Goldstein the fire was not there. The *Woman Voter*, the paper in which Vida Goldstein had inspired a generation of women, was about to close down.[14]

John Curtin stood as the Labor candidate for the seat of Perth. He told the electors he wanted Australians to cease to be the 'blundering puppets' of the 'gang of profiteers and exploiters' that owned and governed Australia. Australians should seize the opportunity to get rid of the men to whom in a moment of folly they had once entrusted their salvation. A change has come over John Curtin. The socialist ideologue of 1916 has turned into the pragmatist of 1919. Australian elections, he now believed, were won not by the men of ideology, but by the men offering sops to the people. In 1916 he called for 'strong and rebellious' men and women who would make no compromise with the capitalist system. He still saw himself as the 'standard bearer of a new order', different from that 'grossly imperfect and foully diseased capitalism'. In 1916 he had believed socialism would usher in a new era in the history of humanity: he now believed a Labor victory would make the world 'a cleaner, sweeter and happier place to live in'. In 1916 he had had a vision of Australia cleansed by the heroes of socialism: now he believed Labor would fashion an Australia where everything was convenient and cosy.[15]

At the start of the election campaign an industrial upheaval erupted in Kalgoorlie. On 6 November an infuriated mob, estimated to number from fifteen hundred to two thousand men assembled at the Boulder Block to listen to inflammatory speeches by officials of the Australian Workers' Union against the non-union workers in the mines. Inflamed by the speakers

[13] *Socialist*, 7 November, 5 December 1919.

[14] Ibid., 21 November 1919; *Woman Voter*, 17 November 1914, 18 December 1919.

[15] *Socialist*, 5 December 1919; *Westralian Worker*, 7, 14, 21, 28 November 1919; Lloyd Ross, *John Curtin* (Melbourne, 1977) pp. 70–2.

the mob chased non-union workers from the mine, kicking, punching and stoning their opponents to the accompaniment of 'torrents of bad language', and 'lurid objurgations on their ancestry'. The Returned Soldiers' League in Kalgoorlie condemned such behaviour. Other returned soldiers held a meeting to condemn the R.S.L. for its reactionary support of the Chamber of Mines in their endeavours to reduce the wages of the miners. The A.W.U. agreed to visit the mines to enrol non-union labour. The ill feeling lingered on, as Hughes shouted louder and louder what he would do to all Bolsheviks.[16]

In the middle of the election campaign the owner of *Smith's Weekly*, James Joynton Smith, offered Hughes a salary of £5000 a year for ten years to edit a daily paper. Hughes declined the offer. Hughes and Joynton Smith had much in common. They were both immigrants: both loners, both haters. They both mocked and snarled at all visionaries as inhabitants of a dung heap and both preached the gospel of work, white civilization, and King and Empire. Both were extremely secretive men. There the similarities ended. James Joynton Smith published the first issue of *Smith's Weekly* on 1 March 1919. In the columns of his newspaper he vilified the Labor Party as the hiding-place for Bolsheviks, Wobblies and Sinn Feiners. He vowed never to be a 'Hebrew's slave'. He announced a campaign against all the 'political pests and poltroons that infest our poor land . . . O.B.U. Bolshevik orators, and bulb-eyed editors, clerical humbugs, business profiteers, wobbly poetical post-mistresses'. The salvation of Australia, he said, would come from the returned soldiers. It was clear that, like Hughes and Norman Lindsay, Joynton Smith saw revolutionaries as the men with the brutish faces, who would usher in an age of barbarism in Australia. Joynton Smith presented Hughes to his readers as the hero of the middle-class larrikins in Australia. That dismayed 'Yarraside'.[17]

On the eve of the election the believers in the Empire had a windfall. On 19 January Hughes offered a prize of £10 000 to the first Australian aviators to fly from England to Australia in a British-made machine. The 'boss sheriffs' of the Australian bureaucracy called the idea 'rather eccentric'. The socialists denounced it as another Hughes stunt to tighten the fetters binding Australians to the British, and to their colonial past. Hughes stood firm. At a quarter to nine on the morning of 12 November 1919 Captain Ross Smith and Lieutenant Keith Smith, together with two mechanics, Sergeants Bennett and Shieres, left England in a British-made Vickers-Vimy machine. They

[16] *West Australian*, 8, 14 November 1919; *Westralian Worker*, 21 November 1919.

[17] *Smith's Weekly*, 29 November 1919; R. M. Ferguson to Lord Milner, 12 October 1919, Novar Papers; *Smith's Weekly*, 1, 8, March 1919; James Joynton Smith, *My Life Story* (Sydney, 1927).

landed at Darwin on 10 December at three-forty in the afternoon. The flight took twenty-eight days.[18]

Hughes was delighted. The *Sydney Morning Herald* shared his enthusiasm. This was a triumph for the Empire, they said. The two ends of the Empire had been brought closer together: the days of Australia's isolation, a prime cause of the inferiority complex, and of all cringing and grovelling were numbered. The *Bulletin* named Captain Ross Smith the Columbus of the twentieth century. In Darwin there were festivities. Hopes were running high for communications by air between Australia and the capital of the Empire. At the close of the Darwin banquet a lady kissed the aviators. Those present cheered. But that night Ross Smith dropped the warning: Australia could now be invaded by air. Australia has won the victory over isolation possibly at the price of her immunity from invasion. The victory in the war was already beginning to be out of date. As the *Daily Telegraph* in Sydney put it, the issues in the forthcoming election were 'like the trivial intangibilities of a child's dream' beside the forthcoming danger from the north. The aeroplane temporarily strengthened the imperial bonds, but in the long run the aeroplane would make obsolete a maritime Empire.[19]

No such doubts crossed the mind of Hughes. Ross and Keith Smith were men after his own heart, disciples of the gospel he had been preaching ever since he entered public life. They were King and Empire men: they were believers in the gospel of work: they believed the world belonged to the brave. Election day on 13 December crowned his joy. In the House of Representatives the Nationalists won thirty-seven seats, the Country groups won eleven (three for candidates of the Farmers' and Settlers' Associations, and eight for the Victorian Farmers' Union). Labor won twenty-six and an Independent one. In the half-Senate election Labor did not win a seat. Hughes and the Nationalists no longer had a majority in the House of Representatives. To govern he must come to some agreement with the representatives of the farmers' organizations in the new Parliament. He must go cap in hand to the men at whose expense he had indulged in the sport which gave him so much pleasure—the sport of mocking those he believed to be his inferiors. John Curtin also had a cross to bear. He had been defeated in the electorate of Perth. He must resume those lonely walks along the

[18] Cablegram of W. M. Hughes to W. Watt, recd 19 February 1919, Aviation Flight to Australia, Correspondence Files of Prime Minister's Department 1919–1920, C'wealth Archives, Item 20/2253; memorandum by G. Swinburne to the Dept of Defence, 7 May 1919, ibid.; Statement with regard to aerial flight from England to Australia, 9 September 1919, ibid.; *Argus*, 13, 19, 29 November, 11 December 1919.

[19] *Argus*, 12 December 1919; *S.M.H.*, 11 December 1919; *Daily Telegraph*, 11 December 1919; *Bulletin*, 18 December 1919.

beach at Cottesloe, brooding over how he could fulfil his destiny. His dark night of the soul was not over.[20]

In the excitement of victory the conservative press attributed Labor's defeat to its failure to distance itself from the Wobblies, Bolsheviks, Sinn Feiners and disloyalists. Labor had a different explanation. The *Australian Worker* was disappointed. Australia was to have the ludicrous spectacle of a Senate composed entirely of supporters of the Government. The Bastilles of Capitalism were intact: not a single brick had been dislodged. There were, they believed, two reasons for this: first, the workers of Australia were not sufficiently intelligent to realize their condition: second, the influence of the 'modern machinery of mendacity'—the press. 'The lying press of Capitalism has . . . buried the brains of innumerable working men and women under immense layers of prejudice and error'. The *Socialist* added to lack of intelligence the apathy of the workers, sectarian divisions, and religious bigotry. Labor must own more newspapers.

No one suggested the role of the spirit of the place in fostering a scepticism and indifference to the fruits of human endeavour. No one blamed the horrors of the war as a source of doubt about humanity's capacity for better things. The optimism of the *Socialist* was not dismissed. It still saw promising signs of a 'bright Red New Year'. Empires were crumbling. The monarchs of Russia, Germany and Austria-Hungary had been deposed. Labor must strive for the time when the workers possessed industrial ownership and political control. Australian workers must be taught the truth about the Australian Labor Party: it was a bourgeois reformist party. The workers must now build a new society.[21]

The *Socialist* had no suggestions on how that might come to be. It copied its ideas from Moscow. It called for the establishment of the dictatorship of the proletariat as the transition stage between Capitalism and Communism. In January 1920 Frederick Sinclaire regretted that Australians of all political persuasions still looked abroad for their ideas. Like the theologians and writers, political radicals in Australia displayed a 'lamentable want of independence'. They were still borrowing words and terms from abroad. Australian radicals boasted they were not British, but instead of talking about being Australians, they borrowed their ideas from the Sinn Feiners, the I.W.W. or the Bolsheviks. Australia would become the 'last refuge of monarchy, the last ditch of capitalism', in which the labour of people would be devoted to the upkeep of a ruling class, mostly resident in England. The time had come for Australians to think for themselves and make an effort to work out their own destiny. The sun, hedonism and the horrors of the war have

[20] *Age*, 15 December 1919; Colin A. Hughes and B. D. Graham, *A Handbook of Australian Government and Politics 1890–1964* (Canberra, 1968), p. 320.

[21] *Australian Worker*, 18 December 1919; *Bulletin*, 11 December 1919; *Socialist*, 9, 16, 23, 30 January 1920.

defeated religion in Australia. The comfortable classes have filled the void with the Union Jack, Anzac Day, Armistice Day, Empire Day, and other symbols of Imperialism. A secular religion has replaced the religion of the spirit. Protestants have removed the crucifix from the sanctuary, and installed the national flag. The Protestants have decorated their churches with the insignia of Imperialism. The people had new idols: the idols of pleasure and comfort. Australians were sailing in the sea of plutocracy, because with the increase in consumer goods the capitalists could toss sops to the hungry and the needy to make them complacent. Talk of a better world made little appeal to a people contented with their lot, a people who believed food, shelter and a bit of fun were all you needed to know on earth. Australians have never been hungry enough, have never suffered enough to inspire them to die for social justice.[22]

The socialists proclaimed a good time was coming. Soon there would be 'Heaven on earth for the people'. Robert Ross, the editor of *Ross's Monthly*, believed a new order was about to begin. On 7 March 1920 Comrade Ross dedicated the new-born baby of Mr and Mrs Heffron to the cause of socialism. The baby lay prettily upon a cushion decorated in red, as Comrade Ross baptized her. The audience then sang the 'Red Flag'. By contrast, the Labor Party was holding progressive euchre parties, with cakes and coffee thrown in, while the socialists sang of the hope that the next generation would be citizens of a 'co-operative Commonwealth'. The time had come to 'put Australia first', the time had come to fan into flame an Australianism which would liberate them from the stigma of inferiority, the stigma of being second-class Europeans. Australians should stop trying to be more English than the English, more Irish than the Irish, or more Scots than the Scots. Christians worshipped and glorified the Man of Sorrows. Socialists celebrated the Man of Smiles. Christians accepted the Cross of Suffering as their symbol, suffering being the beginning of grace, wisdom and understanding. Socialists believed in life, liberty and the pursuit of happiness, in gaiety and the Dionysian frenzy. Christians were straiteners and life-deniers. Socialists were enlargers of life. The Church was the bulwark of vested interests and the main asset of the moneyed classes.[23]

In the *Lone Hand* the editor, A. G. Stephens, told his readers Australia stood in need of a 'healthy encouragement of a virile sentiment of Australianism'. Vance Palmer was propagating the same idea. For years he has rebuked the 'Cultured Philistines' for insisting that nothing in art, literature, music or life was important unless it originated in England, Europe, or classical antiquity. Australia did not need this dead hand of the past: Australia

[22] *Fellowship*, January 1920, p. 95, February 1920, p. 102, April 1920, pp. 131–2; *Ross's Monthly*, 13 December 1919; F. Sinclaire, *Annotations* (Melbourne, 1920), p. 41.

[23] *Ross's Monthly*, 14 February 1920, p. 12, 15 May 1920, p. 11; *Socialist*, 6 February, 12, 19 March 1920.

needed a vital and creative culture of her own. Australians should not waste time reading and studying 'second-rate Elizabethan dramatists' (Palmer graciously excepted William Shakespeare and Ben Jonson). Hughes has shown what manner of man he is: he has said that Australia was as much a part of England as Middlesex. Australia, Palmer said, was not like England: Australia was unique. Her artists, writers and musicians must uncover her uniqueness and the uniqueness of her people to other Australians—the way they spoke, the way they lived, and above all what they lived by.

Australians had a character of their own. The bush, as Henry Lawson pointed out, had been the nursery of a culture. But so far the cities have not developed a culture of their own. The war had left Australia under the sway of a 'rootless politician' and the local jingoes. Having no culture of their own they had been swamped by the new commercial entertainment; the cinema, jazz music, and the 'megaphones of publicity agents'. Australian bookstalls were stacked with 'cheap and nasty' American magazines. The taste of Australian readers, Palmer continued, was being depraved by salacious passages such as: 'Her beautiful, rosy-red bosom was bared now and again as she swayed backwards and forwards in the intoxication of the dance'. There were also descriptions like the one of a lady with 'a silk, softly clinging negligée, showing a little more leg than necessary'. Like his mentor, William Lane, Palmer had lost the faith of his puritan ancestors but not their puritan morality. Like the *Socialist*, Palmer objected to the commercial theatres and picture shows which entertained their patrons with 'nothing but naked women and ribald songs'.[24]

Like Joseph Furphy, Edward Vivian (Vance) Palmer was a boy from the bush, who never broke with his puritan childhood. He was born at Bundaberg, Queensland, in 1885, the son of a schoolmaster with an interest in literature. He was educated at State Schools and at Ipswich Grammar School. He freelanced in London from 1905 to 1908, years in which he absorbed the ideas of the guild socialists and the vitalists, but not their materialism, he remaining all his life a 'burden of the mystery' man. He mixed with the 'future of humanity' men in London and tried unsuccessfully to see Lev Tolstoy. On 23 May 1914 he married in London Janet (Nettie) Gertrude Higgins, the niece of H. B. Higgins of the Commonwealth Court of Conciliation and Arbitration. She, too, was born in 1885, but in her case into a Melbourne patrician family. She had been educated at the Presbyterian Ladies' College and at the University of Melbourne where she graduated as B.A., and then M.A. with honours in Latin and Greek. She was widely read in French, German and Russian literature: she had lived briefly in Berlin, Paris

[24] A. G. Stephens. 'The Nationalism of Australia', *Lone Hand*, 14 February 1920; Vance Palmer, 'Towards a Living Culture', *Fellowship*, May 1916, p. 2; 'Australian Nationalism', ibid., September 1917, pp. 23–5; 'Did We Win The Peace?', *Aussie*, 15 April 1920, p. 9; 'Magazine Morals', *Fellowship*, May 1920, pp. 157–9; *Socialist*, 20 February 1920.

and London. She had published two volumes of poetry, *South Wind* in 1914 and *Shadowy Paths* in 1915.

Before they were married they wrote tender, loving letters to each other. 'If there is a God', he wrote to her, probably in 1911, 'I would never leave off thanking him because he made me a man and you a woman and let our paths cross one another'. It was the same for her: 'Vance', she wrote, 'you're the most inspiring person on earth. I love you on every plane & trust you forever . . . Mate . . . I am yours altogether'. After the marriage in 1914 she found to her dismay he either could not or would not give her what she wanted. He held back as a lover just as he held back as a writer. He was a man of promise, but not of fulfilment. He was an Olympian: she wanted a Byronic lover, a man who was both Apollo and Dionysus. She became his servant. She cooked, washed up, cleaned the house, and made clothes for the two daughters Aileen and Helen. In what time she had left she read and criticized her husband's work, wrote poems and articles, kept a journal and corresponded with a vast number of other writers. Everyone loved her. A. G. Stephens called her 'good, kind, sweet, encouraging Nettie Palmer'. Friends and acquaintances admired Vance Palmer, but something in him checked them from coming near. They loved Nettie: they told her everything.

In 1918 he joined the 18th Battalion of the A.I.F., but arrived in Europe too late to take part in the fighting. In 1919 the family moved to Emerald, Victoria. He wrote articles for weeklies and periodicals, played cricket for Emerald, and corresponded with Bernard O'Dowd, Frederick Sinclaire, E. J. Brady, Katharine Susannah Prichard, A. G. Stephens, Louis and Hilda Esson and Shaw Neilson. She had an even wider circle of letter writers. She wrote to Hugh McCrae, and received in reply the story of the latest woman in his life. No one ever wrote to Vance Palmer the confessions of a passionate heart—either in prose or verse. Vance plugged away with the zeal of a crusader for things Australian. Other writers encouraged him. 'Dear Palmer', wrote Ted Brady, 'get to it'. Hilda Esson asked both the Palmers the question: 'Can't we do anything ourselves as Australians?' Vance Palmer told his readers Europe was doomed: Europe was weighed down by its past. There 'dreams of dead men underground/Trouble the heavy air'. In Australia life 'has scarce begun'. In Australia life 'with a laugh in its mouth/Plays butterfly in the sun'. But something held him back. He was aware of what had happened in Europe: he was aware of 'the dark Somme flowing'. He also had a shy belief in the life of the world to come, a hope that though our bodies may be buried 'our vehement spirits will return'.[25]

[25] H. Heseltine (ed.), *Intimate Portraits: essays and articles by Vance Palmer* (Melbourne, 1969); David Walker, *Dream and Disillusion: the Search for Australian Cultural Identity* (Canberra, 1976); Hugh McCrae to Vance Palmer, 3 March 1920, Palmer Papers, Series 1, Folder 27; A. G. Stephens to Nettie Palmer, 29 March 1920, ibid.; Vance Palmer, 'The Farmer Remembers the Somme', *Ross's Monthly*, June 1920, p. 7; Vance Palmer to Nettie

When the film of the *Sentimental Bloke*, directed by Raymond Longford, was screened in Sydney in October 1919 the *Daily Telegraph* was delighted. It was, it wrote, 'Australian right through'. But the Palmers, the Essons and their circle did not share this delight. Louis Esson did not want Australians to take their entertainment from the sentimentalities of C. J. Dennis. Dennis was an anachronism, a man preaching that those who had wallowed in the city muck would find salvation in the bush. Australia needed a culture for the suburbs. When the film *On Our Selection*, directed by Raymond Longford, was screened later that year in Sydney the press again applauded 'the genuine Australianism', the 'clean, home-made article' so different from 'Yankee trash'. But again the members of the Palmer circle were not happy. They regretted all this nostalgia for an Australia that had ceased to be: they wanted Australians to find other heroes than Dad, Dave, Mother, and the other actors in the black comedy of the 'bush barbarians'. Hilda Esson was disgusted. The Australian cinema, like the American, was fostering the frivolity of the Australian people, a people who found their greatest amusement in picture palaces, dance halls, lying on the beaches in the sun, barracking at the 'footy' and the cricket, or swilling beer on balmy summer nights. So did Vance Palmer and Louis Esson. Vance Palmer played cricket for Emerald, took his children to see Charlie Chaplin films, and barracked for Hawthorn. Louis Esson barracked for Carlton, and loved a chat about who ought to be in the Australian Eleven, and the antics of Warwick Armstrong.[26]

While the Palmers and their circle were on fire with their aim of 'placing ... Australia in the scheme of things', the generals and the conservative politicians were presenting quite a different vision of the future of Australia. On 12 January 1920 General Monash, just back from the war, said at the reception given to him by the Lord Mayor of Melbourne that he thought the only patriotic doctrine for the returned soldier to preach to Australians was that they should be prepared for war. A week later General Birdwood and Admiral Jellicoe had the same message for Australians. 'Birdie', a warm-hearted man who gave a 'digger' a dinkum Aussie firm grip of the hand, not the 'cold fish' handshake, told them it would be the height of folly to rely entirely on the League of Nations. They were all British. They must increase their strength as a united Commonwealth under the British Crown. The Empire must never become decadent. The *Australian Worker* warned its readers against the 'Birdwood boom'. Birdwood was a decoy used by the con-

---

Higgins, n.d., probably 1911, ibid.; Hilda Esson to Vance and Nettie Palmer, 23 April 1920, Palmer Papers, Series 1, Folder 27.

[26] Louis Esson to Vance Palmer, 4 February 1920, Palmer Papers, Series 1, Folder 27; *Daily Telegraph*, 20 October, 3 November 1919; *Lone Hand*, 1 November 1920; *Bulletin*, 28 July, 6 October 1921; Hilda Esson to Vance and Nettie Palmer, 3 February 1921, Palmer Papers, Series 1, Folder 28.

servatives to bind Australia more tightly with the chains and shackles of Imperialism.[27]

Hughes was still the diggers' friend, the man who has promised the ex-servicemen he would give them whatever they asked for. Vain hope. At the beginning of 1920 the soldiers were asking for more than Hughes could deliver: it was no longer in his power. The romantic days were over. In the halcyon days of March and April 1919 the trumpets of triumph had sounded, the drums had rolled. Returning diggers, in the overflow of their hearts, had shouted to the crowds on the wharves and in the streets, 'Good old sunny Australia'. Women, impatient, and unable to restrain the passions coming up from inside them, had jumped the barricades and kissed their soldier sweethearts on the mouth while their mates asked for 'half your luck, sport' or encouraged them, 'Keep going, mate. Y're doin' well'.[28]

By January 1920 much of this 'sweet fraternal spirit' has evaporated. The people found there were 'bad eggs' among the soldiers. Diggers were drinking themselves silly in public houses, reeling round the cities, suburbs or country towns making lewd gestures to women or defiling the air with their talk of what they would do to the first woman who looked as though she too had the same hungers. The earnest women in the Women's Christian Temperance Union wrote thousands of letters to diggers appealing to them 'to be loyal to the principles of morality and temperance in the face of temptation'. Cynics said all the work of the pious women with the knitting needles did not persuade one digger from 'having a lager'. The drunkenness went on. Soldiers fell victims to 'too much hospitality'.[29]

No one knew how to handle these 'broken comrades', these men whose lives have been shattered by the war. Soldiers suffering from shock were observed to act in their sleep as though they were engaged in battle, and went through the pantomime of fighting with bombs, bayonet, machine-gun and rifle. Observers expressed sympathy, but nothing they did seemed to alleviate the suffering of the soldiers. Some suffered from what their contemporaries called 'loathsome diseases'. Numbers had consumption. Hospitals must be built. But where? No suburb wanted a hospital housing 'incurable consumptives'. In August 1919 Dr Cumpston, Federal Director of Quarantine, had published a statement that 55 000 Australian soldiers had suffered from venereal disease during the war. The President of the New South Wales Branch of the Returned Soldiers' and Sailors' League of Australia, Roy Teece, had replied that this was 'slanderous and misleading'. But

[27] *Ross's Monthly*, 12 May 1920, p. 12; *Age*, 13 January 1920; *S.M.H.*, 22 January 1920; *Argus*, 22 January 1920.

[28] *Age*, 4, 23 April 1919.

[29] *Daily Telegraph*, 20 October, 3 July 1919; G. M. Long, 'Our Responsibility to the Living', *Reveille*, 30 November 1929.

the facts could not be overcome by abuse or self-righteousness. Soldiers, it was said, were a menace to health and morals.[30]

There were riots in Melbourne in July 1919: shots were fired: the holy quiet of St Kilda Road was disturbed by drunken hooligans. Spring Street and the Treasury Gardens were vandalized by hordes of angry returned soldiers demanding generous rewards in return for what they had done for their country. Thousands of poor devils who had offered their lives for their country and human liberty did not know where their next meal was coming from. Heroes of Gallipoli, Pozières, Ypres and Passchendaele were walking from house to house selling matches and trinkets to frightened housewives. The Soldiers and Citizens Political Federation drew up a platform. They wanted the maintenance of a White Australia policy, preference in employment for returned soldiers, establishment and encouragement of new industries, a square deal for returned soldiers and their dependants, advances to returned soldiers free of interest for the first five years. They wanted a cash gratuity to returned soldiers and to the next of kin of deceased soldiers. Billy Hughes did not know what to do. The cash gratuity would come to £25 million and the Government did not have it. The soldiers shouted at him at a public meeting on 10 November 1919: 'Get it!' Billy Hughes had the answer. He was not going to be a bald man selling hair restorer. He was not a god. He was a man and he could not perform miracles. The soldiers must be patient.[31]

Promises have been made to the brave men who enlisted. They must be fulfilled. Governments have already laid foundations for the repatriation of soldiers, sailors and airmen. The Commonwealth Parliament put the Australian Soldiers' Repatriation Fund Act on the statute book in 1916, followed by the Australian Soldiers' Repatriation Act in 1917. In February 1916 a conference between the Commonwealth and the States resolved that the seven parties should co-operate in the promotion of a scheme for the settlement of willing and suitable returned soldiers upon the land. In January 1919 the Premiers of the States insisted that the settlement of the returned soldiers was a State responsibility. They jointly agreed to vest the responsibility and control of land settlement in the State authorities, and to give the Commonwealth the responsibility to lend money to the States to enable them to make loans to soldier settlers, such loans not to exceed £625 per settler. On 8 April 1918 the Commonwealth Government established the Department of Repatriation to administer the employment of returned soldiers, the training of discharged soldiers for various trades and callings, assistance both medical and general towards the re-establishment of

[30] *Daily Telegraph*, 23 May, 11 July, 30, 31 October, 5 August 1919.

[31] *Australian Worker*, 9 January 1919; *Age*, 25 February 1919; *Daily Telegraph*, 3, 7, 11, 12, 17 November 1919.

returned soldiers, and provision for the welfare of dependants of deceased soldiers as well as totally incapacitated discharged soldiers and their dependants. The Commonwealth and the States passed Acts to grant preference in employment to returned soldiers. The soldiers called on Billy to soak the war profiteer and give them jobs and money. 'Get it, get it', angry soldiers shouted to Billy Hughes.[32]

Billy replied: 'We have not got the money'. The soldiers retorted: 'You had it for the war. So get it, get it!' But that was the whole bloody trouble. Where was it to come from? Bonds were issued. But that did not satisfy the soldiers. The Government floated a Peace Loan for Repatriation. The 'Big Man Is Coming Home'. Promises to him must be met. That was 'A Point of Honour'. Twenty-five million pounds were raised. But the soldiers wanted more and wanted it now. The soldiers asked in November 1919: 'When will that be?' Hughes replied: 'After the elections', and added, 'I am not God or even Ryan'. Hughes at bay was still superb. The soldiers laughed. The election in December 1919 tied the hands of Hughes. After the polls there was a corner party of eleven members representing the farmers. On 22 January they decided to form themselves into a political party called the Country Party. They also decided to act independently of all other political parties. Billy Hughes was no longer a free agent. At a meeting on 25 February the eleven present elected William James McWilliams as leader and Edmund Jowett deputy leader. McWilliams was chosen as 'provisional leader' because of his previous parliamentary experience in Tasmania. A newspaper proprietor and journalist, he was a stop-gap until such time as a leader emerged. Jowett was from the Grampians in Victoria. He dressed and spoke the part he had always played in life—that of a man on whose properties a million sheep were shorn each year. Billy Hughes rubbed his hands in glee. They were just a party of hayseeds, they were a pushover. He could go on doing what he loved doing, dismissing these country bumpkins as people who did not count, the eternal lightweights of the political world. There was no need to go cap in hand to these nonentities.[33]

Hughes has made the mistake of a lifetime. The Country Party elected Earle Christmas Grafton Page as its secretary. Page was no hayseed. He was

[32] *Daily Telegraph*, 12, 22 August 1919; Report on Losses Due To Soldier Settlement by Mr Justice Pike, *C'wealth P.P.*, 1929, vol. II, pp. 6–8; Australian Soldiers' Repatriation Act, No. 7 of 1916, and Australian Soldiers' Repatriation Act, No. 6 of 1920, *C'wealth Statutes*; Report of the Repatriation Departments, 1919, *C'wealth P.P.*, 1917–18–19, vol. VI, pp. 3–6.

[33] Advertisement for Peace Loan, *Daily Telegraph*, 12 September 1919; *Daily Telegraph*, 11 November 1919; *Argus*, 23 January, 26 February 1920; Ulrich Ellis, Select References and Basic Facts for the guidance of Students concerning the origin of the Federal Country Party (1902–1923), typescript in N.L.A., Canberra; B. D. Graham, *The Formation of the Australian Country Parties* (Canberra, 1966).

'no cocky in appearance'. Captain Bruce of the Nationalists was handsome in a 'dark but bored kind of way'. Dr Page was 'really good looking'. He always wore on his face a 'genial school-boy smile', but no one ever knew what went on behind his 'pleasant man of the world manner'. He was born in Grafton on 8 August 1880, and educated at Grafton, Sydney High School, and at Sydney University where he graduated in Medicine in 1900. He came into the House with three reputations: as a surgeon in Grafton, as a farmer, and as an advocate of country interests. Behind the 'genial school-boy smile' there was also a man with a drive to win, a man who was ruthless with all who stood between him and the fulfilment of his ambition. On the tennis court he was not reliable on whether a ball was 'in' or 'out'. Hughes judged Page by the smile, the sound, sensible exterior he presented to the House, and the pleasing wit of the man about members' frailties. Hughes only discovered the destroyer in Page when it was too late.[34]

Hughes has often had sport with country politicians as 'hayseeds', and men with nothing between the ears. Now he must pay the price for such folly. The Country Party refused to form a coalition with Hughes. Hughes must go it alone as the leader of a minority Government. On 3 February 1920 Hughes announced the members of his new Government. On 10 March McWilliams informed the House of Representatives that the Country Party would support only measures of which they approved. He called for drastic action to relieve the plight of country people. The man on the land was not receiving a return proportionate to his labour: he must be given a standard of living similar to that enjoyed by the city dweller. Page put it more bluntly later: the countryman and the Country Party would no longer be the 'wet nurse' of the Commonwealth Government. To illustrate their power McWilliams announced that the Country Party would limit supply to six weeks.[35]

Labor was uneasy with the Country Party. Frank Anstey was just as contemptuous of their members as Hughes and the Nationalists. They did not stand for the Government: nor for the Labor Party: they stood only for themselves. They were a Party without principles, without policy, without ideas, prepared to stand for nothing, and to desert for anything, to stand up or sit down as the exigencies of the moment demanded. Page did not fly into a rage, nor beat his breast and make a profession of the principles which governed his public life. He was prepared to make a bargain with any individual, any group prepared to work with the Country Party. Hughes was not

[34] Sir Earle Page, Ann Mozley (ed.), *Truant Surgeon* (Sydney, 1963), pp. 54–5, 1–22; *Bulletin*, 9, 16 September 1920; *To-day*, 1 November 1932.

[35] *C'wealth Gazette*, 4 February 1920; *Age*, 4 February 1920; *C'wealth P.D.*, 10 March 1920, vol. 91, pp. 250–2, 15 April 1921, vol. 95, p. 7481.

prepared to do that. The Country Party must find a man among the Nationalists who was prepared to work with them.[36]

Some returned soldiers demanded action against the Bolsheviks. In July 1919 a branch of the Returned Sailors' and Soldiers' Imperial League resolved that it was the imperative duty of Federal and State Governments to take immediate steps against all persons who acted in any manner disloyally to the King and Empire. Hughes, the Nationalist Party and the Country Party could play along with that. The R.S.S.A.I.L.A. also requested that the Federal Government declare 25 April (Anzac Day) a permanent public holiday. Hughes, the Nationalist Party and the Country Party could and did play along with that. The country at large seemed disposed to give the soldiers a 'fair go'. The public, it was said, owed them a debt of gratitude. When six young returned soldiers were tried on 14 February 1920 for tarring and feathering the poet and ex-parliamentarian, J. K. McDougall, for some verses he had written and for his opposition to conscription, the judge of the Victorian Supreme Court, Judge Williams, decided to fine them rather than send them to prison. After all, these young soldiers had had great provocation.[37]

The soldiers wanted more than the sympathy and the concern of the 'tea-ites', and government measures to make loyalty to King and Empire sacrosanct. They wanted jobs and payment in cash. The officials of the Returned Sailors and Soldiers demanded something be done about it quickly. At demonstrations to draw attention to the plight of the returned men, speakers asked for a sustenance allowance, because their wives and children were starving. Beggars appeared in the streets, writing on their placards and collecting boxes pathetic appeals to help a starving digger and his hungry family. Some insisted they did not want 'sustenance': that degraded them. They were men: they wanted jobs: they wanted to be put into the 'cushy' jobs now held by men who have never gone to the war.[38]

The number of unemployed was mounting. In the last quarter of 1918, 16 919 members of trade unions were unemployed; 20 359 in the first quarter of 1919, and 22 186 in the second quarter of 1920. The soldiers still had faith in Billy Hughes. 'Let's talk to Billy', they said. But Billy was no longer master in his own house. Billy now had to seek the approval of the Country Party members for everything he wanted to do. Hughes began to pay the price for indulging in the sport of ridicule. Page had a long memory: there was no art that could read the construction of Page's mind in his face: Page was inscrutable. Hughes would soon learn what went on in the mind of

[36] *C'wealth P.D.*, 15 April 1921, vol. 95, pp. 7483–4.

[37] Memorandum to W. M. Hughes, n.d., probably July 1919, Hughes Papers, Series 16, Box 1, Folder 3; *Age*, 15 February 1920.

[38] *Age*, 9 January, 11 February 1920.

a man whose face was not the mirror either of his thoughts or his passions.[39]

Hughes fondly believed that as long as Labor was divided he was safe. He had grounds for his belief. The Russian revolution has divided the Labor movement. In the early days of the revolution the Labor movement hailed the revolution as the dawn of a new era in the world. At Moscow, on 2 March 1919, the Third International called on communists and socialists throughout the world to distance themselves from 'harmful opportunist and social-patriotic elements'. Moscow appealed to the workers to hasten the victory of the communist revolution throughout the world. The world crisis could only be ended, they maintained, with the help of the dictatorship of the proletariat.[40]

The doctrine of the dictatorship of the proletariat divided the Labor movement. In 1920 Robert Ross, the editor of the *Socialist*, returned to Melbourne after a visit to Moscow. He had much to say to his readers. Australians he said, would not accept the Russian method of 'creating the Kingdom of Heaven by violence'. The dictatorship of the proletariat was not the Australian way. Australians believed in the ballot box, in freedom of expression, in freedom of thought, in freedom of association. The Bolsheviks had a one-party State and had suppressed all other political parties. The Bolsheviks did not permit liberty of the press, liberty of association or liberty of conscience. The Bolsheviks were the spiritual bullies of the post-war world. The Australian tradition was that every man had a right to decide for himself what he would think and what he would do: the Bolsheviks believed liberty of conscience must be sacrificed in the interests of saving the revolution. For them liberty of conscience was a bourgeois self-indulgence.[41]

There were other divisions within the Labor movement. There was the division between those who believed in social change by Parliament, and those who believed in social change by industrial action. The believers in change by industrial action supported the One Big Union movement. The idea has been around for at least a decade. On 6 August 1918 a Trades Union Congress in Sydney passed resolutions to create the One Big Union. Their aim was to abolish capitalism. The class struggle, they declared, must continue until this was achieved. The only way capitalism could be abolished was by 'the workers uniting in one class-conscious economic organisation to take and hold the means of production by revolutionary industrial and political action'. Existing political and industrial methods had been proved to be futile: they had served only to perpetuate capitalism, not to end it.[42]

The *Australian Worker* was delighted with the proposal. A glorious dream

[39] C'wealth Statistics Quarterly Summary, 1919, 1920.
[40] *The New Communist Manifesto of the "Third International"* (Melbourne, 1919).
[41] R. S. Ross, *Revolution in Russia and Australia* (Melbourne, 1920), pp. 45–59.
[42] *One Big Union: Adopted Scheme of the Trade Union Congress* (Sydney, 1918).

looked like coming true: the One Big Union would be launched on a day that would be 'big with destiny', a day that would write a new page in the history of the working class. The One Big Union was the 'doom of Capitalism writ large'. The Melbourne Conference of eighty-three trade unions in November 1918 assented to the proposal. In January 1919 an interstate conference at the Trades Hall in Melbourne accepted the revolutionary preamble of 6 August 1918. They reaffirmed their aim to destroy Capitalism, and establish a 'Co-operative Commonwealth'. To the delegates it was 'so painfully obvious that It Cannot Be Achieved By The Securing Of A Parliamentary Majority'.[43]

J. Mostyn, the President of the Federated Electrical Trades Union, did not agree. Industrial action, he told the Melbourne conference of Trade Unions in January 1919, was a 'Bolshevik tactic'. It was an example of the use of the bludgeon. Beware, he warned delegates, of Bolshevik bully-boys. Beware, he said, of men like 'Jock' Garden, who were the agents of a foreign power. Garden was the secretary of the One Big Union movement. John Smith (Jock) Garden was one of the men who came to prominence in the Australian Labor movement in the turbulent years at the end of the war. He had learned as a boy in Scotland that in the life of the world to come the righteous would be rewarded and the wicked punished. He found it easy to believe that the workers were the righteous, and the capitalists the wicked. He found it even easier to believe that the workers were God's affirming angels and the capitalists God's destroying angels. The hand of the potter had been generous in fashioning Jock Garden. He had the appearance, the manner, the voice and the innate charm to draw all manner of men and women unto him. But the hand of the potter had also faltered: Jock Garden, the mesmerizer, the preacher, the teacher with the message about love and justice and the universal embrace, had the reputation of being 'an unmitigated liar'. Jock Garden was safe with women and alcohol, but, to the dismay of those who admired him, he seemed to believe that one of Christ's commands was 'Render unto Jock Garden the things that are other people's'.

He was born at Nigg, Kincardine, Scotland, on 13 August 1882. Those who observed him in childhood remembered the glow in his eyes in moments of religious ecstasy. That glow was to remain until the day he died. He migrated to Australia with his family in 1904. He was inducted as the minister of the Church of Christ at Harcourt in Victoria in 1906. Three years later he joined the Australian Labor Party. For him Christ was the 'lowly Nazarene' who commanded his followers to fill the hungry with good things and send the rich empty away. Yet to his colleagues in the movement he was an enigma. The man who wept when he told Christians or future of humanity

[43] *Australian Worker*, 15 August, 12 September, 21 November 1918, 16 January 1919.

men that his heart was on fire with love and compassion, was also a liar, a bully and a man, safe with women, but not with other people's property. The Defence Department fined him for improperly accepting a gift from a supplier to the Department. Soon after the Russian revolution of November 1917 he added the teachings of Marx and Lenin to the Sermon on the Mount. He believed it was the historic destiny of the working class to destroy the institutions of the bourgeois state, and create institutions to serve the interests of the working class. In 1918 he became secretary to the Propaganda and Organising Committee of the One Big Union movement.[44]

The pragmatists in the Labor movement laughed at Jock Garden as an 'addle-headed Pommy'. At the Labor Party conference of 1919 the pragmatists moved successfully for the expulsion of Jock Garden and men of like mind from the Labor Party. Labor was interested in the capture of political power. Voltaire Molesworth was one of the new Labor pragmatists. His father was a one-time ideologue who had learned the error of his ways in William Lane's New Australia colony in Paraguay. The son, named Voltaire as evidence of the faith of the father, accepted the father's wisdom. He became a columnist for *Smith's Weekly*. Garden preached world revolution: Molesworth was a nationalist. Molesworth loathed revolutionaries: they were 'cosmopolitan and internationalist'. He believed in racial purity and the maintenance of a White Australia. Garden preached international socialism: Molesworth warned Labor to beware of 'the foreigners in our midst', beware of the 'glib-tongued adventurers from Pommy land'. To the simple-minded, Garden preached the Christian ethic of not resisting evil and fed the superstitions of the wowsers of Sydney. On weekdays Garden preached 'revolutionary opportunism' to the followers of the One Big Union. Molesworth believed Labor must build an Australian culture. Garden and his friends borrowed their ideas from abroad. Garden talked of a 'holy war' for the liberation of humanity: Molesworth wanted Labor to be in power. Garden preached the universal embrace. Molesworth said the universal embrace men were not noted for love of their neighbour. Garden and his followers, he said, 'oozed malignity at every pore, and dripped hypocrisy in every word'.[45]

Labor paid a high price for 'shoving principle into the background'. Labor

[44] *S.M.H.*, 23 January 1919; Bede Nairn, 'John Smith Garden', *A.D.B.*, vol. 8 (Melbourne, 1981), pp. 614–15; Miriam Dixson, *Greater than Lenin?* (Melbourne, 1977), pp. 57–8; Ian Turner, *Industrial Labor and Politics* (Canberra, 1965); Alastair Davidson, *The Communist Party of Australia* (Stanford, U.S.A., 1969); Guido Baracchi, handwritten notes in possession of the author.

[45] Voltaire Molesworth, Notes for a speech, 1919, Molesworth Papers, Mitchell Library; Voltaire Molesworth, *The Bogus O.B.U.* (Sydney, 1919), pamphlet in Molesworth Papers; I. E. Young, 'A. C. Willis, Welsh Nonconformist and the Labour Party in New South Wales', *Journal of Religious History*, vol. 2, December 1963; *Australian Worker*, 23 April 1924.

degenerated into a 'seething mass of vendettas, dogfights and double-crossings with a Kilkenny cat flavour scattered over the *tout ensemble*'. Labor became the hunting ground of the power seekers and the numbers men. John Thomas Lang gave the Party this 'Kilkenny cat flavour'. Like Billy Hughes, Jack Lang learned in childhood all about the jungle of life. He was born in Sydney on 21 December 1876. His mother was a Catholic, his father a pre-marriage convert. Lang supplemented the family income by selling newspapers in the streets. There he learned that to survive a boy had to 'resist the invasion of his pitch with his fists'. His adult life was a fight to keep his place on the pitch—first as an accountant then as a real estate agent. In that profession he amassed a small fortune. On 14 March 1896 he married Hilda Amelia Bredt, the sister of Henry Lawson's wife. Her mother was the wife of the proprietor of McNamara's bookshop in Castlereagh Street, the place where Henry Lawson heard 'a host of Yankee free-thought and socialistic lecturers'. But Lang was never interested in the talk of dreamers and visionaries.[46]

Lang was a mixture, a man of many voices. He was compassionate with all those who did not threaten an 'invasion of his pitch'. He had a charisma for the little people, and a power to attract men and women to his service. There was about him the air of a 'big fella'. He was tall in height, massive in frame, and vast in ambition. He was Christ-like to Henry Lawson. One Friday afternoon in the 1890s (Lang did not give a precise date) he picked up Lawson in Sydney. Henry had been with his mates and was very much the worse for wear. Lang offered to get him home to Newtown. The cab driver wanted fifteen shillings for the ride—a week's wages. Lang agreed. Lawson let the driver 'have it in good ripe Australian oaths'. The driver refused to go further. Lang gagged Lawson. Rumour had it later that either on that occasion or another similar one Lawson rose early the next morning and wrote 'Faces in the Street'. Remorse and guilt may not be good for the soul, but they are often the spur for the person with creative gifts.[47]

The man of compassion, the man who wanted to do something for 'the least of the little ones', kicked back if anyone kicked him. When he became Mayor of Auburn in February 1908 the *Cumberland Argus* noted, 'when he [Lang] cracks the whip, they [the Labor members of the Council] round up'. After he was pre-selected for the seat of Granville in 1913 he said: 'We had the numbers'. By then his real estate agency and money-lending had made him so wealthy the *Bulletin* later labelled him 'the Auburn plute'. When he became Treasurer in the Storey Labor Government in 1920 the Communist

[46] *Bulletin*, 8 April 1926; J. H. C. Sleeman, *The Life of J. T. Lang* (Sydney, 1933); J. T. Lang, *I Remember* (Sydney, 1956), pp. 7–11; marriage certificate of J. T. Lang. Molesworth Papers; Bede Nairn, *The 'Big Fella'* (Melbourne, 1986).

[47] Lang, op. cit., pp. 8–9; Dixson, op. cit., pp. 10– 15; *Cumberland Argus*, 19 January, 6 April 1907; Heather Radi and Peter Spearritt (eds), *Jack Lang* (Sydney, 1977), pp. 7–8.

'MY TRUE NAME IS LABOUR'
James Henry Scullin
Photograph in National Library, Canberra

'DON'T DO IT, JOE,
DON'T DO IT'
Enid and Joseph Aloysius Lyons
Photograph in National Library, Canberra

'THE BIG FELLA'

John Thomas Lang

Photograph in National Library, Canberra

press judged him to be 'not a Labor man at all, but . . . a mere Liberal, a middle-class politician'. His face was generally expressionless, a mask for the man within. It was only when he was either helping the needy and the hungry, or when he was savaging an opponent that his face portrayed animation. Lang enjoyed ridiculing 'do-gooders', and sneering at Jock Garden as the 'parson in politics' and 'the man with the perpetual smile'. He talked of the unity of the human race; but the prospect of an Australia with 'a Black, Brown and Brindle streak right through every strata of our society' made him shiver. He wanted Australia to remain 'a citadel of the white peoples'.[48]

While Labor entered a prolonged 'Kilkenny cat' phase in its history, the 'inexperienced band of Davids' in the Country Party, as Page called them, were 'ready to fling their stones at a numerous legion of highly accomplished Goliaths'. Hughes wanted to attend an Imperial Conference in London. But Hughes was not a free agent: he must get the permission of the Country Party. Page told him in the House of Representatives the Country Party would give him leave for a limited time. Hughes exploded, then sulked as he always did when he could not get his way. But Hughes was not going to go cap in hand to a country doctor. He was not prepared to make Grafton his Canossa.[49]

Hughes was a world statesman. Hughes must have a fight. As a child he fought with the Devil. When he was no longer a child he fought with the Germans. Now he had another fight on his hands. He was fighting Bolsheviks. He was never a half-measure man: he always fought boots and all. He declared that any man or woman who sang 'The Red Flag' in a public place would be prosecuted. That gentle spirit, R. H. Long, who gladdened Nettie Palmer's heart with examples of his wit in verse, a man who took no thought for the morrow, a Francis of Assisi wearing the clothes of an Australian swaggie, was put into gaol for flying the Red Flag. The members of the Palmer circle were shocked. Hughes was alienating middle Australia. The Wobblies, the Socialists and the Sinn Feiners continued to sing their songs of defiance:

'Gone Are The Days' (to the tune of Stephen Foster's 'Old Black Joe')

> Gone are the days when the master class could say,
> "We'll work you long hours for little pay.
> We'll work you all day and half the night as well."
> But I hear the workers' voices calling, "You will, like Hell."

[48] *Cumberland Argus*, 20 November 1909; *Bulletin*, 16 March 1932; Lang, op. cit., pp. 39–40, 43–5, 36; Radi and Spearritt, op. cit., pp. 10–17, 197; *Punch* (Melbourne), 2 April 1925; *Workers' Weekly*, 29 June 1923; *Fellowship*, February 1920, p. 102.

[49] Ulrich Ellis, *A History of the Australian Country Party* (Melbourne, 1963), pp. 52–5; Page, op. cit., pp. 65–75.

Hughes had an answer to that view of the world. He invited His Royal Highness the Prince of Wales to visit Australia. The Prince would say the right things about the King, the Empire and the sedition mongers of Hyde Park and the Yarra Bank. The Royal Family would help to save Australia from the Bolsheviks.[50]

Labor was scandalized. The Prince of Wales was coming, they said, 'for the express purpose of creating a psychology in Australia which was favourable for militarism and capitalism'. Billy Hughes took no notice of them. On 4 June he dined with the Governor-General at Government House. The Governor-General asked him to dance the opening set in the Lancers after the port and the cigars. When the Prince arrived in Melbourne in June he played his part to perfection. He said all the right things. On 16 June Billy Hughes presented him to all 'the leading royals of Melbourne town' as 'the great ambassador of Empire'. The Prince did not let his hosts down. 'And I am quite sure of one thing', he said, 'that as Australia stands by the Empire, so will the Empire stand by Australia for a long time'.

The 'Royals' loved it, and they loved him. Keith Murdoch was lyrical. The Prince, he wrote in the Melbourne *Herald*, had

> a cheerful and boyish nature. He twiddles his thumbs and is keen on exercise . . . He is just lovely, good natured, handsome and kind . . . He bets. He is a thorough sportsman . . . has a clear voice . . . is not boldly handsome . . . is shy and sad, has a wistful look in his eyes. His cap has a suspicion of jauntiness. He might be called Edward the Gay and Gentle . . . He admittedly does not know how to dance the Lancers.

He was 'enormously rich'. The rebels in Australia scorned the Prince as 'Imperialism's Messiah and Capitalism's Jehovah . . . the Imperial Grand Duet of "Unity and Harmony"'. Imperialism and capitalism were in danger: the Prince has come as their saviour. How clever he was: privately he has said all the right things to Billy Hughes, even taking the liberty of congratulating Hughes on his 'utterances against that . . . dangerous Mannix', and expressing the hope that dear Mr Hughes would not let such a horrid man return to Australia.[51]

Before the fervour and the excitement died away the King and Empire men held loyalty demonstrations. They were not ashamed to make a public

[50] *Socialist*, 6 February 1920; Nettie Palmer to Dowell O'Reilly, 13 August 1922, Palmer Papers, Series 1, Box 4, Folder 3; 'Gone are the Days', *Songs of the Industrial Workers of the World* (3rd edn, Sydney, n.d.).

[51] *Socialist*, 13 February, 28 May 1920; *Fellowship*, June 1920, p. 173; *Age*, 17 June 1920; *S.M.H.*, 17 June 1920; R. M. Ferguson to W. M. Hughes, 27 May 1920, Hughes Papers, Series 16, Box 1, Folder 4; Edward, Prince of Wales, to W. M. Hughes, 18 July, 20 August 1920, Hughes Papers, Series 16, Box 1, Folder 5; Everard Cotes, *Down Under with the Prince* (London, 1921).

profession of their creed. Rows broke out in the Hughes Government. Willie Watt, the Treasurer, went to England for financial negotiations with the British Government. Willie Watt took umbrage at Hughes's secrecy and furtiveness. Hughes accused him of suffering from nerves. Willie Watt accused Hughes of 'joking with facts'. The darling of the drawing rooms of 'Yarraside' resigned. Willie Watt's tantrums have finished his rise to the top. 'Yarraside' must find another man to be their political leader. Page was biding his time. Hughes wanted a coalition, but Page played hard to get. Political friends offered to mediate. Hughes preferred to sulk, and so make agreement unlikely. The satisfaction of his passions meant more to him than political survival. Hughes was walking into the night.[52]

The *Socialist* continued to chant that every day the people were one day nearer to socialism. The time was at hand, it kept saying, when the 'cool and calculating, cash-registering, machine-minded, inexorable, ruthless, vampire-souled mere semblances of men and women' lost their power. The years of the 'dry souls' were coming to an end. Socialists in Australia were now like greyhounds on a leash, straining to get away. But the King and Empire men were determined those greyhounds would never even run on to the course. Distinguished army officers, prominent conservative politicians, and men whose social life provided gossip for those with an interest in dinner parties, dances and the balls of those who belonged to the 'social set' in a capital city or a country district, invited all loyal people in Sydney to attend a meeting in the Town Hall on the night of 18 July 1920 to launch the King and Empire Alliance. Scenes of extraordinary enthusiasm marked this overflow meeting. Sir Charles Rosenthal, a general in the A.I.F., was in the chair. On the platform were high dignitaries of the Church of England, many ex-army officers such as Brigadier-General Herring and others of the same rank, colonels, majors, captains and lieutenants, the much decorated brave men back from France and Flanders, but no member of the Labor Party. There were only three women among approximately one hundred and fifty people on the platform.

Proceedings opened with the singing of the National Anthem—the swelling notes of which, in the words of the *Sydney Morning Herald* reporter, 'added impressiveness to the ideals behind the meeting'. So did their rendition of 'Rule Britannia'. That was their faith. They were of British stock, and 'could only feel a tremendous pride in this Empire of ours'. They hoped every Australian child would 'instinctively kiss its hand to the British flag when it saw it'. They reaffirmed their 'unswerving loyalty to the King and Empire'. They decided to join up with the loyalist organizations in Queensland, South Australia, Victoria, Tasmania and New Zealand. They decided to

[52] W. Watt to W. M. Hughes, 7 June 1920; W. G. Higgs to W. M. Hughes, 17, 21 June 1920, Hughes Papers, Series 16, Box 1, Folder 4.

form the King and Empire Alliance to counteract the influence of disloyalty, to build up and maintain a strong national pride of race and Empire, and to oppose strenuously all attempts to introduce and encourage disloyal doctrines. The men wanted the women to help them, knowing as they did what women could do for the King and Empire. Sir Charles Rosenthal concluded the meeting by saying: 'We open our doors to every loyal Roman Catholic to come in and join us in an offensive alliance against all sorts and conditions of disloyalty'. There was tremendous enthusiasm for that. The audience rose to its feet and sang again the National Anthem.[53]

The world which had cradled the mythology of loyalty to King and Empire was passing away. On 10 February 1920 a 36-horse-power motor tractor (truck) arrived in Albury from Sydney *en route* for Melbourne, which it reached the following day. The 'truck' had the capacity to compete with the railway train in the economical transport of goods. The explosion of motor transport has begun. Governments must build roads to carry the cars and the trucks. The age of the horse and buggy and the railway was coming to an end. The aeroplane has transcended distance: the aeroplane and the wireless would end Australian isolation. Federal and State Governments have appointed committees to recommend the cheapest means of supplying electricity to consumers, whether generated from water, coal or other sources, for domestic, industrial and other purposes. All political parties assumed that in Australia services must be vested in a public utility. That was part of the Australian mythology, the assumption questioned only by mavericks, cranks and 'Bolshies'. Governments have initiated schemes for harnessing the waters of the Snowy River, the Clarence River, the Murray River (Hume Reservoir), the Murrumbidgee River (the Barren Jack or Burrinjuck Dam). The Country Party 'new boy' in the House, Dr Earle Christmas Grafton Page, the member with the 'genial school-boy smile', was already busy in the corridors of power in Melbourne buttonholing fellow members for support for his dream of exploiting the waters of the Clarence River.[54]

The electrical firms and gas firms advertised new labour-saving devices. Electrical power held out the promise of reducing domestic drudgery, emancipating women from slavery and giving them leisure in which to pursue careers, hobbies, interests or pleasure. The age of consumerism was about to begin. Entrepreneurs had plans for picture palaces, jazz songs held out a promise of a life of pleasure, or sang of the melancholy fate of men and women without the comforts of the One high on the list of missing persons.[55]

[53] *S.M.H.*, 20 July 1920.

[54] *Argus*, 11 February 1920; Memo by Harold Clapp on Electrical Power Development in Australia, Page Papers, N.L.A., Canberra.

[55] Advertisements for electrical goods, *Bulletin*, 28 June 1923; *Australian Home Builder*, November 1922; Gwen Sergeant White, 'Labor Saving Kitchens, *Real Property Annual*, Melbourne, 1919; *Socialist*, 16 April 1920.

The war has shifted the centre of political power from the States to the Commonwealth. Alfred Deakin has predicted that the financial powers of the Commonwealth would tie the States to its chariot wheels. In the war the defence power has increased the powers of the Commonwealth. Now in peacetime the High Court has put its seal of approval on the increase of federal powers. Bob Menzies has taken a step further along the road for the 'man of destiny'. In the middle of 1920 he was briefed to represent the Amalgamated Society of Engineers in a suit pending before the High Court. Menzies performed with such brilliance in asking the learned judges to recognize the increase in Commonwealth powers that one of the judges asked him: 'Do you realise, Mr Menzies, you are asking the Court to overthrow every decision made in this area since federation? Menzies: 'Yes,your honour, I do'. The boy from Jeparit persuaded the judges to overthrow the doctrine of 'the immunity of instrumentalities', the bulwark of the sovereign independence of the States.[56]

At the University his contemporaries had ridiculed him for his 'gush' about the Empire, and his extravagant professions of loyalty to the King and the Empire. They had also ridiculed his private life by publishing an article in *Farrago* on the 'amazing amatory adventures' of Bob Menzies. But Menzies has had his victory over the mockers. On 27 September 1920 he was married to Pattie Maie Leckie, daughter of a senator and a businessman, in the Presbyterian Church in Kew. *Table Talk* featured it as the wedding of the week. The boy from Jeparit has arrived. John Curtin was still taking lonely walks along the beach at Cottesloe. His lips were beginning to droop, his eyes were looking more and more inward as he asked himself what could a one-time Catholic, Rationalist and Socialist believe now? Bob Menzies was never tormented by doubt: Curtin had doubts about everything.[57]

The Palmers had their faith in Australian culture. Vance was showing the locals he could be cautious and correct with the cricket bat as well as with the pen. He was not a man to 'have a go': he played cricket as he played life, with a straight bat. Nettie, in spare moments between her home duties, was giving comfort to writers and artists embattled by the seemingly all-powerful British philistinism in Australia. Louis Esson, travelling in Ireland, was writing to the Palmers about his hopes for an Australian culture. Bernard O'Dowd recited his poems 'Australia' and 'The Bush' to literary gatherings. Australia, he told the tiny band of pilgrims for the Australia that was coming to be, would soon know her 'quivering dawn': Australia would know 'glory'. Without God, love was the faith by which human beings should live. As

[56] *Age*, 1 September 1920; *C'wealth Law Reports*, vol. 28, 1920–21, pp. 129–77.

[57] R.G.M., 'Of Politics', *M.U.M.*, vol. VI, no. 1, May 1917; S.C.L. (S. C. Lazarus), 'Of Politics', ibid., vol. XI, no. 2, August 1917; *Table Talk*, 14 October 1920; Cameron Hazlehurst, *Menzies Observed* (Sydney, 1979), pp. 33–41; Tom Mann, *Memoirs* (London, 1920), p. 199; J. Curtin to E. Needham, 2 July 1912, Lloyd Ross Papers, Box 33, N.L.A.

Nettie Palmer pointed out, O'Dowd the Rationalist was always kicking the shins of O'Dowd the mystic: O'Dowd was both an artist and a preacher. Rationalism was a faith for mockers and the deprived, not a faith by which the overwhelming majority of humanity could live. In July 1920, when the King and Empire men were shouting themselves hoarse in the Sydney Town Hall, Ted Brady told Vance Palmer, 'the Time is Ripe!'[58]

The King and Empire men and women incorporated Anzac Day into their mythology. On Anzac Day on 25 April 1920 speakers at the ceremonies in cities, suburbs and country towns spoke to those who came to mourn: 'The British Empire is ours', said Lieutenant-Colonel Henley, C.B.E., M.L.A., at a service in Burwood Park, Sydney. 'We belong to it.' 'Ours' was an Empire 'rich in all the sterling qualities that make for human progress and world civilization'. 'Birdie' told the ex-diggers of Bathurst that Australians were members of the British race. 'You boys, I believe . . . will carry on the great traditions of the race.' Clergymen offered divine authority for the old mythology. At the Anzac service in All Saint's Cathedral, Bathurst, Bishop George Merrick Long, the teacher who had encouraged and inspired Martin Boyd at Trinity Grammar School (the 'Mugger' in *The Montforts*) told the people that General Birdwood's visit to their city had 'strengthened the bonds of Empire'.[59]

The socialists and the rationalists warned people against all 'God-botherers'. 'The priest and the parson', wrote the *Socialist* on 4 June 1920, 'are rarely in the van'. Schoolmasters were more valuable to the community than parsons: the things of this life mattered more to the people than the things of the next life. Mannix had been a hero of the people during the conscription struggle, but in the class war Mannix was on the side of the exploiters. Mannix was an enemy of human progress. Australians must be taught to see the parson as a 'parasite' deceiving Australians with an infantile faith and superstition. The parson's work was important for the capitalist and privileged classes: he was their tool. He turned the minds of the people from things that mattered and directed them into channels where all was vagueness, conjecture, myth and unreality.[60]

After the war the Protestant churches became shrines of honour and remembrance for those who had served abroad, and those who had paid the supreme sacrifice. Churches and chapels became places where the worship-

[58] Louis Esson to Vance Palmer, 14 August 1920, Palmer Papers, Series 1, Box 4, Folder 27; Bernard O'Dowd, *The Bush* (Melbourne, 1912); Nettie Palmer to Dowell O'Reilly, 13 August 1922, Palmer Papers, Series 1, Box 4, Folder 29; F. M. Todd, 'The Poetry of Bernard O'Dowd' (C'wealth Literary Fund Lecture, Canberra University College, 1953); W. H. Wilde, *Three Radicals* (Melbourne, 1969), pp. 25–9; E. J. Brady to Vance Palmer, 30 July 1920, Palmer Papers, Series 1, Box 4, Folder 27.

[59] *S.M.H.*, 26, 27 April 1920; *Age*, 26 April 1920.

[60] *Socialist*, 4 June, 9, 16 July 1920; *Ross's Monthly*, 2 October 1920, p. 16.

pers of God could express their patriotism. On occasions such as Anzac Day, Empire Day, Armistice Day, the National Anthem was often sung at the beginning or the end of divine service. The sacrifice of human lives was blessed with the divine approval. The words of the *Book of Common Prayer*, 'that there never may be wanting men to serve Thee in Church or State' acquired a special meaning: it was a message about war and sacrifice. In churches honour boards were put up on which the names of all those who had served abroad were inscribed in gold letters, with special reference to those who had made the supreme sacrifice. Vicars received and blessed regimental flags and placed them in prominent positions in their churches. Clergymen who had served as chaplains and stretcher bearers in the war wore the royal monogram prominently on their vestments during divine worship. On the inside walls of the churches brass plates and marble tablets were erected by relatives and friends to commemorate the deeds of the mighty dead. Soldiers' names appeared below stained-glass windows next to Christ and all the saints of the Church. Soldiers have joined the pioneers of civilization in the mighty bush and the men of renown as heroes to be remembered by worshippers.

In the early years of peace the Protestant clergy interpreted the hymn 'O God our help in ages past' as an assurance that God, like 'Birdie', John Monash, Charles Rosenthal, Brigadier-General 'Ned' Herring, Major Scott, the headmasters of the Public Schools, Bob Menzies, Billy Hughes, Earle Page and others too numerous to mention, was still on the side of the British. 'Abide with me' was still the hymn of resignation and acceptance. But, thanks to being British, resignation to God's will brought many benefits. Congregations meekly kneeling on their knees said a loud 'Amen' after the clergyman had prayed for special grace 'for our sovereign lord, King George, and all other members of the royal family'. In the early years of the white man's occupation of Australia, the clergy had been 'civil servants in cassocks', and God's moral policemen. By 1920 the Protestant churches have often become the spiritual arm of an imperial power.[61]

The churches remained one of the centres of communal life in Australia. There were ladies' guilds, sporting teams for the men and women, and fund-raising evenings. There were church choirs. Stainer's *Crucifixion* was still part of the spiritual food for Protestants in Holy Week, and Handel's *Messiah* at Christmas. *Hymns Ancient and Modern* were still the spiritual food for vast numbers of Australians. Men, women, sensitive boys and girls still responded as the bass sang the words: 'For behold I tell you a mystery . . . The trumpet shall sound, and the dead shall be raised'. Bakers still scooped out of

[61] Plaques on interior walls of St Paul's Church, Carcoar, and Christ Church, South Yarra.

their ovens trays of hot cross buns at Easter. Men, women and children still abstained on Fridays, some holy days, and during Lent. The priests and the parsons still performed ceremonies at three decisive events in the life of a human being—birth, mating and death. The hush still fell in Catholic churches when the altar bell tinkled at the consecration of the bread and the wine. Men and women still believed God would wipe away all tears from their eyes, make the crooked straight and the rough places smooth. But the war has dealt a mortal blow to the credibility of God and the preachers. The people wanted their pleasures. The Catholic and the Protestant papers denounced the cinema, the stage, and certain kinds of dancing, gambling and mixed bathing as influences destroying all moral decency in the community. The parson and the priest stood between the people and the pursuit of pleasure. People never again trusted preachers who had spoken of the war as a cleanser of human hearts. The sufferings and horrors of the war have driven them to reject the fires of Hell and the blessings of Heaven in God's world.[62]

The war has raised again the question of the position of women. The churches for generations have sanctified the doctrine of male superiority and the division of labour between man and woman—man to be the breadwinner, and head of the family, woman to perform home duties and be the heart of the family. In an age of doubt about everything the role of women came up for discussion. Men and women began to talk of the 'liberation of woman from domestic slavery'. Public speakers asked why a woman should be 'subjected to all the little duties about the house which chain her to the kitchen and the nursery, exhaust her primitive and unproductive activity in a series of oppressive and degrading petty tortures'. Jessie MacDonald asked whether a woman was to have the individual right and liberty to control her own body, or was she to be a 'super-rabbit' to breed as long as she was physically capable. She and others advocated education in the use of contraceptives. Women were hopeful:

> I was sad;
> Though far in the future our light would shine
> For the present the dark was ours, was mine.
> I couldn't be glad.

So wrote Lesbia Harford in 1917.[63]

There was a way from the darkness to the light. The Socialist Workers

[62] *Presbyterian Messenger*, 30 November 1923; *Methodist*, 17 March 1923; *Church Standard*, 27 February, 23 September 1921; *Ross's Monthly*, 7 August 1920, p. 6, 2 October 1920, p. 16; personal observation at Cowes and Belgrave 1922–24.

[63] *Ross's Monthly*, 4 September 1920, p. 19, 2 October 1920, pp. 6, 16; untitled poem by Lesbia Harford, published in Drusilla Modjeska, 'Lesbia Harford and her Work, *Overland* 8, 1985.

Women's Rights group in 1919 declared that the oppression of women provided an economic benefit to the capitalists. Women were exploited as wage workers at lower rates than men. Women could be pushed back into the house during an economic downturn. Married women were not entitled to dole payments when they were dismissed from their jobs. In the home women were condemned to domestic slavery. The only solution was the abolition of all forms of exploitation. They demanded an end to all economic discrimination based on sex, equal pay for equal work and maternity leave on full pay without loss of seniority. The division of labour in the home was not, as the defenders of the status quo maintained, a product of the biological differences between men and women. These sex-role stereotypes have been created by society to maintain the second-class status of women. A Socialist society would liberate women from their oppressors.[64]

The churches did not agree. The Catholic Church continued to thunder against the evils of 'race suicide', and to repeat the Pauline doctrine of man as the head of the family. The conservative women's organizations accepted the role of women in the home, while pleading for an end to all ill treatment of and cruelty against women. Labour-saving devices, not political ideology, would reduce the drudgery of women.[65]

Doubt and the questioning of everything has not so far extended to the status of the Aborigine. The Aborigines were still 'the pariah dogs looking for bones and scraps' in the cities, the country towns, and the Australian bush. For some reason the white men and women did not understand, to be born an Aborigine, a 'binghi', was to have the soul of a human being fettered by a 'stunted mind', and to be condemned to 'lead a squalid life in a gunyah'. Aborigines were doomed to spend their lives going round to back doors and pleading with the householders, with a roll of the eye and gestures of helplessness, to 'Gib it tickpen'. Extinction was their destiny. The Aborigines were a dying race. The only thing that could be done for them was to make their passing easier.[66]

The war and the accompanying doubts have not caused the whites to question the assumptions underlying this opinion. At the principal mission stations in the wilderness, at Hermannsburg on the Finke River in Central Australia, at New Norcia and Beagle Bay in Western Australia, and at Port Keats in the Northern Territory, the Aborigines have spurned the gift of European civilization. The Lutheran missionaries have sung Bach cantatas to them, but the Aborigines have responded with a vast indifference. They

[64] *Socialist Workers' Women's Rights Now*, pamphlet of Socialist Women's League (Melbourne, 1919).

[65] Isabel McCorkindale, *Pioneer Pathways* (Melbourne, 1948): G. G. Lather, *A Glorious Heritage, 1885–1965* (Brisbane), 1968); Bessie M. Rischbieth, *March of Australian Women* (Perth, 1964).

[66] Arthur Mee (ed.), *The Children's Encyclopaedia*, vol. 4, p. 2446.

have continued to decay rather than to improve under the influence of the white man's civilization. There were exceptions. Douglas Grant, an Aborigine from Cairns, got round the prohibition on Aborigines serving overseas in the A.I.F. He loved Shakespeare, recited English poetry, and played the bagpipes as well as any Scot. David Unaipon, an Aborigine from the Point Macleay mission station in South Australia, decided by 1920 to use his vast talents to preach the gospel of Christ to his own people. Unaipon taught both blacks and whites the story of the demoralization of the black man since the coming of the European in January 1788. Grant and Unaipon were white men 'encased in a black man's body'.[67]

The scientists and the secular humanists took over from the missionaries as the opinion makers on the Aborigines. They did not challenge the assumption of the missionaries that the Aborigines were 'little children' who must be protected against the white man and against themselves. The Aborigines must have guardians. In the Acts of the five States dealing with Aborigines and in the Acts of the Commonwealth it was decreed that no Aborigine could work for wages without the permission of the State, no Aborigine could marry a non-Aboriginal, or live with a non-Aboriginal without the permission of the State, no marriage of a female Aborigine with any person other than an Aborigine could be celebrated without the permission of the State. Any person other than an Aborigine who cohabited with Aborigines, or cohabited with a female Aborigine was liable to prosecution. Any person who supplied, or caused or permitted to be supplied to an Aborigine or a half-caste any fermented or spirituous liquors or opium could be prosecuted. Any Aborigine who carried any firearm without a licence could be prosecuted. The Aborigine was a permanent child. The Aborigine should be civilized, because his own practices and beliefs were barbarous, but, paradoxically, the Aborigine could not be civilized. The Aborigines must be trained to become persons of 'economic utility' in the white man's society. The Aborigines must be given opportunities to rise to the top in the professions, the business world, entertainment and sport. The white man must decide. The missionaries, the scientists and the secular humanists have not conceded to the Aborigines the right to decide for themselves how they would live and what they would think. Little children had no such rights.[68]

[67] C. Coulthard Clark, 'Aboriginal Medal Winners', *Sabretache*, vol. 18, 1977, pp. 244–5; *British Australasian*, 2 November 1916, p. 15; *Reveille*, 31 January 1932; 'Is the Australian Aboriginal A Degraded Creature?' *A.B.M. Review*, 1 January 1912; James C. Pierson, 'Aboriginal Power and Self-Determination in Adelaide', published in Michael C. Howard, *Aboriginal Power in Australian Society* (St Lucia, 1982), pp. 202–3.

[68] See, for example, An Act to make provision for the better protection of the Aboriginal inhabitants of Western Australia, V Edward VII, No. 14, 23 December 1905, *The Statutes of Western Australia*; W. Baldwin Spencer, Preliminary Report on the Aboriginals of the Northern Territory, contained in report of the Administrator for the Northern Territory for 1912, *C'wealth P.P.*, 1913, vol. 3, pp. 36–41, 42–5.

In July 1920 Henry Lawson was having a spell in the Mental Hospital in Darlinghurst. He had his own problem: how to raise the wind 'to pay for ale now and in the hereafter—if there's any hereafter'. He wondered whether that 'Grand and Glorious Sisterhood', the nurses of Australia, had a hereafter, because in this world the only thing they wanted to know about him was, 'Is yer bowels open?' In August 1920 Hughes decided the Commonwealth Government should pay Lawson a pension of one pound a week. This would at least avoid the 'public scandal' of Lawson being found dead one day on a publisher's doorstep.[69]

While the nurses of Darlinghurst were questioning Henry Lawson on the performance of his bowels men and women influenced by the dream of his youth that the workers of Australia would one day choose between the 'Old Dead Tree' and the 'Young Tree Green' were meeting in Sydney to create the Australian Communist Party. On 30 October 1920 delegates representing the Industrial Workers of the World, the Australian Socialist Party, the Socialist Labour [*sic*] Party and other militant groups met in Sydney and agreed to form themselves into a Communist Party. They agreed with Rosa Luxemburg: capitalist society stood 'shamed, dishonoured, wading in blood and dripping with filth'. They denounced as reactionary and dangerous to the success of the social revolution the hitherto accepted doctrine of Socialist parties that the parliamentary machinery was a 'weapon' which could be used 'by the working class for the positive advancement of its class interests'. They stood for 'the complete overthrow of the Capitalist system, and the destruction of the last vestige of the tyrannical bureaucracy by which it is buttressed and maintained'. Their party was based on the teaching of Marx and Lenin.[70]

Robert Ross and other members of the Socialist Party were disappointed. Once again Australian radicals were looking abroad for their examples. Conservatives strove to be more English than the English. Now some radicals had another orthodoxy: to be more Russian than the Russians. Australia should not always be an 'imitative and second-hand country'. The Intelligence men in Melbourne have also alerted Hughes about a new threat to society. The Communist Party proposed 'the destruction of the whole social and economic structure, and secondly, as a corollary, the abolition of the capitalist and the ravaging of all that the individual possesses'. The gospel of Hughes was under threat: Hughes, the saviour of Australia, the saviour of bourgeois Australia, the saviour of White Australia, must act.[71]

[69] *Ross's Monthly*, 2 October 1920, p. 9; Henry Lawson to Sister Alberta De Villiers MacCallum, 4 July 1920, and Henry Lawson to George Robertson, n.d., probably 5 July 1920, Colin Roderick (ed.), op. cit., pp. 386–7.

[70] *Australian Communist*, 24 December 1920; *Socialist*, 12 November 1920; *S.M.H.*, 2 November 1920; Alastair Davidson, *The Communist Party of Australia* (Stanford, 1969), pp. 10–3; E. M. Higgins, 'The Rise and Fall of Australian Labour', *Labour Monthly*, June 1922.

[71] *Fellowship*, September 1920, pp. 22–3; Memorandum on Communism in Australia, Hughes Papers, Series 21, Folder 2.

White Australia was also under threat. Prophets and soothsayers were drawing attention to the menace of Japan. Japan was the 'Future War Menace'. A day of retribution for the white man's arrogance was approaching. The British were in no position to defend Australia from invasion: in the next war aircraft not battleships would be the invaders. The sympathizers with Sinn Fein were again stirring up sedition and disloyalty. In November 1920 Hugh Mahon told an audience who had assembled in Kalgoorlie to register a protest against the behaviour of the British Black and Tans in Ireland: '. . . the sob of the widow on the coffin would one day shake the foundations of their bloody and accursed Empire'. On 11 November Hughes moved in the House of Representatives that the Honourable Member for Kalgoorlie, Hugh Mahon, 'having, by seditious and disloyal utterances at a public meeting on Sunday last' been guilty of such conduct he was unfit to remain a member of the House. The motion was carried on party lines.[72]

While Hughes was reading the reports of his Intelligence men that Bolshevik rats were gnawing at the pillars on which civilization rested, three days of race riots started at Broome on 20 December 1920. The white inhabitants of the town, the Koepangers and the Manilamen, felt threatened by Japanese competition in the pearling industry. On 20 December two Japanese threatened two Koepangers on the beach. The Koepangers chased a Japanese and stabbed him to death. In retaliation the Japanese bailed up the Koepangers in a house and threatened to hang them from a tree, whereupon the terrorized men were rescued by whites. The white inhabitants formed a vigilante force of three hundred, as the Japanese roved round Broome looking for Koepangers. Business houses and hotels were wrecked. The Riot Act was read: the police and the white vigilantes restored order. For days the riot was blamed for all the 'sins of omission' in Broome. Publicans told the thirsty the whisky had become hot 'because of the riot': one young man who had been celebrating rather unwisely turned up late for his wedding 'because of the riot'. Australians, as usual, make jokes when confronted with a problem they did not want to think about. Laugh on: in just over twenty-one years there would be a terrible retribution on their arrogance to the 'coloured man'. The *Nor' West Echo* called on the white inhabitants to stop fawning on the Japanese. This was a white man's country. White men, said the *Nor' West Echo* must stop treating coloured men as though they were indispensable: traitorous whites should stop embracing coloured men.[73]

[72] George D. Coleman, 'Japan, the Future War Menace', *Socialist*, 2 July 1920; *C'wealth P.D.*, 11 November 1920, vol. 94, pp. 6382–90.

[73] *West Australian*, 22, 23, 24 December 1920; *Nor' West Echo*, 25 December 1920, 1 January 1921; H. P. Colebatch to W. M. Hughes, 8 March 1921, Prime Minister's Department Correspondence File, Pearl Fishing, Broome, 1919–24, C'wealth Archives A 1606, Item SC C 18/1; J. Spry, Report re Fracas between Japanese and Koepangers, 5 January 1921, ibid., Item SC C 18/1; telegram of Premier of Western Australia to Prime Minister of Australia, 21 December 1920, ibid.; personal visit to Broome, 12–14 August 1982.

The Premier of Western Australia asked the Prime Minister to despatch a warship. Hughes agreed. On 23 December 1920 he ordered the warship *Geranium* to proceed to Broome. All through January the trials of the rioters were held in Broome. At public meetings speaker after speaker maintained the whole trouble was that some white men were encouraging the Japanese to believe they were as good as white men: they must be kept in their place. And so it went on. Hughes felt the gospel of all right-minded Australians was being challenged. This new Australian Communist Party was also a threat to the gospel of all true believers in bourgeois civilization. Australia must be kept white and untainted by Bolshevik doctrines. On 3 February 1921 he issued a proclamation prohibiting the importation of certain literature into Australia. Henceforth it was forbidden to import into Australia any literature which advocated the overthrow by force or violence of the established government of the Commonwealth or of any State, or wherein was advocated the abolition of organized government. Hughes was making Australia safe for the bourgeoisie, chaining Australia to the British past.

The Communists called on Australians to fight against 'imperialist barbarity'. Louis Esson told Vance Palmer how sorry he was Australia was so provincial. 'There is no reason', he said, 'why Australia should always be a generation behind'. But Louis Esson did not know Australian history. If he had he might have been able to answer his wife's question to the Palmers earlier that year: 'Can't we do anything ourselves as Australians?' Mary Gilmore had other things on her mind: she saw Christ in the Australian Never-Never. John Shaw Neilson was working as a navvy with men who did not wash their hands before eating, although work had left their hands 'as black as niggers'. Their behaviour reminded him of a saying attributed to an old Catholic priest: 'I can't love the human race, I've seen it'. But Neilson still has his vision. Dear kind Nettie Palmer had written him an encouraging letter. In 'the poor, poor country' he had moments of enchantment, moments which inspired him to sing:

> Let your voice be delicate.
>   The bees are home:
> All their day's love is sunken
>   Safe in the comb.[74]

[74] *Nor'West Echo*, 8 January 1921; *C'wealth Gazette*, 3 February 1921; *Fellowship*, October 1920, p. 37; *The New Communist Manifesto of the "Third International"* (Melbourne, 1919), p. 16; Louis Esson to Vance Palmer, 21 March 1921, Palmer Papers, Series 1, Box 4, Folder 28; Hilda Esson to Vance and Nettie Palmer, 23 April 1920, Palmer Papers, Series 1, Folder 22; Mary Gilmore, 'In Affirmation', *Fellowship*, January 1921, p. 82; *The Autobiography of John Shaw Neilson* (Canberra, 1978), pp. 106–11; John Shaw Neilson, 'Song Be Delicate', A. R. Chisholm (ed.), *The Poems of Shaw Neilson* (Sydney, 1965), p. 65.

5

A HAYSEED TOPPLES THE LITTLE DIGGER

THE YEAR 1921 opened with the same babble of tongues. The 'boss sheriffs' of the Commonwealth Public Service had their satisfaction. They got rid of Walter Burley Griffin, the author of the Griffin plan for Canberra. Once again in the history of Australia the man of imagination was sacrificed on the altar of Australian conformism and mediocrity.

Speaking for the war dead, Vance Palmer condemned those Australians who during the war had watched 'their kindred flesh consumed like grass' and remained dumb. But that rebuke was received with vast indifference. Sir William Irvine again called the socialists and the communists 'wild beasts' and asked that they be silenced. Hughes declared all 'disloyal' and 'disaffected' utterances and publications, and all promotion of 'feelings of ill will and hostility between different classes of His Majesty's subjects', an offence. He promised blood and thunder against Bolsheviks and Sinn Feiners, and threatened to dragoon the working classes and the intelligentsia into 'amiability and goodwill'. The socialists still accused Hughes of plotting to decree that 'no opponent of the Government shall say anything'. A people which boasted of its liberties and its passionate attachment to individualism preferred the quiet life under censorship to the uproar and tumult of liberty. In February, Dando, a half-caste patient of Claremont Lunatic Asylum (Perth) was held by the arms by two attendants while a third punched him in the stomach, head and body until he collapsed, when he was thrown on the bed and told to 'Lie there, you black [bastard]'. He later died of an internal haemorrhage. That event disappeared almost unnoticed into the Australian silence.[1]

The priests and the parsons deplored that God had been shouldered out of Australian life and replaced by paganism. Australians, said Dr James Duhig, the Catholic Archbishop of Brisbane, have become addicts to materialism: they have preserved the cult of 'outward respectability', along side 'religious incredulity'. They preferred the exciting pleasures of the picture show, the dancing hall, the racecourse, the football ground and the beaches to the adoration of the Blessed Sacrament. The sun, as Arthur Adams had said in *The Australians*, had defeated religion in Australia. The *Church Standard* regretted the increase of women drinkers in wine saloons,

[1] Vance Palmer, 'Who, Being Dead', *Fellowship*, October 1920, December 1920, pp. 68–9; *Socialist*, 18 February 1921.

and condemned all pleasure seekers in the bright light of the Australian sun, or the darkness of the picture theatre. Their sweep included 'disgusting literature', lewd conversation in clubs and bars—where, in their words, 'women were discussed in terms one would hardly apply to cattle'—the 'seductive dresses of women', and girls asking librarians and bookshops brazenly for 'something spicy'. The *Methodist* detected a connection between the erotic nature of some of the films, and the erotic dances in the dance halls of the cities. Suggestive clothing, soft lights and sweet music, they said, beckoned young and old on to damnation and ruin. The Presbyterian *Messenger* made the same point: the films were glamorizing and condoning marital infidelity. Priests and parsons and the religious press singled out cheap contraceptives for their wrath and condemnation. Contraceptives, they alleged, opened the door to 'almost unlimited gratification of the senses'. Abstinence, the priests and parsons said, was the only 'moral method of birth control'.[2]

The priests and the parsons taught a gospel of salvation which inflicted an infinity of anguish on human beings striving to achieve the impossible. Humanity, said the secular humanists, would now go forward from that darkness into the bright light of the Australian sun. The Palmers and their circle were hopeful in the late summer of 1921. Louis Esson has just published an edition of his work, *Dead Timber and Other Plays*. As the *Socialist* said of his work, he was alive: he was Australian: 'His atmosphere is a live thing—not merely an Australian setting into which a foreign writer may put American or English ideas and characters, but something essentially Australian throbbing with the thoughts of our own people'. The generation of 'anti-patriots' was passing away, they said, the men and women of the 'King and Empire' persuasion were becoming the darling dodoes of Australia's years as a British colony. The artist would no longer have to stand aside for the stockbroker. The newspapers would not be run by anti-Australian men deliberately hostile to everything Australian except its primary products, those goods that shackled Australia with the imperial chains. Australians were about to explore the mystery of the ancient continent and its inhabitants. The writers must see that Australia did not substitute 'mean-street American' for the old gush and grovel to the British. Esson and his wife would come back to Australia and put Australian characters on the stage.[3]

Thomas Louis Buvelot Esson was born at Leith in Scotland on 10 August

[2] *Advocate*, 3 March 1921, quoted in review of Mark Heathcote, *The Australians* by Arthur Adams, *Fellowship*, October 1920, p. 45; *Church Standard*, 11, 25 February 1921, 17 November 1922; *Methodist*, 10 September 1921, 6 January 1923; *Presbyterian Messenger*, 5 January, 30 March 1923.

[3] Review of Louis Esson's *New Plays* (Melbourne, 1921), *Socialist*, 21 January 1921; Bernard O'Dowd to Nettie Palmer, 20 August 1916; Palmer Papers, Series 1, Box 3, Folder 1; Vance Palmer to Kate Baker, 20 February 1916, ibid., Bernard O'Dowd to Nettie Higgins, 9 November 1911, ibid., Hilda Esson to Vance and Nettie Palmer, 3 February 1921, ibid., Box 4, Folder 28; Louis Esson to Vance Palmer, 21 March 1921, ibid.

1878 and brought to Melbourne when he was three years old. He was educated at Carlton Grammar School and briefly at the University of Melbourne, leaving that institution before he graduated because his subject was life, and the subject of his professors was a lifeless British philistinism. He became a socialist, and a believer in the creation of an Australian culture. He wrote for the *Socialist*, the *Bulletin* and later the *Lone Hand*. He travelled in Ireland in 1905 where W. B. Yeats and J. M. Synge encouraged him to write plays about Australia, plays about a world he knew, rather than ape London drawing room comedies. In 1912 he wrote *The Time Is Not Yet Ripe*, a play which told Australians the truth about their claim to be in the vanguard of humanity. He wanted Australia to be kept 'white', he wanted the 'refuse of Europe' to be kept out of Australia, and he wanted to give 'free expression' to the 'spirit of our own country'.[4]

His second wife, Hilda Wager Bull, a doctor of Medicine, shared his hopes. Writers such as her husband, Louis Esson, and Vance Palmer would rescue Australia from being a 'howling wilderness'. There was no need for Australia to be always a generation behind. In America during the war she and Louis had had their fill of American vulgarity and the worship of the golden calf. In Ireland in 1920 Yeats again encouraged him to put Australians on the stage. Strengthened by those talks he returned to Australia to persuade local theatre proprietors and directors and managers to put on an Australian play rather than one by Arnold Bennett or John Galsworthy. He and his wife joined with Vance and Nettie Palmer, Bernard O'Dowd, Ted Brady, Katharine Susannah Prichard and others to make Australia a place where writers were not condemned to 'useless drudgery', but were creators in a great centre like ancient Rome. For him Australia was a land of resonance, of fantasy, of mystery. He brought with him two long Australian plays he had just finished—but, he added, 'perhaps nobody wants them'.[5]

Composers of music had plans to capture this new spirit of Australia in music. Henry Tate told Nettie Palmer about his new composition, 'Australian Dawn'. In this work he would express in sound and words 'the dawn of Australia's Being as we know it'. The work would begin with bird calls, and then develop the theme of Australia as a country where the people were

[4] Diary of Nettie Palmer, 3, 19 September 1921, Palmer Papers, Series 16, Box 25; David Walker, *Dream and Disillusion* (Canberra, 1976), pp. 16–24; Philip Parsons (ed.), *The Time Is Not Yet Ripe* (Sydney, 1973); Louis Esson to Vance Palmer, 21 March, 11, 20 June 1921, and Louis Esson to Stewart Macky, 8 June 1921, Palmer Papers, Series 1, Box 4, Folder 28.

[5] Hilda Esson to Vance and Nettie Palmer, 3 February 1921, Palmer Papers, Series 1, Box 4, Folder 28; Hilda Esson to Nettie Palmer, 3 April 1917, ibid., Box 3, Folder 1; Louis Esson to Vance Palmer, 21 March, 21 May 1921, Palmer Papers, Series 1, Box 4, Folder 28.

'hanging nebulously between earth and heaven'. The composers would lift up the hearts of Australians, give them the confidence to believe that in their own country they could go for a walk 'in the Paradise Gardens'. Their 'millennial Eden' was here, and the only reason why they did not recognize it was because their eyes were still blinded by the evil Judaic-Christian teaching that human beings had been expelled from the Garden of Eden. The hearts of the sons of men were not in fact filled with evil: madness was not in their hearts while they lived.[6]

The conservatives had their litany. It was enshrined for them in the words of the preamble to the Act of July 1900 creating the Commonwealth of Australia: '. . . humbly relying on the blessing of Almighty God': 'one indissoluble Federal Commonwealth' and 'under the Crown of the United Kingdom of Great Britain and Ireland'. They believed in God, the author of the 'great chain of being': they believed in the federal constitution, the protector of 'interests' and the rights and privileges of minorities against the tyranny of the majority and mob rule: they believed in the King and the Empire as the preservers of order, the emblems of hierarchy, and the means of survival as a white community: they believed that without order, chaos would ensue, and men would descend to the level of the goats and the monkeys. But now God was dead or high on the list of missing persons. Shadows of the evening were stealing across the sky for the British. Australians were to be left alone. The question was, what were they to be? Would they find confidence in being themselves?

Australians must find another myth to replace the British myth. Louis Esson drew strength and inspiration watching the Australian cricketers play the English at Lords. It was a pleasure for him to watch them: they were so graceful in comparison with the English who looked 'so stiff in the joints'. The Australians played a beautiful game. They were like Wagner's Siegfried, god-like in the beauty of their movements, their strength and their power. Warwick Armstrong was someone to be proud of: he had skill, he wanted to win. Nettie Palmer told Australians to be proud of the way they spoke. She held no brief for the Australian 'twang', but every country had its own pests, and the 'twang' was one of Australia's. But, she professed, there was also a 'good Australian accent, something to be proud of and to develop'. It was possible to speak 'good Australian', and, at the same time, to speak well. She was not making absurd claims: Australian English, both spoken and written, was not, so far, as expressive, as rich, as lyrical as American English or English English. But it was right for an Australian—as right as a 'well-cut

[6] Henry Tate to Nettie Palmer, 21 July 1921, Palmer Papers, Series 1, Box 4, Folder 28.

tweed lounge coat'. It was a language, a speech like its people—a people who lounged and lolled in a land of lotus eaters.[7]

This was the age of the rootless man, the age of the kingdom of nothingness. The myths which have sustained human beings for hundreds of years havė lost their relevance. The words of the priests and the parsons no longer fed the hungers of the human heart. A turbulent emptiness was replacing the time when there were 'certain certainties'. Old Australia was becoming a museum piece. The values of 'The Man From Snowy River' and the quest of the Sentimental Bloke for salvation in the country from the city's muck belonged to history. Australians must find out who they are, and what they might be. The Nationalists and the Country Party had no image of the Australian. Billy Hughes has said that Australia was as much a part of England as Middlesex. Bob Menzies has said he was proud of being 'British to the bootstraps'. Labor was the nationalist party. Labor has professed since 1905 to stand for the 'cultivation of Australian national sentiment'.[8]

But Labor was in disarray. The birth pangs of the Australian Communist Party have been followed by bitter exchanges between factions within that Party. At the beginning of 1921 there were two Communist Parties, both adopting the same name and the same principles, both claiming to be 'correct' disciples of the teaching of Marx and Lenin, both more concerned with sullying the reputation of their rival, or exposing the *petit bourgeois* character of the Labor Party than with building a new society. Radical Labor was bogged down in a 'petty, paltry, pitiful squabble'. Between some intellectuals and the communists a bitter debate has begun. Some, like Katharine Susannah Prichard, gulped down communism emotionally. Guido Baracchi believed it was possible to adapt Marxism to Australian conditions. Robert Ross would not shift from the stand he had taken in 1920 that the dictatorship of the proletariat was out of harmony with Australian democratic traditions. The communists wanted to close the mouths of those who disagreed with them. Nettie Palmer wanted the communists to spell out their ideas on the future of Australia. She wanted the communists to tell her how they proposed to prettify the haggard continent. She wanted to know whether culture was their answer to the void created by the death of God. She doubted whether Marxism had any answers to the hungers of the human heart. Christ cursed the moneychangers, and the beneficiaries of the 'kingdom of Shylock'. Christ drove the moneychangers out of the temple.

[7] Preamble to the Act to constitute the Commonwealth of Australia, 9 July 1900, George S. Knowles (ed.), *The Commonwealth of Australia Constitution Act* (Canberra, 1936); Louis Esson to Vance Palmer, 21 May 1921, Palmer Papers, Series 1, Box 4, Folder 28; Nettie Palmer, 'That Australian Accent', *The Home*, December 1920, p. 47.

[8] *Fellowship*, January, March 1921, pp. 83, 115, 119–20; Louis Esson to Stewart Macky, 8 June 1921, Palmer Papers, Series 1, Box 4, Folder 28.

The dry souls of the Enlightenment would never nurture riders in the chariot, or great artists. Marie Pitt, the poet and the journalist, who decided to live with Bernard O'Dowd in 1920, looked forward to the day when in Australia there would be:

> A sun-god race that knows not how to fear,
> A sun-god race to set new slogans ringing.

For her, east from the murk of Europe, in Australia 'breaks the day'. But neither she nor O'Dowd was ever at ease with the spiritual popes of the Australian Communist Party.[9]

The Labor Party was not a group of men and women to usher in that new dawn, that light so different from 'the murk of Europe'. By 1921 the Labor Party resembled more a group of 'wire-pulling politicians' than a 'band of inspired idealists'. To win government Labor was appealing to other sections of the community than the members of the trade unions—the farmers, the petty bourgeoisie, the small shopkeepers, the professional men, and political adventurers. To win a majority at the ballot box Labor must become a party of reformers, a party offering trade unionists and others what they wanted—preference to unionists, equal pay to women for equal work, and the sops of social welfare, pensions for the aged, the disabled and the victims of the wars, unemployment payments, and pensions for widows. The Party was up for grabs by the self-seekers and careerists, who were motivated not by any ideals but by the need to reward their supporters for allowing them to gratify their own lust for power.[10]

Power meant numbers. To secure numbers aspirants to leadership faked ballots, forged tickets, stole ballot boxes and paid bribes. Jack Lang rose to prominence in the Party by buying votes within the Party. By the beginning of 1921 the vendettas, the dog-fights and the double-dealings crescendoed as rival faction leaders quarrelled and struggled to win the right to distribute the 'loot'. While Jock Garden and others sympathetic to the Communists bored away within the Party, the leaders of the factions added their own 'Kilkenny cat flavour' to the Labor Party. Principles were shoved into the background, as questions of procedure took precedence over questions of content at conferences of the Party.[11]

In January 1920 John Bailey was accused of conspiring with others to lodge fraudulent postal votes in an A.W.U. election. Bailey twisted and waxed his moustache so fastidiously that he looked more like one of the

[9] *Socialist*, 28 January 1921; Nettie Palmer to Esmonde Higgins, 10 January, 5 September 1921, E. M. Higgins Papers, Letters from Nettie Palmer to Esmonde Higgins, Mitchell Library; Colleen Burke, *Doherty's Corner* (Sydney, 1985), p. 117, 'The Promised Land II The Fulfilment'.

[10] V. G. Childe, *How Labour Governs* (London, 1923), pp. 54, 62–3, 66–9.

[11] Ibid., pp. 66–7; *Australian Worker*, 16 April 1924, 7 April 1926.

villains of the silver screen than a Labor leader. He made his career in the sheep walks of Australia where the champion 'knuckle duster' was 'cock of the walk'. He gained office in the Australian Workers' Union. He won pre-selection for the seat of Monaro in 1918 by trickery and deceit. He missed out in the Caucus election of the New South Wales Ministry in March 1920, after the Labor victory in that election. That gave him the cue for revenge, the spur to exploit with the parliamentary members and the delegates to the Annual Conference of the Party the dubious devices he had employed to win power in the A.W.U. Labor in New South Wales was split into two factions: a minority faction led by John Storey, and a majority faction led by John Bailey, supported by the A.W.U., Voltaire Molesworth and J. J. McGirr. They muddied the waters of Labor for years in their war of abuse, of charge and counter-charge. So at the beginning of 1921 Labor in New South Wales was a mixture of innocence and corruption. The numbers men threatened to degrade Labor into a party of 'dead bones and whited sepulchres'. The 'light on the hill' men and women belonged to the same Party as the men and the women who seemed hell-bent on making Labor the prime Autralian exhibit of the 'Mammon of unrighteousness'.[12]

Politics was not an occupation for saints. Labor has been no more successful than the Church in its choice of methods by which to guard its members against the corrupting influences of wealth and power. Those who participated in the world must be stained by the world. The conservatives were always realists: they knew what was in man. They had their ideal: loyalty to King and Empire. They had their gospel: work, White Australia and private enterprise. For them political power was a condition of survival. Hughes was an expert in survival. He has survived Labor pre-selections, Labor abuse for his treachery, two conscription crises, the war, and the entry of the Country Party into federal politics. The price of survival was eternal vigilance. There was a shadow line which no conservative could cross. Hughes must not cross it in his handling of the challenge from the Country Party. He had already skated on thin ice with the appointment of John Earle to the Senate in 1917, and the offer of a peerage to John Forrest to get him out of the way. Now at the beginning of 1921 rumour has it that he has offered a knighthood to Edmund Jowett, the deputy leader of the Country Party, on the understanding that he, Jowett, and a colleague would prevent trouble from the Country Party during the current session of Parliament. Jowett's name did not appear in the New Year list of Imperial honours. The

[12] 'War of the Unions', pamphlet in R. S. Ross Papers, N.L.A.; 'The Infamous Iron Hand', pamphlet in ibid.; *Smith's Weekly*, 8 March 1919; 'Dastardly Frame-Up', pamphlet in Lloyd Ross Papers, N.L.A.; *Sunday Times*, 23 April 1922; Miriam Dixson, 'Reformists and Revolutionaries in New South Wales, 1920–1922', *Politics*, vol. 1, no. 2, November 1966; Frank Farrell, *International Socialism and Australian Labour* (Sydney, 1981); Ian Turner, *Industrial Labour and Politics* (Canberra, 1965).

power brokers wanted to know if Hughes still proposed to honour the promise. Hughes was evasive.[13]

The conservatives floated ideas to prevent the members of the Country Party from succeeding in their vendetta against Hughes. Page and his colleagues wanted more than the gratification of personal vanity. They were there to drive hard bargains with the Nationalists, not to haggle over titles for members of their Party. On 5 April 1921 Page was elected leader of the Country Party. Page wanted two things: he knew the drift of population to the cities was eroding the electoral chances of the Country Party, so he wanted an Electoral Act weighted in favour of country electorates. He knew the manufacturers were pressing Hughes and the Minister for Trade and Customs—Massy-Greene—for a high protective tariff. When the tariff schedules were debated again on 7 April 1921, in his first speech as leader Page asked the Government to encourage primary industries by means of bonuses. Hughes has encouraged the production of pig-iron: Page asked him to encourage the production of pigs. Hughes laughed. On 14 April the Labor Party, the Country Party and two Government members combined to defeat the Government in a division. Hughes had one of his tantrums. Page was sensing his power; he explained that the Country Party had no intention of embarrassing the Prime Minister during his visit to the Imperial Conference in London. But the Country Party, he said, was not the 'wet-nurse of the government' and had no intention of giving the Government absolute immunity. Hughes could go for say six weeks. The adjournment notice was carried. Hughes has accepted the humiliation of bargaining with men whom he had once used as whipping boys for his wit. He has made the fatal mistake of treating Page as a lightweight—a 'good doctor but a bad politician', he called him. Hughes was one of those bulls who gored weak men when they were down. But Page was no weakling.[14]

Hughes went off to London in April 1921, hoping that there he would again be received with the enthusiasm of 1916 and 1918–19. The mood of the English has changed. The English were counting the cost of the policies of 'victory at any price', and 'make Germany pay'. Hughes was no longer a hero. Lloyd George, Haig and Hughes were now up for judgement. The men and women of the Jazz Age were now savaging the men responsible for the horrors of the Somme, Ypres, Verdun and Passchendaele. A new group of actors was moving on to the stage of history, and Hughes was being pushed off the edge. The glories of 'yester-year' have vanished. The punishment for the madness in the heart has begun. Unemployment has risen steeply in Great Britain. Germany could not pay reparations in cash and was paying in

[13] H. P. Williams to W. M. Hughes, 5 January 1921, Hughes Papers, Series 16, Box 1, Folder 6.

[14] Sir Earle Page, *Truant Surgeon* (Sydney, 1963), pp. 58–61; Ulrich Ellis, *A History of the Australian Country Party* (Melbourne, 1963), pp. 61–3: *Age*, 6, 8, 15 April 1921.

goods at the expense of British industry. The British were looking for markets and wanted to tighten economic ties with the Empire, to persuade, or entice Australia to buy her manufactured goods, and absorb her surplus population. Britain has won the war on the battlefields, but lost the industrial battle. She was looking to Australia, Canada and New Zealand to regain her position as a world power. In London Hughes was no longer Oedipus Rex: he was Oedipus at Colonus.[15]

At the same time in Australia the Industrial Workers of the World, the Communists and the Sinn Feiners talked of an imminent social revolution. On 1 May 1921 a crowd of two or three thousand marched through the streets of Sydney singing lustily the 'Red Flag', 'Solidarity Forever' and other well-known I.W.W. songs. At the Sydney Domain members of the crowd hoisted a Union Jack on a pole and burned it, tore the remains to shreds and trampled on them. Speakers inflamed the listeners into 'the fever of sedition'. Thomas Glynn of the I.W.W. called on the workers to 'stand together and break up the capitalistic class and demand that the "boss" should give the workers back all he had robbed them of'. A girl of ten or twelve spoke of her training in a Socialist Sunday School and of her determination to stand by the Red Flag and solidarity. The people were on the march.[16]

The *Sydney Morning Herald* was worried. Even if the demonstrations and the disgraceful scenes in the Domain were only 'impudent challenges from a mean minority to a determined, even if slow-moving vast majority', they must be stopped. There was danger in 'allowing such public flaunting of rebellious sentiments'. The Returned Sailors and Soldiers' League agreed. The President and Council of the New South Wales Branch invited all who wanted to 'keep the Union Jack on top' to rally round the flag in Sydney Domain on Sunday 8 May when returned soldiers would prove they did not fight in vain, and that the lives of their comrades had not been laid down in vain to preserve Australia's freedom. Between one hundred thousand and one hundred and fifty thousand people assembled in the Domain to avenge the insult of 1 May to the 'Flag', and demonstrate their 'deep, emotional loyalty'. Amid wild scenes of enthusiasm and exhibitions of patriotic fervour those present unanimously agreed that the Union Jack was the flag for Australia, and that the Red Flag or any other emblem of revolution should not again be exhibited in the State. General 'Ned' Herring said to wild shouts of approval that if Australia was not good enough for 'these people' then let them leave. Sir Charles Rosenthal spoke. So did Major Scott. The flag was the symbol of law and order, of liberty and of opposition to revolution. Just to show what they would tolerate and what they would not tolerate a group of them pulled the speakers off the platform of a rival meeting under the aus-

[15] *Socialist*, 11 November 1921.
[16] *S.M.H.*, 2 May 1921.

pices of the Socialist Labour Party, the Communist Party and the Australian Labor Party, and gave them a rough handling. Jock Garden slipped away before the rough stuff started.[17]

Empire Day on 24 May 1921 was celebrated with marked enthusiasm. The theme was pride in being British. Australia belonged to an Empire which ruled over more than one-fifth of the land surface of the globe. In Sydney and other cities it was marked by an awareness of what the *Sydney Morning Herald* called a 'living, vital force'. Australians were now beginning to reap the benefits of belonging to the Empire. Through that 'great partnership of free nations' Australia was on the winning side in the war. The British Crown was the 'symbol of a great Empire'. Sir Joseph Cook summed up the feelings of all King and Empire men and women at the National Club Empire Day luncheon in Sydney. Australians, he said, did not want to hear all that 'cant and humbug' about the Red Flag. Australians knew that the Red Flag as flown in Australia was 'in bitter antithesis to the Union Jack'. The time was coming, he said, 'when we will have no more of that'. The diners chanted in unison: 'Those who do not like the Union Jack in Australia let them get out'. Loyalty to King and Empire has become the secular religion of Australian conservatism: Australians must conform.[18]

Labor must find a counter-mythology. In June 1921 hundreds of prominent trade unionists assembled in Melbourne for a great congress of unions summoned by the Australian Labor Party. They would answer the 'flag-drunk jingoes, and the brass-brained militarists, and the bitter-hearted sectarians and the lie-spitting newspapers', the servants and lackeys of capitalism and imperialism in Australia. Capitalism was doomed: the workers would be its grave-diggers. Everybody knew that Australia was seething with discontent. Changes were occurring over the whole world: in every country men were deciding to move towards socialization. One problem was to achieve solidarity within the Labor movement. Another problem was to reach agreement on how Australian Labor was to achieve the socialization of industry. There were many views on what should be done. Some wanted action outside the parliamentary system, believing the latter perpetuated capitalism. Jock Garden said that even if they had the opportunity to alter the present society the Labor movement did not have the machinery ready. If the coal miners had the chance to run the mines they would not be able to do it. No one could make a revolution: it had to be born. That was 'the whole bloody trouble'. The trade unions and Labor had neither opinions nor ideas on what to do or how to do it. The moderates in the movement would not accept industrial action alone, because that would hand the movement over to the spiritual popes, the ones who wanted to shut the mouths of all those

[17] Ibid., 4, 9 May 1921.
[18] Ibid., 25 May 1921.

who disagreed with them. So they accepted almost unanimously the compromise motion: 'The socialisation of industry, production, distribution and exchange to be the objective of the Labor Party'. Labor was moving towards a mythology, a creed to set against the loyalty to King and Empire men.[19]

Next the Australian Labor Party must decide where it stood. That would be the task of the Ninth Commonwealth Conference of the Australian Labor Party to be held in Brisbane in October. Hughes has been fighting the battle for the King and Empire men at the Imperial Conference in London, sorting out with his fellow delegates what were the vital needs of the Empire, and arguing that the British only wanted to say what would happen, not to discuss what should happen. He despaired of ever finding a way in which Australia could exercise a real voice in determining the destiny of the Empire. He dismissed as chimerical any idea of leaving the Empire. He now fought the battle for the preservation of a White Australia, telling the British representatives to guard Australia's interests at the forthcoming Washington Conference on naval power in the Pacific. He returned to Fremantle on 22 September 1921.[20]

There had been one good turn of Fortune's wheel for his Party. On 1 August 1921 T. J. Ryan died. Ryan had the talent to restore to the Labor Party some of the brains it blew out in the split of 1916, and also promised to be a most formidable opponent to Hughes. Now he was no more. The Labor Party had lost a gifted advocate for pragmatism, a man who gave the lie to the Hughes claim that Bolsheviks were boring into the Labor Party. Intelligence reports were still feeding the wilder suspicions of Hughes. On 8 August, seven days after Ryan died, Intelligence submitted a memorandum to the Government on the Communist Parties in Australia. Their activities, the memorandum said, were not decreasing. Their leaders belonged 'to the most dangerous class in the community'. They were to be found 'among the Labour [*sic*] ranks'. They had come mainly from ex-I.W.W. men and aliens. They were insidiously pushing Soviet propaganda: they were 'weaning the loyalty of thousands of persons of both sexes in Australia'. Unless measures were taken at an early date the 'loyalty of many others must be severely strained'.[21]

At the Brisbane Conference of the Australian Labor Party beginning on 10 October 1921 the moderates fought to persuade the delegates not to provide ammunition to the flag-waving jingoes and British imperialists who Labor saw as a Trojan horse for a Bolshevik seizure of power in Australia.

[19] *Australian Worker*, 23 June 1921.

[20] L. F. Fitzhardinge, *The Little Digger* (Sydney, 1979), pp. 458–80.

[21] Memorandum: The Communist Parties in Australia, 8 August 1921, Hughes Papers, Series 21, Folder 2, Item 147.

Delegates had before them the recommendation of the Melbourne Trade Union Congress that the objective of the Australian Labor Party should be: the socialization of industry, production, distribution and exchange. Ted Theodore, the Labor Premier of Queensland, was not happy with this. No socialist Labor Party, he said, would ever gain power in a State or the Commonwealth, a socialist programme being electoral suicide. He wanted Labor to declare where they stood, to keep to the monopolies declaration of 1905. The proposed objective could lead only to 'disruption and disunity'. The compromise men had another victory. Maurice Blackburn moved:

> That this Conference declares:
> (a) That the Australian Labor Party proposes collective ownership for the purpose of preventing exploitation, and to whatever extent may be necessary for that purpose.
> (b) That wherever private ownership is a means of exploitation it is opposed by the Party, but
> (c) That the Party does not seek to abolish private ownership of the instruments of production where such instrument is utilised by its owner in a socially useful manner and without exploitation.

The motion was carried by fifteen votes to thirteen.[22]

The socialists at the Conference talked of a sell-out. Robert Ross appealed to the delegates not 'to becloud the whole thing in a world of fog'. The communists cited the decision as further evidence that the Australian Labor Party was what Lenin had said it was, namely, a 'liberal bourgeois party'. The *Socialist* in Melbourne was equally disgusted. The Brisbane Conference, it wrote, has been 'a gathering of the blind and feeble-minded men of organised Labor in Australia'. The more the Bolsheviks and the socialists expressed their anger and contempt, taking on the mantle of the self-appointed Pharisees of all progressive movements in Australia, the more enthusiastic the language of the moderates. The Conference, in the words of the *Australian Worker*, 'did nothing heroic—nothing to make you catch your breath and then burst into cheers'. Australians were not the authors of memorable words, or those words of inspiration which transformed the mundane into the sublime. Australian Labor had no Danton, no Abe Lincoln to say the words which would live on. Ten-bob-a-day socialists did not win places in humanity's portals of fame. To those who had cried 'Rush on!' Labor had responded prudently with 'Take care!' The Conference, the *Australian Worker* said, has 'probably interpreted the mind of the Movement pretty accurately'. Labor has shed an electoral liability at the price of losing the enthusiasm of those who were its conscience. A machine for the capture

[22] Official Report of Proceedings of the Ninth Commonwealth Conference, Brisbane, 10 October 1921, A.L.P. Conference Reports (Melbourne, 1921), pp. iii, 16–17, 35–6.

of political power must be wary of dreamers and visionaries. Numbers men did not lead crusades.[23]

The conservative press was delighted. The lion's skin of revolution, as the *Daily Telegraph* put it, had fallen from Labor to reveal something 'quite harmless'. Communism has fallen over the horizon. Labor has decided in favour of constitutional methods. Labor did not intend to deprive 'a man of his horse and buggy or his motor car'. Labor has recognized that Australia was not Russia. In Australia there never has been any excuse in the political or industrial life of the country 'for the frenzy of the European revolutionary'. The Federal Labor Conference has 'ended in milk and water'. All it had definitely done was to establish clearly the presence in the Labor movement of two parties using different ideas to secure the same end, the capture of power and its emoluments.[24]

Labor has chosen the Australian way. The Communists and the Socialists were disgusted with the Australian Labor Party. It was a bourgeois party, they said, masquerading as the party of the worker. It was a party without an ideology, a party dirtied by 'scabbery, expulsions, ballot-faking and intriguing for offices'. Men scrambling for the crumbs of 'spoils' have been driven to use 'thugs and spielers'. On the day after the Brisbane Conference began there was a debate at the Protestant Church in Castlereagh Street, Sydney, between J. C. W. Baker, the editor of the *Communist*, and Don Cameron, the editor of the *Socialist*. Baker spoke for the affirmative: that the dictatorship of the proletariat was essential if everything was to be brought under the control of the working class: all who opposed the dictatorship of the proletariat must be subjugated. Cameron put the case against the dictatorship of the proletariat. That meant, he said, the centralizing of power in the hands of a few and denying the majority of the workers the right to speak or vote on the determination of the conditions under which they lived. Under the dictatorship of the proletariat workers were expected to be the servile tools of the elected or the appointed few. That was not the Australian way: that was not Labor's way. Labor was a democratic party: Labor believed in the ballot box, in majority rule, not the rule of the one or the few over the many.[25]

Labor's way was change by parliamentary methods. Labor proposed first to create a society in which all adults had an equal right to decide the conditions under which they lived. That meant one man, one vote: that meant the abolition of all undemocratic institutions, such as the Senate and the

[23] V. I. Lenin, 'In Australia', *Pravda*, 13 June 1913, later published in V. I. Lenin, *Collected Works* (Moscow, 1963), vol. 19, pp. 216–17; *Socialist*, 28 October 1921; *Australian Worker*, 20 October, 3 November 1921.

[24] *Daily Telegraph*, 18 October 1921; *Argus*, 19 October 1921.

[25] *Socialist*, 14 October, 9 December 1921.

Legislative Councils in the States. Ever since 1915 the Labor Party in Queensland has looked for ways and means of stopping the 'representatives of vested interests' having 'the power to throttle the democracy of Queensland'. Between February and December 1920 the Labor Government nominated enough members to give the Labor Party a majority in the Legislative Council, intimating that when the proper time came they would provide for the complete abolition of the chamber. The conservatives replied that such a move would not only inflict on Queensland 'the tyranny of the majority', but 'government by the people will be as dead as Caesar, and the country will find itself groaning under the heel of a bureaucratic Soviet of unionist officials, whose machinations have only been checked hitherto by the existence of the sane majority in the Council'. Ted Theodore decided on 24 October 1921, in the wake of the victory for parliamentary methods at the Brisbane Conference, to put an end to the obstruction of the will of the people by this nominated Legislative Council. The conservatives argued that the people did not want abolition: they wanted an elected body to replace a nominated council. Theodore replied by saying the conservatives wanted a council elected on a restricted franchise, a House founded on property franchise. The following day Theodore made it clear that Labor would not compromise. Parliament must give 'free and direct expression to the will of the people'. The Legislative Council had been created in 1859 to be a 'check upon the growing democracy of the people'. If the Council was not an echo of the Assembly, it was an evil: if it was an echo, it was no longer necessary. If the members of the Legislative Assembly flouted the wishes of the people, they could be 'called to book by the people'. Ministers and members were answerable to the people. That was Labor's way. On 23 March 1922 the Governor of Queensland gave the royal assent to the Bill to abolish the Legislative Council of Queensland.[26]

The lion's skin of revolution has fallen from Labor: Labor has entered its 'milk and water' era. Hughes was not fooled. His Intelligence men warned him revolutionaries were still gnawing and boring away like termites at the pillars of society. They must be stopped. On 27 October the Intelligence men sent a memorandum on communism to the Attorney-General's Department. They wrote of a great scheme with world-wide ramifications emanating from Russia and calculated to use unemployment to turn the 'workless into an active revolutionary force'. The unemployed would be used as 'pawns in the Communist game'. On 3 November they wrote another warning about the 'ceaseless Communist propaganda' which was 'making con-

[26] *Qld P.D.*, 8 December 1920, vol. 86, pp. 560–1; *Argus*, 18, 19, 20 February 1920, 21 February 1921; *Qld P.D.*, 24, 25 October 1921, vol. 88, pp. 1729–31, 1773–7; An Act to amend the Constitution of Queensland by Abolishing the Legislative Council, 12 Geo. V, No. 32, Royal assent proclaimed 23 March 1922, *Queensland Acts of Parliament*, Pt 1, 1922 (Brisbane, 1922).

verts all over Australia and luring the unemployed to create a revolution'.[27]

Hughes must strengthen his Government so that it was not vulnerable to the sniping from the 'hayseeds' on the corner benches. Page and company would not be treated as equals: they would be de-fanged. A number of narrow squeaks made talks with Page imperative. In September the Country Party won one more seat in a by-election. Page challenged Hughes to make economies in government expenditure and accused him of doing a 'Rake's Progress' with the taxpayers' money. Hughes was nettled, saying angrily that in all his years in Parliament he had never heard a 'more insulting speech'. Page wondered whether Hughes ever read his own speeches. All Billy's attempts to wheedle the Country Party into the Government failed. When he suggested talks to Page late in October, the latter suspected a 'ruse'. Hughes wanted a coalition to ensure survival. Page wanted guarantees for the Country Party. Talent must be brought into the Government, and the boneheads, the mediocrities, must have their vanity tickled with some public office.

Joseph Cook, the Treasurer, was persuaded to go to London as High Commissioner: Walter Massy-Greene, a power broker in the Nationalist Party, expected promotion. Hughes offered the position to Captain Bruce, the man who had recently distinguished himself as Australia's representative to the League of Nations. Bruce demurred. He asked Hughes whether the feelings of Massy-Greene would not be mortally offended. Hughes was persuasive. Bruce agreed. Other changes occurred. On 21 December a triumphant Hughes announced a major reconstruction of his Government. Hughes had not seen the folly of not coming to terms with Page. Now he had on the corner benches a Party he should, but could not, cultivate. Behind him he had grudge-bearers, 'hosts of Gideon' sitting in the Parliament. What Hughes did not foresee was that observers would soon notice the difference between him and the handsome, well-groomed Captain Bruce. Billy Hughes has dug his own political grave.[28]

At the same time there was great excitement in the Palmer circle. Louis and Hilda Esson returned to Melbourne in September 1921. Louis was looking forward to a 'gorgeous life' in Australia. Australia must build up 'a life of its own'. All the local newspapers dealt 'too much with European, especially English affairs'. He wanted to write plays about Australia, plays that were 'absolutely national and original'. That was what the Sydney *Sunday Sun* was about to offer the children of Australia. They wanted to give them 'an entertaining diversion from the realities of the post-war slump'. So far Amer-

[27] Memorandum on communism for the Secretary, Attorney-General's Department, 27 October, 3 November 1921, Hughes Papers, Series 21, Folder 2.

[28] *C'wealth Gazette*, 21 December 1921; *Argus*, 22 December 1921; Sir Earle Page, op. cit., pp. 70–82; Ellis, op. cit., pp. 63–6.

ican and British comics have predominated, but now, on Sunday 13 November 1921, the Sydney *Sunday Sun* published a cheer-up coloured cartoon called 'Us Fellers'. It was a story about a cricket match between the Kerosene Tins C.C. and the Ashfalt United C.C. The boy who bowled the 'googly', the ball which looked as though it would break one way off the pitch but broke the other way was Ginger Meggs, known to his cobbers as 'Ginge', 'Ginger', or 'Meggsie'. The artist was James Charles Bancks.[29]

Bancks was born in Enmore in Sydney in 1889, the son of an Irish railway worker. As a young man he had impressed the *Bulletin* and the *Sunday Sun* with his cartoons. The *Sunday Sun* invited him to contribute to their new colour supplement each Sunday. Bancks had much in common with C. J. Dennis, the author of *The Sentimental Bloke*. In Australian slang he was 'just a Mick who had lost his faith'. A Merlin, part innocent child and part devil, a gentle spirit, a saint and a larrikin, he took refuge in a world of make-believe, because he had found, like Dennis, there was no salvation in the muck. Ginger Meggs was no more an Australian boy from the suburbs than the Bloke was an Australian larrikin capable of redemption, backslidings, remorse and professions to lead a new life, following the commandments of the 'little woman'. Ginger Meggs was an 'entertaining diversion' from reality.

Ginger was the boy from the suburbs, a street larrikin with a golden heart. He talked big, he talked rough: he was handy with his fists, not afraid of bullies, and never short of a word with which to win an argument. Mum was the Madonna of the kitchen sink, one of the many pack-horses of suburbia. Mum was overweight, her cheeks were puffy, her dresses and her kitchen aprons hanging loosely over her massive frame. Mum had gone to seed, her face and body the victims of a life of drudgery. Mum gave any boy or girl who offended against the lore of the suburbs a cuff on the ear. She ruled the house by her presence, her tongue, and her hand. Mum knew what was in Ginger's heart, but mother and son never really spoke to each other. They were Australians: what mattered most to both of them could never be. Dad was lean and scrawny. He kept the razor-strop in the bathroom cupboard but rarely used it, because Dad was a softie, a man whose only pleasures in life were a quiet read of the newspapers and hearing praise of his son Ginger. The members of the Meggs family had no comforters, no God, and no belief in the capacity of human beings to steal fire from heaven. They took no part in any of the national ceremonies, in Anzac Day, Empire Day, Wattle Day, Armistice Day or the feast days of the Christian year. Bancks was not really interested in answering Hilda Esson's question: 'Can't we do anything our-

[29] Louis Esson to Vance Palmer, 15 September, 20 June 1921, Palmer Papers, Series 1, Box 4, Folder 28; J. C. Bancks, 'Us Fellers', colour supplement to *Sunday Sun*, 13 November 1921.

selves as Australians?' Bancks's answer was: yes, we can all have a good laugh, and provided no one else is looking, a good cry.[30]

For adults the American films offered what *Table Talk* called a 'mad stampede of the emotions'. Early in the new year of 1922 patrons of the Globe picture theatre in Sydney saw on the silver screen an English woman disdain the advances of a demon lover of the deserts of Africa. The would-be lover was the 'Sheikh', played by Rudolf Valentino. The woman rebuffed his first passionate advances by flashing a crucifix in his face. But when she discovered that his 'old folks at home' were really American then all was well. The heroine melted into the arms of the Sheikh and the suburban woman in the audience fulfilled her dream of finding a masterful lover. As a woman she recognized in her heart that she was looking for a master, not a mate or an equal. She wanted Mr Masterful, and she found him in the deserts of Africa. Women and girls crowded into the Globe. The first session started at eleven in the morning. Some queued for the morning session and stayed until the last screening ended at eleven at night. Before the film started a man dressed as the Sheikh walked on to the stage and sang 'Pale hands I loved beside the Shalimar . . . Where are you now, where are you now?' Then the curtains slid back, the column of light lit up the silver screen, and the magical moments began. At Kincoppal Convent school in Sydney one girl built a shrine for Rudolf Valentino. She made a pair of Turkish trousers, draped her room to make it look like a tent, put cushions on the floor and burnt incense. Each night she lit the incense, put on her attire, lay on the cushions and read the book about the Sheikh. That was bliss for her. All over Australia women and girls worshipped at the shrine of Valentino, as did some men, but their fantasies were not quite the same.[31]

While a young girl at the Kincoppal Convent school was decorating her room like a tent to which a Sheikh might come, Archbishop Kelly published in January 1922 a pastoral letter on women's dress. Clothing, he wrote, was given 'for our necessities, not for vanities'. God gave human beings clothing 'to hide the shameful members'. Catholic women, the *Advocate* wrote in January, 'with Mary Mother of God most holy always before them as their Model, should lead the van against everything that tends to lower a high standard of womanly purity'. Catholic fathers, sons and brothers should 'expostulate with flighty daughters, wives or sisters and refuse to escort them thus half dressed anywhere'. Robert Ross was angry with the churches' false doctrine of the sinfulness of man and their teaching that the act of procreation was an evil. There was, he said, 'no room for Mr Grundy' in

[30] John Horgan (ed.), *The Golden Years of Ginger Meggs, 1921–1952* (Medindie, S.A., 1978).

[31] *Table Talk*, 23 February, 2 March 1922; Meg Stewart, *Autobiography of my Mother* (Ringwood, 1985), pp. 93–4.

Australia, 'shuffling along with his umbrella, sniffing into corners, peering with bleary eyes through keyholes in search of sin, desiring to remove all statues from our galleries, advocating the clothing of ballet girls in Victorian costumes; thinking evil of all beauty'. Australian democracy had no place for such a creature. Marie Stopes's book, *Married Love*, has at last been released in Australia. She wanted to teach men 'the sex tide in women'. She wanted men to learn how women could have full sexual satisfaction. But the churches frowned on all this as an appeal to 'the licentiousness and the beast in man'. The minds of Australians, announced Ross, should not be 'befogged and befouled by mediaeval myths and rubbish'.[32]

While the Archbishop and Robert Ross were telling Australians what they should believe, or presuming to answer the riddles of existence, Pastor Carl Strehlow of the Lutheran Mission Station at Hermannsburg was beginning to understand why Christ uttered those words of despair from the Cross: 'My God, my God, why hast thou forsaken me?' In the Australian desert he had heeded for twenty years the precept of his teacher in Germany: 'hold on to Classical literature, or barbarism will come, and to the Bible, or paganism will come'. Now he wondered whether the 'higher civilization' of Europe was the answer for the Aborigines of Australia, whether 'higher civilization' had not robbed them of their most precious possession, the land, the source of their spirituality, their serenity, and the meaning of life. The beginning of understanding between white man and Aborigine, he believed, was for the white man to learn Aboriginal mythology, to learn their myths of creation, to learn their explanation of how the earth, the sky, the sun, the moon, the stars, the trees, the flowers, the birds, the animals, and men and women came to be. The Aborigines were not just the raw material for missionary saviours, or anthropological measurers: they had a wisdom of their own.[33]

While Pastor Strehlow was entering his dark night of the soul ex-servicemen were taking up the blocks of land allotted to them by the Soldier Settlement schemes of the Commonwealth and the States. Governments have responded to the clamour of the soldiers for action. Taking no care to inquire into the capital resources or the previous training of the prospective settler, or into the appropriate size of a home maintenance area; making no provision for any fall in the value of primary produce, the Governments have put men on the land. In the middle of the summer of 1920 one soldier settler arrived at Yenda, in New South Wales, to find that all the stuff he had read in the literature of soldier settlement about being supplied with a tent and a stretcher on arrival was 'hot air'. He and his wife and his two children

[32] *Ross's Monthly*, 21 January 1922, p. 5, 11 March 1922, p. 8, 8 June 1922, p. 6; *Advocate*, 5, 26 January 1922.
[33] T. G. H. Strehlow, *Journey to Horseshoe Bend* (Rigby, Adelaide, 1978), pp. 4–5.

spent the night under the shelter of a big tree. For weeks he and his family had to depend on the hospitality of the ex-diggers for shelter. 'And thank God, the Digger Spirit is very alive here'. With the aid of his fellow diggers he put up a humpy. He had already spent his war gratuity getting started. He was hoping for the 'silver lining'. The *Soldier* reported that many diggers who had gone on the land were in 'straitened circumstances' and 'on the borders of starvation'.[34]

By contrast, over in Western Australia Albert Facey was just as successful in overcoming the difficulties of a soldier settler as he had been in meeting the challenge of early loss of parents, growing up illiterate, being horse-whipped, getting lost in the Australian wilderness, earning a living in a boxing troupe, and surviving the dangers and hardships of a soldier's life on the Gallipoli peninsula. Life had taught him there was no God. 'Anyone', he believed, 'who has taken part in a fierce bayonet charge . . . must doubt the truth of the Bible and the powers of God'. Bert Facey was not a man to cringe or whine or ask either a God or his fellow man to have pity on him, or to lend him a hand. In 1922 he took up approximately twelve hundred acres of land in the Narrogin district of Western Australia. Mr Heuby in the Soldier Settlement Board was a 'very nice, understanding man'. Facey said he had 'a very fair deal from the Board'. Neither he nor his wife knew much about wheat and sheep farming, but they worked hard fencing and clearing the land, sowed wheat, grazed sheep, and made, as he put it, 'quite a lot of money dealing in the buying and selling of sheep'. In Australia the world belonged to the Albert Faceys, the industrious, the sober, and the ones handy with their fists. Again 'knuckle men' became 'cocks of the roost'.[35]

In the meantime as some of the heroes of Gallipoli, Flanders and Picardy worked long hours to win their daily bread from the soils and grasses of Australia, stories were being published in the press about corruption in the Labor Party in New South Wales. Rumour had it that in the elections for the Annual Conference in February 1922 'hidden influences' were at work. Judicious observers said they were unable to say whether or not there had been 'irregularities and corrupt practices'. Others were not so circumspect. John Bailey was accused of having an 'arbitrary Tammany and Czar-like attitude'. He was manufacturing jobs for 'Bailey's good boys'. Labor in New South Wales had surrendered itself to the control of men who were 'insincere, unscrupulous and corrupt'. As members of Parliament, or working in McDonnell House, the Sydney headquarters of the Australian Labor Party, they were lured into running 'after the fleshpots of Egypt for them-

[34] Mr Justice Pike, Report on Losses due to Soldier Settlement, 24 August 1929; *Soldier*, 20 February, 20 July 1922.

[35] A. B. Facey, *A Fortunate Life* (Fremantle, 1981), pp. 317, 297–300.

selves'. To keep such privileges men were prepared to stoop to any device. 'Crook' voters and 'dummies', it was rumoured, had been allowed to vote at the election for the delegates to the Annual Conference. One man testified: 'I want a quid as badly as anyone. I will be back later on'. Some estimated that the number of impersonations was as high as six hundred. All were paid a quid each, and given free meals.[36]

J. H. Catts, a puritan of the old school, a Methodist, a teetotaller and a firm advocate of temperance, and Labor member for Cook, said the time had come to cleanse the Augean stables. Labor, he told a meeting at Sydney University in April 1922, was being destroyed by the Communists and 'a corrupt inner Tammany circle'. He was fighting against the 'mad mullahs' recklessly rushing Australian Labor over the precipice to disaster and ruin absolute and complete. It was not just the Communists and the 'Tammany circle' which was corrupting Labor. The Catholic Church and the liquor interests were also seducing Labor away from its noble aims. He had an idea. He would appeal to Billy Hughes to save Labor. On 9 April 1922 he wrote to Hughes: 'Dear Billy, come back to Labor . . . N.S.W. is ripe for a big sweep back to the old pre-war Labor Party . . . If you returned the country would catch fire with enthusiasm, like a Methodist revival in Wales . . . Come back . . . Conservation [he meant conservatism] does not want you. Labor does. Come back'. But Hughes took no notice of this appeal. He believed he was safe where he was. Labor had already decided on 7 April to get rid of Catts.[37]

The Palmers, the Essons, Frederick Sinclaire and their circle did not lose heart, but interesting Australians in 'things Australian' was an uphill task. Tens of thousands flocked nightly to see British and American plays and pictures, but for an Australian play scarcely a few could be 'scraped together'. Australians read London reviews. This was not, said Frederick Sinclaire, parochialism. This was provincialism, the essence of which he defined as 'looking abroad for standards and sources of enlightenment'. Whatever soul Australia possessed it had at that time no organs of expression, no press, no theatre, no platform. Australians would never contribute to the world's culture until they were aware of their own individuality. They should respond to their own 'call', and not imitate their neighbours or a people over ten thousand miles away. The conservatives had only the hollow

[36] *Australian Worker*, 9 February 1922; 'The Infamous Iron Hand No. 1', pamphlet in Lloyd Ross Papers, N.L.A.; *Sunday Times*, 16, 23 April 1922; T. R. Ashworth, *Politics: the curse of Trade Unionism* (Melbourne, 1922), Pamphlets for the People No. 4, published by the Citizens' League of Australia.

[37] Speech by J. H. Catts at Sydney University, April 1922, and J. H. Catts to W. M. Hughes, 9 April 1922, typescripts in Molesworth Papers, Box 3, M.L.; *C'wealth P.D.*, 6 July 1922, vol. 99, pp. 196–8.

secular religion of imperialism, and loyalty to the British flag, and at the moment Labor had nothing to say.

On 24 April 1922 the Governor of Victoria, Lord Stradbroke, officially declared open the War Museum in the Queen Victoria Building. The idea of a war museum was first put forward by the war correspondent, C. E. W. Bean, after the disasters and horrors of the Somme and Pozières. The soldiers at the front were enthusiastic, encouraging Bean to persuade the politicians to build one of the finest war memorials in the world. At the inauguration ceremony on 24 April 1922 Lord Stradbroke spoke of the collection as a Mecca for Australians. The collection included George Lambert's canvas of the Gallipoli landing, a little watch from the wrist of a fallen soldier, tin crosses tacked onto wooden crosses. In the words of the *Age*, the collection was a record beyond price of 'the shreds of a great tragedy'. On the same day, 24 April, Colin Ross was hanged by the neck for a brutal murder. That was an example of something else which worried them: an example of what the *Age* called 'the sores of civilization'. The war has made some aware of how thin was the veneer of civilization.

Two thousand visited the Museum on Anzac Day 1922. The day was commemorated in all the cities and the country districts with the customary solemnity. The glory of the brave men has not faded. Their unsurpassed bravery has won them a place in the hearts of the Australian people. Their Majesties, the King and Queen of England, sent a message of sympathy and remembrance. Services were held in all the churches. The Dean of St Andrew's Cathedral in Sydney chose words from the Book of Exodus to convey the deep solemnity of the occasion: 'This day shall be unto us for a memorial'. But there was a difference from previous celebrations. This time there were scanty references to the Empire. This time in the Sydney Town Hall an Australian, Roderic Quinn, recited his poem about Australians on that day made sacred by their heroism and their sacrifice. This time there was talk of the role of the Anzacs in the birth of a nation. They were the pioneers of the nation that was to be. As creators of an Australian nation the Anzacs have found their 'Valhallas in the hearts of the Australian people'. It was an occasion when Australians showed their view. At the Soldiers' Club in Sydney some soldiers appealed to Nellie Melba, Australia's Queen of Song, to sing to them. Nellie was coy and played hard to get. A soldier called out in that Aussie combination of cheek and charm: 'Have a try'. Nellie Melba sat down at the piano, and sang to them:

'Mid pleasures and palaces,
Wherever I may roam.
There is no place like Home.
Home, home, sweet, sweet home.
There's no place like home.

There was hardly a dry eye in the room.[38]

In May 1922 D. H. Lawrence arrived in Fremantle on his pilgrimage to find an alternative to the decadence and the despair of the Old World. He stayed for a fortnight just out of Perth. There he sensed a 'queer, pre-primeval ghost over everything'. He sensed, too, that Australia was 'strange and empty and unready'. Then he sailed for Melbourne and Sydney, where he and his wife arranged to rent a cottage at Thirroul, on the coast just over fifty miles south of Sydney. The cottage had an unmistakably Australian name: it was called 'Wyewurk'. He liked the look of the country: 'wonderful sky and sun and air', the 'endless hoary bush', and Sydney Harbour, 'quite one of the sights of the world', and that 'lovely ocean', the Pacific, 'how boomingly, crashingly noisy as a rule' and, at other times, it 'only splashes and rushes, instead of exploding and roaring'. The people he found 'raw, crude and self-satisfied. If every American is King or Queen, I'm sure every Australian is a little Pope all on his own'. He was frightened. In Australia he felt 'the "correct" social world fizzle to nothing'. There was, he sensed, a 'rather fascinating indifference' to what the people of the Old World called 'soul or spirit'. He felt as though he were being resolved back almost to the plant kingdom, before souls, spirits and minds were grown at all. In Australia there was a people with live, energetic bodies and 'a weird face'.[39]

In May 1922 Louis Esson tried to put that 'weird face' on the stage in Melbourne. He and his wife, Stewart Macky, Vance Palmer, Nettie Palmer and others, with the support of Bernard O'Dowd, Frank Wilmot and Katharine Prichard, formed the Pioneer Players. Their aim was to do what William Yeats had encouraged Louis Esson to do, to treat Australians as a 'distinct nationality'. The people of Ireland, Yeats told him, created the sagas in less time than the Europeans had been in Australia. Esson should not let his heart be troubled by the professors, the newspaper editors and literary critics: they would be 'Imperialist and anti-national'. Nor should he be discouraged by surface obstacles such as Australian words: he could make a gully sound as romantic as a glen, and a magpie just as poetical as a nightingale. Yeats felt no lack of atmosphere: so why should Esson?[40]

On 18 May 1922 the Pioneer Players put on Louis Esson's comedy, *The Battler* at the Playhouse in Melbourne. The first-night audience was large and enthusiastic. But then the problems began. The *Age* and the *Argus* were

[38] *Fellowship*, June 1921, p. 164, May 1922, p. 133, June 1922, p. 142; *Age*, 25, 26 April 1922; *S.M.H.*, 26 April 1922.

[39] D. H. Lawrence to Curtis Brown, 15 May 1922, to Mrs A. L. Jenkins, 28 May 1922, and Catherine Carswell, 22 June 1922, Aldous Huxley (ed.), *The Letters of D. H. Lawrence* (London, 1932), pp. 547–50.

[40] Louis Esson, 'W. B. Yeats on National Drama', *Fellowship*, August 1921, pp. 15–27; 'Elzevir', 'Australian Literature', *Argus*, 4 June 1921.

patronizing, the *Age* dismissing the play as 'too slight to make a whole evening's amusement'. Louis Esson complained he was unknown in the *Punch* office. Robert Ross was enthusiastic in *Ross's Monthly*. The play stood, he said, 'for the appreciation of our picturesque hills, gulleys [*sic*] and waterfalls'. It was 'the call to all Australians to make their country the happiest and most beautiful in the world'. In Melbourne there were 'undercurrents against Louis' in the literary world. Sydney, possibly because of a long tradition of treating Melbourne achievements with condescension or indifference, refused to offer a theatre for the performance. The house containing the printing press on which the Pioneer Players had proposed to print editions of their plays was burned down. No one came forward to provide the administrative skills such a company needed. Large audiences patronized the other theatres and the moving pictures. Australians, Robert Ross concluded, preferred 'legs and tinkling music' to the cultivation of Australian sentiment. Within a few weeks Frank Wilmot was telling Louis Esson the Pioneer Players had no need of a chucker-out at the Playhouse: what they needed was a 'chucker-in'. When Stewart Macky's play, *John Blake*, was performed in August the press boycotted it. The *Argus* reported it in what Nettie Palmer characterized as 'its most grumbling granny tones'. Their reporter left well before the end of the performance.[41]

The King and Empire loyalists had no difficulty in exciting support and enthusiasm. On 5 July 1922 a monster patriotic demonstration was held in the Sydney Town Hall to protest against the campaign of murder in Ireland culminating in the assassination of an eminent British army officer, Field Marshal Sir Henry Wilson. Major W. J. Scott possibly took D. H. Lawrence as his guest to the meeting. Sir Charles Rosenthal was again prominent in the proceedings. The meeting expressed its abhorrence at the death of Sir Henry Wilson, and further expressed their 'unabated loyalty to the throne'. They wanted to keep the Empire intact because it meant freedom, prosperity, happiness and progress to all Australians. All the disloyalists should either leave the country or be strung up. Lawrence realized then, or, perhaps later, that beneath the 'long lapse and drift' in Australia, beneath the 'rather fascinating indifference to . . . soul or spirit' there were these ex-diggers who were looking for a leader. Under the surface indifference and the pursuit of independence, there were men who could be savage and monstrous to all who challenged their secular religion. With the help of the ex-diggers, General Rosenthal, Major Scott and men of like mind proposed to stop 'ant-men and ant-women' swarming over Australia. Australia was a country where

[41] Louis Esson to Vance Palmer, n.d., probably May 1922, Palmer Papers, Series 1, Box 4, Folder 28; Nettie Palmer to Dowell O'Reilly, 13 August 1922, ibid., Folder 29; *Argus*, 20 May 1922; *Age*, 19 May 1922; *Table Talk*; 25 May 1922; *Ross's Monthly*, 8 July 1922, p. 5.

eagles flew in the sky, and the tomtits, sparrows and willy wagtails of 'coziness' and 'convenience' would have to 'shut their traps'.

In Sydney a group of these eagles formed the Old Guard. It included businessmen, like Philip Goldfinch, a descendant of Governor Philip Gidley King and now general manager of the Colonial Sugar Refining Company, R. W. Gillespie, a director of the Bank of New South Wales, Sir Samuel Hordern of the retail firm of Anthony Hordern, William McIlwraith, the largest grocer in New South Wales; ex-army officers such as Major-General Sir Charles Rosenthal, Major W. J. Scott and Lieutenant-Colonel Eric Campbell from Young; and members of the old landed gentry such as Brigadier General George Macarthur Onslow of Camden Park, Lieutenant-Colonel Frederic Hinton of Canowindra, and Lieutenant-Colonel Donald Cameron of Scone. They pledged themselves to maintain law and order: they were ready to co-operate in upholding constitutional government: they would expose the demagogues with their malign influence on the masses: they would rid Australia of the foreign element, and put an end once and for all to any attempt to establish in Australia a 'black, brown and brindle autocracy'. They believed in free enterprise, in individualism, not the loss of identity in Fascist or Communist movements. They stood for the Digger tradition, the virtues of Old Australia, for courage, bravery, independence and resource. Australians should beware of 'rule by the multitude'. By the end of 1922 they had 25 000 members in the city and 5000 in the country. In Victoria there was a League of National Security, and in South Australia a Citizens' League.[42]

While the members of the Old Guard and their equivalents in other States were swearing allegiance to digger values and the Empire, Robert Ross published his pamphlet, *Eureka: Freedom's Fight of '54*. He wanted Australians to know more about their democratic traditions. He wanted to rekindle in Australians the Henry Lawson picture of Eureka:

> But not in vain those diggers died. Their comrades may rejoice,
> For o'er the voice of tyranny is heard the people's voice.

There was going to be a 'roll-up of Australians on some dark day to come'. Bernard O'Dowd has published his *Alma Venus* late in 1921, prescribing love to fill the void vacated by the disappearance of God. But unlike Lawson, O'Dowd could never find the memorable words, that felicitous image which would allow his voice to travel 'further than College walls'. Besides the Mr

[42] *S.M.H.*, 6 July 1922; D. H. Lawrence, *Kangaroo* (London, 1923), pp. 121–31; Robert Darroch, 'The Man Behind Australia's Secret Army' and 'Lawrence in Australia', *Bulletin*, 20 May 1980; Robert Darroch, 'The Mystery of Kangaroo and the Secret Army', *Weekend Australian*, 15 May 1976; Andrew Moore, 'Send Lawyers, Guns and Money!' A Study of Conservative Para-Military Organizations, New South Wales, 1930–32, thesis in La Trobe University Library, pp. 25–40.

and Mrs Grundy in the city 'sodden with rectitude', all the respectable people took offence at a poet's laboured attempt to mention the unmentionable.[43]

Lawson had nothing more to say. In August 1922 Vance Palmer stood in awe before the ruins of what had once been the wondrous Henry Lawson. There was a 'look of misery graven deep into his thin hollowed face'. He was found dead on 2 September in the yard of or inside a house in Abbotsford, Sydney. As with the place and circumstances of his birth, the stories of his death varied. Vance Palmer told a friend later than when the body was found, inside his mouth, which was wide open, a blow-fly was buzzing. In the presence of death the respectable people made their somersaults. The widow who had been in his lifetime both his victim and his accuser played the role of chief mourner. Billy Hughes, who had tickled the ribs of the *claqueurs* of Melbourne with stories at Lawson's expense, ordered a State funeral. On 4 September the members of the respectable classes gathered in St Andrew's cathedral for a memorial service. The bush people he had loved were not there. The Reverend D'Arcy Irvine, Anglican Archdeacon of Sydney, preached about God's forgiveness: God, he said, would judge Lawson as Lawson himself had once said God would forgive the drunkard of the Australian bush:

> They'll take the golden sliprails down and let poor Corney in.

Out in George Street a crowd of possibly one hundred thousand people assembled to pay their last tribute. A brass band played the 'Dead March' from *Saul* as the coffin was placed reverently on the hearse, and the procession started on the last journey. At Waverley Cemetery a clergyman of the Church of England recited over the coffin the words which had been spoken over the mortal remains of another of Australia's great native sons just over fifty years before—William Charles Wentworth:

> The days of men are but as grass: for he flourisheth as a flower of the field.
> For as soon as the wind goeth over it, it is gone: and the place thereof shall know it no more.

The words of the Psalmist were borrowed to sum up the life of a man whose 'heart was hot within him'. Near that very vast sea to which so often Lawson had looked in vain for salvation a parson asked Jehovah to spare his wayward, vagrant spirit before he went from hence and was seen no more.

[43] R. Ross, *Eureka: Freedom's Fight of '54* (Melbourne, 1922); Henry Lawson, 'Eureka', *Bulletin*, 2 March 1889; Bernard O'Dowd, *Alma Venus* (Melbourne, 1921); *Fellowship*, March 1922, pp. 112–13; Nettie Palmer to Dowell O'Reilly, 13 August 1922, Palmer Papers, Series 1, Box 4, Folder 29.

He was buried in the same cemetery as J. R. Gribble, 'The Blackfellow's Friend', and Henry Kendall, 'Poet of Australia'.[44]

The literary world was as divided in death as it had been in life about Lawson. Christopher Brennan and Norman Lindsay judged him harshly as a man. Brennan summed him up as a man who had 'sat down with a grievance and let himself be miserable'. Lindsay dismissed Lawson as a nuisance, a blow-fly who had thrown himself away on 'life's rubbish heap'. On Henry as a writer Brennan was equally scathing. Lawson, he said, was a 'fair second-hand' singer of 'emphatic turgid journalese'. Brennan and Lindsay wrote as though the world would now know Lawson no more. There would be, they said, no remembrance of this 'insane genius' with a fatal flaw. By contrast Labor elevated him to the status of minstrel of the Australian people, the apostle of mateship and equality, the man who taught Australians to view all human beings with the eye of pity. Labor elevated him into one of those mighty men of renown who would live for ever.

Lawson had drawn a mantle of majesty and solemn grandeur over the bush people. He had created Mrs Spicer, the woman who told her children to 'Water them Geraniums'; Brighten's Sister-in-Law, the Drover's Wife, Mrs Baker, Jack Mitchell: the 'Giraffe' who passed round the hat to help his mates: the drunk at the bush funeral: Joe Wilson, the man who knew he should never take a glass, but always did, and Mary, his long-suffering wife. Lawson had joined Bold Jack Donohoe, Flash Jack from Gundagai, Ned Kelly, Ben Hall, the Man from Snowy River, Victor Trumper and Warwick Armstrong in the gallery of the heroes of the Australian people. He had been a strange man with many afflictions and few graces. There was the lovable Henry Lawson, the man memorable for his laugh, his handshake, followed by a 'You'll do me'. He was the man with the haunting eyes, which seemed both to dance with joy, and yet to register some ineffable sadness. Henry Lawson had dreamed a great dream, a strange dream and a grey dream, for the man himself had suffered from his own frailties. He knew what he had achieved: '. . . my sins shall be forgiven and my works shall be remembered'. He was right. Early in life he had taken his stance: 'I'll write no more for the cultured fools'. 'Lay out my body decently', he had said, 'before my friends see it, for the soul was great'. The greatest of his dreams had been about the destiny of Australia: 'We are Australians—we know no other land'.[45]

Sixteen days after his death Australians were told the bugles of Old

[44] *S.M.H.*, 4, 5, 9 September 1922; story told by Vance Palmer to C. B. Christesen; *Australian Communist*, 8 September 1922; graves of J. R. Gribble and Henry Kendall, Waverley Cemetery, Sydney, personal visits to site; Psalm 39, vv 3–4.

[45] Axel Clark, *Christopher Brennan* (Melbourne, 1980), pp. 273–5; *Bulletin*, 7 September 1922; Diary of A. G. Stephens, 30 December 1931, MS. in Fryer Memorial Library, University of Queensland; *Daily Mail*, 4 September 1922; *Australasian*, 9 September 1922; *Argus*, 5 September 1922; *Australian Bystander*, 26 October 1922; *Brisbane Worker*, 7 September 1922.

England were calling them again to the service of the Empire. Mustapha Kemal of Turkey has called on the Turks to join him in driving the Allies out of Constantinople. Ever since the fall of Constantinople in 1453 the Greeks have coveted Constantinople as the mother of their religion and the symbol of their past glory. The demands of Mustapha Kemal would mean the reappearance of the Turks in the Balkans: Turkey would again be a European power. On 17 September 1922 Great Britain, France and Italy sent reinforcements to the Near East. Rumours flew that the European Allies were prepared to protect Greece against an attack by Turkey. That day Lloyd George invited Hughes to send Australian contingents to assist the Allies in the Near East tangle. Hughes agreed that the Australians should help the British to ensure the freedom of the straits and the sanctity of Gallipoli, already a shrine in the minds of the Australian people.[46]

The conservatives wanted Australians to 'range their strength behind that of the mother country'. For them the British Empire was that 'great world force' which gave 'humanity hope of a return to reason'. But Australian opinion has moved a long way from supporting the British 'to the last man and the last shilling'. Labor has long since decided the Fisher words were an emotional aberration: unquestioned loyalty led to the disasters and horrors of Gallipoli, the Somme and Passchendaele. Labor advocated a referendum on whether Australian troops should be sent abroad. But Hughes remained an Empire man. Australia would not stand idly by and let the interests of the Empire be threatened. On 19 September he told the House of Representatives a referendum was impracticable. Charlton, for Labor, did not agree. Expeditionary forces meant untold suffering leading not to the birth of a new era but to the impoverishment of Australia. Troops should not be sent abroad without consulting the Australian people. Within two days of the announcement of the Chanak crisis, as it was now called, some conservatives were arguing that Australia's commitment to support the British was not automatic. Page, for the Country Party, said in the House: 'If Great Britain [goes] to war Australia, as part of the Empire, is at war as well'. But that was going too far. By her sacrifices in the last war Australia had won the right to decide whether she would or would not take part in British wars.[47]

A groundswell of opposition developed. Australians were warned to be wary of appeals to defend the solidarity of the Empire, to protect the sacred shrines of Gallipoli against the infidel, and to save Christians from extinction. Behind these laudable intentions there lurked, it was said, the secret aim of British and French imperialists to filch territories on behalf of the capitalists who maintained them in office. Australians should not 'fall down'

[46] *Argus*, 18 September 1922.

[47] *Age*, 19, 20 September 1922; *C'wealth P.D.*, 19 September 1922, vol. 100, pp. 2347–63.

ever again to worship 'the false gods of imperialism', or shed their blood in defence of some chimera. Hughes was prepared to sacrifice Australian lives in a 'sordid squabble'. Now was the time to develop a 'national consciousness' rather than indulge in the sentiments relevant to a world which had ceased to be.[48]

On 23 September 1922, in the middle of the Chanak crisis, Page declared he could see no possibility of satisfactory co-operation with a political opportunist like Mr Hughes. Page said in the House that the role of the Country Party was to switch on the lights when it was known there was a burglar in the House: the Country Party would make the Hughes Government 'drop the loot'. He could see no reason why the Country Party should coalesce with a party in which Hughes was the leader. He has gone close to saying the Country Party would co-operate with a Nationalist Party which had a different leader. Rumours were running along the corridors of power in Parliament House, Melbourne, that the dissident liberals like Willie Watt were looking for a leader who could work with Page and the Country Party.[49]

It was a time for conciliation. But Hughes had never been a conciliator. He was always a fighter, a crusher, never the compromiser. Hughes was not an alcoholic, nor a workaholic: Hughes was a mockaholic. He could not stop. He had mocked Alfred Deakin, Andrew Fisher, Joseph Cook, John Forrest and Willie Watt. In all those cases the indulgence of his passion had ministered to his own personal advancement. Now the mockery of Page and his fellow 'hayseeds' would minister to his political destruction. He continued to mock as he had ever since the Country Party was formed. The policy of the Country Party, he said, was to 'blow hot or blow cold according to the temperature of the political atmosphere'. Page had said the Country Party represented all interests. Well, said Hughes, with one of his well-known leers, if that were the case, they should join the Nationalist Party. Hughes still refused to take them seriously. The 'hayseed', he said, must pay the price for presuming to dictate the policy of the Government of Australia. If there was to be a fight, he said on 27 September, 'I am going to be in it'. He was never a man to turn the other cheek. He would smite Page, he said. He would show the people the Country Party was barren. As for Deakinite liberals like Willie Watt they were all as dead as the dodo. 'Hayseeds', had no chance against an international statesman like himself. He, Billy Hughes, had no reason to fear a lightweight such as Page. He, Billy Hughes, had fought with the Heaven-born Woodrow Wilson, the President of the United States of America.[50]

[48] *Stead's Review*, 30 September 1922; *Australian Worker*, 20, 27 September 1922.

[49] *Argus*, 25 September 1922; Sir Earle Page, op. cit., pp. 83–5; Ellis, op. cit., pp. 74–83.

[50] *Argus*, 28 September 1922; W. M. Hughes, Draft statement for press, 22 February 1922, Hughes Papers, Series 16, Item 473; *Age*, 21 February 1922.

Page was also a fighter who believed he was thrice armed because his quarrel was just. He was crusading for justice for the primary producers of Australia. That was the theme of his policy speech at Grafton on 26 October. The primary producers in 1921, he said, produced £250 million of the £348 million of Australia's total production. Only a warped mind could suggest that country people would support a Government which proposed to increase the burden of the primary producers. The country political movement was a reaction to the centralizing tendencies of the age. The movement of population to the cities had reduced the number of country electorates. Page did not want to impoverish the city dwellers: he wanted the refinement, recreation and employment opportunities of the city to be brought to the country people. Page stood for the suburbanization of Australia.[51]

Hughes strutted on the electoral platforms of Australia like a man confident of victory, unaware of any impending disaster. At Kyneton in Victoria on 3 November he made fun of Page and the Country Party. The Country Party, he said, was 'like a maid entering service for the first time without a character'. Hughes laughed, the audience laughed. Laugh on, laugh on, for retribution is not far away. His Party, the Nationalist Party, represented the middle class, the great mass of the Australian people. With suburbia behind him he and the Nationalists had every reason to feel as Martin Luther felt in the safe stronghold of God: they could not fail. It never occurred to him he might be like Macbeth, waiting at Dunsinane for Birnam Wood to walk towards him. At Castlemaine on the same day he repeated what he had been saying ever since country interest candidates first stood for election in 1919: his Ministry had done everything possible for the primary producer. He would like to know what that 'putty man' Page had done for the man on the land. As for the Labor Party, well they were just a joke, a party imbued with foreign doctrines. There was only one Labor Government left in Australia. That was in Queensland. Even there the floodwaters of change were rising rapidly, but 'there was no ark and no Noah'. Great laughter. Yes, Tom Ryan was dead, but there was another kind of death, and soon Hughes would know why he had spoken so much of death during the election campaign.[52]

Piqued by Hughes's ridicule, the Country Party recommended its supporters not to give their second preferences to Nationalist candidates. Labor might get back on Country Party preferences. Hughes scoffed at that. Labor, he knew, was too discredited by faction fighting in New South Wales to win a Commonwealth election. Besides, their leaders were colourless, nice, kind

[51] W. Massy-Greene to W. M. Hughes, 3 October 1922, Hughes Papers, Series 16, Folder 8; *Farmers' Advocate* (Melbourne), 26 October 1922; *Age*, 26 October 1922.

[52] *Argus*, 4 November 1922.

men, stereotypes for an 'ant-heap' society, not eagles flying in the sky. Hughes did not see that the threat would come from within his own Party. Hughes believed he was indispensable, but no single man was more important than political stability. On 15 November Bruce signalled his intentions: 'As far as I am personally concerned', he said, 'I am prepared to do anything and to make almost any sacrifice to ensure good relations between the Nationalists and the Country Party.[53]

Hughes made no such offer. Sycophants assured him some Country Party members had nothing but the most friendly feelings towards him. Country Party members, he was told, would accept any alternative, even Hughes as Prime Minister, rather than put Labor in office. Hughes should 'lay low' and things would go well for him. The signs were there that the people were behind him. In Melbourne at the Town Hall on 30 November over two thousand people rose to their feet and cheered as he walked on to the platform. But the past would not go away. A voice called out 'Judas' as he rose to speak. He took no notice. He ridiculed the claim of the Country Party that it was the only party representing country interests. He beamed. Hands on hips, he asked his audience to tell him what the Country Party sought. A voice replied: 'To shove you out'. Hughes took no notice. He was middle-class Australia's man. He was their saviour from the menace of Bolshevism. The people, he was sure, would give thumbs down to 'Revolutionary Communists' and their 'Red objective'.[54]

The electors did not shove him out. The poll on 16 December was indecisive. Labor made gains, eleven all told. They had twenty-nine seats, the Nationalists twenty-six, the dissident Liberals in Victoria five, and the Country Party fourteen, with one Independent. The Nationalists have lost their majority. The Country Party was in an even stronger position to be a 'power for mischief'. The Nationalists now could not govern without Country Party support. Hughes was trapped. Page would not budge. He said again he was not prepared to be a member of any Government led by Hughes.[55]

Hughes was in despair. The world was closing in on him. He must pay the price for all his jokes at the expense of Page, for being a little Czar, and for the betrayal of 1916. A daughter of his first marriage, Ethel Hughes, threatened to tell the world he had been 'cruel in every way' to his family. She would tell the world 'the miserable truth' that his conduct had been 'deplorable'. He

[53] Ibid., 16 November 1922.

[54] W. Duncan to W. M. Hughes, 23 November 1922, Hughes Papers, Series 16, Box 1, Folder 8; *S.M.H.*, 1 December 1922; *Age*, 1 December 1922; Advertisements in *S.M.H.*, 15 December 1922.

[55] Colin A. Hughes and B. D. Graham, *A Handbook of Australian Government and Politics 1890–1964* (Canberra, 1968), pp. 325–6; *Age*, 1 December 1922; *Sunday Times*, 24 December 1922; Ellis, op. cit., pp. 87–9; Sir Earle Page, op. cit., pp. 85–9.

should be down on his knees 'asking for our pardon and trying to atone for everything'. 'Why should you be allowed to go on', she asked him, 'as if you were everything that is to be desired in a man, the emblem of greatness?' Why should she and her sisters and her brothers sit down and let him walk over them? He was haunted, too, by those words from his first wife: '. . . once you loved me, Will'. Now it looked as though the people, too, had forsaken him.[56]

Supporters comforted him. Herbert Brookes, the son-in-law of Alfred Deakin, and a member of the 'Yarraside' with whom Hughes had always felt himself to be an eternal outsider, told him to stand firm. Hughes had gone as far as he ought to go in making overtures to the Country Party. The Country Party was now asking for his head on a charger, notwithstanding the fact that Hughes had still the strongest party behind him and that Page's supporters were more or less a rabble. The members of the Country Party were 'Lilliputians masquerading as political Gullivers'. He urged Hughes to forge ahead with his own policy. Let them come cap in hand with terms acceptable to him. Help them to manoeuvre themselves into a position wherein they will have to support Hughes or Labor. George Pearce assured him his indomitable spirit would 'rise above the present reverse'. J. H. Carruthers, a New South Wales conservative, counselled him to lie low for a while: the public would soon want him back, as there was no one equal to him in public life today. That was what Hughes wanted to believe. Brookes advised him to turn the bonnet of his car to Sassafras, lift up his eyes unto the hills, and find the strength to discover 'a happy issue during the New Year out of the new situation that has developed'.[57]

The reverse has not helped Hughes to grow in wisdom. He continued to have his sport with Page. He spoke as though he were still on top. Go on, he said to Page, govern with the support of the Labor Party, and let the people see what manner of man you are. Page treated the proposal with contempt. He has said there could be and would be no bargains between the Country Party and those socialists, and he meant it. Page invited J. G. Latham, the new independent Liberal for the seat of Kooyong, to attend meetings of the Country Party. He agreed. Hughes was not bothered by that. He proposed a meeting between the Nationalists and the Country Party 'to arrive at some

[56] Ethel Hughes to W. M. Hughes, n.d., probably late 1922, Hughes Papers, Series 22, Box 1, Folder 2; for whether Hughes was married to the mother of his first family, see L. F. Fitzhardinge, *William Morris Hughes: A Political Biography. That Fiery Particle 1862–1914* (Sydney, 1964), pp. 9, 177–8; R. R. Garran, *Prosper the Commonwealth* (Sydney, 1958), pp. 235–6.

[57] H. Brookes to W. M. Hughes, 22 December 1922, Hughes Papers, Series 16, Box 1, Folder 8; J. H. Carruthers to W. M. Hughes, 29 December 1922, ibid.; R. W. D. Weaver to W. M. Hughes, 21 December 1922, ibid.

modus vivendi by which the King's Government could be carried on'. Hughes wanted six delegates from each Party. Page insisted on the Country Party sending only three. In his mind he was David fighting Goliath. The delegates met in Melbourne on 17 January. Hughes wanted a debate on policy. Page replied that the first issue to be settled was the office of Prime Minister. The meeting broke up without any agreement. On 19 January Page sent a memorandum to the Nationalist Managers, repeating in writing what he had said at the meeting of 17 January, that the Country Party would 'not support or co-operate with any Government containing the present Prime Minister'.[58]

Hughes refused to surrender. He stalled and played for time. The one gesture he could not bring himself to make was to hold out an olive branch to Page. On 23 January 1923 he made overtures for more discussions. Page was even firmer. 'I insist', he replied on 24 January, 'our Party cannot in any way support a Government containing the present Prime Minister'. Until his retirement was unconditionally guaranteed all negotiations were pointless. Hughes clung on. His own Party was behind him. On 31 January the Nationalists resolved to tell Page and Co. the demand of the Country Party that the retirement of the Prime Minister must precede further negotiations was unreasonable and could not be accepted. They asked the Country Party to join with them in further negotiations to avoid 'the disastrous consequences of possible political turmoil and chaos'.[59]

Page did not budge. He telegraphed Hughes on 1 February that the Nationalist resolutions of 31 January had closed negotiations. That afternoon he published the exchanges between the Country Party and the Nationalist Party in the press. The position of Hughes was now impossible. The solidarity of the Nationalist Party collapsed. Hughes offered to resign. Members commissioned Bruce to resume negotiations. On 2 February 1923 Bruce told Hughes he had seen Pearce and told him he wanted to preserve the National Labor element in the Nationalist Party because without that they were doomed and the future of Australia was 'black indeed'. Bruce hoped he and Hughes could continue to work together. But he wanted Pearce in his Government. He therefore asked Hughes: 'Am I making too great a demand on your generosity if I ask you to advise him to come and help me?' Bruce realized how much he was asking of Hughes. He was asking

[58] J. H. Carruthers to W. M. Hughes, 2 January 1923, Hughes Papers, Series 16, Box 1, Folder 9; W. M. Hughes to E. C. G. Page, 16 January 1923, ibid.; E. C. G. Page, Memorandum for Nationalist Managers, 19 January 1923, ibid.

[59] E. C. G. Page, ibid.; E. C. G. Page to W. M. Hughes, 24 January 1923, ibid.; Resolutions of Nationalist Party Members, 31 January 1923, ibid.

Hughes to make a sacrifice and have the gratification of 'preserving the true spirit of Nationalism in Australia'.[60]

Hughes made the sacrifice. Hughes has been defeated by the class he has served so loyally ever since those talks with Herbert Brookes at Macedon in 1916. In the hour of his great agony Hughes behaved with a dignity he had rarely displayed in office. But he was deeply hurt. For years he was not able to speak to Pearce. He comforted himself with the hope that a day would surely come when he would take vengeance on Bruce for all he had suffered. In adversity Hughes showed dignity, but not magnanimity. This time he went to the hills in Sassafras to watch the mountain ash handle the relentless Australian sun. He, too, had the strength to endure to the end. On 5 February Bruce began his talks with Page. Page asked for a ministry of twelve with the Nationalist and the Country Party both having six portfolios. Bruce demurred. He did not see why a Party which polled just over 12.5 per cent of the votes cast (59.36 per cent of the voters on the roll cast their votes) should enjoy a footing of equality with a Party which had polled 35.22 per cent. Page settled for a six/five distribution, but he persuaded Bruce to give him the key position of Treasurer. On 9 February they published in the press the names of the members of the new Government, and the terms of their partnership in government. The name given to the Government suggested a partnership. The identities of the Nationalist Party and the Country Party were to be maintained. Six members of the Government were Nationalist and five Country Party. Dr Earle Page was to take precedence in the Ministry after the Prime Minister, Stanley Bruce. The Ministry was to be known as the Bruce–Page Ministry.[61]

In the haste to have the new Ministry sworn in, Bruce decided to rush on with the ceremony before Hughes had taken his leave of the Governor-General. That was another slight for which Hughes never forgave Bruce. Bruce, the model of old world courtesy, deeply regretted showing any discourtesy to Hughes. The Governor-General, Lord Forster, asked Hughes to join him at lunch one day the following week. But nothing could console Hughes. The world statesman must now take a seat on the back benches in the House of Representatives. He must endure the mockers of Botany Bay. He must learn to live with the fruits of his own folly.

Page has won. An Australian David has vanquished Goliath. The despised 'hayseeds' have toppled the 'Little Digger'. So Page liked to think in those halcyon days when he and Bruce set out on their journey together. As in 1910 and 1917, and in every crisis in the history of Australia, 'Yarraside' has

[60] Telegram of E. C. G. Page to W. M. Hughes, 1 February 1923, ibid.; S. M. Bruce to W. M. Hughes, 2 February 1923, ibid.

[61] Hughes and Graham, op. cit., p. 326; Sir Earle Page, op. cit., pp. 96–100; *Age*, 10 February 1923; *C'wealth Gazette*, 9 February 1923; B. D. Graham, 'The Country Party and the Formation of the Bruce-Page Ministry', *Historical Studies*, no. 37, November 1961.

won. 'Yarraside' again had one of their own as Prime Minister of Australia. The bourgeoisie and the country gentry still governed the country. Loyalty to King and Empire, and opposition to all those challenging the Australian way of life and the Australian dream have triumphed again. Australia was still chained to her colonial past. The voices of those who wanted to do something about it as Australians have dropped again into the great Australian silence.[62]

[62] S. M. Bruce to W. M Hughes, 9 February 1923, and Lord Forster to W. M. Hughes, 10 February 1923, Hughes Papers, Series 16, Box 1, Folder 9.

6

'AH, QUESTIONS!'

ON 28 FEBRUARY 1923 the Governor-General, Lord Forster, arrived on the steps of Parliament House in Melbourne for the official opening of the ninth Federal Parliament. There was a 'gorgeous setting' of colourful official uniforms. In democratic Australia there was a 'mediaeval frill', redolent of an aristocratic society. There was much bowing of inferiors to superiors. Bruce, the new Prime Minister, was 'immaculately tailored': others, not to be outdone, appeared 'resplendent in frock coats and tall hats'. The costumes of the aristocratic society of the Mother Country have survived the advance of democracy in Australia. Those in power in society still clung tenaciously to a 'gaudy but meaningless ceremony'. A nation of borrowers still crooked the knee to their principal creditors.[1]

As soon as the clerk of the House of Representatives pronounced the final words of the Governor-General's proclamation: 'God Save the King', Labor members responded, 'God save the Government'. Then they asked in unison: 'Where's Billy?' Some sang 'Willie, Willie, we have missed you', as Billy Hughes waited in the corridor outside the Chamber, gathering the strength to face his mockers. The conservatives have dumped him. Labor was about to inflict on him full punishment for being the arch-conspirator in the 'Great Betrayal of 1916'. But Hughes was prepared to wait for a reconciliation with Labor, as his one immediate hope of revenge for the humiliation of that January and February. D. H. Lawrence has said that Australia, the continent, was waiting—but no one knew whether it was waiting for human history to begin, or waiting to hear its history was all over. Billy Hughes was waiting for the chance of revenge. The mighty spirit in the tiny frame would consume itself for years to come in fantasies of revenge while he waited for the call to reconciliation and forgiveness from the victims of the Great Betrayal of 1916.[2]

Labor was in a cheeky, confident mood. The despairs of 1917 have almost vanished. Now there was a Government they could get their teeth into. The Governments of Hughes had had, in their eyes, some of the trappings of respectability. Hughes and Pearce had been Labor men. Now there was a

[1] *Age*, 1 March 1923; *World* (Hobart), 1 March 1923; *C'wealth P.D.*, 28 January 1923, vol. 102, pp. 5–6; *Australian Worker*, 20 December 1922.

[2] *Australian Worker*, 31 January, 28 February 1923.

Government in which, as the *Australian Worker* put it, 'the Sugar Trust, the Coal Vend, the Shipping Combine—all the profiteering fraternity—will settle down with smiling satisfaction to another three years of blissful plunder'. Frank Anstey relished the sport of laughing at the 'immaculately tailored'. Anstey always found it easier to accuse conservatives of their relish for the 'loot of office', to censure the morals of capitalists, or list the evils of capitalism than to affirm what Labor would do. Anstey was the Danton of the Australian Labor Party, an enlarger of life, a lover, a man who paid service with his lips to the Greek ideal of moderation in all things while practising excess in everything in his private life. He spoke with tears in his eyes of the brotherhood of man: yet he loathed the 'little yellow men' and all the 'Shylocks of this world'. As Jack Lang put it later, Frank Anstey's greatest delight was to curl 'the spats off the Bond Street Johnny'. On 1 March, in the House of Representatives, he had his sport with Bruce. A 'cultured Australian', he called him, 'seeking to adapt himself to the manners, customs and fashions of Bond-street and Piccadilly'. Bruce, he said, represented 'that culture which is taught by "big business" in Flinders-lane'—the culture of those who 'struggle for prestige of position in the market places of the world'. He had confidence in the Labor Party: 'The future', he said, 'is ours'.[3]

Dr William Maloney, the Labor member for Melbourne, was angered by all the adulation paid to the Governor-General. Australians, he said, had heard nothing but 'political piffle' from this 'gentleman who holds the highest position which anyone can occupy in Australia, and who represents the head of the British Empire'. Public money was being wasted on ceremonies in which flunkeys paraded in gorgeous uniforms, and brave boys were paid to carry bayonets in front of Parliament House in time of peace. Labor, as the *Australian Worker* has put it on 7 February, believed the Governor-General was 'open to the suspicion' of a 'desire to join with the power-holding and moneyed class to "dish" the Labor Party'. The time would come, Dr Maloney prophesied, when Australia will yet have to 'defend its rights against a Governor-General'. They laughed then, but his words would be remembered later. W. G. Mahony, the Labor member for Dalley, criticized all this 'flummery and ceremonial'. 'Fancy us', he said, 'a democratic community, having our Governor-General drawn through the streets in a State carriage with uniformed postillions in powdered wigs, and with outriders on prancing fiery steeds'. That was going too far: that was just an Irishman letting off steam against the representative of a class which had perpetrated and sustained the 'ancient wrong' against the people of Ireland.[4]

Bruce did not reply in kind. His composure was not disturbed by cheap

[3] *C'wealth P.D.*, 1 March 1923, vol. 102, pp. 70–1, 78.
[4] Ibid., 2 March 1923, pp. 144–54; *Australian Worker*, 7 February 1923.

jokes about his dress, or his 'la-di-da' voice. He always spoke from on high to those below. The honorable member (he meant Frank Anstey) 'did not appear to care for my method of dressing, or my manners, or some quality which he described as culture'. But, Bruce continued, if the honorable member took this as proof that he, Bruce, was a man of 'the good old Conservative mind, or Tory instincts', then he could assure him he was quite wrong. The members of his Government were not Tories. They were progressive men of sanity, men who stuck to the field of the possible. They were realists. Bruce then proceeded to set out his view of the Australian situation.[5]

The survival and material well-being of Australians depended, he argued, on their membership of the British Empire. Bruce was not a man to strike a pose, or to toss off a memorable phrase. There was no poetry in his soul, no gift or taste for talking of being 'British to the boot-straps'. For him it was all a question of common sense. Australia must have a naval defence scheme to resist invasion, or deter would-be invaders. Australia must depend on the British navy: Australia must therefore support 'an Empire naval defence scheme'. Consultation between the Dominions and the Motherland was essential. Some thought because Australia was 12 000 miles from Europe 'that will save us'. No, said Bruce, that was not true: it did not save us in 1914, and would not save us in the future. The safety of Australia depended on her membership of the Empire.

Economically Australia, in his eyes, was also dependent on the Mother Country in two ways. Australia must find markets for her surplus products. 'It is to the Motherland', he said, 'we must look primarily in considering the question of markets and the disposal of our surplus products'. Australia needed population. Australia needed capital: Australia must look to the Motherland to borrow that capital. In the interests of Australia as a whole Australia must have one borrowing authority. So defence, markets, population and capital were 'the great problems of Australia'. As he saw it, the only way to solve them was by entering into a closer relationship with the Mother Country.[6]

The communists disagreed. As they saw it, a period of economic and moral decline was continuing 'the infernal work of the five years of butchery'. Unemployment was increasing, and would continue to get worse for the working class. The only solution was for the workers to take control of industry, and by the establishment of the dictatorship of the proletariat, to overthrow capitalism and establish communism in its place. The question of questions was how the communists could take over the leadership of the Australian workers from the Labor Party. The communists were full of hope. History was on their side: they were the party of destiny. First they must

[5] *C'wealth P.D.*, 1 March 1923, vol. 102, p. 79.
[6] Ibid., pp. 79–91.

unmask the treacherous nature of the leaders of the Labor Party, expose their opportunist rule, and wage a fight against all social traitors of the working class. Second, communists must win decisive majorities in the trade unions. They must join the Labor Party and convince the rank and file that the leaders of the Labor Party would never fight for the interests of the working classes, that the Labor Party was a capitalist party, a party following a policy which bound the workers to the capitalists. Jock Garden has come back from Moscow to preach the new party line. A party of one thousand members has found how to direct over four hundred thousand workers: a party of principle would take over the leadership of the workers from a party 'full of opportunism' and 'directed by reformists'.[7]

The Labor Party would have nothing to do with the communists. The dictatorship of the proletariat was alien to Australian traditions of freedom: the comrades must 'wean themselves from the worship of far-off fetishes'. The Labor Party was committed to the 'maintenance of racial purity'. The communists proposed to abolish White Australia; they were un-Australian. Labor must come up with ideas of its own on the future of Australia, a way forward different from the 'dictatorship of the proletariat' advocated by the communists and from the determination of Bruce and Page to stay within the Empire. That was what Jimmy Scullin tried to do during the debate on Labor's motion of no confidence. Labor, unlike Bruce and the Nationalists, declared Scullin, was no 'champion of British imperialism'. Labor would not call on Australians to co-operate with British capital in the exploitation of the wealth of Australia. As a Labor man of the Irish Catholic variety, Jimmy Scullin was ill at ease with Bruce's desire to strengthen Australia's bonds with the Mother Country. The Australian Labor Party, true to its ideals of justice, was right to express its sympathy with the Irish people in their 'heroic struggle for political and economic freedom'. But Jimmy Scullin was too timid a man to advocate an Australian Boston Tea Party. All he was prepared to say on 1 March 1923 was that Labor stood for the common man and Bruce for the gentleman.[8]

Unlike Frank Anstey, Jimmy Scullin did not have the fly of malice feeding on his heart. By birth and conviction he belonged to a powerful brotherhood within the Australian Labor Party—the brotherhood of Irish Catholics. Frank Anstey was a secular humanist to whom religion was 'mediaeval dirt' and the Church the purveyor of infamy about human depravity. Jimmy Scullin believed in the resurrection of the dead and the life of the world to come. Frank Anstey has waged a crusade against the 'Kingdom of Shylock': Jimmy Scullin wanted Australian Labor to address the ancient wrong committed by the English against the Irish. He was born at Trawalla, Victoria, on

[7] *Australian Communist*, 23 February 1923; *S.M.H.*, 16 February, 13 March 1923.

[8] *Australian Worker*, 3 January, 14, 21 February 1923; J. H. Scullin, *A Nation's Agony: the Labor View of the Irish Question* (Bathurst, 1921), p. 2.

18 September 1876, and educated at Trawalla State School. Just as Henry Parkes grew up in the shadow of Kenilworth Castle, so Jimmy Scullin grew up in the shadow of Ercildoune, the seat of the Learmonth family. His politics he learned from the Utopian socialists, the Sermon on the Mount, and the poems and stories of Henry Lawson. He was a gentle spirit who had worn the hobnailed boots, and the bowyangs of the Australian bush worker. He had the soul of a John Shaw Neilson, and the oratorical gifts of a Daniel O'Connell. A Catholic puritan, he was a follower of Father Thomas Mathew on the temperance question, and a man who had been taught that adultery was a greater sin than murder. Frank Anstey agreed with the *Soldier* that Marie Stopes's book, *Married Love*, would 'remove many misunderstandings from the minds of mates'. Jimmy Scullin agreed with the bishops of his Church that Marie Stopes was spreading the knowledge of contraception among the wives of the poor 'in a monstrous campaign against decent instincts'. Frank Anstey believed the only peace a man ever knew was in the arms of a woman. Jimmy Scullin believed only the peace of God passed all understanding. So a man with the image of Christ in his heart became the Labor member for Corangamite in April 1910. In the House of Representatives he was soon known as the 'hurricane orator', and the man whose heart was on fire over the wrongs of Ireland and the poor.[9]

By contrast the communists wanted to enlighten the masses on the brutal nature of capitalism. They wanted to teach the workers not to regard Parliament with 'supernatural awe, a form of idolatry'. It was a period of moral decline. It was a year of shabbiness, shabby cities, shabby buildings, shabby parks, and shabby seats in the theatres. In the eyes of the communists, capitalist society was in its shabby period, its period of decay. They would bury capitalist society. But in its death throes the workers and others were attracted to quack religions and odd superstitions. In what the communists called the 'great shambles' there was a tendency to break away from religious orthodoxy and to substitute for the 'unadulterated superstition' of the Christian faith odd religious revivals.

Faith healers, with their 'insipid inanities' were making their appeal to the 'semi-imbecile victims' of a 'decadent civilization'. James Hickson arrived on a healing mission in the churches of Sydney and Melbourne and other places in March 1923. To the communists he was just another of 'those medicine men' exploiting the neurotic in a corrupt and decadent society. To the congregations which filled the churches to capacity, Hickson was the man who with God's help made the blind to see, the lame to walk, and the deaf to hear. Hickson asked the people to believe there was no limit to what God could do

[9] John Robertson, *J. H. Scullin* (Perth, 1974), pp. 1–27; *Soldier*, 20 February 1923; *Advocate*, 1 March 1923; personal visit to Trawalla, 11 September 1986.

for sick and crippled people. The communists advised the people not to be fooled by 'master class dope'.[10]

The captains of industry were not dismayed by this talk about the plight of capitalist society. For them it was a time of promise, a time of hope. The 'Sleeping Beauty of the South Seas', as the employers' magazine, *Business Efficiency*, called Australia, was about to wake and find herself a princess. Electrification and harnessing of water power would 'free Australia from the hampering traditions of the past' and launch Australia on a 'rising tide of progress'. That was the Bruce–Page vision: that was their answer to the gloom and doom men of the Left, the self-appointed preachers at the graveside of capitalist society. A new era was about to begin. The 'vital spark' of electricity was working a silent revolution in transport, communications, the factory and the home.[11]

In May 1921 the Victorian Railway commissioners published their plan to electrify the Melbourne suburban railways by 1923. The Railways Department in Sydney had a similar plan. The States had plans to supply cheap electric power for street lighting, factories, and private houses. In the forests of Australia trees were felled to make poles to carry wires transmitting electricity from power station to consumer. Pylons like miniature Eiffel Towers appeared in the countryside to the anger of some and the delight of others. Electric power promised to be a remedy for that 'welter of discontent'. It restored the 'dignity of useful work' by reducing drudgery. Electric power expanded the class of skilled workers, the class which owed its privileged position to the expansion of capitalist society. Electric power speeded up the bourgeoisification of the worker.[12]

Electric gadgets promised the Australian housewife relief from drudgery. The *Australian Home Builder* claimed electrical appliances removed the dirt at a very low cost. The electric iron meant 'cleanliness', no 'soiled clothes' and no 'annoying delays'. The electric vacuum cleaner was more efficient than the carpet brush or the carpet sweeper. The electric kettle, the electric stove, the electric toaster and the electric boiling ring were cheaper and cleaner than gas or wood or coal. So were electric hot water services. Electric radiators brought warmth into the home just by turning on a switch. The electric refrigerator preserved milk, vegetables, fruit, cream, and chilled drinks without the slops from the ice chest, or the dependence on the ice-man, carrying the huge slabs of ice on his shoulder, and dirtying kitchen floors. Electric appliances did not liberate women from the home: they provided

[10] *Australian Communist*, 23 February, 2, 9, 16, 23 March 1923; *S.M.H.*, 6, 10, 13 March 1923.

[11] 'The New Outlook', *Business Efficiency* (Sydney), May 1923.

[12] *Table Talk*, 2 January 1922; 'Electricity—the Power Behind the Worker', *Australian Home Builder*, May 1924, p. 25.

women with more leisure. Even ironing and pegging out clothes lost some of their burden. Humanity, or rather middle-class humanity, was marching towards a cleaner way of life. Electric power promised not only to relieve human beings of the labour of cleaning their teeth, but also promised in the future 'the electrically groomed man and the electrically beautiful woman'.[13]

The aeroplane would end the isolation of Australia from the rest of the world, the fate of being 'down under'. Aviation would end the differences between town and country. The motor car was already making a contribution to that revolution. Sales were increasing. The number of registered motor vehicles in Victoria rose from 21 772 in 1920 to 144 596 in 1930, and in New South Wales from 25 197 in 1920 to 197 550 in 1930. There were similar increases in the other States. Cars were not cheap. Like electrical labour-saving devices they were for the beneficiaries of middle-class affluence in Australia. The cheapest Chevrolet cost £325, the Essex £475, the Wolseley (British) £430, and the Packard £975. Hitching posts in the cities became relics of the horse and buggy age; water troughs ceased to slake the thirst of horses and became troughs in which the bourgeoisie dumped the members of their class who had behaved in ways displeasing to them. The age of the gadget and the petrol engine increased comfort but did not liberate Australia from the tyranny of bourgeois ideals of correct behaviour.

Bruce and Page were a Government of developers. The motor car needed roads. Bruce and Page proposed to pay the States the money with which to build the roads. That might mean borrowing from London. The new industrial revolution would increase Australia's dependence on the Mother Country. Money for roads could also be provided by a roads tax. At the Premiers' Conference of June 1923 the Bruce–Page Government promised to pay £500 000 to the States on condition that the States contributed on a pound-for-pound basis. On 22 June 1923 Bruce introduced the second reading of the Main Roads Development Bill in the House of Representatives. The proposal, he said, was 'a practical means of aiding the development and progress of the country generally'. Bruce and Page have committed Australia to material progress.[14]

People moved from the country to the city to benefit from the higher wages, the better facilities and the higher standard of living. In 1911 38.03 per cent of the population lived in the seven capital cities; in 1921 43.01 per cent of the people lived in the seven capitals. The 1920s witnessed another

[13] *Australian Home Builder*, 15 July, 15 December 1924, 15 June, 15 August 1925; *Punch* (Melbourne), 30 August 1923; Gwen Sergeant White, 'Labor Saving Kitchens', *Real Property Annual* (Melbourne, 1919).

[14] *C'wealth P.D.*, 22 June 1923, vol. 103, pp. 311–13; An Act Relating to Main Roads Development, No. 2 of 2 July 1923, *C'wealth Acts*, 1923.

suburban sprawl. Municipal councils built roads: contractors hastily built houses: States and municipal councils supplied electricity, water and sewerage. It was the age of reinforced concrete, asphalt, brick veneer and weatherboard, galvanized iron and asbestos sheeting. The suburbs of Australian cities became 'a litter of bungalows . . . scattered for miles and miles'. The front lawn, the car in a garage, the wireless aerial, the front entrance to the house became measuring rods of status and respectability. For the bourgeoisie it was the age of 'jazz style', the age of the gramophone, the ebony elephant and the cocktail cabinet at which the hostess or a uniformed maid mixed the cocktails—the 'Temptation', the 'Devil's Kick', and 'High Stepper' for the guests at a cocktail party. The creedless puritans of the previous decade shed some of the restraints inherited from the past. For the working classes it was the age of the weatherboard villa, the interior decoration of which lacked the conspicuous waste and display of the bourgeoisie. On the walls of the family room a ghoulish painting of the sufferings of Christ on the Cross often looked down on the menfolk as they ate their prawns and drank their beer and yarned about the 'footy', or Australia's chances in the next cricket tests against the English, while Mum knitted patiently and waited for the signal from Dad to bring in the supper.[15]

Entertainment must be provided for the leisure hours of the city dwellers. Picture palaces were hastily put up. Plans were announced for bigger and more gaudy palaces expressive of the extravagance characteristic of the age. On 27 July 1922 the chairman of Amalgamated Wireless (Australasia), Ernest Fisk, informed the Commonwealth Government he would build a broadcasting station transmitting news, information and entertainment to people in town and country. Fisk was an Englishman who wanted all the senior positions on the technical side of his company to be filled by Australians, and all wireless parts to be made by Australians with Australian materials. Yet it never occurred to him that the programmes should have an Australian bias. The leaders of economic nationalism in Australia were still chauvinists for British culture.[16]

When other companies applied for broadcast licences the Postmaster General summoned a conference of all parties interested in broadcasting on 23 May 1923. They decided to introduce the sealed set system under which listeners used wireless sets capable only of receiving the company to which

[15] G. W. Mitchell, 'Genesis and Development of Reinforced Concrete in Australia', *Transactions of the Institution of Engineers in Australia*, vol. 3, 1922, pp. 172–6; J. C. L. Laing, 'The Principles of Reinforced Concrete', *Australian Home Beautiful*, 1 November 1928; 'Concrete Cottages—Doing Without Bricks', *Industrial Australian and Mining Standard*, 24 February 1921, and 'Concrete for Road Making', ibid., 4 January 1923; *C'wealth Year Book*, No. 22 (Melbourne, 1922), p. 890; D. H. Lawrence, *Kangaroo* (London, 1923, 1950 reprint), p. 24; Robin Boyd, *Australia's Home* (Melbourne, 1952), ch. 8.

[16] I. Mackay, *Broadcasting in Australia* (Melbourne, 1957), pp. 16–17; K. S. Inglis, *This is the A.B.C.* (Melbourne, 1983), pp. 5–6.

they were subscribers. Between November 1923 and June 1924 the Government licensed four companies: two in Sydney, one in Melbourne and one in Perth. A revolution was about to begin. Advertisers in newspapers, weeklies and trade journals promised purchasers of sets that they and their families would keep in touch with the world, that wireless would overcome loneliness in the backblocks, flatten out the differences between town and country, and end Australia's isolation from the rest of the world. A crystal set cost between £3 and £5, a one-valve amplifier on a crystal detector £7 to £10, a two-valve amplifier £12 to £16, a three-valve set £30 to £35 and a four-valve set capable of picking up inter-state stations over £50. Like the motor car the wireless promised to be both a social leveller and an endorser of the existing social order.[17]

In preparation for the first wireless broadcast, newspapers published diagrams of circuits for the home builder. Trade journals offered advice on circuits and parts. Aerial poles, white insulators, and aerial copper wire appeared in the gardens of the suburbs and the country districts. Rooms in houses were taken over by zealous amateurs, who filled them with sheets of bakelite, coil wire, insulators, valves, transformers, earphones and loudspeakers. Disturbing the cat's whiskers, wantonly wasting batteries, forgetting to change batteries, or fiddling with the equipment became grave offences, especially if they deprived Dad of the only news that mattered—who won the 'footy'—or Mum of the women's programme and the kiddies of the children's hour.[18]

Universal education and mass culture were producing a community of good bourgeois, and loyal sons and daughters of the Empire. Of the annual public holidays two—Easter and Christmas—came from the Christian religion, two—Anzac Day and Empire Day—came from the secular religion of loyalty to King and Empire, and one—Eight Hours Day—from the veneration of democratic traditions, the idea of Australia as the vanguard of human progress. Except for Anzac Day, no day of special significance to Australia was the occasion for a holiday. The States have not agreed on which day should be Australia Day or which event the people should commemorate. Anzac Day and Empire Day were occasions for public professions of faith in and loyalty to the King and the Empire. On Anzac Day 1923 the Governor-General, Lord Forster, spoke in Sydney of 'the purifying power of sacrifice' known by those who had been prepared to lay down their lives for the King and the Empire. But at that ceremony a woman handed out sprigs of rosemary, for Anzac Day was also a people's day of grief. In the country districts army officers and local mayors spoke of the 'gallant lads'

[17] I. Mackay, op. cit., pp. 17–21; *Bulletin*, 25 September 1924; *Australian Home Builder*, May 1924, p. 17, 15 December 1924, pp. 19, 31.

[18] Personal memories of many years as an amateur builder of crystal and valve (first battery then electric) sets.

who had gathered to the side of the Mother Country to defend all that the British flag represented. At Emerald in Victoria on 22 April 1921 Nettie Palmer heard Jack Mahony, successful real estate agent and President of the Shire, make what she found an 'awful speech' about the 'disloyal elements in our midst'. Children noticed that their fathers wept. This was a day of grief, a day of loss, but no one ever explained why this was so. Anzac Day was about something too deep for words.

In the Public Schools, University Colleges, the Royal Military College at Duntroon, Canberra, and the Naval College at Flinders initiations gave the members of those communities an early lesson in the duty to conform, and the expectations of their elders that they would be loyal to the prevailing virtues. In the State Schools, the *School Papers* and the teachers introduced the children to English heroes such as Lord Nelson and the Duke of Wellington, and to their good fortune in belonging to an Empire on which the sun never set. Each Monday morning in term time the children were lined up around a flag pole, asked to place their right hand on their left breast and recite with the teacher a promise to obey their parents and their teachers, and to be loyal to their King and their Empire. To honour the Anzacs and the Empire verses were added to some school songs. At Melbourne Grammar School these verses were added:

(sung to the tune of 'Men of Harlech')

Some, in strife of sterner omen,
Faced the Empire's stubborn foemen;
Fought as erst their sires—her yeomen;
Won the deathless name.
Praise ye these who stood for Britain,
These by foreign marksmen smitten;
Praise them for their names are written
High in storied fame.

None their ranks could sunder;
Who could shirk or blunder
So stood they true
To the old Dark Blue,
And all their foes went under.
Honour ye the old School's story
Heroes who—her sons before ye—
Died or lived, but fought for glory,
Honoured evermore.[19]

Out of school boys read the *Boys' Own Paper*, the *Gem*, the *Magnet, Chums*, and

[19] *S.M.H.*, 26 April 1923; *Phillip Island Standard*, 2 May 1923; *Ferntree Gully News*, 3 May 1924; personal memories of ceremony at Cowes, Phillip Island, 25 April 1923; *School Paper* (Victoria), 1 May 1924; Diary of Nettie Palmer, 22 April 1921, Palmer Papers, Series 16, Box 25; Additional verse and chorus of Melbourne Grammar School song quoted in Chester Eagle, *Play Together, Dark Blue Twenty* (Melbourne, 1986), pp. 94–5.

the *Union Jack*. Girls read the *Schoolgirl's Annual, Chatterbox*, the *Girl's Own Paper*, the *Australian Girl's Annual*, and *Cassell's Australian Girl's Annual*. Boys and girls read the novels of Mary Grant Bruce, in which the 'goodies' were Wally and Jim, two of nature's gentlemen who were safe anywhere with girls, and never even thought of looking into the wine cup when it was red. The 'baddies' had been to State Schools, wore shoes or boots with pointed toes, brown footwear with blue suits, were Trade Union agitators and grass and woolshed burners during the strikes of 1890 and 1893–94. Girls read *The Girls of Dormitory Ten* and Louisa M. Alcott's *Little Women*. The boys received both entertainment and instruction in the male virtues of courage, daring and endurance, and in loyalty to King and Empire. The girls were entertained, but their instruction was different. They were told their duty was to prepare themselves for the role God had allotted to women. They were to be the servants of and partners of their husbands, and mothers of law-abiding Christian children. Both boys and girls were indoctrinated in the advantages of being British. Foreigners were introduced as cowards, cads, tempters, temptresses, betrayers, cheats at sport and pimps.[20]

On 28 August the Herald and Weekly Times published the first edition of 'an Australian paper for Australian boys'. It was called *Pals*, the price threepence per copy. Readers were urged to do their duty to their King and their Empire. They were entertained with stories of the heroic deeds of the men who won the Empire, men such as James Cook, William Charles Wentworth, Robert Falcon Scott, Horatio Nelson and the Duke of Wellington. They were introduced to the heroes of the sporting field, batsmen such as Victor Trumper, fast bowlers like Ernie MacDonald, and all-rounders such as Warwick Armstrong. 'Pals' were advised to buy British cricket bats because they were like stout British hearts: they never cracked, unless they were mishandled by someone not worthy of being a 'Pal'. There was advice on how to breed mice, how to make crystal sets, stamp collections, boxing gloves and mouth organs. There were tips on manliness and courage, and many tips on what was expected of a 'Pal'. 'Pals' were advised not to have anything to do with Aborigines as they were 'a miserable specimen of humanity': they were dirty: they speared cattle: they were not really British. Nature had not fashioned them to be 'Pals'. They were not the ones:

> To set the cause above renown;
> To love the game beyond the prize.[21]

It was the age of the pictorial press. The Sydney *Sun* increased its circulation from 25 000 in 1914 to 148 000 in 1920. On 11 September 1922 the

[20] Advertisements in *Australasian*, 4 December 1920, 2 December 1922, 16 December 1922, 8 December 1923.

[21] *Pals* (Melbourne), 28 August, 11, 25 September 1920; Vane Lindesay, 'Cartoon Annuals', *This Australia*, Autumn 1985.

Sun-News Pictorial was first published in Melbourne with service as its slogan and success as its aim. It was the first daily pictorial in Australia. The paper was to be a 'sounding-box for Empire affairs'. Nothing in the daily lives of the people would be omitted, and naught set down in malice. Their reporters had an eye for the sensational. On 14 September 1922 there was a news item on disgraceful scenes at the Sydney Artists' Ball. Whisky has been poured into the claret cup in such quantities that by the early hours of the morning there were such goings-on that a police report on the attempts of the artists to maintain the centre of gravity was marked 'confidential' and not shown to reporters. To attract more readers both papers had a coloured weekend supplement, with coloured cartoons designed to amuse, to distract but never to alarm. While the intellectuals were discussing the decline of the West or searching for the 'roots that clutch' and the branches that 'grow out of this stony rubbish' the people at large were being nourished on a diet of pleasure.

The portable gramophone was the new fun-maker. In 1923 they were being sold for £5 5s, ten-inch records for 4 shillings and twelve-inch discs for 6 shillings. The new fun-maker could be played on the beach, in the bush, on the front lawn, in the back yard, on the verandah or on any flat surface. The moralizers protested that questions of high seriousness were being trivialized. Love was being debased to the level of 'When my sugar walks down the street' or 'Nobody knows what a red-hot Momma can do', or 'We'll build a dear little, cute little love nest', or 'Nothing can be finer than to be with Carolina in the mor-or-or-ning, Nothing could be sweeter &c.'. The dreams and hungers of humanity were reduced to the inane words: 'I'm forever blowing bubbles, pretty bubbles everywhere'. The people kept on doing what they were doing although frowners, straiteners, spoil-sports and spiritual bullies warned them such delights were leading them to ruin. They had been doing it for a very long time, long before their ancestors had planted their civilization in the ancient continent of Australia.[22]

The dance halls were the pleasure palaces for the masses, the cabaret for the comfortable classes. At the cabarets of Sydney and Melbourne everyone who appointed themselves to be 'anyone' or attached importance to being seen, and later in the evening to being heard, was there. Alcohol was forbidden, but human ingenuity, generous lengths of table cloth, and wide table legs helped patrons to evade the law, and provided places in which to conceal the precious bottles with their promise of making good night a certainty. At the cabaret one-time scholarship boys, and aspirants to social and public preferment, were seen 'rubbing elbows with the rich, with those millionaires'. The curious and the pryers received information on who was dancing cheek to cheek with whom in Melbourne and Sydney town. As with

[22] *Sun-News Pictorial*, 11, 14 September 1922; *Table Talk*, 24 December 1924; *Catalogue* of the Columbia Gramophone Company (London, 1923, 1924).

the dance music on gramophone records the moralizers likened the entrances to the cabaret and the dance palace to the 'doors of Hell', and named the time after midnight the 'danger hour', when the back seats of taxis and hansom cabs became 'brothels on wheels'. As with mixed bathing, the priests and the parsons prophesied that if more female flesh were exposed to the lascivious eyes of hungry men there would soon be no more womanly modesty and reticence left in Australia.[23]

The people discovered a new race of heroes. In the nineteenth century the heroes of Australians differed from class to class. The heroes of the comfortable classes had been the mighty men of renown in the British armed forces, the Elizabethan sea dogs, the navigators such as Captain Cook, army officers such as the Duke of Wellington and naval officers such as Lord Nelson. The explorers of the ancient continent had also won a place in the portals of renown—Captain Sturt for his heroic row upstream on the Murray, Edmund Besley Court Kennedy and Jacky Jacky for their heroism when surrounded by savages, and Robert O'Hara Burke and William John Wills for crossing the continent from south to north. The bush people had different heroes in their temple of fame—the men and the women who had defied the oppressors of the people: Jim Jones of Botany Bay: Bold Jack Donohoe: the wild colonial boy: Ned Kelly, the advocate of the life of the 'fearless, the free and the bold': Adam Lindsay Gordon who on his horse had jumped the gap at the Blue Lake at Mt Gambier, in an act of bravado, one of those daredevils the bushmen admired—a man of physical courage who defied the laws of nature.

Now the people have found on the sporting field the heroes who seemed to defy even the laws of gravity. The people warmed to the men who were cheeky to the Englishmen claiming the right to define the rules and conventions of every sport. In 1921 in England Warwick Armstrong, the captain of the Australian cricket team, had annoyed the English by encouraging the two Australian fast bowlers, Jack Gregory and Ernie MacDonald, to aim at the ribs of English batsmen. Armstrong had worn shirts with extra-long sleeves to conceal the spin his fingers were imparting to the ball. The people worshipped him: they called him affectionately 'Warwick', the giant of the cricket field who stood well over six feet in his socks, and weighed well over twenty stone. The English described Armstrong and his team as 'hard-bitten', 'grim' and 'pitiless'. The English believed gentlemen always defeated 'cads': this time the cads from 'Down Under' won easily. Louis Esson admired Armstrong and his team. They were not pleasant, he told Vance Palmer, but they had 'a touch of genius' about them.[24]

[23] *Table Talk*, 7 May, 3 September 1925.

[24] *The Times*, 6, 11 August 1921; *Daily Herald* (London), 11, 15 August 1921; K. Dunstan, *The Paddock That Grew* (Melbourne, 1962); R. Grace, *Warwick Armstrong* (Camberwell, 1975); *Table Talk*, 6 January, 3 March, 25 August, 1 September 1921; Louis Esson to Vance Palmer, 1 June 1921, Palmer Papers, Series 1, Box 4, Folder 28.

On the football field the heroes of the people also defied the laws of gravity. Roy Cazaly habitually took such a prodigious leap for a mark that as soon as he began his run the crowd would chant: 'Up there, Cazaly' or, more affectionately, 'Up there, Cazza boy'. The moralizers denounced the 'footy' as a circus in which civilized men behaved to each other like savages towards members of other tribes. As Louis Esson told Vance Palmer later, football was 'taken with high seriousness in Carlton'. Any 'weakening of the Old Blues' was regarded as a national calamity. Defeat on a Saturday afternoon meant 'a black night in Carlton'. Eighty thousand attended the four matches in the opening round of the Victorian Football League in 1921. That year the V.F.L. hoped for a hundred thousand attendance at the Grand Final. They got forty-three thousand. Songs were composed to commemorate the exploits of players. Carlton had a song about their champion centre half-forward, Horrie Clover, the man who became god-like at Princes Park on alternate Saturday afternoons in winter:

> Oh Mr Gallagher,
> Yes Mr Sheahan.
> I think I know the player that you mean.
> It isn't eight or nine,
> And it isn't Pat O'Brien.
> It isn't Duncan, Mr Gallagher,
> No. It's Clover, Mr Sheahan.

Geelong had a warm, cosy song about the feats of their players:

> Any plum, any pud
> Any wee Georgy Wood [a reference to a popular comedian]
> Are the Geebungs any good?
> For they met the old Tigers [Richmond] in 1922
> They met the old Tigers and put them in the zoo.

And so it went on: boastful, cheeky songs of a people contented, as the popular song put it, with 'the little things in life', a people with a rich larrikin tradition.[25]

Publicly the Communist Party leaders sang their aria about the imminent end of capitalist society. Privately some of their members were becoming disenchanted, because the party had not blossomed into a mass movement. They were breaking up into little cliques, each claiming to be the only correct interpreter of the teachings of Marx and Lenin. Some were put off by the 'humourless seriousness' of party members presenting themselves as the 'self-appointed instruments of a new way of life'. The brother of Nettie

[25] *Table Talk*, 19 October 1922; *Argus*, 27 October 1923; *Australasian*, 27 October 1923; Louis Esson to Vance Palmer, 21 September 1925, Palmer Papers, Series 1, Box 4, Folder 33; Leonie Sandercock and Ian Turner, *Up Where, Cazaly?* (London, 1981), ch. 8.

Palmer, Esmonde Higgins, who had entertained such high hopes in 1920, was taking to frivolity. He proposed to learn dancing steps with the assistance of a gramophone to lift him out of his 'hellish gloomy' mood. He was pondering again over his sister Nettie's remark about people who accepted the Marxist philosophy as an explanation of life. He remembered her comment that life was not as simple as calling Mannix a 'fat prelate'. Marx had a simplistic view of salvation: life was much more complex than that. Inside the Labor Party the factions were still fighting over the spoils of office. Faction leaders were still levelling against each other charges of bribery and ballot rigging. The pamphlet war was still raging. One faction revealed in May 'More Aspects of Dooleyism'. Another asserted there was not a scrap of evidence against John Bailey. Factions used the language of the gutter rather than the language of brotherhood in their exchanges.[26]

While Labor consumed energy arguing over 'More Aspects of Dooleyism', Stanley Bruce had been doing some thinking. His departure for an Imperial Conference gave him the chance to tell Australians what was on his mind. He believed, he told the House of Representatives on 24 July 1923, in 'the maintenance of a united and strong British Empire', and that therefore, as 'true partners in the Empire', Australia should be given a proper opportunity to express an opinion upon imperial policy before the course to be taken by Britain was determined. That was one question he would take up with the British during the Imperial Conference in London. Australia should remain a member of the British Empire for two reasons. 'We must', he told the House, 'have regard to the position of Australia as it really is. I would ask those people who contend that Australia must provide for the defence of her own territory, how that is to be done?' Every one of Australia's capital cities, where manufacturing was centred, was situated on the coast. Australia did not have a naval force to repel an attack. Any attack from the sea on those centres would quickly drain away 'the life's blood of the country'. Australia must have an ally. There was only one natural ally for Australia and that was the rest of the British Empire.

The other reason was trade. Bruce has been doing a lot of thinking about the problems of Australian trade. Australia produced huge surpluses of wool, wheat, dairy products, meat and dried fruits, to mention only the principal commodities. She needed markets. British industry, falling behind in the race to compete with European and American manufactures, needed markets for her goods. The Mother Country was suffering and Australia too needed markets for her surplus production. He now believed in Imperial preference. So, he hoped and believed, did the British. That was what he

[26] E. M. Higgins to Dear Old Harry, 22 March 1925, E. M. Higgins Papers, Mitchell Library; Nettie Palmer to E. M. Higgins, 5 September 1921, ibid.; 'More Aspects of Dooleyism', *Australian Communist*, 4 May 1923; *Australian Worker*, 3 October 1923.

would advocate in London. 'The ties of Empire', he concluded, 'are really those of kinship and of a common sympathy arising out of mutual interests, certain ideals, and the great history of our race'. In London he proposed to 'strengthen the links of sentiment, self-interest, and self-defence'. For him Imperial preference meant more than 'the mere material advancement of different parts of the Empire'—Australia's future and Australia's greatness would be 'best served by remaining within the Empire.[27]

Jimmy Scullin, speaking in reply for the Australian Labor Party, could not go as far as that. He warned the Prime Minister and other 'swashbuckling Imperialists' that Australian Democracy would stand by the 'silken ties of kinship; which would last, but would not consent to 'the cast-iron bonds of Imperialism', which Labor believed would break. Labor feared that closer ties for defence and trade were not in the interests of the Australian people, and did not trust the British. Australia should not sacrifice the 'clean, honest lives of its men in a dishonest capitalistic intrigue'. Australia was the Brolga, the innocent New World country: Britain the Buln-Buln, the liar, the corrupt Old World country. Australia was the 'Young Tree Green', Britain the 'Old Dead Tree'. For Jimmy Scullin, the boy from the Australian bush, that Imperialist, George Arnot Maxwell, the Nationalist member for Fawkner, had uncovered the difference between the 'ties of Empire' men and the Labor believers in the cultivation of Australian national sentiment. Maxwell had said the Prime Minister is 'going Home'. But, said Jimmy Scullin, probably he meant that the right honorable gentleman was 'leaving home'. For the Nationalists and the Country Party, Britain was 'Home': for Labor, Australia was home. But timid Jimmy Scullin did not want to cut the painter, to cut loose. Labor wanted Australians to develop their own country. 'Politically, militarily, and diplomatically', he said, 'we shall mind our own business'.[28]

The Essons and the Palmers had plans to do something about Australia. But, like the conservative politicians, they had a double loyalty. Nettie Palmer wrote letters of encouragement to Australian writers. In her spare time she read Goethe's *Wilhelm Meister* in German, and Marcel Proust's *Du Côté de chez Swann* in French. The serious-minded still looked to the literature of the Old World for wisdom and understanding. In the nineteenth century the Russian intellectuals said: 'I am a Russian, but my religion is Greek'. In the twentieth century the Australian intellectuals could say: 'I am Australian, but my ideas come from Shakespeare, from Milton, from Dostoevsky, from Tolstoy. No Australian writer has taught me how to think or how to live'. The writers behaved like members of an embattled society of human beings.

[27] *C'wealth P.D.*, 24 July 1923, vol. 104, pp. 1478–94.
[28] Ibid., 31 July 1923, pp. 1876–85.

They were bitchy to each other. Hugh McCrae called another writer a 'strumpet for the butcher'. Dowell O'Reilly told Nettie Palmer that John Le Gay Brereton, the one-time Bohemian now dispensing sweetness and light behind 'College walls', had a cruel mouth, that he had understudied Christ all his life, with occasional lapses from the ideal. The writers stood for nothing. As Hilda Esson put it, 'no clear aim animated us'. Often they did not like Australians. 'I don't care for its people', Louis Esson wrote later to Vance Palmer. He did not like Melbourne either. Melbourne, he told Palmer, was 'a wowser, bourgeois town, without an idea of any kind, and intensely bored with its respectability and stupidity'.[29]

The prominent painters also had a love-hate relationship with the country and its people. Arthur Streeton, the innocent who had created *Purple Noon's Transparent Might*, was now selling his paintings for huge sums at exhibitions in Melbourne and Sydney. Commercialism and money values have blunted his sensibilities. Tom Roberts returned to Melbourne in February 1923 and settled down in the Sherbrooke Forest near Sassafras, painting the majestic mountain ash. He still wanted to convince himself and Australians that the gum tree was not 'an uninteresting excrescence on the face of the earth'. But he still did not know where he belonged—to the top hat and white tie Government House society, or to the bush people, the wearers of the bowyangs and the moleskins.[30]

William Baylebridge, poet and essayist, put forward a national religion for Australians, a religion which would lead to their 'transmutation to a higher form of life'. The battle between riches and poverty had been finalized: the battlefield was now the heart of man. God was dead, or had disappeared. Men had to decide what they were going to place between themselves and death. The improvers have argued that in a more just society human behaviour would improve, that bad conditions had made evil men and women, good conditions would make good men and women. The conservatives, led by Bruce and Page, believed their kind of material progress would increase happiness and well-being. Baylebridge rejected the assumption that material well-being was an essential condition of human happiness. He wanted Australians to know 'a higher form of life'. But he had few followers. Nettie Palmer lent him her ear, and replied in detail to all his witty letters on the

[29] Hugh McCrae to Vance Palmer, n.d., but probably 1923, Palmer Papers, Series 1, Box 4, Folder 30; Nettie Palmer to Dowell O'Reilly, 7 March 1923, ibid.; Dowell O'Reilly to Nettie Palmer, 30 August 1923, ibid.; Hilda Esson to Vance Palmer, n.d. probably 1923, ibid.

[30] Lionel Lindsay, 'Twenty-Five Years of Australian Art', *Art in Australia*, no. 4, 1918; *Bulletin*, 29 November 1923; Virginia Spate, *Tom Roberts* (Melbourne, 1972), pp. 126–7.

influence of a man of letters in a society where 'grocerdom' and the 'money-changers' set the tone of life.[31]

In his paintings and cartoons Norman Lindsay wanted to save Australians from the dark world of the parsons and the priests, but uncovered instead the darkness within himself. He wanted to form in Australia 'some sort of a place for art'. He believed, as he put it in a letter in 1922, the 'space is cleared and if cows and bagmen choose to dance upon it, at least the grass is kept from growing there, which is so much gained'. In his cartoons he portrayed Australians as ugly, ape-like creatures grunting after petty pleasures. He painted women as obscene vultures threatening to devour and swallow men. Anti-Christ had some private hell in his heart. He believed a society of 'bagmen' lacked the capacity to share in the artist's view of the world. For him humanitarianism and meliorism were just mawkish sentimentality. They were like religion: they were an opiate for the people. He believed there was no future for the masses. They belonged in the 'human ant bed': they went back to the mud from which they came. The 'great souls' turned the beauty and the terror of the world into art. There was an aristocracy composed of those who knew 'Beauty, Gaiety, Uprightness'. Lindsay was a bit of a puritan, and no devotee of the Dionysian frenzy. The great souls lived on in their art, mastered death. The Faun, the symbol of desire and poetry, and not the 'pale Galilean' would 'sound his pipes to call man to his high task'.[32]

The same ideas were put forward in the magazine *Vision*, edited by Norman Lindsay's son Jack, Kenneth Slessor, the poet, and Frank Johnson, publicist and critic. In their foreword to issue No. 1, May 1923, they proclaimed their intention to vindicate the youthfulness of Australia by being alive. Their ideal was beauty: they would deny 'all imagery that touches the body with disgust and ridicule'. *Vision*, they wrote, had its 'roots deep in life and sensation'. They would wage a war on the idea of evil preached by the priests and the parsons. Evil depressed the energy of Life by debasing the image of Beauty. In Australia the proportion of Ugliness was vastly in excess of Beauty. They would stimulate Vitality in Life.[33]

The master, Norman Lindsay, worked in his studio at Springwood in the Blue Mountains from dawn to dusk, and often far into the night. The master

[31] William Baylebridge, *This Vital Flesh* (Sydney, 1961), pp. xx–xxii; Noel Macainsh, *Nietzsche in Australia* (Munich, 1975), pp. 2–57; Judith Wright, 'William Baylebridge and the Modern Problem', *Southerly*, 3, 1955; letters of William Baylebridge to Nettie Palmer during 1923, Palmer Papers, Series 1, Box 4, Folder 30.

[32] Norman Lindsay to Hugh McCrae, n.d., probably 1922, R. G. Howarth and A. W. Barker (eds), *Letters of Norman Lindsay* (Sydney, 1979), p. 204; Norman Lindsay, *Creative Effort* (Sydney, 1920), pp. 1–4; Fergus Farrow, Norman Lindsay: an exercise in the history of ideas (thesis in Monash University Library, Clayton, Victoria).

[33] Foreword to *Vision*, no. 1, May 1923; Norman Lindsay, 'The Sex Synonym in Art', *Vision*, no. 1, May 1923.

preached 'Uprightness', discipline, self-restraint, and moderation in all things. The disciples were often libertarians. The master taught that God was dead: the disciples took this to mean that everything was allowable. The master preached that surrender to the wild passions in man led to terror, hate and destruction. The disciples believed there was 'precious metal in the dirt'. The master believed no artist should attempt to shout a message to humanity above 'the noise of men and trams'. The disciples loved 'the sights that dazzle' and the 'tempting sounds' of the cities. The father believed in the act of faith and virtue which creates great Art. The son, Ray, frequented the Bohemian haunts of Sydney. He liked watching the face of 'an old bitch named Rose Rooney . . . [an] arrogant fat old slut, with dyed ginger hair, her great dewlap of a throat encircled with jewelled necklaces and her fingers gleaming with diamonds'. He enjoyed listening to the latest story of the strange capers of the poet Christopher Brennan and his daughter Anne. The father had a desire and a longing for the beauty of the lotus flower: the son found the roots of the lotus flower in the mire of Sydney.[34]

As Stanley Bruce prepared to set out for London to assert the rights of Australians as 'true partners in the Empire', the Pioneer Players opened a short season of five one-act plays on 16 August—*Mates*, by Frank Brown, *The Great Man* by Katharine Prichard, *The Black Horse* by Vance Palmer, *The Trap* by Stewart Macky and *The Bishop and the Buns* by Ernest O'Ferrall. The weekly press, especially the *Bulletin* and the *Australasian*, were enthusiastic. The *Age* and the *Argus* either ignored the production or were condescending towards an Australian work. After the first night the numbers in the audience declined. Once again Frank Wilmot told Louis Esson what they needed for serious Australian plays was not a chucker-out, but a chucker-in. To the dismay of the Essons huge crowds roared with delight every night at the performance of Dennis's 'Sentimental Bloke' at the Theatre Royal in Melbourne. Each night audiences rocked with laughter when 'Erb los' his forlse teeth'. Louis Esson concluded that that was what the pioneer Players should expect from a society which had gone in 'heels up' for the world of 'grocerdom'. Hilda Esson confessed to Vance Palmer: 'what we have done is so much less than what it should be'. She and Louis did not know whether the failure was due to Melbourne's 'respectability and stupidity' or moles in their own beings.[35]

In the Labor movement there was also an ever-widening gap between the

[34] Norman Lindsay to A. G. Beutler, March 1922, R. G. Howarth and A. W. Barker (eds), op. cit., p. 203.

[35] *Bulletin*, 9, 23 August 1923; *Australasian*, 25 August 1923; Stewart Macky to Vance Palmer, n.d., probably August-September 1923; Hilda Esson to Vance Palmer, n.d., probably August-September 1923, and Louis Esson to Vance Palmer, 19 February 1924, Palmer Papers, Series 1, Box 4, Folders 30–31.

nobility of the conception and the ugliness of the creation. Men who believed 'My true name is Labour, though priests call me Christ' spoke of each other in the language of guttersnipes. The opponents of John Bailey, it was said, were still 'bubbling with fury' because he had been exonerated from charges of ballot rigging. The *Australian Worker* described Bailey's opponents as 'Pitiful specimens, with flaming eyes and poison-spitting lips, and intellects sodden with bitter bias . . . a species that is capable of sinking so low . . . howlers of hate'. In 1920, the year of the foundation of the Communist Party, there was 'the thrill of enthusiasm in the air'. The grand ideal of solidarity was the dominant factor of the day. Now in 1923 the radicals, including the communists and the supporters of the One Big Union, have to face a painful truth: radicalism has failed: the masses have not rallied to their support. In their anguish radicals blamed the failure not on what they stood for, or any aspect of their own behaviour—their humourlessness, their spiritual popery and bullying—but on the 'apathy, indifference and ignorance of the mass of the workers'.[36]

In 1923 the tactics of the communists changed. Hitherto they had abused the Labor Party as the buttress of capitalism: now they proposed to woo the Labor Party. Instructions have been issued in Moscow that the communists should seek to be admitted into the Labor Party. Hitherto they have treated the members of the Labor Party with 'aversion and contumely'. Now they were all 'seductive smiles' as they spoke of the virtues of a 'United Front'. The members of the Labor Party were warned to be on their guard. H. E. Boote in the *Australian Worker* on 10 October presented the case against the 'comrades'. Communists, he said, in the interests of the 'Cause', practised 'barefaced dishonesty'. For communists, obedience to Bolshevik authority (the Comintern in Moscow) differed very little from the prostrations of superstition. The communists believed in dictatorship, the rule of a minority imposed by force: Labor, by contrast, was democratic to the core, and repudiated 'with loathing the principles of terrorism when deliberately inculcated as a method of government'.[37]

On 19 October 1923 the State Executive of the Australian Labor Party in New South Wales decreed that no individual who persisted in the retention of his or her Communist Party membership could remain a member of the Australian Labor Party. All high-sounding talk by the communists about a united working-class front was 'the veriest and the vilest of hypocrisy'. Labor was not going to be tricked into allowing the communists treacherously to exploit the Labor Party for the 'accomplishment of their nefarious purposes'. Jock Garden was disappointed. The communists, he said after the decision was announced, would continue to fight for their right to be mem-

[36] *Australian Worker*, 10 October 1923; *O.B.U.: Why It Failed* (Sydney 1924), p. 3.
[37] *Australian Worker*, 10 October 1923.

bers of the Labor Party until the next Annual Conference gave its decision or until the Labor Party became 'clean'. The Labor Party bosses, he added, were afraid of the communists because they knew that they, the communists, wanted a 'cleaning up', and the 'loot men' wanted a cover-up, wanted corruption, chicanery, ballot rigging and 'Dooleyism' to go on for ever.

Jack Lang, the leader of the Labor Party, was delighted. Labor has suffered from the 'machinations of a handful of crooks during the past few years'. They should not take on men and women whose anti-Christian sentiments were utterly incompatible with the methods endorsed by the Australian Labor Party. The communists would turn Labor into a party of warring factions at a time when they should be a party united in opposition to the Nationalist Governments of most States and the Commonwealth. P. F. Loughlin pointed out in his pamphlet, *Ten Reasons Why Labor Should Continue to Exclude the Communist Party*, that the communists taught that religion was a poison which was still being instilled into the people. Under communism the shackles of religion, of a morality enslaved to private property, of a corrupt press and lying education would be thrown off. Out of their own mouths and pens the communists have shown they were enemies of liberty and of religion. The communists replied that a small army of capitalist-minded politicians, trade union officials and middle-class leaders of Labor had again blocked the advance of the Australian working class. These 'cowards and weaklings' who hounded down the militant workers were protecting the capitalist class. Their leader in New South Wales was Mr Jack Lang, a man who openly declared he did not know the meaning of the objective of the Australian Labor Party.[38]

Meanwhile Bruce was socializing with the Marquises and the Dukes, the Earls and the Lords, at the Imperial Conference in London. Bruce was not present at the opening of the Conference on 1 October, but attended all meetings of delegates after his arrival in London on 5 October. The British were most accommodating to the wish of W. L. Mackenzie King of Canada, W. M. Massey of New Zealand, and J. C. Smuts of South Africa that Dominions be consulted in any negotiations by the British Government for a treaty. The delegates agreed that before negotiations were opened to draft any treaty steps should be taken to ensure that any of the other Governments of the Empire likely to be interested were to be consulted. Bruce was also delighted with the role the British were assigning to Australia for the revival of British industry. He asked English businessmen to recognize that the only way to develop the Dominions was by finding a market for what

[38] *Australian Worker*, 24 October, 14 November 1923; *Smith's Weekly*, 24 November 1923; P. F. Loughlin, *Ten Reasons Why Labor Should Continue to Exclude the Communist Party* (Parramatta, n.d.); 'The Political Labor Conference in New South Wales', *Round Table*, September 1923; *Workers' Weekly*, 19 October 1923.

they produced. He told the businessmen of London: 'You brought us into existence. You have some responsibility for us and you cannot shirk it'. He was ready to go back to Australia with a message of hope: Australia could absorb some of Britain's surplus population: Australia could buy British manufactured goods, and Britain buy Australian primary produce.

Bruce was not intimidated by any Bolshevik talk accusing him of committing Australia to the role of lackey of British imperialism. He shared to the full the sentiments of affection and respect for His Majesty expressed by the delegates at the end of the Conference. He agreed with them that 'amid the economic and political convulsions which have shaken the world, the British Empire stands firm and that its widely scattered peoples remain one in their belief in its ideals and their faith in its destiny'. That was his faith. On his way back to Australia he visited Gallipoli. He stood there on the beach where the Australians had landed on 25 April 1915, and drew strength to face the future. He did not want Australians ever to lose the spirit of 'Lest We Forget'. He was on holy ground. Gallipoli was a shrine for those who believed in the King and the Empire. Anzac and the Empire were now part of the creed of Australian conservatism, part of the secular religion.[39]

Before Bruce whispered 'Lest We Forget' on the beach at Gallipoli the commotion he and his fellow conservatives dreaded occurred in Australia. Riot and anarchy broke out in the streets of Melbourne. For years the Victorian police had sought redress for their grievances. They had sought to achieve this by constitutional means, but officialdom had turned a deaf ear. They were not allowed to form a trade union or join another trade union, and seek redress through the Arbitration Court: they were not permitted direct access to Parliament: they were refused publicity for their grievances in the newspapers. They wanted an increase in their pay of at least one shilling a day, which would still have left them with wages lower than those paid to police in other States. Exasperated by the Minister's parsimony and cheese-paring policy, the rank and file became desperate. In this delicate situation the Chief Commissioner introduced a system of plain-clothes police supervisors. The men, promptly nicknaming them 'spooks', demanded they be withdrawn. The Chief Commissioner refused. On 31 October the night constables refused to go on duty. The Victorian Government told the men they must either return to work or be dismissed. The men refused. On the night of 2 November, with a much depleted police patrol, there were acts of hooliganism. Neither side would give way. General Monash phoned the Naval and Military Club and called for volunteers. At a ball on the eve of the

[39] Summary of Proceedings of Imperial Conference, Commons Papers, Reports from Commissioners, 1923, vol. 12, Cmd. 1987, pp. 13, 24; Cecil Edwards, *Bruce of Melbourne* (London, 1965), pp. 102–4.

Derby Sir William Glasgow took a number of young men aside and warned them 'things were very serious'. They assured him they were ready to serve. The Chiefs of the Army, Navy and Air Force held a conference and decided to cancel all leave.[40]

The following day, Derby Day, 3 November 1923, Page caught the morning express from Sydney to Melbourne. A crisis was imminent. That evening, mobs of thugs and hooligans gathered in the centre of Melbourne after the races. Drunk men stood in front of trams and forced them to stop. The driver of one tram was hauled from his cabin, thrown on the ground, and trampled on to the cheers of a drunken mob. The window of the Ezywalkin boot and shoe store in Bourke Street was smashed with bricks. Looters began to fill their sacks and bags. Within minutes the windows of the Leviathan, London Stores and Dunklings were also smashed and the looters were scrambling for jewellery, furs, sporting goods, musical instruments, tobacco, safety razors, cameras, and men's and women's clothing. There were fights. A lad wearing a Scotch cap performed a wild dance on the top of a tram car. Hooting, shouting, laughing, singing broke out amongst the crowd of five thousand. Not a policeman was in sight. A clergyman produced a Bible and, holding it aloft above the crowd, endeavoured to quieten the noisy masses, just as, in the Psalms, Jehovah had once stilled the madness of the people. A drunken man, using, it was said, the 'language of the sewer', commanded the clergyman to shut up, but when the latter refused the drunkard knocked the clergyman to the ground and trampled on him. The voices of the respectable were heard complaining that the mob had taken the side of the strikers. The mob cheered those sentiments to the echo.

The cry went up: 'Where are the police? We want the police'. It was not till 7 p.m., two hours after the riot began, that a small contingent of police arrived to assist the sailors in restoring order. But still the vandalism and the looting continued. At 9 p.m. the looters went to work at the intersection of Bourke and Elizabeth Streets. 'Window after window fell with a resounding crash to the footpath', as the *Age* described the scene, and the contents were quickly snatched by the bands of insane hoodlums, who were assisted in their work by a fleet of waiting motor cars. Jewellery was their chief object, but articles of all descriptions were taken by thousands of people.

Within an hour all the shopfronts in Bourke Street between Elizabeth Street and Swanston Street were a mass of ruins, denuded of their goods. A howling riotous mob inflamed to fury by strong drink and the hope of loot

[40] 'The Victorian Police Strike', *Round Table*, vol. 14, no. 54, pp. 385–91; 'The Melbourne Police Strike', *Stead's Review*, 24 November 1923; *Argus*, 1, 2 November 1923; Andrew Moore, 'Send Lawyers, Guns and Money!' A Study of Conservative Para-Military Organisations in New South Wales, 1930–32, thesis in La Trobe University Library, pp. 122–30.

roamed up and down Bourke Street. The management of picture theatres in the city and the suburbs flashed on the screens:

> 'The Ministry asks all returned soldiers to rally round General ('Pompey') Elliott at the Melbourne Town Hall to enrol as special constables, and assist in preventing further looting in the city.'

Soon at the Town Hall there were scenes reminiscent of the Great War in the early months of recruiting, as young, old and middle-aged men enrolled as special constables ('specials'). Leading commercial and professional men took the oath. Victorian and interstate graziers in Melbourne for the Cup took the oath and marched out with the squads. One Danish citizen volunteered but was rejected because he could not take an oath to the British King. 'I am sorry', he said, as boisterous, happy diggers grabbed their truncheons and marched off to give a lesson to all looters and hooligans. The police arrived. Arrests were made—55 all told. The imminent departure of the last trams and trains thinned the mob. Theatre crowds poured into the streets to see the damage done while they were enjoying themselves. But well after midnight there were still cries of 'After him' as yet another looter made his dash for safety.

On that Saturday night and the following Sunday, 4 November, what the *Age* called the 'cream of the manhood of the metropolis' volunteered to serve as 'special constables'. They were determined that 'Victoria's name shall not be further stained by the vicious deeds of the community'. Five hundred enrolled on Saturday. By Sunday evening two thousand had enrolled, some estimates putting the figure as high as six thousand.

In the eyes of the good bourgeois the 'worst elements' in Australia had a long history of antagonism to the police. It had begun in the convict period, been sanctified in popular tradition by the exploits of the bushrangers Ben Hall and Ned Kelly, and strengthened during the strikes of the 1890s. 'Yarraside' must stand firm. Sir Arthur Robinson, the Victorian Attorney-General, announced that the police who had mutinied would never be re-engaged. They had been found lacking in the high ethical standards 'Yarraside' demanded of the guardians of the public peace. They could never be trusted again. Those who had stood loyally by the State would be treated 'in a manner advantageous to them'. An influential citizens' committee was formed.[41]

On Sunday afternoon, there was a confrontation between twenty 'specials' and a number of young fellows outside Scots Church in Collins Street. Insults and obscenities were exchanged. The 'specials' called on the youths to disperse. The youths refused. The 'specials' swung their batons and charged. The youths fled for safety. Someone in the Congregational

[41] *Age*, 5 November 1923; *Argus*, 5 November 1923.

Church turned on the switch, and the electric cross shone out in the Melbourne Sunday gloom. The crowd dispersed. But 'hooligans' from the working-class districts continued to jeer at any man or woman from a class different from their own. The 'specials' and the Light Horse men terrorized the 'hooligans', who were driven off the streets. The city's property was guarded all night by companies of 'specials'. 'Fascisti', in the words of the *Workers' Weekly* were driving round the streets of Melbourne guarding the property of the bourgeoisie: the motor car has become a weapon in the class war.

General Monash, who was entrusted by 'Yarraside' with the task of restoring law and order, had his usual victory. An army officer asked General Monash to form some League which would be at the service of the Government to maintain law and order. There was talk of a White Guard. But the traditional Melbourne bourgeois calm-down soon removed the need for armed protectors of bourgeois society. In Australia riots never blossom into revolution, and there was no tradition of the army as an overt arm of government. The police strikers sought reinstatement. The Government replied with an uncompromising 'No'. The strikers have committed the sin against the Holy Ghost in the bourgeois world: they have exposed property to the hungers of hoodlums and hooligans. The safety of property was the supreme law. No violation could be pardoned. The cheese-parers of Melbourne have won. Bourgeois society has been saved from the mob.[42]

On 23 November, after the return of calmer days, Station 2SB broadcast the first Australian radio programme from a room in the *Smith's Weekly* building in Sydney. The programme consisted of classical and popular music, stock exchange and market reports, news items, weather information, special talks for women with emphasis on fashion and personal hygiene, and bed-time stories for children told by Mr Sandman. Wireless broadcasting promised to keep the people in their homes and off the streets. Radio was like the press: it was a purveyor of bourgeois respectability. Even artists were conforming. Arthur Streeton, the painter in 1888 of *Golden Summer* has become a successful businessman. In Farmer's Exhibition Hall in Sydney in November 1923 his paintings were sold for six times the price they fetched in 1888. As the *Bulletin* put it, 'the pound sterling has trailed her glittering robe on the front page' of a catalogue of an artist's works.[43]

Things were still going well for Bob Menzies. He became the father of a son that year. He had a weekend house at Macedon next to Staniforth

[42] *Table Talk*, 8 November 1923; *Australian Worker*, 7, 14 November 1923; John R. Haughton James, 'The Guardsmen are Born', *Nation*, 11 March 1961; K. Amos, *The New Guard Movement 1931–1935* (Melbourne, 1976), pp. 10–11; *Age*, 6 November 1923; *Workers' Weekly*, 16 November 1923; Andrew Moore, op. cit., pp. 129–30.

[43] *S.M.H.*, 24 November 1923; *Bulletin*, 29 November 1923.

Ricketson, stock-broker of Melbourne and future power-broker of Australian politics. Menzies was climbing to the top. He became a director in the firm of J. B. Were and Son, the Australian Foundation Investment Company, and the National Reliance Investment Company. Success in the world has not mellowed him. Despite the warning that anyone who said of another 'Thou fool' would be in danger of hell-fire, Menzies still enjoyed ridiculing men of weak intellects for presenting arguments in the form of 'tripe'. He still asked them insolently whether they had anything between their ears. With Bruce and Page in power and 'Yarraside' in the saddle it was a promising time for King and Empire men. John Curtin was going for solitary walks on the beach at Cottesloe looking for answers to questions which concerned him as a Labor man: could Labor be pragmatic without becoming corrupt? Must Australia always be dependent on the British Navy for the defence of her shores? How could he overcome the weakness which stood between him and the fulfilment of his destiny as a Labor leader? He has not lost his faith. For him Labor was still the 'great cause'. He has not forsworn the hope, or become cynical. There was a man within, whom those privileged to know never forgot. He had a power to make people worship and idolize him.[44]

At year's end copies of the novel, *Kangaroo*, by D. H. Lawrence arrived in Australia. In the letters he had written earlier from Australia to his friends overseas, and in this novel, he wrote that he was puzzled by the spirit of the place. The Australian bush was 'biding its time with a terrible ageless watchfulness, waiting for a far-off end, watching myriad intruding white men'. His eye has noticed 'the wonderful Southern night-sky, that makes a man feel so lonely, alien'. The terror of the bush had overwhelmed him in Australia. 'He looked at the weird, white, dead trees, and into the hollow distances of the bush. Nothing! Nothing at all.' In Australia he had known the 'deep mystery of joy' sitting on the edge of the bush as twilight fell. The bush had a 'deep mystery for him'.

About the people and their future he was not so sure. He was appalled by Australian slovenliness. He wondered whether the people, with their vast indifference, would ever waken this ancient land, or whether the land would 'put them to sleep, drift them back into the torpid semi-consciousness of the world of the twilight'. He was puzzled by the '*vacancy* of this freedom' in Australia, 'this new chaos', 'this Englishness all crumpled out into formlessness and chaos'. Australia, he found to his dismay, was a country with no inner life, no interest in anything, a country where the people loved the sense of release from old pressures and old tight control, from the old world

[44] Cameron Hazlehurst, *Menzies Observed* (Sydney, 1979), pp. 35–43; Lloyd Ross, *John Curtin* (Melbourne, 1977), pp. 75–7; *Westralian Worker*, 22 December 1922.

of water-tight compartments', a country where the people were 'working without any meaning' and 'playing without any meaning'. He wanted to know why so far in Australian history there had not been an 'earthquake that would capsize a tumbler of hot punch'. He heard from the angry men on the Right and the angry men on the Left their ideas on what to do about the 'emptiness' in Australia. He wondered how long a people without any opinions, without any ideas, without any feeling for what the people of the Old World called 'spirit' or 'soul' could survive. He asked himself the questions: 'Is it merely running down, however, like a machine running on but gradually running down?' He asked how long 'the heavy established European way of life' would last in Australia.[45]

The Australian reviewers did not even discuss the questions Lawrence had put. The *Bulletin*, in its most complacent, patronizing mood, saw no point in trying to 'probe into Mr Lawrence's heart'. Anyhow, they continued, 'he has written a very beautiful book that is full of the sunshine and flowers of Australia, with many quiet little gibes at our peculiarities at which nobody could take offence unless he is determined to take offence'. *Stead's Review* observed that Mr Lawrence had 'a very rare gift for catching atmosphere', but found much of the work 'tedious and vague', and the main character, Richard Lovat Somers, the man of Derbyshire, 'mean and little of soul'. Later A. G. Stephens dismissed Lawrence as an author of 'over-sexed earlier novels . . . heavy with English summer farmyard odours; effective in creating a thick atmosphere of rutting swine'. *Kangaroo*, he wrote in one wild swipe, was a novel of 'fantastic dullness'. On Lawrence's other book on Australia, written in collaboration with Molly Skinner, *The Boy in the Bush*, Vance Palmer was 'breathless with astonishment at the book's badness'.

Bruce and Page carried on as though the British were still the 'heroes of humanity'. Page was not interested in all this concern about an absence of 'spirit' or 'soul' in Australia. He was a partner in 'an essentially practical government'. The London experience has strengthened Bruce's faith in the 'Imperial firm of wealth, progress and opportunities unlimited'. In China Mao Tse-Tung was asking: Who rules over man's destiny?—and dreaming of setting the people of China afire with words of revolution, and teaching the people to count 'the mighty no more than muck'. In the Rhineland D. H. Lawrence, with the eye of the prophet to see into the heart of the matter, predicted that the Ruhr occupation and English nullity would drive Germany back to 'the destructive vortex of Tartary', that the 'heroes of human-

[45] D. H. Lawrence, *Kangaroo* (London, 1923, reprint of 1950), pp. 9–10, 24, 398, 198, 387, 187, 18–19.

ity' were hatching a brood of 'dangerous, lurking barbarians' in Germany. In Australia men and women were singing around the pianola:

> Oh I wish I had someone to love me,
> I'm tired of living alone.

Life is immense.[46]

[46] *Times Literary Supplement*, 20 September 1923; *Bulletin*, 13 December 1923; *Age*, 12 December 1923; *Stead's Review*, 12 January 1923, pp. 65–6; *Bookfellow*, 29 November 1924; Nettie Palmer to Esther Levey, 19 December 1924, Vivian Smith (ed.), *Letters of Vance and Nettie Palmer 1915–1963* (Canberra, 1977), pp. 23–4; D. H. Lawrence, 'A Letter From Germany', in Edward D. McDonald (ed.), *Phoenix* (London, 1936), pp. 107–10; Robin Boyd, *Australia's Home* (Melbourne, 1952, Penguin Books edn, 1968), p. 92; Mao Tse Tung, 'Changsha', *Mao Tse Tung Poems* (Peking, 1976), pp. 1–2.

7

THE GREAT IMPERIAL FIRM OF WEALTH, PROGRESS AND OPPORTUNITIES UNLIMITED

IN THE NEW YEAR OF 1924 Bruce came back from the Imperial Conference in London strengthened in his resolve to shape Australia's future as a partner in the British Empire. In March 1924 Vice-Admiral Sir Frederick Field, the commander of the British fleet (including the battleships *Hood* and *Repulse*) then visiting Australia, told the Commercial Travellers' Club in Melbourne that trade was the father of the British navy. The provision by Great Britain of better markets for Dominion products would result in Empire prosperity that would make Empire defence comparatively easy. The British were the 'great commercial travellers of history'. Bruce heeded 'His Master's Voice'. At the opening of the Royal Show in Sydney on 16 April he spoke of the duty of Australians to develop 'the most potentially rich, uninhabited country on the face of the globe'. To carry out this great task, he continued, 'we must increase our man power, expand our financial resources, and secure ever-widening markets for our production'. 'Men, money and markets' became the slogan of the Bruce–Page Government.[1]

Australia needed men. The five and a half million people in Australia were not enough to carry out the great task. Australia needed men and women of British stock. Bruce and Page and all right-minded people agreed on that. The *West Australian* said Australia needed 'millions of Australians . . . to uphold the Union Jack of Empire'. The 'land of freedom and sunshine' could be defended only with a larger population. A larger population would provide more markets for Australian industry. Australia needed 'all the British blood she could get'. The United Kingdom had a surplus population; Australia had the empty spaces. All the people in high places agreed that as far as possible the newcomers should be Britishers. Migration from the British Isles would promote what they all wanted to promote: 'The Great Imperial Firm of Wealth, Progress, and Opportunities Unlimited'.[2]

Some intellectuals had their doubts. Louis Esson thought Melbourne was already too much a 'wowser, bourgeois town' in which he was 'intensely bored'. Melbourne, and indeed Australia, did not need more of the same.

[1] *Argus*, 19 March 1924; *Business Efficiency*, May 1924, p. 813.
[2] *Argus*, 12 May 1923; *West Australian*, 23 March, 16 April 1923.

Melbourne needed variety, men and women who knew the Dionysian frenzy, not these cosy crumpet eaters, these British Philistines. The Palmers have had letters from friends overseas about a degenerate Europe. The Palmers thought they needed less, rather than more, of the spirit of Old England in Australia. A few years previously two members of the Railways Union in Melbourne had been dismissed for calling the 'Black and Tans' in Ireland 'hired assassins'. Nettie Palmer was reading *Babbitt* by Sinclair Lewis. The Protestant Federation in Melbourne already aped Babbittry. They had a resolution on their books: 'No head of a Department ought to be a Catholic. No good Protestant ought to have to serve under a Catholic'. The suburban intelligentsia wanted liberators from Babbittry, not reinforcers.[3]

Bruce had again committed Australia to British migrants at the Imperial Conference in October and November 1923. After consultation with the Dominions the British Government had drafted the Imperial Land Settlement scheme in 1922. The idea was for the British, the Commonwealth and the six States to join in a scheme for the settlement of people of British stock in British Dominions overseas. On 19 February 1923, during the negotiations for the formation of the Bruce–Page Government, the Governments of New South Wales, Victoria and Western Australia signed agreements with the Commonwealth and the British Governments to carry out the scheme. Yeomen from Devon would create another Devon in the Australian wilderness: the men of Somerset, where the cider apples grow, would plant another England in the land of sunshine and freedom. The Government of Western Australia agreed to take seventy-five thousand British migrants and settle them on the land. They agreed to provide three days of hospitality for them, place them in suitable employment during a probationary period, and then help them to begin farming on their blocks. Migration literature read like an invitation to a walk in the Paradise Gardens.[4]

One migrant from Devon found to his dismay that he and his family were housed in tin sheds near their blocks until they built a house of their own. They had expected a stone cottage with vine leaves covering the walls. When his wife saw their future house was a tin shed, her 'heart was up in her mouth straight away'. She told her husband she had come to the end of her days. There was worse to come. In the block ballot he got a swamp on his farm. After a few weeks working to clear the land his hands were 'red raw with blisters'. To drain the block he worked at times with only his head and

[3] Louis Esson to Vance Palmer, 19 February 1924, Palmer Papers, Series 1, Box 4, Folder 31; Diary of Nettie Palmer, 16, 17 March 1921, Palmer Papers, Series 16, Box 25; Nettie Palmer to Esmonde Higgins, 10 June 1923, E. M. Higgins Papers, M.L.

[4] *West Australian*, 28 February, 18 May 1923; L. Hunt, Group Settlements in Western Australia, *University Studies in Western Australian History*, vol. 3, no. 2, October 1958; First Annual Report of the Development and Migration Commission, *C'wealth P.P.*, 1926–27–28, vol. 5.

shoulders above the water. There were no schools, no shops, no churches, nothing of what he and his wife understood by civilization, only the vast indifference of the bush, and the immensity of the sky above. He was paying a high price for sunshine and freedom. In June 1924 he heard the Premier of Western Australia, Philip Collier, say on the first broadcast from Perth that the radio would bring the comforts and pleasures of city life to the country. There would be 'opportunities unlimited' in Western Australia for those prepared to work. But that was small comfort to a man from Devon who got up six days of the week at four in the morning and 'slaved his guts out', and was called a 'bloody Pommy' or a 'whingeing Pom' if he risked opening his heart to any Aussie on what he and his wife had to endure.[5]

Another woman in England read greedily the literature in Australia House about the group settlements in Western Australia. She persuaded her husband to sell all they possessed, including her engagement and wedding rings, 'make a break' and start a new and better life near Albany. There in the bush there were no lavatories, no roads, no doctors, no hospital, no beds, no milk, no fruit. She and the children slept on the bare earth, sometimes in a tent, sometimes in a tin shack, while her husband slept under the sky. She missed the familiar sights, smells and sounds of civilized life—the pubs, church bells, factory sirens, the roar of a football crowd, and the uproar of the music hall. Instead she had to endure the silence of the Australian bush, and the pitiless Australian sun which shone down on her from that very vast sky with often not even a cloud to add variety to the scene. As compensation she had what the migrant literature had called 'the freedom to roam wherever the spirit moved her'. But the questions were: where? and: how and when would they be rescued from the hell they were enduring? To add to her misery, by day she was plagued by flies, and by might by mosquitoes: by day and night both, there were fleas.

Within a year her burdens were eased. Cows were in milk, pigs slaughtered for meat, vegetables grew, crops were sown, schools and churches were built. The Government planned to build a railway line, and to build roads and bridges to allow motor cars to come into the district. The wireless reduced the isolation and the loneliness, while feeding the restlessness. Like the selectors, the closer settlers and the soldier settlers, the 'groupies' ran up debts to the nearest store-keepers on the security of their 'blocks'. Within two years the store-keepers threatened foreclosure against hopeless debtors. By April 1924 when Bruce was telling his audience at the Sydney Show how the man on the land in Australia had been 'bountifully blessed by Nature' 32 per cent of the immigrant group settlers and 42 per cent of Australian-born 'groupies' have walked off their blocks. In Australia the world belonged to

[5] Anon, 'Warning to migrants from one with nearly twelve years' experience, quoted in G. C. Bolton, *A Fine Country to Starve In* (Perth, 1972), pp. 40–1.

the tough. But the promises of the politicians continued. The British had fought the fight against the German menace and would win another victory over the Australian bush. So while the 'groupies' got up at crack of dawn and slaved all day, Sir Joseph Cook, the High Commissioner in London, told prospective migrants that Australia was 'the land of the better chance'. There was 'sunshine and laughter' in Australia.[6]

On King Island in Bass Strait the soldier settlers and migrants suffered the same fate as their counterparts in other areas. The first white inhabitants on the Island late in 1888 had come to a place where there were no roads, only bush tracks, no shops, no schools or churches. The only communication with Tasmania was the lighthouse boat which called once every three months with supplies. The first houses were built of timber washed up on the shore from passing boats. The survivors had the qualities of the Australian bush-man, the heroic qualities which contributed to the Digger legend—the courage, the physical strength, the enterprise, the daring and the toughness to survive even the mud of Flanders or a winter on the Somme. The number volunteering between 1914 and 1918 was high, and so was the number eligible for soldier settlement on the Island. Fifty farm sites were allotted. From 1917 to 1924 men and women slaved to clear the land, and build a dairy of green poles with a dirt floor. The cows carried bells around their necks, as the paddocks were still covered with scrub. The cows were milked by hand, and the women made their own butter and carted it to the township of Currie, as Bruce held out that ray of hope at the Sydney Show that his Government would find markets for Australian produce.

The bush legend was still very much alive. On 21 March 1924 a very large gathering of people watched their local member of Parliament, A. H. Grimm, M.L.A. for Murrumbidgee, unveil a memorial obelisk to Henry Lawson on the site of his birth at Grenfell, New South Wales. To great cheering he quoted from the Henry Lawson poem: 'Said Grenfell to my spirit'

> You were born on Grenfell goldfield
> And you can't get over that.

Lawson's poems, he said, were Australia's history, the history of the bush. But when they sang, they sang a well-loved English song: 'Home, Sweet Home'. A trumpeter sounded the 'Last Post'. Henry Lawson's widow and her daughter thanked the people of Grenfell for their kindness. Five gum trees were planted around the obelisk. The bush people were honouring the man who had looked on them with the eye of pity and understanding.[7]

[6] G. C. Bolton, op. cit., pp. 43–7; Report of Royal Commission on Group Settlement, *V. & P.* of the Legislative Assembly of W.A., vol. 1, 1925; *West Australian*, 19 February 1923; *Soldier*, 20 June 1923.

[7] C. Sullivan, *King Island* (Currie, King Island, 1979), pp. 43–8, 81–3; *Argus*, 22 March 1924; personal visit to Henry Lawson obelisk at Grenfell, 20 October 1986.

Bruce was himself a businessman. In his private life he followed the way of life of those who believed in conspicuous consumption. For a pre-breakfast gallop on the tan in the Melbourne Domain he wore riding breeches and woollen socks, tan brogue shoes, a Viyella shirt and an elegant, unobtrusive bow-tie. On formal occasions he wore a swallow-tailed coat, striped trousers and black shoes, sometimes partly covered by spats. He had the appropriate motor car for every occasion, always driven by a uniformed chauffeur, who touched his cap to his master with the elegance of the chauffeurs of London's West End.

Frank Anstey made political capital out of Bruce's connection with the 'rag-trade'. Bruce, he said, posed as an Australian Scot—a member of one of those Presbyterian families which had created Melbourne, the city 'sodden with rectitude', uprightness and respectability. But, said Anstey, if you looked at the portrait of Bruce,you would see his family came from the East End of London, and made a fortune in the rag trade in Flinders Lane. Bruce was not a man to lose his composure when the tormentors of Melbourne tried to cut him down. Bruce was an enigma, the soul of courtesy, the man with the public face. He never let anyone see his private face, though observers with the eye of pity were intrigued by the becoming melancholy, the sad eyes, and the charm of the smile, which was all he ever let anyone see of the man within. Clothes were part of the wall he built to protect himself against intruders. When he wrapped the muffler of a Cambridge Blue around his neck, it was not just to keep out the cold.[8]

As a businessman Bruce understood the problem of finding markets. Australian producers, he knew, must find customers both for the products of industry and the produce of the man on the land. The task of government, he said on 16 April, was to see clearly on what principles they should act in rendering assistance to finding markets for Australia's own secondary industry producers. That was one of the tablets of the law in Australia. He did not propose to challenge it, even though he knew protection would probably increase the costs of production and so make Australian goods uncompetitive in foreign markets. The problem was how to assist the primary producers—all those industries which must 'seek their necessary markets overseas'. It was inequitable to help the secondary producers to markets, and do nothing for those who had to find their outlets overseas. The Government has committed itself to bringing more primary producers to Australia: there must be markets for their produce. The answer, he said, was to give the primary producers a measure of assistance equivalent to what had been done in the tariff for secondary producers. Much has to be done. Marketing systems must be devised. The discussions on Imperial preference

[8] Cecil Edwards, *Bruce of Melbourne* (London, 1965), pp. 82, 105–6; Louis Esson to Vance Palmer, 21 September 1925, Palmer Papers, Series 1, Box 4, Folder 33.

begun at the London Conference of October 1923 must be continued. Bruce was moving inexorably towards binding Australia in an Imperial vice. His Government, he believed, was setting 'the foundations of a great democracy . . . [to] populate and develop our great empty spaces, and realise the full destiny that lies before Australia'.[9]

Australia also needed money. Threadneedle Street in London must do for Mr Money Man what Dooley Street did for the big butter and egg men of Australia: the little old lady of Threadneedle Street must be their saviour. The British must invest their capital. In return prosperous Australians would buy British goods: Australia and New Zealand must revive 'the sick man of Europe'. For generations to come there would be more than 'the silken threads of kinship' binding Australians to the King and the Empire: there would be economic ties. But one day borrowers must repay the bond-holders. Borrowers might one day have their lives controlled in part by the bond-holders. It never occurred to Bruce, the Cambridge Blue, the captain in the Royal Fusiliers, that the little old lady of Threadneedle Street might turn into a tyrant. It never occurred to him that Australia was pawning her independence. He was the Chairman of the 'Great Imperial Firm of Wealth, Progress and Opportunities Unlimited'.[10]

Labor was harmless. The communists have not blossomed into a mass movement. Publicly in the *Workers' Weekly*, on the Sydney Domain and on Melbourne's Yarra Bank on Sunday afternoons, their members still prophesied the day of reckoning for capitalist society was at hand. They were evangelists singing the well-known hymn: 'Tell me the old, old story':

> Tell me the story often,
> For I forget so soon.
> The early dew of morning,
> Has passed away at noon.

Privately their leaders were asking themselves why they had failed to develop into a mass movement. They were already pointing an accusing finger at the apathy and ignorance of the Australian working classes. Like prophets of the Old Testament they savaged the very people they hoped to redeem.

Within the Australian Labor Party in New South Wales there were still Kilkenny cat fights between the factions as believers in 'Fraternity' accused their rivals of deeds of moral turpitude, just as those other professors of the universal embrace, the Christians, found the difficult thing was to love one another. Unseemly scenes occurred at the Easter Conference of the New South Wales party. One hundred men stormed into the Conference of the Australian Labor Party, doorkeepers were overpowered, delegates were

[9] *S.M.H.*, 17 April 1924.
[10] Ibid.

beaten and women badly scared. Bruce and Page were paragons of civilized behaviour: Labor was a bear-pit, in which the strong and the cunning overpowered the weak. In the Federal sphere, ever since Labor 'blew out its brains' in November 1916, Labor leaders have been distinguished by a dullness so deep that no one could fathom it, or by the brilliant malice and mockery of Frank Anstey.[11]

At the same time Bruce and Page took steps to ensure that Labor remained in opposition for a long time. On 1 May 1924, in a speech in Adelaide, Bruce suggested that the two coalition partners should discuss the terms for an electoral agreement. They must prepare for the elections due in 1925. Discussions were held. On 29 May the terms of a new pact were announced. The two parties agreed not to contest each other's seats at the forthcoming election. All seats held by the Nationalists would be contested by the Nationalist Party, and all seats held by the Country Party by the Country Party. In seats held by neither, both sides could field candidates but every effort would be made to reach agreement between the Parties on which of the two was most likely to win the seat. They agreed there should be an exchange of preferences between the two Parties. For the Senate a group of candidates should consist of two Nationalist candidates and one Country Party nominee. Within both Parties there were misgivings. Neither Party could now increase its numbers except at the expense of the Labor Party and, with Labor getting slowly stronger, that seemed unlikely. The radical wing of the Country Party fumed about this sell-out to Australian conservatism. Some Nationalists said the arrangement for the Senate elections was too high a price to pay for remaining in office. Conservatives have agreed to surrender much to Page and his 'hayseeds' to keep Labor out. Pride, vanity, and many other things must be subordinated to that 'great, good thing'.[12]

At public ceremonies loyalty to the Empire was presented as 'the great, good thing'. On Anzac Day, 25 April 1924, speakers told their listeners they were there to honour those who had proved that Australians were worthy of belonging to the British race. Australians had won the right to emulate that 'hardy, free-born race . . . under the cloudless skies of the Southern Cross'. On Empire Day, 24 May, the children in the State Schools were told: 'Great deeds won your Empire; and great deeds alone can keep it'. The Empire had its own code of behaviour: 'play the game', 'to seek, to strive and not to yield', 'work is worship' and 'love is service'. Children of the British Empire should follow the splendid example set by their King: he was an early riser: he read the Bible every day: he went to church every Sunday.[13]

[11] *S.M.H.*, 19 April 1924; *Australian Worker*, 16, 23 April 1924.

[12] *Argus*, 2 May 1924; *Age*, 30 May 1924; Ulrich Ellis, *A History of the Australian Country Party* (Melbourne, 1963), pp. 121–2.

[13] *School Paper* (Victoria), Grades VII and VIII, 1 April 1924, p. 34, and Grades V and VI, May 1924, p. 51, 2 June 1924, p. 65.

Australia was about to enjoy 'Opportunities Unlimited'. On 4 June 1924 the first aeroplane providing an airmail service between capital cities landed at Mascot in Sydney after flying from Adelaide, taking a day longer than the planned one-day journey. But the pilot, Lieutenant F. S. Briggs, was confident that next time they would do the trip in one day. *En route* they picked up the mails from Mildura, Hay, Narrandera and Cootamundra. Earlier in December 1921 Perth and Derby had been linked by air, and in December 1922 Charleville and Cloncurry. The aeroplane has begun to transcend distance and isolation.[14]

In mid-July 1924 Senator H. J. M. Payne introduced into the Senate a Private Member's Bill to make voting compulsory in elections for the House of Representatives and the Senate. Registration on the electoral roll had been compulsory since 1911 for all adults except Aborigines and Torres Strait Islanders. Queensland had introduced compulsory voting for the Legislative Assembly in 1915. In the election of 1922 only 57.95 per cent of those registered had voted—and that was not the lowest percentage in recent years. In introducing the Bill on 17 July Senator Payne explained that compulsory voting would ensure that laws would in future be enacted by a majority of electors represented by the majority of members in the Parliament. He believed Parliament should force those who lived under a democratic form of government to see that it was democratic 'not only in name, but in deed'. The proposal roused little interest. The Senators and the Representatives treated it as the great yawn of the Parliamentary year. Members of both Chambers stayed away in droves. The three political parties made no decision either way. The Bill was rushed through. Bruce and Page did not oppose it. There was an idea abroad that the indifferent, if compelled to vote, would be conservative. The Act received the royal assent on 31 July 1924.[15]

Women were also demanding an opportunity to play an active role in Australian public life. The first Electoral Act of 1902 gave women the right to vote and the right to be elected. But, as with the radicals in the Labor movement, the women have decided that the ballot box was not the key to power in Australia. Women wanted 'other things'. Article 7 of the Covenant of the League of Nations declared that all positions in the Secretariat of the League should be open to both men and women. Women demanded that Australia should honour its obligations as a member of the League and its obligations to women. In 1921 at the Conference of the Australian Federation of Women Voters the delegates agreed to ask the Commonwealth

[14] *S.M.H.*, 4 June 1924; *Sky Riders, A Book of Famous Flyers* (London, 1940), pp. 52–65.

[15] *C'wealth P.D.*, 17 July 1924, vol. 107, pp. 2179–82; An Act to amend the Commonwealth Electoral Act 1918–1922 for the purpose of making provision for Compulsory Voting, 31 July 1924, No. 10 of 1924, *C'wealth Acts*, vol. XXII, 1924.

Government to include a woman in the Australian delegation to International Conferences. The following year the Commonwealth Government appointed Mrs Margaret Dale of Sydney as an alternate delegate for the third meeting of the Assembly of the League of Nations in Geneva.

But women wanted more than political participation. Women were enfranchised: they wanted to be emancipated. Women must learn how to exploit their enfranchisement to give them the freedom to decide for themselves how to use their bodies, and, in general, how to live their lives. Women were divided on the means to be adopted. At the triennial conference of the Australian Federation of Women Voters in Adelaide in March 1924, the delegates professed their faith in emancipation by political means: baptism in politics would be followed by salvation from male domination. Being British, being members of the British Empire, would mean that women would soon win 'political honors' and after 'political honors' would come 'equality of opportunity' and after that their right to decide for themselves, and the opportunity for fulfilment. The radicals did not agree. They believed that the overthrow of capitalist society was essential to their emancipation. The private ownership of the means of production, distribution and exchange was the prime cause of the subordination of women to men. Women were not biologically inferior to men: the teaching of the Church was just another example of how 'spook men' provided arguments for the gaolers and oppressors of women.[16]

The Aborigines were still fighting for survival. No power of princes, philosophy or Christianity, as the *Australian Board of Missions Review* put it, has been able to avert 'their proudly gloomy progress towards a certain and utter extinction'. No one, either white or Aboriginal, has shown how the Aborigines could be rescued from the degradation they had suffered ever since the coming of the white man. The mission station, the Aboriginal reserve, fringe dwellers in the country towns, or inhabitants of city ghettos—were all characterized by squalor, listlessness and despair. The ruthless argued for force. The only way to convert an Aborigine, they argued, was with a Winchester rifle. The white man should use the boot and the whip: that was all the Aborigines understood. 'Kick a nigger', some white men said, 'and he becomes almost tolerable'. But for God's sake drop all the twaddle about the 'uplifting of the colored man'. Being British, Australians were 'hogs for morals and humanity', but members of the British race were great realists: they should draw the line at the Aborigine.[17]

Nettie Palmer put Australia first. Louis Esson agreed, but he was a bit of a

[16] Bessie M. Rischbieth, *March of Australian Women* (Perth, 1964), pp. 70–1.

[17] *A.B.M. Review*, 7 October 1920, pp. 118–19, 7 March 1921, pp. 7–8, 7 May 1922, p. 40.

backslider. He had other things on his mind: he was telling Vance Palmer that Warwick Armstrong would still be worth a place in the Australian side. No wonder Katharine Susannah Prichard thought Louis Esson needed 'a bit of a shove'. She was determined to get Australia on the printed page. Let the English publishers remind her as much as they liked of her errors in grammar and punctuation: what did it matter if she was wobbly on the two uses of the colon in punctuation? She would not stand or fall by her grammatical imperfections. It was what she had to say that mattered. The problem was how to persuade readers, theatre-goers and picture-goers to take interest in Australian works. The Pioneer Players had talent and enthusiasm, but no audience. In Melbourne, as they stayed away in droves from the performances of the Pioneer Players, huge crowds were packing the Princess Theatre each evening for a 'sumptuous, super attraction', the 'Latest and Greatest Song and Dance Show', the *Rise of Rosie O'Reilly*. At the Theatre Royal, Harry Weldon was giving gloom the K.O. twice daily. At the new Palace patrons were enjoying London's greatest actor, Seymour Hicks, in his impersonation of 'Ole Bill' in Bruce Bairnsfather's *Old Bill, M.P.* Alan Wilkie's Company was performing Shakespeare's *The Taming of the Shrew*. There was also Somerset Maugham's *East of Suez*. The audiences were Australian: their culture at the theatre was British.[18]

At the dance halls teachers illustrated the latest London dances. At the picture palaces the audiences gaped at American conspicuous wealth, conspicuous consumption, and conspicuous waste. Forty hairdressers, twelve wardrobe mistresses and five special makeup experts groomed the four thousand extras in Norma Talmadge's starring vehicle, *Ashes of Vengeance*. Audiences flocked from the suburbs to the cities each night to fill the picture palaces. In 1921 the proprietors of a proposed new picture theatre in Melbourne, the Capitol, commissioned Walter Burley Griffin to draw plans. The Capitol was to be the work of the designer of Australia's capital. Sumptuousness was his commission. The man who drank carrot juice and practised all kinds of asceticism and meditation to free himself from worldly ties and dependence on creature comforts, was engaged to design an architectural extravaganza. The carpets were gorgeous: the ceiling passed through all the colours of a rainbow in succession while a man playing a Wurlitzer organ whisked patrons off into the land of make-believe. The first film, Cecil B. De Mille's *The Ten Commandments* which opened on 7 November 1924, was an extravaganza. In a secular temple, to a surge of the Wurlitzer organ or, at sessions when the orchestra performed, to a roll of the drums, ending

[18] Louis Esson to Vance Palmer, 12 January 1924, and Eileen Duggan ('E.D.') to Nettie Palmer, n.d., probably early 1924, Palmer Papers, Series 1, Box 4, Folder 31; Katharine Susannah Prichard to Vance Palmer, 15 September 1925, ibid., Folder 33; *Table Talk*, 2, 9, 16 October 1924; *Daily Telegraph* (Sydney), 4, 11 October 1924.

with the 'drumstick's whack', men and women who still followed the puritan morality long after the faith had disappeared, were presented with the silver screen's version of how humanity acquired the laws which caused them such an infinity of suffering.[19]

On 13 November 1924 Nellie Melba ended her operatic career singing Mimi in Puccini's *La Bohème* at His Majesty's Theatre. The 'greatest singer of a century and perhaps of all time' was ending her public career in her native city. The Prime Minister, S. M. Bruce, was there, dressed immaculately in white tie and tails. At the end of the last act, when the beautiful tones had died away, the riotous cheering had subsided, and all the bouquets had fallen on the stage, the curtain went up once again, revealing Melba alone in a perfect garden of flowers. Behind her was emblazoned in electric lights the words: 'Australia's Greatest Daughter, Our Melba'. Nellie then spoke: 'My heart is breaking', she said, 'but I am happy. I am happy to think the darling soldiers who gave their all to the Empire will receive from us a wonderful sum of money . . . I cannot say much. You don't want me to break down'. Mr Bruce, who had walked on to the stage, thanked her for what she had done for Australia, and then with one of those gallant gestures even the imperturbable one indulged in, he kissed her hand. For Mr Bruce was not just the head of a businessman's government: he was a man, too.[20]

Australia had 'Opportunities Unlimited'. The performance of *La Bohème* was broadcast over land and sea to different parts of Australia, and to faraway places in the Pacific. The following morning the *Age* informed its readers that the broadcast had been heard on the coast of California. The Government, it was said, felt that this 'important innovation meant a great deal to the widely-separated settlers in Australia'. The days of Australia's isolation were drawing to a close. Nellie Melba has put Australia on the cultural map of the world. Wireless will put her on the maps of every country.[21]

Culture was still British. On the opening night of 7LL, the Hobart wireless station, on 17 December 1924 a school choir sang 'Drink to me only with thine eyes', 'Lead Kindly Light' and 'Come to the fair'. Mrs Gordon Harris sang 'Daffodils are here' and 'Coming through the Rye'. Two young soloists sang 'Somewhere a Voice is Calling' and 'I Passed by Your Window'. George Wright, a guest artist from South Australia, sang 'The Trumpeter'. The announcer attempted an English accent. The men wore dinner suits and black ties, the women evening dresses. The wireless transcended distance and promised an end to isolation, but it did not liberate the people from

[19] 'A Beautiful Picture Theatre', *Australian Home Builder*, 15 November 1924, pp. 61–2; *Age*, 8 November 1924; *Argus*, 8 November 1924.

[20] *Age*, 14 October 1924.

[21] Ibid.; *Argus*, 14 November 1924.

their cultural past: it was a preserver and sanctifier of that past. It conferred the prestige of modernity on the dead hand of the past.[22]

In the meantime Bruce was discussing with his advisers how Australia could achieve an effective voice in Imperial decisions on defence and foreign policy. In February 1924 he had asked Allen Leeper, the son of that fanatical upholder of the Protestant ascendancy, Dr Alexander Leeper, the first Warden of Trinity College, Melbourne, to advise him on such questions. By June, Leeper had a question for Bruce: did Australia want 'a foreign policy distinct from that of H. M. Government?' That was what John Curtin was brooding over during those lonely walks on the beach at Cottesloe. Or did Bruce want to 'link up more closely with H. M. Government on all matters of Imperial relations with foreign countries'. Of course Bruce said 'Yes' to that, because that was what he had worked for so patiently ever since he took over from Hughes in the preceding February. Well, then, said Leeper, as the answer to that question was yes, then he would recommend the appointment of an Australian liaison officer to the Foreign Office in London. Bruce nominated Richard Gardiner Casey, a young man of promise, one of those men known to his friends as a man of infinite desire and limited capacity. Casey belonged to the landed families of Queensland, the Australian robber barons of the nineteenth century. Like Bruce, Casey's education had been English—Melbourne Grammar School and Cambridge. His manners were impeccable, his clothes straight from Bond Street, and his voice from the Old Country. Like Bruce, as a boy Casey had sung with fervour of his desire to 'bear the dark blue flag to glory/Grammar to the fore!' Now he would bring Australia and the Empire 'to the fore'.[23]

Bruce was also giving much thought to how a 'businessman's government' could succeed in Australia. He had a problem. To compete for markets, Australian workers must accept lower wages. To carry out such a policy would provoke industrial unrest. Unrest might be exploited by the Bolsheviks for their own ends, for the overthrow by violence of the existing society. Bruce wanted material progress, harmony between classes, the rule of law, independence of the judiciary, individual liberty and toleration. The problem was: could those features survive if the Bolsheviks used those liberties to rouse a mass movement in favour of revolution? Bruce was impressed with the 'possibilities and resources of Australia'. On 8 April 1924 he announced he had negotiated successfully with the British Government for the provision of money at a nominal rate of interest to the States to carry out

[22] *Mercury* (Hobart), 18 December 1924; *Argus*, 28 January 1924; *School Paper* (Victoria), 1 May 1924; R. R. Walker, *The Magic Spark* (Melbourne, 1973), pp. 12–14.

[23] J. R. Poynter, 'The Yo-Yo Variations: Initiative and Dependence in Australia's External Relations, 1918–1923', *Historical Studies*, vol. 14, no. 54, 1970, pp. 248–9; *The Times*, 31 December 1924.

the developmental works which would increase Australia's power to absorb migrants. The future of Australia, Great Britain and the whole Empire depended upon 'a redistribution of its white population'. But Australia could absorb British migrants only if assured of a market in the United Kingdom for her own products. Britain had made £1 million available to stimulate the consumption of Dominion products in Great Britain. Australia, tied to the Empire, could look forward 'with confidence to the great destiny that lay before it'.

The conservatives, through their control of the press and the new medium of radio broadcasting, have established for generations to come a picture of Australian politics. The Nationalists and the Country Party, they said, were the prudent parties: Labor was the prodigal party. Labor governments were 'prodigally spendthrift governments' that tapped every conceivable source of taxation to pay for their reckless expenditure. Australian radicals had no 'creative faculty'. They had 'no ideal of noble achievement'. They had nothing but the 'gorilla idea' of using the proletariat to destroy brains and capital and authority and order. The Labor movement, conservatives said, was composed of two wings. One was working for a 'vampire-like sucking of the people's life-blood'. They would thieve the property of the prudent and industrious to pay for their extravagant schemes. They promoted the careers of individual demagogues such as Jack Lang. The other wing of Labor, the communist wing, was working for a 'violent, mad-dog revolution'. Their symbol was the Red Flag, the 'flag of treason'. Communists hated the British Empire. Communists had as little respect for the King of England as they had for human life and private property.[24]

Communists were also undermining the morals of the people. Atheism, agnosticism, hedonism, sexual licence, pornographic literature and lascivious paintings were being used by communists for their own devilish purposes. Disloyalty, treason, insults to the flag, disrespectful remarks about the King and the Empire grew rank in minds which had rejected conventional morality. The churches preached the old morality: they must be encouraged. The *Freeman's Journal* in Sydney, the voice of the Catholic Church in New South Wales, expressed its concern at women arriving half-naked at dances, of men eyeing lasciviously women in wet bathing gowns on the beaches of Sydney. The Protestant parsons wanted to preserve the tight little world of the Ten Commandments and the savage judgements of the Apostle Paul on those who succumbed to the 'sinful lusts of the flesh'. The press published the moral teaching of priests and parsons, but gave no space to those advocating a morality free from the Christian infamy of original sin,

[24] *Argus*, 9 April 1925; 'Taxation—A contrast. The Premier's Promises and All Carry the Brand', *Australian National Review*, 13 March 1925.

and the impotence of human beings to change human behaviour. The parsons and the priests asked their congregations to turn to God for help: 'Have pity on us, Lord, for our great folly. For thou alone canst remove all the evil in the world'.

The faith of the fathers known of the old might well be becoming more feeble, but the sons enforced the morality of a decaying faith with all the zeal of the moral improvers of humanity in previous generations. On 2 June 1925 the wife of Christopher Brennan, the Associate Professor of German and Comparative Literature in the University of Sydney, petitioned for judicial separation from her husband. Colleagues of Brennan at the University of Sydney have been embarrassed by stories of his wayward behaviour. While giving a public lecture he has fallen flat on his face, leaving the listeners in the front row the massive task of getting him upright again. There were stories, too, of his cavalier attitude to punctuality at lectures, and to the marking of examination papers. But Brennan was a mighty spirit, idolized by his students, a man with an international reputation, employed in one of Australia's temples of British Philistinism. On 15 June 1925 the Senate of the University of Sydney discussed the Brennan affair. Professor Sir Mungo William MacCallum, formerly Professor of English and now Vice-Chancellor, himself quite a toper and *bon viveur*, and a brilliant exponent of the art of not being found out, addressed the members with tears rolling down his cheeks. He admired Chris Brennan. But Brennan must go. He has offended against the lore of the tribe: the Senators could not overlook his offence, because it has become public. Some mercy was shown. Brennan was not dismissed. He was given leave of absence on full pay for the rest of the year on the understanding that he tender his resignation as Associate Professor as from 31 December 1925.[25]

The win for Labor in the New South Wales State election on 30 May 1925 alarmed the conservatives. Lang was no menace to the morals of society, or to the existing social order. He was a pragmatist, not an ideologue. But he was also a demagogue, a man who roused the passions of the people by posing as their saviour. The people had a hero. 'Lang', as the slogan put it later, 'is greater than Lenin'. Lang had ideas on social reform. That, too, had its dangers. Social welfare—widows' pensions, sickness payments, unemployment benefits—could only be paid for by increased taxation. Lang would not be prudent: Lang would be prodigal, a spendthrift. The conservatives in the Legislative Council should emasculate Lang's legislation. Lang, the demagogue, would stir up public opinion: the Legislative Council might be abolished, as in Queensland. That was one of the planks in Labor's plat-

[25] *Freeman's Journal*, 5, 19 March 1925; Axel Clark, *Christopher Brennan* (Melbourne, 1980), pp. 252; John Thompson, 'Christopher Brennan', tape in A.B.C. Library, Sydney.

form. Failing that the Legislative Council might be rendered impotent, or simply a mirror of the Legislative Assembly. The last of the bulwarks William Charles Wentworth had proposed for a lasting constitution—'a conservative one—a British not a Yankee constitution'—would be swept away. It would lead to what Wentworth had also prophesied, 'the severance of our allegiance from the mother country, and of our loyalty to the throne . . . the severance of that ancient and glorious tie which binds us to our fatherland—that golden link which, I trust, will ever bind us to it'. Lang must be watched.[26]

The communists branded Lang as a capitalist politician masquerading as a Labor man. The *Workers' Weekly* was full of righteous anger: it proposed to rip the mask off the face of this opportunist and traitor to the working class, and expose the true role of the Labor leaders in New South Wales and Australia. The victory of Lang has brought new life to the Communist Party. They wrote and talked as though it were their turn next—their turn after they had rescued the workers from being duped by Labor Party leaders. If the Labor Party failed to fulfil their promises the workers would not revert to Nationalism: they would move further to the left and support the Communist Party. Bruce must take action. Bruce must save Australian bourgeois society from those Bolsheviks and wreckers, who were stirring up trouble on the waterfront, in the coal mines, and in transport.[27]

Ever since 1917 there has been conflict on the waterfront. The great betrayal by Hughes had intensified the suspicions and resentments of the waterside workers. Since the seamen's strike of 1917 labour on the waterfront was recruited from the Shipping Labour Bureau. Only 'loyalists' and returned soldiers or sailors could be registered with the Shipping Labour Bureau. The waterside workers argued that the membership restrictions were a strike-breaking weapon. On 20 October 1923 they announced they would strike unless the Government agreed to abolish the Bureau. By 17 November 1924 they had won their point. In the beginning of 1925 they demanded changes to the system of 'picking-up' crews, which had many of the features of a slave market. They demanded the 'pick-up' places should be the union offices on the wharves: the ship owners suggested the Mercantile Marine Offices. The Union said no. All interstate shipping was held up pending the settlement of the dispute. On 29 January the Commonwealth Court of Conciliation and Arbitration gave a final warning to the Union. The Union accepted the award. The strike was over, the differences remained.[28]

[26] *S.M.H.*, 1, 8 June 1925; *Australian Worker*, 3 June 1925; *Workers' Weekly*, 5 June 1925; *S.M.H.*, 17 August 1853.

[27] *Workers' Weekly*, 12 June 1925.

[28] 'The Waterside Disputes', *Round Table*, vol. 15, 1924–25, pp. 283–7; A. N. Smith, *Thirty Years: the Commonwealth of Australia 1901–1931* (Melbourne, 1933), p. 261.

Bruce decided to divide the moderates from the militants on the waterfront. In February 1925 the Attorney-General indicted Tom Walsh, the President of the Seamen's Union, for inciting the men to strike. He was fined £150, and asked to pay costs of 50 guineas. Bruce believed that punishment would scare the moderates. Vain hope. Tom Walsh, briefly, became a hero of the Australian working class. Tom Walsh was from County Cork in Ireland and known as the man who was 'born in struggle, reared in strife, agitator all his life'. He was married in Melbourne on 30 September 1917 to Adela Pankhurst by the Reverend Frederick Sinclaire at the Free Religious Fellowship, with Robert Ross, the editor of the *Socialist*, as his best man. She had a hankering to get away from the 'silly political game' and a wish to go away from Australia. She will have her satisfaction but only after Bruce has used her husband as his whipping boy. Jacob Johnson (Johannsen) said he was by birth a Hollander who arrived in Australia from New Zealand in July 1910. By an odd irony these two believers in the brotherhood of man loathed each other. Bruce wanted the workers to see Tom Walsh and Jacob Johnson/Johannsen as aliens threatening the Aussie way of life, the family, the footy on Saturday arvo, a few quick snorts with the mates before six o'clock closing, and an occasional trip to the beach or the mountains with the wife and the kids. '*La Patrie*' was not '*en danger*', but Aussiedom and mateship were. Bruce, the patrician, would save the worker from the foreign seducer.

Bruce knew that the moderates believed militants gave Labor a bad name with the electors. This was an election year. Labor would not fall into the trap of supporting disloyalists, traitors to the King and the Empire. John Curtin was deeply troubled. In April 1925 he wrote to Frank Anstey that the central question of the time was 'the use to which mass forces shall be put'. They should not be exhausted in incessant strikes for the modification of wages and conditions. He was convinced of the 'futility of such enterprise'. They must all take care that the army of Labor did not march in the wrong direction: they must not allow their captains to commit grievous blunders. The cause of Labor must survive all mistakes. They were all, as he put it later, 'standard bearers in a holy war'. Bruce believed pragmatists like Scullin and Curtin would understand, and would in part agree with him.[29]

On 25 June 1925 Bruce introduced into the House of Representatives a Bill to amend the Immigration Act 1901–1924. Bruce was in a hurry, and he told the House why. He has come to the conclusion, he told the House, that the threat to Australian society was coming from aliens, the people who were

[29] *Socialist*, 5 October 1917; Adela Pankhurst to Tom Walsh, n.d., probably 1918, Adela Pankhurst Papers, N.L.A., Box 7, Folder 61; *S.M.H.*, 8 April 1943; *Argus*, 8 April 1943; information on Johnson in files of Department of Home and Territories, copy held in N.L.A.; John Curtin to Frank Anstey, 3 April 1925, 8 November 1934, Lloyd Ross Papers, Box 33, N.L.A.

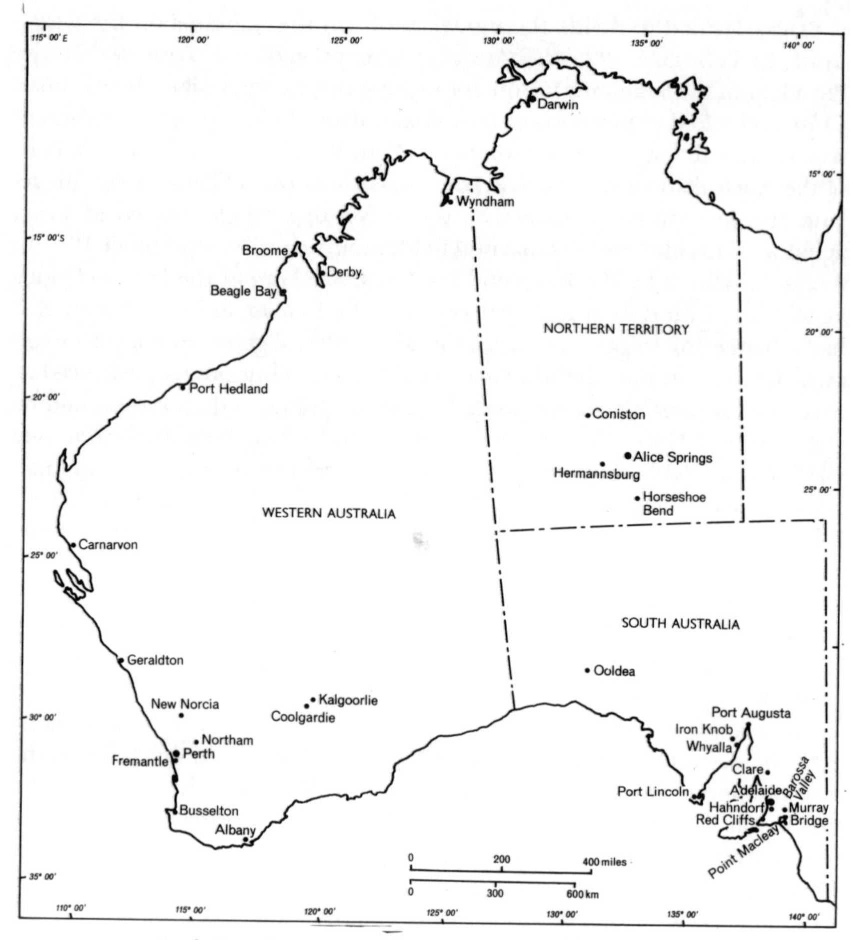

South Australia, Western Australia and the Northern Territory

not British. Australians, he said, were proud of being more British than the British. Aliens threatened 'our racial purity'. This Act would enable Australians to retain their racial purity and remain 'essentially and basically a British people'. There were in Australia a number of persons of alien race and blood who had refused to become Australians. They were not imbued with the spirit of loyalty: they had 'false doctrines and ideas'. As they refused to become Australians the Government had decided to return them to the country from which they came. Australia would then be free of the poisonous propaganda of these men. Free of alien agitators, Australia would not have half the trouble it was having today. He therefore proposed that if at any time the Governor-General believed serious industrial disturbance prejudiced or threatened the peace, order or good government of the Com-

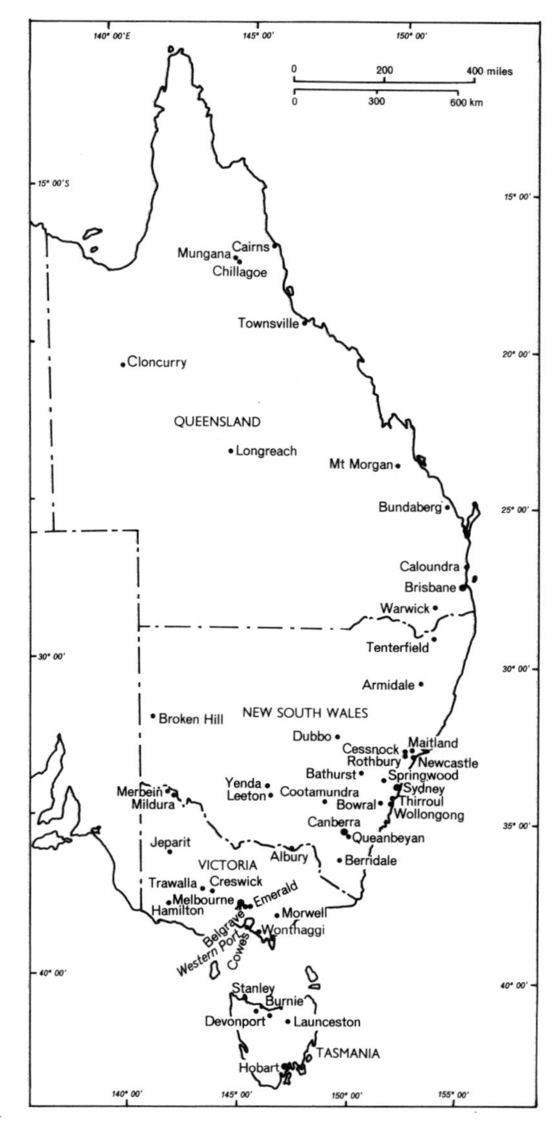

Queensland, New South Wales, Victoria and Tasmania

monwealth he might issue a Proclamation ordering the deportation of any person not born in Australia whose presence was deemed to be injurious to the peace, order or good government of the Commonwealth.[30]

Bruce succeeded only in increasing the uproar the Act was designed to

[30] *Age*, 26 June 1925; *C'wealth P.D.*, 25 June 1925, vol. 110, pp. 456–63; An Act to amend the Immigration Act 1901–1924, 20 July 1925, No. 7 of 1925, *C'wealth Acts*, vol. XXIII, 1925.

reduce. Bruce has united the two wings of the Labor movement. Matthew Charlton, the leader of the Australian Labor Party, was roused to an unwonted passion. The Act, he said, aimed a direct blow at the trade union movement in this country. The *Workers' Weekly* said the same thing. The Act, they said, was a declaration of war on the bosses of the trade union movement of Australia. The Act could be used against reformers of any kind, even against those who exposed graft and corruption. Bruce has become the ogre of all those who believed in Australian ideals—the Mr Bad Man threatening the liberties of the Australian people.[31]

Bruce took no notice of all the tumult and the shouting. As soon as the Act passed through the Houses of Parliament he rushed the printed text out to Government House in Melbourne for the assent of the Governor-General, Lord Forster, on 20 July. The ink was barely dry on the viceregal signature when the Minister of State for Home and Territories, G. F. Pearce, on 24 August proclaimed there was a serious industrial disturbance prejudicing or threatening the peace, order or good government of the Commonwealth.

On 18 November the Solicitor-General, Sir Robert Garran, announced that the Deportation Board had recommended the deportations of Thomas Walsh and Jacob Johannsen for being concerned in acts directed towards hindering or obstructing the transport of goods or the conveyance of passengers. On 20 November they were taken quietly into custody on Garden Island in Sydney Harbour. Neither offered any resistance. Acting on instruction from their solicitors, their barrister, Dr. H. V. Evatt, asked for their release, in a case before the Supreme Court of New South Wales. The case was transferred to the High Court on 30 November. On 11 December the judges of the High Court handed down their judgment. They had been asked to decide whether the Commonwealth Parliament had the constitutional power to pass such legislation, and whether in the Constitution Act of 1900 general power over the liberty of the subject was transferred from the States to the national Parliament. The majority said Parliament had not legislated according to its powers. The appellants, Walsh and Johnson, were released.[32]

The learned and venerable judges of the High Court, generally so far removed from the public gaze that they resembled statues rather than full-blooded human beings, became the heroes of the people. Old men were

[31] *C'wealth P.D.*, 1 July 1925, vol. 110, pp. 567–71; *Age*, 2 July 1925; *Workers' Weekly*, 3, 10 July 1925.

[32] *C'wealth Gazette*, 24 August 1925; *S.M.H.*, 21 November, 12, 14 December 1925; Ex Parte Walsh and Johnson; in re Yates, *C'wealth Law Reports*, vol. 37, 1925.

metamorphosed into John Hampdens of the liberty of the individual in Australia. Judges of the High Court have ruled that the offensive clauses of the Immigration Act were 'quite out of line' with the ideals of the Australian people. This was a 'landmark in Australian history', like the landmark of the conscription campaigns. Toasts were drunk to their Honours in the pubs of Woolloomooloo and Port Melbourne. Encomiums were lavished upon them in the Trades and Labor Councils and the editorial offices of the Labor press. The *Workers' Weekly* was ill at ease with all this drivel about British justice and liberty and equality. It was the strategy of Australia's 'Imperial masters', they said, to propagate such illusions. They, the communists, the saviours of the Australian workers, could save them from this 'poisonous bourgeois ideology', and all the filth the masters' press was spewing forth. The master class has not been defeated. They could not be defeated until the Communist Party, as the vanguard of the proletariat, abolished the private ownership of the means of production, distribution and exchange.[33]

Bruce did not lose heart. In the forthcoming election on 14 November 1925 middle-class Australia, immigrant Australia, petty-bourgeois working-class Australia would assert itself at the ballot box as it had asserted itself at the election of May 1917 after the defeat in the referendum. Bruce would prove that Labor was tarred with the communist brush. Bruce would present his Government as a government of law and order. The paramount issue in the campaign, he said, was the maintenance of Law and Order, and the supremacy of Constitutional Government. He asked the electors of Australia not to let wreckers plunge Australia into chaos and misery in a period of great prosperity. He appealed to the electors to vote Nationalist or Country Party and 'save Australia from the Extremists'. Defeat the Reds and keep Australia White. That was his policy.

Labor fell into the trap. Charlton promised that Labor would deport all law-breakers. Lang denounced all communists as a 'criminal element' in the community. Charlton and Lang rejected the class war and competed with Bruce in their professions of loyalty to King and Empire. Once again Labor presented itself as a reformist party humanizing capitalist society. Labor would create a cosy world, a world in which everything was convenient. Labor would show it was just as efficient as the conservatives in running the capitalist state.[34]

In the election of 14 November 1925 the Nationalists won thirty-six seats,

[33] *Argus*, 12 December 1925; *Australian Worker*, 16 December 1925; *Workers' Weekly*, 18 December 1925.

[34] *S.M.H.*, 16 November 1925; *Age*, 14 November 1925; *Workers' Weekly*, 13 November 1925.

and had the promise of the support of one Independent. The Country Party won fourteen seats, and Labor twenty-three. The swing of the pendulum was against Labor. The *Sydney Morning Herald* congratulated the Bruce–Page Government on a 'great and well-deserved success'. Once again in a crisis the electors have chosen the conservatives.

The *Australian Worker* was not disheartened. History, they believed, was on the side of Labor. Labor has suffered a reverse, but it could not be vanquished. The *Workers' Weekly* used the defeat of Labor as yet another occasion to take a 'holier than thou' stance. The Labor Party, they said, had succumbed to the despicable lying and calumnies of Bruce. They had lost yet another opportunity to take the side of the workers against the oppressors. A 'swarm of aspiring lawyers and middle-class candidates' has fastened on the Australian Labor Party. The Communist Party was the conscience of the Australian worker. The Communist Party was the 'pure, unspotted' one, which alone could liberate the workers.[35]

The result plunged Louis Esson into a mood of despair about Australians. He assumed conditions in Australia must be so generally tolerable that people had no desire to risk a change. He could understand a people being opposed to change, but he could not understand a people accepting deportation. If Australians accepted that, they could stand anything. There was hope for God, but there was no hope for Australians. The trouble was, as Katharine Prichard pointed out, the people did not care for 'Australian stuff'. As Frank Anstey was fond of saying, Bruce posed in public as an Australian Scot when the truth was his family came from a 'rag shop' in the East End of London. The only subject Australians took with 'high seriousness' was football. Esson's neighbours in Carlton were more cast down by 'any weakening of the Old Blues' than the defeat of the Australian Labor Party. He wondered whether they would ever do anything about it 'as Australians'.[36]

During the election campaign the first copies reached Australia of *The Way Home*, the second volume of the trilogy, *The Fortunes of Richard Mahony*, by Henry Handel Richardson (Ethel Florence Robertson, elder daughter of Dr Walter Richardson). It was a major contribution to the literature of 'exiles' in

[35] *S.M.H.*, 16 November 1925; *Australian Worker*, 18 November, 2 December 1925; *Workers' Weekly*, 13, 20 November 1925; Colin A. Hughes and B. D. Graham, *A Handbook of Australian Government and Politics, 1890–1964* (Canberra, 1968), pp. 331–2; *Age*, 16 November 1925.

[36] Louis Esson to Vance Palmer, 21 September, 23 November 1925, Palmer Papers, Series 1, Box 4, Folder 33; Frank Anstey, *The Kingdom of Shylock* (revised edn, Melbourne, 1917); Hilda Esson to Vance and Nettie Palmer, 23 April 1920, Palmer Papers, Series 1, Box 4, Folder 27; Katharine Susannah Prichard to Vance Palmer, 4 October 1925, Palmer Papers, Series 1, Box 4, Folder 33.

Australia; but it was more than that. It was the story of a man who had so relished life in Australia free from the restraints of the Old World that he could never enjoy heart's ease again in the British Isles. It was the story of the complex fate of a man whom the spirit of place in Australia and the spirit of its society would never allow to be at ease there. It was a work about the corrupting influence of money values—an Old Testament prophet's judgement on a society run by the money-changers. It was a moral tale for a society obsessed with 'Men, Money and Markets'—a society in love with 'Wealth, Progress and Opportunities Unlimited'. The reception of the first part of the trilogy—*Australia Felix*—had not been kindly. The *Bulletin* had awarded the author the prize for long-windedness. Nettie Palmer discovered in the work only a 'rather faded kind of charm'. Together with its predecessor, *Australia Felix*, she found *The Way Home* 'a solid achievement in the direction of a background for Australian life of the present day'. Australians did not want to be disturbed. As with D. H. Lawrence's *Kangaroo* they preferred to pull down the blinds, rather than look into the dark side of the human heart, let alone ask what a human being could live by in a world in which God was dead.[37]

The Jeremiahs have prophesied about a day of reckoning. In his book, *Money Power*, published in 1921, Frank Anstey warned Australians there would one day be a terrible retribution because the money men in Australia were piling debts to British financiers higher and higher. Australians, he said, would one day pay a high price for the Bruce policy of borrowing money in London for development. The money men have not heeded the warning. They have recklessly borrowed more, laughing at the Jeremiahs. But, Anstey insisted, a gale would blow. Financiers and bourgeois politicians were dragging Australia towards the abyss. A day of reckoning would come. Above the uproar in the stock exchanges of Sydney and Melbourne, Anstey heard the 'drum beat of the Armies of Revolution'. He prophesied they would beat louder and louder. No nation would escape the catastrophe. But Australians sat on Bondi Beach, or went to Luna Park: Just for Fun.[38]

The priests and the parsons reminded their congregations of the comforting words Christ had said to all those who believed in Him: Come unto me all ye that travail and are heavy laden and I will give you rest. In the world human beings would know tribulation and sorrow. But with Christ they could overcome the world. Donald Baker, the Church of England Bishop of Bendigo, assured believers there was no need to be alarmed. There would be no revolution in Australia, there would be no blood in the

[37] Henry Handel Richardson, *The Way Home* (London, 1925); Nettie Palmer, 'Henry Handel Richardson', *Bulletin*, 15 October 1925.

[38] Frank Anstey, *Money Power* (Melbourne, 1921), pp. 11, 138–9.

streets because the people were not materialists and atheists. The hymns they sang were so reassuring:

> We have Christ's own promise
> And that cannot fail.

So: onward Christian soldiers marching as to war, with the cross of Jesus going on before! The manager of the Myer Emporium, Lee Neil, spoke of Australia as 'a veritable Utopia'. The proprietors of Rexona soap told the women of Australia:

> Be Pretty! Be Dainty!
> Be Attractive!
> Be a Rexona girl!

There was glad news for the women of Australia at the beginning of 1926. Thanks to electrical power it was possible to 'ease the burden of the wash-up'. Domestic gadgets would help women to keep their charm. There was a new popular song about the things that mattered in life:

> If you knew Susie,
> Like I know Susie,
> Oh, oh, oh, what a thrill!

The beer was good: prawns were cheap: the surf was good. The Aussie cricketers were doing well. Alan Kippax of New South Wales, a batsman in the Victor Trumper tradition, has just scored 271 runs. Policemen in Melbourne controlling the traffic at peak hours still wore shiny black helmets and white gauntlets. Things were still the same as ever both in the cities and out in the Never-Never.[39]

At the Australia Day celebrations in Sydney on 26 January 1926 Bruce exhorted his audience to take no notice of the 'croakers'. Australia would have a great and marvellous future. Australia was on the threshold of a great leap forward. Australians would reap the harvest of loyal sons of the King and the Empire. Soon there would be an All Red (Empire) Air service between Australia and Great Britain. Bruce did not mention then the price Australia might have to pay for patching up the antiquated British economic and social system. He was not a man to see the need for or the imminence of any 'cleansing fire'.[40]

It was a dry year. The bush was as dry as tinder. Louis Esson found it a 'dreadful season', a depressing time for those who had dreamed dreams of a glorious future for humanity. In Soviet Russia, to his dismay, he found the grand dukes and capitalists had been replaced by union secretaries, 'the

[39] *Age*, 1, 26, 27 January, 2 February 1926.
[40] *S.M.H.*, 27 January 1926; *Age*, 27 January 1926.

universal spouters who boss everything on committees'. Organizing society was a hard job. He was inclined to give it up. There was no point in listening to the 'drum beats of the Armies of Revolution', if they were to be followed by 'spiritual popes'. In Australia there was the menace of the mighty bush, always threatening to wipe out all human hopes and aspirations. As Mary Gilmore pointed out at the beginning of the year, Henry Lawson had had the sense of pity for all of us in our great folly, our great madness: but Lawson was dead.[41]

Now the mighty bush was ablaze. Fires were raging on a five-mile front near the junction of the Cotter and Murrumbidgee rivers. Canberra was threatened. On 27 January 1926 the bush around Belgrave was turned into a 'scene of desolation'. Burnt trees, and the entire absence of undergrowth in one day changed a place of beauty into a 'forlorn spectacle'. There was worse to come. On 31 January the temperature reached 104° Fahrenheit in Melbourne. Fires again swept the Dandenong Ranges. Weekend houses were destroyed. The wives of settlers stood with their children where only the chimneys of their weatherboard cottages were left standing after the 'ravenous conflagration'. Orchards were destroyed. Church bells were tolled to summon more volunteer fire-fighters. Equipment and water were scarce. Men beat the edge of the fire with strips of hessian attached to long poles, or with saplings with a bushy head of leaves. The ladies of the district provided tea, sandwiches, cakes and encouragement. Church services were abandoned, clergymen took off their 'dog-collars', butchers and bakers took off their aprons: schools were closed. Young boys ate what the fire-fighters did not consume, and swallowed cups of tea like grown-ups. The grown-ups, even in the presence of danger, took special care the young folk did not get any of the 'cold tea'. In Australia 'cold tea' was strictly for the menfolk.[42]

At the same time in Melbourne Bruce and Page took measures to stamp out a different sort of fire. Jock Garden has let the cat out of the bag: he boasted that the shadow of communism was over the Labor movement, that white ants could do more to a building than all the winds that blow. The electors, Bruce claimed, had given the Government a mandate to deal with the communist threat to law and order. He had asked the people to choose between 'Democracy and Communism' and the people had chosen Democracy. Now he was taking action to preserve his version of democracy in Australia. On 28 January, the day after the first of the disastrous fires, John Latham, the Attorney-General, opened the debate in the House of Representatives on the second reading of the Crimes Act Amendment Bill. He was

[41] Louis Esson to Vance Palmer, 29 March 1926, and Mary Gilmore to Nettie Palmer, 5 January 1926, Palmer Papers, Series 1, Box 4, Folder 34.

[42] *Age*, 28, 30 January, 1, 2, 6 February 1926; personal memories of fires at Belgrave, 27 January to 6 February 1926.

there, he said, to fulfil 'a clear and definite mandate of the people' given to the Government at the last election. 'The mandate of the people', he said, 'was clear and unmistakable'.[43]

John Greig Latham, like Bob Menzies, was a one-time scholarship boy who rose to high places by his talents and his determination. He was a man of parts who excelled in many fields. Born in Melbourne on 25 August 1887, educated at State Schools, Scotch College and the University of Melbourne, he graduated in Arts in 1897 but, to his mortification, not in the first place. That was won by an eccentric young man of talent, who had the brains, but neither the stamina nor the temperament to last the distance in a city of rectitude. Latham graduated in Law in 1902. To his contemporaries he was an enigma. He was secretary of the Education Defence League, but a great believer in Public Schools. He was a Rationalist and a Conservative. Belief in God, or belief in the perfectibility of humanity were for him evidence of the stupidity of the great mass of human beings. Latham was a vain man. He brushed his hair with the care of a man who had taken literally Christ's remark that the very hairs of his head were numbered. He stood always aloof, always separate, his one pleasure in life seeming to be in listening to or relating stories of weakness and folly. Himself a man of moderation in all things, he nevertheless derived deep satisfaction as a voyeur at those gatherings when men in high places indulged in the 'divine excesses'. He seemed a cold man. Yet in his younger days he had written beautiful love letters to the woman he married, Ella Tobin. And it was the same for her. She found him 'the dearest old fellow anywhere'.[44]

Unlike Bob Menzies he was no showman. No one ever said of John Latham that he was a man with a shopfront but no factory. In his practice at the Melbourne Bar he was successful, but there were no stories of ripostes to pompous judges, or the bullies of the Bar. Frederic Eggleston admired Latham's 'hard brain capable of immense effort without feeling fatigue'. But he did not warm to him. Latham, he found, was a 'non-stop talker', one of those intellectuals who appointed himself a super-maestro among the maestros. But there was something about Latham then which would come between him and his ambition to be number one in Australia. He was a very fine logician and controversialist. He won all the arguments. But he was deficient in everything which depended upon the instincts or the imagination. He had a sense of humour, but it was of the mirthless kind. He giggled at other people, but he never laughed with them. Unlike Bob Menzies he was no lover of the 'chuckle', nor a 'cuddly' man, not even to the members of his

[43] *Age*, 29 January 1926; *C'wealth P.D.*, 28 January 1926, vol. 112, p. 457.

[44] Biography of J. G. Latham in Latham Papers, Box 1, N.L.A.; Ella Tobin to J. G. Latham, 11, 12 February 1904, ibid., Box 2, Folder 1; J. G. Latham to Ella Latham, 11 December 1929, 27 July 1930, ibid., Folder 17.

family. Eggleston noticed that Latham's self-respect was not strong enough to protect him against the 'ordinary temptations of snobbery and influence'. Eggleston found him an 'advertiser and an egotist'. In 1922 Latham won the federal seat of Kooyong as a progressive liberal, though no one quite knew what he stood for. In 1925 he joined the Nationalist Party. After the election of 14 November 1925 he became Attorney-General in the second Bruce–Page Government.[45]

On 28 January this rationalist rose in the House to tell members the step the Government proposed to take against atheistic communism. With every hair of his head neatly in place, John Latham presented it all as a theorem in geometry. The people have given the Government a mandate to protect them against those who threatened to disturb the peace, order and good government of the Commonwealth of Australia. Therefore the Government had introduced the Crimes Bill to declare all those who advocated the overthrow by violence of the existing governments of Australia guilty of a crime punishable by imprisonment or a fine. The communists have professed their intention to use violence. Marx and Engels in the Communist Manifesto have said no social improvement could be obtained 'save by violent revolution and force'. Latham was a lawyer: Latham quoted his sources: 'They [the communists] openly declare that their ends can be obtained only by the forcible overthrow of all existing social conditions'. There was no need for windy rhetoric or verbal extravaganzas, no need to talk of corrupt hearts worshipping false idols or humanity bowing down to strange gods. In his mind it was as lucid and as beautiful as one of Euclid's theorems.

The following were declared unlawful associations: Any body of persons which advocated the overthrow of the Constitution of the Commonwealth by revolution or sabotage, the overthrow by violence of the established Government of the Commonwealth or of a State, the destruction or injury of the property of the Commonwealth or of a State, any body of persons which by its constitution advocated or propagated the doing of an act of sedition, any person who by speech or writing advocated any of the above acts, any person who gave or solicited money for unlawful associations. Books advocating the use of violence for political ends were not to be transmitted by post, and all books and literature of unlawful associations were to be prohibited. Anyone guilty of these offences could be imprisoned for one year or six months.[46]

Matthew Charlton did not know what to say. To oppose the Bill would be electoral suicide for the Labor Party. To support it would provide proof for

[45] F. W. Eggleston, Confidential Notes, typescript in Menzies Library, A.N.U., Canberra; Warren G. Osmond, *Frederic Eggleston* (Sydney, 1985), pp. 46–8, 86–9.

[46] *C'wealth P.D.*, 28 January 1926, vol. 112, pp. 457–60; An Act to amend the Crimes Act 1914–1915, 16 March 1926, No. 9 of 1926, *C'wealth Acts*, vol. XXIV, 1926.

the communist argument that Labor leaders were defenders of capitalist society. So Matthew Charlton tried to have it both ways. Persons, he said, who advocated the overthrow of government by violence or revolution deserved punishment, but the Australian workers were in a different category, because they were law abiding. Government should not penalize them: Government should speed up access to the Arbitration Court and so avoid delays which drove moderates at times into the camp of the militants. The Labor press was angry. Mr Bruce, the *Australian Worker* said on 3 February 1926, was trying to 'cure deep-seated economic evils with a bludgeon'. His efforts were not likely to be any more successful than those of his predecessors. The Communist Party again knew the answers. Theirs was the righteous cause. They would carry on the work for the emancipation of the working class from wage slavery. That was their mission. They were the vanguard of the proletariat in their progress to revolution, socialism and communism. They would lead humanity towards that time when history would end, and the 'freedom of each would be the condition of the freedom of all'. The Crimes Act Amendment Act, the *Workers' Weekly* said, was a sure sign 'of the decadence of Capitalist democracy'. Bruce might arrest communists: he could not resist the flood of ideas. 'Forward', the *Workers' Weekly* called, 'to a Workers' Republic—and Communism'.[47]

Vain hope. The Communist Party still has not become a mass movement. As Nettie Palmer's brother, Esmonde Higgins, put it in March 1925, the Communist Party was only 'a few little cliques' with no chance of organizing 'any left-wing opposition let alone a revolution'. Members squabbled with each other on the interpretation of Marx and Lenin. Everyone in the Party, according to Higgins, was 'nervy & suspicious & chattering'. Their activities were waning. The Saturday dances were getting 'less lucrative'. 'My own outlook', he told his sister, is 'hellish gloomy'. He was uneasy with the 'humourless seriousness' which pervaded gatherings of party members. Others, like Nettie Palmer herself, were put off by party members posing as the self-appointed creators of a new way of life, by the arrogance of men and women who knew what others did not know, the offensiveness of claiming to be always 'correct'.[48]

Higgins and others were just as doubtful about the role the Australian Labor Party could play in Australian society. John Curtin believed it was possible for the Labor Party to be pragmatic without being unprincipled and opportunistic. The *Bulletin* did not agree. As they saw it, Labor had acquired political strength at the price of moral weakness. Labor had won victories at

[47] *C'wealth P.D.*, 10 February 1926, vol. 112, pp. 838–9; *Australian Worker*, 3 February 1926; *Workers' Weekly*, 5, 12, 19 February 1926.

[48] Esmonde Higgins to 'Dear Old Harry', 22 March 1925, E. M. Higgins Papers, M.L.

the ballot box in New South Wales and Queensland by shoving ideals and principles into the background. The price for this was that Labor had fragmented into factions fighting for their share of the loot. Labor parties were beset by struggles between one 'crafty, audacious and desperate gang' against another of the same kind, for who was to receive the 'many and varied pecuniary benefits arising out of control of a well-organised industrial-political machine'. The men who believed in 'the cause' were being replaced by demagogues and charlatans. The annual conferences of the Labor Party in New South Wales have long ceased to be occasions for inspired idealists and men of faith to preach the gospel of Labor. They have degenerated into 'a seething mass of vendettas, dog-fights and double-crossings'. The cry of 'Solidarity forever, for the union makes us strong' has become a mockery, an aspiration, not an ever-present reality.[49]

Bruce continued to speak of Australia as the country of 'Opportunities Unlimited'. Capitalist society would deliver the goods: capitalist society would provide opportunities for all those with talent, industry and moral fibre. To aid the primary and secondary industries of Australia he introduced into the House of Representatives on 26 May 1926 the second reading of a Bill to create the Council of Scientific and Industrial Research (to be known as the C.S.I.R.). Science, he said, could better the conditions of the workers and bring greater prosperity to the Australian people. The scientific organization created by Hughes in 1916 had been too narrowly restricted to the war: the organization of 1920 had had limited powers. Australia must catch up the ground it had lost by following slavishly the English curriculum designed for the education of a governing class. The Council of Scientific and Industrial Research would encourage that capacity for invention which had made Australia a pioneer in the fields of agricultural machinery, gold mining, wheat breeding and dry farming. There would be a Central Council of three members appointed by the Commonwealth Government, and Chairmen of the State Committees.

The first three nominees were George Alfred Julius, a mechanical engineer and inventor and Englishman, the son of a clergyman who migrated to Australia. George Julius, like Bruce, had been a Melbourne Grammar boy. There was David Rivett, the son-in-law of Alfred Deakin, and brother-in-law of Herbert Brookes and Tommy White, a member of the 'king-makers of Yarraside', and A. E. Y. Richardson. They were three men who wanted to fight prickly pear, to root out diseases in sheep and cattle, and to find how to grow crops in the dry years as well as in the green. The engineers and the scientists would be the servants of bourgeois society. The Act to amend the

[49] *Bulletin*, 8 April 1926; Demand for Special Conference, 16 April 1926, Broadsheet in R. S. Ross Collection, N.L.A.

Institute of Science and Industry Act was assented to on 21 June 1926.[50]

Bruce also had plans to take the sting out of the socialist condemnation of capitalist society as the cause of the moral infamies of exploitation, poverty and unemployment. Early in 1926 he appointed a Royal Commission of six members under the chairmanship of Senator J. D. Millen to inquire into and report upon National Insurance as a means of making provision for casual sickness, permanent invalidity, old age, unemployment, maternity allowance, and pensions for the destitute. In two Reports they put forward recommendations to minimize the risks of unemployment and to relieve the distress of the aged, the sick and the disabled. Labor leaders wanted more. Communist leaders and journalists denounced the Reports for putting up schemes to dampen the revolutionary ardour of the workers. Bruce believed that Government could give capitalist society a human face. The coalition Government would see that Australia enjoyed material well-being without the moral odium of unemployment or the loss of individual liberty inherent in any socialist or communist utopia.[51]

In Melbourne at this time the Russian bass singer, Feodor Chaliapin, was lifting his listeners into quite another world. As he sang, his eyes seemed on fire with the hope of a life quite different from the petty-bourgeois values of a Bruce or a Page. He sang of a temple within whose sacred walls men did not know revenge: he sang of love: he sang of a world where men and women, exalted by music, loosened the chains of ignorance and superstition. Louis Esson was carried away. Tolstoy had testified to the terrible things music could do to a man. Esson sat there in awe and wonder that music could mask the otherwise dissipated face of Chaliapin with an air of 'Shakespearean serenity'. The man who knew the lower depths, the man who had searched in vain for salvation in the muck was redeemed by his art. But Esson still went to the football every Saturday afternoon that winter. A loss by the 'mighty Blues' had the same effect on him as the squabblers in the Communist Party had on Esmonde Higgins: it made him 'hellish gloomy'.[52]

While Chaliapin's voice was making tears roll down the cheeks of Australian concert-goers Bruce left for London to attend the Imperial Conference. As in 1923, the delegates gathered first in Westminster Abbey to ask Almighty God to pour down upon them the continual dew of His blessing so that virtue and morality might abound, wickedness and vice be punished, and Christ's Kingdom might spread. There were other pre-conference

[50] *C'wealth P.D.*, 26 May 1926, vol. 113, pp. 2330–4; An Act to amend the Science and Industry Research Act, 1920–26, 21 June 1926, No. 20 of 1926, *C'wealth Acts*, vol. XXIV, 1926; G. Currie and J. Graham, *The Origins of C.S.I.R.O.* (Melbourne, 1966).

[51] First and Second Progress Report of Royal Commission into National Insurance, July 1926, *C'wealth P.P.*, 1926–28, vol. 4, pt 2.

[52] Louis Esson to Vance Palmer, 15 July 1926, Palmer Papers, Series 1, Box 4, Folder 35.

gatherings to inspire confidence in the 'Imperial Firm'. Bruce was present in the Albert Hall on 17 October 1926 when Sir Alan Cobham, the aviator, described to twelve thousand children his flight to and from Australia. Bruce told them it was open to every one of the boys present to go to Australia—the most democratic country in the world—and come back to speak in the Albert Hall as Prime Minister of Australia. He had in his Cabinet a man only forty years old who began life selling newspapers on the steps of the Federal Parliament House in Melbourne. The feats of Ross and Keith Smith, Lieutenant Parer and Alan Cobham proved the British race still possessed 'the virtues of courage, endurance, enterprise, a love of adventure and the determination to overcome difficulties'. Everyone must now see that the Empire was supreme in the air as it had been with its navy and mercantile marine.[53]

The delegates believed in the role of the British in promoting material well-being and freedom in the world. They discussed at length how the resources of the Empire could be so organized that prosperity would abound. They talked of the need to encourage a redistribution of the white population within the Empire. They never doubted that what was good for the Empire was good for the world. They discussed the problems of freedom and unity. They came up with a resolution which breathed the very spirit of the British genius for compromise. The Dominions, they agreed, were 'autonomous communities within the British Empire equal in status, in no way subordinate one to another in any aspect of their domestic or external affairs, though united by a common allegiance to the Crown, and freely associated as members of the British Commonwealth of Nations'. There had been an Empire: now there was an Empire and a Commonwealth. As an essential consequence of the equality of status among all members of the British Commonwealth, delegates agreed that the Governor-General of a Dominion was the representative of the Crown, holding in all essential respects the same position in relation to the public affairs in the Dominion as 'held by His Majesty the King in Great Britain, and that he is not the representative or agent of His Majesty's Government in Great Britain or of any Department of that Government'.[54]

The *Sydney Morning Herald* was delighted. Every self-governing Dominion as now master of itself without endangering its commitment to the integrity of the Empire. Australians, it said, were prepared 'to sink or swim with the Empire. Advertisers agreed: 'Yes, Mr Bruce', one advertisement read, 'we will buy within the Empire'. The equality of Britain and the Dominions

[53] *Age*, 18 October 1926; *Worker* (Brisbane), 27 October 1926.

[54] Summary of Proceedings of Imperial Conference, 1926, Commons Papers, reports from Commissioners, vol. eleven, paper no. 13; Report of Inter-Imperial Relations Committee, ibid., pp. 14–16.

has been given a formal recognition. The 'Imperial Firm' has been strengthened. Bruce said they now had 'an Empire of completely self-governing nations, jealous of their autonomy, yet proud of their imperial unity'.

The *Australian Worker* did not agree. The Dominions, it said, were now 'more securely harnessed to the chariot of Imperialism'. British capitalism was 'slipping down hill at a terrific rate'. The Dominions were to be exploited to 'stay the rush'. The British had tricked the Australians and the other delegates into supporting the dope of 'A Strong British Empire Atmosphere'. The workers of the Empire were to be duped, sweated and fleeced so that the British could win back 'the industrial position lost during and since the world war, and [promote] the further strengthening of the predatory forces of Imperial Capitalism'. All this talk of 'every Dominion [as] a self-governing member of the Empire, and master of its destiny' was simply 'political humbug'. Political independence was of no value when Australia was to be throttled financially and economically by the Shylocks of Great Britain. So long as British Money Power had this stranglehold over Australia, Australia could never be master of its destiny. This charter of political independence was not worth the paper it was written on. The British still wanted to be Dives: the British were not troubled that Australia should be Lazarus, picking up the crumbs from the rich man's table. John Curtin pondered how Australia could be economically a free nation without risk to its security, how Australia could be the 'Young Tree Green', and not be tied forever to the 'Old Dead Tree'. Bob Menzies and Bruce, by contrast, were happy. For them the Conference had been an 'epoch-making advance'.[55]

Louis and Hilda Esson continued to despair of Australians ever doing something as Australians. Australian works were often greeted with 'stupid, catty' comments by other writers. Louis Esson believed Australia was perhaps the only country in the world that was not ashamed of its provincialism. Shifting dislikes and loyalties were threatening to disintegrate the Pioneer Players. The Essons wanted to know why 'morons' had such power in the Australian theatre, and why Australians seemed to have no interest in seeing their own life portrayed on the stage. Percy Grainger had his faith: the time would come when Australia produced a music which had something 'big and simple and democratic about it'.The poet Hugh McCrae was confiding to Nettie Palmer that he was quite incapable of remaining faithful to any woman. He was likely to have an affair with the next attractive woman he saw. The Palmers have gone to Caloundra on the Queensland coast, where Nettie cooked, sewed clothes for her daughters, wrote letters and articles while Vance sat on the veranda, gazing at that very vast sea, musing on the lives of the locals who accepted the spirit of the place, and on those who were

[55] *S.M.H.*, 22, 23, 24 November 1926; *Australian Worker*, 27 October 1926; *Worker* (Brisbane), 27 October 1926.

the robbers and the fleers. Louis Esson found consolation in the performance of the Australian cricketers. Early in December in the match between Victoria and New South Wales W. H. Ponsford ('Ponnie') smashed all records with an innings of 334 not out. Esson was delighted. 'Ponnie', to him, looked 'just as masterful and dominating as Macartney. At the moment he may be the greatest bat in the world'.[56]

While Nettie Palmer gave her magnificent witness that Australia was a place for things of the spirit as well as the concerns of the sheep walk, the cattle run, the horse races, the 'footy' and the cricket, copies of Katharine Susannah Prichard's work, *Working Bullocks* reached Australia. It was a story of men and women who had no yearning for higher civilization or for England's green and pleasant land, who did not see themselves as 'exiles' in Australia. Australia was all they knew. It was a story of the lives of the men and women who worked in the forests of south-western Western Australia. There was nothing noble or exalting in their work: the men were chained to their labour and the local pub, the women to the home. They had no hope of anything better either in this world or in the world to come. For them there was no rainbow, no vision of a new heaven or a new earth. They had their own lore: a man must not deceive a woman nor betray his mates. It was a man's world. They took no interest in redemption, salvation or forgiveness. The trees dwarfed the men: the sky dwarfed the trees. Nature was all-powerful. When a parson offered words of Christian hope to the wife of a man crushed under a tree, she did not take the words in a spirit of meekness: 'Blast 'im! If that's 'is way of doing things . . . makin' bloody pulp of my Bill, blast 'im!' When an intellectual from the city introduced them to the ideas of Karl Marx they were not interested.

Life was struggle: life was cruel. When the hero and heroine of *Working Bullocks* were finally married they too went into the forest, into the jungle of life, to the laughter of a butcher-bird, melodious and cruel. Australians must face the truth about life: the most beautiful song-bird in the forest, the bell-bird, was the most cruel. Love was the only comforter against a malevolent nature, the vast indifference of the sky, and the wild passions in the human heart. Australians were not sojourners here, men and women who would go from hence and be seen no more. They belonged here. They should cultivate the 'Young Tree Green' in 'the land that belongs to you'.[57]

[56] Vance Palmer to Nettie Palmer, 16 September 1926, Hilda Esson to Vance Palmer, n.d., probably 1926, Hilda Esson to Nettie Palmer, 6 October 1926, Louis Esson to Vance Palmer, 15 November 1926, 2, 28 December 1926, Palmer Papers, Series 1, Box 4, Folder 35.

[57] Katharine Susannah Prichard, *Working Bullocks* (London, 1926), see especially pp. 245 and 316; Hilda Esson to Nettie Palmer, 6 October 1926, and Louis Esson to Vance Palmer, 15 November 1926, Palmer Papers, Series 1, Box 4, Folder 35.

8

THE IMPERIAL FIRM PAYS DIVIDENDS

ON 7 FEBRUARY 1927 Bruce arrived back in Australia. On 3 March he submitted to the House of Representatives a report upon the work done at the Imperial Conference in London. He was well pleased with the Imperial Firm of Great Britain and Australia. It had been a gathering, he said, at which much was accomplished 'to cement the unity of the Empire and promote amongst its constituent parts a broader spirit of co-operation than has existed in the past'. Australia had got what she wanted: absolute autonomy without violating or weakening the ties of Empire. Australia was safe from attack. Co-operation between members of the Empire would be such that no part of the Empire would be imperilled. But Bruce did not answer the charge that he had sanctioned the throttling of Australia, financially and economically, by the Shylocks of Great Britain. Australia, he believed, was now 'assuming the obligations of nationhood'.[1]

Australia was still mainly a province of British culture. Fourteen days after Bruce spoke in the House of Representatives the *Bulletin* published an article on the failure of the Pioneer Players to put Australian life on the stage. When the Pioneer Players started in 1922 the atmosphere of Australian life was 'a complete stranger to the Australian stage'. This led to bizarre situations in the world of the theatre. In any British drawing room comedy played on an Australian stage a butler or a country house was a fixed convention, accepted cheerfully by an Australian audience most of whom had seen neither. Yet young Australian repertory actresses would faint, and need a reviving whiff of the smelling-salts bottle or a mouthful of 'something stronger' if they were asked to play the part of a woman from Fitzroy in an Esson play. They would be mortally offended if they were asked to act the part of an Australian dairy maid, straight from the cow-sheds of Gippsland or the Bega valley. Yet they would, as the *Bulletin* put it, 'leap at the chance of representing Lady Flapdoodle' in a Milne or Pinero play. For the Australian public five lines of an Esson or a Palmer play was more than enough. The reading public wanted fashion notes. They wanted to know what women were wearing, not what creative people in Australia were thinking. In March, Melbourne was getting ready for football: as Louis Esson, a lifelong addict

[1] *Age*, 8 February 1927; *C'wealth P.D.*, 3 March 1927, vol. 115, pp. 62–79.

with no intention of reforming, said: '[Football] is the most serious matter in the State'.[2]

In Australian public ceremonies nothing has changed. Canberra, for many years the joke of Australians and visitors from overseas as 'mostly a city of foundation stones' was about to become the seat of the Parliament and Government of Australia. The Parliament House overlooking the lovely meadow of the Molonglo River and St John's Church, was to be opened on 9 May 1927. Twenty-six years earlier on 9 May 1901 the first Parliament of the Commonwealth of Australia was opened in Melbourne by a member of the royal family, the Duke of York. Now his son, also a Duke of York, was to open Parliament House in Canberra. In 1901 the Governor-General belonged to the British aristocracy: in 1927 the Governor-General still came from the British aristocracy. In 1901 there were 'royal times' for the 'cuff and collar push', 'lots of dreary drivel and clap-trap', and the leading Australian politicians were dressed in English formal dress. In May 1927 the Prime Minister of Australia, Stanley Melbourne Bruce, was dressed like 'a Bond Street tailor's dummy'. In 1901 there were 'carriages in waiting for the swells from overseas'. In 1927 the carriages for the 'swells' were drawn by horses over the lovely valley of the Molonglo. In 1901 no one spoke of the wonder that was Australia. In 1927 again no one spoke of 'the wide brown land', of the fragile beauty of the haggard continent, or of any 'vision splendid on the sunlit plains extended'.

It was one of those days when the air was 'clear as crystal'. The autumn sun soon dissipated the fog over the river valley. One of the heartlands of Old Australia provided the setting for the social customs of the Old World. To the disgust of those who believed Australia was different from the Old World there was much 'bowing and scraping' as men in cocked hats and plumes arrived at Parliament House, where representatives of the 'cuff and collar push' greeted them.[3]

The royal couple travelled in cars from Government House, Yarralumla, to the Prime Minister's Lodge. From there two State carriages, each drawn by four horses, mounted by liveried postillions with white powdered wigs and attended by two footmen, transported their Royal Highnesses and their party to Parliament House. Guests sat in improvised stands in front of the steps. A solitary Aborigine sat on the grass. Australia's 'Queen of Song', Dame Nellie Melba, stood on the steps of Parliament House, in front of a microphone, and sang the five petitions—one to God to save their gracious

[2] *Bulletin*, 17 March 1927; Louis Esson to Vance Palmer, 10 March 1927, Palmer Papers, Series 1, Box 4, Folder 36.

[3] *S.M.H.*, 10 May 1927; *Canberra Times*, 13 May 1927; Henry Lawson, 'The Men Who Made Australia', Henry Lawson, *Children of the Bush* (London, 1902); A. B. ('Banjo') Paterson, 'The Man From Snowy River', *Collected Verse of A. B. Paterson* (Sydney, 1946), p. 5.

and noble King, a second to give the King a long life, a third to 'send him victorious', the fourth to render him 'happy and glorious' and the fifth to let him 'reign over us' for a long time.

Nellie Melba was Australia's own, the star of the world's opera houses, the friend of the crowned kings of Europe but no longer the Nellie Mitchell who had once been very 'Aussie' on the banks of the Yarra River near Richmond. Mr Bruce handed the Duke a golden key and invited him to open the doors of the building. He told the Duke the King was the 'symbol of our unity, the centre of all our loyalties'. He asked the Duke of York to convey to His Majesty 'the devoted homage' of the Australian people and their 'loyalty and affection to his Throne and person'. The royal Duke turned the key in the door and, as it opened, cheer after cheer broke out, flags were waved, as a surge of 'heartfelt emotion' swept like a tide over the assembled multitude. The Duke of York then spoke.

He told the audience it was peculiarly fitting they should celebrate the birth of this new capital city just after the close of an Imperial Conference, the beginning, he said, 'of another chapter in our Empire story'. He expressed the wish that the ceremony would inspire in them a 're-dedication of this Commonwealth to those great ideals of liberty, fair-dealing, justice, and devotion to the cause of Peace for which the Empire and all its members stand. We turn to-day a new page of history. May it be a page glorious for Australia and the whole Empire'. The clergy of the main Protestant churches —the Anglican, the Presbyterian and the Methodist—joined in dedicating the building 'to the glory of God and to the service of the people'. Led by the Canberra Philharmonic Choir and the New South Wales Military Band, the crowd sang 'O God, our help in ages past'. The Lord's Prayer was recited and the Anglican Primate, Dr Riley, pronounced the benediction. The royal party entered the building, and when they later left the scene, cheers again rent the air. The people of Australia had once more freely and generously made their 'expressions of loyalty'.[4]

The Labor press was disgusted. The *Australian Worker* complained that the past had 'brooded over the scene with sombre visage'. What should have been an Australian ceremony was lost in a vulgar imitation of the 'encrusted customs and hoary conventions' of their British past. Australia had once again been presented, not with a national ceremony but a 'tony picnic'. The *Workers' Weekly* was even more angry. Australians have again prostrated themselves before 'a pair of royal clowns'. Australians in high places have received a 'royal circus' with 'slavish servility'. The British have cunningly sent a pair of 'royal parasites' on a tour to strengthen a shaky capitalist society. Labor one day must put an end to these 'dope carnivals'.[5]

[4] *S.M.H.*, 10 May 1927; *Canberra Times*, 13 May 1927.
[5] *Australian Worker*, 11 May 1927; *Workers' Weekly*, 29 April, 3 June 1927.

Two days later, on 11 May, delegates from trade unions met in Melbourne to discuss ways and means of increasing the effective use of unions in the conduct of industrial disputes, and the more efficient rationalizing of trade union functions. The giddy days of 1917–21 when members of trade unions held congresses to discuss ways and means of replacing capitalist society by a socialist society were over. The moderates have beaten the militants in the contest for power. The 'not a penny off the pay, not a minute on the day' men have beaten the visionaries and the revolutionaries. The Council of Action, appointed by the Melbourne Congress of 1921 to devise ways and means for the socialization of the means of production, distribution and exchange has atrophied, it was said, because of the apathy and ignorance of the Australian working classes. Membership of trade unions has increased from 54 888 in 1891 to 433 224 in 1912 and 911 652 in 1927. Other institutions have federated—the political parties, the manufacturers, the businessmen, the cricketers, the golfers, the tennis players and the swimmers— but not the trade unions.

The revolutionary fire has not all turned to ashes. Jock Garden, still at heart a preacher and a prophet of a new heaven and a new earth, opened proceedings by leading the delegates in the singing of the 'Red Flag'. But once the serious business began, the moderates had the numbers. There was to be no revolutionary preamble, no ringing words about the role of the workers in creating a new world. There was to be an Australasian Council of Trade Unions. Congress was to meet biennially. The day-to-day business of the Council was to be conducted by an Executive. There was to be a Bureau of Peace charged with the duty of keeping in touch with the working class of all nations, to prevent war, and to promote world peace. The A.C.T.U. undertook to develop working-class educational facilities such as Labor Colleges in which men and women would be educated in the working-class view of history, economics, literature and art.[6]

In Canberra on 11 May the Australian Labor Party began its 11th Commonwealth Conference. Labor had an opportunity to show they had an alternative to the 'Bond Street tailor's dummy' and the flag-wavers of the Molonglo Plains. Australia and Labor could show they would shock the ghosts of the past back into their graves. The mummies exploited by Bruce would be stowed away in the museums of antiquities. Or so it was hoped. But the delegates spent six days and nights trying to resolve the internecine faction fights in the New South Wales Branch of the Party. Resolutions were submitted, amendments were promptly moved, the chairman was asked to rule on points of order. Delegates squabbled, shouted, roared, and

[6] 'The Australasian Council of Trade Unions', *Economic Record*, May 1928, pp. 107–10; *C'wealth Year Books*, 1901–1913, p. 906, and 1928, p. 577; *Australian Worker*, 11 May 1927; *Age*, 9, 10 May 1927.

exchanged insults. Two days later delegates agreed that the Federal Executive should have power to take whatever steps it might deem necessary to ensure a satisfactory settlement of the existing difficulties in the Labor movement in New South Wales. Labor had a chance to put its house in order. Delegates then discussed the objective of the Party. But the damage had been done. Labor was still a party in which rival factions were contending for the right to distribute the loot of office.[7]

Bruce and Page believed in efficient government, in a businessman's government. Bruce summoned the Premiers of the six States to a conference in Melbourne, beginning on 16 June 1927, to discuss the adjustment of Commonwealth and State financial relations. Bruce knew how to handle men. In his opening remarks he said it was desirable that the people should thoroughly understand the complicated and difficult problems. 'What do you say, Mr Lang?' Lang: 'I agree'. Bruce knew what manner of man Lang was. He went on to say the Government was anxious to put the financial relations of the Commonwealth and the States on a permanent basis. Both possessed sovereign powers: it was most undesirable that there should be hostility. He wanted to remove from the minds of the State Premiers the suspicion that the Commonwealth wished to aggrandize itself at the expense of the States. He wanted the Commonwealth to stop suspecting that the States were unreasonable in their demands or their expectations. Nice Mr Bruce would smooth things over, just as he had smoothed over the troubles with that stormy petrel, Billy Hughes, and relations between the Nationalists and the Country Party. They were all British: all decent chaps. 'Is that right, Mr Lang?'

The Commonwealth Ministers were there with open minds. He would summarize the proposal for the Premiers. He was always very helpful. The Commonwealth would take over the whole of the existing debts of the States: the Commonwealth would pay a fixed annual contribution towards meeting the interest on that debt, equivalent to the 1926–27 *per capita* payments, until the debt had been extinguished: the Commonwealth would contribute to a sinking fund to be established for the extinction of this debt, the amount of 2s 6d for every £100 of debt, continuing these payments until the debt had been extinguished: the Commonwealth would contribute to a sinking fund to cover the future borrowings by the States: a Loan Council, on the lines of the present Loan Council, would be established with a defined status in the scheme of public borrowing for the Commonwealth and States. By regulating the extinction of the present debt and by avoiding competition between the Commonwealth and the States for loan money in London they would all obtain better terms for loans, and effect a tremendous saving to the

[7] *Official Report of Proceedings of the 11th Commonwealth Conference of the Australian Labor Party* (Canberra, 1927).

Australian taxpayers. 'This', he concluded, 'would promote the general prosperity of the whole country'. Efficient handling of State debts and loan money would be another Commonwealth contribution to the great 'Imperial Firm' which they had toasted that night on the Molonglo Plains.[8]

Lang was not happy. The end of *per capita* payments would not be fair to New South Wales. If the Commonwealth abandoned such payments, to which the States had an undoubted right, then the Commonwealth Government should vacate that field of direct taxation which it had invaded during the war. There must be an end to the vicious principle of one authority raising by taxation money for another authority to spend. But Bruce had no intention to compromise on this point. The financial powers of the Commonwealth have tied the States to the chariot wheels of the Commonwealth: he would not loose them. Lang would not agree to bind New South Wales to a Loan Council. That would, as he put it, 'betray the sovereign rights of the State of New South Wales'. Lang was not an anti-Empire man: he was just as pro-British as Stanley Bruce or Billy Hughes, or Willie Watt, the boy from Phillip Island, or the young Bob Menzies. But Lang suffered from the Anstey paranoia about the Shylocks of Threadneedle Street. Lang wanted to have sovereign rights for New South Wales in dealing with those seen as scoundrels by all true Labor men—the bond-holders of London.[9]

Joseph Aloysius Lyons, the Labor Premier and Treasurer of Tasmania was most accommodating. In his experience as State Treasurer he had found no antagonism either between the States, or between the States and the Commonwealth. He also had to admit that in his experience it was better to have one borrower than to have two. There was already a major difference of opinion between the Catholic Labor Premier of New South Wales and the Catholic Labor Premier of Tasmania. Lyons was already a man of experience in the field of public finance. He has learned his politics in the backblocks of Tasmania, Lang in Sydney, where a man must fight to keep his pitch in the streets. The Conference of Premiers amended the Bruce proposals and agreed that Section 105A of the Constitution should now read:

105A (1) The Parliament may, for carrying out or giving effect to any agreement made or to be made between the Commonwealth and the States, make laws with respect to the public debts of the States, including—

(a) the taking over of such debts by the Commonwealth;

[8] Adjustment of Commonwealth and State Financial Relations, Conference of Commonwealth and State Ministers, Melbourne, 16 June 1927, *C'wealth P.P.*, 1926–28, vol. 5, pp. 381–2, 386.

[9] Ibid., pp. 386–9.

(b) the management of such debts;
(c) the payment of interest and the provision and management of sinking funds in respect of such debts;
(d) the consolidation, renewal, conversion and redemption of such debts;
(e) the indemnification of the Commonwealth by the States in respect of debts taken over by the Commonwealth; and
(f) the borrowing of money by the States, or by the Commonwealth for the States.

(2) The powers conferred by this section shall not be construed as being limited in any way by the provision of Section 105 of this Constitution.

As from 1 July 1927 all public borrowing by Australian Governments would be arranged by the Commonwealth in accordance with the decisions of the Loan Council. The States were being tied more firmly to the chariot wheels of the Commonwealth. Lang, who belonged to a party which wanted to abolish the federal Constitution, was not happy about this. He believed in the sovereignty of the States, because he did not want New South Wales to have to wait for 'little Tassie' or the 'sand gropers' of Western Australia or the 'banana benders' of Queensland to catch up. Lyons welcomed a 'truly Australian Loan Council'. They would confront each other again.[10]

Lyons did not look like a man moved by a revolutionary passion, or the hope of better things for humanity. Lang was a fighter, a dour man with his mouth clenched tight, and his big hands ready for combat. Lyons was a cheery soul. Lang was an Australian Ishmael, a man whose hand was raised against every man because he believed every man's hand was raised against him. Lyons held out his arms as though he wanted every man and woman to come to him. Lang belonged to the pavement, first as a newspaper boy, then as a real estate agent in Auburn, and then as a 'numbers man' in the Labor Party. Lyons was a teacher of loving kindness, and doing things for 'the least of the little ones'. When he attended his first Premiers' Conference in Sydney in 1915 the *Bulletin* described him as a man 'with hair that stood up like the bristles of a doormat'. They described his wife as 'a pretty girl with fluffy hair blown by a rude wind'. They looked like innocents wandering in the streets of a modern Babylon. Like Jimmy Scullin, Lyons was a man of deep religious faith, a man who looked with confidence to the resurrection of the dead and the life of the world to come, who found himself in a society of money-changers and measurers. Lyons was a smiler, a lover: Lang was a scowler and a hater.

Joseph Aloysius Lyons was born on 15 September 1879 at Circular Head (the Nut), Stanley, the headquarters of the Van Diemen's Land Company in

[10] Ibid., pp. 395–6, 402–3.

north-western Tasmania. He spent his childhood in the company of aunts. His private life was always in the world of women, his public life always in the world of men. He was often like a man with a private face who found himself in a public place. He was educated at Catholic and State Schools. He was educated, too, in the bush of Tasmania, the nursery of eccentrics and outsiders, the school for training men and women in adversity, courage, kindness and the will to endure. In 1895 he became a pupil teacher. At Smithton he helped to form a branch of the Tasmanian Workers' Political League. At that time he was more interested in the wrongs of Ireland than the condition of the working classes. Unlike Jimmy Scullin and John Curtin, Lyons was never a voracious reader, or a man with a lively curiosity. As an Irish Catholic he opposed conscription. On that issue he was in the eyes of his colleagues in the Labor Party a 'clean skin', not one of the 'rats' of 1916. The year before, in 1915, he had married Enid Muriel Burnell, the pretty girl with the fluffy hair, a member of the social class his aunts had taught him to respect and imitate. Lyons began to rise out of the working classes into the middle classes.

Joe Lyons, the genial gollywog from the Nut, changed the apron strings of his aunts for the apron strings of his wife. He believed in prayer: he turned to God in all the crises of his life: the sisters of the local convent school prayed for him. Women prayed for him. God and the Holy Mother gave him the strength to climb higher. The promises of Christ and the love of his family always meant more to him than the dreams of the believers in the brotherhood of man. In 1909 he was elected to the Tasmanian House of Assembly as the Member for Wilmot. In 1914 he became a member of the Labor Government of Tasmania. It was perhaps a hint of things to come that when asked to form a Labor Government in 1923 he sought advice from Sir Henry Jones, Chairman of IXL, the 'knight of the jam tin', rather than from his colleagues in the Labor Party. He asked his wife: he also prayed. In his house at Home Hill there was a print of Fra Angelico's *Mother and Child*, but no sign that its distinguished inhabitant ever sustained hopes for the future of humanity.[11]

While Lang and Lyons were sizing each other up at the Premiers' Conference in Melbourne, Bob Menzies was confiding to his friend, S. H. Ricketson of J. B. Were and Company, that he needed a wider stage on which to perform than a law court, or the dining table of a club. John Curtin had plans to stand for Fremantle in the next Commonwealth election.

Over in Belgium, on 24 July 1927, at the Menin Gate of the city of Ypres a distinguished gathering, including King Albert of the Belgians, watched Lord

[11] Enid M. Lyons, *So We Take Comfort* (London, 1965), p. 45; *Mercury* (Hobart), 3 July 1908; *Standard* (Hobart), 13 April 1939; *Australian Worker*, 19 April 1939; P. R. Hart, 'Lyons: Labor Minister—Leader of the U.A.P.', *Labour History*, October 1969; personal visit to the Nut, Home Hill and Devonport, 5–10 May 1983.

Plumer unveil the memorial to the thousands of the Empire's sons buried in nameless graves around Ypres. The Governments of every nation in the British Commonwealth had contributed to the memorial. Lord Plumer said relatives of loved ones whose bodies had never been found could now say to themselves: 'He is not missing. He is here'. King Albert of the Belgians, speaking in English, delivered a speech with many 'unforgettable passages'. 'If blood shed in a noble cause sanctifies the ground where it is spilt, no ground in the world is more sacred than the Ypres salient . . . Its name will stand for evermore as the symbol of British courage and endurance'.

Sir Granville Ryrie, the High Commissioner for Australia in London, laid a wreath in memory of 6200 Australians whose bodies lay somewhere close to the heroic city of Ypres. The wreath was inscribed: 'From the people of Australia'. Sir Granville Ryrie came from the Monaro, down Kosciusko way. A message from General Douglas Haig was read out in which he expressed grief for all those men cut down in the prime of life. Tears streamed down the faces of the spectators. Some asked God to spare humanity from again enduring what they had been through. Some asked God to have pity on them all for their great folly. Some just shook and wept. Will Longstaff, a war artist, was so exalted by the ceremony and the nearby war cemeteries that he could not sleep. As he walked entranced in the moonlight, he saw the mighty dead in steel helmets rising out of the poppy fields of Flanders: he saw them as a 'deathless army'. That night he began to transfer his vision into paint. He called the work *The Menin Gate at Midnight, 24 July 1927*. Charles Bean had a similar vision. He wanted the War Memorial in Canberra to be a building which would evoke for visitors the phantoms of the men who had suffered and died so that others might live.[12]

Around Ypres every tombstone in the war cemeteries spoke of somebody's loss, somebody's grief, somebody's hope. Some died 'that we might live': some were 'not dead, but gone before', some 'gone but not forgotten': some received a 'Tribute to a devoted son and a brave soldier by his parents': some received words of praise:

> On Honor's Field
> His Body Lies
> In God's Just Cause
> No Soldier Dies.

There were words of praise for heroic men. One epitaph read:

> He fell a hero in the strife
> For King and Country he gave his life.

[12] *S.M.H.*, 26 July 1927; personal visit to Menin Gate, 13 April 1985; text of telegram by Haig, 20 July 1927, in Ypres Museum; Will Longstaff, *The Menin Gate at Midnight, 24 July 1927*, A.W.M., Canberra.

Another was 'Worthy of everlasting love'. Some testified resignation to and acceptance of the divine will: 'Thy will be done'. Some had hopes of meeting son, husband or lover beyond the grave: 'God be with you till we meet again'. Some were unmistakably Australian, saying simply, 'From Mum and Dad'. Some were tombstones for those who were not found or not identified. On those tombstones were Rudyard Kipling's words, 'Known Unto God'. In Passchendaele the villagers put up a stone statue of Christ on the Cross. It was the Christ of the sorrowful countenance, the Christ who was sad because hundreds of thousands of human beings had died to capture one very slight rise. On the same day as the unveiling of the Menin Gate American and Japanese scholars held a seminar at Honolulu to discuss possible remedies for the problems of unemployment and over-population in Japan. The madness might start again.[13]

Back in Australia Norman Lindsay and Hugh McCrae were discussing how to prevent the poet Christopher Brennan from sinking 'down to the gutter through drink'. Brennan, Lindsay said, was an Irish peasant, and doomed to a peasant's end. 'A potent belly', Lindsay added, 'is a terrible Nemesis'. Norman Lindsay was also musing on what would happen if all great minds produced work to the limit of their capacity. There would be nothing left for great minds in two hundred years. So perhaps it was just as well friends bought a drink or two for 'poor old Chris. Brennan'. William Baylebridge told Nettie Palmer that to attempt to climb to any plane of the spirit was impossible for the lords of the market place in Australia. Any touch of the divine simplicity, Baylebridge added, had no interest 'for the gross stomachs' of the money-changers of Australia. Louis Esson thought Australians were 'too frightened of life'.

Writers and artists could always mix with the people of the circus, for there they found people of like mind—people who believed everything was allowable. Circus people could join with them in their revolt against middle-brow British Philistinism. In October Will Dyson, J. C. Bancks, the creator of Ginger Meggs ('Us Fellers'), Tom Roberts and other highbrows had a party in Sydney with trapeze artists, bear-tamers and lion-tamers from America, Germany and Denmark. Much sparkling hock and whisky was drunk. Dyson disguised himself as a wombat-tamer.

Esson had hopes of raising the minds of Australians to higher things. He was writing a play with Quiros as the hero. The man with the dream of Australia as the land of the Holy Spirit would be presented as an alternative to the good burghers of 'Yarraside' and the raucous chanters of 'Play Together, Dark Blue Twenty'. Mary Gilmore was telling Nettie Palmer the

[13] Personal visit to war cemeteries near Ypres, 13–14 April 1985, and to Passchendaele, 14 April 1985; *S.M.H.*, 26 July 1927.

time had come for the white man to take an interest in the myths of the Aborigines. To give Australian and New Zealand writers more recognition, the Australian Literature Society proposed to hold a plebiscite to obtain some expressions of opinion on the merits of Australian and New Zealand writers. The *Bulletin*, believing Australia to be rich in short stories but to suffer from a 'great dearth of full-length Australian novels', and that the book stores were stacked with novels published elsewhere, announced in August 1927 a competition for prizes of £500, £125 and £75 for a long story or a novel.[14]

Labor had a chance to present an Australian alternative to the Bruce–Page 'Imperial Firm' and the promise of 'Opportunities Unlimited'. But the Communist Party said nothing about what Australia would come to be in a socialist or communist society. They went on chanting the litany of Marx, Engels, Lenin and Stalin. Esmonde Higgins thought he and his fellow communists were in a 'spiritual muddle'. At the birth of the Party in 1920 there was enthusiasm. Now, as Higgins put it in a letter to his sister, Nettie Palmer, 'the sugar is wearing off'. The Central Executive was 'set firm in a damned sectarian attitude' and 'afraid of touching anything that might soil our precious purity'. Members were falling back on generalities and jargon learned from ideas applicable to European conditions. Here it was 'cant'. Nettie Palmer still felt that the communists simplified human behaviour. The question put in Job should be put to these communists with their claim to have all the answers: what knowest thou which is not in us?

Within the Labor Party factional leaders muddied the reputations of their rivals. Labor leaders were like whores: they were up for sale to the highest bidders. Labor, it was said, was a 'rare whore' who could 'misrepresent, lie, slander, vilify, calumniate and do anything but tell the truth'. Labor pretended to have a soul above money. The truth was that for Labor, as for the conservatives, money was 'my saviour, my God and my King'. The people in the suburbs were like the Swiss in Goethe's description of them. They were 'ensconced behind their walls and imprisoned in their customs, their laws, the opinion of their neighbours, and their Philistine suburbanism'. Frank Anstey has heard the drum-beats of a revolution which would put an end to bourgeois society, but very few others have heard those beats. During walks on Cottesloe beach John Curtin's mind was working on how Labor could 'spread the gospel', and what that gospel would now be. He once had faith in a workingman's paradise, and was a soap-box orator for socialism: now he

[14] Norman Lindsay to Jack Lindsay, 1926, and Norman Lindsay to Hugh McCrae, 1926, R. G. Howarth and A. W. Barker (eds), *Letters of Norman Lindsay* (Sydney, 1979), pp. 258–62; William Baylebridge to Nettie Palmer, 25 September 1927 or 1928, Louis Esson to Vance Palmer, 6, 29 October 1927, and Nettie Palmer to her mother (Mrs Higgins), 29 November 1927, Palmer Papers, Series 1, Box 4, Folder 37; *Argus*, 9 August 1927; *Bulletin*, 18 August 1927.

was the pragmatist of the suburbs. The one-time idealists were losing heart. Louis Esson had once had hopes of 'doing something as Australians'. Now he was indulging in 'Hamlet-like meditations on the futility of human existence' in his room in Carlton.[15]

Even the suburbs were no longer safe and cosy. On 28 October 1927 John Theodore Leslie ('Squizzy') Taylor and John ('Snowy') Cutmore, members of underworld gangs, shot each other in a house in Barkly Street, Carlton. The event troubled the *Argus*. The progressives, the improvers of humanity, they said, believed in mankind's upward march, believing a time was coming when it would be possible to 'let the ape and tiger die'. The shoot-out in the suburbs has exposed this as dangerous sentimentalists' wishy-washy. Men and women who taught that everything was allowable were themselves instruments in letting loose this 'flood of anarchy and lawlessness'. The time had come to break with 'pseudo-humanitarianism', and all 'looseness in thinking'. Nihilism ended in shoot-outs in the suburbs.[16]

Bruce was not troubled. He had his faith. Man delighted him. He agreed with Hamlet: 'What a piece of work is a man, how noble in reason, how infinite in faculty'. He believed in the Empire: he believed in the British race: he believed in the courage, endurance, resource and love of adventure of Australians. He was preoccupied with the problem of the financial relations between the Commonwealth and the States. On 14 December 1927 he explained the problems to the members of the House of Representatives. He told them how the founding fathers had agonized over the means by which the Commonwealth could have adequate financial resources without weakening the financial security and independence of the States. The result was a compromise, generally known as the 'Braddon blot', under which three-fourths of the customs and excise revenue collected by the Commonwealth was returned to the States. Until 1910 the requirements of the Commonwealth had been small. When the question was reviewed in 1910 it was agreed that the Commonwealth should pay to the States 25 shillings per head of their population. These payments suited the more populous States but not States such as Western Australia and Queensland with huge areas and a sparse population. The demands on the financial resources of the

[15] E. M. Higgins to Harry ——, 30 August 1926, Letters by E. M. Higgins 1903–60, E. M. Higgins Papers, M.L.; Nettie Palmer to Esmonde Higgins, 5 September 1921, Letters from Nettie Palmer to Esmonde Higgins, 1921–1960, ibid; Edward Ernest Judd, The Brisbane Street Whore. Broadsheet in R. S. Ross Collection, N.L.A., Canberra; Goethe, 'Briefe Aus Der Schweiz, Erste Abteilung', quoted in Richard Wagner, *My Life* (London, 1911, reissue of 1963), p. 642; Lloyd Ross, *John Curtin* (Melbourne, 1977), pp. 84–6; C. Hartley Grattan, 'The Australian Labor Situation', *Nation* (New York), 19 October 1927; Louis Esson to Vance Palmer, 6 June 1928, Palmer Papers, Series 1, Box 5, Folder 38.

[16] *Argus*, 29 October, 5 November 1927.

Commonwealth had been increased by the introduction of old age and invalid pensions.

Then with the war the Commonwealth found it needed large revenues for war purposes. In 1919, 1923 and 1926 the wit of man found no solutions agreeable to all parties. Under the federal Constitution one Government raised revenue by means of taxation and another spent it. Ever since the beginning of the war of 1914–18 there had been duplication in taxation. So in June the Commonwealth had submitted its proposals to the States, which had agreed to them. The Commonwealth Government was now asking the Parliament to ratify that agreement, and to agree that the consequential need to amend the Constitution be submitted to a referendum by the electors. Bruce believed it was a 'harmonious settlement', an agreement which would enable them to make loan arrangements upon more favourable terms than had hitherto obtained. Australia's credit would be enhanced in the money markets of the world.[17]

Matthew Charlton, the leader of the Labor Party, thought there had been too much trickery and bargaining. He was a wise man and a kind man. He wanted harmony, not bludgeoning and threats. He believed in the slogan, 'One people, one destiny'. But Matthew Charlton was worried: Bruce and Page have asked a committee to report on ways and means of paying child endowment and widows' pensions. The expenses of the Commonwealth must increase, as Governments assumed responsibility for social welfare. Unemployment payments were on the way. The Commonwealth would be forced to drive harder and harder bargains with the States. Harmony would go. Jimmy Scullin also wanted harmony. He did not like the resentment that was stirred up in the breasts of the people. Jack Lang was angry: Jack Lang was enraged. The people of Australia were being enslaved to the bondholders of London. The Shylocks of London would throttle the liberties and the independence of the Australian people. But Bruce took no notice. He believed in the 'Imperial Firm' as the source for Australia of men, money and markets.[18]

Men of heroic ingredients were crossing the oceans by air, flying from continent to continent, just as Vasco da Gama, Ferdinand Magellan and Captain Cook had explored the oceans of the world, and Charles Sturt, Edward Eyre, Robert O'Hara Burke and William John Wills the deserts of Australia. In May 1927 Captain Charles Lindbergh, an American airman, flying alone, started from Roosevelt Field on Friday morning 20 May and arrived at Le Bourget, France, on Saturday 21 May. Man and his machines

[17] William Shakespeare, *Hamlet*, II, 2, 323–4; *C'wealth P.D.*, 14 December 1927, vol. 117, pp. 3178–87.

[18] *C'wealth P.D.*, 7 March 1928, vol. 118, pp. 3624–7, 16 March 1928, ibid., pp. 3924–34.

could meet any challenge. Lindbergh and his plane had even weathered the violent sleet storms in the Atlantic. The flight lasted thirty-four and a half hours. Lindbergh was twenty-five years old. But the British could do it too. There had been an impression the British race was lagging behind in the conquest of the air. On 8 January 1920 R. J. Parer and J. C. McIntosh took off from Hounslow in England in a DH9 monoplane to fly to Australia. Seven months later on 2 August they arrived in Darwin. Alan Cobham arrived in Darwin on 5 August 1926 to finish the first solo flight between England and Australia. The men of the bulldog breed have shown they were just as good in the air as on sea or land.[19]

Civil aviation developed rapidly in Australia. On 16 November 1920 the Queensland and Northern Territory Aerial Services Limited was registered in Brisbane for passenger and postal services at the Top End. Hudson Fysh was one of the pilots. The company was known by the trade name of QANTAS. Western Australian Airways (W.A.A. and later West) was registered in August 1921. On 4 December 1921 it began the first civil air service, planes flying between Geraldton and Derby. Charles Kingsford Smith ('Smithy') was one of their pilots. In 1924 they extended their service from Geraldton to Perth. In 1928 they began the Perth–Adelaide passenger and mail service. On 7 February 1928 Bert Hinkler set out from Croydon in England to fly to Bundaberg. On 27 February a crowd of twelve thousand broke into frenzied excitement to welcome him there. Pipe and brass bands played. Two boys climbed up a telegraph pole in a nearby paddock. The firebell rang in Bundaberg. Church bells joined in. Shops were closed. Everyone flocked to the airfield to give a hero's welcome to the boy from Bundaberg. He had taken sixteen days to fly solo from London to Darwin.

Herbert John Louis Hinkler was born in Bundaberg on 8 December 1892. He was thirty-six in the year of his great achievement. He was the son of a German-born father, and a mother whose father had been a prospector on the Gympie goldfields. Machines were the great passion of his life. He had tinkered with bicycles in his younger days, and then experimented with gliders. When he addressed the crowd on the airfield at Bundaberg he spoke with passion about the behaviour of his machine during the flight, and all the attention he had given it. He was interested in gadgets. Bruce and others expanded on the significance of the flight. Bruce sent a telegram of congratulation and a cheque for £2000 from the people of Australia. Hinkler's feat, he said, was no stunt or freak performance. He took great pride in the fact that Hinkler was an Australian. Hinkler had the qualities which had made this nation great during the war, and would make her great in peace. That day it was announced that Hinkler would speak by wireless to both

[19] *Argus*, 23, 24 May 1927; *S.M.H.*, 25 February 1928.

British and Australian listeners. The aeroplane and the wireless were transcending distance: they were putting an end to Australian isolation.[20]

Everyone was proud of Bert Hinkler. The British claimed him as one of their own. The King sent him a message of congratulation. The Governor-General congratulated him on his 'splendid achievement'. The *Australian Worker* saluted him as the son of a pioneer woman worker on an Australian goldfield, and a member of a family of 'solid Laborites'. A boy from the Australian bush has shown he was 'entitled to be ranked with Columbus, Cook, Stanley, Lindbergh and other intrepid men who have added fresh pages to the records of great deeds'. 'Hooray, Hinkler', said the *Bulletin*. An Australian was the first to do it alone. But, despite all the flattery, the praise and the applause, Bert Hinkler did not let anyone know what was going on inside him. He enthused over his gadgets, over his machine. The *Bulletin* was puzzled by this 'natty little airman, remarkable for the width of his forehead, the directness of his eyes and the smallness of his hands', who did not let anyone know what was going on in his mind.[21]

On 11 March 1928 thousands of sightseers flocked to Mascot aerodrome in Sydney to catch a glimpse of him. There were Hinkler balloons for sale, Hinkler buttons and booklets. There were ice-creams, cigarettes and soft drinks. Loudspeakers roared out jazz tunes, stunt planes performed overhead as photographers and cinematographers jostled for the best position on the landing field. Shortly after three in the afternoon cheers and shouts from eighty thousand throats, together with the tooting of motor horns, heralded the hero's arrival. Hats were thrown into the air, handkerchiefs were waved frantically, voices chanted 'We want Bert. We want Bert'. But Hinkler was not a man of words, he was the man of action. 'My heart', he said, 'is too full for many words'. That evening Hinkler and his mother were introduced to the Governor of New South Wales, Sir Dudley de Chair, and his wife. At night they were supper guests of the British Imperial Oil company, who had decorated the dining room at the Wentworth Hotel with the words: 'See the conquering hero comes'.[22]

In March Bruce welcomed Hinkler to Canberra and invited him to enter the House of Representatives as a mark of honour. On 15 March the Speaker, Sir Littleton Groom, said to the members: 'I desire to inform honourable members that a highly distinguished aviator, Captain Herbert Hinkler, A.F.C., is within the precincts of the House'. Bruce spoke of Australia and the Empire. Hinkler said not a word. Later the Governor-General,

[20] *S.M.H.*, 25, 28 February 1928; Ian F. McLaren, *Australian Aviation: A Bibliographical Survey* (Melbourne, 1958); Stanley Brogden, *The History of Australian Aviation* (Melbourne, 1960); R. D. MacKenzie, *Solo: the Bert Hinkler Story* (Brisbane, 1963).

[21] *S.M.H.*, 25 February 1928; *Australian Worker*, 29 February 1928; *Bulletin*, 29 February, 14 March 1928.

[22] *S.M.H.* 12 March 1928.

Lord Stonehaven, saluted him as a hero. Hinkler explained to the Governor-General the mechanism of his machine. That was the great passion of his life. He did not belong to what the *Bulletin* called 'the select band of pony-raising and picture show and "suburban estate" knights' honoured by Bruce and Page. Hinkler's subject was the machine.

In Melbourne thousands of members of Christian churches were shocked that the Hinkler Welcome Committee had arranged to welcome him to Melbourne on a Sunday. After the welcome on 20 March the Royal Aero Club entertained him at the Princess Theatre. All the high-ranking officers in the Australian Imperial Forces were there, including Sir Harry Chauvel, the hero of the Palestine campaign, and Rear-Admiral Napier. So were captains of industry such as C. N. McKay of the Sunshine Harvester Company. The military and the captains of industry were allies in Australian public life. Amid great enthusiasm a baritone sang Jack O'Hagan's song specially composed for the occasion: 'Hustling Hinkler, here I come'. But being an object of worship to the men in high places was not what Bert Hinkler craved. He wanted to build a machine which would cross all the oceans of the world, and survive all storms. He wanted his name to live on in the story of the conquest of the air.[23]

In Canberra another drama began. On 29 March 1928 Matthew Charlton, the leader of the Australian Labor Party, informed the House of Representatives that due to failing health, he was resigning from the office of leader of the Australian Labor Party. Charlton was the last of the leaders who had come to prominence after Labor had 'blown out its brains' during the imbroglio over conscription. Everyone liked him. Members on both sides of the House praised him for his years in office. For Charlton was a most honourable man, a most virtuous man. He had won the loyalty and esteem of his colleagues. No one would stoop so low as to stab Mattie Charlton in the back. But no one could remember what he had done, or what he had stood for. For Charlton was also a very dull man.

The Party must now elect his successor. Jimmy Scullin was widely expected to win the vote in Caucus, which met on 26 April 1928. In the first ballot Scullin had a substantial margin over other candidates, including Ted Theodore. The latter then moved, seconded by G. E. Yates of Adelaide, that Scullin be declared the leader of the Party. This motion was carried unanimously. Nearly one half of the voters in Caucus belonged to the Catholic Church. To the surprise of the press and other observers, Arthur Blakeley defeated Ted Theodore in the ballot for the deputy leadership. Labor has again 'played safe'. The Party has preferred a party faithful with a long period of service to the brilliant new boy from Queensland. Within a week

[23] *C'wealth P.D.*, 15 March 1928, vol. 118, p. 3844; *Argus*, 16, 21 March 1928; *Bulletin*, 21, 28 March 1928.

the old guard in the Party wrote to Scullin accusing Theodore of bribing W. G. Mahony, the former member for Dalley, to resign so that he, Ted Theodore, could have his seat. The Lang faction, with the support of Jock Garden, wanted a safe seat for J. A. Beasley, a Langite and President of that testing furnace for human strength, the Trades and Labor Council of New South Wales. The Langites have cast a shadow over the celebrations at the beginning of Scullin's leadership. Jack Beasley and Lang would cast a darker shadow later, when Catholic would stab Catholic. Men who kneeled at the same altar to receive the gifts of divine love looked on each other in the Labor Party with 'undying hostility'. The faction brawls and talk of corruption have muddied the waters again just as Jimmy Scullin, the high-minded man and believer in the 'cause', took over the leadership. Opponents mocked him as the 'Mannix man', or the political voice of the Bishop of Rome. Over in Perth John Curtin, another believer in the 'cause', was preparing to stand for Fremantle in the elections due at the end of the year.[24]

Bruce was courteous to the new leader of the Labor Party. He addressed him as he addressed all other Labor men, calling him 'Scullin', never 'Mr Scullin', or 'sir'. Bruce had other things on his mind. He was anxious to promote 'confidence and good will' between the Nationalists and the Country Party. He wanted to stabilize the financial arrangements between the Commonwealth and the States. While Labor men were posing as redeemers of humanity but fighting each other like wild beasts over their prey, on 2 April the Governor-General assented to the Act to approve an agreement between the Commonwealth of Australia and the States of New South Wales, Victoria, Queensland, South Australia, Western Australia and Tasmania, or the Financial Agreement Act. So while Lang, Theodore, Jock Garden and Jack Beasley were alarming poor Jimmy Scullin, the Commonwealth acquired the legislative powers to discipline recalcitrant State Premiers. The financial powers of the Commonwealth might make and unmake State governments.[25]

Bruce wanted to end the communist menace. Australia must be made safe for the bourgeoisie, the farmers and the graziers. Members of Trade Unions were still circulating revolutionary propaganda. They were talking of the workers of Australia combining together 'in a solid working-class phalanx, to ensure to all workers the full product of their labour'. On 2 April 1928, the day the Governor-General assented to the Financial Agreement Act, the first number of the *Pan-Pacific Worker* was published in Sydney. It was the official

[24] *C'wealth P.D.*, 29 March 1928, vol. 118, p. 4307; *Australian Worker*, 4 April 1928; John Robertson, *J. H. Scullin* (Nedlands, 1974), pp. 114–15, 131–3.

[25] *Argus*, 21 March 1928; An Act to approve an agreement between the Commonwealth of the First Part and the States of New South Wales, Victoria, Queensland, South Australia, Western Australia and Tasmania, 2 April 1928, No. 5 of 1928, *C'wealth Acts*, vol. XXVI, 1928.

organ of the Pan-Pacific Secretariat formed at the Pan-Pacific Trade Union Conference held at Hankow, China, in May 1927. This group believed only the militant action of the working class on an international basis would enable the workers to frustrate the predatory plans of the imperialists. They resolved to support actively the liberation movements of the oppressed peoples and exploited classes in China, India, Indonesia, Korea, the Philippines and Latin America. For them the class struggle, not creed, nationality or race, was the sole means to the liberation of the workers. The Labor Party distanced itself from the movement. The Pan-Pacific Trade Union Secretariat threatened White Australia: Labor would have nothing to do with 'coloured gentlemen'. Bruce agreed. Bruce and the Labor Party would work together against 'coloured gentlemen' and the would-be destroyers of White Australia.[26]

In December 1927 amendments to the Conciliation and Arbitration Act were drafted. Bruce defended his proposals as a move to preserve industrial peace, a move to stop the militants bullying the moderates in the key transport unions. The communists had a different explanation. 'As capitalism develops', the *Workers' Weekly* wrote on 23 December 1927, 'and class clashes become sharper, the parasite class is compelled to tighten its legal chains on the working class'. That, they said, was the purpose of the amendments to the Conciliation and Arbitration Act. The workers must fight Bruce's 'bludgeon bill'. Bruce has decided to kill working-class resistance to 'boss-class oppression'. The Labor movement must present a united front. Labor politicians must be compelled to oppose the Bill.

The moderates in the trade unions and in the Labor Party believed Bruce would represent their opposition to the Bill as evidence that Labor was soft on the 'reds'. All through the first half of 1928 the Communist Party appealed to the working class: away with this indecision: beware, Bruce wants a huge unemployed army. Labor was trapped. The communists appealed to the workers not to fall for Bruce's 'dope' about Anzac Day because that was 'designed to idealise the last blood-bath'. The workers must be taught there would be no relief from the struggle until capitalism was overthrown and the working class itself took control of the means of life. There must be a 'mass challenge to capitalism'. Bruce stood firm. On 7 June he told the House of Representatives the time had come for a showdown with the unions.[27]

The following day, 8 June, Charles Kingsford Smith and Charles Ulm landed their Fokker monoplane, the *Southern Cross*, at Brisbane. They had flown the Pacific. 'Smithy', as he was known to his friends, was a man after Bruce's own heart: a hero of aviation during the world war, one of those war

[26] *Pan-Pacific Worker*, 2 April 1928.
[27] *Workers' Weekly*, 23 December 1927, 20 January, 16 March, 27 April 1928.

heroes who believed that Australia was a place where only eagles flew in the sky. Like his illustrious namesakes Keith and Ross Smith, 'Smithy' was a King and Empire Alliance man, a man who believed Australia belonged to the fearless, the free and the bold. He was one of those daredevil pilots of the war, one of those men of British race whom Bruce believed to be the salt of the earth, the hope for the future of humanity. On 25 April 1928, Bruce had appealed to the youth of Australia to appreciate the significance of Anzac Day in the annals of the Empire and in the history of the British race. Now 'Smithy' has given the example for youth to follow. As a member of the Royal Flying Corps he had been awarded the Military Cross for 'exceptional bravery' when engaged in a 'merry dogfight' with four German planes. His foot was smashed and he lost consciousness as his plane nose-dived. By grit and determination he had managed to regain control in time. Doctors cut off two toes: ground staff picked bullets out of the plane. After the war 'Smithy' made a living as a stunt pilot in America. All his life he was plagued with the 'getting and spending' problem. After returning to Australia he flew aeroplanes for companies providing airmail services. In 1926 he flew round Australia with Charles Ulm.[28]

Now, just over four hundred years after Magellan had asked the Holy Mother of God to watch over them during their voyage on that 'very vast sea', Kingsford Smith, Ulm, and their two American companions set out from San Francisco on 31 May. 'Smithy' had his own superstition: he had a rabbit's paw in his pocket. On 9 June they landed at Eagle Farm, Brisbane. Five thousand motor cars tooted a welcome, onlookers cheered, tossed hats in the air and waved handkerchiefs as 'Smithy' gave them a smile, one of those smiles which endeared him to the hero-worshippers. Bruce gave him and his companions a cheque for £5000 for their 'epoch-making flight'. 'Smithy', Bruce added, demonstrated that the spirit which animated our troops in battle still survived. The identification of Australia with the wonderful exploit filled him with pride. The Governor-General thanked 'Smithy' for rendering 'great service to the Empire'. The Returned Sailors and Soldiers' League tendered the warmest congratulations of the diggers to their brother digger and his gallant companions. 'Smithy' said it was a big moment in their lives: it was 'the fulfilment of my life's ambition'.[29]

Two hundred thousand people welcomed them at Mascot aerodrome in Sydney when they landed there on 10 June. Young girls were there to pour out their adoration for 'Smithy': photographers begged him to stand still, just for one moment, please: mayors ran excitedly after him bearing their illuminated addresses: voices shouted out above the never-ending roar of the crowd: 'Don't you remember me, Smithy?': autograph hunters scrambled

[28] *S.M.H.*, 2, 4, 7, 9 June 1928.
[29] Ibid., 11 June 1928.

with each other: pressmen tried to keep their pencils poised over the blank pages in their reporter's books: onlookers shivered: thousands coughed and spluttered on the damp ground, waiting for just one fleeting glimpse. The Mayor of Mascot managed to tell 'Smithy', 'we proudly greet you as an Australian and one of ourselves'. 'Smithy' modestly said the praise belonged to Charlie Ulm and their two American 'pals'. Without them, he said, we would all have been drowned. Ulm spoke of their plans for the future. There was talk of a flight round the world, of a flight across the Tasman Sea to New Zealand. 'But you can take this as definite', Charlie Ulm added, 'Smithy and I will never be finished with flying'.

Two Australians have proved that the widest ocean in the world could be traversed by air, and, as the *Sydney Morning Herald* put it, 'the fury of the storms outstayed and conquered'. Most important, two Australians have been associated with two Americans. Australia and America were 'the two great white English-speaking guardians of the Pacific'. The airmen have added 'immensely to the ties which a common blood and a common tongue and a common heritage have already forged'. That collaboration was the promise for the future. The association between the two nations was designed by Providence to be indissoluble. 'Smithy' has strengthened the hope for that indissolubility. The flight was part of the destiny of Australia, and 'Smithy' was the agent of destiny. 'Smithy' could not kiss all the girls who offered their lips to him. But he has shown one great thing: the qualities that made the digger the remarkable soldier and the bushman the wonderful mate have made the Australian successful in the air. 'Smithy' was the spirit of Australia. Now 'Smithy' must shorten the air voyage from Australia to England: that would bring Australia nearer to the centre of the Empire: that would 'forge another link in the Imperial chain'.[30]

While 'Smithy', during storms over the Pacific Ocean, was having his fantasies about what he would do to those Bolshie bludgers, the intellectuals and writers in Australia were thinking of quite different things. William Baylebridge wanted to know why Australia was such a 'makeshift world', a world in which every man who thought and felt deeply enough was 'bound in some measure to become a spiritual outcast'. Martin Boyd was brooding over the complex fate of being a person with a fine conscience and delicate sensibilities in a society where conversation was about the affairs of the sheep walk, the oscillating fortunes of the moneychangers, the 'good oil' on the 'gee-gees', and gossip about the cricket and the 'footy'. Martin Boyd has tried many things—pleasure, beauty, art, life in an Anglo-Catholic monastery, music, literature, drawing-room talk, the life of the country gentry in England and Australia, and the love between two boys. He was also a pilgrim in search of the means of grace. He was not sure where he belonged. The Old

[30] Ibid.; *Bulletin*, 13, 20 June 1928; *Daily Telegraph*, 21 June, 13 July 1928.

World had culture, elegance and refinement but no human warmth. The New World was coarse, vulgar and common, but abounded in warmth. He was not sure what he believed—being drawn to both the Greek and the Christian views of the world.

There were many voices inside Martin Boyd. In his work, *The Montforts* he wrote of how richness of spirit could not exist in a country little more than one hundred years old, of the power of British Philistinism in Australia, of living in a country designed by nature for the Greek ideals of beauty and harmony, but which placed its inhabitants in the straitjacket of Victorian-age puritanism. He believed pleasure to be the important thing in life, but pleasure could not be pursued in Australia because of the power of the puritans and the wowsers. He wrote of the Australian as having the 'face of an angel and the heart of a beast'. He wrote of his fear of some future 'parvenu flood' which would drown what little there was of taste and civilized values in Australia. The novel was perilously close to a Henry James assault on the vulgarities of the New World. It reminded Nettie Palmer of the exchange between Henry James and W. D. Howells. When Howells read Henry James's long list of what was missing in the New World, followed by the James question. 'What then remains?', Howells replied: 'Why, the whole of life'. But, so far, no one had put on paper or canvas, or into stone, or on a music sheet the 'whole of life' in Australia. No one wrote 'We Australians . . .' as Thomas Mann wrote 'We Germans . . .', because no one knew who the Australians were, or what had made them what they were.[31]

Prime Minister Bruce was an Empire man, a believer in Australia as a province of British civilization. As he saw it, the British came to Australia as conquerors and subduers. The previous 'tenants of the soil', the Aborigines, were swept aside. By 1928 the resistance of the conquered was confined to the northern and inland parts of Australia. In the winter of 1928 at Brooks' Soak, near Coniston in the Northern Territory, a white dingo trapper, Freddie Brooks, asked an Aborigine to let his wife wash his clothes. The Aboriginal woman did not return to her husband. Two Aborigines, Padygar and Akirkka went to Brook's camp and asked to see 'white feller'. Accounts given later differed on what then happened. One Aborigine testified that Brooks 'givem cheek', so Aborigine 'puttem [boomerang] right through Brooks' throat' and cut him with a stone knife. Another Aborigine testified that two Aborigines murdered Brooks with a yam stick and a tomahawk. A half-caste reported the murder of Brooks to Mounted Constable William George Murray.

[31] W. Baylebridge to Nettie Palmer, 25 July 1928, Palmer Papers, Series 1, Box 5, Folder 39; Martin Boyd ('Martin Mills'), *The Montforts* (London, 1928); P. A. Dobrez, Martin Boyd, thesis in A.N.U. Library; Nettie Palmer in *Brisbane Courier*, 8 September 1928; *Age*, 26 May 1928; *Bulletin*, 8 August, 10 October 1928.

TWO BOYS FROM THE BUSH

Donald George Bradman,
the Boy from Bowral

Stanley Joseph McCabe, the Boy from Grenfell

Photographs in National Library, Canberra

A SON OF THE ENLIGHTENMENT

Herbert Vere Evatt

Photograph in National Library, Canberra

Murray was a hero of the white population of Central Australia. He had all the virtues and qualities of the bushman. He could tame wild horses, repair the engine of a car, be brave in the face of a foreign foe (he had been a digger) or the assaults of nature, but was painfully shy and tongue-tied in the presence of women. He believed in revenge, in the Old Testament lore of an eye for an eye, and a tooth for a tooth. When he and his party surprised the Aborigines near Brooks' Soak on 7 August 1928 he, in the words of an Aboriginal witness, 'bin shootem whole fucking lot . . . gatherum up, ridem, and . . . shootem all fucking lot . . . All t' people, all, like bullock . . . big mob, woman, kid, man . . . too much blackfeller'. Probably twenty-eight were massacred.

Missionaries, moral improvers and humanitarians asked the Government to charge Murrary with murder. Men like Murray, they said, were speeding up the 'gloomy progress towards a certain and utter destruction' of the Aborigines. White settlers in the Northern Territory, in Alice Springs, Katherine, Daly Waters and Darwin replied that the bullet and the whip were the only way to make 'black fellows', 'abos' and 'goons' give up these barbarous deeds of revenge against the white inhabitants. Having heard from white settlers about the barbarous practices of the Aborigines they would not listen to any charge of brutality. Progress meant development for the white man and forfeiture for the black man. The black man should either be quietly incorporated into the white man's world, or retreat further into the desert. Might was right. Bruce must decide. He made the standard response of those in power to a problem to which there was no answer which would satisfy both sides. He appointed a commission to inquire into the killing of natives in the Northern Territory. The question was: whose story would be believed? The reply to that question depended upon the values of the men giving the answer. No Government dared to appoint to such a commission men or women who would give credibility to the evidence of one of the 'original tenants of the deserts of Australia'.[32]

British civilization must prevail. That was Bruce's view. That was also the view of Bob Menzies. He was, as he put it later, 'enthusiastically for the British character'. He has said so during the war. For him the British flag was 'the glowing emblem of liberty, and hatred of all tyranny and oppression'. The British flag was 'the gleam of truth and righteousness'. During the war when the 'Bugles of death' and the 'wild, barbaric drum' sounded, he was sustained by his faith in 'the ancient pride of blood and race'. Now in 1928 he proposed to serve the British people in public life. He has decided to 'throw

[32] J. and P. Read (eds), Eyewitness Accounts of the Coniston Massacres, typescript in possession of editors; *Northern Standard*, 9 November 1928; *Northern Territory News*, 14 August, 13 November 1928; F. E. Baume, *Tragedy Track* (Sydney, 1933), pp. 85–6; *A.B.M. Review*, 7 May 1922, p. 40.

his hat into the political ring'. He has decided to stand for election for the province of East Yarra to the Legislative Council of Victoria.[33]

The shadows from the past were still there. He wanted two contradictory satisfactions: the sport of scoring off his inferiors, and the fulfilment of his ambition to be number one. He has called the men on whom he depended for a start in his political career 'the boneheads of Spring Street'. The shadow cast by the war would also not go away. On 16 May an elector asked the question: where were you during the war? Why was it that you, Bob Menzies, having trained in the militia, having passed all your examinations at the University, being unmarried at the time and in sound health, did not volunteer for service in the Australian Imperial Force, and fight for the King, the Empire, and for Australia? Menzies said he was not seeking a political career for personal comfort, profit or advancement. His mind was on higher things. But still the shadow would not go away.

Another elector called for an explanation. Menzies must answer. And so he did on 29 May 1928. He held a public meeting in Hawthorn. Speaking with the emotion of a man of great human warmth and passion, he explained why he had stayed at home. At a family council of all the Menzies' sons it had been decided that two should go, and one remain at home. His brothers had insisted he be the one to stay at home, he being the youngest. But the shadow would not go away. The cruel undergraduate joke that the brilliant military career of Bob Menzies was cut short by the outbreak of war was still hounding him. Men judge each other harshly. He has done that for which he would never be forgiven, for which there could be no expiation or atonement. Behind the mask of overbearing pride and arrogance which he put between himself and the world there was a man wanting to be loved, who feared he would win from other human beings only the consolation prize of admiration. That year he had one satisfaction. The electors in the province of East Yarra voted for him to join 'the boneheads of Spring Street'.[34]

Others were on the way up. David Unaipon appealed to the white man to help the Aborigines until such time as the Aborigines could help themselves. David Unaipon was a member of the Ngarrindjeri tribe. He was born in 1872 at the Point McLeay Mission Station near the mouth of the Murray River in South Australia. He excelled in many fields: as a musician, a scientist, an inventor and a preacher. In his lifetime he was called the Leonardo da Vinci of the Aboriginal people. But he was sustained, too, by the image of Christ in his heart. He wanted the Aborigines to blend the white man's science, the

[33] Robert Gordon Menzies, *The Forgotten People* (Sydney, 1943), pp. 46, 78–9; R.G.M. (R. G. Menzies), 'What Are We Fighting For?', *M.U.M.*, May 1916, p. 15.

[34] *Herald* (Melbourne), 16, 17 May 1928; *Age*, 30 May 1928; *Argus*, 30 May 1928.

white man's religion, with the skills of the Aborigines as food gatherers, observers of nature, and their spirituality. He set out to prove that the Aborigine could rise to the top in any field of human endeavour, that Aborigines were not condemned to be forever nomads of the desert, fringe-dwellers in the white man's towns, or stockmen, boxers, footballers, trackers, kitchen hands, cooks, wood-choppers, cadgers and cringers on the edge of the white man's world. David Unaipon wanted the white man to cease patronizing the blackfellows as 'little children' who had a chance in the kingdom of heaven, but drew blanks and never prizes in the white man's world.

The white man should be shown that the Aborigine was not a Caliban on whom nurture did not stick, not 'this thing of darkness'. Like the white man the Aborigine could 'seek for grace'. White men and women were also undergoing a sea change. Hitherto anyone who believed that the Aborigine could teach the white man wisdom and understanding was dismissed as a 'hairbrained fool'. Now Mary Gilmore was telling the Palmers the bread of life would be won by listening to the Aboriginal stories of the creation of the world. Margaret Preston wanted artists to stop condescending to Aboriginal art 'from the heights of a school of design education'. She wanted the white man to cease thinking of Aboriginal art as 'these primitive efforts'. She wanted him to see the world through Aboriginal eyes. The Aborigine had an answer to the decadence and the doubts of the white man.[35]

Women also wanted a change in men's behaviour and hearts. The Women's Christian Temperance Union, founded in 1887, had three aims: world prohibition, world peace and world purity. They wanted to rid men's minds of the delusion that alcohol was just another beverage. They wanted to persuade men that gambling was a perversion of the instinct to make riches. The Housewives' Progressive Association, founded in 1917 as the Housewives' Association and renamed in 1928, wanted to protect women from being exploited by tradesmen—from buying adulterated fruit, from being victimized by cunning store-keepers with their dirty trick of selling cold-storage eggs as fresh-laid eggs. The Women's Equal Citizenship Federation and the Adelaide Social Purity Society wanted women to have a role in deciding Australian domestic and foreign policy, and to secure equality of opportunity with men.[36]

Women played many roles. In the heart of 'Yarraside' Ivy Brookes, daughter of Alfred Deakin, wife of Herbert Brookes, the king-maker of

[35] *A.B.M. Review*, 12 October 1925; personal talks with David Unaipon, Belgrave, 1927 and 1928; Mary Gilmore to Nettie Palmer, 7 April 1928, Palmer Papers, Series 1, Box 5, Folder 38; Margaret Preston, 'The Application of Aboriginal Designs', *Art in Australia*, March 1930.

[36] *S.M.H.*, 3, 4, 6 May 1927; Bessie M. Rischbieth, *March of Australian Women* (Perth, 1964), pp. 59–60, 73, 127–8.

1916–17, presided with grace and distinction at the gatherings of the patricians of South Yarra and Toorak. She served soft drinks to her guests because she believed alcohol deprived men of the divine gift of reason and reduced them to the behaviour of the goats and the monkeys. She was sensible in her religion. She rejected the ritualism of the Church of Rome and of the High Anglicans as idolatrous and superstitious. She thought the absence of vestments in the dissenting churches led to anarchy and unbelief. Like her illustrious father, Alfred Deakin, she believed the Anglican Church was evidence of the British genius for compromise. She knew Christ had warned that it was easier for a camel to pass through the eye of a needle than for a rich man to enter the kingdom of heaven. She took comfort from Christ's rider, that with God all things were possible. She believed God had a plan, and that the British were the instruments of Divine Providence. Australia mirrored God's plan. There was no need for any change in society: the industrious, the talented and the frugal could rise to the top in Australia. Australia was a New Britannia, built on British ideals of liberty, the rule of law, tolerance and fair play. She was not bothered when the vicar of Christ Church, South Yarra, read the passage in the Book of Isaiah prophesying that Jehovah would take away the ornaments with which women decorated themselves. She thought some modern women went too far with their jewels, their powder and their painted pomp. Christ Church, South Yarra, was what Christian churches should be, a temple which reminded worshippers of British achievements and British glory.[37]

Annie West was the wife of a chicory farmer, Charlie West, a descendant of one of those families who had taken up small selections on Phillip Island not long after the proclamation of the Selection Act in 1865. Years of hard work in the house, the dairy and the chicory field and of bearing children had wrecked her body. She walked with the permanent stoop of a victim of drudgery at the cow bail, the wood heap and the kitchen sink. She had a ravaged face, the lines bearing testimony to the hard years. She had the light in the eye of a woman whose mind was single, and whose heart overflowed with love and charity to all those afflicted or distressed in mind, body or estate. She was a mighty spirit encased within a tiny frame. Without protest or complaint she accepted the place in life which God had allotted to her, never speaking as though things could be any different. She enjoyed her chats with Mrs Archie Findlay, a mountain of flesh with a heart to match, Mrs Bert Jones, one of the best, and other women who fought the good fight with all their might. She loved to stand in the schoolroom at Ventnor and join with a tiny band of worshippers in singing hymns such as:

[37] Rohan Rivett, *Australian Citizen: Herbert Brookes, 1867–1963* (Melbourne, 1965), pp. 36–7, 49–51, 78–82, 113–14; Herbert Brookes Papers, N.L.A., Canberra.

Abide with me,
Fast falls the eventide,
The darkness deepens,
Lord with me abide.

She knew that other helpers might fail, as she knew what was in man. She found it comforting to hear that some things, like the sea, the sky, and the sou'westerly wind were from everlasting and would never change. She found it comforting to know there was a being who had pity on all of us, who was the 'help of the helpless'. That gave her the strength to continue.[38]

Nettie Palmer was having long talks about life on the veranda of their home at Caloundra. She found to her delight that visitors were more likely to unbutton themselves in the country than in the town. She liked to watch the fishing boats return at sunset and the swans flying in formation. She was the Martha and the Mary of the Australian literary world. Like Martha she was 'much cumbered' with the life of the tea-towel, the kitchen stove, the sink and the wash-tub. Like Mary she was mindful of the one big thing—that Australians should discover who they were. She was like Nina in Chekhov's *Seagull*. She was growing in spirit every day that passed. She believed that what really mattered was not fame, or glamour, or things people dream about when young, but knowing how to endure, how to bear one's cross, and to have faith. Aware as she was of her vocation and her role in Australia, she was not afraid of life. She knew that what mattered was work, not talk about what would be in a work about Australia if one were to write a book about Australia. Vance Palmer had moments of penitence, moments of insight into women as 'pack-horses'. 'This continual cooking and washing up', he told her, 'you have too much of it, especially when you're doing so much other work beside. I've a deep-seated feeling that I've been letting you carry the heavy end of the log . . . I can examine myself and see what a hog I've been as soon as you go away'. She had her compensations. Bernard O'Dowd told her how much he loved her: 'I cherish above most facts the fact that I've known you'. Hugh McCrae told her A. G. Stephens continued to be cruel to him. She was the great life-affirmer, the giver of the waters of life. She wanted to slay the giant of British philistinism in Australia: she wanted to liberate women from their servitude. Ivy Brookes did not think either was necessary. Neither idea ever occurred to Annie West. Nettie Palmer wanted both but was beginning to wonder whether in Australia what mattered most would ever be.[39]

[38] Conversations with Annie (Mrs Charlie) West, Phillip Island, 1922–44.

[39] Anton Chekhov, 'The Seagull', Elisaveta Fen, *Plays of Anton Chekhov* (Penguin edn, London, 1971), p. 181; Vance Palmer to Nettie Palmer, n.d., probably mid-1928, Palmer Papers, Series 1, Box 5, Folder 39; Hugh McCrae to Nettie Palmer, August 1928, ibid.; Bernard O'Dowd to Nettie Palmer, 31 July 1928, ibid.

The Militant Women's Group believed they had the answer. They believed the day would dawn when the workers of Australia, both men and women, rallied to resist Bruce and his capitalists. Then capitalism would be overthrown and the working class would take control of the means of life. The Militant Women's Group wanted first to liberate the minds of women from the delusions which gave life meaning to Ivy Brookes and Annie West. Religion was a false comforter, the propagator of the cruel lie of rewards in heaven for the sufferings in this world, the origin of that odious idea that there was a divine sanction for the inferiority of women, and the teacher of that reactionary doctrine that God alone, not fallen man and fallen woman, could remove all the evil in the world. The exploitation and drudgery of women, the legal, economic and social inferiority of women, could be ended only by the destruction of capitalist society and the creation of a society based on the common ownership of the means of production, distribution and exchange. There must be a 'mass challenge' to capitalism.

The problem was how to rally the masses to what the Militant Women's Group and the communists believed to be a noble cause. The call has been made. The response was feeble. Some blamed this on the apathy and the ignorance of the Australian working classes, some on the bullying, the self-righteousness and the humourlessness of those preaching this doctrine of salvation, and some on their alien ideas borrowed from other countries, ideas which did not grow out of the experiences of humanity in Australia.[40]

The people now had another 'dope'. That was the ever-expanding world of entertainment, which offered escape and pleasure at prices everyone could afford. The proprietors of the Regent Theatre in Sydney told the people of Sydney to be sure to see two films at their theatre, Charlie Chaplin in *The Circus*, and *Metropolis*. *The Circus*, their advertisement said, 'Absolutely instills joy into your soul'. It was the 'Greatest Show of Mirth, Gaiety, Wit, Genius'. *Metropolis* was 'An Abounding, Profoundly Moving Play, crammed full of Amazing, Beautiful, and Magnificent Features'. The attention of ladies was drawn to the morning session which they could attend at surprisingly low admission prices.

At the Capitol Theatre in Sydney patrons could sit in surroundings 'more dream-like than anyone's dream gardens', a 'glorious temple', dedicated 'to you and to art'. There on Sydney's 'New Bright Way' patrons could see the 'most spectacular romantic and sensational Master Picture', *His Lady*, with John Barrymore and Dolores Costello. They could hear Ted Henkel and his band of twenty players, and Fred Scholl and his mighty Capitol Wurlitzer organ, the largest ever to leave America. At 10.30 a.m. shoppers could

[40] *Woman's Road to Freedom*, Pamphlet of Militant Women's Group (Sydney, 1927); *Workers' Weekly*, 27 April 1928.

inspect the art treasures of the Theatre on display in the foyer. At 11 a.m., at prices anyone could afford, they could hear Leslie Waldron at the same organ. At the morning session a seat in the front stalls cost one shilling, the back stalls and dress circle two shillings, children ninepence and one shilling respectively. Evening prices were two shillings in the front stalls, three shillings in the back stalls and dress circle and four shillings in the reserve section. Crowds flocked to the ticket office: queues wound down George Street and Pitt Street, as the *Workers' Weekly* called on the men and women of Australia to mount a 'mass challenge to capitalism'.[41]

Musical comedies also enticed theatre-goers into a land of make-believe. In 1927 and 1928 *The Student Prince*, *The Girl Friend*, *Good News*, *The Desert Song* and *Rio Rita* were staged in the capital cities. The beautiful girl won her prince charming: the man in the desert, the outsider, won the heart of the beautiful woman. There was hope for everyone. Musical comedy trivialized the human situation by satisfying the desires and longings of all the 'lonely hearts' of the suburbs, and putting on a 'good show' for all those down from the bush for Show Week, the Sydney racing carnival, the Caulfield Cup, the Derby, the Melbourne Cup and the Grand Final. Bathroom baritones and tenors were heard singing of their hopes and their longings for one of those magical nights they would probably never know when:

> Overhead the moon is beaming,
> White as blossoms on the bough.
> Nothing is heard but the song of a bird
> Filling all the air with dreaming.

In *The Desert Song* patrons heard the hero sing:

> One love alone
> Is *not* for *men*.

The men were pleased, the women pained. It was a man's world. Even musical comedy conferred its blessing on that. Musical comedy was hopeful about the relations between men and women: musical comedy knew nothing of the fret and fever of two human beings living together. Musical comedy assured people:

> Rio Rita,
> Life is sweeter
> Rita
> When you are near.

There were moments when the shadow fell. There was the moment in *Good News* when a soothsayer made the disturbing remark: 'Lucky in cards,

[41] *Daily Telegraph*, 4 May, 5 April 1928; *Workers' Weekly*, 27 April 1928.

unlucky in love'. But the pretty girl promptly scotched that dark thought. Looking most fetching, she sang with a husky voice:

> Lucky in love. Lucky in love,
> What else matters if you're lucky in love?

What indeed! Only the whole of life. So what did it matter if a man was a green-horn at euchre or poker or five hundred, or even bridge, if only he was lucky in love? That was the 'Good News'. That was the message to take away on a rain-sodden Melbourne night:

> Good news is *welcome* to me (sung *fortissimo)*
> Bad news is *Hell* come truly (sung *pianissimo)*

Besides, for men, life was all summed up in the popular song:

> So if the girls don't seem to fall for you,
> There's just no hope at all for you.
> You've either got,
> Or you have not
> Got IT.

The atmosphere was frothy. Theatre patrons were told the important thing in life was 'Getting Gertie's Garter', or hearing Gladys Moncrieff ('Our Glad') sing of a woman's life and love.[42]

The *Pan-Pacific Worker* and the *Workers' Weekly* continued to lecture the workers on the class struggle. The capitalists, they said, were determined to reduce the standard of living of the working class. The clash of class interests was now 'perfectly visible' in Australia. The time has come to strike a blow for the 'exploited masses'. The crisis of capitalist society was at hand. On 22 June Bruce proclaimed the 'bludgeon act', the Act to amend the Commonwealth Conciliation and Arbitration Act. The workers must be vigilant: compulsory arbitration must be stopped. Bruce was promoting 'class collaboration'. Bruce was dampening the fighting spirit of the workers. Workers must stand firm: workers must be united.[43]

On 21 August 1928 Judge Beeby brought down an award on working conditions on the waterfront designed to 'lay a new foundation for better relationships on the waterfront'. George Stephenson Beeby entered public life as an advocate of the cause of moderation in the Labor movement and an opponent of all revolutionary doctrines. He was a man of parts, an author of

[42] *Just It* (Sydney), 11 August 1927; *Table Talk*, 10 November 1927, 3 May, 21 June, 20 September 1928; *Australasian*, 12 November 1927; personal memories of *Good News*, *Desert Song*, *The Student Prince* and *Rio Rita*; C. Hartley Grattan, 'Antipodal Theatres', *New York Times*, 12 August 1928.

[43] *Pan-Pacific Worker*, 15 May, 15 August 1928.

plays, a writer of bawdy verses, a sybarite and a wine bibber. He saw himself as an Erasmus in the Australian industrial jungle. He was such a wise man, Judge Beeby, a man who knew what it was like to be a waterside worker and an employer. In the clubs in Melbourne and Sydney he said many wise things over the port and the cigars. He wanted both sides to be reasonable, just as he was reasonable. He believed in kindness, and people being nice to each other. He found the militancy of the Waterside Workers' Federation quite distasteful. He wanted the employers to stop their 'litigious spirit'. In the interests of industrial peace he was prepared to make what he called 'most generous concessions' to the Waterside Workers. He conceded the central pick-up system which the men had been demanding ever since 1917. He awarded two 'smoke-ohs' to men working 'bulk' or shovelling cargoes. He awarded double time to the men on the night shift. Judge Beeby understood: Judge Beeby, rich though he was, has shown he had a warm and understanding heart.[44]

The Waterside Workers' Federation was not impressed by all this 'blah blah' about harmony and reconciliation. Capitalist society has entered a period of crisis. Prices have begun to fall. Employers and governments, the servants of their capitalist masters, were conspiring to slash wages and smash trade unions. The *Workers' Weekly* chanted their requiem for capitalist society. Bruce's 'bludgeon act' must be repealed. The workers must present a united front. The obnoxious clauses in the Beeby award—the provision for two pick-ups a day—must be changed. The days of the slave market on the waterfront must be brought to an end. The Beeby award means slavery: there must be no servile peace, no capitulation to the ship owners: class solidarity would break the bosses' attack. On 10 September the men on the Sydney waterfront boycotted the afternoon pick-up. The shipping companies threatened to employ 'free labour' if the members of the Federation continued to boycott the afternoon pick-up. The Federation stood firm.[45]

Bruce, Latham and Page appealed to the people of Australia to defend White Australia against the Reds. Jimmy Scullin and the Labor Party did not know what to do. An election was due at the end of the year. Support for the strikers aroused the 'hectic fear' of losing seats. Opposing the strikers exposed the members of the Labor Party to the offensive moralizing of the 'comrades', and accusations by the 'Reds' that Labor leaders were trying to outdo the conservatives in protestations of their 'lily-white Australianism'. Labor leaders and the Labor rank and file were being trapped into posing in

[44] *S.M.H.*, 22 August 1928.

[45] Ibid., 11 September 1928; W. Jethro Brown, 'The Strike of the Australian Waterside Worker: A Review', *Economic Record*, May 1929, pp. 22–33; *Workers' Weekly*, 21 September 1928.

public as the 'only-and-true defenders of the white-Australian faith', becoming defenders of the Bruce bludgeon.[46]

The *Australian Worker* was worried. A big strike at this juncture, they said on 12 September 1928, would 'disastrously prejudice the prospects of Labor at the polls'. This did not bother the *Workers' Weekly* or the *Pan-Pacific Worker*. For them Parliament, constitutionalism, ballot boxes and law courts were all shams. But the workers should beware, the *Australian Worker* continued, 'lest they too play into the hands of capitalistic conspirators'. A Labor triumph in the constituencies was what mattered. Every grievance of the workers, they argued, should be subordinated to that 'supreme object'. Jimmy Scullin did not know what to say. He offered to use his influence with the men in the interests of industrial peace if Bruce used his influence with the employers. He wanted industrial harmony for Australia: he wanted that before the elections.[47]

On 16 September the *Sydney Morning Herald* jubilantly announced the strike had been declared off: the men had capitulated. Two days later they announced there was still trouble on the waterfront in Melbourne. The owners had tried to use free labour. At Brisbane and Adelaide all work on ships was declared 'black' until such time as that pernicious clause in the Beeby award was struck out. Jimmy Scullin was distressed. Once again he offered to serve as an agent of peace. The militants disowned him. The *Workers' Weekly* called on the men to stand firm: victory was not far off. The moderates with political aspirations wanted industrial peace quickly. The militants, they said, were putting a trump card in Bruce's hand. Communists wanted revolution, not a Labor Government. Bruce threatened to invoke the Crimes Act against the union leaders. The Labor moderates accused the communists of plotting to slaughter the W. McCormack Labor Government in Queensland and Labor's chances in the forthcoming federal election. The communists counter-charged, accusing Labor of being hand-in-glove with Bruce and his capitalistic masters. Jimmy Scullin suggested a peace conference: the communists snorted with disgust. The election was drawing nearer, with Labor putting on yet another Kilkenny cat brawl.[48]

John Curtin was also baffled in his search for an answer. For years he has been convinced of the futility of exhausting mass forces in the Labor movement in 'incessant strikes for modifications of wages and conditions'. The army of Labor must not commit such 'grievous blunders'. With an election imminent it was foolhardy to go in for a long strike. It has been a hard year

[46] *Pan-Pacific Worker*, 15 August 1928.

[47] *Australian Worker*, 12, 26 September 1928; *C'wealth P.D.*, 11 September 1928, vol. 119, pp. 6563–5; Robertson, op. cit., pp. 142–4.

[48] *S.M.H.*, 16, 18 September 1928; Robertson, op. cit., p. 144; *Australian Worker*, 19 September 1928.

for him. Ever since the middle of 1927 he has been a member of the Royal Commission appointed by Bruce to report on whether the Commonwealth should introduce a scheme of child endowment, and, if so, how this should be done. The communists belted into him as one of those Labor men prepared to introduce 'sops' to dampen the revolutionary ardour of the workers. On the Commission he soon found himself ill at ease with the conservative members. They were measurers, walnut-hearted men who had no idea of the cause he served. During long absences from Fremantle he missed his wife's cooking. Life in hotels was too much for him. He broke down: he reached for his crutch. The shadow fell across his path on the road to destiny just as another shadow fell across the path of Bob Menzies. He played billiards: he saw his beloved Carlton play football: he read 'wild Westerns'. But men have seen his fatal flaw. Now in September just as he and Mrs F. M. Muscio submitted their minority report on child endowment his own behaviour and this futile strike were damaging his chances in the electorate of Fremantle.[49]

The communists continued to call on the workers to use the strike on the waterfront for a 'mass challenge to capitalism'. Bruce decided to ask Parliament to grant his Government greater powers over the transport workers. On 20 September, with the men still out on Brisbane, Adelaide and Melbourne waterfronts, Bruce asked leave to bring in a Bill for an Act relating to employment in relation to trade and commerce with other countries and among the States. The second reading was on 21 September. The Bill gave the Governor-General power to make regulations with respect to the employment of transport workers, and the licensing of persons as transport workers and for regulating or prohibiting the employment of unlicensed persons as transport workers, and for the protection of transport workers. Bruce was the saviour of Australia from the communist wreckers. Labor was outraged. The proposed Act was nicknamed the 'dog-collar' Act. The communists called for a united front, and lectured the Labor Party on its moral duty. Jimmy Scullin was horrified. The Bill, he told the House of Representatives on 21 September, was the 'proclamation of industrial martial law'. The Government was deliberately throwing the 'apple of discord into the industrial arena'. The cry went up: trade unions are in danger. Bruce was exploiting a strike to smash the unions. But Jimmy Scullin was not only a saint, one of the pure in heart. He had the native cunning of his people, the cunning of a box of monkeys in the presence of a threat to life. Jimmy Scullin sensed that Bruce's extremism would antagonize middle Australia, that

[49] John Curtin to Frank Anstey, 3 April 1925, Lloyd Ross Papers, Box 33, N.L.A., Canberra; Minority Report of Commissioners Mrs F. M. Muscio and John Curtin, 3 September 1928, *C'wealth P.P.*, 1929, vol. 2; Lloyd Ross, op. cit., pp. 85–6.

there were possible electoral gains for Labor in tempting Bruce into further onslaughts on the trade unions. The Bill was read a third time on 22 September, went to the Senate the same day, was rushed through that Chamber, and received the assent of the Governor-General on 24 September.[50]

Licensing of waterside workers began as soon as the Act was proclaimed. Fearing the Act would deprive many unionists, especially those known to be militant, of their means of livelihood, the unions decided to 'fight the Act to the last ditch'. Plans were laid to extend the strike on the waterfront. Bruce, in a conciliatory gesture, promised that licensing of workers would not be enforced at any port where the workers accepted the clauses of the Beeby award. The prevailing unemployment gave the employers plenty of labour ('free labour') to work the ships in port. Clashes occurred between unionists and non-unionists on the Melbourne and Adelaide waterfronts. By the beginning of October there were rumours that the South Australian Government had issued rifles and bayonets to a volunteer body of five hundred men. In Melbourne the homes of a couple of stevedores who had helped to work some of the ships were damaged by bombs. On Friday 12 October, as Thomas Warne, a foreman stevedore, prepared to go to bed, he heard a thud on his veranda followed by scampering feet and a terrific explosion. Warne escaped death. Windows of nearby houses were blown out. Ned Hogan, the Labor Premier, expressed his horror. The *Workers' Weekly* said it was treachery to tell the workers at such a time not to act because it might interfere with the federal elections. Any election campaign based on 'an appeal to the cowardice of the workers' was 'a sign of black reaction'. Jimmy Scullin condemned all proposals to extend the strike, and accused the militant section of the unions of urging men to do certain deeds they themselves were not prepared to do. Any extension of the strike, he added, would have the most disastrous effects upon the prospects of the Party at the federal elections.[51]

Jimmy Scullin delivered his policy speech on 4 October 1928. Like John Curtin in Fremantle, Scullin believed Labor must be pragmatic: Labor must not be a party of ideologues but must attract the swinging voter, the middle group of the uncommitted which was decisive in Commonwealth elections. In the Richmond Town Hall Scullin was strong on details, Scullin was down to earth, but never the missionary or the visionary, or the apostle of 'the noblest cause of all'. He set out in detail what Labor would do. He never said what Labor stood for. Labor would reduce 'the appalling number of unemployed': Labor would review the finances of the Government: Labor

[50] An Act relating to Employment in relation to Trade and Commerce with other Countries and among the States, 24 September 1928, No. 37 of 1928, *C'wealth Acts*, vol. XXVI, 1928; *C'wealth P.D.*, 20 September 1928, vol. 119, p. 7010, 21 September, pp. 7072–171, 22 September, pp. 7172–225; Robertson, op. cit., pp. 143–4.

[51] *Australian Worker*, 3, 17 October 1928; *Workers' Weekly*, 28 September 1928.

would afford the fullest possible protection to Australian primary and secondary industries: the Australian market would be protected for Australian producers: the sugar industry would be preserved: Labor would increase the responsibility of the Commonwealth for social welfare: Labor would meet Australia's obligations to the Aboriginal race: Labor would ask the people to vote 'Yes' in the referendum to amend the Constitution to give the Commonwealth the power to carry out the Financial Agreement between the Commonwealth and the States: Labor would repeal the Transport Workers' Act. Labor believed in reason for the settlement of industrial disputes.[52]

The *Workers' Weekly* denounced Scullin as a petty bourgeois politician, who was a lackey of the capitalists. The sole concern of Scullin and other Labor members of Parliament, they said, was 'the securing of their return to the seats of the Federal parliamentary chamber'. All that Scullin could talk about was the national debt, the government deficit and taxes, at great length. The reformists of the Australian Labor Party had no policy in opposition to Bruce. Once again the communists presented themselves as the ones with all the political virtues. 'Christ', said the *Workers' Weekly*, 'had only one Judas, but the Labor Movement has its hundreds'. Bruce rested on the achievements of his Government, and the need to preserve law and order. He and Page were the promoters of the 'Imperial Firm', the Firm which has delivered 'Men, Money and Markets' to Australia. The people must decide whether they wanted the British version of law and order, or the anarchy and lawlessness which would prevail under Labor. Only a coalition Government of the Nationalists and the Country Party could offer Australia the necessary stability.

The strike was still off again and on again. On 17 October 1928 the waterside workers decided to resume work and register under the Transport Workers' Act, and the seamen decided to man the ships. The communists tried to persuade the Sydney waterside workers to keep up the struggle. The moderates chucked them out of the meeting and made it clear they did not intend to take orders from any communist organization. In Melbourne the battle between the militants and the moderates flared up. Jock Garden tried by intimidation to prevent men from returning to work. The shipping companies decided to use volunteer labour. On 2 November volunteer labourers were signed on to work the mail steamer *Chitral*. When they arrived at the Port Melbourne wharf they were protected by twenty-five policemen. Two thousand unionists were there to stop them boarding the *Chitral*. They threw stones at the police and the volunteer workers. The police drew their revolvers and fired blanks. The unionists attempted to board the *Chitral*, but a policeman stood on the gang-plank and threatened to shoot any unionist

[52] *Age*, 5 October 1928; *Argus*, 5 October 1928.

who attempted to walk up it. Fierce fighting broke out. The police fired, and four unionists dropped wounded on the wharves.

The riots stopped. Law and order were restored. Bruce said his Government was determined to give adequate protection to the volunteer waterside workers and prevent any further intimidation. In the Victorian Parliament the Premier, Ned Hogan, offered a reward of £1000 to anyone giving information leading to the conviction of the bomb-throwers. Speakers warned of worse to come. Italian volunteer workers, they said, carried knives: there would be more bloodshed. The Waterside Workers' Federation announced that every branch had decided to observe the awards of the Arbitration Court. But still the victimization by employers continued. In Melbourne 3300 lost their jobs, 1700 in Adelaide, 1400 in Brisbane, 600 in Queensland's northern ports, and 300 in Newcastle.[53]

As election day approached Labor's hopes were high. Bruce's 'bludgeon acts', Labor believed, had shocked middle Australia. Labor's campaign was going well. Over in Fremantle John Curtin spoke for one hour and a half on 23 October to a large and enthusiastic audience. Labor was about to acquire in Canberra one of the greatest public orators of the day. Curtin had the power to grip an audience from start to finish. He had something to say. He spoke of dependence on the British for defence as a 'sham', and of ways and means of promoting industrial peace. Labor was still divided. Jack Lang, the Labor leader in New South Wales, advised electors to vote 'No' in the referendum on the Financial Agreement. He feared that Commonwealth financial power might be used to dictate policy to a State Government. Jack Lang has explained why he was a 'No' man—he feared the London bond-holders. John Curtin said 'Yes' to the referendum. For him all members of the Labor Party were 'standard bearers in a holy war'. Jimmy Scullin also said 'Yes' to the referendum.[54]

The results of the referendum and election on 17 November were decisive. The 'Yes' vote received majorities in all the States, and the majority of the people required by the Constitution. For the House of Representatives the result was also decisive. The Nationalists won twenty-nine seats, the Country Party thirteen, the Country Progressives in Victoria one, the Independents one, and Labor thirty-one. Bruce and Page still had a comfortable majority. In the Senate the Nationalists won ten, the Country Party two and Labor seven. Labor has added to its ranks the men of destiny. John Curtin won Fremantle by a narrow majority: Joseph Benedict Chifley, a 'light on the hill' man, won Macquarie from the Nationalists: Rowland ('Rowley') James replaced Matthew Charlton in Hunter: J. A. Beasley, who has learnt his poli-

[53] *Workers' Weekly*, 12, 26 October, 16 November 1928; *Age*, 18 October 1928; *Argus*, 18 October 1928; *Australian Worker*, 24 October 1928.

[54] *Westralian Worker*, 26 October 1928.

tics in the Sydney Trades and Labor Council, won West Sydney. The actors in the drama to come were moving on to the stage.[55]

Bruce was delighted. He had asked the electors to endorse his stand for law and order: they did just that. The *Sydney Morning Herald* was pleased that Australia would be free of Caucus domination for at least another three years. Jimmy Scullin took comfort from the increase in Labor's overall voting figure: he was also glad to see a revival of Labor's old-time 'fighting spirit'. The *Pan-Pacific Worker* was sarcastic. Bruce, they said, 'was the re-elected State Manager of Australian Capitalism, and loyal agent of British imperialism'. The Australian people have again voted for the Imperial Firm, for King and Empire, and for the existing society. Defeat at the ballot box, they maintained, was not all that important. Communists must rally together for the 'complete victory for the Australian working class'. Louis Esson was just as depressed as he had been after the election of 1925. He was thinking a lot about death. He was also picking out the names of the men he would choose for the next test match against the English cricketers. The electors have not voted in favour of what D. H. Lawrence called 'making a hole in the bourgeois world'. Lawrence wondered whether Australians would ever do that. '. . . you Australians', he told P. R. Stephensen in December 1928, 'seem to believe in squandering, which is a pity, because squandering, like drink, is only a form of evasion—mere evasion of life. To live one has to live a life-long fight'. Squanderers believed in nothing. Once again Australians showed no desire to risk a change.[56]

Australia has again chosen the Imperial Firm. Australia has accepted the Stanley Baldwin statement that the major responsibility in matters of foreign affairs and defence still rested with the British. Singapore was Australia's fortress and the British Navy the bastion of her defence. But already prophecies were being made of the use to be made of aircraft in any future war. A foreign power could occupy a strip of the Northern Territory: air bases could be built from which the cities of Australia could be bombed. There were 800 million people on the shores of the Pacific, of whom 600 million were Asiatics. The problem was how to preserve white domination. British power was declining. That left America and Australia: they needed each other. But Bruce and Page, the young Bob Menzies, and all right-thinking people in Australia still believed in the Imperial Firm, never fearing it might go bung. So long as Australia leaned on the Imperial Firm, they saw no contradiction in being Australian by birth or adoption, and British in culture. Henry Tate

[55] Colin A. Hughes and B. D. Graham, *A Handbook of Australian Government and Politics 1890–1964* (Canberra, 1968), p. 337; *Westralian Worker*, 23, 30 November 1928; *West Australian*, 1 December 1928; Robertson, op. cit., pp. 147–8.

[56] *S.M.H.*, 20 November 1928; *Pan-Pacific Worker*, 15 January 1929; D. H. Lawrence to P. R. Stephensen, 20 December 1928, Craig Munro, 'The D. H. Lawrence–P. R. Stephensen Letters', *Australian Literary Studies*, vol. II, no. 3, May 1984.

has put forward ideas for an Australian line of expression in music. The Essons and the Palmers wanted to do something as Australians. But that was something to which Australians have so far shown a vast indifference. War would persuade them to reconsider their position. The election of November 1928 has sent to Canberra the man who would help them to change their minds. He was John Curtin, the man who had dreamed a great dream.[57]

In that year, popular music was not about the destinies of the Australian people. The people were still singing about one of the great agonies in the human situation:

What'll I do
When you
Are far away
And I am blue
What'll I do?

Everyone wanted to know what to do when there was 'no one there to tell my troubles to'. Popular music was replacing hymns as a medium in which to express the hungers of the human heart. Popular music has come up with the same truth about the human situation as the Preacher in the *Book of Ecclesiastes*: 'There is one *alone*, and there is not a second'. Popular music was all about love or making money or wallowing in the titillation culture of the day. The Australian people wrote no songs about making a new heaven or a new earth.[58]

[57] C. Hartley Grattan, 'Australia and the Pacific', *Foreign Affairs*, vol. 7, October 1928; Henry Tate, *Australian Musical Resources* (Melbourne, 1917); *Bulletin*, 21 November 1928.

[58] Irving Berlin, 'What'll I Do?' (New York, 1924); *Book of Ecclesiastes*, IV, 8.

9

THE IMPERIAL FIRM GOES BUNG

BRUCE BELIEVED Australia should maintain the British character of the population. Australia was 98 per cent British. He was determined that it should remain so. The ceremony at the opening of the new Parliament on 6 February 1929 was British. The Governor-General wore British ceremonial dress. The beautiful Lady Stonehaven was dressed as a consort to a member of the British governing classes. The Prime Minister of Australia, Stanley Melbourne Bruce, wore a swallow-tailed coat, striped trousers, a butterfly collar and a cravat. He looked as though he were clothed, not by Fred Hesse, the people's tailor in Melbourne, or in one of the Myer Emporium's ready-made suits, but in a suit tailored in Bond Street, London. Postillions clothed in knee breeches and hose, and silk coats, attended the Governor-General. He spoke of those 'sentiments of enduring loyalty and affection' which united Australians to the Crown. The financial position, he added, was sound. There were 'encouraging indications' that the coming year would witness a return to prosperity. All was well.[1]

Yet all the pointers were ominous. The King was gravely ill. Medical bulletins were being issued in London. The condition of the King was unchanged after a quiet day. The economy, too, was sick. At the Premiers' Conference in Canberra on 9 January 1929 those present were told of the contents of the report by the members of the British Economic Mission on the Australian economy. Australia, being a vast country, needed to raise large sums of capital for development. That has been done. But, the report continued, those development schemes should become self-supporting within a reasonable period of time. This has not happened. The States and the Commonwealth were now carrying 'the dead weight burden of debt'. Government debts led to increases in taxation and the cost of living. Revenue from all State-owned projects such as railways, tramways, irrigation, soldier settlement, and closer settlement was falling. The total number of assisted migrants from the British Isles fell from 26 645 in 1923 to 22 394 in 1928. Export prices were falling. Unemployment rose from 7 per cent in 1927 to 10.8 per cent at the beginning of 1928. Beggars were becoming common in the streets: tramps were knocking on the back door in the

[1] *Age*, 25 June 1928, 7 February 1929; *C'wealth P.D.*, 6 February 1929, vol. 120, p. 6.

suburbs and in the country asking for a feed in return for chopping wood or mowing the lawn, or digging in the garden. Hawkers tried to persuade housewives to buy boxes of matches or other trifles: charity workers asked passers-by in the street to drop a coin in their collection boxes.

The behaviour of the people was disturbing to some. It was the age of jazz, the age in which the words sung to the popular dance music held out promises of delights for the body. It was the age of the flapper in which women exposed more and more flesh to the lascivious gaze of hungry men. As in all previous ages the self-appointed guardians of the people's morals chastised both sexes for wallowing in such sport. Priests and parsons warned their followers of the peril to their immortal souls to be encountered in flats, solemnly declaring that adultery was more probable in a flat than in a house. But the priests and the parsons, with few exceptions, did not ask their flocks to examine the causes of the mood of the times. For them human nature was still the prime suspect, not the society in which some amassed huge fortunes from the commercialization of fun. Dance on, dance on. Rail on, rail on. Mock on, mock on. Jazz ages are like the grasses of the field. They have their moment before they are thrown into the cleansing fire and consumed. They live on in the record books of human folly.[2]

There were already sporadic outbreaks of violence on the waterfront. On 14 January 1929 at Port Adelaide a riot broke out when supporters of the waterside workers confronted the volunteers who were attempting to load the A.U.S.N. Company's steamer *Mareeba*. One thousand men rushed the shed where the volunteers were sheltering, and then climbed on the ship. The police fired revolvers at the waterside workers, the latter retaliating with stones. The police drove the rioters off the ship. Mounted police then drove them off the wharf to hooting and jeering. Some waterside workers tried to push a car owned by one of the volunteers into the sea: the windscreen of another volunteer's car was smashed. The waterside workers retreated and assembled for a meeting where the angry men accused the owners of 'putting in the dirt' and Bruce of being the accomplice of the enemies of the working class. On 22 January there was further waterside trouble at Port Adelaide when five hundred waterside workers, some of their supporters and fifty women rushed the Corporation Wharf where the steamer *Lanena* was being loaded by non-union labour. Other rushes were made towards the motor ship *Minnipa* and the steamer *Rathlin Head*, where non-union labour was employed. The police restored order.[3]

It was one of those times in human affairs when respect for those in power was dropping fast. The image of the conservatives has been irrevocably

[2] *S.M.H.* 10 January 1929; L. J. Louis and I. Turner, *The Depression of the 1930s* (Melbourne, 1968), pp. 24–5; Second Annual Report of Development and Migration Commission, *C'wealth P.P.*, 1929, vol. 2, p. 1584.

[3] *S.M.H.*, 15, 23 January 1929.

blackened. Jack Lang had told his people so often that Bruce was selling Australia into bondage to Mr Money Man in London in return for development loans, that some now believed him. Frank Anstey and others characterized Bruce as the 'anti-Australian Prime Minister', the man with aristocratic pretensions who ordered the people of Australia to

> 'Bow, bow, ye lower middle classes,
> Bow, bow, ye tradesmen and ye masses.

Australians still loved that sort of mockery, that taking of the mighty down from their seat. To the communists Bruce was the 'State Manager of Australian Capitalism, and loyal agent of British imperialism'. He had once sunk so low as to send Australian troops to join the Imperial Powers fighting against the first Workers' Republic in Russia. Nothing Bruce could do could stop the flow. A tide in human affairs was moving towards the shore.[4]

The economy, like the morals of the people, was sick. The export of coal from New South Wales was declining, because the production cost was too high to compete in foreign markets. The price must come down. The premier of New South Wales, Tom Bavin, and the coal owners met in Sydney on 21 January 1929, to discuss a scheme to reduce the price of coal sufficient to check the drop in external trade, and to stimulate consumption within the State. Like Bruce they believed that the standard of living in Australia must be reduced if Australian products were to compete successfully in overseas markets. But the miners would not listen to the proposals. To them this was proof that capitalist governments, especially the Nationalist Government of New South Wales and the Nationalist–Country Party Government of the Commonwealth were plotting an assault on the living standards of Australian workers, and on the trade unions. The New South Wales Government asked the men to accept a small reduction in pay. The men said no wages cuts would be permitted. Owners and managers foretold 'grave industrial trouble'. Militants in the Labor movement called on workers to stand firm against all 'cowards' and 'shirkers'. On 22 January 1929 the representatives of the miners rejected the scheme for the rehabilitation of the industry.[5]

In the timber industry, by 30 January 1929 the managers of timber yards and saw-milling interests were preparing for a strike. The men were unhappy with Judge Lukin's award for timber workers. They wanted a working week which did not include work on Saturday morning. On 3 February three thousand men employed in five-day timber shops in New South Wales refused to work on Saturday morning. Within a week the

[4] *S.M.H.*, 19 November 1928; *Labor Daily*, 30 October, 9, 16, 19 November 1928; *Pan-Pacific Worker*, 15 January 1929.

[5] *S.M.H.*, 22, 23, 24 January 1929; *Workers' Weekly*, 18, 25 January 1929; Robin Gollan, *Revolutionaries and Reformists* (Richmond, U.K., 1975), pp. 19–23.

majority of timber workers in New South Wales and the adjoining States were idle. Jock Garden was threatening to extend the strike by calling out the men employed in country sawmills. Workers in Australia in the key industries of power and transport were on strike. Things were slipping away for Bruce and his Ministers.[6]

In politics, too, there was the same ferment and unrest. The euphoria of 1923 has given way to suspicion and back-biting. The British were letting Bruce down. The Commonwealth Line of steamers has been sold to the British firm of Kylsant's White Star Line in August 1928, it being Government policy to end government involvement with the production and distribution of wealth. Early in the new year the company announced an increase in outward freight rates to Australia as from 19 January. Bruce cabled Dick Casey, the Government's liaison officer in London, to put pressure on the company to delay carrying out the decision. He feared a censure motion in the House. The Labor Party might attract Hughes, who has been waiting for six years for a chance to avenge the humiliation of February 1923. Hughes might attract other disgruntled members of the Nationalist Party, especially those who feared future electoral consequences from the Bruce 'bludgeon' and the grovelling to the British money-lenders. The Government might be defeated. Hughes and Labor might form a minority Government, ask for a dissolution, hold an election and win a majority.[7]

At the pre-session meeting of the Nationalist Party on 5 February criticisms were made of the electoral pact with the Country Party. Henry Gullett, the Member for Henty, a prince of good fellows, but inclined to be extravagant in his choice of words about the Country Party, labelled Page 'the most tragic Treasurer Australia has ever struck'. Inside the Party room verbal brawls broke out on the choice of a Speaker. Bruce wanted J. G. Bayley, the Nationalist member for Oxley in Queensland. Bayley would know what to do in a crisis. Others wanted the retiring Speaker, Sir Littleton Groom, to be nominated. Bruce was not sure of Groom: the man was nursing a grudge for being dismissed from the Ministry in 1925 for his unsatisfactory handling of the Walsh and Johnson affair. Groom was known to be a wobbler on the tough industrial legislation and Bruce's talk about a root and branch reform of the arbitration system. Groom thought of the 1904 Conciliation and Arbitration Act as one of the 'tablets of the law' in Australia. It was like White Australia, Protection, the federal Constitution, and loyalty to the Crown—one of the untouchable conventions sanctified by the passage of time. A majority insisted on Groom's name going forward. Hughes wore the smile of a man watching his enemies walking towards a trap. In the Party room Hughes delivered an all-out attack on the Bruce–Page coalition, and vig-

[6] *S.M.H.*, 31 January, 4 February 1929.
[7] Cecil Edwards, *Bruce of Melbourne* (London, 1965), pp. 147–8.

orously denounced those who had not observed closely the terms of the electoral pact with the Country Party. The Party unanimously passed a vote of confidence in Bruce. Bruce said ruefully, 'to have a vote of confidence passed on one is certain evidence that there is some lack of it'. The light came back into the eyes of William Morris Hughes. The opportunity to take revenge for the wounds of 1923 was not far away.[8]

Rumblings of dissatisfaction were heard in the Country Party room. At the end of the pre-session meeting in January Dr Page told the press, 'the utmost harmony had prevailed'. Everyone knew what that meant. By contrast, in the Labor Party room there was a feeling that the thirteen years in the political wilderness were coming to an end. There were not enough chairs in the room to seat all the members. Jimmy Scullin was bubbling over with confidence. The Party has at last answered the slur that in 1916 it had blown out its brains. Ted Theodore was elected deputy leader of the Party. In John Curtin—one of Australia's great orators, a thinker, what Australians called a 'thoughtful customer'—and in Ben Chifley—a quiet man, but strong as the rock of ages—the intellectuals and the Australian nationalists had two heroes who warmed their hearts.[9]

In the House of Representatives on 7 February 1929 Jimmy Scullin accused the Government of being incapable of 'handling the problems that confront us to-day'. Hughes and Labor were on the attack. When the Public Service Arbitrator made an award, the Public Service union asked that it be disallowed. When a Labor member asked Bruce on 13 February what he proposed to do, Bruce moved that he be no longer heard. Scullin asked how he, Bruce, could take that stand, and at the same time profess his faith in arbitration. Bruce at bay was making mistakes. Bruce explained more fully why he supported the Public Service Board's ruling. Bruce tried to gag the debate. Motions of dissent were moved. After heated exchanges Scullin said he would withdraw his motion that the papers be printed, if Bruce promised to give members an opportunity to debate the question. Labor was getting cheeky—Labor members taunted Bruce: 'You're a coward', 'You're a bushranger'. The tide was swinging Labor's way: Labor has regained its confidence. Bruce refused. A vote was taken. Hughes and three other disaffected Nationalists voted with Labor. Some members were absent. The vote was tied—35 all. The Speaker, Sir Littleton Groom, gave his casting vote to save the Government. But Bruce knew he could not always rely on Groom. Hughes and Groom had the most powerful reason of all to bring him down. Bruce had made the fatal mistake of wounding the pride of two men who never forgave and never forgot.[10]

[8] *S.M.H.*, 6 February 1929; Edwards, op. cit., pp. 148–52.

[9] *S.M.H.*, 6 February 1929; *Age*, 6 February 1929.

[10] *C'wealth P.D.*, 7 February 1929, vol. 120, p. 75; *S.M.H.*, 14 February 1929; *Age*, 14 February 1929; Edwards, op. cit., pp. 151–3.

Bruce did not heed the warning. On the following day, 14 February, he reminded the House of Representatives that the people had given the Government a mandate to ensure peace on the waterfront, in the coal mines and in the timber industry. The people have endorsed their methods: the Government must be obeyed. Ted Theodore, one of the great debaters in Parliament and at public meetings, asked the question: what sort of endorsement was Bruce talking about when the electors had reduced his following from fifty-one to forty-three? Bruce did not answer. The prospects for industrial peace were bleak. Each day the crisis became more grave. On 1 March twelve thousand men stopped work on the northern coal fields. The prospects were that there would be a long period of idleness. The men had all gone fishing: that was ominous. The *Workers' Weekly* told its readers that capitalism itself was the enemy: the industry must be 'freed from the control of profit seekers before there can be security for the toilers'. The slogan for the miners must be: 'Not a penny off the pay! Not a minute on the day!'[11]

The Bruce 'bludgeon' has given his enemies in the Nationalist Party a high-minded motive to work with the Labor Party for the destruction of his Government. Bruce has clothed their amibitions with the mantle of respectability. Bruce did not know what to do. In an evil hour for himself he decided to follow the example of Pontius Pilate, one of the world's most notorious liberals. He would wash his hands of the whole business, by taking the Commonwealth out of the field of industrial relations, and handing it over to the States. That had its dangers. That would give Hughes the chance he was looking for: he could have revenge by taking a stand on principle. He could pose as the defender of the rights of trade unions and the Australian tradition of settling industrial disputes by conciliation and arbitration.

Things were getting out of hand. Militants were insulting judges: respect for authority was being undermined. On 27 March riots broke out in the city of Sydney. Stirred up by communist agitators a crowd of angry men demonstrated against Judge Lukin's award. Outside the Trades Hall they burned union ballot papers and sang revolutionary songs, such as 'We'll hang Judge Lukin to a sour apple tree'. In Hyde Park they burned the effigy of Judge Lukin. Speaker after speaker inflamed their passions. Mr Fitzgerald told them the workers were in for a long bitter fight to prove that the workers who produced the wealth, and not the employers, must control it. Jock Garden told them Judge Lukin could not rob the workers of their right to a 44-hour week, as soon the workers would win a 40 hour week. Another

[11] *C'wealth P.D.*, 14 February 1929, vol. 120, pp. 258–9, 260–6; *Age*, 15 February 1929; *S.M.H.*, 15 February, 2 March 1929; *Workers' Weekly*, 8 March 1929.

speaker said: Judge Lukin was put there to do the 'dirty work of his class'. The workers must get rid of him and of all who stood in their way. If the law stood in their way they must change the law.[12]

As Alfred Grace, a 'free labour' timber worker, left his place of employment with other 'loyal' timber workers on 8 April four men sprang from the shadow of a building in Young Street, and seized him. One of the assailants said: 'You dirty scab, we'll fix you up'. Grace was then felled by 'a savage blow at [the] jaw'. He was admitted to the Balmain hospital suffering from a fractured skull and numerous bruises. These sporadic acts of violence might develop into a threat to the existing society. Governments must quickly restore industrial peace.[13]

Discussions must be held quickly. On the day of the assault on the 'free labour' men Bruce held a conference of representatives of the coal owners and the Miners' Federation in Sydney. He appealed to both sides to reopen the mines and settle their disputes afterwards. The situation was serious. The wives and children of the men were suffering: the owners were losing. Without adequate supplies of coal there would be a curtailment of the industrial life of the country, leading to an increase in unemployment and more suffering and distress. The Government would appoint a Royal Commission to report on the problems in the coal industry. In the meantime he asked owners, managers and miners to be reasonable. To promote peace the Government had withdrawn the prosecution of John Brown and Company for a lock-out. The *Workers' Weekly* whooped with joy: here, it said, was final proof, if any further proof were needed, that Bruce was a bosses' man.[14]

By an odd irony, on the day after the conference in Sydney, the Home and Territories Department published its memorandum on the shooting of Aborigines by Police Officer Murray and others near Coniston in Central Australia. In February the Board of Inquiry had exonerated Murray. The Australian Board of Missions had accused the Board of Inquiry of bias, and of accepting uncritically the accusation of wrong-doing by the Aborigines while omitting to make any comment upon provocation by the white man. The Home and Territories Department agreed with the Board of Inquiry. There had been, they said, no provocation given by white men which could 'reasonably account for the depredations by Aboriginals and their attacks on white men in Central Australia'. The Board of Inquiry had not shown bias. In the white man's courts, and in the white man's law the white man was not guilty. The time would come when the white man would stand accused before the bar of history. But in April 1929 the white man was like the

[12] *S.M.H.*, 28 March 1929.
[13] Ibid., 9 April 1929.
[14] Ibid.

Pharisee: he has gone into the temple and thanked his God he was not as other men: he was not a sinner.[15]

The people had other things on their minds. On 12 April a delegation of unemployed ruffled the temper of the Governor of New South Wales, Sir Dudley de Chair, by casting aspersions on the conservative Premier of the State, Tom Bavin. Sir Dudley promptly left the room. The Labor press knew all about these imported English governors. In their eyes they were all bosses' men trying to conceal their class loyalties under all that verbiage about impartiality and being above the struggle.

'Smithy' was missing. He had set out to fly the *Southern Cross* from Sydney to London, but was believed to have made a forced landing near Wyndham on the coast of Western Australia. Search parties were organized. Rumours were flying that it was all a publicity stunt by 'Smithy' to boost his sagging fortunes. Then on 13 April the press announced all was well. The captain of the aircraft *Canberra* reported sighting the *Southern Cross* and its crew on marshy ground near the Glenelg River, twenty miles south of the Port George Mission Station. That was not the end of the story. Keith Anderson, who had left Alice Springs in the *Kookaburra* to search for 'Smithy', was now missing. Nine days later, on 22 April, the press announced that the *Kookaburra* aeroplane was found at a spot equidistant from Alice Springs and Wyndham. There was a dead man under the wing of the plane. It looked like Lieutenant Anderson. The other man was missing. It was desert country. The ancient continent has claimed another victim. Bruce expressed 'extreme gratification' on hearing the news that 'Smithy' was safe.

Louis Esson was still worried about the collapse of the Australians in the final test at Brisbane. Australia needed another Warwick Armstrong, another hero of the cricket field: Carlton needed another Horrie Clover.[16]

Australia was a country where the people believed in the superiority of the white race. The Prime Minister has often declared that the White Australia policy was one of the basic principles of the country. The Australian Labor Party wanted to cultivate an enlightened and self-reliant community based upon the maintenance of racial purity. No one must question that article of faith: it was one of the sacred tablets of the law. In 1928 Katharine Susannah Prichard submitted her novel, *Coonardoo*, for the *Bulletin* prize for Australian fiction. The *Bulletin* announced on 22 August that she and Barnard Eldershaw shared first prize. Barnard Eldershaw's novel was *A House is Built*. Vance

[15] Memorandum on Shooting of Aboriginals, Central Australia, Home and Territories Department, Attacks on White Men by Natives, The Killing of Natives, Central Australia 1928–29, Australian Archives C.R.S. Item 50/2768.

[16] *S.M.H.*, 13, 22 April 1929; Louis Esson to Nettie Palmer, 15 January and 5 March 1929, Palmer Papers, Series I, Box 5, Folder 40.

Palmer won third prize for *Men Are Human*. *Coonardoo* was the story of the tragic love of a white man for an Aboriginal woman who was not only 'black and comely' like the daughters of Jerusalem in the Love Song of Solomon. She also had a mind and a soul, and a warm, loving heart, capable of inspiring tenderness in a white man. The *Bulletin* published it as a serial between 5 September and 12 December 1928. It was published in book form in London in 1929. The *Bulletin* was not happy with *Coonardoo*. It was too 'morbid', and its theme, the love of a white man for a black woman, such that the Australian public would not stand it. They were not the only ones to feel uncomfortable, or to recoil when they read the work. Mary Gilmore found it 'appalling . . . vulgar and dirty', a work which has 'disgusted everyone'. Fancy the *Bulletin* giving £500 for a love story about a white man and a black woman. After their disastrous experience with *Coonardoo* the *Bulletin* told Vance Palmer in May 1929 they could not print his work. *Men Are Human*. The *Coonardoo* episode has shown that the Australian public would not stand stories based on a white man's relations with an Aboriginal woman. 'There is no chance, I suppose', the editor wrote to Vance Palmer, 'of your whitewashing the girl'. Palmer refused. *Men Are Human* was quietly buried by the opinion makers of White Australia.[17]

Australia was white: Australia was British. Keith Hancock, a clergyman's son, a scholarship boy at Melbourne Grammar School, and Trinity College, and then a Rhodes Scholar at Balliol College, Oxford, a kind man, a warm-hearted man with a shy hope in the resurrection of the dead, sent drafts of his book on Australia to Nettie Palmer. He promised her he would look over his 'rather hysterical phrasing about the abos.'. He was not keen on improving cultural relations with America because, as he put it, 'what we get culturally from America is second hand Europe and America'. Men took the risk of showing their hearts to Nettie Palmer: Hugh McCrae told her that winter: 'How alive you are! How you make people live, and want to live! It's a great gift, surely'. C. Hartley Grattan, a promising young American writer whose articles have already appeared in serious American journals, tried to interest Australians in the shift of American opinion on the origin of the war. Americans, he told the Palmers, had been fooled by British propaganda. But Australians were not ready for such talk about the British. Australians were not interested in listening to Americans. When Grattan tried to talk seriously to C. J. Dennis, he found to his disgust that Dennis was in fancy dress and, as

[17] *Pan-Pacific Worker*, 1 May 1929; Louis Esson to Nettie Palmer, October 1928, Palmer Papers, Series 1, Box 5, Folder 39; Mary Gilmore to Nettie Palmer, 28 November, 18 December 1928, ibid., *Bulletin*, 22 August 1928, and 5 September, weekly to 12 December 1928; S. H. Prior to Vance Palmer, 9 May 1929, Palmer Papers, Series 1, Box 5, Folder 40; Katharine Susannah Prichard, *Coonardoo* (London, 1929); Vance Palmer, *Men Are Human* (London, 1928).

Grattan put it, a 'bit boiled'. Perhaps Australians could not be serious about life?[18]

The militants believed the decisive hour was approaching. Leaders of the workers were making wild speeches. The timber strike was still on. At Yallourn on 7 May Jock Garden struck terror into the hearts of the bourgeoisie by speaking of a night of pillage. 'One night of darkness in Melbourne', he said, 'and there would be a few new suits in the city. The workers would have a few gold watches, too. One night of darkness would be more than enough, and that would be all we require of you'. Was it coming to that? Was there soon going to be anarchy and lawlessness in the cities? Was property no longer safe? Must the law-abiding tremble in their beds, fearful lest they not survive the night? On the same day as the Garden words were published the Melbourne and Sydney press carried a story reporting 'remarkable disclosures' about the members of the strike committee directing the timber workers. They were 'uncompromising extremists', neither timber workers nor Australians. Aliens, not people of reliable British stock, were about to begin an era of revolutionary terror in Australia. At the northern coal mines of New South Wales the militants were talking of using force to compel the bosses to open the mines on existing wages and withdraw the lock-out notices. The militants were forming rank and file organizations to conduct the fight: the workers were being trained to take over the mines: miners would begin industrial democracy in Australia.[19]

Bruce remained confident. The upper-class habit of lecturing the lower orders on the error of their ways was ingrained in him. It never left him. It was a temptation he could never resist, even though the price of indulgence might be the loss for ever of the chance to employ one talent he had in abundance, the talent for administering the affairs of the bourgeois state. He could not resist. On 17 May 1929 he issued a statement on the errors of the strikers. The timber workers' strike, he said, like the waterside workers' strike, was against an award of the Arbitration Court. '. . . I would ask unionists', he continued, 'to consider the full significance of their action'. It was the Melbourne Grammar headmaster's argument to the non-conformists: 'You know you are doing wrong: why do you do it?' Why indeed? Like a headmaster, Bruce wagged a reproving finger, and uttered a threat: did they not realize the consequences of their folly? The workers were discrediting and imperilling the whole arbitration system. To save them from such folly and madness, his Government might be forced to deprive them of the boon of arbitration. The men were the dupes of the wicked communists and mili-

[18] W. K. Hancock to Nettie Palmer, 27 September 1929, and Hugh McCrae to Nettie Palmer, 16 October 1929, Palmer Papers, Series 1, Box 5, Folder 41; C. Hartley Grattan to Vance and Nettie Palmer, 6 August 1929, and C. Hartley Grattan to Nettie Palmer, 4 December 1929, ibid.

[19] *S.M.H.*, 8 May 1929; *Workers' Weekly*, 17 May 1929.

tants. To save the men from their seducers the coal owners have wisely offered to meet the men, provided the union officials were not there. Bruce would save the workers from destruction.[20]

Bruce needed to be saved from himself. All the warning signs were there. The eyes of Billy Hughes were shining: Labor was bubbling over with confidence. In the John Brown case Bruce has shown his double standards: he had one way of treating Labor, and another way of treating capital: the would-be wreckers of society must be punished

For his speeches and his behaviour on the day when the workers burned the effigy of Judge Lukin, on 20 May the magistrate lectured Jock Garden for 'striking a vital blow at the safety and security of society'. Garden replied that in the University song-book there were 'parodies derogatory to many public men'. The magistrate was not impressed: 'That', he said, 'is the work of young men who have not yet felt the responsibility of life'. Garden has offended against the laws of the majority and must be punished. Garden was fined £10, in default one month's imprisonment. He refused to pay, so Garden became a prisoner in Long Bay Gaol. The laws of the land were now gaoling the advocates of the workers.[21]

The union leaders spoke of a fight to the finish: the communists spoke of a crisis in capitalist society, a crisis which could only end with the cleansing fire of revolution. The advertisements in the press beckoned people to spend their time in the picture palaces for 'A Laugh, A Scream, A Riot. Book Now and Avoid the Crush'. Better still: 'Attend the Early Shoppers' session'. It was the golden age of the picture palaces. The State Theatre was opened on 15 March 1929, the Plaza Theatre on 10 May 1929, both in Melbourne. They were both 'gala openings', opportunities for men and women—but mainly men—in high places to show what they stood for. The State Theatre was for 'the amusement-loving people of Melbourne'. Parsons and priests grieved that the cinema aroused the sinful lusts of the flesh, and encouraged people to lust after the pomps and vanities of this wicked world. But the Church's world of sin and punishment and guilt was passing away. Australians were a people who knew happiness without guilt.

The State Theatre in Melbourne, like the other new picture palaces, was the quintessence of the tinsel and glitter of capitalist society. It had many spendours. It was Saracenic in design. The auditorium resembled a Florentine garden in which stone statues were placed in prominent positions to remind patrons of the glory that was Florence at the time of Dante. Glorious Diana was there in a niche close to the source of the music pouring forth from the Wurlitzer organ. Everything was on the scale of Grand Opera. Clouds floated across the deep blue ceiling of the theatre, dotted with pin

[20] *Age*, 18 May 1929; Edwards, op. cit., pp. 158–60.
[21] *S.M.H.*, 21 May 1929.

pricks of light like stars to remind patrons of the canopy of heaven, for patrons had the hungers of the soul as well as the appetites of the senses. In the men's retiring room the crests of the public schools—what Barry Humphries later called 'Grammar and that sort of thing'—hung on the walls. In the ladies' retiring room the decoration was in the style of the period of Madame Pompadour. There was nothing Australian either in design, ornament or entertainment. The first film shown was about the American fleet, starring Clara Bow, she of the cute, kissable lips, and the shy, winsome smile. The next week there was a thriller, *Laugh, Clown, Laugh*, with Lon Chaney. There was the giant Wurlitzer organ: there was the theatre orchestra. There were the boys in uniform, bearing trays and calling: 'Sweets, Ices, Drinks'.[22]

On 31 January 1929 the proprietors of the Athenaeum Theatre had news for motion picture enthusiasts in Melbourne. 'Be Not Misled', they informed the public. The first talking film in Melbourne would be presented at the Athenaeum on 2 February at 11 a.m. for four sessions a day, and thereafter, daily except on Sunday, the Lord's Day. Patrons would 'see and hear' Al Jolson talk and sing on the screen in Warner Brothers Vitaphone drama, *The Jazz Singer*. This film, the advertisement added, would never be seen and heard in any other theatre in the city or suburbs of Melbourne. So hurry, hurry, hurry. Giovanni Martinelli would also sing an aria from *I Pagliacci*. There would be other attractions. The press was not happy with Al Jolson. The story was dull, and his singing 'a grievous disappointment'. But Martinelli—well, if you closed your eyes, you might imagine you were at the Grand Opera. *The Jazz Singer* was the story of a Jewish boy who broke his mother's heart by leaving home to become a jazz singer. But, of course, he had kept his love for his mother alive in his heart. He expressed it in a tear-jerking rendition of 'Mammy', the big tears rolling down his cheeks, and the audible sob in his voice uncovering what was in his heart.

Not to be outdone the State Theatre announced that 6 April would be 'a momentous day in the theatrical life of this great city' of Melbourne. On that day, patrons would not only see, they would also hear 'amazing confessions' in *The Doctor's Secret*. In Sydney the State Theatre offered 'Entertainment Stupendous, Dazzling, Bewildering'. They were keeping all the old favourites of the silent picture days. There was Will Prior and his State Orchestra, Price Dunlavy playing The Largest Organ That Ever Came Out Of America, the State Theatre's 'Permanent Beauty Ballet, The Most Beautiful and Talented in Australia'. Patrons would also see a talking picture. As the advertisement

[22] *Daily Telegraph*, 24 May 1929; 'The State Theatre, Sydney', *Building*, 12 March 1929; Beatrice Tildesley, 'The Cinema in Australia', *Australian Quarterly*, 15 December 1930, no. 8; Andrew Pike and Ross Cooper, *Australian Film 1900–1977* (Melbourne, 1980); *Table Talk* (Melbourne), 28 February, 27 June 1929; *Daily Telegraph*, 22 May 1929; *Age*, 25 February 1929; *Argus*, 25 February, 16 March, 11 May 1929; *S.M.H.*, 8 June 1929.

said, there was never 'Any Theatre Quite So Wonderful As The Splendid State'.[23]

In July 1929 the Capitol Theatre in Melbourne screened *The Broadway Melody*, the 'One Hundred Per Cent All Talking, All Singing, All Dancing Show'. Gorgeous ballet girls were seen on the screen: comedians cracked jokes: men and women sang of happy days. They advised their viewers:

> Don't bring a frown to old Broadway,
> For you must clown on Broadway.
> Your troubles there are out of style,
> For Broadway always wears a smile,
> A million lights they flicker there,
> A million hearts beat quicker there.
> No skies are grey on that great white way.
> That's the Broadway Melody.

They sang of love, just as the stage musical comedies sang of love. The talking pictures were now setting the pace, and establishing the fashions. All over Australia lovesick men sang, with an optimism the situation probably did not warrant:

> You were meant for me
> I was meant for you
> Nature fashioned you
> And when she was done
> You were all the sweet things
> Rolled up in one.
> You're like a plaintive melody
> That never sets me free
> I'm content
> The angels must have sent you
> And they meant you
> Just for me-ee.[24]

The King and Empire men were uneasy. American domination of the world was imminent. The Americans were seducing Australians into imitating their 'nauseating, nasal and inane way' of pronouncing the English language. The horrors of the Australian accent were giving way to the even greater horrors of the Yankee drawl. Australians were developing 'a rash of

[23] *Australasian*, 9 February, 30 March 1929; *Age*, 4, 25 February 1929; *Table Talk*, 24, 31 January, 7 February, 28 March 1929.

[24] *Advocate*, 4 July 1929; *Australasian*, 20 July 1929; *Bulletin*, 7 August 1929; *Table Talk*, 18 July 1929.

stars and stripes'. American films were making Australians into vulgar Yankees. British influence was waning. 'America has hustled', said *Table Talk*, 'England has yawned'. The priests and the parsons were also alarmed. American talking pictures were depraving the morals of the people: American films were suggestive in 'language, costume and situation'. After God there was nothingness, a nothingness filled by the titillation culture. But there has been a great change. More and more people saw the priests and the parsons as spiritual bullies trying to frighten the people from doing what they wanted to do with warnings about a Hell for transgressors.[25]

Things have gone hardly for A. H. Davis ('Steele Rudd'), the creator of Dad, Mother and Dave in *On Our Selection* and its many sequels. Davis has sunk into a profound melancholy. He told Nettie Palmer he was 'like a wounded sulky eagle desiring only to claw the Almighty for his false idea of justice and mercy'. For Ethel Florence Robertson ('Henry Handel Richardson') the 'long years of neglect and oblivion' were over. *Ultima Thule*, the third volume of the trilogy on *The Fortunes of Richard Mahony*, was acclaimed in London and New York in 1929. She needed, she told Vance Palmer, a 'little success' if she were not to lose heart altogether. Nettie Palmer hailed it as a 'work of genius', a possible Nobel Prize winner, 'like a dream come true for us all', i.e., those, like herself, who had believed that one day somebody would make a mark as an Australian. The reception in Australia was not so enthusiastic. The Melbourne *Herald* found it 'too gloomy' and doubted whether it would have a wide public. Australians were not interested in one man's quest for salvation or for the means of grace. Australians had no interest in the sufferings of a 'wayward, vagrant spirit'. The world belonged to the brave, not to those eccentrics and queers who held conversations with the dead. Katharine Susannah Prichard had her doubts. She told Nettie Palmer later she found *Ultima Thule* a 'great and fine piece of work. Utterly beautiful'. But she still felt Henry Handel Richardson wrote of Australia as 'a stranger—not one of us really'. Like Marcus Clarke she had 'an alien psychology on us'. Henry Handel Richardson felt so superior to the people. She lacked the 'soil besottedness'. Katharine Prichard could not 'quite believe in her [H. H. R.] as an Australian'.

That was the theme developed by Bruce at the inauguration of the War Memorial in Canberra on Anzac Day, 25 April 1929. In 1923 the Bruce–Page Government had decided that the site for any War Museum or Memorial should be in Canberra at the foot of Mt Ainslie. A competition was to be held for designs for a building to be called the Australian War Memorial. The War Memorial Act was passed in 1925, unopposed, Matthew Charlton taking the opportunity to say Labor wanted the War Memorial to train young minds 'in

[25] *Table Talk*, 14 March, 23 May, 18 July 1929; *Bulletin*, 27 February 1929.

the paths of peace'. As with the design of Canberra, the boss sheriffs found it difficult to agree on the design for the building. They settled for a compromise, asking the two best entrants to work together on a new design. John Crust was a migrant from Yorkshire, Emil Sodersten a Sydneysider. Once again there were to be no religious emblems, not because of sectarian differences or any reluctance to offend those groups which did not accept the divinity of Christ, but because most soldiers did not believe in the resurrection of the dead. Once again Australians borrowed voices from abroad to express their deepest feelings. On the Stone of Remembrance at the foot of the proposed Memorial they carved the words from Ecclesiasticus in *The Books Called Apocrypha*: 'Their Name Liveth For Evermore'. On the programme for the inauguration ceremony they printed words from the Funeral Speech by Pericles at the end of the first year of the Peloponnesian War: 'They gave their lives. For that public gift they received a praise which never ages and a tomb most glorious—not so much the tomb in which they lie, but that in which their fame survives, to be remembered for ever when occasion comes for word or deed'. The programme also printed a verse from Laurence Binyon's poem 'For the Fallen', and some words by Rupert Brooke. No words by an Australian author were quoted.

But this time there was a difference. Bruce did not dwell on the glories or benefits of belonging to the Empire. Speaking with unwonted passion he told the audience that the war had created the Australian nation. He was there, he said, to inaugurate the memorial of the Australian people as a nation. They were there to commemorate the sacrifices and sufferings of those who had created this Australian nationhood. A nation, he said, must have both tradition and sentiment. Australians have inherited the traditions of the nation from which they sprang. Australians have also built traditions of their own. All those who saw the Memorial would be inspired with the great ideals of service to Australia. This would be a lasting and enduring memorial of what Australia stood for. Australia now had a shrine.

There was still a gun salute for an English Governor-General. Australians still sang of their dependence on God. God had been their help in ages past: God was still their hope in years to come. But Australians were beginning to talk on public occasions of what they stood for. That night in the Albert Hall Charlie Bean, the war historian, spoke of the 'spirit of comradeship' which transcended all creeds, classes and conditions. He spoke too of the Australian conviction that there was something to admire in every man—and every woman, too, because women have proved themselves as 'the sisters of the A.I.F.'. Australians, he said, were all of the same type which had made the A.I.F. They had the spirit of comradeship; they had the bravery; they had the audacity and the resource.

Anzac has made Australians more aware of themselves. They were not Australian Britons; they were Austral sons of British sires. But events in

America and Great Britain would soon deal a setback to that development. Bruce has discovered Australia, but not how to make Australia free.[26]

Bruce had other things on his mind. Thousands of pounds were being lost every day because on the coal fields the miners have not returned to work. Unemployment was slowly increasing: communists were inciting the workers to sedition and disaffection. The soldier settlement schemes conceived and planned in a wave of patriotic enthusiasm have proved no more successful in putting people on the land than the selection acts or the closer settlement acts. By 1929 the enthusiasm has been replaced by searches for what went wrong. Some attributed the losses to lack of business acumen and the extravagances of State governments in providing services to such settlers. There were losses on the railways which had been extended for the purpose of soldier settlement, losses on irrigation works and other public utilities provided by the States. Other factors were the want of capital, the want of an adequate home maintenance area, the unsuitability of the settlers and their lack of training, and the drop in value of primary products, chiefly in irrigation areas.

To discuss the crisis Bruce summoned representatives of the States to a conference in Canberra. They met on one of those golden mornings in late May 1929 in a part of Old Australia which has bred the men and women of heroic ingredients, the ones who would never give in. Bruce told them the situation confronting Australia was one that could not fail to cause anxiety to every thinking citizen. Australia has known depressions in the past, but they were now threatened with a monster depression. Prices for the staple commodities of wool and wheat have declined: the sale of the surplus products of most of Australia's other primary industries have become unprofitable: the position of Australia's secondary industries was becoming more and more difficult because of competition from overseas. The rise in unemployment was the cumulative effect of all these developments. In measured words he told them there was 'something wrong somewhere in our national economy'. His Government therefore proposed to take measures to halt the slide towards an even greater depression. His Government has decided that the duplication and overlapping of the industrial powers of the Commonwealth

[26] Arthur Davis ('Steele Rudd') to Nettie Palmer, 29 April 1929, Palmer Papers, Series 1, Box 5, Folder 40; Katharine Susannah Prichard to Nettie Palmer, 20 May 1930, ibid., Folder 43; Louis Esson to Nettie Palmer, 5 March 1929, and Henry Handel Richardson to Vance Palmer, 8 May 1929, ibid., Folder 40; Nettie Palmer, 'Henry Handel Richardson', *Australian Women's Mirror*, 5 March 1929; *Canberra Times*, 26 April 1929; K. S. Inglis, 'A Sacred Place: The Making of the Australian War Memorial', *War and Society*, vol. 3, no. 2, September 1985; programme for Inauguration of the Australian War Memorial, Canberra, 25 April 1929, Australian War Memorial Stone of Remembrance, Australian War Memorial, Canberra; *Ecclesiasticus*, ch. 44, v. 14, *The Books Called Apocrypha* (Oxford University Press edn, n.d.).

AN 'UNCLE TOM'
OR A TEACHER OF THE
ABORIGINAL PEOPLE?
David Unaipon
Photograph in Australian Institute of Aboriginal Studies, Canberra

THE PROPHET
FROM
CUMEROOGUNGA
William Cooper
Photograph in Australian Institute of Aboriginal Studies, Canberra

'LAY OUT THE BODY DECENTLY
BEFORE MY FRIENDS SEE IT
— FOR THE SOUL WAS GREAT'

Henry Lawson

Charcoal drawing by Noel Counihan

and the States were retarding national progress and preventing industrial peace. They have therefore decided to repeal the federal arbitration legislation, retaining for the Commonwealth control only over shipping and the waterfront industries.[27]

The eyes of Billy Hughes gleamed. Bruce, Hughes sensed, has dug his own grave. The members of the Nationalist Party with a grudge against Bruce, or misgivings about the electoral consequences of his policies, now had the pretext to take a stand as defenders of the tablets of the law in Australia. The unions were divided. Those governed by federal awards feared a loss of power. Those governed by State awards welcomed the proposal at first. Bruce took heart. The communists were still angering some members of the Labor Party by their assumption of political virtue, by their claim to know what was good for the working class, and by their humourless smugness. Bruce would isolate the militants. He would take a leaf out of the textbook of the British governing classes on the government of inferior people: he would divide and rule.[28]

Vain hope. On two things the Labor movement was united. They did not want this pseudo-Englishman, as they saw Bruce, to invite another British Economic Mission to tell Australians how to run their country. This was just further proof that Bruce felt unequal to the task of governing. Labor did not want any more English financiers attending a number of banquets, chatting with 'captains of industry' and then having the impertinence to lecture Australians as though they were little children. The owners have locked out the miners to force a reduction of wages upon them. On that question, too, Labor was united. Government should step in and take possession of the coal in the name of the sovereign people. In the age of faith people sang: 'The earth is the Lord's, and the fulness thereof'. Now, in the twentieth century, in a secular age, Labor said the coal belonged to the people. Nature, as the *Australian Worker* put it, 'gives coal as a free gift to the whole of the community'. John Brown and the other coal owners could not say in the twentieth century: 'This coal belongs to us'. John Brown and Co. could not 'sweat and starve the men who wrest it from the caverns of the earth for them'. The miners would not acquiesce peacefully in their unemployed position. Councils of action were being formed on the northern coal fields. The miners would fight: there would be no more cowardice. The owners would not be permitted to starve the miners into submission. The solution was simple: the workers would take the coal from them.[29]

Faced with such revolutionary talk, Bruce announced the Government's

[27] *S.M.H.*, 29 May 1929; Mr Justice Pike, Report on Losses Due to Soldier Settlement, 24 August 1929, *C'wealth P.P.*, 1929, vol. 2, pp. 13, 23.

[28] *S.M.H.*, 29 May 1929.

[29] *Australian Worker*, 12 June 1929; *Workers' Weekly*, 14 June 1929.

decision on 13 June. Duplication of power between the Commonwealth and the States on industrial matters has played into the hands of the extremists and the agitators, and enabled them to 'generate ferment and create unrest in industry' and affect the whole nation. The present strikes were plainly controlled by the extremist elements. The Government would withdraw the Commonwealth from the field of conciliation and arbitration. Eliminate the extremist, he said, and the way was open for a better understanding in industry. There would be peace in industry, and with it a chance for what he believed in: prosperity and progress. Bruce has made a fatal error of judgement. He hoped to divide Labor. Instead he has united Labor. Nine days later, on 21 June, at a conference of delegates from all Australian unions held in the Melbourne Trades Hall, Jimmy Scullin declared that the Bruce proposals would be fought in the Federal Parliament. The political and industrial branches of Labor would present a united front to defeat them. The conference appointed a committee to organize an Australia-wide campaign against the proposals. In Bruce Nature had 'made a fair creature', a man of talent, an Australian version of the Renaissance man, a man with a fine brain who also excelled in athletics. But Fortune, or some flaw in his clay, has decreed that even he must 'fall into the fire'. Nature had given Bruce the wit to 'flout at Fortune', but Fortune would prove too strong.[30]

On the northern coal fields militants lectured moderates for their cowardice and their confusion. Working through the councils of action formed by the rank and file, they called on them to force the officials of the Miners' Federation to stand firm. Militants praised the women for being more militant than their husbands and their sons. The *Australian Worker* called on the Government of New South Wales to open the mines. Their refusal to do so provided more evidence that the Government had implicated itself in 'a wicked wage-reducing conspiracy which is reacting with damaging effect upon the whole community'. Bruce believed capitulation could not be delayed much longer, as the miners and their families were being starved into submission. After the suffering there would be a feast of reconciliation for all except the extremists and the trouble-makers. Bruce had faith in the good sense of Australian working men. He saw himself as their saviour, it never occurring to him that he himself, not the Australian worker, was in need of a saviour.[31]

There was a diversion. The Labour Government in the United Kingdom threatened to abolish imperial preference. This provoked an outcry from all parts of the Empire. Bruce cabled London saying that the abolition of such preferences would be a great blow to Australian industries. The sugar and

[30] *S.M.H.*, 14, 22 June 1929; W. Shakespeare, *As You Like It*, Act I, sc.ii, 42–3.
[31] *Workers' Weekly*, 5 July 1929; *Australian Worker*, 31 July 1929.

dried fruits industries would lose £850 000 a year. Bruce believed in the trinity of men, money and markets and in Empire trade. Now that was slipping away. Imperial preference was not just a pounds, shillings and pence question: imperial preference was ' a manifestation of sympathy . . . for a more intimate inter-Imperial relationship'. Imperial preference was a question of the heart as much as of the pocket. Abolition of imperial preference would have a disastrous effect on the minds of people in Australia. It would foster doubts about the wisdom of loyalty, the wisdom of Australia being tied economically and by sentiment to the 'Imperial Firm'.

For Bruce much was at stake. He believed in the Empire as the market for Australian goods and in the efforts of the Empire Marketing Board in London to persuade the British public to buy Empire goods. That Board advertised: 'Have an Empire Christmas Pudding'. The ingredients, they said, were from countries of the Empire—Canadian flour, Australian or South African raisins, Australian sultanas, Australian currants, Demerara sugar, chopped mixed peel, English or Scottish beef suet, breadcrumbs, English cooking apple, Indian pudding spice, Jamaican rum and an English threepenny bit for luck! The British would enjoy it all the more because by using Empire fruit, rum and sugar to make it they were 'giving a helping hand to the thousands of British settlers overseas—most of them ex-Service men and their families'. So buyers should ask: is it British? Bruce found that Empire trade was slipping away, just as British ideas of fair play in relations between capital and labour were slipping away in Australia and being replaced by the law of the jungle.[32]

Bruce observed a precept of the British governing classes: in time of trouble, arrest the trouble-makers, and be generous to the rank and file. On 22 July detectives arrested seven trade union leaders, including Jock Garden, and charged them with having conspired unlawfully and by violence to prevent persons employed in the timber trade in Sydney from exercising their lawful trade or occupation, and having conspired to 'riotously assemble together, and, with persons unknown, to assault workmen employed by George Hudson Ltd.'. But Bruce took no action against the colliery proprietor John Brown for the lock-out on the northern coal-fields. Labor believed they had Bruce on the run. The miners declared on 29 July they were as strong as on the day they were locked out, and as determined not to accept any reduction of wages unless this could be proved to be warranted. Labor talked of a day of reckoning. John Brown had callously closed down his mines, and thereby sentenced a whole community to 'hunger, suffering and ruin'. Bruce supported John Brown: '. . . it is written in the Book of

[32] *S.M.H.*, 13 July 1929; advertisements for the Empire Marketing Board, reproduced in W. Hudson and Wendy Way (eds), *Letters from a Secret Service Agent* (Canberra, 1986), inside cover.

Retribution that the Bruce–Page Government shall perish of John Brown'.[33]

Labor decided to censure the Bruce–Page Government for withdrawing legal proceedings against John Brown for the lock-out. On 15 August in the House of Representatives Ted Theodore led the attack on the Government. John Brown, he said, the millionaire political financier of the Government, had some mysterious influence over Bruce, an influence which enabled him to laugh in the face of the law. But beware, Theodore continued, a day of reckoning was at hand. Jimmy Scullin, who believed that the wicked would be punished and that the hungry miners would be filled with good things and that rich men like John Brown would be sent empty away, thought Labor was again the standard-bearer in a holy crusade. So did John Curtin, the new member for Fremantle, and Ben Chifley, the new member for Macquarie. Labor was again the conscience of the nation. In his reply Bruce denied that his Government was vindictively persecuting the trade unions. But it was clear that law and order could not be restored by the imposition of penalties. Something else must be done. Rowley James, the Labor Member for Hunter, warned Bruce his Government had lost the confidence of the people of Australia. Hughes accused him of committing a 'blunder of the first magnitude'. Bruce, he said, has provided the enemy (Labor) with much ammunition. The people would turn away from the Nationalists in thousands because Bruce had one way of treating labour and another way of treating capital. The Labor benches called out 'Hear, hear. Hear, hear'.[34]

Bruce took no notice of the warning. On 19 August the prosecution of Garden and six others for their alleged intimidation of timber workers was resumed. Bruce declined to stop the prosecution of the workers although he had dropped the prosecution of the millionaire, John Brown. The capitalist press gloated over what was dredged up and presented as evidence against the union leaders. Garden, it was alleged, had boasted there would be a 'street of blood' in Australia. Some of the bourgeoisie were trembling: some were arming and drilling in the Old Guard. Bruce would be their saviour. The Labor press condemned Bruce with an air of righteous indignation. The people must punish the evil-doer; they must use the ballot box to pass judgement on the transgressor. Again Bruce took no notice of the drift in public opinion or the erosion of support within his own party. The critics must be disciplined. On 22 August he took retaliatory action against W. M Hughes and E. A. Mann for indulging in hostile criticism of some of the actions of the Bruce–Page Government. Neither was permitted to attend meetings of the Nationalist Party.[35]

[33] *S.M.H.*, 23, 31 July 1929; *Australian Worker*, 28 August 1929.

[34] *C'wealth P.D.*, 15 August 1929, vol. 121, pp. 7–26, 34–44; *S.M.H.*, 16 August 1929; *Age*, 16 August 1929.

[35] *S.M.H.* 20, 23 August 1929.

The following day, 23 August, Bruce introduced in the House of Representatives the second reading of the Arbitration Abolition Bill, a Bill to give effect to his announced intention to withdraw the Commonwealth from the field of industrial regulation save in respect of the shipping and maritime industries. He went over the familiar ground. Australia was in a serious economic position: public finance was 'in a condition of serious embarrassment': loans for developmental purposes were more and more difficult to raise: unemployment was rife: the markets for Australian primary and secondary products were shrinking. Strikes were compounding the economic ills of the country. They must be reduced. One way of alleviating that situation, he believed, was for the Commonwealth to vacate the field of industrial regulation. They have heard it all before. The Labor members again put on the armour of righteousness as defenders of the tablets of the law. The Labor press, both moderate and militant, girded themselves. The day of reckoning was at hand, when the people would smite their enemy. Three days later Billy Hughes, one of the early advocates of arbitration, took up the theme. It was not for Mr Bruce, he said, to settle this question. It was for the people: they had the last say. Bruce has forgotten that, but the people will give him a rude awakening.[36]

Bruce was confident. There was, he said, no schism in the Federal National Party. The Government was going right ahead, and it was certain to win out. It would win in the House, but, in the unlikely event of being beaten in the House it would win in the electorate. The Government was not about to 'go over the top'. It had already been over the top and had done it very successfully. At public meetings Bruce was reassured by the ovations he received. Bruce lacked the art to read the signs of the times. The ground swell in the electorate was not noticed in the dining rooms and smoking rooms of clubland or the drawing rooms of 'Yarraside' and Vaucluse. But the people would have their chance. Billy Hughes has read the signs of the times. On 5 September he told the House of Representatives he would move in committee that the Maritime Industries Bill should remain in abeyance until such time as the people had been consulted. The people would be in the instrument of his revenge on Bruce for the humiliation of February 1923. The people, not God, would be Hughes's avenging angels. Bruce and Page were not worried. They, too, were crusaders for a righteous cause: they were saving the people of Australia from what Page called a 'generation of Communistic poison'.[37]

On 8 September in the House of Representatives things went well for Bruce and Page. The Maritime Industries Bill was passed on the second

[36] Ibid., 24 August 1929.

[37] *C'wealth P.D.*, 22 August 1929, 5, 7, 10 September 1929, vol. 121, pp. 187, 596–605, 825–6, 841–50, 867; *S.M.H.*, 23, 26 August, 3, 6 September 1929.

reading with a margin of four votes, even though three Nationalists, W. M. Hughes, G. A. Maxwell, and E. A. Mann, voted with the Labor Party. But the real test would be when the Bill reached the committee stage. Hughes has declared his intention to submit an amendment that the Bill should not operate until it had been submitted to the people. On 10 September Billy Hughes had the satisfaction he had been waiting for. He submitted his amendment. Bruce warned the members he would interpret the passing of the amendment as a vote of no confidence in his Government, and that he would ask the Governor-General for a dissolution. Hughes accused Bruce of holding the sword of Damocles over the heads of members of the Nationalist Party. 'Let us go before the people and fight this battle once and for all'. Then, he prophesied, those who stood for this measure will disappear. The amendment was carried by 35 votes to 34. Bruce announced he and his Ministers wished to consider the position. Labor was jubilant. The people, they believed, would return Labor.[38]

On 12 September Bruce advised the Governor-General to grant a double dissolution of the House of Representatives and the Senate and Lord Stonehaven agreed. The election, it was hoped, would be held on 19 October (later changed to 12 October). Bruce was confident the people would approve of the steps his Government had taken to put an end to the evils that resulted from the present dual control of industrial regulation. Page was proud of the loyalty of his men. Both men were proud of the achievements of their partnership. The people would, they believed, again endorse the 'Imperial Firm', the creators of 'Men, Money and Markets'. Bruce underlined his position in his policy speech at Dandenong on 18 September. There was only one issue in the election: the people must decide whether they approved of the policy of his Government to promote peace in industry, continuity of employment and the highest wages and best conditions that industry could provide. He spoke as a man who believed material well-being was the essential condition of human happiness, as a man who believed that the efficient bookkeeping of a counting-house would satisfy the hungers of Australian hearts. 'The future greatness of this country', he declared in his peroration, 'depends entirely upon the unrivalled opportunities for national progress with which we have been blessed in our great natural resources and climatic advantages, and the energy, skill and intelligence of our people'.[39]

At the Richmond Town Hall on the following night, 19 September, Jimmy Scullin spoke with moral fervour. Beware, he told an overflow audience, 'of the powerful commercial and financial forces behind the Government' that would seek to dictate the policy of the nation, and would at this moment in Australia's history put the clock back thirty years and more to repeat again

[38] *S.M.H.*, 9, 11 September 1929.
[39] Ibid., 3, 19 September 1929.

the evils of the nineties. It was out of the terror and travail of those times that the Labor Party was born. Those days would not return because the people of Australia have resolved that the men 'who spent their lives in fighting for the righting of our wrongs shall not have fought and suffered in vain'. Labor has regained its soul, once again has a righteous cause. But when Jimmy Scullin set out in detail what Labor would do, he too spoke the language of the measurers and the money-changers. He spoke not as a man who believed Australians could steal fire from heaven, not as a man with fire in the belly for an Australians' Australia as distinct from the Imperial Firm of John Bull and Co. in which Bruce, Page and Bob Menzies placed their trust.

Labor, he declared, would put an end to the era of 'reckless finance' presided over by Dr Page. Labor, he continued, would put Australia back on the plane of 'sane finance', and would review all the methods of 'getting and spending'. Labor would show it could run the bourgeois state more efficiently than a coalition of Nationalist and Country Party politicians. Labor would introduce a programme of public works, a better telephone system, a better water supply. There would be no 'wasteful expenditure'. Jimmy Scullin made no mention of a 'better society', a more just society, equality of opportunity, or careers open to talent. The people were being asked who would be the more efficient administrators of things as they were, not to choose between 'the Old Dead Tree' and 'the Young Tree Green'. Since the days when the world was wide Labor has tasted the fruit of the Forbidden Tree of the knowledge of good and evil. Labor has lost the charm of the years of innocence and become a party of mature and gifted men, determined to give capitalism a human face. To stand for anything more would mean banishment to the political wilderness for a long time. Labor would see to it that the British would still enjoy an 'Empire Christmas Pudding'.[40]

On 9 October, three days before the election, Bob Menzies told the diners at an Old Trinity Grammarians' luncheon that what was wanted in Australia was 'the maintenance of the public school spirit and ethics in after school life'. But it was too late. Australia has left that world behind. When counting of votes ceased at midnight on Saturday 12 October it was clear there had been a massive swing to Labor. Subsequent counting confirmed this swing. Labor polled nearly 49 per cent of the vote, the Nationalists less than 34 per cent, and the Country Party 10 per cent. Labor had forty-six seats, the Nationalists fourteen, the Independent Nationalists (Hughes, Marks and Maxwell) three, the Country Party ten, and the Country Progressives one. In the Senate Labor had only seven seats, and the Coalition twenty-nine. Curtin and Chifley increased their majorities. Bruce lost the seat of Flinders by 305 votes to E. J. Holloway, a Melbourne trade unionist, one of those moderates whom Bruce had hoped to wean away from the militants. Page's

[40] *Age*, 20 September 1929; *S.M.H.*, 20 September 1929.

confidence in the loyalty of the country districts of Australia was proved to be misplaced. Labor made huge gains in the country electorates at the expense of the Country Party.[41]

Labor was jubilant. Jimmy Scullin found the result 'exhilarating'. As Ted Theodore heard on Saturday night of 'success beyond his wildest dreams', he beamed broadly. Labor men spoke of a 'new era for the great mass of the people in Australia'. The people, said the *Australian Worker*, have sent up a 'thunderous shout': there was to be no reduction in wages, no lengthening of hours, no 'murderous hand upon the arbitration system'. John Curtin was confident he and his colleagues would be 'standard-bearers in a holy war'. Hughes was delighted. 'The result', he said on Monday 14 October, 'is a veritable triumph for the people' and has sounded the death knell of the party machine and the reactionaries who directed and financed it'. The Bruce–Page Government has come to 'an inglorious end': Hughes has had his satisfaction. Joe Lyons, the new Labor member for Wilmot, received scores of enthusiastic letters. Tasmanians had great confidence in Joe Lyons, confidence in his faith and power to do something for 'little Tassie', and confidence in his loyalty to Labor. If anyone could obtain justice for 'little Tassie', their Joe 'would do it'. Joe Lyons would never 'forget the ranks from which he came'. Or so his friends in the Labor Party believed.[42]

Bruce accepted the defeat of his Government and his own defeat in the electorate of Flinders with the dignity and generosity which had conferred a distinction on his eleven years in the House of Representatives. 'Mr Bruce', wrote the *Sydney Morning Herald*, 'leaves his high office with the demeanour and record of a statesman and a gentleman'. He had one regret. His exclusion from the Parliament and public life of Australia had occurred at a time when the economic and industrial life of the nation was beset with so many difficulties. He did not waste his time or blacken his reputation by words of vulgar abuse of those who had despitefully used him. He used his own humiliation to grow in wisdom and understanding. With the passage of time he accepted without indulging in self-pity or attributing blame to others one lesson of those years, namely, that it would be difficult if not impossible for him ever to regain the confidence of the Australian electors. But, as he told George Pearce, he did not propose to give way to pessimism. The moment the people realized, he told Pearce, how greatly they have been

[41] *S.M.H.*, 14 October 1929; *Age*, 14 October 1929; Colin A. Hughes and B. D. Graham, *A Handbook of Australian Government and Politics, 1890–1964* (Canberra, 1968), p. 342.

[42] John Robertson, *J. H. Scullin* (Nedlands, 1974), pp. 167–9; *S.M.H.*, 14 October 1929; *Australian Worker*, 16, 30 October 1929; *Newcastle Morning Herald*, 14 October 1929; *Pan-Pacific Worker*, 2 December 1929; John Curtin to Frank Anstey, 8 March 1934, Lloyd Ross Papers, Box 33; G. Drakeford to J. A. Lyons, 14 October 1929, W. M. Hughes to J. A. Lyons, 16 October 1929, J. A. Lyons Papers, Box 1, Folder 1, N.L.A., Canberra.

deceived and how 'impossible of redemption' were the promises that were made, there would be 'a tremendous revulsion of feeling in our favour'. Labor, he predicted, would destroy themselves by their own actions and their own failures. Bruce knew how to be gracious in defeat. He thanked his colleagues. He thanked George Pearce in a letter which showed Bruce had a heart. 'No one', he told Pearce, 'has ever had a wiser counsellor loyaler colleague or truer friend than you have been to me'. From that time he began to serve Australia outside the glitter, the limelight and the flickering fortunes of party politics. With time he came to see that his faith in the harmony of British and Australian economic interests and in the intention and capacity of the British to provide for the defence of Australia was misplaced. Bruce had the wisdom to turn a public defeat into a personal victory, to use his own pain and suffering to begin a journey of discovery of the truth about Australia.[43]

In the years to come there would not be much evidence of a new era in the history of the people of Australia. During the whirlwind time of the last months of the Bruce–Page Government the American musical comedy, *Show Boat* was first performed at His Majesty's Theatre in Melbourne on 3 August, and later in Sydney. It was a story about a great river—the Mississippi—and about the relations between negroes and whites in the period after the Civil War in America. It was about the love of a woman for a no-hoper white man. She put with passion a puzzle in woman's love life. She could find no reason why she should love such a man. She only knew the one big thing:

> Fish got to swim, and birds got to fly
> I got to love one man till I die
> Can't help lovin' dat man of mine.
>
> . . .
>
> Tell me he's lazy, tell me he's slow
> Tell me I'm crazy, maybe I know
> Can't help lovin' dat man of mine.
> Oh listen, sister, I love my mister man
> And I can't tell yo' why
> Dere ain't no reason why
> I should love dat man.

There were other songs about love—'Make Believe', and 'Why Do I Love You?' There was the song about the Mississippi—'Ole Man River'. The *Bulletin*, which had already asked Vance Palmer to 'white-wash' the Aboriginal

[43] *S.M.H.*, 18 October 1929; S. M. Bruce to G. F. Pearce, October 1929, quoted in Edwards, op. cit., pp. 194–6; two letters of S. M. Bruce to G. F. Pearce, 17 November 1929, G. F. Pearce Papers, N.L.A., Canberra.

woman in his novel *Men Are Human*, was not impressed by the 'creoles, mulattos and other sun-burned elements' in *Show Boat*. Australians, it said, were not interested in the life of 'niggers'. Nothing has changed.[44]

During the election campaign Jean Devanny, a communist novelist, announced her intention to give a public lecture on 'companionate marriage'. The Government prohibited the lecture. The Communist Party was uneasy too, they being just as prudish and conformist on questions of behaviour as the bourgeois politicians. In the things of the mind and the spirit the descendants of the men and women who had planted civilization in the Australian bush have again displayed the spirit of the 'suburban old maid'. The ghosts of the past still haunted the brain of the living. Children in Sunday Schools still sang each Sunday:

> Hurry pennies quickly,
> Though you are so small
> Help to tell the heathen
> Jesus loves them all.

Out in the Never-Never things were still the same as ever. A very vast sky, and an inhospitable environment, spoke not of any new eras in the history of the ancient continent, but of all those things which were from eternity and would not change. In the Old World prophets came out of the deserts. In Australia the question was whether prophets would ever arise out of the deserts of suburbia.[45]

[44] *Australasian*, 10 August 1929; *Bulletin*, 7 August 1929; *Show Boat*, Music by Jerome Kern, Book and Lyrics by Oscar Hammerstein (New York, n.d.), pp. 67–83.

[45] Mary Gilmore to Nettie Palmer, 21 December 1929, Palmer Papers, Series 1, Box 5, Folder 41; Nettie Palmer, *Fourteen Years* (Melbourne, 1948), pp. 53–4.

10

AN AUSTRALIAN IN THE PALACE OF THE KING-EMPEROR

LABOR HAS GAINED 'a glorious triumph'. But by the end of October 1929 the drums of celebration have ceased to beat, the flags of triumph have been rolled up. The time has come for Labor to show what it stood for. Jimmy Scullin warned the people of Australia not to expect Labor to 'usher in the millennium'. The *Australian Worker* wanted Labor to place the interests of Australia first. England did not own the Dominions: England should not be able to do what it liked with Australia. Australia was not a place with unlimited space for English factories, workshops and people. The English were so mischievous they had lost America, and then turned Australia into a penal settlement. Labor must not allow the English to engage in their 'stupid meddlesomeness'. A Labor Government must not allow Australia to be enslaved to the English bondholder.[1]

On 22 October the Labor Caucus assembled in Canberra to elect the Ministry. Hope was in the air. Jimmy Scullin was elected leader unanimously, followed by cheers. Tears came to the eyes of Jimmy Scullin, the hurricane orator, the man who believed Labor's role was to 'satisfy humanity's yearning for a fuller and better life'. He told his colleagues that it was 'the proudest moment of his life'. Ted Theodore was elected deputy leader. That too was carried unanimously, followed by cheers. Theodore thanked the members. He was not a man to wear his heart on his sleeve, or let anyone know what touched him deeply. Theodore was an enigma. He belonged to the same Church as Jimmy Scullin. He, too, looked for the resurrection of the dead and the life of the world to come. But no one knew what he stood for in politics. The events leading to his election to the House of Representatives muddied his reputation. There were rumours of money passing hands. His was an odd career for a Labor leader. In his youth he had had the aim of becoming 'disgustingly rich'. He had tramped around the goldfields of Western Australia in a vain search for such riches. He had always been on the fringes of 'tainted money'. Yet, paradoxically, while seemingly a slave to the 'unholy hunger', he also won a reputation as an excellent organizer of the Amalgamated Workers' Association of Queensland.

[1] *Australian Worker*, 16, 23 October 1929.

He was born at Port Adelaide on 29 December 1884, the son of a Roumanian immigrant and grandson of a priest of the Orthodox Church. His mother was a Methodist who had been converted to the Catholic Church. Theodore was both a Labor man, and a man who searched all his life for a place where the rocks were full of 'spangles of gold'. Like Job he was on the watch for 'something precious'. But unlike Job he never seemed to be bothered by the question: 'Where does wisdom come from? Where is understanding to be found?' He preferred fishing to talking with metaphysicians or ideologues. He had no sympathy with revolutionaries or communists or the adoption of the socialization objective at the Brisbane Conference of the Australian Labor Party in October 1921. He believed in politics without doctrines and never spoke of Labor as a standard-bearer in a holy war. He wanted a society where men of enterprise and vision could find their gold mine. He believed in cheerfulness, a yarn about fishing, and other related matters. He was a silver-tongued orator, a magnificent figure of a man, a glamorous man, a man with an aura about him, a man without a political faith who believed that those with the daring to go into the jungle would one day come out rich. He and Bruce had a supreme confidence in 'their superiority to the worms around them'. Theodore had bulbous lips, and much hair on the back of his hands. He loved to indulge in cold, calculated vituperation of those who opposed him: he smoked his pipe, he plotted, but he never dreamed a great dream.[2]

Frank Anstey, the Minister for Health and Repatriation, was a visionary. He had a compass, he said, which could guide Labor through the storm that was brewing, but he was never able to be explicit on the direction in which the needle of the compass was pointing. He has prophesied a day of reckoning for capitalist society. But he doubted whether Labor intended to be its grave-digger. He was afraid the war of 1914–18 had 'chloroformed' the radicals in the Labor movement. Anstey wanted Labor to abandon 'Viceroy Bruce's slogan: 'Follow Britain'. He wanted Australians to laugh at the advice of the parsons and the priests to be content with the station in life in which God had placed them, and all that 'crawlsome obedience to one's betters': he wanted Australians to 'see it was time for a change'.

His colleagues did not share his views. James Edward Fenton, the Member for Maribyrnong and Minister for Trade and Customs, was a loquacious man, one of Australia's many non-stop talkers, with one great passion: the growth of Australian industry. He was determined that Australia should develop into a manufacturing country. The Chambers of Manufactures

[2] Minutes of the Federal Parliamentary Labor Party, 22 October 1929, Patrick Weller (ed.), *Caucus Minutes* (Melbourne, 1975), vol. 2, 1917–1931, p. 348; Irwin Young, *Theodore, His Life and Times* (Sydney, 1971); Warren Denning, *Caucus Crisis* (Parramatta, 1937), pp. 23–6; *Book of Job*, XXVIII, 6–12 (Jerusalem Bible).

agreed with him. He was never heard to utter a word about Labor's mission to the afflicted and distressed. Joseph Aloysius Lyons, the Post-Master General, and Minister of State for Works and Railways, had beautiful blue eyes, and a Roman nose slightly out of line. Everyone liked Joe Lyons. One supporter sent him '8000 Hoorays'.

John Albert Beasley was to be a member of the Federal Executive Council. Beasley was a Lang man. Born at Werribee in Victoria on 9 November 1895, he moved to Sydney when young, worked as an electrician for the Sydney County Council, rose to prominence in the Electrical Trades Union, and was President of the Trades and Labor Council from 1921–1928. In 1928 he was elected the member for West Sydney in the House of Representatives. He was a shy man, an unassuming man, a man of tireless efficiency, with a capacity to take pains. Like Scullin he belonged to that generation of Irish Catholics in Australia who were shocked by the British butchery of the Irish leaders after the Easter Rising. Like Lang his mind was stuffed with all the talk in the Labor Party about that bogy man, Mr Money Man, and the other villain, the British bond-holder. No one suspected that this 'gentle creature', this shy man, had the inner strength to destroy reputations and governments. John Curtin was not elected to the Ministry. He must pay a heavy price for his failure to overcome his 'strange infirmity'. Men judge each other harshly.[3]

They were like a happy band of pilgrims on 22 October 1929 when Lord Stonehaven administered the oaths of office to them at Government House. Labor had hopes of its men. 'No body of men', the *Australian Worker* wrote, 'were ever better qualified for the task that confronted them'. Two days later on 24 October, on the picturesque lawn of the courtyard of Parliament House, Jimmy Scullin introduced the members of his Government (except for Lyons and Anstey) to Australia and the world through a Fox Movietone News camera. It was a historic moment, the first time an Australian Prime Minister had used the 'talkies'. The days of the stump orator and the platform politician were drawing to a close: the days of the talking picture politician and the radio politician were beginning. The *Sydney Morning Herald* was impressed: Labor Ministers acquitted themselves 'creditably': Labor men could bow to the public 'in an impressive and dignified manner'. Jimmy Scullin spoke of his hopes for disarmament, immigration and peace. Ted Theodore promised to face the problems of unemployment and an empty Treasury with 'optimism and even with enthusiasm'. There were beaming smiles: under the 'flowering pagoda' of the courtyard and in the sparkling

[3] Frank Anstey to Harry Maddison, n.d., Anstey Papers, N.L.A., Canberra; V. Molesworth to Frank Anstey, 13 October 1917; *S.M.H.*, 3 September 1949; *C'wealth Gazette*, 23 October 1929; *Australasian Manufacturer*, 26 October 1929.

October air everything seemed possible to these members of a 'great Movement'.[4]

On the same day as the Scullin Government was sworn in, hectic scenes occurred on the floor of the New York Stock Exchange. Brokers were frantic. Wave after wave of selling stocks and shares slashed prices. Traders surged about the brokerage offices, watching their holdings wiped out. Bankers held meetings to stem the tide of offerings, but nothing they did stopped the flood. A rumour ran round the business houses of New York that the Stock Exchange had been forced to close. The entire fabric of capitalist society threatened to come down. On 27 and 28 October there was again frenzied trading on the New York stock market. Panic spread quickly. Even the stocks of the wealthier class were slashed. The Australian press was not unduly worried. This was a stock exchange crash, not a commercial crash, not a crash affecting what the *Sydney Morning Herald* labelled 'productive capacity'. Three days later they were saying that the 'insensate optimism' of the decade had been replaced by a 'dire pessimism'.[5]

Already there were victims of the financial crisis. According to Australian tradition, it was the churches and the benevolent societies that ministered to the needs of those who were in any way afflicted or distressed in mind, body or estate. These bodies now redoubled their efforts. Dr Mannix, the hero of the Irish in Australia, distributed charity to the inhabitants of the 'lower depths'. As he passed through Collingwood on his daily walk from 'Raheen' in Kew to St Patrick's Cathedral, the hungry went down on their knees and begged him for the love of Christ to spare a coin for themselves and their starving families. The Archbishop blessed them and gave them a coin. Dr Dale, the Melbourne City Health Officer, published a daily diet which was cheap and would sustain life. Charity was not enough. Australians wanted their traditional diet of bread, soup, meat, vegetables, pudding and tea. All over the country charity workers strained every nerve to relieve suffering and hunger. Australians wanted not charity, but work. They did not want to sink into despair.[6]

The Government must do something for those out of work. But no one had a clear idea on the duty of government towards the workless. No one wanted to condemn the unemployed to 'the torments of dire poverty'. Humanitarian instincts pleaded for help. But the Australian bourgeoisie has inherited a tradition contrary to any 'wasteful expenditure' and believed in self-help. Government hand-outs were both wasteful and degrading. Labor was not a revolutionary Party. Labor believed in putting Australia first:

[4] *C'wealth Gazette*, 23 October 1929; *Australian Worker*, 23 October 1929; *S.M.H.*, 25 October 1929.

[5] *Argus*, 26, 30 October 1929; *S.M.H.*, 26, 28, 30, 31 October 1929.

[6] *Bulletin*, 5 June 1929.

unlike the Nationalists, Labor did not believe in England doing what it liked with Australia. But all this meant was that Labor supported Australian capital against British, American or German capital. Labor would continue to act in the interests of the ruling classes in Australia. Any welfare policy, any help to the unemployed and their families, must meet with the approval of the governing classes. Labor might try to patch up capitalism, but to do that they must have the approval of the capitalist.[7]

Even on questions of political convention Labor was timid. In opposition they spoke of their intention to strip away all the outward and visible practices copied from class-dominated British conventions. Labor speakers ridiculed the flunkeys attending the Governor-General on State occasions, the appointment of a member of the British governing classes as Governor-General, the wig and gown worn by Mr Speaker and the President of the Senate. But at the ceremony for the opening of the first Parliament under the Scullin Government on 20 November 1929 there were only minor changes. The Governor-General, Lord Stonehaven, arrived at Parliament House with all the pomp and ceremony conservatives observed for the representative of the King-Emperor. Mr Speaker did not wear a wig, but he opened the session with prayers for the King and 'all those placed in authority over us'. The Governor-General's speech did not foreshadow any radical changes. One speaker said the Mace was 'nothing but a relic of barbarism'. The Opposition was scandalized. In the debate on the Address-In-Reply one Labor speaker, J. C. Eldridge, made the 'thunderous declaration' that the Government should 'absolutely insist' on the appointment of an Australian Governor-General. He also added that there should be no discrimination against women in the choice of the most suitable person. That was too much for the House. Both sides collapsed into hilarity. But Eldridge stood his ground. Members should remember, he said, that half the voters in Australia were female. As Barry Humphries was to make Colin Cartwright say later, 'Times change, brother! Times change!' Fifty-seven years later the appointment of a woman as Speaker of the House was no longer a subject for male hilarity.[8]

In opposition, Labor speakers such as Frank Anstey and Maurice Blackburn had called on the Bruce–Page Government to modify the censorship of books, pamphlets and films on the grounds that they were either seditious or likely to deprave and corrupt the morals of the people. Lenin's *Imperialism* and Stalin's *Theory and Practice of Leninism* were both banned, as was James Joyce's *Ulysses*. John Anderson, the Challis Professor of Philosophy at the University of Sydney, called on the new Labor Government to review the

[7] *Age*, 1 November 1929; *Workers' Weekly*, 25 October, 1, 8 November 1929.

[8] *C'wealth P.D.*, 20 November 1929, vol. 122, pp. 6–8; *Canberra Times*, 21 November 1929; *S.M.H.*, 22 November 1929.

formidable list of banned books, to end the censorship of political literature, and to admit all books of proven literary merit. Nettie Palmer hoped Labor would remove from Australia the stigma of being a society of old maids in things of the mind. A deputation called on J. E. Fenton, the Minister for Customs. He told them there would be no wholesale lifting of the ban, but cases would be considered on their merits. Books advocating extreme revolution and bloodshed would certainly not be admitted. Nettie Palmer and her circle were disappointed. The *Workers' Weekly* was self-righteous. Labor, it said, was an imperialist government, seeking to blind Australian workers to world developments and in particular to the danger of an imperialist war.[9]

On the economy Labor believed there must not be extravagance. Labor was not a team of spendthrifts. Jimmy Scullin told the press on 22 October 'this was no time for luxuries'. He would set an example. He and his wife would take rooms in the Hotel Canberra, instead of living in luxury in the Prime Minister's Lodge in Canberra. To ensure privacy he asked the manager of the Hotel Canberra to screen his wife and himself from the other diners. But that was as a gnat to a elephant. Labor wanted to cure the ills of capitalist society, without creating a new society. Labor must solve unemployment, the lock-out in the coal mines, the timber strike, and the threat of strikes on the waterfront without inciting radicals to revolution, or provoking extreme conservatives to armed resistance.[10]

Unemployment confronted the Government with a problem. Labor's solution was public works. Public works meant loan money. Loan money entailed dependence on the British money-lender. Jack Lang and his followers in New South Wales were uneasy about that. Jack Beasley, a member of Jimmy Scullin's Government, was a Lang man. There might be trouble: Labor in Canberra, like Labor in New South Wales, might split into factions. The Government was not a free agent, lacking as it did a majority in the Senate. The division of powers between the Commonwealth and the States made it difficult for a government to regulate the economy. Jimmy Scullin must walk warily. He was like a man jumping from stone to stone to cross a swiftly flowing river: one false step, and he might be swept into the deep water. Jimmy Scullin was a timid man, but brave. He suggested a conference to talk about the problem of unemployment, and this was held in Melbourne at the end of October. Those present appointed a committee to discuss ways and means of alleviating unemployment. They met at the Melbourne Town Hall on 1 November. All the right-minded people were there —representatives of governments, trade unions, returned soldiers, charity organizations, Douglas Copland, an economist from the University of Mel-

[9] *Workers' Weekly*, 8, 15 November 1929.
[10] *Canberra Times*, 23 October 1929.

bourne, and Mrs G. M. Woinarski from the Melbourne Ladies' Benevolent Society. They appointed committees to make a detailed investigation of the causes of unemployment and to plan for relief works. The keynote of their meeting, according to the *Age*, was 'earnestness and an intense desire to accomplish practical results'. But good will and charity could do little to tame the monster of unemployment.[11]

On 5 November thirty women representing twenty women's organizations asked the Premier of New South Wales, Thomas Bavin, to take pity on the plight of the unemployed. Thomas Bavin was not lacking in compassion: he was no Mr Gradgrind of Australian public life: he was also not all heart, having a cool head. Bavin was a Methodist by birth and a Low Church Anglican by conviction. He gave the appearance of having the heart of a measurer, and the mind of a man who expected little but madness and folly from his fellow human beings. Christ's Kingdom, he believed, was not of this world. His finishing school in the matter of wisdom had been the Law School of the University of Sydney. For him life was a 'high adventure', the goal of which was virtue, not happiness or pleasure. Men and women must accept the fate God had allocated to them as best they could, because through suffering and sacrifice people increased in wisdom and understanding. He told these women of Sydney it would be disastrous if the State accepted responsibility for the welfare of their families. He was not lacking in 'humanitarian' sympathy with their plight, but there was nothing to prevent a man in Australia earning as much as he wanted to. 'But', said one member of the delegation, 'there is no opportunity'. Well, said Bavin, you must find one.[12]

On the disputes between capital and labour Jimmy Scullin believed in reaching agreement by discussion. On the coal dispute, on 30 October he announced that his Ministry believed it would be possible to reach a settlement by conciliation. He proposed to summon a conference so that such a settlement could be reached. There would be a compulsory conference between representatives of the mining unions and the mine owners. He believed in collaboration and was willing to confer at any time with the miners and the owners. The *Workers' Weekly* called on the mine workers to 'refuse to again be a party to class collaboration designs of the employers and the reformists'. The only way to achieve peace in industry was by the abolition of the capitalist control of the industry. Imperialism and capitalism were dying and decadent. The class war was being intensified. The workers should be on their guard against those reformists in the Australian Labor Party who were attempting to patch up capitalism and betray the workers to

[11] *Age*, 2 November 1929.
[12] *S.M.H.*, 6 November 1929.

their class enemies. Don't fall for 'Scullin's wiles'. Build councils of action! Prepare to meet the scabs! Prepare to meet the boss![13]

The conference met with high hopes in early November. Jimmy Scullin's wife sent a bouquet of roses as a gesture of good will and he himself spoke the language of conciliation and harmony. All to no avail. Neither side would budge. The conference broke up without achieving any result. But some coal workers drew one conclusion from the efforts of Scullin and his Ministers. Labor had promised the electors there would be no reductions in wages. Now they seemed quite flagrantly to be departing from that principle. What was worse was Bavin's response to the failure of the conference to reach a settlement of the dispute on the northern coalfields. On that very day, 14 November, Bavin announced it was the intention of his Government to take over three of the collieries and to run them, if necessary, with non-union labour. Production of coal was vital to the community. The *Australian Worker* promptly warned Bavin he had blundered badly: he would rouse the entire Labor movement of Australia into action. The cheap coal scheme of Premier Bavin, they said, was doomed to failure. The *Workers' Weekly* appealed for solidarity: miners should not be seduced by the cowards among the officials of the Miners' Federation. They must fight and expose the Left-Wing Reformists, fight against scabs and wage cuts, join rank and file action committees. On to victory![14]

On the northern coalfields a rumour was circulating that the Bavin Government was about to withdraw sustenance allowances from all those who refused to work in the mines. The workers were to be starved into submission. The *Workers' Weekly* called on the workers to tighten their belts, and never surrender. Victory was at hand. Jimmy Scullin prayed. Bavin announced that the mine at Rothbury would be opened. On 20 November R. W. D. Weaver, the State Minister for Mines, declared Rothbury would be worked even 'if the heavens fall'. Neither he nor the other members of the Government were going to be 'dominated by a mob of miners'. Rothbury would be worked by unionists or by free labour. He would not leave the coalfields until coal was mined at Rothbury.[15]

Tension mounted. The *Sydney Morning Herald* on 26 November called the miners' policy 'bushranging upon the industry'. Unemployment has risen from 9.3 per cent in the first quarter of 1929 to 12.1 per cent in the third quarter. The Government's answer was a palliative. Jimmy Scullin decided to provide £1 million for relief work. That would be the Government's

[13] *Australian Worker*, 6 November 1929; *Workers' Weekly*, 8, 15 November 1929.

[14] *S.M.H.*, 15, 19 November 1929; *Australian Worker*, 20 November 1929; *Workers' Weekly*, 22 November, 6 December 1929.

[15] *Australian Worker*, 27 November 1929; *S.M.H.*, 21, 25 November 1929.

Christmas gift to the workless. Jimmy Scullin was still able to laugh: the troubled look on his face was not always there. At the celebration of the silver jubilee of the women's central organizing committee of the Australian Labor Party in New South Wales on 1 December he was in his element, cracking jokes about why there were no women in the House of Representatives. 'It might be said', he quipped, 'that the women do not vote for one of their own sex because the men tell them not to'. (Laughter) 'The reason why women do not rule in Parliament is because they rule in the home.' There was more laughter for that. Jimmy Scullin was gracious and generous to Jack Lang, the leader of the Labor Party in New South Wales: Jimmy Scullin said New South Wales was the backbone of the Labor Party and had saved Australia from conscription. Lang beamed. A beautiful smile passed over the face of Jimmy Scullin, because the only happiness he ever knew was when people were being nice to each other, and he was able to say nice things about the great partner of his life—his wife.[16]

The communists pilloried him as a traitor to the working class. The *Labor Daily*, which was pro-Lang, was needling away at the Scullin Government. Jimmy Scullin had a 'poisonous opponent' in Sydney. The heady days of late October were over. Even within the Labor Party questions were being asked. That prince of story-tellers, 'Rowley' James, the Member for Hunter, that fair dinkum friend of the workers, has lost his faith in Jimmy Scullin. On 3 December he told his colleagues in the House of Representatives why. He had a duty to perform for his constituents, he said, and he was going to perform it, even if in doing so he damaged the Labor Government. 'Rowley' James was worried. The Labor Party stood for no reductions in wages: they won the elections partly on that pledge. He, James, had often condemned Bruce and Page for being traitors to Australia, but there was one thing that could be said for them, at least they were loyal to their class. But the Government of Jimmy Scullin has betrayed the people that sent them to Canberra. 'My people', he said with fervour and a catch in the voice, 'were deserted by the party which proposed to protect them'. He had more to say. The song of revolution and militancy has become weaker: soon 'we shall finally hear them no more. I say further that this is a time when we should have strong men in the Labour [*sic*] party'. Jimmy Scullin has learned at his mother's knee to bless those who persecuted him, to be loving and forgiving to those who despitefully used him. He excused the honorable member for the tone in which he had spoken. He, Jimmy Scullin, knew that the constituents of the honorable member had suffered much. The honorable member had seen men, women and children suffer in their fight for the defence of

[16] *S.M.H.*, 26, 27, 30 November, 2, 10 December 1929.

the principle. Jimmy Scullin understood. But Jimmy Scullin could do nothing.[17]

The unemployed members of the trade unions discussed their plight with Tom Bavin on 5 December. He was full of understanding: he was full of compassion. He knew, he told them, that the unemployed were having 'a very rough spin'. But they too must understand that the Government did not have a 'bottomless purse'. He would never surrender to agitators and militants. On 9 and 10 December Jock Garden exhorted the miners at Cessnock to disregard the officials of the Miners' Federation, those cowardly, lily-livered traitors to the working class, and to set up rank and file committees to take over control of the dispute. Garden was carrying out the Moscow policy of white-anting the Miners' Federation as a step towards creating Soviets in Australia. Bavin took action. On 10 December his Cabinet announced they would open the Rothbury mine forthwith. They planned to build a camp to accommodate the free labour needed to work the mine. Ample police protection would be provided. Work would be offered to the men previously employed in the mine. If men refused to work then the Government would cut off their sustenance payments.

Coal would be mined: the miners would be starved into submission. The rates of pay would be the rates the officials of the Miners' Federation had been advising the miners to accept. The Government and the moderates would isolate the militants: sanity would prevail. The men were not intimidated. The Labor Council of New South Wales recommended that the miners declare a general strike in the mining industry throughout the Commonwealth unless the proprietors agreed to reopen the mines on conditions prevailing before the lock-out. Depression or no Depression, there must be not a penny off the pay, and not a minute on the day. The managers were optimistic. The opening of the mine, they prophesied, would be the signal for a 'stampede back to work'. The mine would be reopened on 16 December.[18]

There was a stampede to the site of the Rothbury mine, but it was not the stampede of men returning to work. It was a stampede of miners on strike preparing to confront free workers. On the Sunday, the day before the mine was due to be reopened, motor cars, lorries, buses, bicycles, motor bikes, jinkers, buggies and drays carried a crowd of eight thousand miners to the mine site. In the heat of a summer's night they sang revolutionary songs round the camp fires. As the sparks from the fires flew upwards they sang with fervour, 'Solidarity Forever, for union makes us strong'. Billies boiled, 'cold tea' was handed around to those who cared for something stronger.

[17] *Labor Daily*, 2 December 1929; *C'wealth P.D.*, 13 March 1931, vol. 128, p. 247; John Robertson, *J. H. Scullin* (Nedlands, 1974), pp. 188–9; *C'wealth P.D.*, 3 December 1929, vol. 122, pp. 576–80; *Age*, 4 December 1929.

[18] *S.M.H.*, 6, 11 December 1929; *Australian Worker*, 11 December 1929.

There were jokes: there were more songs, all the old favourites, and that new song of the workers born out of their present struggle: 'We'll hang Judge Lukin . . .'. At dawn on the following morning, Monday 16 December, three thousand of the campers smashed down the gates in the fence around the mine, and forced the police to retreat towards the pit-head. The police counter-charged. The miners threw stones. The police fired their revolvers into the ground. A policeman shouted, 'Out with your guns and into them'. Another policeman shouted, 'No, don't fire'. But it was too late. Three men were injured. Men batoned by the police lay moaning on the ground. The tactics of the police aroused the men to 'sheer bloody passionate hatred'.[19]

A mass meeting of the men was called. Angry speeches were made. The moderates pleaded with the men to avoid further violence, as the police were armed with guns and the miners had only sticks and stones. A voice was heard to call out, 'Why don't you lead us?' But the miners had no agreed leadership—only two factions pulling them in different directions. The rank and file turned on the journalists and told them to get off the bloody field, quick smart, mate. A howling mob of youths followed one journalist down the main street of Rothbury and shouted at him to leave the town. When another newspaper man stopped he was surrounded and threatened with being kicked to death. He left. The mob then turned its wrath on a stationary motor car owned by a press photographer, and threatened to overturn it. The photographer pleaded with them not to harm his car as it was his only means of earning his living. The mob turned in fury on the cameras in the back seat and smashed them to pieces. Then a detachment was sent to tear up the railway line to the colliery. Armed with sticks and picks they tore up two lengths of rail before the police arrived and drove them off.

While these youths were tearing up the railway line a misunderstanding near the mine head ended in tragedy. A car arrived at the gate seeking entrance. One picket called out that he could see 'that bastard Weaver, (R. W. D. Weaver, New South Wales Minister for Mines) sitting in the car. In fact it was an Inspector of Mines. The pickets became angry. They surged around the car. The police ran towards the mêlée. The men threw stones and the police drew their revolvers. The men refused to move. The police fired. The men retreated. There were three bodies on the ground. They were taken to Maitland Hospital. One of those shot, Norman Brown, died. On that day one man had died, nine miners had been wounded, and seven policemen were wounded. There were about twenty-five minor casualties.[20]

The officials of the Miners' Federation expressed their horror. The attempts, they said, by the New South Wales Government to use free labour have now caused bloodshed, 'something unusual in Australian industrial

[19] *Australian Worker*, 18 December 1929.
[20] *S.M.H.*, 17 December 1929; *Australian Worker*, 18 December 1929.

history'. Blood has stained the wattle. The executive of the Labor Party in New South Wales hoped the Federal Government would take strong action to prevent the Bavin Government forcing miners to work for less than the award wages. In the New South Wales Parliament Jack Lang asked the House to deplore the behaviour of the Bavin Government in shooting down the miners. Angry words were exchanged. One Labor member was removed from the House for calling Weaver a murderer. Thirty thousand unionists attended a mass meeting in Hyde Park. When they attempted to march on Parliament House the police blocked the way with batons. Mines in Queensland and Victoria were closed as a protest against the shooting of the miners at Rothbury.

The *Australian Worker* warned the conservatives: 'the hour of retribution will come'. Moderate Labor feared the militants might incite the miners into more violence. The workers must be 'alert to the danger' from the militants, because that would only lead to more bloodshed. The *Workers' Weekly* lectured the cowards and traitors in the camp of the moderates on their 'effeminacy' and their cringing in every crisis. They agreed with a lone voice on the day of battle: 'Lead us over the wall'.[21]

At the funeral of Norman Brown at Greta on 17 December 1929 the miners, the people of the district, the police and the ministers of Christ's Church gathered to express sorrow rather than join in any cry for vengeance. A piper played 'A Lament'. Massed bands rendered 'Abide with me'. The Bishop of Newcastle, Dr G. M. Long, told them Norman Brown was a 'clean-living, straight-going and loving man'. If, the Bishop continued, Norman Brown were to reappear among them, 'he would urge them to abstain from any cry of vengeance'. They should all leave this scene of sorrow with their minds purged of passion, and a determination that their minds should be guided by righteousness'. Brown wished to live 'peacefully with all men'.[22]

The militants and the communists despised this appeal by Bishop Long to the miners to 'turn the other cheek'. The priests and the Australian Labor Party were 'the vigilantes of capital'. The Communist Party and the Communist Party alone could respond to that lone voice on the coal fields: 'Lead us over the wall'. Norman Brown would be elevated into a hero of the Australian working class. A song was later written:

> Oh Norman Brown, oh Norman Brown, the murdering coppers they shot you down,
> They shot you down in Rothbury town, to live forever, Norman Brown.

[21] *Australian Worker*, 18 December 1929; *Workers' Weekly*, 20 December 1929.

[22] *S.M.H.*, 18 December 1929; Romans, XII, 18; personal visit to Greta, 7 April 1987.

The workers must be armed: only by armed force could they overcome the armed attack of capital. The workers must prepare immediately to form and maintain their own armed defence force as this was the only way to prevent their being forced further and further back into slavery. A Workers' Army should be formed.[23]

At the Strand Theatre in Cessnock on Sunday 12 January 1930 the oaths of membership of such an army were solemnly administered to a number of men. Each swore:

> That I . . . a member of the working class do hereby solemnly swear to protect the working class against armed and other aggression of our capitalist class enemy . . . should I betray the trust imposed upon me I will receive the scorn and contempt of the entire working class.

That evening the newly sworn-in members of the Labor Defence Army provided a bodyguard for the miners' wives as they marched down the main street of Cessnock bearing banners calling for the intensification of the struggle against the rotten system of capitalism. Labor's Defence Army was, as the communists saw it, the only fitting reply to Bavin's capitalist 'thuggery'. The Labor Defence Army would be the beginning of the end of capitalist society. It would provide the revolutionary leadership to carry through the fight until capitalism was overthrown and communism established, and so end the exploitation of man by man.[24]

The past, the vast sky, and the spirit of the place whispered 'Not now'; or faintly, to the comfort of 'Yarraside' and the impotent fury of the revolutionaries: 'Maybe, never'. A society of immigrants and their descendants; a working class wedded to the bourgeois ideas of the ownership of property, and an affluent middle class, have chained Australia to the existing order of society. Besides, Australians had their minds on other things that year. Van Eyke the evangelist visited Cessnock in December 1929 to baptize men and women into the 'fellowship of the saved'. Adela Pankhurst, the one-time orator at the Socialist Hall in Melbourne, preached industrial peace to the miners of Cessnock: 'The lion', she said, 'should lie down with the lamb'. In Melbourne Bob Menzies urged every Victorian politician to pin above his shaving mirror the words: 'How can I do a better job in the next twelve months?' He was still fighting the battle ''twixt damnation and impassioned clay'. Nettie Palmer was helping Keith Hancock to write his book on Australia and comforting Martin Boyd because the Australian literary reviewers, in their best mocking tradition, had accused him of writing 'clumsily'.

Hundreds of thousands were singing the new song of resignation, 'Ole

[23] *Workers' Weekly*, 22 November, 20, 27 December 1929; Dorothy Hewett, 'Norman Brown', published in *Australian Tradition*, November 1965; personal visit to Cessnock, 7 April 1987.

[24] *Workers' Weekly*, 17, 24 January 1930.

Man River'. Men and women in lonely rooms were singing to themselves:

> Wondering where you are
> And if you are
> All alone too.

Members of the sporting public had matters of great moment on their minds. Teams were announced for the Test trial cricket match at the Sydney Cricket Ground in December. Bert Ironmonger was not chosen. That gave the know-alls and the experts in the low-down a field day. Bert Ironmonger, they said, was socially not presentable, not the right sort of man to play for Australia against a team captained by that nice gentleman Arthur Gilligan. Others posed the question they obviously proposed to answer. 'You know why Bert Ironmonger's been left out. Don't yer? Well, I'll tell yer in case yer want to know. Bert's an elbow bender—not the sort of elbow bending we're doing here. But I tell yer when Bert bowls his faster ball, he's a chucker, and the selectors know it'. As ever in the summer, much of the sporting talk was about the 'footy', as the enthusiasts argued who was the better full-forward—a high flyer like 'Nuts' Coventry of Collingwood, or a goal sneak like Jack Moriarty of Fitzroy, or a player who could kick a torpedo punt seventy yards like Lloyd Hagger of Geelong.[25]

Australians believed in sacrifice of life for King, Country and Empire. They did not believe in spilling human blood for the sake of some future harmony. Human blood was not the manure for some future happiness. They were men and women with a long tradition of making do with what they had. They were patchers-up, not visionaries, not creators of either a new heaven or a new earth. Jimmy Scullin believed it was possible to patch up capitalist society, and solve unemployment and stimulate production by a programme of public works. But there was the rub. Public works required loans. Reports from financial advisers in London showed that conditions in the overseas markets were not favourable for any Australian borrowing. What was he to do? As a palliative, he made funds available for relief work as a Christmas present to the unemployed. Jimmy Scullin had compassion. Despite the sneers of the communists and the doubts of Rowley James he still commanded great respect. Louis Esson told Vance Palmer at year's end: 'It seems to me the best [government] Australia has had'.[26]

[25] *Age*, 26 November 1929; *S.M.H.*, 10 December 1929; Wendy Lowenstein, *Weevils in the Flour* (Melbourne, 1978), p. 80; *Age*, 10 October 1929; *Herald* (Melbourne), 6 December 1929; Keith Hancock to Nettie Palmer, 12 June, 27 September 1929, Palmer Papers, Series 1, Box 5, Folders 40 and 41; Martin Boyd to Nettie Palmer, 27 November 1929, ibid., Folder 41.

[26] *S.M.H.*, 10 December 1929; Louis Esson to Vance Palmer, 27 November 1921, Palmer Papers, ibid.

The sufferings of the unemployed were drawn more and more to the attention of the public. On 3 January 1939 Robert Leverton, an unemployed labourer, was charged at Parramatta Court with attempting to take his own life. When asked by the magistrate why he had swallowed poison he said: 'I was out of work. I have a family of ten to keep, and I had a lot of pigs which I could not afford to feed'. On 5 January at Newcastle several unemployed men, weakened by months of semi-starvation, collapsed in a crowd rushing to apply for work at a local labour bureau. Those present cursed the conservative Government of New South Wales for supporting businessmen at the expense of the 'unfortunate, down-trodden unemployed'. Every day in Sydney thousands of what the *Labor Daily* called 'ill-dressed, sad-eyed and gaunt-faced men' gathered outside the Government Labour Bureau in Sydney to collect their ration order. With their tickets they moved to the grocery department where they filled their suitcases or sugar-bags with their supplies. It was the same in all the other cities. On the northern coalfields the Bavin Government refused to pay the dole to any family which had received money from the Federal government's £1 million Christmas gift to the unemployed. The Scullin Christmas cheer for stricken families was almost snatched away by another Government. Those affected were angry: any more of such destitution, it was said, and there would be insurrection on the coalfields. There was to be more tightening of the belts on those fields. Early in January 1930 the Chief Secretary of New South Wales prohibited the distribution of food to anyone who took part in unauthorized drilling.[27]

The uproar at Rothbury continued. Volunteer labour produced coal and rail trucks arrived at the mines to transport it. Militants fumed and talked of the cowardice of the officials of the Miners' Federation. On 10 January a number of pickets challenged a number of volunteer workers on their way to the Ashtonfields Colliery near Maitland. The pickets manhandled the volunteers, stripped them naked and chased them into the bush. A mob of pickets burned a sulky in which a father and son were going to work. They flogged the horse and drove it into the bush. On the same day in Cessnock the members of the Labor Defence Army sang militant songs in the main street. Special contingents of police arrived from Sydney and order was restored. The Labor Defence Army continued to drill. The pickets became more and more aggressive. Fearful for the safety of their men, the Federated Engine Drivers' and Firemen's Association withdrew the safety men from the pits. Rothbury and other mines ceased to work. Bavin countered by issuing instructions that food relief was to be withheld from all law-breakers.[28]

At a special conference on 22 January 1930 in the Trades Hall in Sydney, convened by the executive of the New South Wales Branch of the Australian

[27] *Labor Daily*, 4, 6, 9 January 1930; *Daily Telegraph*, 15 January 1930.
[28] *S.M.H.*, 11, 15, 28 January 1930.

Labor Party to discuss the crisis on the coalfields, the Federal Government was censured for its lack of 'firmness, initiative and ability' in handling the dispute. Other decisions were reached. The Government of New South Wales must disarm the police on the coalfields: the Federal Government should prosecute the Government of New South Wales for aiding and abetting the lock-out; the Federal Government should impose a prohibitive duty on imported and bunker coal produced by volunteer labour. Jack Lang made a fiery speech in which he called on Scullin to act in the tradition of Henry Parkes, who had prohibited 'coolie' labour: Scullin should prohibit volunteer labour, even if that was a breach of the Constitution. A. J. Macpherson went further: he advocated the socialization of the mines without compensation by the next Labor Government in New South Wales, the dismissal of all police officers who had been brutal to miners, and the removal to the country of all rank and file policemen who had ill-used the miners. The Federal Government should seek to gain by referendum the necessary industrial and economic powers to handle the crisis. His proposals were rejected.[29]

The numbers of the unemployed grew each month. The amount of money paid in unemployed sustenance increased each month. The Commonwealth and State Governments complained of lack of funds. The churches protested they could not meet the demand for free meals. In Brisbane the Church of England Men's Society announced in the middle of January they were being called upon to supply one hundred more meals each week. They did not know where the money would come from. In the same week the Government of New South Wales announced that the relief of the destitute was costing the taxpayers £2 million a year. The *Daily Telegraph* put the question: 'How long can this continue?' But the unemployed clamoured for the politicians to do something. A member of a delegation from the One Big Union of Unemployed said to the Minister for Labour and Industry in Brisbane: 'Put your "nuts" together and stop it'.[30]

No one knew how to do that. All sorts of solutions were advanced. The *Daily Telegraph*, the self-appointed watch-dog over the taxpayers' money, wanted the unemployed to be taught 'a deeper sense of individual responsibility, a stronger resolve to stand on [their] own feet'. That, it said, would be an immense benefit to New South Wales. All the conservatives said 'Amen' to that. The *Labor Daily* said the slogan of the hundreds of thousands who wandered hopeless around the dreary streets of Sydney, some of them homeless, was: We Want Work. They drew the attention of the Governments to the transcontinental railway: it was now paying its way. It was not

[29] Ibid., 23 January 1930.

[30] *Brisbane Courier*, 8, 17 January 1930; *Age*, 8 January 1930; *Daily Telegraph*, 21 January 1930.

built with foreign borrowed money, and 'has not had to pay the debenture holders their boodle first'. The transcontinental railway was built out of paper. A note issue. 'Well', said the *Labor Daily*, a mouthpiece for the ideas of politicians like Jack Lang and Jack Beasley, 'what's wrong with doing this again?' So an idea was floated, an idea germinating in the Labor Party of New South Wales 'to help Labor defeat its old bogey man, Mr Money Power'.[31]

Some had hopes for arbitration. On 23 January before the Commonwealth Court of Conciliation and Arbitration in Melbourne Judge Beeby considered the log of claims submitted by the Australasian Coal and Shale Employees' Federation, in which they asked for an increase in the rates of pay. Bob Menzies, representing the Northern Colliery Proprietors' Association, presented the case against the miners' claims. Judge Beeby suggested that, pending a final award by the Court, work be resumed in the idle collieries on the wages and conditions of work set out in the last awards of the tribunal. Bob Menzies intimated his clients would appeal—that was the whole 'bloody' trouble. Both sides accepted the judgments of the Court only when they were favourable, but not otherwise.[32]

The Government of New South Wales came up with a solution. The Minister for Mines, R. W. D. Weaver, known to the militants as the murderer of Rothbury, suggested every miner's lodge should be given an opportunity to take a secret ballot on whether they were prepared to return to work on terms and conditions prevailing before the lock-out. There had been votes taken at meetings, but there the moderates had been terrorized by the militants. In a secret ballot the moderates would have a majority. The militants would be angry, but the moderates knew that if the 'Reds' had their way the miners would be on shorter commons than ever. The Government might cut off food relief if the miners were not permitted to return to work. The Government could starve them into submission. The *Workers' Weekly* bolstered the spirits of the men and their families with the promise of a bright dawn after the black night of suffering and deprivation.[33]

The Bavin Government continued the pressure. On 4 February 1930 they announced that as from 5 February the State dole would not be paid to miners involved in the lock-out. These instructions were to be carried out until the 'black bans' were lifted. The miners held meetings to consider the effects of the move on their families. At Weston, miners suggested their children refrain from attending school until such time as they were properly fed. Committees were appointed to administer relief to starving families. The miners were determined not to be starved into submission. For eleven

[31] *Daily Telegraph*, 21 January 1930; *Labor Daily*, 30 January 1930.
[32] *S.M.H.*, 24 January 1930; *Age*, 24 January 1930.
[33] *S.M.H.*, 3 February 1930.

months now the miners in the northern collieries have endured 'the pangs of privation'. Victory alone could confer a meaning on their suffering.[34]

Jimmy Scullin was ill at ease with suggestions that the problems of Australia could be cured by 'funny money'. He was an honourable man, a man of his word. So were Joe Lyons and James Fenton. They were all honourable men, though Jack Beasley was conspicuously silent whenever the idea of 'funny money' was up for discussion. Jimmy Scullin did not believe industrial disputes should degenerate into violence. He believed in agreement, in the ballot box and the rule of law. If the law of the Constitution rendered the Commonwealth Government impotent then the Constitution should be changed. Great was truth: the people would see the truth and support it with their votes. A Bill for a referendum to change the Constitution would be submitted to the House of Representatives. The people would be asked to grant full legislative powers to the Commonwealth Parliament, and, especially, to confer on the Commonwealth full industrial power. Armed with these powers, and acting within the law, the Scullin Government could then proceed to alleviate the sufferings of the unemployed, and foster industrial peace.[35]

Something must be done quickly. The familiar faces of the poor at the fruit and vegetable markets in Sydney filling their bags have disappeared. God knows where they were now getting their food, now that they had no money. They must join the army of beggars, the army of the forgotten men tramping around the countryside. The Labor press implored their readers not to accept the capitalist lie that depressions were part of the scheme of things. On the contrary, they insisted, depressions were 'directly traceable to the absurd anomalies of the capitalist system and the gross incompetence of the capitalist class'. Labor would honour all its obligations. Rumours were abroad in London that a Labor Government would not pay the English bond-holders. Jimmy Scullin gave the lie to that. In a joint statement with Ted Theodore he scotched the anxiety in London. It was 'absolutely unthinkable', they said, that there would be any possibility whatever of Labor postponing or cancelling interest payments to foreign investors. Interest would be paid with unfailing regularity.[36]

The rank and file of Labor became restive and fretful. They wanted the bread of work: Scullin and Theodore were offering them the stone of financial respectability, of winning the approval of Labor's traditional villain, Mr Money Man in London. On 10 February a special conference of the Labor Party metropolitan provincial group was held in Sydney. Ted Theodore was

[34] *Labor Daily*, 4 February 1930.

[35] *S.M.H.*, 8 February 1930.

[36] *Labor Daily*, 5 February 1930; *Australian Worker*, 5 February 1930; *S.M.H.*, 7 February 1930.

there to tell them what the Scullin Government was doing to settle the coal dispute. Tempers were frayed. Theodore shouted: 'There is one man who could have ended the trouble months ago and could do it now. That man is Bavin'. There were cries of 'rubbish' and 'cut it out'. Donald Grant, imprisoned for sedition in 1916, said simply, 'The Federal Government has not got the courage to act'. To the dismay of Theodore those present adopted the report of the Party's executive, which recommended the commandeering of the mines, the disarming of the police on the coalfields, the prosecution of the coal owners and the State Ministry and the payment of the basic wage to the unemployed miners. One delegate dropped the ominous remark that if Scullin and Theodore could not do anything, then 'the sooner they [the Government] go out the better'.[37]

Jimmy Scullin did not heed the warning. The Government of New South Wales showed no signs of caving in. On the contrary Weaver, a 'murderer' to the militants of the northern fields, was the hero of the bourgeoisie of Sydney. At Strathfield on 17 February he moved to the attack. Volunteer workers, he said, were earning high wages—up to £15 a week—working under the reduced wages scheme. He listed the losses to the coal miners through these 'illegitimate stoppages'. The law was on the side of the Government,and he would enforce the law. The socialists and all the other 'peripatetic reformers' were busy all the time 'devising new restraints, restrictions, limitations, prohibitions, strangulations, and doing everything in their power to prevent the making of more wealth'. The trade unions were multiplying the 'shall nots'. That was killing industry. They must be stopped. The burghers of Strathfield cheered him to the echo. They, too, were engaging in their own holy war, the war to save bourgeois civilization from the destroyers and the wreckers.[38]

Bourgeois politicians were not the only ones to lecture the trade unions on their folly, and urge them to mend their ways. In the third week of February Judge Beeby delivered a homily to the representatives of the metal trades. Judge Beeby was not by inclination or public profession a 'bosses' man'. He began public life as an advocate for the Labor Party and the trade unions. His sympathies were known to be with the 'underdog'. Judge Beeby now told organized Labor it was wrong—disastrously wrong. Labor, he said, must grasp a few fundamental facts. The slump in the prices of wool and wheat was not seasonal, but, with slight variations, it was likely to remain. Australian credit on the money markets was exhausted. Unionists must cooperate with employers to reduce the cost of production, or a huge reduction in wages would occur. Under existing conditions the closing down of public works was inevitable, because they were dependent upon non-exis-

[37] *S.M.H.*, 11 February 1930.
[38] Ibid., 18 February 1930.

tent loan money. To avoid these consequences members of the trade union movement must agree to a change of methods, or a reduction in wages was inevitable. The unions must accept progress.[39]

Mr Justice Beeby paid a price for these words of good sense: his name was added to the long list of villains and traitors in the Labor version of Australian society. Fence-sitters, Pontius Pilates, social scientists, economists and lawyers were all villains if they did not toe the Labor or union line. This was no time for one of those wise men who understood everything, and forgave everything. The unemployed did not want forgiveness or charity: they wanted bread: they wanted work. The situation was desperate. On 24 February the Government of New South Wales decided it could not continue indefinitely to hand out the dole for the relief of unemployed miners on the northern coalfields. Payments would be withdrawn. The men would be starved into submission. The Government proposed to hold yet another conference of all the parties to the dispute. It was not certain the miners would agree to attend under such a threat of intimidation. The Bavin tough line provoked wild scenes in Sydney. On 26 February the city's unemployed attempted to interview the Premier at Parliament House, wondering whether they were the next to be struck off the dole list. They were told they could not interview the Premier. Communists called on them to stand firm. The police charged them and quickly cleared the street.[40]

Opinions differed on what should be done. A committee appointed by the All-Australian Trade Union Congress to report on unemployment and immigration said it was the primary duty of Australian Governments, Federal and State, to provide adequate food, clothing and shelter in default of remunerative employment for any member of the community able and willing to work. The conservatives did not agree. The dole, they said, corrupted morale, and withered individual initiative. The churches spoke of the duty of their members to distribute charity. They had Christ's injunction to feed the hungry, and fill them with good things. The communists feared that the dole and charity might blunt the revolutionary enthusiasm of the workers. For them the beggars and tramps who knocked on suburban back doors were 'scabs', corrupted human beings who indulged in 'a profusion of thanks and grovelling'. Every self-respecting comrade felt ashamed to allow 'such a contemptible, crawling scab near the place'. Such 'scabs' rarely had a union card. Then there were the insurance agents who were driven by their circumstances to extravagant flattery and persistency. These door-step human beings must be taught that capitalism was the cause of their suffering and their humiliation. Capitalism has degraded them into such pitiable creatures. They should fight the battle for socialism, not the verbal battle of the Aus-

[39] 'Judge Beeby's Warning', *Australasian Manufacturer*, 22 February 1930.
[40] *S.M.H.*, 25, 27 February 1930.

tralian back door, trying to persuade housewives with very little housekeeping money to spend a shilling 'for the sake of the kiddie that is arriving', or some other pathetic reason.[41]

The situation was 'ghastly, simply ghastly'. In all the cities scarcely a week passed without a procession of the unemployed. During the marches they shouted and sang songs, and held aloft banners drawing attention to their plight. Scuffles with the police were common, accompanied by cries from forgotten and embittered men and women such as 'Why not take the lot of us?' (i.e., to gaol). Jimmy Scullin hoped the £1 million donated by the Commonwealth Government would help, but even that ran into the old problem of rivalry between the Commonwealth and the States. The workers wanted a reduction of hours. Employers replied that shorter hours would increase the costs of production, which would mean less consumption, and therefore reduce employment. Increased production would come from harder toil. Bob Menzies agreed. He was saying then what he was to say all his life, that the Australian workers needed to 'get up a good sweat'. Against this policy Labor recommended higher wages and increased production by setting the unemployed to work.

Professor Fritz Hart and Professor Bernard Heinze announced their intentions to give concerts to aid all those musicians unemployed through the advent of talking pictures. Even the pianist who for a generation had provided the music to accompany the silent films has become redundant. The *Australian Worker* was confident it knew the source of the trouble, and its cure —big business claimed to provide work for all the members of the community. It has miserably failed. 'For the vast army of workers it can provide no means of earning their living.' The solution, as they saw it, was simple: 'An extensive programme of public works, backed by a nation-wide scheme of Unemployment Insurance is urgently needed'.[42]

But there was the rub. Governments were facing deficits. Loans could not be raised unless Governments reduced their expenditure and increased their revenue. Jimmy Scullin decided that Australian industry needed protection against foreign competition. On 3 April 1930 he announced what the *Sydney Morning Herald* called: 'Sensational Tariff Proposals'. There was to be a total prohibition on the import of some articles, and a partial prohibition of others. Spirits, beverages, textiles, metals and machinery, oils, paints and varnishes, earthenware, cement, china, glass, stone, toilet preparations, wood, wicker, cane, jewellery and fancy goods, hides, leather, rubber, paper

[41] *Labor Daily*, 1 March 1930; Mrs F. Jackson, 'Door Knockers', *Pan-Pacific Worker*, 1 March 1930.

[42] *Labor Daily*, 5 March 1930; *West Australian*, 2 April 1930; *Age*, 12 March 1930; *Australian Worker*, 12 March 1930; 'Work is the Cure for Australia's Ills', *Australasian Manufacturer*, 8 March 1930; *Australian Worker*, 19 March 1930.

and stationery, vehicles, musical instruments and miscellaneous articles were all to pay a duty of 50 per cent in addition to the duties already imposed. Imports would be reduced by £40 million, and Customs revenue would be increased from £10 million to £12 million. Labor was the party of economic nationalism: Labor believed in the maintenance of racial purity, and therefore in excluding cheap Asian goods. Jimmy Scullin has protected Australian industrial practices and Australian wages at the cost of removing incentives to experiment and improvement.[43]

Six days later, on 8 April, Bavin swung the axe. He announced that his Government would reintroduce the 48-hour week, or payment for time actually worked if the 44-hour week was maintained. He introduced a system of payment by results and bonuses for speed workers, a levy on wages, salaries and earnings of all kinds to provide funds to carry out works of a reproductive character, and the appointment of a committee representing employers and employees to ensure that such funds were administered in the most economic manner. Bavin believed in salvation by the endeavours of the individual. Bavin was dismantling many of the schemes introduced by the Lang Labor Government to cotton-wool the workers against capitalist greed and oppression. Bavin had already reduced the salaries of Ministers and Members of Parliament by 15 per cent and of public servants by 10 per cent. But still Labor shouted long and loud that the workers were making all the sacrifices, and the capitalists were not being asked to shoulder any burdens. The communists declared this was a 'wholesale onslaught'. Arguments, they said, never won any battles in the class war. The workers should ask 'the loquacious politicians, pudgy beneficiaries of industry, the capitalist press, and arbitration court judges' who were singing in unison their chant: lower wages, longer hours, harder work: 'When will the vultures be satiated?' The workers must stop crafty men lowering the workers' standards of living.[44]

Capitalist society, said the *Workers' Weekly*, was mortally sick. Customs officers (the servants of capitalists) banned books which might take the blinkers off the eyes of Australians, and tell them the truth about the world they were living in. In 1929 Erich Remarque's novel, *All Quiet on the Western Front*, was banned because of its tendency to 'deprave and corrupt' the morals of the people. But Remarque's high purpose was, in part, to teach his readers the horrors of war. Australians must not be told the truth about the war. They had their myth about the victory of right over might, about sacrifice of life and suffering as a source of wisdom and understanding. Masterpieces of world literature were banned because they might induce in

[43] *S.M.H.*, 4 April 1930.

[44] *Australian Worker*, 2, 16 April 1930; *S.M.H.*, 26 March, 9 April 1930; *Pan-Pacific Worker*, 1 April 1930.

their readers a state of doubt about the old puritan morality, about the lore of the tribe of the British in Australia. Yet no one called in question the large number of American films which showed how small-town American vaudeville troupers could rise to the 'glittering heights of Broadway', and a life of conspicuous waste. On the way up these heroes enjoyed themselves, as presumably did the film-goers in Australia, gaping at ballet girls undressing and making up off-stage. Australians complained that the actors and actresses spoke through their noses in slang which was ugly, raucous and often unintelligible. The characters, the Australians found, were 'cheap and vulgar'. Conservative governments did not find those values immoral. Conservatives wanted Australians to see British films because they portrayed that genteel English life which Australians should copy. But Australians shunned this effete gentility, with its whiff of death. Australians were enjoying the brash confidence of that magnificent negro Louis Armstrong singing in his gravelly voice:

> 'Cos my teeth are pearly
> 'Cos my hair is curly.
> Just because I always wear a smile
> Like to dress up in the latest style
> That's why they call me Shine.[45]

It was a time when not even a swansdown feather thrown on the bosom of the sea could indicate the movement of the tide of public opinion. In South Australia on 5 April the conservative government was defeated by the Labor Party. In Western Australia on 12 April the Labor Party was defeated. On the coalfields the long-drawn-out dispute was coming to an end. On 26 March the officials of the Miners' Federation recommended the men return to work on the terms of the November agreement, provided this was approved at mass meetings of the miners. At five aggregate meetings on the northern coalfields on 7 April the terms were rejected by four of the five. The moderates were dismayed. The Miners' Federation had only enough funds to keep their members on the existing scale of rations for another six weeks. The starved would be forced to accept less favourable terms. The Communist Party, sniffing revolution in the air, savaged all the moderates and the Federation officials as 'contemptible, crawling scabs'. The *Workers' Weekly* called on the workers to fight 'the fascist terror of capitalism, uniformed police, the scolding of the parsons, the lies of the capitalist press, the introduction of scabs' and all those 'social fascists in the Labor Party and the Miners' Federation who were conniving with the coal barons'.[46]

[45] *S.M.H.*, 10 March, 17 April 1930; James Lincoln Collier, *Louis Armstrong* (New York, 1983); personal memories of hearing Louis Armstrong sing.

[46] *S.M.H.*, 7, 14 April 1930; *Labor Daily*, 5 March 1930; *S.M.H.*, 22, 28 March, 8 April 1930; *Pan-Pacific Worker*, 1 March 1930; *Workers' Weekly*, 23 May 1930.

The situation was desperate. The capitalist state was heading for bankruptcy. At the Sydney Royal Show luncheon on 17 April 1930, Theodore gave the facts. Exportable products had declined by £40 million the previous year, due partly to drought, but mainly to the fall in the market value of such exportable products. Despite this decline in the national income Australians continued to buy goods from overseas. It was not possible to go to London for loan money for public works or development. Australia has been borrowing too freely for years—often beyond her capacity to meet her obligations to repay the loans. Australia must become more independent, must put her financial house in order. The question was how? The Government had already had discussions on what to do. Ted Theodore had his hopes: 'ultimately', he said, 'things will go along swimmingly'. The Government had already asked the British Treasury for advice on how they could obtain credit to pay the £2 770 000 owing to the British Government. In February the Government asked the High Commissioner in London to make discreet inquiries. Labor has opted for financial respectability. On 21 April Jimmy Scullin said it was his proud boast, as an Australian, to say that Australia would pay her debts. Paying the debt must precede helping the unemployed, or any social reform.[47]

In that same month of February in which Jimmy Scullin, Joe Lyons, Jack Beasley and their colleagues decided to ask the British money men for advice, Jimmy Scullin was refusing to grovel to the British governing classes about the appointment of a new Governor-General. The term of Lord Stonehaven was due to expire during 1930. In February Cabinet discussed possible candidates. John Monash, the hero of the Great War, was probably too ill to be considered. Some men of distinction were too closely identified with the conservative side in politics. Cabinet decided at the end of March on Sir Isaac Isaacs, the Chief Justice of the High Court of Australia. Isaacs had much to recommend him to a Labor Government. He had risen from obscurity to fame. The son of a tailor in Beechworth in Victoria, he eventually held one of the highest offices in the land. Born in Melbourne on 6 August 1855, he had spent his childhood in the goldmining town of Beechworth, living through those stirring times when Dr Walter Richardson, the father of 'Henry Handel Richardson', became 'peculiar' at nearby Chiltern, and the countryside harboured bushrangers like Ned Kelly, who was eventually locked up in Beechworth Gaol. He became a pupil teacher, and then a student of the law. While other youths whiled away their time he improved himself. There were stories of prodigious feats of memory. Yet in the world of men he was the perpetual outsider. Mr Deakin did not like him. To Deakin, Isaac Isaacs' face

[47] *S.M.H.*, 18, 22 April 1930; Robertson, op. cit., pp. 242–5, C. B. Schedvin, *Australia and the Great Depression* (Sydney, 1970), pp. 132–5; Frank Anstey, Transformation, MS. in Lloyd Ross Papers, Box 33; *Pan-Pacific Worker*, 1 July 1930.

was not handsome, his figure was ungainly, and his nostrils quivered when men said unpleasant things to him. Deakin disliked the man's egotism and his ambition, an ambition too marked for him ever to become a popular figure. But the exclusion from 'Yarraside' and clubland (Isaacs' faith debarred him from ever becoming a member of the Melbourne Club) was one of the many qualities which commended him to a Labor Government. Labor had a never-ending quarrel with those who believed the government of Australia belonged naturally to an alliance of businessmen and landed proprietors.[48]

Jimmy Scullin forwarded the name of Isaac Isaacs to the King. The King was not amused. Cables were exchanged. Through his private secretary the King wanted to know who Isaac Isaacs was. The King wanted to retain his right of choice: he wanted a list of names from which he would make the final choice. Ramsay Macdonald asked Jimmy Scullin to wait until he arrived in London for the Imperial Conference. But Jimmy Scullin did not bow to all this pressure. In cables to the private secretary to the King he informed his most Britannic Majesty that Isaac Isaacs had had 'an exceptionally long and honorable public career', that he was a 'man of splendid qualities', that his probity and impartiality have earned for him the unstinted admiration and respect of his fellow citizens. The manner of his private life afforded 'additional reassurance that his elevation to the high office of Governor-General would occasion no offence to any section in the community'. Jimmy Scullin did not want to do anything 'which might occasion His Majesty any difficulty or embarrassment'. The King would not budge: Jimmy Scullin would not budge. The man who has grovelled to Mr Money Man would not grovel to the titular head of the British governing classes.[49]

He was just as firm with the King and Empire men in Australia. On 1 April Henry Gullett asked in the House of Representatives if it was true the Government intended to appoint an Australian. Jimmy Scullin did not apologize or cringe. He asked whether there was anything wrong in appointing an Australian. 'I have yet to learn', he said, 'that it has been laid down that an Australian may not be recommended for the position'. On 24 April the Opposition returned to the attack. John Latham, the leader of the Federal Opposition, said the question was not whether an Australian could discharge

[48] *S.M.H.*, 2 April 1930; *C'wealth P.D.*, 1 April 1930, vol. 123, pp. 704–6; Herbert Brookes (ed.), *The Federal Story of Alfred Deakin* (Melbourne, 1944), pp. 67–8; *Bulletin*, 30 April 1930; Zelman Cowen, *Isaac Isaacs* (Melbourne, 1967), ch. 1; Robertson, op. cit., pp. 238–9.

[49] Exchange of cables between J. H. Scullin and Secretary of State for Dominion Affairs, copies in Scullin Papers, N.L.A. Canberra; L. F. Crisp, 'The Appointment of Sir Isaac Isaacs as Governor-General of Australia, 1930', *Historical Studies*, vol. 11, no. 42, April 1964.

the duties of the position: the question was whether it was wise or right to change, particularly at the present time, the relations now existing between the Empire and the Commonwealth. The conservatives did not wish to encourage any 'strident and narrow Australian jingoism'. The conservatives, as ever, were 'not now' or 'some other time' men. Outside the House of Representatives those who opposed the appointment of an Australian maintained the proposal would be interpreted as an attempt to break away from the Empire. The President of the Royal Empire Society, Sir James Barrett, expressed concern. The Victoria League was unhappy. Jimmy Scullin stood firm. The tradition which laid it down that Government House should be occupied by amiable men from the British aristocracy was coming to an end.[50]

On economic questions Jimmy Scullin continued timid and unadventurous. Australian economists had ideas for the solution of the Government's problems. On 28 April the newly appointed Ritchie Professor of Economic Research, L. F. Giblin, in his inaugural lecture at the University of Melbourne, addressed himself to the question: 'How are we going to pay our way?' He was an eccentric: his coat had no lapels, his shirt sleeves were cut off at the elbow: his boots were massive, his pipe equally so. He preferred a hurricane lamp in his bedroom to an electric light. He did not walk: he shambled. His face was a map which no one ever read, the lips were bulbous, the eyes deep-set, but rarely visible to the observer. By birth Giblin belonged to those families who had fashioned the Tasmanian version of the bushman's bible. He devoted his vast talents and industry to the preservation of that society, whose way of life was the very stuff of life for him. Giblin had had many adventures. Born in Hobart on 29 November 1872, he was educated in a public school, Hutchins School, at the University of Tasmania and King's College, Cambridge. He served with distinction in the war. He prospected for gold in British Columbia after the war, partly for adventure, partly because one part of him knew all about the 'unholy hunger', but no one ever knew what went on in his heart. His friends called him affectionately 'Gibbie', but he checked them if they risked coming too near. He had a twinkle in the eye whenever the subject of love was mentioned. He was generous to promising young men, but no one was allowed to know what went on inside the mind and the heart of this giant of a man.[51]

He shared the view of J. M. Keynes that the role of economists was to

[50] *C'wealth P.D.*, 1 April 1930, vol. 123, pp. 704–6; *S.M.H.*, 23, 25 April 1930; *Bulletin*, 30 April 1930; telegrams of Royal Empire Society and Victoria League to J. H. Scullin, reproduced in exchange of cables between J. H. Scullin and Secretary of State for Dominion Affairs, April–May 1930, Scullin Papers.

[51] An address by Sir Roland Wilson, Canberra, 29 April 1986, privately printed; D. B. Copland (ed.), *Giblin: the Scholar and the Man* (Melbourne, 1960); personal observation of L. F. Giblin.

shield bourgeois society against revolution. He warned his audience at the University of Melbourne that unless wages were reduced in Australia the unemployment figures would rise steeply. There would be famine, bloodshed and class hatred in the land. It would be the end of the Australian dream of a society in which equality of opportunity did not impinge on the liberties of the individual. He believed capitalist society could be patched up. There was no need for the 'cleansing fire' of revolution. There must be sacrifices, after which Australia would emerge, he believed, on the 'right side'. Giblin believed in the world of 'chaps': that those with the 'head piece clever', their heart in the right place, and the right ideas on economics would save Australia from social revolution. He and Douglas Copland, another Professor of Economics at the University of Melbourne, were already writing to Joe Lyons to tell him what ought to be done.[52]

Something must indeed be done. Men and women, mad with hunger, were ferretting about in gutters and garbage bins in Sydney for scraps of food. To collect the dole, men and women stood for hours in chilly, draughty places herded like wild beasts. Government officers mocked them. The unkind branded them as the 'sussos'. The coal miners and their families on the northern coalfields were close to starvation. One unemployed ex-digger handed back the medal he had received from a 'grateful country' for his service in the war. Albert Jacka, a winner of the Victoria Cross, was knocking on suburban doors, and pleading with housewives to buy his soap. The *Workers' Weekly* called on the members of the Labor Defence Army to prepare to defend the interests of their class by force. The *Labor Daily* warned Scullin that the suffering workless were being driven to link up with the militants. The *Australian Worker* counselled the workers not to listen to all this pernicious talk by capitalists and economists about 'rationing' and reduction of wages: that was only a dodge to conceal the capitalist crime of unemployment.[53]

The plight of the miners and their families on the northern coalfields became so desperate that the officials of the Miners' Federation discussed terms of a settlement. On 22 May the miners agreed to return to work under the terms and conditions of the award of 1929. The capitalist press was jubilant. The officials of the Miners' Federation said there was nothing ignoble in defeat. The *Workers' Weekly* said the capitalist class had forced the comrades of the workers to 'bow to the slave terms'. The workers had not been strong enough to defeat the 'social fascists', the officials of the Miners' Federation and the Australian Labor Party. The fight would go on. Under

[52] *Age*, 29 April 1930; P. Hart, J. A. Lyons: A Political Biography, thesis in Menzies Library A.N.U., pp. 63–8.

[53] *Pan-Pacific Worker*, 1 May 1930; *S.M.H.*, 5, 23 May, 7, 13 June 1930; *Labor Daily*, 2, 12, 13 May 1930; *Australian Worker*, 21 May 1930.

the leadership of the Communist Party the workers would receive the 'correct working class leadership' which would lead the miners to final victory over the capitalist exploiters. There were sufficient brains in the working-class movement to beat these 'social fascists'. They would build a militant leadership: they would build the Workers' Defence Army to meet the Bosses' Fascist Forces: they would give a revolutionary lead to the miners. Forward to victory![54]

There were distractions. At 3.55 p.m. on Saturday 24 May 1930 Amy Johnson made a graceful landing at Darwin in her plane, *Jason's Quest*, in which she had flown solo from England to Australia in nineteen days of 'peril and anxiety'. A woman has shown she could endure the dangers of the air as well as a man. For weeks crowds gathered at every airfield in Australia where she landed. 'Waiting for Amy', it was called. Songs were composed in her honour. The bar-room wits fabricated stories about one aspect of her life not discussed in the press or the pulpit. She said all the right things, including the remark about how pleased she had been to arrive in Australia on Empire Day. She also publicly professed her love for Australia and its people. 'I love Australia and its people', she told a cheering crowd at Mascot. They loved it.[55]

The cricket news from England was just as exciting. Don Bradman, the boy from Bowral, scored one thousand runs in May. Australians in England experienced 'a mad frenzy of delight'. A month later Henry Handel Richardson talked with pride about the achievements of Bradman to Vance Palmer. He found she was much more patriotic than he had expected. In Australia Louis Esson, a man no longer dreaming of castles in the air, was so excited he left the house every day to find out the cricket score: nothing else got him out of the house except the cricket and the football. Helen Palmer was writing letters to her father about Don Bradman, and the long uphill struggle of Hawthorn to get off the bottom of the premiership ladder in the Victorian Football League competition, and how much Hawthorn owed to Bert Hyde and 'Tich' Utting.

Bradman was a strange man to become a hero of the Australian people. In sport he was like Isaac Isaacs in law and politics: he was a loner. Like Isaac Isaacs he spent much of his childhood perfecting himself to fulfil the great passion of his life—success in his chosen field. Isaac Isaacs worked on the use of the English language: Don Bradman worked on how to play a ball to any part of the field he chose. Donald George Bradman was born in a private hospital in Adams Street, Cootamundra, New South Wales, on 27 August

[54] *Labor Daily*, 12, 13 May, 15 July 1930; *Australian Worker*, 21 May 1930; *Workers' Weekly*, 23 May 1930.

[55] *S.M.H.*, 26 May, 5 June 1930.

1908, and lived for two years in a slab hut near Stockinbingal. When he was two the family moved to Bowral. Thus he became known as the 'boy from Bowral'. Like Bob Menzies and John Curtin he was to rise from obscurity to fame, to rise from the slab hut to riches. He had the qualities Australians admired in a sportsman. He defied the conventions on how to bat and succeeded. He was like the pony ridden by the Man from Snowy River:

> He was hard and tough and wiry—just the sort that won't say die.
> There was courage in his quick, impatient tread;
> And he bore the badge of gameness in his bright and fiery eye.
> And the proud and lofty carriage of his head.

After a disastrous debut in test cricket in the match against England in Brisbane in 1928, he had gone on to glory in the third, fourth and fifth tests. By 1930 he challenged the position of Bill Ponsford as Australia's most prolific run-getter. By June 1930 his achievements in England have shaped the question Australians now habitually asked each other: 'Is he out?' Everyone knew who 'he' was.[56]

Nettie Palmer had other things on her mind. That private ache in her heart would not go away. 'It's all very well for you', she told her husband in May 1930, 'to be patriarchal and sensible. I don't look on you as the head-of-the-house but as a lover . . . I'm middle-aged and plain I know', she wrote, 'but then I never had any looks to lose & I oughtn't to be just a woman who runs a house. (I'm not very brilliant if that's my calling!) . . . Your letters [are] not the letters of anyone who could imaginably be a lover of the person to whom they are written'. She added as a postscript: 'Some day you'll write me a love letter & I'll be natural again. Some wretched formalism in me forbids me to unbend till then'. Vance Palmer never wrote the letter she so desperately needed. By contrast Hugh McCrae was never short of objects for his affection. While Nettie Palmer was making the confessions of a passionate heart, Hugh McCrae had his own confessions to make: 'I know', he told her in July, 'I can't be true to any single person. I dote on somebody fresh every fresh second. Last night it was the North Shore Bridge, but I couldn't persuade her to come home to bed with me'. He added that he had been visiting Lady Stonehaven ('by command, as they say'), and liked her so much he had asked her to run away with him. But alas, she thought he was joking. 'She is', he added, 'as kind as kind as kind, with beautiful Scotch eyes, clear and bright'.[57]

[56] Helen Palmer to Vance Palmer, 8 June 1930, Palmer Papers, Series 1, Box 5, Folder 44; personal visit to Bradman house, Temora Museum, Stockinbingal, and Adams Street, Cootamundra, 22 November 1986.

[57] Nettie Palmer to Vance Palmer, 14 May 1930, Palmer Papers, Series 1, Box 5, Folder 43; Hugh McCrae to Nettie Palmer, 15 July 1930, ibid., Folder 44.

At the same time workless men tramped the city streets. As in 1891 and 1892 there were again 'Faces in the Street' in Sydney:

> Drifting past, drifting past,
> To the beat of weary feet—
> . . .

and on their faces were stamped 'the marks of want and care'. The communists prophesied the time was at hand when the streets of Sydney would feel 'Red Revolution's feet'. Every day in Sydney scuffles between the unemployed and the police broke out in the streets: punches were thrown, and men were bundled into the police wagons for a night in Darlinghurst Gaol. The moralizers lectured destitute girls on the consequences of not resisting the temptation to 'hawk the bod' in the streets of Sydney. A ragged army of human beings tramped country roads. They were called the 'Soldiers of Despair'. There were boys, there were men with grey hair in this 'unhappy band of human beings'. The *Workers' Weekly* chanted that capitalist society would never provide them with a job.[58]

Jimmy Scullin believed Australia's financial position required the use of the best brains the nation could bring to its solution. Labor believed Australians should provide the answer to their own problems. But Jimmy Scullin and Ted Theodore have already asked the High Commissioner in London to sound out the British Treasury. They sent him on to the Bank of England. The Bank of England said it wanted to know more. Telegrams have been exchanged. Dr Page has been saying the financial crisis might easily bring about Labor's end. Frank Anstey and Jack Beasley have told Jimmy Scullin to beware of Mr Money Man—beware of the Bank of England, that Shylock in modern dress. Jimmy Scullin, ever the pragmatist, wanted the right man for the right position. The Bank of England suggested a team of three should go to Australia to report on what should be done—Sir Otto Niemeyer, a Director of the Bank of England, J. E. Gregory, Professor of Banking in the University of London, and R. N. Kershaw, an Australian economist on the staff of the Bank of England.[59]

On 19 June 1930 Jimmy Scullin announced the appointment of the economic mission in the House of Representatives. John Latham said the news of the appointment had 'created a good impression in the city'. The Labor press was apprehensive. 'Bankers', the *Labor Daily* told its readers, 'can make and unmake Cabinets'. The *Australian Worker* wanted to know whether a

[58] Henry Lawson, 'Faces In The Street', *Bulletin*, 28 July 1888; *West Australian*, 5, 6, 11, 12, 14 June 1930; *Labor Daily*, 11 August 1930; *Workers' Weekly*, 13 June, 1 August 1930.

[59] *C'wealth P.D.*, 19 June 1930, vol. 125, pp. 2933–4; *Age*, 30 June 1930; Frank Anstey, op. cit., *Pan-Pacific Worker*, 1 July 1930; E. O. G. Shann and D. B. Copland, *The Crisis in Australian Finance, 1929–1931* (Sydney, 1931), pp. 35–6.

British lord of finance could tell Australians what they did not know already. Australian must learn that London was no longer the Mecca of those who worshipped the great god Cash. Britain has ceased to be the dominating Money Power. The devotees of wealth now piously turn their eyes to New York when they say their prayers. Within a few months the *Labor Daily* became scurrilous. The Scullin Government, it said, was 'being bluffed, well and truly' into handing over 'our present and future into the clutch of the foreign Jews'. 'Australia', it continued, 'can stand on its own sturdy legs—any time—anywhere'. The *Labor Daily* was the voice of Jack Lang. The first shots in the Lang war against the interest payments to British financiers were being fired.[60]

Jimmy Scullin, as the *Workers' Weekly* said, was now in danger of agreeing with the Australian capitalists and the British financiers that the solution to Australia's problems was to bring wages down, and make Australian workers produce more. Like Billy Hughes in April—June 1916 Jimmy Scullin was in danger of becoming a hero of the traditional enemies of Labor, and an object of suspicion to the idealists and visionaries within his own political party. The face of Scullin began to show the strain of the times. Rumours circulated that he was not well: doctors were summoned: they shook their heads gravely, and spoke of the need for rest. For Jimmy Scullin was a sensitive and vulnerable man. But, unlike Billy Hughes, his eye was single. No flattery or courting by Labor's foes would ever persuade him to give up the convictions of a lifetime. He shared John Curtin's view that they were all taking part in a 'holy crusade'. He had faith to sustain him: 'And my true name is Labour, though priests call me Christ'. He would go to London to the Imperial Conference in August. The sea and his faith would give him the strength to endure. Jimmy Scullin believed the words of St Paul: 'It is required of stewards that a man be found faithful'. He would be faithful unto death.[61]

Not all those close to him enjoyed the reputation of being unblemished. There had been a question mark against the reputation of Theodore ever since the stories of his connection with the Mungana scandal, and the alleged bribery to buy him a safe seat in 1928. On 28 February 1930 the Nationalist Government of Queensland had commissioned Mr Justice Campbell of the Supreme Court of New South Wales to report on certain matters relating to the Chillagoe mines and smelters, the Mungana leases, the Fluorspar Mining Company, and the Argentum Mining Company, and the conduct of any Minister of the Crown in relation to these matters. On 4 July 1930 Mr Justice

[60] *Labor Daily*, 23 June, 18, 22 July, 23 August 1930; *Bulletin*, 25 June, 30 July 1930; G. L. Wood, 'Threadneedle Street's Emissaries', *Stead's Review*, 1 August 1930; *Australian Worker*, 25 June 1930; *C'wealth P.D.*, 19 June 1930, vol. 125, p. 2934.

[61] *Workers' Weekly*, 29 August 1930; Robertson, op. cit., pp. 227–56; Victor Daley, 'The Sorrowful One'.

Campbell reported that Messrs Theodore, McCormack, Goddard and Reid were guilty of fraud and dishonesty in persuading the State of Queensland to buy the Mungana Mines for £40 000, and that Theodore was guilty of the grossest impropriety in becoming secretly associated with Goddard in the other mining companies. On 6 July Theodore announced his intention to ask Scullin to relieve him of the position of Treasurer. He declared he had a complete answer to the allegations made by Mr Justice Campbell, and characterized the report as 'dastardly partisanship'. Theodore publicly protested his innocence until the day he died.[62]

As ever, the Nationalists preached the morals of the Pharisee. Latham said that whatever happened the honour of Parliament must be upheld. Labor was divided. Lang observed silence, the silence of a politician when a competitor for prominence is reported to have a blot in his copy-book. Labor, too, had a plethora of the righteous, of those who thanked their God they were not as other men. The President of the Labor Party, J. J. Graves, and Jock Garden strongly defended Theodore. So did Jimmy Scullin. Mindful of that most difficult command, 'Judge not', he spoke in the House of Representatives, on 8 July 1930, on the achievements of Theodore. 'I feel', he said, 'that I would be falling short of my duty if I did not bear public testimony to the loyalty, courage and ability with which the late Treasurer has discharged his most exacting and responsible duties'. Theodore, who was greeted with cheers of approval from his colleagues and Billy Hughes, began by thanking Scullin graciously for the generous tribute. He then delivered an impassioned speech in which he asked his calumniators to draw up an indictment so that he might answer it. He insisted he was 'the victim of a hired assassin.'[63]

Jimmy Scullin announced he would administer the Treasury until he left for the Imperial Conference. Those close to him wondered whether his health would endure the strain for much longer, but there was a mighty spirit within his fragile body. The righteous in the Labor movement urged the Government to clear up the scandal, and 'fix the stigma of infamy where it justly belongs'. Labor had business of great moment on its hands. The press, the professors and the parsons continued to deliver unctuous homilies to the workers, explaining to them that because Australians had been living beyond their means the workers must agree to wholesale reductions in wages and an increase in hours. 'Gibbie' (Professor L. F. Giblin) recommended the same remedy in a series of letters to 'John Smith' published in the Melbourne *Herald*, starting on 10 July and finishing on 18 July. Everyone,

[62] *S.M.H.*, 5, 7 July 1930; Report of the Royal Commission on Mungana, Chillagoe Mines etc., 4 July 1930, *Qld P.P.*, 1930, vol. 1.

[63] *S.M.H.*, 8, 9 July 1930.

he said, wanted higher wages and a higher standard of comfort. The only way to get them was either by 'greater efficiency of production or at the cost of unemployment'. Without greater efficiency there must be a reduction in wages. Waving banners would get the workers nowhere. Men and women were neither angels nor devils.[64]

It was all good sound common sense at a time when misery was stirring the madness in the blood. But words of economic wisdom brought no comfort to starving men and women. Men herded like wild beasts to receive their dole tickets or their sustenance payments, starving women, children who were grateful for crusts to gnaw, and all the members of the desolate army of tramps were wanting something more than a professorial lecture, or a talk by one of the measurers on the laws of political economy. Circumstances have given the economists a central place on the stage: they would have their moment of satisfaction. Far away in London, Sir Otto Niemeyer gave the first of his lectures to a captive Australian audience on 13 July. Australians, he said, were about to reap the fruits of the very bad seed that they had long persisted in planting, despite all the warnings. The seed has struck deep at the roots of the economic system. Politicians thought they were wiser than the economists. They borrowed wantonly. Now they must reap the harvest of their folly. The unemployed, in his eyes, were guilty of a supreme folly: at a time when sacrifice was called for, they were asking for higher payments.[65]

The achievements of Don Bradman provided one answer to all these English lectures about Australian foolishness. In the second Test at Lords he made 254. In the third Test at Leeds he made 334. Vance Palmer asked his wife Nettie to tell his daughter Helen that the whole street where he was staying in London was vibrating with news about Bradman. Nettie had to feed on that in her heart by faith with thanksgiving instead of the love letter she still hoped to receive from Vance. Henry Handel Richardson was so excited by the performances of the boy from Bowral she scarcely talked of anything else when Vance Palmer called on her. Jack O'Hagan wrote a song about Bradman:

> Our Don Bradman,
> Now I ask you: is he any good?
> . . .
> For when he goes in to bat
> He knocks every record flat . . .

[64] *S.M.H.*, 9 July 1930; *Australian Worker*, 9 July 1930; *Age*, 9 July 1930; *Pan-Pacific Worker*, 2 June 1930; L. F. Giblin, 'Letters to John Smith' (Melbourne, 1930) and *Herald* (Melbourne), 8, 9, 10, 11, 12, 14, 15, 16, 17, 18 July 1930.

[65] *Labor Daily*, 15 July 1930; *Age*, 9 August 1930; *S.M.H.*, 14 July, 13 August 1930.

The Australian newspapers exhausted their supply of superlatives in eulogies of the Don.[66]

Sir Otto Niemeyer arrived in Fremantle on the liner *Cathay* within a day of Don Bradman playing all those fancy strokes against the English bowlers on the Headingley ground at Leeds. He spoke to Australians like a messenger of death chilling the hearts of revellers. Australia's position, he said, was difficult. It could not be righted by waiting for something to turn up. Australia could not escape from the conditions affecting the other parts of the world. Australia, he implied, was in for punishment: the day of retribution for past extravagances, for transgressing the rule: thou shalt not live beyond thy means, was at hand. On 21 July Jimmy Scullin met Sir Otto in Sydney, together with the Premier of Victoria, Ned Hogan, the Premier of New South Wales, Tom Bavin, officials of the Treasury and the Commonwealth Bank. Jimmy Scullin explained part of the problem: Australian governments had previously raised loan money in London to meet their interest payments on previous loans. That was no longer possible. That day Sir Otto began his examination of the financial situation in Australia.[67]

Two days later, on 23 July, the Minister for Labour in New South Wales, E. H. Farrar, announced that all relief works in Sydney would be closed down because of the strike of the unemployed against the re-introduction of a 40-hour week for men on such relief work. The works would be re-opened with other workers the following week. Those men who refused work would not be given food rations. The strike, he said, was the work of communists. The ragged army of hungry men continued to tramp along the country roads in search of casual work in return for a feed. They were known as Australia's 'Soldiers of Despair'. They had two needs: to avoid starvation; to avoid loneliness. Municipalities built camps to provide shelter for the unemployed single men. The grocers of Melbourne had schemes to relieve the distress of the hungry. The combined choirs of the churches of Brunswick (all Protestant because not even the Depression transcended sectarianism in Australia) sang Handel's 'Hallelujah Chorus' and other works in the Brunswick Town Hall to raise money for the relief of citizens in distress that winter.[68]

While they were singing about the 'kingdoms of this world' and professing their faith in God's world, over which 'He shall reign for ever and ever, Amen', Sir Otto was dining at the Melbourne Club with Richard Penrose Franklin, the headmaster of Melbourne Grammar School. That afternoon he had had talks on the Victorian budget with J. M. Niall of Goldsbrough, Mort and Co., and with E. R. Pitt, the Under-Treasurer of Victoria. The next

[66] *S.M.H.*, 14, 15 July 1930; *West Australian*, 14, 15 July 1930.
[67] *S.M.H.*, 15, 22 July 1930.
[68] Ibid., 24 July 1930; *Labor Daily*, 11 August 1930; *Age*, 11 August 1930.

day he saw the heads of the Commercial Bank of Australia, the English, Scottish and Australian Bank, the National Bank and the Bank of Australasia. He had seen the head of the Bank of New South Wales in Sydney. Sir Otto was increasing in wisdom about Australia. He now knew:

> . . . nothing ever matters, and nothing ever fails,
> As long as nothing happens to the Bank of New South Wales.

In the next few days he spoke to senior officials, played golf at the Metropolitan Club, talked again with J. M. Niall, met Maie Casey, the wife of that promising young man Dick Casey, went to the races at Flemington, dined with Clive Baillieu, and went for a drive to Ferntree Gully and Sassafras, the retreat in the hills for the patricians of Melbourne.[69]

On 21 August Sir Otto addressed a conference of the Prime Minister, the Premiers and Treasurers in Melbourne. His speech made a deep impression on those present. Sir Otto warned them they were faced with a serious problem, the practical solution of which was not rendered any easier by the natural optimism of the Australian. Australians must learn there was not an unlimited market abroad for Australian goods: they must be stripped of the delusion that something would turn up. They must find the answers to many problems: the deficits in government budgets; the floating debt of about £3 million; how to service the external debt; the balance of trade; the low ebb of Australia's credit; the decline in the price of staple products. Australia, he summed up, was 'off Budget equilibrium, off exchange equilibrium'. Australia was faced by considerable unfunded and maturing debts, both internally and externally, in addition to which she had on her hands a very large programme of loan works for which no provision had been made.

Those present were penitent. They had sinned against the laws of political economy through their 'own most grievous fault'. They swore to try, with Sir Otto's help, and the help of the Bank of England, not to sin again. They would do their penance. They agreed it was time for Australian governments to enter that period of 'amendment of life'. They declared their 'fixed determination' to balance their respective budgets for the financial year 1930–31, and to maintain balanced budgets in future years. The Loan Council would raise no future loans overseas until after the short-run indebtedness had been completely dealt with. They would not give approval to the undertaking of new public works which were not reproductive in the sense of yielding to the Treasury concerned within a reasonable time revenue at least equal to the service of the debt. All interest payments were to be paid to a special account in the Commonwealth Bank to be used solely for the payment of interest. The Commonwealth and the States were to publish

[69] Extracts from Sir Otto Niemeyer's Australian Diary, 13–18 August 1930; *Historical Studies*, vol. 20, no. 79, October 1982.

monthly a statement showing their Budget revenue and expenditure. The Australian extravagants have confessed their sins to the vicar of the Bank of England and vowed not to sin again.[70]

Jimmy Scullin believed what they had done was for the good of Australia. Tom Bavin expressed his 'profound satisfaction'. Bertram Stevens was delighted. Dr Page expressed pleasure. Sir Otto has known how to appeal to Australians, he has flattered them for their 'sturdy resolution and self-reliance'. The conservatives and Jimmy Scullin were drawing closer together. One section of Labor was dismayed. The Scullin Labor Government, said the *Labor Daily* on 23 August, was 'being bluffed, well and truly, into handing over our present and our future into the clutch of the foreign Jews'. A Labor Government has pledged itself to 'fight for and protect the interests of money power'. They called for an Australia-wide conference to plan a campaign for the people to have their say. To Hell with capitalist howlers. Australia could 'stand on its own sturdy legs, any time—anywhere'. Don't let the English capitalists reduce the wages of the Australian workers to the level of the lowest Hindu or coolie Chinese. 'Hail, Sir Otto with the Kaffir outlook!' The *Australian Worker* was angry: 'Our workers', they wrote, 'spilt their blood to save England's war lords. Now they must go hungry to fatten England's money lords'. All this has been consented to by a Labor Government. Don't let the 'great Labour Movement of Australia . . . be reduced to a tragic futility' by England's money lords![71]

By then Jimmy Scullin was travelling on the *Orama* to London for the Imperial Conference. He looked very pale and very worried. The doctors on board found him to be 'extremely fatigued and exhausted'. Jimmy Scullin was upset. Divisions have appeared within his Government. The bliss of October 1929 has vanished. Jimmy Scullin has asked two men of like mind to his own to occupy key positions during his absence. J. E. Fenton was to be Acting Prime Minister, and J. A. Lyons to be Acting Treasurer—both men he could trust to carry out the Niemeyer remedies. Frank Anstey was already joining the group of critics of the resolutions in Melbourne. A serious split in the Labor Party was threatened. In Sydney a Labor committee resolved that Federal Labor members should repudiate the agreement reached at the Melbourne Conference under threat of expulsion from the Party. Jack Lang was making wild statements about repudiating the London debts. Jack Beasley was close to Lang. Lang might soon be Premier of New South Wales. What then? To add to his anxiety he received reports of wild scenes on the wharves at Port Adelaide: waterside workers had intimidated 'scab' labour.

[70] *S.M.H.*, 22 August 1930; *Age*, 22 August 1930.

[71] *S.M.H.*, 28, 29 August, 4 September 1930; *Labor Daily*, 23 August 1930; *Australian Worker*, 27 August 1930.

Police charged with batons. Australia was still on the verge of an industrial uproar. The Communist Party again put itself forward as the true working-class party, the only party capable of leading the workers in their struggle against capitalism.[72]

In the election campaign in New South Wales Jack Lang announced his stand against the Niemeyer proposals. On 22 September 1930 in the Auburn Town Hall Jack Lang told an enthusiastic audience London financial interests were plotting to 'degrade, by economic pressure, the Australian standard of living to the level of agrarian Argentina and industrial Germany'. He would save the Australian standard of living. That was more important than paying money to the English bond-holders. The audience clapped and stamped, Jack Beasley smiled in approval. The conservatives were shocked: Lang, they said, was being irresponsible. The communists were disgusted. A demagogue, they said, was fooling the workers with 'vote-catching propaganda'. But Lang knew what he was doing. He was appealing to Australian mythology: Australia was the chosen home of a free people, who prided themselves on being liberated from Old World poverty. Australians had a destiny of their own. Australians had the courage and the strength to resist this brutal English attack on wages and hours. Labor was the representative of the Australian legend: Labor was the conscience of Australia.[73]

Middle-class Australia took fright. In Sydney a thousand ex-Public School boys were drilling secretly in preparation for an armed defence of bourgeois society. Lang went to Canberra to stiffen the opposition of Jack Beasley and Frank Anstey to the Niemeyer proposals. Beasley and Anstey had been prepared to keep quiet about Lang's intentions until after the election at the end of October. But an audience was always a temptation to Frank Anstey. On the night of 1 October at Queanbeyan he threw discretion to the winds. He spoke of 'these cormorants and vultures of finance', who were grinding down the workers of the world. The audience loved it as he vigorously denounced any form of wage reduction. Jack Beasley was on the platform with him. As ever, he was gentle and seemingly innocuous, as he told the audience it was his duty as a Labor man to denounce Niemeyer. Jimmy Scullin was troubled. The furrows cut deeper into his fine brow. A gentle spirit has to tame the wild men of Labor.[74]

Federal Labor did not bend to this wind. The following day Federal Cabinet decided to recommend to Caucus the reduction of Commonwealth expenditure by £4 million, a reduction in Ministers' salaries, in members'

[72] *S.M.H.*, 28, 29 August 1930; *Workers' Weekly*, 29 August 1930; *Pan-Pacific Worker*, 1 September 1930.

[73] *S.M.H.*, 23 September 1930; *Workers' Weekly*, 26 September 1930; *Pan-Pacific Worker*, 1 October 1930; *Australian Worker*, 15 October 1930.

[74] *Stead's Review*, 1 October 1930; *S.M.H.*, 2 October 1930.

salaries, and in public servants' salaries on a graduated scale from 2½ to 15 per cent. Caucus was to discuss the proposals on 27 October 1930.

There were distractions. 'Smithy' flew from England to Australia in ten and a half days, reducing the record for the flight by five days. His average speed was ninety-three miles per hour. But this time the heroics of 'Smithy' had to take second place. The business houses were nervous. Stories were going about that if Lang were successful Australia would receive a setback which would make the present Depression pale into insignificance. Federal Labor must not compromise with Lang. Vain hope. On 25 October Labor swept to victory in New South Wales, winning fifty-two seats to the Nationalists' twenty. The Country Party won twelve and six were doubtful. Lang said it was a victory for Australian ideals, a victory for those determined not to allow the British to whittle down the Australian standard of living, or dictation by an outsider in Australia's domestic affairs.[75]

Strengthened by the victory, at the Caucus meeting on 27 October Jack Beasley moved a motion, seconded by Dr Maloney, that 'this party disagrees with the tariff and industrial policy enunciated by Sir Otto Niemeyer . . . and affirms that the tariff and industrial policy of Australia are domestic matters to be determined by the people of Australia'. Fenton and Lyons spoke against the resolution, arguing that, if passed, it would have a damaging effect on Australia's credit abroad. It would also be a breach of the pledges given at the Melbourne conference. Labor men must not break their word. Fenton and Lyons were moral men. They were sure Jimmy Scullin would be on their side. R. A. Crouch, the Member for Corangamite, joined them. But Jack Beasley stood firm: Niemeyer, he said, had interfered with the financial affairs of Australians. The resolution was carried unanimously. Fenton, Lyons and Crouch did not vote. Caucus was also unhappy with the decision of the Government to reappoint Sir Robert Gibson as Chairman of the Commonwealth Bank Board. Sir Robert was no friend to Labor: Sir Robert must go, but Labor wobbled. Scullin has accepted Niemeyer: now he has given a Labor Government's approval to an enemy of Labor. The following day, 28 October, there were angry exchanges in Caucus between Fenton and Theodore. Theodore wanted the Government to have control over the Commonwealth Bank: Lyons and Fenton did not. Lyons and Fenton again saw themselves as fighting a battle for moral responsibility. They were the reliable men.[76]

Lyons received a large fan mail from people thanking him for the stand he had taken against the Labor extremists. Letter writers planted in his mind the idea that he had a role to play as the saviour of Australia from moral and

[75] *S.M.H.*, 3, 20, 27 October 1930.
[76] Ibid., 28, 29 October 1930; Patrick Weller (ed.), op. cit., pp. 390–1.

economic disgrace. A Toorak matron told him her prayer: 'God give us men a time like this demands'. Others praised his courageous stand against the repudiationists. Australia, one said, had 'found a real man'. Joe Lyons was finding new friends and admirers, not sensing, as his wife did from that time on that both of them 'never again would . . . know peace'. Lyons said he would have to consider his position: he said he might resign: Federal Labor was cracking up.

Lyons made the first of those historic journeys to Melbourne during which he agonized over whether to resign or not. He decided to talk things over by wireless telephone with Jimmy Scullin. Scullin persuaded him not to do it. For him the movement was greater than the pride and scruples of the individual members. Jimmy Scullin was firm: 'Joe, don't do it'. It was the first time Lyons was asked not to do it. This time he agreed not to betray the friends of a lifetime. Jimmy Scullin was no Billy Hughes: Jimmy Scullin was a believer. Lyons agreed to stay on. In Melbourne Bob Menzies and Staniforth Ricketson were having talks on what to do to save Australia. The times were serious. The Communist Party was exhorting the workers to mobilize for some sharper mass fights. The conservatives must have contingency plans if things got out of hand, if the streets and not Parliament become the centre of power in Australia. Australia's credit might suffer irreparable damage if Federal Labor got behind the irresponsible promises of Jack Lang to resist reductions in wages, and supported that wild talk about Australia becoming an Argentine Republic.[77]

In the middle of all this fear and suspicion Don Bradman returned to Australia with the Test team. Bradman was now a people's hero. His were the achievements that tickled Australian pride. The team arrived in Fremantle on 28 October, 1930. Bradman was the stuff of which Australian heroes were made. He stood alone, 'fearless, free and bold'. He was not the prisoner of convention or of English ideas on how to make runs. He made them in his own way, a law unto himself. He travelled alone in the train across the Nullarbor Plain. In Adelaide on 30 October the welcoming group was so dense troopers and foot police had to force a passage for Bradman through the crowd. Bradman, or 'the Don', as he was coming to be called, was something special.

He arrived in Melbourne by air one day earlier than the rest of the Australian team. At the Town Hall reception the Lord Mayor, Councillor Harold Luxton, said that listening to the description of the Tests on the radio had taken their minds off the Depression. At a function in the Tivoli Theatre the

[77] *S.M.H.*, 30, 31 October 1930; *Australian Worker*, 12 November 1930; *Workers' Weekly*, 31 October 1930; Mrs D'Ebro to J. A. Lyons, 7 November 1930, A. K. McElwee to J. A. Lyons, 10 November 1930, Lyons Papers, Folder 3, N.L.A., Canberra; Dame Enid Lyons, *So We Take Comfort* (London, 1965), p. 146.

Don was given a cheque for £100 by his Melbourne admirers. It was presented by Earl Beauchamp, one-time Governor of New South Wales, who had once been warm and friendly to Henry Lawson when he needed it. Don's mother was given a bouquet of roses by the singer, Ada Reeve, 'from the mothers of Melbourne'. Ada Reeve kissed the Don fair and square on the mouth. In Bowral they proudly welcomed him as 'the same carefree, unassuming, clear-eyed boy' they had known. In Sydney on 5 November General Motors gave him a car. The Chief Secretary, Mr Gosling, said: 'Bradman is the Phar Lap of cricket'. If Jack Lang and Joe Lyons were looking for new taxation schemes they ought to 'make Don pay a super-tax on every second century'. They all laughed, Australians believed it did you good to 'have a good laugh'. A laugh a day, as the advertisement ran, keeps the doctor away.[78]

At the same time Joe Lyons announced his intention to fight the mad proposals of the Caucus majority. He stood, he said, where Scullin stood at the Niemeyer conference in Melbourne. The Labor Premiers of Victoria and South Australia agreed with him. Lang would be a lonely figure if he stuck by his 'fantastic scheme'. Ben Chifley also agreed with him. There was a confrontation at the meeting of the Loan Council in Canberra on 11 November. Lyons proposed the issue of a £28 million loan. Lang, the opponent of payments to bond-holders, threatened to take New South Wales out of the Loan Council.

While Lang was making his gesture on the Limestone Plains for the financial independence of Australia, Jimmy Scullin was pleading the case for an Australian Governor-General at the Court of the King-Emperor in London. The King, through the Secretary of State for the Dominions, J. H. Thomas, has informed Jimmy Scullin that His Most Britannic Majesty would not accept Isaac Isaacs as Governor-General. So on that 11 November, the day Joe Lyons and Jack Lang clashed over the financial power of the British in Australia, Jimmy Scullin met Lord Stamfordham, the Private Secretary to the King. Scullin had faith and courage. He has told his Labor colleagues and brothers in London he would not be able to return to Australia if the King declined to appoint Sir Isaac Isaacs. Stamfordham was brusque and condescending. The Australian Prime Minister, he complained, had pointed a pistol at the head of His Majesty. Gentlemen, he implied, did not do that sort of thing. When Stamfordham said of an appointment to South Africa that at least he was an Englishman, Jimmy Scullin replied firmly: 'your real objection . . . is that Sir Isaac Isaacs is an Australian'. Stamfordham tried other arguments. Jimmy Scullin would not budge. He told Stamfordham he would

[78] *West Australian*, 29 October 1930; *Argus*, 1, 3, 4 November 1930; *S.M.H.*, 6, 7 November 1930.

hold an election on the issue if the King did not agree. Jimmy Scullin must see the King-Emperor.[79]

First he went to Mother Ireland where he met relatives and found the strength to stand by the faith of his fathers. But he had to interrupt this refreshment for the soul at the waters of life. The King-Emperor has asked to see him. They met at Buckingham Palace on 29 November, only a few hours after Jimmy Scullin had bidden an emotional farewell to his relatives in the village of Ballyscullin. The King said he wanted to say something to the Australian Prime Minister: '. . . we have sent many Governors, Commonwealth and State, and I hope they have not all been failures'. Scullin said 'No', they had not all been failures. He then unfolded the reasons why they had nominated an Australian. It was clear Jimmy Scullin was not going to make any concessions. It was fourteen years since Billy Hughes, another Labor Prime Minister, had been a guest at Buckingham Palace, fourteen years since the *Labor Call* had exclaimed, 'Ye gods!' But this time no Labor man need have any qualms about treachery or betrayal. This time the King-Emperor gave way. After explaining to Mr Scullin that the last thing he wanted as King was to be the centre of a public controversy, the King said: 'I have been for 20 years a monarch, and I hope I have always been a constitutional one, and being a constitutional monarch I must, Mr Scullin, accept your advice which, I take it, you will tender me formally by letter'. The interview ended. Jimmy Scullin has not grovelled to the English governing classes. An Australian was to be Governor-General. The conservatives accused an Australian Labor Prime Minister of being guilty of an act of discourtesy to the King. Jimmy Scullin has not spoken for *their* Australia, the Australia of the King and the Empire. Jimmy Scullin has spoken for the Australia that was coming to be.[80]

The conservatives did not rejoice. The *Sydney Morning Herald* was worried about the break with tradition. A heavy blow, it said, has been dealt at the sentimental fabric of the Empire. Australia's loyalty to the King and the Empire has been weakened: Empire sentiment in Australia would be weakened. Labor supporters were delighted. An Australian Labor leader has persuaded the King-Emperor to recognize that Australians were qualified to hold the highest place in the land. The claims of the Dominions to equality have been accepted. The Scullin Government has put at least one plank of the Labor Party's platform into place. The *Labor Daily* gloated over its enemies. The King and Empire men, it said, 'soaked in class-selfishness, blind partisanship', and the traditions of subservience, have failed to realize their contemptible cowardice, their destitution of national outlook and the disgust

[79] *West Australian*, 29 October 1930; *Argus*, 1 November 1930; John Robertson, op. cit., pp. 286–8; The typescript report of these exchanges is in Scullin Papers, N.L.A.

[80] Robertson, op. cit., pp. 285–7; *S.M.H.*, 4 December 1930.

it excited among real Australians. Australian national sentiment has had a great boost. It did not matter if His Majesty, in announcing the appointment, did not say as usual, that he had been 'graciously pleased to appoint', but had just said that 'on the recommendation of Mr J. H. Scullin' he had merely 'approved' of the appointment. The conservatives were the parochial-minded ones: Labor was liberating Australia from its colonial past.[81]

On 3 December Jimmy Scullin left England for a visit to the Australian battlefields in France. That night he heard a bugler sound the 'Last Post' at the Menin Gate. The following day he went to the fields near Pozières where, with the larks ascending, he stood on that mound of earth where boys from the Australian bush had known 'Hell itself' in 1916, and seen death grinning at them, and where brave men had been driven 'stark, staring mad' and had wandered about 'crying and sobbing like children, their nerves completely gone'. There he heard French school children sing in French 'Australia will be there'. Jimmy Scullin was so moved he could not speak.

He did not know that as he stood there in that moment of tragic grandeur, back in Australia Herbert Gepp was writing to Lord Somers that the time had come to form a National Government in Australia. Gepp hoped to persuade the Governor-General designate, Sir Isaac Isaacs, to throw in his influence and 'appeal for action on non-party lines for the sake of Australia'. While on board the *Ormonde* on the voyage back to Australia Jimmy Scullin heard that in his absence his colleagues had appointed H. V. Evatt, a Labor Member for Balmain from 1925 to 1927, and E. A. McTiernan, the Labor Member for Parkes, to be judges of the High Court. Jimmy Scullin was shocked: 'no suspicion of political influence', he said 'shall surround an appointment to the High Court'. Staniforth Ricketson, the stockbroker of J. B. Were and Co., was talking with Joe Lyons in Melbourne about a National Government. Bob Menzies was talking with Staniforth Ricketson. Jimmy Scullin could not believe any Labor Party man would betray a Labor Government. He believed in Christ. He believed in Labor. How could there be a Judas?[82]

[81] *Australian Worker*, 3, 10 December 1930; *Labor Daily*, 5 December 1930; *S.M.H.*, 4 December 1930.

[82] *Argus*, 9 December 1930; Robertson, op. cit., pp. 283, 288–9; Bill Gammage, *The Broken Years* (Canberra, 1974), pp. 165–7; H. Gepp to Lord Somers, 10 December 1930, Pearce Papers, N.L.A., A. J. Nettlefold to J. A. Lyons, 7 November 1930, Lyons Papers, N.L.A.; *S.M.H.*, 5, 19 December 1930.

11

AN IRISH CATHOLIC TO THE RESCUE OF BOURGEOIS AUSTRALIA

WHEN JIMMY SCULLIN arrived in Fremantle on 6 January 1931 his friends and supporters were delighted to see him. Jimmy Scullin had such debonair manners: he was so gentle, he charmed everyone who ever spoke to him. A smile even lit up the sad face of John Curtin that day in the bright light of the Australian sun. Jimmy Scullin looked refreshed. Supporters turned to him, hoping their beloved leader would point the way forward. But Jimmy Scullin warned them not to expect too much. 'I have limitations', he said. He added, 'It will require strong effort, and it will require united effort if Australia is going to get on to the high road of prosperity'. He also said: 'I do not believe that we will solve the problem of unemployment by tearing down the standard of living in Australia'. Some cheered: some hooted. The unity of Labor has disappeared.[1]

Lyons and Fenton welcomed the reference to a 'united effort'. On 1 September 1930 his old Tasmanian friend, Professor Giblin, had told him he, Lyons, was 'about our last hope of a peaceful solution'. Were it not for Joe Lyons there would be 'a bad smash with a chance of revolution and chaos'. Giblin had thought then that the breakup of the Labor Party was inevitable. Giblin and Copland have already presented to Lyons a plan for economic recovery, a plan which included a 10 per cent cut in wages, and a recommendation for bank advances provided the security was sound. Lyons has agreed. Lang and Theodore have rejected such a plan. Lang has said he would never preside over the lowering of the standard of living in Australia. Lyons has said in December 1930 that he had long wanted to 'put the interests of Australia before those of party'. When Latham had suggested on 9 December the formation of an all-party advisory council to deal with the Depression, Lyons said: '. . . drop Party'. By then Lyons was telling his wife how 'heavenly' it would be to get away from political life.[2]

Lang and Theodore welcomed Jimmy Scullin's undertaking not to solve

[1] *Argus*, 7 January 1931; *Age*, 14 January 1931.

[2] L. F. Giblin to J. A. Lyons, 1 September 1930, Lyons Papers, Box 2, Folder 14; D. B. Copland, E. C. Dyason and L. F. Giblin, Plan for Economic Adjustment, 18 September 1930, typescript in Lyons Papers, ibid.; *C'wealth P.D.*, 4 December 1930, vol. 127, p. 1000, 9 December 1930, ibid., pp. 1141–2; see also the excellent thesis by P. Hart, J. A. Lyons: A Political Biography (in Menzies Library, A.N.U., Canberra).

the problem of unemployment by tearing down the standard of living in Australia. Within the Federal Labor Party opposition to the professors and the bankers has stiffened. Frank Anstey, the man who called the bankers and bond-holders 'Shylocks' has come up with a counter-slogan to the professors' pleas for wage cutting: 'Default and be damned'. Theodore has had talks with R. F. Irvine. A passionate man was Irvine, no walnut heart in him, no reverence for the measurers and the money-changers, a man whose heart was hot within him. He was the first Professor of Economics at the University of Sydney, but was forced to resign in 1922 because of acts of adultery. Some said the Senate was really dismissing him for his radical ideas. He has converted Theodore to the case for bank credit. Under Irvine's influence Theodore has said on 12 January, 'Australia to-day needs not £20 000 000 but £120 000 000 extra credit'.[3]

Jimmy Scullin has said there would be no repudiation, that there was no easy way. At Ashfield on 15 January 1931, when opening the Labor campaign for the by-election for the seat of Parkes he said:

> I do not want to deceive the workers that there is an easy road to millions that will lead them to emancipation. Do you think I would refuse an easy road if it was there to travel? There is a danger in the relying on the printing of notes, because that leads to wild inflation.

That reassured Lyons and Fenton and others of like mind. But something must be done. Disturbances were breaking out all over Australia. Some conservatives were forming a private army of their own. The communists were calling the workers to join the Labor Defence Army, to drill and prepare for a showdown. Adelaide had the worst riot in its history on 9 January 1931, when one thousand unemployed marched into Victoria Square to protest against the withdrawal of beef from the ration issue. They stormed the Treasury building. The police drew their batons: the unemployed used iron bars and sticks. Several bodies fell to the ground with blood streaming from wounds: hats, coats and placards were strewn all over the footpath and the road. The riot lasted for an hour.[4]

On 22 January Sir Isaac Isaacs was sworn in as Governor-General of Australia. He took the oath on a Bible given to him when he first entered the Federal Parliament in 1901—a Bible which bore the signatures of the Duke and Duchess of York. The ceremony was conducted in Melbourne in the presence of many of the distinguished men of Australia, what Henry Lawson had angrily called the 'Cuff and Collar push', and the gold lace brigade. But the people who made Australia were again not there. The only innovation Labor made in the ceremony was that for the first time in history the docu-

[3] *Labor Daily*, 7 January 1931; *S.M.H.*, 13 January 1931.
[4] *S.M.H.*, 10, 16 January 1931.

ment was signed by the Prime Minister of Australia by authority of the King. But the people still loved Jimmy Scullin. They crowded round him with such enthusiasm outside Parliament House that he needed a police escort to get him to the Hotel Windsor. Jimmy Scullin was still the people's man.[5]

Many ideas were tossed up to solve the antagonism between social classes. Businessmen held meetings in Sydney and Melbourne. In Sydney the Sane Democracy League held meetings to discuss ways and means of fighting communism. In January Lord Somers, the Governor of Victoria, held another camp at Somers, on Westernport Bay, for boys from both sides of the Yarra. The idea was 'to get the other fellow's point of view'. Lord Somers believed in class collaboration, not class antagonism. He wanted the leaven of his 'Power House' Scheme to bring 'to a happy medium the present extremes of thought in the community'. Lord Somers believed in love. On the last day of the camp he read to the boys from Toorak, and the boys from Carlton and Collingwood, the words of St Paul in the 12th chapter of the Epistle to the Romans:

> If it be possible, as much as lieth in you, live peaceably with all men . . . if thine enemy hunger, feed him; if he thirst, give him drink; for in so doing thou shalt heap coals of fire on his head. Be not overcome of evil, but overcome evil with good.

That January the *Workers' Weekly* told the workers the one thing that stood between them and plenty was the 'parasitic capitalist class and their agents of the calibre of Scullin, Beasley, Martin, Lang, Garden'. The masses must fight to obtain a living *Now*.[6]

Joe Lyons believed Jimmy Scullin shared his view that St Paul was right. Labor should live peaceably with all men. But at the meeting of the Labor Caucus in Canberra on 26 January Jimmy Scullin shocked Joe Lyons. He recommended that Theodore be reappointed Treasurer of the Commonwealth. Scullin had never believed any of the charges against Theodore. Lyons was always uneasy about him, partly because of the Mungana scandal, and partly because of Theodore's apparent conversion to the 'funny money' solution to the economic depression. Theodore had these ideas from Irvine, and Irvine was one of those Bohemians of Sydney, an advocate of the morality that everything was allowable. Or so Joe Lyons feared. Lyons was scandalized. At the Caucus meeting he moved for a spill, but sensing the majority were against him, he withdrew the motion. Caucus then reinstated Theodore by twenty-four votes to nineteen. The conservatives raised the question of morality: the Scullin Government, Henry Gullett said, had estab-

[5] *Age*, 23 January 1931; *S.M.H.*, 23 January 1931; Henry Lawson, 'The Men Who Made Australia', *Children of the Bush* (London, 1902), p. 289.

[6] *S.M.H.*, 22 January 1931; *Argus*, 12 January 1931; *Epistle to the Romans*, chapter XII, vv 18–21; *Workers' Weekly*, 23 January 1931.

lished new standards in public life. Archdale Parkhill said it was monstrous to suggest the country could not be governed without a man of Theodore's record. The conservatives were on the march: the conservatives were the guardians of Australia against the men of shabby morals.[7]

The following day Moses Gabb, the Member for Angas, resigned from the Labor Party, David Charles McGrath, the Member for Ballarat, announced his intention to resign, but decided not to. It was that sort of time in the affairs of men. Lyons and Fenton also did not know what to do. As always in a crisis in his life Lyons sought advice and guidance from his wife. While these two were agonizing over whether to abandon the friends and convictions of a lifetime, the Group of Six in Melbourne again got in touch with Lyons. On that day Theodore threw down the gauntlet to Lyons and Fenton. He told a meeting in Ashfield he had been advised there was a power vested in the banks to control credit: by extending credit he hoped to 'stem the tide of adversity'. Latham warned that Theodore would do 'grave injury to the credit and reputation of Australia'. Sir Robert Gibson has said the Loan Council could only advance finance which all banks could see their way to discount at any given period. Well, Theodore has said, 'The Government will take control over the banks'. Lyons and Fenton agreed with Latham. On 29 January they resigned from the Government.[8]

Lyons was 'at his wit's end to know where to turn and which course to follow'. The decision was taken out of his hands. He was approached by Staniforth Ricketson, a director of the stockbroking firm of J. B. Were and Co. Ricketson and Lyons had been friends since meeting in Tasmania in the 1920s, both being Tasmanians. Ricketson had already had talks with T. S. Nettlefold, another successful businessman. Another member of 'The Group' was Robert Gordon Menzies, who had a holiday house at Macedon next to Ricketson's weekender. In the Group they were joined by Charles Arthur Norris, General Manager of the National Mutual Life Association, John Higgins, Chairman of the British and Australasian Wool Realization Association, and Ambrose Pratt, who had been a journalist on the *Age*. They had already been of service to Lyons. In December 1930 they had helped Lyons in the Commonwealth Conversion Loan.

Now they were engaged in a much more formidable task. They had to persuade Lyons to leave the Labor Party, and Latham to hand over the leadership of any future conservative party to Lyons. Latham, they have decided, was not capable of leading the party to victory and government. He had neither the magnetism that was required, nor a real grasp of affairs. They must appeal to the electors as the 'party of political morality'. They

[7] *S.M.H.*, 27 January 1931; Patrick Weller (ed.), *Caucus Minutes*, vol. 2, *1901–1949* (Melbourne, 1975), pp. 410–11.

[8] *S.M.H.*, 20, 28, 30 January 1931.

must create a public image of Lyons as 'Honest Joe', the man who left the Labor Party because of Theodore's shabby finances and shabby public behaviour. The Group chose Bob Menzies to persuade Latham to abandon the great ambition of his life, and to make way for a man who held beliefs he despised. Latham was a rationalist, Lyons was a devout Catholic. Latham believed in government schools, Lyons in Catholic education. Bob Menzies was asking an Irish Catholic, a man said to be wobbly about the King and the Empire during the war, to rescue bourgeois Australia.[9]

On 7 February the Group invited Lyons to meet them in the office of J. B. Were and Co. in Melbourne. The boy from Stanley entered the portals of high finance, just as in 1925 he turned to Sir Henry Jones of the I.X.L. Company for advice and guidance. The Group was in a confident mood. The electors were on their side: the tide has changed. On 31 January in the by-election for Parkes, C. W. C. Marr, a former Minister in the Bruce–Page Government, regained the seat with a majority of at least 8833. 'The voice of Parkes', said Henry Gullett, 'may be taken as the voice of Australia'. The result was also an indignant moral vote against Theodore as Treasurer. Lyons was reassured. Labor was no longer a party of men of rectitude. Labor has muddied its garments. The conservatives were now wearing the mantle of purity Lyons had once believed was the robe of Labor. The conservatives were the party for a man with his morals.

On 7 February 1931 the Group asked him to leave the Labor Party, and become the leader of the Nationalists. They offered him electoral immunity, but no financial bribes. He would be Australia's 'Honest Joe', the voice of moral Australia denouncing those wicked men who proposed repudiation and the issuing of 'funny money'. He was interested, he said, but first he must consult his wife. She saw him as an 'Aaron holding up the Prophet's hands'. He was going to do something to protect the future of his children. 'And by heaven', he told his wife, 'no one is going to spoil this country for them as long as I can lift a finger to stop it'.[10]

Lang's behaviour showed Lyons the path the righteous should tread. At a conference of Commonwealth and State Ministers in Canberra on 9 February Lang submitted a plan advocating that the Governments of Australia should decide to pay no further interest to British bond-holders until Britain has dealt with the Australian overseas debt in the same manner as she settled her own foreign debt over America. He also advocated that Australia should break away from the gold standard of currency, and set up in its place a currency based on the wealth of Australia. This meant, Lang claimed, there

[9] Keith Officer to R. G. Casey, 16 June 1930, Keith Officer Papers, Series 1, item 147, N.L.A.

[10] *S.M.H.*, 10 February 1931; Hart, op. cit., pp. 88–93; Dame Enid Lyons, *So We Take Comfort* (London, 1965), pp. 170–2.

would be an immediate release in Australia of millions of pounds which were now sent overseas. Lang must be stopped. Lyons must play the man of destiny, the saviour of Australia. The conservatives renewed their call for a 'Government of all the talents'. Australia should dissipate the odour of Mungana, and all the wild talk about 'funny money', if they did not want to become 'rickshaw-men'. Leagues and organizations advocating political purity were mushrooming all over the country. On 3 October 1930 a group of businessmen in Adelaide formed the Citizens' League of South Australia. They had as their slogan: 'More business in government, and less government in finance'. They wanted 'sound finance'. On 11 February 1931 they appealed to Lyons to lead a party to defeat Scullin. They had a slogan: 'Scullin must go, Lyons must lead, Latham must support'.[11]

On 12 February there were scenes of great enthusiasm at a public meeting in Killara (Sydney) called to ask those present to 'purge politics'. Purity was the 'great, good thing' amongst conservatives. Norman Cowper, a Sydney lawyer—great-grandson of William Cowper, the chaplain whose other-worldliness had contrasted so sharply with the 'Feed my sheep' Christianity of the Reverend Samuel Marsden, and grandson of Charles Cowper, an early Premier who had forged the long-lasting alliance between the country gentry and the patricians of the cities—told them they had gathered there 'to clean up politics'. Cowper belonged to a class with a long tradition of service and high-mindedness, flavoured with wit and warmth of heart. His wife was the daughter of Hugh McCrae, the poet and friend of Nettie Palmer, the man who had been kind to Henry Lawson in his long agony in Sydney. A businessman told the meeting they were there in a spirit of patriotism, determined to 're-establish the integrity and prosperity of Australia'. Their platform read like a list of the commandments of the business community of Australia: restoration of national credit: Government economy: balanced budgets: creation of unity of purpose: the joining of producing and consuming interests: co-operation between class and class. They had their own crusade: to nullify the communist gospel of class hatred.[12]

The Australian Citizens' League held their first meeting in Melbourne on 19 February 1931. Like the similar organizations in New South Wales and South Australia their members were full of fervour for a united Australia, in which there was co-operation between class and class, in which government finances were above suspicion and politics were pure. They, too, put Australia first. The conservatives were moving towards the unity of a class faced with a dangerous enemy. By contrast Labor was falling into disarray. On 15 February representatives of the Federal Government—the Scullin–

[11] *S.M.H.*, 10 February 1931; *Bulletin*, 11 February 1931; Hart, op. cit., p. 104.
[12] *S.M.H.*, 13 February 1931.

Theodore faction—and representatives of the New South Wales Labor Government—the Lang–Beasley faction—met in the Commonwealth Bank Building in Sydney to decide the financial policy to be presented to the electors in the East Sydney by-election. The State Branch of the Australian Labor Party has already endorsed E. J. Ward as the Labor candidate. Ward was a follower of Jack Lang. Jimmy Scullin wanted the Sydney conference to instruct speakers to advocate the Theodore rather than the Lang policy. But it was easier to prise a limpet off a rock than to persuade Eddie Ward or the New South Wales faction to suppress their opinions.

Edward John ('Eddie') Ward was a stubborn man. He was a boxer entering a different sort of stadium—the political stadium for faction fights in the New South Wales Labor Party. He pummelled political opponents with the same wild glee with which he hit opponents in the ring. Eddie Ward was born at Darlington, Sydney, on 21 March 1899. By birth and temperament he was attracted to Lang's 'simplistic' and 'populist' solution to the economic crisis. For him the world was divided into 'baddies', the Money Men who were generally liars, fornicators and drunkards, and the 'goodies', like Lang, who wanted to relieve the sufferings of the people. Like Lang and Beasley he was Catholic by religion, inheriting from his parents and his teachers the myth of an Irish working class condemned to the ghetto of the slums of Sydney by those greedy, brazen hypocrites, the Low Church Anglicans of Sydney. Like Lang he was malicious in his references to his opponents, and lacking in charity when judging their motives and their behaviour. He had the appearance and the vocabulary of one of nature's haters. In his speeches he concentrated on the 'low-down' about his opponents. No one would guess that the man who poured forth a never-ending torrent of abuse believed he had a mission to lead the workers out of the wilderness of capitalism into a land flowing with milk and honey. He had the thin lips of the hater, the scorn in the eye for all opponents of his class, and the gestures of the mocker. For the mockers he was a hero of the Australian working class. He spoke as though he believed that the members of his faction represented a righteous cause, and that all those who opposed it must be crushed as boys squash flies on blowzy Australian summer days. He was the man of virtue: virtue in politics, virtue in his private life, virtue in his abstention from alcohol. An Irish Catholic puritan flowered into a puritan of the Australian Labor Party.[13]

The State President of the Australian Labor Party, J. J. Graves, announced on 15 February that Lang's financial policy would be presented to the elec-

[13] Ibid., 16 February 1931; *Bulletin*, 25 February 1931; Elwyn Spratt, *Eddie Ward: Firebrand of East Sydney* (Adelaide, 1965).

tors in the East Sydney by-election. No advocate of the Scullin–Theodore policy would be allowed to speak from any Labor platform during the election campaign. Four days later at a meeting of the Federal Caucus in Canberra those present carried a resolution that Federal Labor members would advocate the Federal Labor policy in the East Sydney by-election. The motion was carried fifteen to nil, but three members abstained, and Jack Beasley, Moses Gabb and four others did not attend. State Labor now supported the Lang plan, Federal Labor the Theodore plan. Labor leaders were wrangling over financial policy while men, women and children lived on the Outer Domain in Sydney in shelters built from canvas and potato bags sewn together. Out at Cowra the town's unemployed asked the local Council for permission to use the cattle stalls at the showground as a camping place.[14]

The angry men had their day. On 18 February Colonel Eric Campbell, Major W. J. Scott and six other ex-officers of the Australian Imperial Force met in the Imperial Service Club in Sydney and decided to form the New Guard under Campbell's leadership. Their aim was not to revive the digger spirit in a time of crisis, but rather to protect what they understood by Old Australia. They wanted to stop British-Christian Australia from being destroyed by Langism, Bolshevism, Jewish corruption and the immorality of those who believed everything was allowable. Campbell, a lawyer by profession, was fashioned in the Australian countryside at Young in New South Wales. He proposed to recruit men mainly from the suburbs into a private army. He was asking the ordinary citizen to join with him in keeping the world as it was, against the foreigners and the Jews who promised the Paradise of Communism. Campbell asked his members to take an oath of loyalty to the throne, to pledge themselves to the slogan of 'All for the British Empire', to suppress any disloyal and immoral elements in government, industrial and social circles, to abolish machine politics, and to maintain the full liberty of the subject. In his mind Labor and the communists threatened the most precious thing in life—the individual human soul. Labor and the communists wanted the human ant-heap: Campbell wanted the free individual, the Ned Kelly life of the 'fearless, the free and the bold', without the Ned Kelly murderous criminality. Campbell had the same values as Latham, Bavin, Stevens, Menzies, and Hughes. He differed on how to preserve the Australia they believed in. They believed in British institutions, the ballot box, and parliamentary government. Campbell believed in the British tradition, in individual freedom, honesty, courage and self-sacrifice. He was a moral man. He would fight all those self-seeking people who had made laziness the law of the land. He differed from the conservatives in his ideas on

[14] *S.M.H.*, 16, 25 February 1931; *Caucus Minutes*, pp. 414–15.

how to save Australia from the corrupters. He, too, believed that Labor and the communists threatened morality.[15]

It was a time when men and women were looking for a saviour. The idea was in the air that Labor had had its chance and had muffed it. Niemeyer and the Premiers have pointed the way out of the Depression. Now Labor was squabbling and returning to its Kilkenny cat mood. Australia, conservatives insisted, must regain its confidence, because then it would get help from London. That was what Australia could not do without. During this great war of words on what should be done, on 23 February 1931 Nellie Melba, Australia's queen of song, died in St Vincent's Hospital Sydney. The Australian press gave prominence to the English words of praise. They quoted with pride the eulogy in the London *Times*. That paper in turn had quoted Massenet's name for Melba: 'Madame Stradivarius'. Hers, it said, was 'one of the finest voices ever granted to woman'. It was not easy to believe, it added, that Melba would never sing, laugh or talk again. Other English papers were just as generous. Her personality, her voice, and her 'queenly presence' were gone. Australians basked in the praise. Melba was one of the last of the great exiles. She had disproved the warning that all those who lived abroad were in a dream. Fulfilment for an Australian singer was still at Covent Garden. The English still awarded the prizes and the blanks to gifted Australians.[16]

The fight was on between the Lang and the Theodore supporters. On 26 February at the Premiers' Conference in Melbourne, Theodore submitted a plan for a fiduciary note issue of £24 million of which £6 million would be used to assist the wheat farmers. Jimmy Scullin explained it was futile to enter the money market for a loan, because the public utterances of Mr Lang would ensure the complete failure of such a move. The conservative Premiers presented the case for orthodox finance. Joe Lyons was dismayed. On 2 March the Theodore proposals were placed before the Labor Caucus in Canberra. Some New South Wales members demurred. A heated debate ensued. Lyons was more aware than ever that a man with his principles was powerless to have an effective voice in the Labor Party. He told the press it was pointless for him to attend a Caucus meeting. He decided to go to Melbourne for more discussions with members of the Group. In conversations with this Group, Keith Murdoch of the Melbourne *Herald* came up with the suggestion that his paper would present Lyons to the electors as

[15] Phyllis Mitchell, 'Australian Patriots: A Study of the New Guard', *Australian Economic History Review*, vol. 9, no. 2, September 1969; Keith Amos, *The New Guard Movement, 1931–1935* (Melbourne, 1976), pp. 10–12; New Guard Movement, copy of Police Reports in Regard To, And Its Objects, N.S.W. *P.P.*, vol. 5, 1930–32; 'New Guard', in Humphrey McQueen, *Gallipoli to Petrov* (Sydney, 1984), pp. 199–217; Andrew Moore, 'Send Lawyers, Guns and Money!' A Study of Para-Military Organisations in New South Wales, 1930–31, thesis in La Trobe University Library.

[16] *Bulletin*, 4 March 1931; *S.M.H.*, 25 February 1931.

Honest Joe, the moral man, the man who could be trusted, the good Australian, in contrast to Lang, the would-be repudiator, the blemisher of Australia's reputation and advocate of 'funny money'.[17]

Events moved swiftly. Wild rumours were abroad. In the Wimmera and the Mallee the word passed from farm to farm that the communists had seized Sydney. There was another story that communists from Mildura were marching on Melbourne. The know-alls dismissed such talk as 'childish and absurd rumour', but the members of the secret armies were drilling just in case. The conservative politicians believed they did not need the services of the secret armies. Australia had no tradition of that sort of thing, no record of military coups, or of the people being deluded by demagogues or political mountebanks. The conservatives had other methods: they made bargains with disgruntled Labor leaders. It had worked in 1917. The Group would make it work again. So while the extremists drilled, the Menzies group had their talks with Joe Lyons.

No financial bribes were offered: Honest Joe was offered the Prime Ministership of Australia. Latham must be persuaded to put Australia before personal ambition. Menzies has begun his talks with Latham. Latham would not go quietly. Later rumours grew in profusion. Latham, it was said, was offered the bait of appointment as Chief Justice of the High Court. He had not lost all hope and he wrote letters to his wife telling her of his prospects. Her Jack was no pawn in any political game of chess. Joe Lyons was asking his wife what to do. Latham moved in the House of Representatives on Friday 6 March that 'the Government no longer possesses the confidence of this House'. He was doing this, he said, because he believed 'the best thing we could do for Australia would be to put the present Government out of office'. But Latham had miscalculated. The Labor dissidents did not cross the floor. That was his last chance. Those talks in Melbourne were making his position untenable. Latham must go: the conservatives had no further use for him. Lyons and Menzies drew closer.[18]

The electors were ahead of the politicians. On the following day, Saturday 7 March, Eddie Ward won the seat of East Sydney, but the Labor majority was reduced by at least 10 000 votes. Lang claimed it as a victory for his policy. Bavin claimed the Nationalists had won a moral victory. That was what the conservatives stood for—the old morality, the old moral values. Latham, too, believed the electors had delivered Scullin and Theodore a 'moral rebuff'. At the declaration of the poll Eddie Ward refused to shake hands with his Nationalist opponent. In Caucus on 12 March Jimmy Scullin

[17] *Canberra Times*, 27 February 1931; *Caucus Minutes*, 2 March 1931, pp. 416–19; *Herald* (Melbourne), 2 March 1931; Hart, op. cit., pp. 96–8.

[18] *C'wealth P.D.*, 6 March 1931, vol. 128, p. 11; Hart, op. cit., pp. 96–100; Moore, op. cit., Stuart Macintyre, *The Oxford History of Australia*, vol. 4, 1901–1942 (Melbourne, 1986), pp. 264–6.

moved that any member elected on any policy other than that of the Federal A.L.P. could not attend Caucus meetings. That was carried, despite opposition from Jack Beasley. There was now a Labor man in Canberra who did not attend Party meetings. Jack Beasley opposed Jimmy Scullin, accusing him of 'vindictive spleen'. Scullin, he said, had joined the bankers, the capitalist press and all the reactionary forces. Within the Party there was an enclave of Lang followers.

Menzies and Lyons continued their talks. Latham had made the greatest political mistake of his life. When the vote was taken on the no-confidence motion, Lyons, Fenton, Gabb and Co. voted with the Opposition, but Beasley, Ward and the other Lang men voted with the Government. The Government survived. But that was not the real Latham blunder. Latham gave Lyons the chance to make the speech of his lifetime. Labor members accused Lyons of having attempted to form a coalition government. Lyons replied: '. . . there is only one answer to that. It is a contemptible lie'. Under attack from his one-time friends, Lyons showed his mettle. In a voice trembling with emotion he told the House that to break deliberately with the associations of a lifetime was a step that no man who was not utterly bankrupt of sensibility could take without deep pain and sharp mental suffering. He could not accept the Theodore plan. Only the Creator could make something out of nothing. He believed that men should make bread in the sweat of their brow. He was a moral man. It was because he had been a Labor man all his life that he desired to protect the workers from the misery and destitution that would befall them. Nationalist members of the House, men such as Henry Gullett, who had wondered whether there was anything more to Lyons than these public professions of honesty and sound finance, shed all their misgivings. Joe Lyons was an orator, a man of passion. Poor John Latham was a cold fish, on whom nature had played a cruel trick, inflicting him with a slight impediment in his speech. Australia had a new leader.[19]

Buoyed up with the confidence and knowledge that he could bring all manner of men unto him, and nettled by Labor cries of treachery and betrayal, Lyons set off for Melbourne for more talks with his wife and with the Group. His mind was now made up. His old Labor colleagues appealed to him: 'Don't do it, Joe. Don't do it'. But, armed with a sense of his own righteousness and his own powers, he caught the train to Melbourne. On the Spencer Street platform the wife of a Labor Minister turned her face away as Joe Lyons and his wife passed. This was the beginning of what he and she had to endure for the rest of their lives. Labor men and women shunned them like pariahs, and added him to the list of traitors to be treated with undying hostility.

[19] *Caucus Minutes*, 12 March 1931, pp. 421–2; *Canberra Times*, 13 March 1931.

Lang must be stopped. Lang was still calling on Australians to fight 'the usurious demands of the hungry money-mongers'. Labor radicals, like Donald Grant, were making wild speeches: the revolution, said Grant on 15 March, would be a godsend if it pulled the unemployed out of the mire. Lang has repeated his pledge to oppose payments on the interest bills due in London. Australia, he has said, cannot and will not pay. This gave Lyons, Menzies, Richardson, Nettlefold and their associates a sense of urgency. Menzies had more talks with Latham: all the groups opposed to Labor were to be persuaded to unite into one political party under the leadership of Lyons.[20]

There was much to cheer Lyons on. D. C. McGrath, the Member for Ballarat, resigned from the Labor Party on 16 March. He had had enough. But a band of five or six Labour renegades could not bring down the Scullin Government nor get rid of Lang. Lyons said he felt like a free man, but that sort of freedom did not bring power, nor rescue Australia from dishonest politicians. He must unite the Opposition parties and persuade them to accept him as their leader.

Labor was again tearing itself asunder. The State Conference of the Australian Labor Party expelled Theodore, and began to discuss whether the other New South Wales federal members who had followed the Theodore policy should be expelled. The Federal Conference of the Australian Labor Party expelled the New South Wales Executive for having refused to acknowledge and accept the Federal Platform and Consitution. Inspired by Bob Menzies, the Young Nationalist Organisation called on the various groups which made up the Federal Opposition to agree on concerted action 'under the direction of a common leader acceptable to all'. That was, they believed, the only way to defeat 'the unsound financial proposals now being made by Labour'. That was on 27 March 1931.

Two days later in Sydney the convention of the All For Australia League decided to organize a political movement under the leadership of Joe Lyons. Those present saw themselves as a 'great moral force', fighting the cancer of repudiation which was the brain-child of those disrupters, the communists. They would drive the communists out of the country. Unity was the order of the day, the prime necessity for the salvation of Australia. In such a crisis the country was not against the city. The country believed in 'getting together'. The following day the prospective saviour delivered his message to the people of New South Wales: 'Tell them', Lyons said, 'that just as I have broken associations of a lifetime and abandoned party for country, so they too must act if they truly and sincerely desire to serve Australia effectively in its hour of greatest need'. To which a one-time Labor supporter added, 'God bless you, Joe', and another well-wisher said, 'You're the leader we want'.

[20] *Canberra Times*, 16 March 1931; Dame Enid Lyons, op. cit., pp. 170–2.

Lang stood firm. The policy of the Labor movement, he said, was to challenge the overseas financial interests which were burdening Australia.[21]

The people had other interests. The Davis Cup matches were about to be played. A monoplane, the *Southern Cloud*, was missing on a flight from Sydney to Melbourne. 'Smithy' was reluctantly forced to the conclusion there was no chance of finding any of the crew or the passengers alive.

To the alarm of all right-minded people the New South Wales State Conference of the Australian Labor Party at its Easter Conference passed resolutions which committed the Party to a Soviet-style five-year plan of socialization. Lang and Garden voted against the scheme, but the radicals persuaded delegates that reformism and capitalism had failed the workers. The time had come to change society fundamentally. To the dismay of all lovers of the Empire, the Education Committee of Conference recommended that Empire Day be no longer observed in the schools of New South Wales, and that the weekly ceremony of saluting the flag be discontinued. Imperialist bias was to be removed from the textbooks, and more attention was to be paid to the struggles of the working class. Other delegates wanted less homework to relieve the nervous strain on the children. No one put in a plea for the teaching of Australian history or Australian literature.[22]

Labor leaders accused Lyons of being a 'rat', a leader of a tiny group of Labor men who had 'sold out as shamefully as any body of men ever sold out of the Labor movement'. The workers would judge them. The great tide in the affairs of men and women has begun to flow in the other direction. Joe Lyons has begun to appeal to the people, and the people were on his side. The campaign began in the Adelaide Town Hall on 10 April 1931. At a monster meeting he told a huge, enthusiastic crowd he was setting out on a mission to repair the damage that had been done to Australia. He and his colleagues would succeed by following the lines that made for success in business. He would run the country on business lines. He would encourage private enterprise, because the only way to employ people was to get them producing something worthwhile. Time was running out for Latham. Honest Joe Lyons had a huge following among the Australian people. His wife, Enid, was a great asset. She had a homely charm. In Adelaide she said the women of Australia had to save Australia today. Women had equal rights with men, and the responsibility for Australia's position was equally theirs. They should get behind her husband. Honest Joe Lyons has launched a successful crusade for the salvation of Australia.[23]

[21] Hart, op. cit., 100–8; *Age*, 16, 17 March 1931; *Argus*, 17 March 1931; *Canberra Times*, 28 March 1931; *Report of Federal Conference of the Australian Labor Party, Sydney, 27 March 1931* (Sydney, 1931); Dame Enid Lyons, op. cit., p. 174.

[22] *S.M.H.*, 4, 6, 7 April 1931.

[23] Ibid., 11 April 1931.

Respectable people began to isolate Lang. The Melbourne City Council refused his request for permission to speak in the Melbourne Town Hall. The trustees of the Exhibition Building also refused him permission to speak there because he had 'acted in a dishonourable manner in wilfully defaulting in the payment of interest due to British bond-holders'. By contrast Honest Joe was going from strength to strength. Unlike that repudiator Jack Lang, or that financial wizard Ted Theodore, he was just a plain man. 'I am no orator like Mr Scullin', he told an audience in Ballarat on 12 April, 'I am no financial genius as is Mr Theodore; I am just a plain, blunt man with a simple, straightforward story to tell of what seems to me to be the position in Australia to-day . . . I bring a message of hope to the people of Australia'. His wife told the audience what manner of man her husband was: '. . . one day he said to me: 'Look, my girl, we have no money, and I suppose we never will have any, but we have our children. We have nine of them, you know, and they are going to live in Australia when you and I are no longer here, and, by heaven, I am not going to allow anyone to ruin Australia if I can lift a finger to prevent it'.[24]

Latham must do his duty for Australia just as 'Honest Joe' Lyons was doing his duty. The times required a man to put country above party, to do, as urged by the name of one of their organizations, 'All For Australia'. Another crisis was brewing. The Chairman of the Commonwealth Bank, Sir Robert Gibson, informed Ted Theodore in April that a point was being reached beyond which it would be impossible for the Bank to provide further financial assistance to the Commonwealth and State Governments. Theodore accused the Bank of arrogating 'to itself a supremacy over the Government in the determination of the financial policy of the Commonwealth, a supremacy which, I am sure, was never contemplated by the framers of the Australian Constitution, and has never been sanctioned by the Australian people'. The Board of the Commonwealth Bank and the Senate now stood as guardians of the financial reputation of Australia. But the Group and Joe Lyons must act quickly. Scullin has announced that if the Senate did not pass the Fiduciary Notes Bill then he would recommend a double dissolution. There were three months to go, three months in which to plan for the defeat of Labor.[25]

Prominent public figures pressed Latham to make up his mind. Bob Menzies and the Young Nationalists announced that the time had come for all parties to unite under a common leader. Keith Murdoch continued his campaign in the Melbourne *Herald*. Walter Massy-Greene said the same. Bob Menzies spent the weekend in the middle of April with Joe Lyons at Mount

[24] Ibid., 11, 13 April 1931; *Age*, 11, 13 April 1931.
[25] *S.M.H.*, 18 April 1931.

Macedon. He told him the people were behind the 'saviour of sound finance'. All eyes were on Latham: he must do his duty. Latham was, in their eyes, worthy of the hour. Things have gone badly for him. In February he had been full of hope, confiding to his wife that he had a chance of winning. Now the ambition of a lifetime was forever beyond his grasp. He announced his decision on 17 April. 'In view of the desperate national emergency', he said, the Nationalist Party was prepared to join with Mr Lyons and his supporters in forming a united party in the House of Representatives and in the country under the leadership of Mr Lyons. It was for Lyons to say whether he accepted the offer. Lyons accepted, thanking Latham for subordinating 'self and self-interest in the belief that by this action he is serving the nation'. He called on all sections to follow the lead given by Latham and meet together in a common desire to do something to end the present misery and want in Australia.[26]

Page and the Country Party stood aside. Page had a long memory. Bob Menzies, one of the architects of the drive for forming a single opposition party, was a notorious Country Party baiter, a man with a reputation for insufferable arrogance towards the men of the sheep-walk and the wheat farm. As Page saw it, the men behind the Lyons–Nationalist coalition were all 'big Melbourne manufacturers and stock brokers' who would have no more mercy on Country Party men than on Latham, whom they had buried alive. The Country Party would stand alone. On 19 April the big decision was made in Melbourne. Representatives of the Group, Joe Lyons, and officials from the National Union, the Citizens' League of South Australia, and the All For Australia Leagues, met in Melbourne. They decided to form a United Australia Party by amalgamation of the Nationalists and the other organizations present at the meeting. The United Australia Party was not, in their eyes, just another name for the Nationalists. It was a new Party, composed of Labor men and women, conservatives, and liberals—all those who were dedicated to sound finance and the salvation of Australia from repudiationists, 'funny money' men, communists and all those who sang 'The Red Flag' rather than 'God Save the King'. Joe Lyons would be the leader. Latham refused to be the deputy leader. Now it was time for the Nationalist members of Parliament to act.[27]

On 20 April Jimmy Scullin broadcast to the Australian people. He asked them not to be fooled by the attacks on the Fiduciary Notes Bill. True, it was

[26] Ibid.; *Argus*, 17 March, 18 April 1931; *Sun-News Pictorial*, 2 April 1931; J. G. Latham to J. A. Lyons, 15 April 1931, Lyons Papers, Box 1, Folder 8; Memorandum by J. G. Latham, 15 April 1931, and J. G. Latham to E. Latham, 28 February 1931, Latham Papers, Series 1, Folder 49.

[27] Minutes of Conference, 19 April 1931, Bagot Papers, N.L.A.; *Age*, 20, 23 April 1931; Hart, op. cit., pp. 114–21.

not backed by gold. But it was backed by the credit of the nation. Don't be fooled by those critics who were saying that Australia was bankrupt, that its capacity to maintain its population in the necessaries of life was exhausted. Such a policy of despair could only lead to default. Australia was not bankrupt: he had faith in the people of Australia. Mr Lyons has said that when he became Prime Minister there would be an ample supply of money. Well, said Jimmy Scullin, let him tell the people where it would come from.

But the tide flowed on. Rumours were floating about in Sydney of heavy withdrawals from the Government Savings Bank of New South Wales. On 22 April the President of the Government Savings Bank announced that the Bank would cease operations as from the morning of 23 April, and would remain closed until further notice. The Labor press said this was a capitalist plot to force Lang to resign. The *Sydney Morning Herald* has let the cat out of the bag. 'Mr Lang must resign and the State must secure a stable government with the least possible loss of time'. The closing of the Bank, the *Labor Daily* argued, was a 'calamity, deliberately brought about by disgruntled politicians for purely political purposes'.[28]

For the bourgeoisie salvation was at hand. On 27 April supporters of Honest Joe and his plan for a united Federal Opposition Party flocked to the Sydney Town Hall. The meeting had all the fervour of a religious revival. There was much cheering, much waving of patriotic flags, handkerchiefs, hats, scarves, much whistling. Tears rolled down the cheeks of the good burghers and matrons of Sydney as Joe Lyons, the boy from Stanley, now grown in wisdom and understanding, was introduced as 'the leader of this country and the leader of this movement'. The huge crowd rose to its feet and stamped, and shook hands, and embraced. Honest Joe told them they were there because they wanted to abolish antagonism between classes. Two days earlier they had seen the Anzacs march: now he was there, with Jim Fenton, Guy and Price, to confront another great crisis. He stood for the old Labor Party. But what, he asked, have we got now? The crowd yelled, 'Bushrangers'. That was the whole point as he saw it.

He was the leader of a band of pilgrims who would rescue Australia from these bushrangers, these men who had put themselves outside the moral law. He was the good shepherd. Joe Lyons had the charisma to make people follow after him and the values of Old Australia. We must, he said in conclusion, turn a deaf ear to those who would have us believe that the road to recovery could be accomplished by means of the printing press, rather than by our own efforts. They were dedicated men. At lunch on the same day, Dr Page, for the Country Party, said they would be prepared to co-operate.

[28] *S.M.H.*, 21, 22, 23 April 1931; *Labor Daily*, 23, 24 April 1931; *C'wealth P.D.*, 21 April 1931, vol. 128, pp. 1086–94.

Latham called on them all to get together, to sink personal antagonism for the sake of their common cause. Rid Australia of the incubus of the present Governments of the Commonwealth and New South Wales. They were evangelists for bourgeois Australia, for the Australia of King, Country and Empire. They were not explorers of the way forward: they were imploring Australians to remain loyal to their past.[29]

Labor had no ideas on the way forward but was tearing itself apart. The Lang group was feuding with the followers of Scullin and Theodore. The New South Wales Labor Party was at war with the Federal Labor Party. The Scullin Government now depended for its survival on the votes of the Lang group. The Commonwealth Bank and the Senate stood between the Scullin Government and the execution of its policies. But Jimmy Scullin has not given way to despair. He had his faith: no Labor man would destroy a Labor Government.

Nettie Palmer has not lost her faith. Miles Franklin thought that the Australian nation was being degraded by 'talkies and football and tin hares in pandemoniac plenitude', but she still believed the future lay with that 'far, lone, siren land that enthrals us'. A. G. Stephens was still giving advice. 'What you want, you old dog', he told that gentle spirit, John Shaw Neilson, 'is three bottles of sound old wine under your belt . . . after a good dinner of beef and greens'. Then Neilson would write 'a lusty joyful full-mouthed stanza . . . [about] sturdy breasts and loving bosums' (*sic*). Do not be niggling over the physical side of love-making. Above all: 'Don't be ashamed of life'.[30]

The popular songs from America conveyed a variety of emotions. There was much about love. Irving Berlin, the author of 'What'll I Do?', was now asking another disturbing question for a man worried about what love was doing to him:

> All of me
> Why not take all of me?
> Can't you see
> I'm no good without you.

Con Conrad had some astonishing advice for lovers:

> Bend down, Sister
> Bend down, Sister
> If you want to be loved.

[29] *S.M.H.*, 28 April 1931; *Age*, 28 April 1931.

[30] B. B. B. (Miles Franklin) to Nettie Palmer, 8 May 1931, and A. G. Stephens to J. S. Neilson, 18 August 1931, Palmer Papers, Series 1, Box 5, Folder 47.

Another advised young women:

Take care of all those charms
And you'll always be in someone's arms
Keep young and beautiful
If you want to be loved.

Being loved was one of the great good things. Al Bowley sang about it in such a soothing, saccharine way:

Goodnight, Sweetheart
All my prayers are for you.

The song-writers even had a word of advice for those whose desires were infinite, but whose results were disappointing:

Put a Marcel wave in your hair.

There were other possibilities. A man might have the same experience as Billy Rose and Mort Dixon.

I found a million dollar baby
In a five and ten cents store.

The song-writers knew all about failure in love:

You didn't have to tell me,
I knew it all the time.

They also spoke to those who did not expect much from life. There was Rudy Vallee to tell a man or a woman:

Life is just a bowl of cherries,
Don't take it serious
It's too mysterious.
You work, you slave you worry so
But you don't get your dough,
When you go, go, go.

But life had its moments, moments such as:

When I take my sugar to tea
All the boys are jealous of me
'Cos I never take her where the gang goes,
When I take my sugar to tea.

Advertisers offered relief to those afflicted or distressed in mind or body. Anxious mothers were assured, that 'some little fellow will sleep better' if she rubbed his chest with Vick's Vaporub. Heenzo was a 'Wonderful Family Remedy For Banishing Coughing'. Headache sufferers were told some good news: 'Aspro will not fail you'. Mothers were warned not to ignore cuts in the flesh of their children. There was danger in that cut! Avoid the danger: 'Remember Rexona'—the ointment that heals. On most suburban railway stations there was an advertisement to help people make up their minds about which brand of ham and bacon to buy: 'Don't argue', it said, 'Hutton's hams and bacons are best'.[31]

Labor had put forward no alternative to the tinsel and glamour of capitalist society, or its money values. Labor was locked into a debate within its own ranks and with the conservatives on the answers to unemployment, and the financial problems of Australian governments. A crowd of five to six thousand assembled in the West Melbourne Stadium on the night of 3 May 1931 to hear Ted Theodore present the Federal Labor view. He spoke for two hours. Members of the age group identified by the *Book of Common Prayer* as 'such as are of riper years' already spoke of Theodore as one of the greatest orators Australia had produced, more passionate than the ethereal Mr Deakin, and having more substance than Willie Watt. Federal Labor, he said, would never repudiate the debt to England. 'Having invited England to lend us money for the development of the country, we should not be so mean-spirited as to say "We will not pay you". It would be to the eternal disgrace of Australia'. Some cheered, some hooted. For Labor was divided. Theodore and Jimmy Scullin wanted unity. Labor's enemy was now 'the banks'. He appealed to Lang to join with Scullin and marshal all Labor forces 'in a common fight against the banks'. Labor was involved now in what he called 'a life-and-death struggle with organised capitalism'. Lang was attacking the Party in the rear. They must stand together as a Labor movement.[32]

Jack Lang ignored the appeal. Jack Beasley, Eddie Ward and the other three stood firm. The conservatives presented themselves as the champions of sound and honest finance against the Labor cads, the men with big brains who wanted to play tricks with money. The Nationalists summoned Sir Robert Gibson to the bar of the Senate on 6 May. He was the man whom Jimmy Scullin had insisted should be reappointed as Chairman of the Commonwealth Bank. Now Sir Robert stood there to testify on behalf of sane finance and doing the 'right thing'. Sir Robert was cautious and shrewd. He made it clear that the Commonwealth Bank Bill had never been sent to the Bank for advice, and that the Bank had never sent any official communication to the Government on the subject. He made it clear that no Government could dictate to the Bank and that in his opinion Australia should not default. He made it clear that for him England was 'Home'. On the same day Bob Menzies put the case for 'honest finance' to the electors at Launceston in

[31] Julius Mattfeld, *Variety Music Cavalcade* (3rd edn, New York, 1962), pp. 463–7; personal memories.

[32] *Age*, 8 May 1931.

Tasmania. It was, he said, a 'big thing' to be honest at a time when the honesty of some politicians was, to say the least of it, 'under suspicion'. Hard work and honesty of purpose were 'the essentials of the remedy for Australia's ills'.[33]

The following day, 7 May, the parliamentary members of the Nationalist Party agreed to form themselves into the United Australia Party under the leadership of J. A. Lyons, with J. G. Latham as deputy leader. Latham has decided his pride must be subordinated to the interests of Australia. Lyons and the other ex-Labor men then entered the room, followed by W. M. Hughes and the other members of his Australia Party. Conservatives were now united: their next task was to bring down the Scullin Government and the Lang Government. They were as excited as the members of a football team about to run a lap of honour after victory in the Grand Final on the Melbourne Cricket Ground. Joe Lyons, with a becoming pride and a new confidence, told the House the same day that he had been elected Leader of the Opposition, and Latham had been elected Deputy Leader. He then moved a vote of no confidence in the Government. Labor members ridiculed Joe Lyons. He had been running around the country, the member for Corangamite said, posing as a Daniel:

> Dare to be a Daniel
> Dare to stand alone.

But the people would one day put him up for judgement.

This time Labor remained united. The no-confidence motion was lost by thirty-two votes to thirty-four. Outside the Parliament, Labor supporters remained confident. The future, the *Australian Worker* declared, 'belongs to the people'. The *Workers' Weekly* dismissed Joe Lyons as a 'mullet head'. Vain words! Labor's confidence in the people was misplaced. The following day, 9 May, in the Tasmanian election, Nationalists won nineteen seats, Labor ten and an Independent one. The electors have voted for the Niemeyer policy, for honest finance. The Tasmanians have shown, Joe Lyons declared, they would have nothing to do with 'fiduciary currencies or policies of repudiation'.[34]

The movement against Labor developed into a crusade about morality. The clergy joined in, conferring divine blessing on the political ambitions of 'Yarraside' and their new recruits, especially Honest Joe Lyons. Politicians, said the Anglican Dean of Newcastle, the Very Reverend W. H. Johnson,

[33] *C'wealth P.D.*, 6 May 1931, vol. 129, pp. 1615–31; *Examiner* (Launceston), 7 May 1931.

[34] *Age*, 8 May 1931; Hart, op. cit., pp. 120–1; *C'wealth P.D.*, 7 May 1931, vol. 129, pp. 1690–1; *S.M.H.*, 11, 12 May 1931; *Australian Worker*, 13 May 1931; *Workers' Weekly*, 5 June 1931; *Examiner* (Launceston), 11 May 1931.

were bringing disgrace upon Australia by 'evasive, dishonest and dishonourable financial schemes'. Australia was facing economic chaos and social disruption because of its neglect of morals and religion. The conservatives would help Australians to be 'reconciled to God'. Australians must be moral: Australians must be honest. As Senator George Pearce put it: Australia could not borrow any more abroad until it proved it was living within its income. That was what the conservatives would do.[35]

Lang again pledged himself to put the standard of living of the workers above the claims of the London bond-holders. The supporters of Scullin and Theodore in the Labor Party in New South Wales revolted against the pledge. Labor in New South Wales was split and in disarray. Jimmy Scullin pleaded with his colleagues to show the people that Labor was just as honourable as the money-changers of Melbourne, or the members of the Melbourne Club. The Prime Minister and his loyal Treasurer, Ted Theodore, met the Premiers in a momentous conference in Melbourne on 25 May. They had before them the report of the special sub-committee of the Loan Council on what should be done. The sub-committee had followed the Niemeyer Plan for Australia. Jimmy Scullin was grave. The position of Australia was parlous. There was the growing question of unemployment: there was the question of government expenditure: there was the fact that the Banks have informed governments they could not carry them any longer. It was not a time for Labor to 'make and unmake social conditions'. It was a time for economy, a time for sacrifice. They talked for many days, while the wits and know-alls of Melbourne argued in pubs about Reg Hickey and 'Tich' Utting, and why it was that Tommy O'Halloran, the full forward for the Tigers, could take such towering marks but could not be relied on to kick straight, even when he was inside the ten-yard square.[36]

Jimmy Scullin was determined Labor would go 'straight'. The plight of the unemployed has become desperate. On 1 June Jack Beasley spoke at the opening of a soup kitchen in Glebe, Sydney. He said he was not prepared to draw the emoluments of Cabinet rank while people were starving and his leader, Mr Scullin, had done nothing about it. As a Christian it was his [Beasley's] duty to do everything to feed hungry people. The Reverend R. B. S. Hammond opened a hostel in Sydney for those who had 'lost out in the worst possible way'. Another hostel was opened for the homeless at Darling Harbour. The forgotten men would not be pampered: no intoxicating liquor was permitted on the premises: no political or religious subjects were to be discussed: the men would be given one pyjama suit which they must wear after a bath: their ordinary clothes would be fumigated. Cleanliness and moral decency were the rule of the house. There were camps for

[35] *S.M.H.*, 11 May 1931; *C'wealth P.D.*, 13 May 1931, vol. 129, p. 1800.
[36] *S.M.H.*, 26 May 1931; *Age*, 26 May 1931.

the unemployed on the fringes of the city, tent dwellers exposed to the wind and the rain, victims of those deluges which fell from time to time on rich and poor alike. But the unemployed insisted they could not live on the dole.[37]

At the end of days of torrents of rain, and with news of violent communist riots in Sydney hitting the headlines in the press, Jimmy Scullin announced the decisions of the Premiers' Conference. There was to be a reduction of 20 per cent below the standard of 30 June 1930 in individual wages, salaries, pensions and similar payments by all governments: a reduction of 20 per cent below the standard of 30 June 1930 in the minima of wages and salaries fixed by or pursuant to any statute: a reduction of 22½ per cent by legislative direction or pressure in all interest payments in respect of fixed-term money obligations: a conversion loan, the details of which had not been worked out, but which would certainly require legislative action: the Fiduciary Notes Bill was to be dropped.[38]

Some members of the Labor movement were stunned. Jimmy Scullin, the leader of a Labor Government, has sentenced all those in the community on miserable pittances, helpless widows, the blind and the maimed, to 'slow but certain death'. Thousands of unemployed would be deprived of their means of support. Angry words were spoken when Jimmy Scullin introduced the Premiers' Plan to members of Caucus in Canberra on 11 June. Some members wanted to exempt old age pensions, invalid and war pensions from the economy measures. Jimmy Scullin ruled there could be no amendment to the Plan. The following day, 12 June, the vote was taken: Caucus approved the Premiers' Plan by twenty-six votes to thirteen. John Curtin voted against the Plan. One lone voice called out as the vote was taken: 'The most pitiful sight I ever knew in the history of the Labour Party'.[39]

Two days later, on 14 June 1931, Ted Holloway resigned from the Government. Labor was losing the confidence and faith of the visionaries and the missionaries. Riots of the unemployed assumed a note of desperation. Four hundred rushed the side gate to Parliament House in Sydney on 11 June. On 17 June forty policemen fought a pitched battle with sixteen men defending a barricaded house at Bankstown. Anti-eviction riots erupted in all the cities. Ted Brady, the poet, one of the many men who had tried in vain to persuade Henry Lawson to stop drinking, told Bertha Lawson, Lawson's daughter, the 'Capitalist System' was in 'its death throes'. He found the voice of Jack Lang refreshing 'after the mewlings of the moderates'. 'Scullin', he told her on 7 July,

> makes me sick. He has all the virtues of the *petit bourgeois*. I can always

[37] *S.M.H.*, 2, 9 June 1931.
[38] Ibid., 3, 8, 10 June 1931.
[39] *Pan-Pacific Worker*, 8 June 1931; *Caucus Minutes*, pp. 431–2; *S.M.H.*, 13 June 1931.

> vision him in a nightgown and slippers winding up the clock and putting the cat out before saying his prayers. People who believe the story of Noah's Ark & the Creation as given in Genesis are almost certain to fall down on the job.[40]

Frank Anstey was disillusioned. Scullin, in his eyes, has betrayed Labor and formed an alliance with the Nationalists and the Country Party. The three of them were now 'linked in unholy matrimony'. Jimmy Scullin, a Labor Prime Minister, has inflicted crucifixion on the mass of men and women in Australia. Anstey could understand it, he told the House on 8 July, if that came from the enemies of Labor: but this stab was coming from their companions. 'What would Christ have thought as He hung on the cross if the nails that pierced His hands and feet had been hammered in by His friends; if the sponge of vinegar had been held to His lips by His friends'. Today a Labor Government was crucifying the very people who had raised its members from obscurity and placed them in power. He was appalled that a Labor man should even contemplate doing such a contemptible thing.[41]

The communists said the Labor endorsement of the Premiers' Plan had completely justified their analysis of the role of the Labor Party in the capitalist crisis. Labor, as they had predicted, had supported 'Niemeyerism', the attempt to stabilize and perpetuate capitalism by reducing wages, extending hours, and worsening living conditions. Labor leaders such as Jimmy Scullin, Jack Lang, Ted Theodore, Ned Hogan and Lionel Hill (Labor Premier of South Australia) were the 'demagogues of Social Fascism'. They were advocating a capitalist way out of the present crisis. Even the schemes over which Labor had divided—the Lang scheme and the Theodore fiduciary notes scheme—were dropped when their capitalist bosses cracked the whip. Now Lang was whipping up a sham parliamentary battle with the Legislative Council of New South Wales.[42]

Lang has said the battle was between the people and the privileged few. Lang has called himself the people's man, the friend of the people. Eviction riots were still going on. The communists were the champions of the people against the police. But Lang was, he claimed, the true friend of the people. In the Legislative Council on 29 June the conservatives turned down his taxation proposals. Lang asked the Governor to nominate enough new members to give the Lang Government a majority in the Council. The Governor, Sir Philip Game, demurred. Lang spoke in public on the rights of the people. The Governor must, he said, accept the advice of the government of the day: that was his 'bounden duty'.

[40] *Age*, 12 June 1931; *S.M.H.*, 15, 18 June 1931; E. J. Brady to Bertha Lawson, 7 July 1931, Henry Lawson Papers, Supplementary, M.L., Sydney.

[41] *C'wealth P.D.*, 8 July 1931, vol. 130, pp. 3559–65.

[42] *Pan-Pacific Worker*, 10 July 1931.

Jimmy Scullin appealed to all classes to make the conversion loan a success. With 360 thousand men out of work, Australia was facing the gravest financial crisis in its history. Lang appealed to the Federal Government for financial help. Lang appealed to the people. He told a crowd of at least fifty thousand in the Sydney Domain on 26 July they had to decide whether they would fight to be Australians, and to claim nationhood for Australia. They must decide who governed Australia: the people or Bavinism. He wanted to relieve unemployment, but Bavinism has said 'No'. The people must decide: either the elected representatives were to govern, or a nominee Governor could come here and rule Australians. A voice was heard to say: 'Send him home again'. But in clubland another voice was saying: the Governor must dismiss Jack Lang. Colonel Campbell was saying his men were ready to get rid of Lang.[43]

On 28 July 1931 the Governor of New South Wales unveiled the memorial statue of Henry Lawson by George Lambert in the Sydney Domain. The poet's widow, Mrs Bertha Lawson, was accompanied by her sister, Mrs Jack Lang. Bishop D'Arcy Irvine and Professor J. Le Gay Brereton sat on the platform together with the Vice-Chancellor of the University of Sydney, Sir Mungo MacCallum, the man who had wept when the Sydney University Senate dismissed Christopher Brennan. Jim Graham who had camped on the banks of the Murrumbidgee with Lawson in 1916 was there. All was not lost. Even an English Governor spoke warmly of 'mateyness'. Lawson's words and Lawson's spirit have not been forgotten. Henry Hauptmann, a pupil of Sydney High School, recited Henry Lawson's poem, 'Waratah and Wattle':

> Though poor and in trouble I wander alone,
> With a rebel cockade in my hat;
>
> . . . And I love the great land where the waratah grows,
> And the wattle bough blooms on the hill.[44]

There was no 'mateyness' in the politics of the day. A litigant has sued Ted Theodore and three others for damages. The case opened on 22 July 1931 in Brisbane before the Chief Justice of Queensland. Theodore was not only the advocate of 'funny money': he was, in the eyes of the conservatives, the practitioner of 'dishonest finance'. To the conservatives Ted Theodore was a shabby man whose personal life was like his public policy. He was not reliable; there was, they believed something not quite right about him. Theodore's reputation supported their contention that Labor could not be trusted

[43] *S.M.H.*, 20, 30 June, 1, 7, 27 July 1931.

[44] Ibid., 29 July 1931; Henry Lawson, 'Waratah and Wattle', Colin Roderick (ed.), *Henry Lawson, Collected Verse*, vol. 2, 1901–1909 (Sydney, 1969, reprint of 1981), p. 126; Amy Lambert, *Thirty Years of an Artist's Life* (Sydney, 1938), pp. 191–205.

to administer the affairs of the bourgeois state. Under Labor things fell apart. Under Labor, men, women and children could not ever be certain of their daily bread. On 3 August the Master Bakers' Association in Sydney refused to accept dole coupons in return for bread. Two days later the Lang Government announced that their Treasury was empty. There was consternation in the public service. Something must be done. The communists accused the bourgeoisie of planning to inaugurate a time of 'Capitalistic Terror' in Australia as a prelude to the abolition of democracy. They portrayed Lang as a leader of 'Social Fascist gangsters' splitting the working class to pave the way for the imposition of a bloody Fascist dictatorship in Australia.[45]

Strong words. But the storm clouds disappeared without even a clap of thunder. Australia was like that. The Commonwealth Government, through the Loan Council, made £500 000 available to New South Wales to enable the salaries of the public servants to be paid. On 24 August the jury in the Mungana case found in favour of Theodore and the three others accused of conspiracy. Jimmy Scullin sent Theodore a telegram of congratulation: he and the Labor Party have been vindicated. He had always believed in Ted Theodore. Now they must work together for the salvation of Australia. The August session of Parliament began. Labor must unite, must not be destroyed from within. On 27 August a special Federal Conference of the Labor Party was opened in Melbourne. Jimmy Scullin wanted to heal the divisions within the Party over the Premiers' Plan. The disillusioned wanted the supporters of the Premiers' Plan to be expelled from the Party. John Curtin seconded a motion re-stating the hostility of the Labor movement to the reduction of wages, pensions and social services, and their determination to resist any such proposals. But Conference stopped short of expelling supporters of the Premiers' Plan. Reduction was not part of Labor's policy. But unity has been preserved.[46]

Jimmy Scullin had his faith: the unity of Labor was the hope of the world. The bourgeoisie had faith in Joe Lyons: he was the 'strong and faithful soul' the bourgeoisie needed to march 'steadily and bravely to victory'. The communists bullied the workers into not hoping for anything from those social fascists in the Labor Party with all their words about parliamentary government: parliaments were impotent. The hungry sheep of Australia, it was said, were looking up to their political leaders but they were not being fed. Colonel Campbell told an audience at Bondi on 7 September what the New Guard would do. A member of the audience asked him whether the New Guard could not 'get rid of this pack of dingoes—these Communists—by putting them on a boat and sending them back to where they came from'.

[45] *S.M.H.*, 23 July, 4, 6 August 1931; *Pan-Pacific Worker*, 5 August 1931.
[46] *S.M.H.*, 10, 25, 28 August 1931; *Australian Worker*, 2 September 1931.

The Colonel said the trouble with Australia was that they had governments who seemed to look with absolute pleasure upon the actions of those communist scoundrels. Australians would get rid of those governments: Australia must not leave the affairs of the State 'in the hands of men of very doubtful morals'. He would clean up the Reds.[47]

Jimmy Scullin was like the Russian 'Eternal Husband': he did not notice what was happening before his eyes. Everyone was getting angry: everyone was becoming extreme, and some even 'bloody' and 'murderous'. The conservative women of Sydney met in the Town Hall on 9 September for an anti-communist demonstration. Mrs Marion Pickett called on those present to fight communism: 'a beastly, horrible, damnable worship of a thing that was evil', she said. The meeting closed with an enthusiastic singing of the National Anthem. Jimmy Scullin did not heed the warning that conditions in Australia were turning women into shriekers and gesticulators. Jimmy Scullin wanted money for the Government. He would raise it by a loan. The banks have promised to advance £3 million to enable the Government to complete public works and assist the wheat growers.[48]

Jimmy Scullin wanted more: he wanted the people who had supported him in 1929 to renew their faith in him. But that was something which had gone for ever. Men and women of vision have lost their faith in the Labor Government. Labor has promised much, but delivered little. The conservatives within the Labor Party have deserted him. The radicals have deserted him, and drifted into cynicism and bitterness. Only Theodore and a hard core of Labor faithfuls were still with him. Even they were divided between supporters and opponents of the Premiers' Plan. The Government had to rely upon the support of the Beasley (pro-Lang) group of five.

In Labor circles a most insidious idea was abroad. It no longer mattered whether an action damaged the Labor Government. It was no longer the great thing to save Labor. Jimmy Scullin no longer spoke the language of the missionary. He now spoke as the apologist for Niemeyer, the banks and the Premiers' Plan. The man who once stood before the King-Emperor like David before Goliath, and knocked him down with one stone from his sling, was now bowing to the traditional enemies of Labor. On 17 September he told the House he had again asked the banks for finance to expand industry and increase employment. But the banks have turned him down. Jimmy Scullin was no David before the Banks: he would consider, he said, what steps could be taken to 'relieve distress and avert disaster'.[49]

Impatient as ever, on 16 September Colonel Campbell told his followers in

[47] Ambrose Pratt to J. A. Lyons, 18 May 1931, Lyons Papers, Box 1, Folder 2; *Argus*, 2 September 1931; *S.M.H.*, 8 September 1931.

[48] *S.M.H.*, 5, 10 September 1931.

[49] *C'wealth P.D.*, 17 September 1931, vol. 132, pp. 53–6.

the Sydney Town Hall how he would get rid of Lang and Scullin. There were storms of applause when the Colonel presented his answer to the political problems of the day. On a given day every town, village and district should hold a public meeting, and pass a resolution that the present Government (i.e., the Lang Government) had lost the confidence of the people. The New Guard would protect such meetings. Delegates from such meetings would present a petition to the Governor, Sir Philip Game, requesting the dismissal of Lang. Sir Philip, Campbell believed, would do his duty. The people and the New Guard would save civilization, and provide the bulwark against the 'cherished designs of the organised Soviet supporters of this State'. He believed in the right of personal freedom, the sanctity of the home and the family, not the domination of the country by a 'self-appointed minority of scoundrels'.[50]

Lang was not cowed. He believed Labor had effected a revolution in New South Wales. He had said before and he said it again on 4 October that the system of currency was crushing the people. Labor in New South Wales has searched for a currency which would serve the people. He claimed they had found one, though he did not say what it was. Labor, he said, had found a people's currency, not a financiers' currency. Labor in New South Wales has inspired other countries to search for a currency which would serve the people and not the financiers only. Labor in New South Wales has brought about a revolution—not by violence, not by barricades in the streets, but by a revolution in the British way, that is, by Act of Parliament. Labor in New South Wales has attacked, he claimed, the citadel of the financiers' power. Lang, as the slogan put it, was always right. Lang was 'greater than Lenin'. Lang was more important than the survival of the Scullin Government. Megalomania has made compromise between Lang Labor and Federal Labor improbable.[51]

The militants in the Labor movement have lost interest in the survival of the Scullin Government. The communists have taught them that both Lang and Scullin were the lackeys of capitalism, that Lang was a demagogue, and poor Jimmy Scullin a God-botherer, a man who believed in such fairy stories as Noah and the Ark. The militants have ripped away the aura from Jimmy Scullin. Page, on 24 September, has suggested a coalition government. Scullin has said he would never back away from the great Labor movement and from Labor principles: 'I may be forced by circumstances to do certain things; but I shall never break away from the Party and the movement to which I belong'. He still had his faith. Labor, he said, would ride the economic storm.[52]

[50] *S.M.H.*, 17 September 1931.
[51] Ibid., 5 October 1931.
[52] Ibid., 25 September 1931; *C'wealth P.D.*, 24 September 1931, vol. 132, p. 1332.

Jimmy Scullin either could not or would not believe that Labor men would destroy a Labor Government. The signs were ominous. On 20 October the seamen refused to accept the decision of the Conciliation Commissioner, E. H. Conybeer, that the right of employers to select their crews be recognized. The moderates wanted the men to accept the terms. The communists and the militants persuaded the rank and file to ignore the pleas for agreement by union officials. Jimmy Scullin wanted the men to return to work. The New Guard offered to protect volunteer labour from the basher gangs on the wharves—to protect the people of Australia from the agents of Moscow in Australian ports. The New Guard offered to help every seaman to maintain his independence. The militants mocked at Jimmy Scullin, and called him a liar. Labor was tearing itself to pieces. Jimmy Scullin was a man of peace. When Eddie Ward asked him in the House of Representatives whether the Government was taking steps to smash the 'militaristic body which aims to set up an armed dictatorship', Jimmy Scullin said his Government would allow no organization which used force to operate. He was not a Pontius Pilate. He wanted all men to live in love and fellowship with each other.[53]

Jimmy Scullin believed in Parliament. The trouble was that the Commonwealth Parliament did not have the power to do what he wanted it to do. So he decided early in November to ask the people to give the Commonwealth Parliament complete powers. He had faith in the people: tell the people the truth, and they will want to follow that truth. But it was too late. Jack Beasley had other ideas. Rumours have already started in the corridors of Parliament House that Jack Beasley would move on 25 November that as a matter of urgent public business the House of Representatives should discuss the 'methods adopted by the Federal Government in the employment of men under the recent Commonwealth grant' to relieve unemployment. Jack Beasley was a moral man: he was outraged to find the grants had been used to employ pro-Federal Labor voters and not Lang Labor voters. But Jimmy Scullin could not believe that a Labor man would destroy a Labor Government over such an issue. Rumours have fomented an 'atmosphere of sensationalism'. Lyons has left nothing to chance: he has telegraphed all members of his Party to be in the House on 25 November.

Rumours flew round Canberra that Beasley and Lyons were having secret talks. Lang Labor and the United Australia Party would combine to bring down the Government. But Jimmy Scullin could not believe it: not Jack Beasley, the man who, like himself, believed that he would one day have to give an account of all he had ever said or done before the throne of Almighty God. Such a man could never put a knife in the back of a Labor Government.

[53] *Age*, 24 November 1931; *S.M.H.*, 24 November 1931.

On 25 November Jack Beasley moved the adjournment of the House to discuss a matter of definite public importance: 'The method adopted by the Government in the selection of men to be employed in connexion with the recent federal grant for the relief of unemployed'. He spoke with passion, with moral indignation. Persons, he said, had been thrown out of work to make the Commonwealth money available for electioneering purposes in certain Sydney electorates. He was against 'sharp practice' and 'preference to the political heelers of Commonwealth Ministers and Government supporters'. Latham, the rationalist, was also full of moral indignation. He was a man of principle: the only qualification for unemployment relief should be hunger, not political conviction. Jimmy Scullin did not believe that Beasley and the Opposition would push the matter to a vote. In a dramatic moment he challenged them: If you want to take business out of the hands of Government you can have an election. But it is a mighty poor issue—the hunger of the people. But that was what they wanted. The division was taken. The Ayes had thirty-seven votes and the Noes thirty-two. The Lang group—Beasley, Eldridge, James, Lazzarini and Ward, all Labor men—voted with the Opposition. Fenton, Gabb, Lyons and McGrath had previously joined the Opposition. Lang members joined with the Opposition in cheering when the result of the division was announced.[54]

Jimmy Scullin sought an audience with the Governor-General, and advised him to dissolve the House of Representatives and hold a half-Senate election as soon as practicable. The Governor-General, Sir Isaac Isaacs, agreed. Scullin blamed the defeat of the Government on the followers of Lang. Lyons was jubilant. Now the people had a chance to remove political uncertainty in Australia and prepare the way for political stability. The bully-boys of the bourgeois world had been hunting in packs for years. They had a chance now to hunt a quarry as sensitive as a new boy in a boarding school. They had a long experience in knowing what to say to the inhabitants of suburbia.

Life went on. Hugh McCrae was not interested in who was in and who was out. He has found another enthusiasm: he has decided to read Montaigne 'all the days of my life'; he also asked the gods to bless all good cooks, and all talented blenders of wine. Nettie Palmer was waiting for a word of love from her husband, Vance Palmer, that word which he either could not or would not give her to comfort and relieve her. Henry Handel Richardson was hoping the Nobel Prize for literature would come her way. Guido Baracchi has just read the manuscript of a novel by a Melbourne boy, Judah Waten, which used some language 'to make the hair curl on the first page'. Guido

[54] *C'wealth P.D.*, 25 November 1931, vol. 132, pp. 1888- 1906; *Age*, 26 November 1931; *S.M.H.*, 26 November 1931; *Australian Worker*, 2 December 1931.

Baracchi wanted Vance Palmer to stop pathetically trying to 'stimulate Australian literature with invalid stout'.[55]

On 1 December in his policy speech, broadcast over 3LO and other stations, Jimmy Scullin offered Australians 'invalid stout'. Australia has been sick. His Government has succeeded in restoring Australia to health. Australians had to decide whether they would support a coalition whose medicine had been so disastrous they had brought the country to the edge of ruin, or whether they would support the remedy which had already stopped the drift and averted a national calamity. Jimmy Scullin had nothing to say. The Messiah of October 1929 has become the man with the petty-bourgeois values of duty and obligation. He was talking like the Sandman on the evening wireless programme for children. He was talking of putting out the light, and sleeping tight. He had no vision of an independent Australia, of a different Australia. Lang was a demagogue, but at least he spoke to the hearts of the people: he gave the little men and women hope. So did Honest Joe Lyons. Honest Joe told the people in the Sydney Town Hall on the night of 2 December 1931 that the old ways were the best. 'Follow the example of Britain', he said to thunderous applause. 'Do not be tempted or seduced by financial tricks and devices'. Honest Joe, the one-time Labor man from Tasmania, now believed the only way for Australia was the way of the businessman. Private enterprise, production on the land, and measures to deal with the Communist Party were the only way. Honest Joe would keep Australians loyal to the faith of their fathers: he would bind Australians to their past. 'Follow the example of Britain'. Do as Britain did: vote for a truly national government. That was 'the grand example'.[56]

The Labor press howled about treachery and betrayal, about the knife in the back from one of its former members. But the life has gone out of Labor. The enthusiasm, the fervour, the missionary zeal of October 1929 have evaporated. The shell was still there, battered and reduced: but the light was no longer in the eye of Jimmy Scullin. He spoke like a man who had been betrayed, like a sacrificial victim. He spoke of his own ache, but the people had no interest in private aches. They wanted bread. Lyons was offering it to them, telling them they were like lost sheep who had gone astray: they must return to the fold of Britain, to the old ways, the ways their fathers had trod. It was the turn of conservatives to use the language of righteousness.

The *Australian Worker* warned Australians not to substitute for men of capacity and courage such as Scullin and Theodore a 'poor weak copy-dick

[55] *S.M.H.*, 26 November 1931; A. G. Stephens to John Shaw Neilson, 18 August 1931, H.H.R. to Vance Palmer, 28 January 1932, H.H.R. to Nettie Palmer, 10 November 1931, and Guido Baracchi to Nettie Palmer, 8 October 1931, Palmer Papers, Series 1, Box 5.

[56] *S.M.H.*, 2, 3 December 1931.

like Lyons and a dull pedantic wayback like Latham—mere puppet politicians, wire-pulled by the Banks and the Bosses'. Australia should stop all this grovelling to the British, and go forward to the creation of an enlightened democracy.

Labor might win all the arguments, but the glamour of October 1929 has vanished. Poor Jimmy Scullin was now greeted with cynical laughter when he spoke of Labor's plans for the unemployed. The people have a new hero: Joe Lyons, the man of honesty, the man of 'pulsating sincerity'. On the Depression he was like Abe Lincoln on slavery: he has touched the conscience of the nation.[57]

In the election on 19 December the Australian Labor Party received a crushing defeat. Twenty-two Federal members and three Lang Labor men were defeated. The anti-socialists had forty-six or forty-seven seats, and the combined Labor Parties (Federal and Lang Labor) only eighteen. Five Ministers—including Ted Theodore and Ben Chifley—lost their seats. Eddie Ward was defeated in East Sydney and John Curtin in Fremantle. Labor, said the *Australian Worker* on 23 December 1931, was the victim of the Jack Beasley stab in the back. Labor has been 'politically rent asunder' in the most populous State of the Commonwealth. The unscrupulous propaganda, the moral assassination, and the exploitation of 'timorous intellects' and 'nervous dispositions' by wild exaggeration about the Red Menace and the link of the Labor Party with the Communist Party have fooled the people. The *Workers' Weekly* said the two years of a Labor Government had taught the workers the impotence of the parliamentary weapon: the only weapon the Labor Party had, reformism, was now completely exposed. The masses must prepare for mass action against capitalism, under the revolutionary leadership of the communists.[58]

John Curtin did not lose heart. He went back to his work on the *Westralian Worker*. His task, he said, was to 'rally the fainthearts', and continue the fight for the Federal Labor Party against Lang and his intriguers. The workers needed a leader, someone to give them hope and guidance. He walked again on Cottesloe Beach. His destiny was ahead. No movement, he knew, could rally without a leader—a Christ, a Mahomet, a Washington, a Robespierre, a Lenin. His time would come. He must win a victory over the 'strange infirmity'. He must find something to say, something about Australia as an alternative to the conservative 'Follow Britain'. Jack Lang said the people

[57] *Australian Worker*, 9 December 1931; *S.M.H.*, 10 December 1931; *To-day*, 12 December 1931.

[58] *S.M.H.*, 21 December 1931; *Age*, 21 December 1931; Colin A. Hughes and B. D. Graham, *A Handbook of Australian Government and Politics, 1890–1964* (Canberra, 1968), pp. 346–7; *Australian Worker*, 23 December 1931; *Workers' Weekly*, 25 December 1931.

were giving the private banks a last chance to justify themselves. He was delighted his party had won, he claimed, at least ten seats.

Jimmy Scullin was stunned. The people had delivered Labor a 'staggering blow'. He regretted the loss of 'earnest and able colleagues'. Jimmy Scullin never recovered from that 'staggering blow'. From that day he was never able to speak a word to Jack Beasley. He had been told by his mother to love his enemies, and bless those who persecuted him. But from that day Jimmy Scullin turned his back when Jack Beasley entered a room. He still had his faith. He would never leave the Australian Labor Party. He still had a role to play: he could pass on the wisdom he had learned in those two years to those who came after him. He was to become a revered figure in the Labor Party. Members turned to him for advice: those in trouble were advised to talk it over with Mr Scullin.[59]

Ted Theodore decided to retire from politics. He was going to occupy himself in other fields. Unlike Jimmy Scullin, whose eye was always single, and whose whole body was always full of light, Ted Theodore always had other ambitions. For him there was a lure other than politics. He believed there was a place where the rocks were 'set with sapphires, full of spangles of gold'. He always believed that man could discover under the earth 'secrets that were hidden'. Somewhere over the horizon there was a gold mine and he would discover it. He would have his satisfaction. But it might be doubted whether he used the occasion to make the other journey for a man: the journey to find the answer to the question: 'Where does wisdom come from? Where is understanding to be found?' Mungana would haunt him until the day he died. But about Mungana and the other secrets of his heart he spoke to no man or woman.[60]

Joe Lyons was delighted. The people, in their wisdom, have accepted his advice to 'follow Britain'. The Sisters of Mercy at Deloraine, Tasmania, have told him that God's cause was his cause. He agreed. When Enid Lyons heard of the great victory she spoke to the press with tears streaming down her face. They were tears of joy. There were celebrations in Devonport and in Melbourne. There were dinner parties and dances. She saw something again of Bob Menzies. With a woman's gift to sense the shape of things to come she felt a chill in the heart. In the midst of all the gaiety and the laughter she had intimations of some future pain, some future disaster. She knew the truth of what had been said of old: in my beginning was my end. A time would come when she would weep tears of sorrow. A time would come, too, when Bob Menzies would weep, for he would pay a terrible price for marching behind

[59] Lloyd Ross, *John Curtin* (Melbourne, 1977), pp. 130–3; Warren Denning, *Caucus Crisis* (Parramatta, 1937), pp. 98–9; *Bulletin*, 23 December 1931.

[60] Lloyd Ross, op. cit.; *Book of Job*, XXVIII, vv 1–12.

the slogan, 'Follow Britain'. But at the time the mood of all of them was like the mood of the theme song from the musical comedy film, *Sunnyside Up*. It was their time to sing:

> Keep your sunny-side up, up
> Hide the side that gets blue, blue
>
> . . .
>
> Stand upon your legs
> Be like two fried eggs
> Keep your sunny-side up.[61]

[61] Dame Enid Lyons, op. cit., p. 190; Andrew Clark, Interview with Dame Enid Lyons, transcript in possession of the author; 'Sunny-side Up', 1929, *New York Times Film Reviews*, vol. 1., 1913–1931, 4 October 1929 (New York, 1970).

12

'TUNE IN WITH BRITAIN'

THERE WAS A TIME when Frank Anstey had made 'pulses surge by the sheer force and passion of his language'. Those days were now over. The behaviour of the Australian Labor Government disillusioned him. The Scullin Government capitulated to all the demands of the banking power. In a crisis the Scullin Government recanted from the faith its members had preached for a lifetime. In a crisis Jimmy Scullin and Ted Theodore preached the capitalists' and the professors' doctrine of lower wages with all the fervour of men who had just seen a great truth. A Labor Prime Minister preached the doctrine of 'cheaper living' and 'more work'. Labor was defeated because its own leaders looked for salvation in anti-Labor doctrines. In both England and Australia Labor governments were defeated by 'showing the white flag to the banking power'. Frank Anstey decided he was finished. The hopes he had set his heart upon have turned to ashes, and everything was sour in his mouth. Frank Anstey became very sad —not angry with God, because ever since his youth god had been high on his list of missing persons. Frank Anstey was angry with humanity. Deprived in childhood of the myth of the life of the world to come, and in his riper years of the myth of humanity's capacity for better things, Frank Anstey became a citizen of the Kingdom of Nothingness. He found no 'Young Tree Green' to replace the 'Old Dead Tree' of Joe Lyons, Bob Menzies, and all those who were chanting 'Tune in with Britain'.[1]

John Curtin was not disillusioned. Labor would find the way forward for the masses, would find the answer to the two questions of how to mobilize the masses, and how to defend Australia without the help of the British. Unless Labor found an answer to the defence question Australia would never break with the 'Old Dead Tree', but remain condemned to a dependence on British capitalism. Australians would live in Australia, but their culture would be British, European or American. Curtin was the man of destiny. He would overcome the strange infirmity which had stood between him and the fulfilment of his dreams. But first he must find something to say,

[1] *S.M.H.*, 9 July 1931; Frank Anstey, 'The Belly Walkers', typescript in Lloyd Ross Papers, Box 33; Frank Anstey, 'The Dead End', ibid., Frank Anstey, 'Red Ned', ibid., Frank Anstey, 'Bible Lessons', ibid.

some message of hope to inspire the masses after the terrible humiliation of December 1931. Curtin could never become a citizen of the Kingdom of Nothingness. Ted Theodore has decided that 'one or two little business interests' would keep him 'out of mischief'. But that could not be the answer for John Curtin. All his life he had been a missionary—for the Salvation Army, for socialism, for anti-conscription, for rationalism. Now he would make himself worthy of being a missionary for Labor in the days when doctrine was a hindrance, and pragmatism an electoral asset. He would find salvation without doctrines. The election has left Federal Labor 'moribund'. He would 'rally the faint hearts'. Being a missionary had always been his role.[2]

Honest Joe Lyons was enjoying one of his freedoms in the United Australia Party. He did not have to go any more, cap in hand, to any party caucus. He could choose his Ministers himself. Never again would he have to put up with the dictation by colleagues practised by the Labor Party. He had talks with Page about a coalition government. But Page wanted too much: he wanted to be Minister for Trade and Customs. Henry Gullett has warned Honest Joe to beware of the Country Party. They were, he said, 'the untouchables of Australian politics'. They were 'filthy foes & will stab you all the way from the corner'. The Country Party accused him of ingratitude. J. A. J. Hunter, the Country Party member for Maranoa, accused him of being 'drunk with success' and greedy for 'place and power and pay for his own supporters'. The pre-election unanimity was wearing thin. Lyons, they said, had handed the Country Party 'a pretty raw deal'.

The Government was sworn in on 6 January 1932. Lyons had Latham as his deputy, Bruce as honorary minister, but third in seniority because of his 'ripe and rich' political experience and his high qualifications, Pearce as his Minister for Defence, Gullett in Customs and Fenton as Postmaster General. It was like the Hughes Government after the election of 1917. It was a combination of three ex-Labor men and ten conservatives. All the States were represented in the Government. The conservatives were staking their claim to be the natural government of Australia.[3]

Except for the fear that those 'filthy foes', the Country Party, would stab them from the corner, things looked well for Lyons and the United Australia Party. The banks offered their co-operation. The business community was delighted. At its first meeting the new Government reappointed Mr Claude

[2] Lloyd Ross, *John Curtin* (Melbourne, 1977), pp. 130–2; Irwin Young, *Theodore, His Life and Times* (Sydney, 1971), pp. 55–6; John Curtin to E. G. Theodore, 30 September 1932, and E. G. Theodore to John Curtin, 14 October 1932, Theodore Papers, Box 1, Folder 2, N.L.A., Canberra.

[3] H. Gullett to J. A. Lyons, 24 September 1931, Lyons Papers, Box 1, Folder 2; *S.M.H.*, 1, 7, 12, 22 January 1932; *C'wealth Gazette*, 6 January 1932.

Reading to the Commonwealth Bank Board. Lyons was full of praise for Latham for his act of 'selfless patriotism' in stepping aside from the leadership. 'No man', Lyons said of Latham, 'could have desired a more loyal or able colleague'. Frederic Eggleston made some sour remarks about Lyons, saying that he had contributed nothing to the victory and was never more than a figurehead. Ex-Labor leaders, Eggleston said, always were an embarrassment to conservatives. Hughes had been a disaster. Beware, he warned the conservatives, lest Lyons introduce 'bits of socialistic policy'. The United Australia Party must encourage the old Liberalism, the Liberalism of Deakin and Bruce, to reassert itself. Beware, too, of the agrarians, with their parochialism and their incompetent leaders.[4]

Honest Joe has promised the electors he would get rid of Lang in New South Wales. Colonel Campbell offered to help him with his New Guard. The victory of Lyons has strengthened the Colonel's resolve. The members of the New Guard, he told his followers at a meeting of the Lane Cove division of the New Guard on 11 January 1932, have pledged themselves to 'rid the State of a nasty tyrant'. The New Guard would see that the bushfire of Langism was stamped out. All those who, like himself, believed in the 'basic pledges of personal integrity', 'individual security' and the 'sanctity of contract' would not tolerate the State of New South Wales being left in charge of a 'defaulting trustee'. The buffoon must not be left any longer at the head of affairs. Lang must go. The question was: how? The Colonel proposed a giant petition of the citizens of New South Wales to the King, humbly praying that his Majesty would be graciously pleased to cause the dissolution of the present Legislative Assembly of New South Wales, so that the electors might 'decide the question of dealing with disloyalists and Communists'. One thing was certain: the man who had dragged the honour of New South Wales in the mire would not open the Sydney Harbour Bridge.[5]

Honest Joe did not need any private army like the New Guard to get rid of Jack Lang. The capitalists encouraged a flight of capital from New South Wales. Banking deposits were transferred from Sydney to other capital cities. Lack of capital would starve Lang out. The police would break up all communist demonstrations. In British societies the law was there to curb all extremists. Campbell's way was not the British way. The law would curb the tongue of this angry Colonel. At that meeting on 11 January in the Lane Cove picture theatre the Colonel had called Lang a 'buffoon', a 'tyrant' and a 'scoundrel'. He said Lang was like a bull the farmer had got sick of: it was

[4] *S.M.H.*, 7 January 1932; F. W. Eggleston, 'Reflections on the Election', *To-day*, 9 January 1932.
[5] *S.M.H.*, 12 January 1932.

quite legitimate to take the family meat-axe to him and chop off his head. Campbell must be shown that the law did not permit a man to speak like that in British communities. Campbell must be charged before a magistrate. The law could handle Colonel Campbell.[6]

The law, with the help of capital, could handle Lang. Lang has said he was a man of principle: he would never change his attitude to repudiation. The answer was simple: the Commonwealth Parliament would make repudiation by a State a breach of the law. Respectable people in Sydney and Melbourne have promised they were ready to co-operate in upholding the Constitution and the law under which they lived. Lang always feared that the financial powers of the Commonwealth might be used to interfere in the political affairs of a sovereign State. Lyons would give substance to his fears.

The Lyons Government was confident. Australia was stirring again. The election has been followed by a greatly increased business turnover. Lyons would use the law to get rid of Lang. The people would understand. On 15 January 1932 he explained to the people that the Financial Agreements Enforcement Act would compel all Australian governments to meet their financial obligations. The conservatives took heart. With men of the honesty of Joe Lyons chairing meetings of the Loan Council Lang would soon be rendered impotent. Lang must either obey the law and betray his principles, or break the law and be dismissed. That was the law and the Constitution. A Governor of a State had the power to dismiss any Minister who broke the law. Capital, the law and the Constitution would soon get rid of Lang. Lang was the odd man out. In New South Wales the basic wage had not been reduced as much as in other States: in five of the States the weekly hours of work were forty-eight, in New South Wales forty-four. New South Wales must be made to conform. Joe Lyons made this plain at a meeting of the Loan Council in Melbourne on 28 January. The Premiers' Plan must be observed: the only alternatives to it were default or inflation. His Government would not permit either. He was saying to Lang what Bruce had said, more politely, to Lang in 1926: 'What do you say, Mr Lang?'[7]

The Langites laughed at poor Jimmy Scullin in Sydney. On 27 January 1932 he spoke with passion, and some of the fire of his old days, as Labor's 'hurricane orator' in the campaign for the East Sydney by-election, caused by the death of the successful U.A.P. candidate at the election of December 1931. He was greeted with wild, derisive laughter. But the mockers could not

[6] Ibid., 14, 16, 25 January 1932; *To-day*, 23 January 1932; Andrew Moore, 'Send Lawyers, Guns and Money!' A Study of Conservative Para-Military Organisations in New South Wales, 1930–1932, thesis in La Trobe University Library, pp. 16–18.

[7] Financial Agreements Enforcement Act, No. 3 of 1932, 12 March 1932, *C'wealth Acts*, vol. XXX, 1932; *S.M.H.*, 16, 25, 29 January 1932; Moore, op. cit., pp. 23–7.

silence Jimmy Scullin. He still had his faith. 'Those who desert the Labor Party', he said,

> are still deserters whether they go to the right or to the left. The Labour movement is not a one-man movement. (Uproar) The Labour policy is not a one-man policy (renewed uproar). The Labour movement is the growth of men and women in every State. The Labour party will come again. I hope you will weigh up the position carefully.

That night there were cheers and hoots for Jimmy Scullin. John Curtin would take over his vision: but first there must be the years in the wilderness, the years in which Labor must regain its soul, and come up with a vision of Australia.[8]

Lang would not bow before all the bluster and moralizing by Joe Lyons. At the Loan Council on 29 January he asked the members to approve his application for £500 000 to enable New South Wales to meet the overseas interest. The Loan Council, chaired by Lyons, refused. Lang replied that if he did not get the money he would default. Tom Bavin said: if a Government did not carry out its obligations the Governor had the right and the duty to see that there was in office a Government that would do so. Lang told his *claqueurs* that a Governor must act on the advice of his Ministers. That was the constitutional convention. Lang was the 'Big Fella': no one could bring him down. Overweening pride and arrogance blinded him to the trap which had been set for him: his very confidence was enticing him to spring the trap. Lang saw himself as the defender of the little people against the rapacious, inhumane bond-holders. In his mind the Commonwealth was forcing New South Wales to stop paying the motherhood endowment. 'Not even the most soulless bondholder', he told the Loan Council 'would snatch his interest out of the mouths of the undernourished children of the State'. The Big Fella was the moral man: the Big Fella had a warm capacious heart. The people, he believed, were on his side. The Commonwealth Government said 'No'. The question then was: would New South Wales default? The other question was: what would the Governor of New South Wales then do?[9]

That was on 31 January. Two days later, on 2 February, the Commonwealth Government announced it would seek a writ to force New South Wales to pay the £958 763 due to the overseas bond-holders. Lang replied he would negotiate direct with the overseas bond-holders to arrange a moratorium. The Commonwealth Government said if Lang did not meet his overseas commitments they would withhold from the Government of New South Wales that portion of the loan money allocation to which it would otherwise have been entitled. The Commonwealth would dictate the policy and behaviour of a State. Lang replied with a bitter attack on the Com-

[8] *S.M.H.*, 28 January 1932.
[9] Ibid., 30 January, 1 February 1932.

monwealth Government, accusing it of putting workers out of employment. So two sides confronted each other, each believing it was morally superior to the other. The upholders of the morality of financial honesty confronted those who proposed to feed and clothe the hungry. The economists, the lawyers and the measurers confronted the men and women who were all heart, the men and women who believed they were the enlargers of life, the ones with compassion. The upholders of financial decency confronted those who professed to care for 'the least of the little ones'.[10]

No one could be certain how the electors would judge the two sides. Colonel Campbell, like Mr Passion in Bunyan's *Pilgrim's Progress*, wanted everything 'Now'. The conservatives did not think they needed him: they wanted men with cool heads, not men of passion. The communists talked of a revolutionary situation but, again to their dismay, the workers showed no signs of developing the necessary 'revolutionary consciousness'. Eddie Ward scraped in with a majority of under five hundred in East Sydney, riding to victory on the back of the second preferences of the communist candidate. Lyons took the vote as proof that Labor would be easily defeated in an election in New South Wales. Lang must be forced to the polls, must be enticed into the trap he has set for him, and spring it. Then the Governor of New South Wales must do his duty on behalf of all those bourgeois virtues he and the U.A.P. were upholding against this wild man from Auburn.[11]

On 10 February Lyons announced that Bruce would be stationed in London as resident minister to carry out financial negotiations on behalf of the Commonwealth Government. It was assumed that Bruce would replace Major-General Sir Granville Ryrie when he retired as Australian High Commissioner in London. Once again both sides took a different view of the new arrangements. To Lyons and his new friends in 'Yarraside' Bruce was obeying the higher call of duty, sacrificing personal comfort and ambition to the service of his country. To Labor a pseudo-Englishman, an Australian dressed in English tweeds, has responded to the glamour of London. Bruce, they said, was going to the heart of the Empire because he liked the world of 'gold lace and epaulettes'. The conservatives have again entrusted Australian interests to the man with the 'great imperial outlook'. Bruce, the imperialist, would try to checkmate A. C. Willis, the New South Wales Agent-General, in the latter's attempts to achieve a moratorium in London. The conservatives were using the Shylocks of the Empire to defeat a people's hero.[12]

Lang promised to protect the people against their oppressors. He had a mission to the people, and he would neither betray them, nor let them down. At the meeting of the metropolitan conference of the State Labor Party on 15 February the hotheads passed resolutions calling on the Labor

[10] Ibid., 3, 4 February 1932.
[11] Ibid., 9 February 1932.
[12] *Labor Daily*, 11, 15, 16 February 1932.

Government to socialize industry in New South Wales. Lang would have none of this. The *Workers' Weekly* sneered at him as a reformist and a tool of the capitalist. But the Big Fella would have nothing to do with the extremists: he would never surrender to the great spiritual bullies of the twentieth century. He had always been a fighter, ever since he had fought for his pitch as a newspaper boy in the streets of Sydney. This time he said, to thunderous applause, that he would fight to the last ditch and win. He liked his daily clap: he was a human being. The issue was clear: 'It is your children', he said, 'or those overseas creditors of Australia'. It is a 'fight between the people and those who would oppress them'. He would fight for the right of the people to be fed.[13]

Colonel Campbell also took a stand. If governments, he said, would not move against Lang, disloyalists and extremists, then he and the members of the New Guard would give the 'Commos' a hiding. Rumours flew around Sydney that the Colonel had a plan to kidnap Lang and hold him in captivity until someone 'respectable' opened the new Harbour Bridge. The 'buffoon', he swore, would never cut the ribbon: the Colonel promised to save the people of New South Wales from that disgrace. The verbal war intensified. Name calling became a national sport. The *Labor Daily* called the New Guard the 'Boo Guard'. Labor supporters laughed. The Colonel promised they would soon be laughing on the other side of their faces. The *Workers' Weekly* ridiculed Campbell as 'chicken-hearted'. Members of the New Guard and communists brawled with each other at public meetings, like boxers in the preliminary fights in the Sydney Stadium, preludes to the 'big stoush' between the heavyweights. But this was Australia. Here there were only preliminary skirmishes: a show-down would never begin.

At Bankstown on 26 February 1932 a communist speaker ridiculed the New Guard as clowns 'racing about in Yankee cars, filling the air with poisonous fumes from Yankee petrol, and smoking Yankee cigars'. The communists, he said, would restore Australians to the days of innocence, the days before they ate of the fruit of the tree of capitalist greed and capitalist corruption. A New Guard man knocked the communist off the speaker's table. The members of the New Guard then sang 'God Save the King'. The communists tried to drown them with a lusty performance of 'The Red Flag'. The police arrived: the crowd dispersed. Such goings-on occurred not far from that place on the south arm of Botany Bay where the Aborigines had waved their darts at Lieutenant James Cook and made it plain, in Cook's words, that they [the Aborigines] 'want us to be gone'. But the white man was still living out the consequences of that 'inequality of condition' which distinguished his society from the society of Aborigines.[14]

[13] *S.M.H.*, 5, 16 February 1932; *Workers' Weekly*, 8 January 1932.
[14] *Labor Daily*, 16 February 1932; *S.M.H.*, 27 February 1932.

Lyons had no need of the Colonel and his team of muscular Christians. Lyons was like the apologists for a new religion: he was full of righteousness: he was convinced of his own moral superiority. Ever since he had entered the Commonwealth Parliament, and probably earlier, people have told him he was the instrument of a higher power. Now on 3 March he wrote to Lang and lectured him on his financial morals, or lack of them, telling him that if he, Lang, could not get things straight, then there was no further role for him, Lang, in bourgeois Australia. In just this way Dr Thomas Arnold of Rugby told Flashman that because he had lied to him, there was no further place for him in Rugby School. But Lang was not the Flashman of *Tom Brown's Schooldays*. He defied Lyons. He took up again the position he had taken all through the controversy: he represented the people of New South Wales, not English money-lenders. Colonel Campbell had another emotional tantrum. Lyons, he said, must stop acting like a cissy, or he would step in and cleanse the Augean stables of New South Wales.[15]

On 12 March Lyons rushed through both Houses of the Commonwealth Parliament the Financial Agreements (Commonwealth Liability) Act. This removed doubts about the liability of the Commonwealth for the debts of the States. An Act of Parliament would be the British way of getting rid of trouble-makers. Lyons believed his own slogan: 'Tune in with Britain'. The British way was the only way. The Colonel was offering a foreign solution, something essentially un-British. Lang was not cornered: he took evasive action. On 13 March his Government withdrew more than £1 million from two banks. The Colonel was just as cocky. If Lang tried to open the Bridge, he told his followers on 14 March, he would give Sydney 'a gladiator tournament that will be the best show you have ever seen'.[16]

The iron span linking the city of Sydney with the north shore has been finished. The skill and courage of Australian workers has fulfilled the dream conceived as long ago as 1815 by the convict architect Francis Greenway. Lang was to open the Bridge to traffic on 19 March. In the eyes of Labor the Bridge was the quintessence of Australian democracy: it knew no class distinctions, it knew no social barriers. The Bridge was a 'sacrificial offering' laid upon the altar of Australian 'manhood, womanhood and childhood'. The two physical halves of the great city of Sydney have been joined together. The two parts of the society could not be so beautifully joined into one. This was to be a people's occasion. This time the Governor-General was an Australian, and the Premier of New South Wales was an apologist for the men and women who made Australia.[17]

[15] *S.M.H.*, 4 March 1932.

[16] Financial Agreements (Commonwealth Liability) Act, 12 March 1932, No. 2 of 1932, *C'wealth Acts*, vol. XXX, 1932; *S.M.H.*, 14, 15 March 1932.

[17] *Australian Worker*, 16 March 1932; *Labor Daily*, 19 March 1932; *Australasian*, 19 March 1932.

Jack Lang made a speech in which he declared the Bridge open to traffic. He was no revolutionary. He spoke of the achievement by all concerned in bulding a bridge spanning the world's most beautiful harbour and linking two sections of the greatest city in the southern hemisphere. Jack Lang knew Australians would be tickled by a good old boast. Lang went on to say that the Bridge was symbolic of what Australians stood for but so far had not attained. The Bridge would unite people with similar aims and ideals. It was a happy example of the blending of English and Australian resources. The engineering brains and the finance had come from the centre of the Empire: the skill, the labour and the determination had come from the Australian people. The Bridge was therefore both an adornment to a beautiful Australian city, and a source of pride to the whole British Empire. Now Australians would build another bridge: the bridge of common understanding to serve all the people. The Australian people would build this bridge of common understanding to carry them to the glorious destination everyone knew was in store for them. He declared the Bridge open to traffic, and pressed a button which unveiled a tablet recording the fact.[18]

The crowd applauded, and clapped and whistled. The people's man then stood before the ribbon stretched across the width of the bridge. The scissors were placed in his hand. Suddenly there was a commotion. A rider on a horse, dressed in the uniform of an officer of the King, advanced towards the ribbon. The horse, borrowed for the occasion, stood still. The man's sword would not reach to the ribbon. Frantic, he spurred the horse on as the police closed in on him. He slashed, but the blade of his sword fell short. He slashed again, and stood up triumphant in his stirrup irons and cried out: 'On behalf of the decent and loyal citizens of New South Wales I now declare this bridge open'. Like Eilert Løvborg in Ibsen's *Hedda Gabler* the rider has not done the deed 'beautifully'. The police dragged the man from the horse and took him into captivity, as an Australian voice cried out, 'Take him away'. The man on the horse said: 'You can't take me. I'm a Commonwealth officer'. A policeman replied: 'So am I'. A fresh ribbon was stretched across the Bridge. Lang cut it. The people's man had opened the Bridge.[19]

The man on the horse told the police his name was Edward De Groot. He claimed he had been an officer in His Majesty's Hussars. As he was driven away in a police car sections of the crowd booed him. He became an object of hatred for Labor men and women, and a goldmine for the bar-room wits. The State President of the Returned Soldiers' League apologized for the insult offered to the elected representative of the people by one of their members. The *Labor Daily* detected something odious in the 'Boo Guard'

[18] *S.M.H.*, 21 March 1932; *Labor Daily*, 21 March 1932.
[19] *S.M.H.*, 21 March 1932; *Australasian*, 26 March 1932.

choosing a man with a Dutch name to perform this 'scurrilous business'. There was something sinister, they suspected, behind the act of madness on the Bridge. Was the affair part of a general attack planned by the 'Boo Guard', possibly with the connivance of 'Honest Joe', on the State of New South Wales and its Labor Government? The *Labor Daily* was pleased the police proposed to charge Francis Edward De Groot before the Lunacy Court on 21 March with being 'an insane person not under proper control'. The *Workers' Weekly* accused Colonel Campbell of resorting to the stunt of sending De Groot to cut the ribbon because he was unable to fulfil his boast that he would raise 100 thousand men to stop Lang opening the Bridge. Campbell and others, they continued, had wanted a prince of the Blood Royal to fawn on. The opening of the Bridge was not, they said, of any consequence to the working class. Right opposite this huge bridge was a Sydney slum created by capitalism.[20]

Colonel Eric Campbell told the *Sydney Morning Herald* De Groot had acted 'with the full approval of the executive council of the New Guard'. The *Australian Worker* wanted to know whether a 'shoddy collection of stage-strutting warriors' was trying to determine what should and what should not be done in New South Wales. De Groot, it appeared, was not insane. De Groot would be prosecuted for offensive behaviour. Australians could neither start a Paris Commune, nor toss up a leader for the reactionaries. De Groot and Colonel Campbell were harmless. Australians soon turned the whole episode into a joke. Tooheys, the brewers of beer, coined a new slogan: 'I'd sooner open a bottle of Toohey's Pilsener any day'. The creators of the Bridge were laughed at as the men who had built the 'largest coat-hanger in the world'. Margaret Preston, the artist, who had been looking for 'one form' which would 'suggest Australia in some way', dismissed the Bridge as 'Meccano Art'. The fierce judges of humanity took the occasion to rail against the pleasure-hungry in Australia. Australians have built a bridge, but they have not paid for it. Australians were living riotously on borrowed money. A day of reckoning would come. But the people laughed on and mocked at the local Jeremiahs.[21]

Believing he was one of God's chosen vessels, on 6 April Colonel Campbell telegraphed Lyons offering 'any number of thoroughly trustworthy reputable men highly organised in units under known commanders who would be ready on two hours' notice'. Lyons thanked him for his offer of help, but said again that he deprecated the use of organized forces to solve political questions. Latham agreed. People kept writing to him (Latham) for advice on how to deal with the spread of communist tentacles in the Australian bush.

[20] *S.M.H.*, 22 March 1932; *Labor Daily*, 21, 22 March 1932; *Workers' Weekly*, 25 March 1932; *Australian Worker*, 23 March 1932.

[21] *Australian Worker*, 23 March 1932; *To-day*, 2 April 1932; *Bulletin*, 16 March 1932; Elizabeth Butel, *Margaret Preston* (Ringwood, 1985), pp. 46, 52.

Latham had the same recipe as Lyons for extremists either of the Left or the Right. He thought a general improvement in the conditions of the people as a whole, towards which a wise general policy could assist, would 'provide the most effectual answer to any propaganda of a really revolutionary character'. That was the British way. An Australian government did not need a Colonel Campbell. The British way would combat successfully any 'insidious propaganda'.[22]

The conservatives acquired a new leader in New South Wales. That majestic experience of fishing for trout in the rivers down Kosciusko way persuaded Tom Bavin there was more to life than defending bourgeois society in the bear-pit in Macquarie Street, Sydney. He has decided to resign as leader of his Party. On 5 April his colleagues chose Bertram Stevens as party leader. Stevens was not a man to allow a nonconformist conscience to temper his political passions, nor was he a sensitive soul who needed to be revived by wading in the cleansing waters of the Goodradigbee or the Crackenback. Stevens was a tough Sydney public servant who had learned what Australians were like in the rough and tumble of the New South Wales Treasury. For him law and order took precedence over compassion and mercy. Lang learned to be tough on a newspaper boy's pitch: Stevens learned about his fellow men and women in a Government Counting House. Stevens knew more about finance than Lang. Two ruthless men now confronted each other. Lang's harshness was softened by compassion for the hungry and the homeless. Stevens believed no leader of men should ever feel a twinge of conscience about the victims in the never-ending war of survival.[23]

Australians were not just political animals: they were sports lovers. On 6 April the death of a horse captured the nation's attention. The mighty Phar Lap, twice winner of the Melbourne Cup, the performer of miracles on the race track comparable with Don Bradman's performances with the cricket bat and Nellie Melba's with the human voice, died that day in a stable in California. Phar Lap followed the Australian way for those who were driven to board the train which 'goes on to glory'. He went abroad, where he found not glory, but death. The veterinary surgeon reported that he died from a surfeit of fresh lucerne. But that was no hero's death. The popular imagination was soon busy at myth-making: Phar Lap suffered 'murder most foul' at the hands of envious Americans. Phar Lap was poisoned, just as another hero of the people, Ben Hall, was 'butchered by cowards in his sleep' out on the Lachlan plain, and Les Darcy, the boxer, was murdered by

[22] Telegram of E. Campbell to J. A. Lyons, 6 April 1932, and J. A. Lyons to E. Campbell, 7 April 1932, Lyons Papers, Box 1, Folder 4; H. Gregory to J. G. Latham, 10 October 1932, and J. G. Latham to H. Gregory, 13 October 1932, Latham Papers.

[23] *S.M.H.*, 6 April 1932.

envious Americans. Australians would remember for generations those two years when Phar Lap won the Cup. That was, for sportsmen, a way of identifying a year. His body was brought reverently back to Melbourne, stuffed by a taxidermist, and placed in a glass case in the Victorian Museum for future generations to observe and revere, just as the skull of Ned Kelly was on display in the Institute of Anatomy in the nation's capital.[24]

While Phar Lap's stable hand was lavishing tender loving care on a thoroughbred horse in California, fiery speeches were being made at the Easter Conference of the New South Wales Labor Party. S. A. Rosa asked delegates to request Lang to pass an Act compelling every local government body to provide work for the unemployed, and that the unemployed be allowed to purchase any commodity. Rosa was a 'heels up' man, who wept in his cups when professing his faith in the day when all men would be brothers. The times gave birth to madcap schemes and wild speeches. M. Lawrence, of the St George Council, called on delegates to smash the capitalist system. 'Jock' Garden, now in the 'calm-down' years of his political life, denounced the communists and the New Guard. Both, he said, were shouting 'Overthrow Jack Lang and the system'. Others declared that the Australian Labor Party would never make any headway in this country until it joined forces with the militant minority movement. But the majority in Labor has always consisted of men and women of common sense, believers in and supporters of 'Socialism without Doctrines'. Doctrine was an inhibitor of thinking, an electoral liability. Mr Maloney was a 'dinkum Aussie'. 'I am not going to have my head smashed for nothing', he said. 'Winter is coming on. There is not likely to be a revolution before winter, so let us find work for the unemployed'. So they went home to their boiled eggs, their toast, maybe a crumpet or so, their tea, or something stronger for the menfolk. Dr Johnson has said: claret was for boys, and brandy for heroes. The Australians were prepared to lay down their lives for King, Country and Empire. They were not prepared to sacrifice their lives for the sake of some future harmony. Part of the mythology of Labor was that blood should never stain the wattle.[25]

Returned soldiers were now talking nostalgically of the need for a diggers' political party. The soldiers missed the digger spirit, that comradeship which made divisions between classes and sects seem trivial and superficial. At unit reunions around the country digger leaders called for a revival of the comradeship they had experienced under fire. That was a spiritual experience no words could describe. Look, diggers, Colonel E. Martin said at the reunion of the 34th Battalion in Sydney on 27 March 1932, at the muddle in Australia today. Six and a half million people were being governed by about two

[24] Ibid., 7 April 1932.
[25] Ibid., 26 March 1932.

thousand men. That, diggers, was far too many. Australia needed the right man for the job. Australia needed a G.O.C. (General Officer Commanding) just as the Australian diggers had needed a G.O.C. A really good man with a staff of twelve men about him could run this country. They cheered, they whistled, they coo-eed, they cried, as the vision of all of them marching again to glory flashed before their eyes. The arrival of Major-General Sir Charles Rosenthal, off-sider to General Monash and advocate since 1920 of kicking all 'Commos' out of the country, brought them again to their feet. There were cries of 'Good old Rosy'. He reminded them of what soldiers could do. At Messines, he said, £3 million worth of artillery ammunition had been 'sent over' in a day and a half. That was the spirit of the troops: that was the spirit they needed in Australia. At the end of the meeting they repeated the sacred words; the words which always moved them to tears: 'Lest we forget. Lest we forget'. But after the tears and the brotherly embraces, they went back to their homes in the suburbs in time for a good night's rest to prepare them for 'the trivial round and the common task'. Australians did not want the glory the diggers had known. Nor were politics an occasion for the mystical brotherhood the diggers enjoyed with each other.[26]

The conservatives also had a sacred mission. Bourgeois society must be preserved. 'Lang must go'. At the first general convention of the United Australia Party in New South Wales on 31 March 1932 Joe Lyons solemnly promised that the Federal Government would fight Langism 'to the finish'. The United Australia Party, he said, was the coming together of all those opposed to extremism in politics. The United Australia Party was middle Australia. That was why his Government was in conflict in principle with Lang. That was why Lang must go: that was why Lang would go. Bourgeois Australia would overcome Lang just as it had overcome the challenge of 1916–17 and the turbulence of the Scullin years.[27]

Tension was mounting. When De Groot arrived at the Central Police Court in Sydney on 1 April to face charges for slashing the Harbour Bridge ribbon, scuffles broke out between members of the New Guard, the police and the communists. Police reinforcements pushed the Guardsmen away and restored order. There were bizarre scenes each night outside Lang's house in Auburn. The police were taking special precautions to prevent New Guard members kidnapping Jack Lang. Suspicious characters hid in shop doorways. Down-and-outs lay drunk in nearby gutters. Police patrolled the streets to keep an eye on the movements of any loiterers. Rumour had it that the puritan of Auburn was an addict to the bottle and the bed, and it was said in Melbourne that the Melbourne University Rifles would deal with Lang if he went too far. It was a strange time in the affairs of humanity in Australia.

[26] Ibid., 28 March 1932.
[27] Ibid., 1 April 1932.

More reliable rumour had it that the wild man of Australian politics was plotting the assassination of Lang. Australia had a long tradition of violence. There had been the violence against the land, violence against its original inhabitants, and against the convicts. Now class struggles were threatening to explode into violence. Lyons must act before the violence spread. The Governor of New South Wales must do his duty. Thousands of middle-class Australians were ready to follow a leader. But Campbell was a braggart, a strutter and a limelighter. Campbell talked too much—he was all talk. The setting required a mob orator, but Campbell was no mob orator, no Mark Antony. The times required a passionate speaker. Campbell was an 'iceberg orator'. Campbell was something of an Australian Hamlet, a man with the cue for revenge, but not the single-mindedness.[28]

Lyons and his advisers were not strutters and boasters. They were men of action. On 7 April proclamations in the *Commonwealth Gazette* directed that New South Wales Income Tax, exclusive of the unemployment relief, should be paid immediately to the Commonwealth. One of the proclamations requested the Government of New South Wales to pay the income tax direct to the head office of the Commonwealth Bank in Sydney. On that day Lang made no comment. For six years Lang has crusaded against interference by the Commonwealth in the affairs of a sovereign State. Now in a show-down the Big Fella was silent, dropping from a roar to a whisper. The Big Fella was cornered. He has had enough. Lyons knew Lang would not do anything desperate. He had been advised confidentially by someone who knew Lang well that he, Lang, was looking for a peaceful way out of the legal maze in which the wily men of Canberra entangled him. He would not appeal to the masses, would not go out on to the streets. There would be no civil war. Lang would go quietly. That was the British way. The streets of Sydney would not hear 'Red Revolution's feet'. Lang wanted the people to indulge in the cosiness to which they were enslaved without bloodshed. Bloodshed might be the prelude to what he hated and dreaded far more than the money-changers, the bond-holders, the Otto Niemeyers and the Robert Gibsons. He would rather surrender to a renegade Labor man and an English Governor than join forces with the militants and the communists to begin a revolution. Lang was ready to negotiate a settlement: Lang would go quietly.[29]

Publicly Lang kept up the bravado of defiance. On 8 April he responded to the Commonwealth's move to collect State income tax by ordering the police to block off access to the three floors of the building of the Taxation Department in Sydney. On 15 April he told his fellow Premiers and the

[28] Ibid., 2 April 1932; *To-day*, 2 April 1932; personal memories of rumour in Melbourne.

[29] *C'wealth Gazette*, 7 April 1932; *S.M.H.*, 8 April 1932; H. Campbell Jones to M. Threlfall, 12 May 1932, Lyons Papers, Box 1, Folder 4.

Prime Minister that their wage cuts and pension reductions could be enforced only by the policeman's baton. He would have none of that. The Premiers should say: 'We will not move one inch further along the road we have been going'. Officials at the Trades Hall in Sydney offered to form a Red Army, composed of ex-soldiers with working-class views, to play their part in the fight that was impending. But again Lang gave them no encouragement: that was not the Big Fella's way. The Labor Party in New South Wales was becoming more and more divided. There was a 'Militant Minority Group': there was a Moderate Majority. They showed no signs of sinking their differences to confront a common enemy. Colonel Campbell called on 'all courageous souls' in Australia to join him in 'cleansing the political life of the country'. The new leader of the Communist Party, Lance Sharkey, denounced Lang on May Day for engaging in a sham fight with Lyons. This was only a smoke-screen to hide the great betrayal of the workers. Lang was helping the capitalist system just as Scullin and Theodore had. Radicals were becoming more and more outspoken. At a teachers' conference in Sydney on 10 May some speakers proposed the abolition of Empire Day.[30]

The Federal Government's proclamation requiring accounting officials of certain State departments to transfer moneys received from the State's taxpayers to the Commonwealth Bank came into effect on 11 May. State taxation officials were waiting philosophically, it was said, for something to happen. Their wait was not a long one. Lang ordered the offices of the Taxation Department to be locked. Lang had a counter. Slavery, he said, had been abolished in the British Empire: therefore, civil servants should not work without pay. He issued an order that they be paid. On 12 May the Governor, Sir Philip Game, asked Lang for a copy of the circular. Lang promptly replied, enclosing a copy of the circular. On the same day the Governor asked the Premier by letter either to show proof that the instructions in the circular were within the law or, if they were not, to have them withdrawn. He insisted on a firm reply by 11 a.m. on Friday 13 May. On 13 May the Governor received a letter from the Premier refusing to withdraw the circular. The Governor then asked the Premier to call on him at Government House at 3 p.m. After the interview the Governor wrote to the Premier: 'If Ministers are not prepared to abide by the law, then . . . it is their bounden duty to tender their resignations'. The Premier replied: '. . . you are hereby informed that your request is refused'. Late that afternoon the Governor replied. 'I feel it is my bounden duty to inform you', he told Lang, 'that I cannot retain my present Ministers in office, and that I am seeking other advisers. I must ask you to regard this as final'.[31]

When Lang read the letter he let slip how he was feeling in his comments

[30] *S.M.H.*, 9, 16, 18 April, 2, 11 May 1932.

[31] Ibid., 12, 13, 14 May 1932; *Australian Worker*, 18 May 1932; supplement to the N.S.W. *Government Gazette*, 16 May 1932.

to the gentlemen of the press. 'Well, I am sacked. I am dismissed from office. I am no longer a Premier, but a free man'. That was the point: he was a free man. Publicly he criticized the Governor for sacking a constitutionally elected Government which still had eighteen months to run. But he made no move to appeal to the people not to allow an Englishman to decide who was to be Premier of the State of New South Wales. The Federal Labor members declared that Lang had received his just deserts for wrecking the Labor Government in Canberra. The *Labor Daily* was angry: 'A usurper', it wrote on 14 May, 'rules over our land and its citizens, and our freedom has been blotted out'. The *Australian Worker* said the whole responsibility lay with the Garden–Graves faction, the Lang men, in the Labor Party. The communists asked again why the Australian workers had never developed a revolutionary consciousness, why they meekly allowed an English gentleman to resolve their political differences.

The conservatives were delighted. A learned professor in England said the Governor was constitutionally justified. Conservatives in Australia have always had a tendency to enthuse over the reserve powers of the Crown. Businessmen said Lang had to go. As John Latham told them: every time Lang opened his mouth Australian stocks in London went down. If Lyons had allowed Lang to default, Australia would sell few apples and little fruit, wine, butter and meat in London. The chairman of the Associated Banks of Victoria said the dismissal would engender confidence and assist trade. The banks would do their part to assist recovery. In Vaucluse, Wahroonga, and 'Yarraside' celebrations went on into the night. In the eyes of their residents decency, honesty and respectability had triumphed over the shabby and disreputable. All those who observed the virtues of bourgeois Australia, those who worked, those who saved, those who built houses, those who played the game of life cleanly, those who loved cosiness, doing the right thing and never mixing with the wrong element felt they had been refreshed by a southerly buster after a hot, sticky summer's day in Sydney.[32]

For them there was better to come. On Saturday 14 May 1932, the day after the Lang dismissal, the Labor Party was decisively beaten in the election for the Legislative Assembly of Victoria. The United Australia Party won thirty-three seats, the Country Party thirteen, Official Labor fifteen and Labor supporters of the Premiers' Plan two, and one seat went to an Independent. Victoria also was safe for bourgeois society. Australia could now 'Tune in with Britain'. Men of the families who had pioneered Australia, such as J. V. Fairbairn and E. A. Austin, were now in the Legislative Assembly. Labor paid a price for degenerating into a party of factions and

[32] *Australian Worker*, 18 May 1932; *Labor Daily*, 14 May 1932; *Pan-Pacific Worker*, May 1932; *To-day*, 28 May 1932; J. T. Lang, *The Great Bust* (McNamara's Books edn, Katoomba, 1980); J. G. Latham to G. F. Pearce, 21 April 1932, Pearce Papers, N.L.A., Canberra; Bede Nairn, *The 'Big Fella'* (Melbourne, 1986), pp. 258–61.

bosses. The workers of Australia were thinkers, not 'mere faggots' to be manipulated by the political machine men. Bob Menzies was elected to the Legislative Assembly. He thought of challenging Stanley Argyle for the leadership of the United Australia Party in Victoria. Some said that if he did, he would be putting personal ambition before the interests of party. Some warned him to take care not to give offence to small men in the Assembly because they would take delight in thwarting him. The little men will one day inflict the great wound. But not then. Bob Menzies was getting closer to the fulfilment of the prophecy by his father's friend that Robert might be 'one of our future Prime Ministers'.[33]

The New Guard was jubilant. Colonel Campbell urged his members to dedicate their lives to the defence of all that was worth while. In his paper, *Liberty*, he promised to conduct a 'new inspiring fight against low-brow oppression'. He would unite all 'courageous souls who prize their just and proper rights, their own self-respect and Australia's good name'. He wanted the 'cleansing of political life in this great country . . . the regeneration of decent, national principles . . . the preservation of liberties regained'. He wanted the end of what he called the Soviet 'Anti-Christ depravity'. Australians should be washed clean, not in the 'blood of the Lamb', but in their own hearts and minds. There must be no more spreading of that 'anti-religious disease' in Australia. The New Guard believed in its mission to help Australians find their soul.

Anzac Day was not a day for the waving of flags: Anzac Day was a 'holy day', a day on which Australians bore witness to their loyalty. As the King's colours passed the Cenotaph in Melbourne on 25 April 1932 one man in the crowd did not take off his hat. It was taken off for him. Anzac Day was a day for reverence. On Empire Day, 24 May, the Union Jack was flown from public buildings: miniatures of the flag appeared in windows of shops and on the windscreens of cars. All the loyal societies, the Australian Women's National League, the Empire League, the Navy League, held special meetings. At a function organized by the Overseas League, Bob Menzies presented the case for loyalty to the Empire. The Empire, he said, stood for justice, the right of every man to a fair deal, self-government, and a sense of moral judgement when dealing with other parts of the world.

Membership of the Empire satisfied one of the great hungers of the Australian bourgeoisie. It made them feel morally superior to all other people. With other British people they could draft the commandments which all human beings should observe. The secret delight of being British was that it made you feel good, it made you feel superior. The Empire gave Australia progress 'in a constitutional manner' and material advantages: the Empire

[33] *Age*, 16 May 1932; *Argus*, 16 May 1932; *To-day*, 28 May 1932; Cameron Hazlehurst, *Menzies Observed* (Sydney, 1979) p. 19.

saved Australia from invasion. The only assistance Australia could count on in the event of invasion was from fellow members of the Empire, and especially from 'the centre and head'. Schoolchildren were taught to be proud of how much of the world was 'tinted red' on the map. In South Africa, they were told, there were ripening oranges and lemons, in India peasants were sowing the seeds of jute for corn-sacks. No doubts were expressed on Empire Day 1932 of the price Australians might one day pay for accepting such an idyll.[34]

Labor did not offer an alternative to this Arcadia. No one was speaking of 'The Young Tree Green'. Lang in New South Wales has become what his enemies said he was: a buffoon. On 26 May 1932 Lang opened his campaign for the elections in the Auburn Town Hall. Banners were on display: 'Lang' they read in huge capitals, 'is right'. When he entered the hall the crowd went wild with excitement. They sang 'For he's a jolly good fellow'. They did not sing about the people or about Australia. It was an adoration of one man. He said the Labor movement was a Christian movement. He would express that in a paraphrase from the Bible: 'The people giveth; the Government taketh; blessed be the name of the people'. The people had overcome nearly all their enemies—the newspapers, the courts, the governments of other States, the Legislative Council. The people were just about to enjoy the fruits of the victory when the hand of the assassin struck, swift and unerring. But on any vision of the future of New South Wales Lang said not a word. He was the thorough demagogue, the past master of phrase mongering, a man who employed his powerful personality to entice the masses towards a mirage.[35]

Lyons spoke like a man who believed that God, history and the people were on his side. Everywhere he went during the campaign he spoke as the morally superior person. 'Mr Lang', he told an audience in Goulburn on 27 May, 'could not borrow a bob because no one would lend it to him'. The people of New South Wales had to decide whether they wanted order in their finances, or proposed to continue a 'pawnshop policy'. They must decide whether they wanted rehabilitation, restoration and honest government, or to allow Lang to bring Australia to ruin. Stevens repeated everywhere the same arguments and put the same question: did the people want a regime of 'orderly, constitutional government, or another period of chaos and turmoil, leading to despair and desolation?' The people of New South Wales must have no more to do with politicians who ought to go back

[34] *Liberty*, 21 May 1932; *Age*, 26 April 1932; *Argus*, 25 May 1932; *School Paper*, Department of Education, Grades III & IV, Melbourne, May 1930; *S.M.H.*, 26 April, 24, 25, 26 May 1932.

[35] *S.M.H.*, 27 May 1932; *Australian Worker*, 25 May 1932; *Workers' Weekly*, 5 February 1932.

to the sewer where they belonged. The Labor press warned the workers that a victory for Stevens would mean they would 'dance to the wirepulling of Big Business and High Finance'. Stevens would mean lower wages. Stevens was Bavin with the gloves off; a man who had neither pity nor mercy for the victims of the depression.[36]

The verdict of the people was clear. On 11 June more than thirty followers of Lang lost their seats. The United Australia Party won forty-two, the United Country Party twenty-four, and Lang Labor twenty-four. Stevens and the U.A.P. had a chance to prove the capitalist system could bring prosperity. It was a verdict for those values Lyons and Stevens had espoused, a verdict for 'honesty and living within one's means'. The people have decided Lang was not quite right, that he did not get things straight. Lang has been weighed in the balance and found wanting. With the dignity which characterized him on great occasions Lang accepted the verdict without whining or blaming others for his misfortunes. The people, he said, had given their judgement, and he accepted their verdict. The Federal Labor supporters attributed the defeat to factionalism, the chief villain responsible being John Thomas Lang. He has paid a terrible price for indulging in the 'insane folly of faction fighting', which has killed the soul of Labor. Something better must be born: redemption must come from within. First, there must be solidarity. That was what Jimmy Scullin and John Curtin wanted so passionately. But Labor must stand for something more than just 'phrase-mongering'. The Victorian elections have given Bob Menzies his chance. The New South Wales election could be the chance for John Curtin. Stained though he was by his past, the shadow that would not go away, on one question he was a 'clean-skin': he has not supported the Premiers' Plan.[37]

Queensland was a ray of hope for Federal Labor. On the same day as Lang Labor was routed in New South Wales, the Australian Labor Party won the election for the Legislative Assembly of Queensland by a majority of two. As a bonus the two Lang Labor candidates secured only 559 votes between them. Labor owed its success in part to its leader William Forgan Smith. He had none of the arts of the demagogue, or the hungers of the megalomaniac. He did not thirst for his daily clap, or the praise of his admirers. His speeches were not interrupted by outbursts of hatred, or exalted by expressions of compassion. He laughed little and wept not at all. He held out no promise of better things for humanity and never promised with a tremble in the voice to make 'the rough places plain'. He was not a man for Schilleresque senti-

[36] *S.M.H.*, 28 May, 10 June 1932; *C'wealth P.D.*, 12 May 1932, vol. 134, p. 669; *Australian Worker*, 8 June 1932.

[37] *Australian Worker*, 15 June 1932; *Bulletin*, 15 June 1932; *To-day*, 25 June 1932; *S.M.H.*, 13 June 1932.

ments about all men being brothers, and a 'loving Father' presiding over the universe. He spoke of public works. Power has already finished off what nature had begun. He never forgave any critic, any doubter, or anyone who stood in his way. He was known as 'Foregone', the political bully. The bar-room wits made another play on his name, but they had to be careful lest he discover the word-coiner, because he was not only the uncriticizable: he was also an Irish Catholic puritan, a Jansenist, for whom the procreative parts of the body were 'taboo'. He was not able to describe his position in politics, because he did not know himself what he stood for. Forgan Smith was to prove by a record term in office that pragmatism was one way for Labor to win a majority.

Forgan Smith was born in Scotland on 15 April 1887, just two years after John Curtin. He migrated to Mackay in Queensland where he became President of a local branch of the Australian Workers' Union. In 1915 he became the Labor member for Mackay in the Legislative Assembly of Queensland. In 1916 and 1917, like John Curtin and Jimmy Scullin, he campaigned against conscription. Billy Hughes cracked one of his jokes at his expense, calling him that 'Mr Hogan [*sic*] Smith, an Irishman from Glasgow', who talked 'Gaelic treason'. On conscription he spoke with passion, but not so on the life of the toiling multitudes. In his union days and in the Legislative Assembly he used the language of the bookkeeper. He spoke like the Nationalists and the U.A.P., promising that a Labor Government would be as efficient as any bourgeois government, and, as a bonus, more humane. His obsession with the problems of the bookkeeper, with profit and loss, credit and debit, made him sound tedious, dour and stubborn to those who listened to him. His dullness was relieved at times by a 'pawky sense of humour'. He presented Labor as an alternative committee to administer the affairs of the bourgeois state. The people accepted him as the new 'depression period' Labor leader, the successor to the hurricane orators, the spell-binders, the missionaries and the gospellers who had preached a faith and held out a promise of secular salvation. There was about him none of the tragic grandeur of a Tom Ryan or a Ted Theodore. The age of the tragic heroes was over: after the giants the levelling flood has swept the country.[38]

Mass production of consumer goods was replacing the individual craftsman. Advertisers were becoming the hidden persuaders, deciding what people would eat, drink, do, how they would amuse themselves, and how they would safeguard their health. Men of Melbourne town were urged:

> Be smart, be dressy,
> Be clothed by Fred Hesse.

[38] *S.M.H.*, 13 June 1932; *To-day*, 9 July 1932.

Furniture seekers in Melbourne knew:

There's a Maples store,
Right near your door.

The advertisers still exploited the fears of the buyers. Sundry soaps and mouthwashes protected women from being 'always the bridesmaid and never the blushing bride'. The advertisers were prepared to tell what no one else would:

'Your best friend won't tell you, but we will'.

Men were advised how much more attractive they would be to women if their socks were kept neat by the right pair of suspenders. Peace of mind and strength of body were guaranteed to the drinkers of Bournville Cocoa and Bovril, the swallowers of Doan's Backache Pills, Dr Wood's Great Peppermint Cure, and De Witt's Kidney Pills. Ladies were advised that those things they did not dare to speak about to anyone could be written down, placed in an envelope, and sent to an address where they would be treated in the strictest confidence. Men who worried about their virility were also advised to write, phone or call to a certain address where they would be told something to their advantage.[39]

Popular songs were gradually replacing hymns as the means of expression for the hungers of humanity. Previous generations put their faith in Christ:

If I ask Him to receive me
Will He say me nay?
Not till earth, and not till heaven
Pass away.

This generation had different passions:

I couldn't aspire
To anything higher
Than fill a desire
To make you my own.

There was the song for those who had such a hungry yearning 'burning inside of me':

Night and day you are the one
Only you beneath the moon and under the sun
Whether near to me or far

[39] *Age*, 18, 21, 26 May, 7 June 1932.

It's no matter darling where you are
I think of you
Night and day.

There was the song for lovers who had to deal with the 'frigid Friedas' of the lovers' walks of Australia:

Please, tell me that you love me.

There was the song for the lover tormented by jealousy, of some past or present lover, real or imaginary;

People say that you've
Found somebody new
And it won't be long before you leave me
Say it isn't true
Say that everything is still O.K.
That's all I want to know
And what they're saying
Say it isn't true.

There was advice for husbands:

She may be weary
Women do get weary
Wearing the same shabby dress
And when she's weary
Try a little tenderness.

There were outlets for boasters:

Now I'll have you know it's understood
Whatever I do I sure do good
(So)
How'm I doin'? (Hey, Hey!)[40]

The farmers of Australia were told in June they would do just fine if they continued to 'Tune in with Britain'. Henry Gullett, the Federal Minister for Customs, and Stanley Bruce, the High Commissioner-elect in the United Kingdom, were about to go to Ottawa to put the case for Imperial preference in trade policies. On 21 June 1932, in an interview with the Australian papers, Gullett indicated the 'peculiar and vital importance' of the British market to Australian farmers. Great Britain bought from Australia produce for which there was very little demand elsewhere in the world. Britain pur-

[40] Nat Shapiro (ed.), *Popular Music: An Annotated Index of American Popular Songs*, vol. 4, 1930–1939 (New York, 1968), pp. 67–87; memories of an incurable romantic and crystal-set listener, Belgrave, 1932.

chased 89½ per cent of Australian butter, 76 per cent of Australian lamb and other meat, 76 per cent of Australian apples, 75 per cent of Australian dried fruits, 70½ per cent of Australian canned fruits, and 94½ per cent of Australian wines. Negotiations at Ottawa would give a 'healthy stimulus' to almost every branch of Australian farming, and 'a great accession of new wealth and increased prosperity' to all Australians. Bruce would have talks with British military chiefs about defence. Britain was Australia's market and Australia's shield. The Ottawa Conference would not be just a 'glorified commercial travellers' convention'. Bob Menzies and others reminded Australians that the Empire was also an association of peoples sharing a common morality. The essence of this morality, as Menzies saw it, was to consider not only one's own point of view, but 'that of the other fellow also'.[41]

On 17 May the Governor-General gave his assent to the Act creating the Australian Broacasting Commission. The Act created a Commission consisting of five commissioners, one of whom should be the Chairman, and one the Vice-Chairman. The Chairman was to hold office for a period not exceeding five years, the Vice-Chairman for not more than four years, and the other three for not more than three years. They were to receive salaries and allowances—the Chairman's not exceeding £500 a year, the Vice-Chairman's not exceeding £400 a year, and the other commissioners' not exceeding £300 a year. The Act authorized the Minister responsible for the Commission to direct the Commission to transmit any matter the transmission of which was deemed to be in the public interest. The Commission should not broadcast advertisements. The Commission might collect in such a manner as it thought fit news and information relating to current events. The Commission was to give encouragement to local talent and was to establish and utilize in such manner as it thought desirable groups of musicians for the rendition of orchestral, choral and band music of high quality. There was to be an Australian Broadcasting Commission fund made up of a portion of the fees paid for listeners' licences. The Minister could prohibit the broadcasting of any matter and would have the power to determine to what extent and in what manner political speeches might be broadcast.[42]

The Act was a model of the British genius for compromise. Just as the *Book of Common Prayer* contained within its majestic prose the compromise between the Catholic and the Protestant teaching on the Eucharist, so this Act produced in the legal language of the day a compromise between the rights of the State and the liberties of the individual. The Act encouraged local talent, the performance of music in Australia, the development of

[41] *S.M.H.*, 29 June 1932, *Age*, 29 June 1932.

[42] Australian Broadcasting Commission, 17 May 1932, No. 14 of 1932, *C'wealth Acts*, vol. XXX, 1932.

independent news services and commentaries. But what the Act gave it often took away. The broadcasting stations of the Australian Broadcasting Commission were not permitted to broadcast material which might give offence to any section of the population. All that some sections of the population held to be sacred, and therefore unmentionable, was not to be heard on Australian air.[43]

The broadcasting stations of the Australian Broadcasting Commission became media for the dissemination of the opinions and ideas of those Australians who were 'dyed in the wool British'. The first Chairman of the Commission, Charles Lloyd Jones, a businessman, was an Australian-Briton, a man with a nostalgia for England's green and pleasant land, rather than any passion for the 'wide, brown land' of his native country. At the opening of the broadcasting stations of the Australian Broadcasting Commission on 1 July, Lyons spoke of their task to minister to the 'culture, as well as the gaiety of the nation'. Eleven days later, on 12 July, the Chairman revealed what the Commission understood by culture. The Commission proposed to emulate the example and the experience of the British Broadcasting Corporation. They proposed to co-operate in every way possible for the benefit of the Commonwealth and the Empire. For an Australian, he said, London was 'the Mecca of all artists of outstanding ability'. The Australian Broadcasting Commission would steer a judicious course between the Act's instruction to encourage local talent, and the engagement of 'visiting artists of distinction'.[44]

The studios of the Australian Broadcasting Commission became a schoolroom and a theatre for the education and entertainment of Australian-Britons. Announcers imitated an English accent when presenting programmes and news services. For the evening programmes male announcers and artists wore dinner suits, white shirts and black bow-ties; women wore long evening dresses. Out on the 'sunlit plains extended' the spiritual heirs of Bold Jack Donohoe, and Flash Jack from Gundagai heard the bloodless voices of the over-civilized sing of the charms of Annie Laurie, whose brow, unlike theirs, was 'like the snow-drift'. The programmes of the Australian Broadcasting Commission catered for a society of creedless puritans, conforming to the lore of the society to which they belonged; men and women skilled in the use of 'snow language'. They never raised the questions middle-class Australians did not want to hear. Australians, as D. H. Lawrence discovered, were accustomed to leaving seven-tenths of themselves out when they spoke to each other. They were uneasy unless they were permitted to present a blank to most of the great questions.

The Australian Broadcasting Commission had the same high-minded

[43] Ibid.; K. S. Inglis, *This is the A.B.C.* (Melbourne, 1983).

[44] *Age*, 2, 13 July 1932; *S.M.H.*, 2, 13 July 1932; K. S. Inglis, op. cit.

aims as the British Broadcasting Corporation: they were conveying to their listeners 'whatsoever things that are sincere and beautiful', encouraging them to incline their ears to those things which would persuade them to follow 'the path of virtue and wisdom'. It was a British path of virtue and wisdom, not a vision of a society which might banish from under its 'bonny skies' the old world errors and lies. The Australian Broadcasting Commission assumed the task of giving life to the 'Old Dead Tree': it was a time when faith in 'The Young Tree Green' was in eclipse.[45]

The commercial broadcasting stations entertained no such high-minded aspiration. Dependent on advertising for revenue, they found that popular music, comedy and sport attracted audiences in the numbers their sponsors expected. 3AW listeners breakfasted with the 'Happy Man', shopped with Susie, heard advice to housewives, lunched to light music followed by an afternoon session for women: then came 'Chatterbox' Corner for the kiddies, dinner music, an evening programme of music, talk, racing, 'footy' talk, news, weather (what humanity would have to put up with in Melbourne, and those areas south of the Divide). The long day ended with Al Bowley singing 'Good-night, Sweetheart, all my prayers are for you, Good-night, Sweetheart, I'll be watching o'er you', followed by a reminder to put out the cat, yes, and the milk bottle too. A soft and soothing voice wished all listeners 'sweet dreams'. So, 'close your eyes' and 'sleep tight'. Other commercial stations ended their programmes with similar invitations to a land of make-believe, and a resounding playing of 'God Save the King'. The commercial stations prospered by feeding the greed and the thirst for reassurance in their listeners. Radical politics, an alternative morality to the moribund puritan morality, and even the limited aspirations of the secular humanists were all 'taboos'. They were classified as 'not really suitable'. Australians must not be disturbed.[46]

The Lyons Government put into a statute the guiding principles on what could and what could not be read or said in Australia. The Police Offences Acts of the States imposed penalties for blasphemy, obscenity, and anything likely to deprave or corrupt the morals of a listener or a reader. The War Precautions Act extended the area of forbidden topics to cover sedition. After the war those clauses were amended and extended in a series of Crimes Acts. The conservatives declared illegal the dissemination of ideas calculated to secure the overthrow of existing society by violence. On 30 May 1932 the Governor-General assented to an Act to amend the Crimes Act, 1914–1928. The Justices of the High Court were empowered to declare what was an 'unlawful association' within the meaning of the Act. Newspapers could be

[45] A.B.C. radio programmes, *Age*, 1, 13 July 1932; D. H. Lawrence, *Kangaroo* (Heinemann edn, reprint of 1950), pp. 39–41.
[46] *Age*, 1 July 1932.

deregistered for advocating the overthrow of the existing society by violence: the Postmaster-General could withdraw the licence of any broadcasting station for the same offence: all members of an unlawful association were to be disqualified from voting: all blasphemous, indecent or obscene books were declared again to be prohibited imports. Australia was to be sanitized against the devils within and the devils without. The law was the instrument of bourgeois conformism.[47]

Loyalty to the King and the Empire was the only way. The communists were circulating the insidious doctrine that Empire trade did not represent the way out for the working class. The communists were preaching that there was only one way out of the crisis for the workers, and that was the road shown to Australians by the Russian working class in 1917, who had solved the crisis of capitalism by revolutionary mass action. They must be silenced. That was not the Australian way; that was not the British way. The communists wanted to abolish censorship of literature, puritans though they often were themselves. The communists wanted to defeat Lyons in his moves to have the Communist Party declared illegal. All the institutions of the bourgeois state: the Parliament, the High Court, the Supreme Courts of the States, the army and the bureaucracy were being used to preserve bourgeois conformism in Australia.

At a ceremony to lay the foundation stone of the Anzac Memorial in Hyde Park, Sydney, on 19 July 1932, the Lord Mayor of Sydney, Alderman Walder, exhorted those present to preserve the traditions of British people in the ancient continent of Australia. The sons and daughters of the Anzacs must never degenerate into a 'pampered, lazy and dishonest people'. Being British was something special, something which distinguished them from all other human beings. The fifteen thousand people present sang with fervour the well-beloved petition to God, their 'help in ages past', their 'hope for years to come'. God, not man, would shelter them from the 'stormy blast'. God was their 'eternal home'. They sang Rudyard Kipling's 'Recessional'. They believed in the 'Lord God of Hosts'. He would be their shield and buckler so long as they behaved. They meant the words: 'Lest we forget'. Of the sunlit plains, the wide brown land, the haggard continent and its people they said and sang not a word. They were among the guardians of the heroic tradition of the British Empire.[48]

Half a million men were unable to obtain work. Their families were surviving as best they could on sustenance payments in money or kind. In Cairns on 17 July 1932 a pitched battle was fought by the police and some citizens of the town against the nomadic unemployed. In all the cities evic-

[47] An Act to amend the Crimes Act, 30 May 1932, No. 30 of 1932, *C'wealth Acts*, vol. XXX, 1932, *C'wealth P.D.*, 20 May 1932, vol. 134, pp. 1140–8; Brian Fitzpatrick (Council for Civil Liberties). *Six Acts Against Civil Liberties* (Melbourne, 1937).

[48] *Workers' Weekly*, 25 March 1932; *S.M.H.*, 20 July 1932; *Liberty*, 15 July 1932.

tion riots occurred almost every day, often accompanied in Sydney by clashes between the New Guard and the 'Labor Army'. Lyons and Latham hoped the return of prosperity would usher in another great bourgeois calm-down. The Labor leaders in New South Wales denounced Bertram Stevens as a latter-day Moses leading his followers to the Promised Land of Lower Wages. Bruce and Gullett were at Ottawa bargaining with the British and leaders of the other Dominions. Bruce was finding to his dismay that the British were quite cynical in their exploitation of Australian gush about the Empire. The British called him 'Bruce, old boy', or 'my dear chap', and all the other endearments used by superiors when addressing their inferiors. Bruce wanted the British to impose a duty on foreign meat to protect Australian cattle-men and sheep-men against competition from Argentinian beef and mutton. The British were very ingratiating. They put their arms around him and told him: 'You know, old boy, we cannot afford to offend the Argentinians: our people want cheap meat'. Bruce wanted the British to agree to Imperial preference. Gullett, too, found that in talk about British economic interests the mask of urbanity slipped off.

On defence the talks with the British were no more comforting. Conservatives have insisted for generations that Australians have agreed to unite in 'one indissoluble federal Commonwealth under the Crown' because that was the only way Australia could be secure from invasion. Economic interests and sentiment played a part, but defence was the main reason for the Imperial show in Australia—the Governor-General, the State Governors, Empire Day, the weekly professions of loyalty in the schools, and the professions of hope and faith each Anzac Day. At Ottawa British defence chiefs have not given the undertakings the Australians wanted to hear. Once again the whole world was rushing towards a crisis. The Japanese already had a foothold on the mainland of China and plans for expansion in the south Pacific. Mao Tse Tung was talking of the awakening of the workers and peasants of China in their millions, to fight as one man under 'the riot of red flags'. Moscow radio began its daily news bulletins with the words: 'The crisis of capitalism deepens every day'. Adolf Hitler, the leader of the Nazi Party in Germany, was making angry speeches about the shameful Treaty of Versailles, and his intention to start a war against Bolshevism to rescue Germany from the corrupting influences of international Jewry and international communism. Wild men were saying that in the course of the war against Bolshevism England and France would disappear from the map of the world.[49]

[49] *Australian Worker*, 13 July 1932; *S.M.H.*, 18 July 1932; S. M. Bruce to J. A. Lyons, 23 August 1932, Lyons Papers, Box 1, Folder 4; R. G. Menzies to J. A. Lyons, 21 December 1932, ibid.; Mao Tse Tung, *Against the First Encirclement Campaign*, Mao Tse Tung, *Poems* (Foreign Language Press, Peking, 1976), p. 10.

Bruce persuaded the British to make concessions. At the plenary session of the Conference in the House of Commons in Ottawa on 20 August 1932, the delegates accepted Imperial co-operation through preferential treatment of Empire products. Britain agreed to enforce restrictions on the import of Argentinian beef, mutton and lamb. Britain had granted new preferences on dairy products, fruit and wine, but not on sugar and tobacco. The King was delighted with the prospects for trade within the Empire. Stanley Baldwin was poetic. The British Empire, he said, had moved yet again 'out of darkness through fire into the light'. Bruce was not quite as lyrical. Just as the founder of the Christian religion knew what was in man, so Bruce has discovered in weeks of hard bargaining what was in the British. His comment was that of a man who had had quite a shock. The Ottawa Agreement, he said, was a 'fair, just and equal bargain'.[50]

Opinion in Australia was divided. Lyons and the conservatives were delighted. Lyons said a foundation had been laid to further good will and co-operation between Empire countries. On his return from Ottawa on 26 September Henry Gullett said the bonds of Empire had 'emerged incomparably stronger than before'. James Fenton, always a strong supporter of Australian industry, said he would resign. He did so on 5 October. Dr Page congratulated the Australian delegation. Jimmy Scullin did not know what to say: he was still in the dark. He was worried that Ottawa had condemned Australia to remain a servant of British imperial interests, that the agreements might blight the development of Australian industry. The *Australian Worker* said that in an excess of imperialistic fervour the 'calamitous' Mr Bruce 'sold our secondary industries to Britain for a mess of primary pottage'. Labor believed Australia must develop and encourage her manufacturing industries. Without secondary industry Australia could never rise to greatness and become famous in the arts and sciences and creative graces that constituted civilization. Australia, under Labor, must oppose the policy of imperialism. Australia must not be in economic subjugation to Great Britain. Australia must fight those 'greedy interests reaching out clutching fingers from the banks of the Thames to make the world their oyster'.[51]

While the conservatives were selling Australia to the British for a 'mess of primary pottage', and enthusing over the strengthening of the bonds of the Empire, Douglas Jardine, the probable captain of the next English test team in Australia, A. W. Carr, the captain of Nottinghamshire, Harold Larwood, and William (Bill) Voce, both fast bowlers, dined at the Piccadilly Hotel Grill Room in London early in August1932. They discussed how to dismiss Bradman cheaply in the forthcoming Test series in Australia. Carr was not fond of

[50] *S.M.H.*, 22 August 1932.

[51] Ibid., 23 August, 1, 2, 27 September, 6 October 1932; *Australian Worker*, 12 October 1932.

Australians. He said of the previous Australian Test side in England that he would not invite one member of it to his home. Douglas Jardine lacked what Bob Menzies called 'the juicy humanity of cricketers': unlike Bob Menzies, Douglas Jardine was not a man for a good, hearty chuckle. Jardine believed that under the stress of physical danger the Australians would crack, because they were 'yellow'. The problem was how to make the Australians afraid. That night Jardine and Carr explored 'the field of the possible', while Larwood and Voce, good professionals that they were, assumed the role of servants to gentlemen. So two English gentlemen began to hatch a scheme to humiliate the vulgar, over-confident Australians, while the politicians of Australia agreed to allow their country to be a 'vast field for imperialist exploitation'.[52]

The first confrontation between Harold Larwood and Don Bradman was to occur at the Melbourne Cricket Ground on 19 November 1932. Ten days before that, P. R. Stephensen, in an article in the *Bulletin*, exhorted Australians to stop apologizing for their land and for their literature. Australians, he said, must stop repeating the Englishman's view of Australia, stop paying reverence to the Old Country. Australian writers must drop the 'nostalgia of the exile' and remove the stigma of 'colonial' from the inhabitants of Australia. There was no need to apologize for being Australian. The historians and the legend-makers must cultivate a growth of national consciousness. Australian authors must not concede the Englishman's view that Australia was deficient in culture. Australians should show the English they knew what was what.[53]

Ever since he had walked on to the stage of public life in Maryborough as an anti-conscriptionist in the world war Stephensen had been a missionary for the cause of culture, spiced, as he put it, with a passion 'to beat the burghers'. He had aspired to live the life of a tragic hero: more often than not he found himself acting the role of the clown in a comic opera. Born in Biggenden, Queensland, in the year of the death of Queen Victoria, he consumed much of his energy fighting the relics of the Victorian age in Australia and England. He was the school prefect who handed out anti-conscription literature to the citizens of Maryborough. He was the student at the University of Queensland who, in company with Jack Lindsay, searched for salvation in the muck. He called on the professors to join him in the pleasures of the Dionysian frenzy. Fred Paterson and Herbert Burton urged him to stop, but he was 'one-and-twenty/No use to talk to me'. No burgher

[52] Michael Page, *Bradman* (Melbourne, 1983), p. 189; H. Larwood and K. Perkins, *The Larwood Story* (Penguin Books edn, Ringwood, 1984), ch. 8; D. R. Jardine, *In Quest of the Ashes* (London, 1983); Laurence Le Quesne, *The Bodyline Controversy* (London, 1983), pp. 8–16; Philip Derriman, *Bodyline* (Melbourne, 1984), pp. 39–40.

[53] P. R. Stephensen, 'Australian Books', *Bulletin*, 9 November 1932.

would ever stamp out the huge fire alive in him. He was never still: he rarely sat down: he rarely stopped talking.

As a Queensland Rhodes Scholar at Oxford he fell foul of those in high places because of his support for revolution in India. Later in London, in collaboration with Jack Lindsay, he published Nietzsche's *Anti-Christ*, and Jack Lindsay's translation of the *Lysistrata*. He also organized an exhibition of the paintings of D. H. Lawrence. He wanted humanity not to be afraid of the light, to liberate itself from the Christian libel on the body as the instrument of sin. He believed puritanism was the enemy of all the enlargers of life. He was a bundle of contradictions: he was an anti-Semite shouting Schilleresque sentiments about the brotherhood of man: he was both a Nietzschean and a believer in the bushman's version of equality. He believed one blast on the trumpet of Australian cultural chauvinism would cause the walls of British philistinism in Australia to tumble down. Taken all in all, he was a man. He reminded those who knew him of Hamlet's exclamation: 'What a piece of work is man'. While milking a cow with a frenzy which left the cow restless in the stall, he would speak with wonder of the stars in the sky, of Luther and the German Reformation, and then in a fit of the sillies add, as a cloud passed over his eye: 'Of course, *they* paid him!' A wild man has put himself forward as leader of a movement to express the Australian character and landscape in writing and painting.[54]

Just as 'Inky' Stephensen was exhorting Australians to develop a national consciousness, Dr Paddy Moran, to his great joy, heard Christopher Brennan 'uttering in clear and fervent tones' the responses to the priest's prayers in Lewisham Catholic Hospital on 5 October 1932. Father Eris Michael O'Brien, historian, a leader of a movement to have native-born Australians raised to episcopal office, was also moved to tears when he heard that booming voice ask the Holy Mother of God to pray for him in the hour of his death. That night Brennan died of cancer of the stomach. He was the finest flower of the school of thought which saw Australia as a province of European culture in the south-west Pacific. But he was more than that. Like Henry Lawson he was a mighty spirit brought to destruction both by the flaws in his own clay, and the secular priests in the temple of British philistinism in Australia. After the coffin was lowered into the grave in the Catholic section of the Northern Suburbs Cemetery, A. G. Stephens shouted in anger: 'Why the hell can't he [J. Le Gay Brereton, the Professor of English and funeral orator] say what a man he was, what a man. Just that. And how the Senate [of the University of Sydney] kicked his teeth in just to save Mungo MacCallum's senile respectability. To hell with this burble'. But the 'burble' of respec-

[54] Craig Munro, *Wild Man of Letters* (Melbourne, 1984), pp. 1–122; conversations with P. R. Stephensen, Bethanga, near Albury, May 1952.

tability would live on in Australia, and claim other victims among its gifted sons and daughters.[55]

On 19 November a crowd of 53 916 entered the Melbourne Cricket Ground to see another of Australia's gifted sons, Don Bradman, face Harold Larwood, the Notts bowler reputed to be as fast as 'greased lightning'. That winter Roy ('Mo') Rene, as the innocent boy from the Australian bush, and Sadie Gale as his equally innocent wife, had audiences at the Melbourne Tivoli in fits of laughter as they fought to preserve their virtue against the temptations of a decadent, drunken, morally dubious Englishman played by Gus Bluett. That was the world of fantasy, the world of make-believe. Now a boy from the bush was to face the Old World in a contest between one man with the bush virtues, and another employing the cunning, deviousness and tricks of an old and corrupt civilization.

Bradman came to the crease when the Australian score was 1 for 84. Like Betsey Bandicoot of old, he was the daredevil. Just as the Man from Snowy River was game enough to take his horse where all others feared to ride, so Bradman square cut the first ball he received from Larwood for four. The crowd bubbled over with delight. The second ball from Larwood flew high over Bradman's head. He ducked. The crowd simmered, like a crowd at a prize fight. The third ball was hooked by Bradman for four. The crowd went wild with excitement. The boy from the bush was making a monkey of these clever men from the British Isles. But when he reached 36 Larwood trapped him 'Leg Before Wicket'. The contest has been indecisive. That day Douglas Jardine was fishing for trout on the Kiewa River in Victoria. There had been no sign of how the Don would respond to bowling directed at his body. That day there was no need to test whether Australians were 'yellow'. They got themselves out to a man who bowled with great speed. Both the Don and Harold Larwood were at the height of their powers. In the second Australian innings Larwood bowled Bradman for thirteen. The English believed Larwood's demon speed had solved the Bradman problem: the Don, they said, disliked 'supercharged fast bowling'.[56]

The dole riots continued. The Lyons Government prosecuted communists. 'Inky' Stephensen appealed to Australian writers to let him publish their manuscripts. But for the moment all eyes and ears were on the cricket. On the eve of the first Test there was a sensation when the announcers on the evening news informed their listeners that Bradman was in such a seriously run-down condition he would not play in the first Test on the Sydney Cricket Ground beginning on Friday 2 December. There was consternation on the first day. Larwood and Voce rocked their deliveries in at high speed.

[55] Axel Clark, *Christopher Brennan* (Melbourne, 1980), pp. 294–6; personal talks with Archbishop E. M. O'Brien and Professor A. R. Chisholm.

[56] *Age*, 21, 23 November 1932; *S.M.H.*, 21, 23 November 1932.

The batsmen ducked, but often they were too slow. The short, rising balls struck the batsmen on the body. Jardine placed six fieldsmen close to the batsman on the leg side. The crowd on the hill let the Englishmen know what they thought of such tactics. When Jardine swatted the flies on his face one wit on the Sydney Hill called out: 'Leave our flies alone, Jardine'. Jardine took no notice. That was what he expected from Australians: when they were down they whinged and whined like ill-bred curs, or made jokes at the expense of their superiors. With 4 wickets down for 87 runs Australia was in a desperate situation. There was no boy from Bowral to rescue them.

That was the task of the boy from Grenfell, Stan McCabe, and the buccaneer from Adelaide, Victor Richardson. The latter made 49 before falling to Larwood in the leg trap. He was also limping from a blow on the leg from a ball by Larwood. But Richardson did not put on black looks, or scowl at the Notts genius. That night McCabe was 127 not out. The following day a packed ground rang to 'an ever-increasing crescendo' as their hero Stan McCabe despatched both fast and slow bowlers to all parts of the boundary. Leg theory had no terrors for him. Like another boy from Grenfell, Henry Lawson, he was savouring that majestic moment 'when the world was wide'. He drove, cut, hooked, glanced and pulled the ball with the authority and skill of a veteran. The crowd was in a state of 'delirious joy'. He was 187 not out when the innings closed. His performance passed into the folklore of Australian sport. For generations it would be a mark of distinction to have been there when Stan McCabe hooked Harold Larwood for four on the Sydney Cricket Ground. Despite a beautiful six by Stan McCabe off Bill Voce in the second innings Australia was defeated easily.[57]

The Australians did not like it. A letter writer to the *Sydney Morning Herald* accused the English bowlers of deliberately bowling at the batsman. If this went on, he said, then all the beautiful strokes of cricket would be eliminated, and the game would come to resemble baseball with players wearing padding and helmets. In a cable to London one journalist shortened the phrase 'on the line of the body' to 'bodyline'. The term stuck. Australians now had a word with which to communicate their reactions to the English tactics. Jardine put on an air of innocence. At Launceston he told reporters leg-theory (he was careful not to use the Australian term 'bodyline' which implied condemnation) had had its birth in Australian newspapers. 'We know nothing about it . . . The practice is nothing new, and there is nothing dangerous about it. I hope it goes on being successful'.[58]

Australians were still dreaming of the return of the halcyon days before the Depression. Billy Hughes came back from England on 22 December, and

[57] *To-day*, 1 December 1932; *Australian Worker*, 2 November, 7 December 1932; *S.M.H.*, 3, 5, 7 December 1932.

[58] *S.M.H.*, 7, 8, 16 December 1932; Philip Derriman, op. cit., pp. 62–4.

delivered the message the conservatives liked to believe was true. The only hope for Australia, he said, was that England should give a lead to the world. Well, here in Australia England was giving a lead on the cricket field and Australians did not like it. There were other things besides bodyline and imperial preference. Dr Mannix spoke that December like the prophets of old. He told Australians that millions of men and women in the world were starving while the world was full of wealth. So long as wealth was concentrated in the hands of the few the multitude were left without the wherewithal to pay for the goods that were being produced. More motor cars were being produced than the people could buy, and there was more of everything than the people could purchase. He hoped some means would be discovered to put an end to such an evil society. Socialism or communism was not the solution, being based on the false philosophy of atheistic materialism. Enemies as they were of God, the family and private property, they must never be allowed to obtain a foothold in Australia. But he hoped human beings under divine providence would find a better system than the capitalist system. If they did not, he prophesied the slow suicide of humanity.[59]

At year's end Australians were told a story of human heroism in the wilds of Australia. On 14 May 1932 a young German pilot, Hans Bertram, and his mechanic, Adolf Klausmann, took off in the seaplane *Atlantis* from Koepang in Timor to fly to Darwin. They were on a flight from Germany to the Far East to stake a claim for German aviation in the forthcoming competition for control of passenger and freight air traffic between Europe and the East. Losing their way on the flight between Koepang and Darwin, Bertram landed the plane on the desolate, rocky north-west coast of Australia near Wyndham. Forty days later, at the point of death by starvation, Aborigines found them, gave them food and water, cared for them, and informed the white officials searching for them of their whereabouts. Klausmann never recovered from the ordeal. Bertram became the darling of Australian hostesses. The Aborigines have succeeded where the white man with all his science and his inventions has failed. Bertram never forgot his debt to these nomads of the deserts of Australia. Yet soon after his return to Germany early in 1933 he fell under the spell of Adolf Hitler, the apologist for the Germans as a 'master race'. He believed in this man. He believed that only those with an iron will and an unbreakable faith could survive.[60]

The Aborigines were making a new move in their struggle for survival. Enraged by the reluctance of the white man to bring the Coniston murderers to justice, and by the inhumanity of the policy of separating Aboriginal

[59] *S.M.H.*, 23 December 1932; *Advocate* (Melbourne), 8 December 1932.

[60] Hans Bertram, *Flug in die Hölle* (Berlin, 1933), see especially p. 204; Hans Bertram, *Flight Into Hell* (South Yarra, 1985).

children from their families to educate and raise them in the ways of the white man, the Aborigines were beginning to combine. That year William Cooper formed the Australian Aborigines League. William Cooper was a half-caste Aborigine who had lived through all these experiences. Born on the tribal territory of the Joti-Jota at the junction of the Murray and the Goulburn rivers in about 1861, he was forcibly taken from his family to work on a white man's station in the district, and later removed to Melbourne to work as a coachman for Sir John O'Shanassy. Later he wandered around the shearing sheds of the men of broad acres. By the 1920s William Cooper decided the time had come for the Aborigines to take charge of their own lives. The Aborigines must liberate themselves from their white guardians, must no longer accept the role in which the white man has cast them—the permanent little children on the fringe of society and on the lower rungs of the white man's ladder. The Aborigines must decide for themselves their way of life. To help them William Cooper wanted an Australian Aborigines League to seek direct representation in Parliament, the franchise, and land rights for Aborigines. The seeds for a great change were being sown.[61]

At the same time a cricket ground provided the setting for the white man's growth in national awareness. On Friday 30 December 1932 a world record crowd for a cricket match of 63 993 poured into the Melbourne Cricket Ground to watch the start of the second Test match. Once again there had been doubt up to the last moment whether Bradman would play, because he had breached the player-writer rules drawn up by the Australian Board of Control. But that was not what caught the attention of the crowd when the game was about to start. A gasp was heard all around the ground as the names of the English bowlers were placed one by one on the score board—Larwood, Voce, Allen, Bowes—all fast bowlers but no slow bowlers such as Hedley Verity, or medium-pace swing bowlers like Maurice Tate. The English were up to their tricks again. Larwood and Voce opened the bowling to Bill Woodfull and Jack Fingleton. As soon as enough of the shine was off the ball, Jardine clapped his hands and six English fieldsmen took up their positions close to the batsman on the leg side. A hush fell over the ground. Larwood was as graceful and light in his movements as a ballet dancer, indeed so light that the umpire at the bowler's end had to turn round to see whether he had started his run. It was too early in the day for the contents of the Gladstone bag or visits to the bar to whip the spectators into a fury. Besides, there were odd ironies. Allen, the only non-bodyline bowler in the English battery, took the first wicket. The second, that of Leo O'Brien, a plodder but game as they came, was a run-out.

[61] D. E. Barwick, 'Coranderrk and Cumeroogunga', published in T. S. Epstein and D. Penny (eds), *Opportunity and Response* (London, 1972); M. T. Clark, *Pastor Doug* (Melbourne, 1965); *Argus*, 5 December 1934.

As Don Bradman came in to bat, the onlookers cheered, then fell silent while the Don took his guard and examined the position of the six fieldsmen crouching close to him on the leg side. Bowes bowled a short-pitched ball. Bradman attempted to hook it, but the ball glanced off his bat on to his stumps. The mighty Don has been bowled for a duck. In the silence which fell over the ground, Bowes put his hands on his hips, turned to the umpire at the bowler's end, and made to him a remark as earthy and memorable as the remark of his illustrious fellow-Yorkshireman, Captain Cook, on the Aboriginal women of New Holland. Another Yorkshireman became part of the folklore of Australia on that day.

It was a low-scoring game. The Australians made 228. England was dismissed on the Saturday for 169, due to a magnificent spell of bowling by 'Tiger' Bill O'Reilly, a leg spinner, one of the old school, and, of course, being Australian, not a pupil of the Jardine school of dirty tricks. On Monday, the New Year's holiday, yet another record crowd—68 188— was in the ground to see the next contest between Bradman and Larwood. They were not disappointed. The Don finished with 103 not out. The Don's was still 'the world's greatest wicket to get'. The boy from the Australian bush could bat under any conditions, on a wicket crinkled like corrugated iron, or against all the tricks the crafty English could devise, and still make runs. The challenge of 'bodyline', and the tactics of Australia's one-time Imperial master have been overcome. Australia won the second Test.[62]

On Christmas Day 1932 the parsons and the priests preached as usual on that event in Bethlehem when the shepherds watched their flocks and the angel of the Lord came down, and glory shone around. On that day, they said, God had assumed the shape of a man. It was an occasion for rejoicing. The parsons told their flocks of how Tiny Tim Cratchit in Charles Dickens's *A Christmas Carol* hoped people saw him in church on that day, because he was a cripple. 'It might be pleasant to them', he told his father, 'to remember upon Christmas Day, who made beggars walk and blind men see'. Australians still celebrated an English Christmas. On a day when the temperature in many parts of the continent rose to over 100 degrees, and with the perspiration running down their cheeks and dampening dresses, shirts and blouses, they sang of how the snow lay deep and crisp and even. They decorated their table settings with the holly and the ivy. They sat down to a hot roast Christmas dinner, topped off with a steaming Christmas pudding, laced generously in homes not controlled by a puritan with wine or brandy. On the wireless there were carols and much music from the British Isles. The Watchman assured his listeners they could go to bed in peace, thanks to the

[62] *Age*, 31 December 1932, 2, 3, 4 January 1933; *Australian Worker*, 4 January 1933; personal memories of the game.

'THE ONE WHO PUT AUSTRALIA FIRST'
Nettie Palmer
Photograph in National Library, Canberra

'WE HAVE BEGUN THE SPIRITUAL ADJUSTMENT TO OUR SURROUNDINGS'

Vance Palmer
Photograph in National Library, Canberra

THE CREATOR OF
RICHARD MAHONY
'Henry Handel Richardson'
(Ethel Florence Richardson)
Photograph in National Library, Canberra

THE CHILD OF
THE HURRICANE
Katharine Susannah Prichard
Photograph in National Library, Canberra

protection of a strong British navy and a strong British Empire. The British God was still in the Australian heaven: all seemed right with the world.[63]

Adelaide was the setting for the third Test. In Adelaide, England, for many, was Home, and a standards laboratory for what the comfortable classes understood by 'good form'. The rules of cricket were like the rules of life: they were drawn up by the English. There was the letter of the law: there was the spirit of the law, which was all very vague, but everyone seemed to know what they meant when they said of an action in the field or in life: 'That's not cricket'. The people of Adelaide were reluctant to believe English gentlemen such as Douglas Jardine, Bob Wyatt, 'Gubby' Allen or 'Plum' Warner would do anything which was not 'cricket'. That was unthinkable. On Friday 13 January 1933, and till lunchtime of the Saturday, they watched the Australians dismiss the Englishmen for a modest 341. The ball-by-ball description of the play at the Ground kept everyone in the city, elsewhere and all round Australia in touch with what was going on. In hotel bars men drank their ice-cold beer as they listened to the scores, and the feats performed by their heroes under a hot sun beating down out of a brassy sky.[64]

After lunch on Saturday the Australian batsmen again faced the music, when Woodfull and Fingleton walked together into the bright light of the Adelaide sun. Larwood began his run. Woodfull was struck over the heart by a rising ball. As he collapsed to the ground Jardine was heard to say, 'Well bowled, Harold'. He clapped his hands. Six fieldsmen crouched close to the batsmen on the leg side. Larwood was to bowl 'bodyline' to a wounded batsman. That was in the eyes of the Australian players 'a dreadful display of heartlessness'. As Larwood began his majestic run-up to the wicket the crowd counted 'one, two, three, four, five . . .', reaching ten in a deafening crescendo. Jardine's face remained expressionless, though perhaps the man within was pleased to see Australians behaving as he had predicted they would: they were squealing. Disasters followed for the Australian batsmen. Allen bowled Woodfull, having previously had Jack Fingleton caught behind for a duck. There was worse to come. Larwood had Bradman and McCabe caught in the leg trap for low scores. Only Bill Ponsford and Vic Richardson defied the onslaughts of ball on bat and body. Both were bruised.[65]

Hearing that Woodfull was in a 'distressed condition', the manager of the English team, 'Plum' Warner, breezed into the Australian dressing room, hoping for one of those heart-warming exchanges so dear to 'sporting

[63] Charles Dickens, *A Christmas Carol*, published in Charles Dickens, *Christmas Books* (O.U.P. edn, Oxford, 1954), p. 45.

[64] *Australian Worker*, 18 January 1933; *Advertiser* (Adelaide), 14, 16 January 1933.

[65] *Australian Worker*, 18 January 1933.

chaps'. 'Plum' was one of those cheerful souls, who greeted fellow cricketers with a double handshake, an elbow squeeze, and a straight look in the eye. Woodfull, who was known to his friends as a 'steadfast man', said

> I don't want to speak to you, Mr Warner. Of two teams out there, one is playing cricket, the other is making no effort to play the game of cricket. It is too great a game to spoil by the tactics you are adopting. I don't approve of them and never will. If they are persevered in it may be better if I do not play the game. The matter is in your hands. I have nothing further to say. Good afternoon.

'Plum' Warner went back to the English changing room, slumped into a chair, and said: 'He would not speak to me'.[66]

On Monday 16 January the Australian popular press rebuked the English for their use of 'basher tactics'. Various versions of what Bill Woodfull had said to 'Plum' Warner were published. They had one point in common. Woodfull had said there were two teams out there and one of them was not playing cricket. The Labor press has already exposed the English for their standover tactics at Ottawa, saying Australian industry has fallen a victim to the greed and the power lust of the British imperialists. According to the Labor press, Australian cricketers were becoming the victims of English ruthlessness and cunning. To fuel the rising anger on the Monday morning when the game was resumed, Bert Oldfield, the Australian wicket-keeper, a prince of good fellows, and a real white man if ever there was one, was struck on the forehead when he tried to hook a rising ball from Larwood. One more sacred convention of the game has been flouted by the Englishmen: it was not 'done' for a fast bowler to deliver a 'bouncer' (bumper) to a tail-ender. Oldfield was helped from the field. To his credit he blamed himself, saying he, not Larwood, was to blame for his injury. 'I made a mistake', he said. He retired hurt for 41: soon after Australia was all out for 222.[67]

The shufflers, or slow movers, in the Australian team called for a ban on bodyline. Those who believed in drawing yet closer the links between Australia and the Empire wanted cricket to be 'saved'. Arthur Mailey, one-time Australian leg-break bowler, and now a cartoonist in the daily press, was shocked. Bob Menzies wanted something to be done. The English popular press mocked at the Australians. The *News Chronicle* had some advice: Australia should find quickly some batsmen quick enough to handle the English onslaught. The *Daily Herald* was disgusted by the 'undignified snivelling' of

[66] Ibid.; *Advertiser*, 16 January 1933; there are many versions of what W. Woodfull said to P. J. Warner and many accounts of who told the press what W. Woodfull and P. J. Warner said to each other; 'Tiger' Bill O'Reilly, *60 Years of Cricket* (Fontana Books edn, Sydney, 1986), pp. 91–3.

[67] *Advertiser*, 16, 17 January 1933; *Australian Worker*, 18 January 1933; *S.M.H.*, 18 January 1933.

the Australians because the English bowling tactics had beaten their best batsmen. That, the English believed, was the point: the English had won, and the Australians did not like it. The Australians demanded an end to bodyline bowling. Believing the Australian sporting public was behind them, on 18 January 1933 the Australian Board of Control sent a cable of protest to the Marylebone Cricket Club. 'Body Bowling', they said, was menacing 'the best interests of the game and causing intensely bitter relations between players as well as injury'. Body bowling was 'unsportsmanlike'. They concluded: 'unless stopped at once, [it] is likely to upset friendly relations existing between England and Australia'.[68]

The cable exasperated Englishmen. The *Evening Standard* thought it was a 'drastic thing publicly to accuse one's opponents of unsportsmanlike conduct'. Other writers in England made fun of the Australians, advising them in their own interests to learn to play leg theory quickly or play cricket with tennis balls. That fine old English literary gentleman, J. C. Squire, a connoisseur of the late cut, asked:

> Where is that tough Australian grin?
> When comrades did you learn to faint?
> Can you not take without complaint
> A dose of your own medicine?
>
> Finish this futile brawl to-day
> We won't believe the paradox,
> A whining digger funking knocks,
> Come on one up and two to play.

The British were only giving Australian batsmen what those demon Australian bowlers, Ernie McDonald and Jack Gregory, had given the English batsmen in 1921. This was a tit for tat. Come on: play up, play up, and play the game.[69]

The members of the Australian team were divided. Woodfull wanted a protest. Don Bradman and Jack Fingleton were opposed. Victor Richardson, who had learned to take harder knocks without squealing as an Australian Rules footballer, thought the cable was 'undignified and humiliating'. Imminent defeat was humiliating enough. Why expose the players to the charge that they 'couldn't take it'? Arthur Gilligan, a former captain of an English Test side, another prince of good fellows, and believer in the world of 'chaps', suggested a committee of international players should meet. Those who understood cricket understood each other. The great game must not be degraded by the ballyhoo of exchanges between administrators. 'Chaps'

[68] *S.M.H.*, 19 January 1933.
[69] Ibid., 23, 25 January 1933.

would soon fix things up. But it was not the time for an Erasmus in the world of cricket. The Marylebone Cricket Club did not apologize, nor make concessions. They replied on 24 January 1933 that if the Australians wanted to cancel the tour they would consent but with great reluctance. P. G. H. Fender said the Australian protest was not surprising: what else could an English gentleman expect from a team in which only one or two could be accepted as Public School types? A. W. Carr agreed. The members of the Australian team could not be invited to the home of any gentleman.[70]

Cricket was casting a shadow over the relations between Australia and England. The times were too serious to allow a sporting contest to jeopardize Australia's relations with the Empire. The Labor press has been critical of British imperialism in Australia, declaring the interests of Australian industry to be irreconcilable with the interests of British industry. The Labor press was most vocal of all in the denunciation of the English tactics as 'unsportsmanlike'. The Labor press has spoken up for Australia against the 'sneers and jibes' of the English press against Australia's champion, Don Bradman. Labor was again assuming the role of champion of Australian nationalism. Labor was moving towards an alternative to the King and Empire men and women. Labor was on the march again in Australia. At a meeting in the Sydney Town Hall on 30 January 1932 to protest against the suspension by the New South Wales Director of Education of a teacher because she had given a public address on conditions in Russia, a huge crowd sang 'The Internationale'. Labor was regaining its soul. Conservatives were putting blinkers on the eyes of the Australian people, not wanting them even to see the conditions of life in a Socialist country.

On 30 January President Hindenburg invited Adolf Hitler, the leader of the German National Socialist Workers' Party, to form a Cabinet. Hindenburg has accepted the inevitable: the alternative was civil war. The Socialists and the Communists in Germany announced they would offer decisive resistance to any attempt to create a dictatorship hostile to the workers. Australian reaction was cautious. The conservatives hoped Germany was about to achieve political stability. The Labor press was not alarmed. There would be a rude awakening.[71]

The cricketers must be reconciled. Cricket must be like a Charles Dickens Christmas, full of the spirit of forgiving and forgetting. 'Plum' Warner offered the hand of forgiveness to Bill Woodfull, and all was well between them. Bill Woodfull was received back into the world of 'chaps'. The Australian Board of Control offered the olive branch to the Marylebone Cricket Club, saying, of course it did not want to cancel the series. The Marylebone

[70] Laurence Le Quesne, op. cit., pp. 42–3; *S.M.H.*, 19, 23, 25 January 1933; *Australian Worker*, 25 January 1933; *To-day*, 1 February 1933.

[71] *Australian Worker*, 8 February 1933; *S.M.H.*, 31 January 1933.

Cricket Club was delighted. More cables were exchanged. Both sides agreed the tour should go on. Messages were exchanged between the British and Australian Governments. There was to be no Boston Tea Party. For Australians any extremism was like Heaven or Hell: Australians did not believe in either place. The English continued to bowl bodyline. The crowd in Brisbane was restrained. In Sydney during the fifth and final Test, between 23 and 28 February 1933, which the English won, the crowd rose to its feet to cheer Harold Larwood as he walked off the ground after making 98. Australians had the generosity and the magnaminity to recognize genius and grace on the sporting field.[72]

Under conservative leadership Australians have been committed to 'Tune in with Britain'. The Australian Broadcasting Commission has established Empire broadcasting from England by the British Broadcasting Corporation. These programmes have been received with enthusiasm. The Australian Broadcasting Commission programmes were the right alternative to 'treasonable and imported agitation'. On 26 March Sir Charles Kingsford Smith flew across the Tasman from Thirty Mile Beach in New Zealand to Mascot Aerodrome in Sydney. 'Smithy' was again a hero. Women fought with each other to touch his garments. The way to get anywhere, he told them, was to fly. Australians were playing a role in bringing the parts of the Empire closer together. This was a British achievement.[73]

For Australians, England was still the 'Land of Hope and Glory', still the 'mother of the free'. In the School Papers published by the Education Departments of the States the children, as they learned to read, were indoctrinated in the double loyalty. They were enjoined to devote their energies to strengthening the bonds of the Empire. They were told to count being British as a great blessing. They were given curly questions to discuss with their teachers, such as: who was sorry when the Prodigal Son returned? What kind of fruit did Noah take into the Ark? should a woman get a man's wages? should you go to church with a cough? They were also encouraged to notice and enjoy the beauty of Australia, to savour the stately redgums near the banks of the Murray River, down-river from Albury, and enjoy the flight of the bronzewing pigeon. They were told to buy Australian goods: they were told Australian goods were as good as any they would find elsewhere in the world. So: 'Every day in every way—Australian raisins'. Support all those industries, all those farms, 'carried on by Australians for Australians.[74]

In April 1933 an advertisement in the Sydney press and later in Mel-

[72] Laurence Le Quesne, op. cit., pp. 69–74; *To-day*, 1 February 1933; *Australian Worker*, 8 February 1933; *S.M.H.*, 20, 21, 23 February 1933.

[73] *S.M.H.*, 27 March 1933.

[74] *School Paper*, Education Department of Victoria, Grades VII & VIII, 1 May 1933, pp. 53, 63, 1 June 1933, p. 67, 1 July 1933, passim, and 1 September 1933, p. 124.

bourne papers informed readers that the British had the answer to the uncertainties of the day. 'In a world distressed', the advertisement ran, '—amid the whirling chaos of three decades—while ideals crumble and manners decay', an English mother would make for picture patrons 'a strange heaven out of an unbelievable hell'. Noel Coward's masterpiece, *Cavalcade*, had the answer Australians were looking for. The English had the answers. The world was in a mess:

> In this strange illusion,
> Chaos and confusion.
> People seem to lose their way
> What is there to strive for,
> Love or keep alive for?

The film had an answer to such despair. Above this 'twentieth century din' the British Empire stood for decency, the domestic virtues and for courage, loyalty and sacrifice. British ideals and the British way of life were the answer to the 'twentieth century blues' At the end of the film the survivors drank a toast, 'To England. Let us drink to the hope that this country, which we love so much, will retain dignity and greatness and will find peace again'. England had the answer to 'moral drift and decay', and the 'decadence and unrest of the twentieth century'. The toast to Old England rang forth triumphant over the Babel of the modern world, all the frantic pursuit of strange gods, and the worship of idols by corrupt hearts.

The film reviewer for the *Sydney Morning Herald* was carried away. The film reminded him, he wrote, of the Pilgrim's Chorus from *Tannhäuser* rising triumphant over the sensual sty of the Venusberg. Winston Churchill said that England was the best country for a duke or a dustman to live in. In England a man could assert the rights of an individual, and criticize the government without being disloyal to the King. England would keep the glories of her past, and Australia would follow in her train. Australian conservatives agreed. Labor feared England had her soul in the past. If they followed down that path, Australians would be chained to the fading glories of an imperial past.[75]

Time was running out. On 9 April 1933 the Chancellor of Germany issued a number of decrees which history was to know as the April Laws. Administrators with dictatorial powers were appointed in all the German states. Books deemed seditious or depraved were burned. Trade unions were abolished and replaced by State-controlled unions. Jews were no longer eligible for positions in the civil service, the army, the schools or the universities. Jews were segregated into a debased order in society. Hitler has reverted to what the *Sydney Morning Herald* called 'the militant and intolerant bigotry of

[75] *S.M.H.*, 15, 17 April 1933; *Bulletin*, 19 April 1933; *Table Talk*, 1 June 1933; *Australasian*, 3 June 1933; *The Times*, 25 April 1933.

bygone times'. Communists, Socialists and Jews were incarcerated in concentration camps. Strident voices were heard. Germans were singing with exuberance and fervour of a day of reckoning against the 'Red Front' and 'reaction', a day when comrades would march together with ranks closed, and smash Bolshevism, liberalism, socialism, and the shameful Treaty of Versailles. *Kameraden* (comrades, or in the Australian language, 'mates') looked at each other with laughter in their eyes as they marched together in this 'revolution of nothingness'. Australians were alarmed. All shades of political opinion denounced the attack on the Jews. Bertram Stevens said that to deny Jews the right to full citizenship and the right to observe the laws of the country was tantamount to saying they had no right to live. That idea was repugnant to the Australian sense of fair play. Germany was menacing the peace of the world.[76]

The conservatives were in a dilemma. A barbarian was threatening the very foundations of society, but the barbarian might have his uses. He was offering to wipe Bolshevism off the map of the world: he was already destroying trade union power: in a most brutal and barbarous fashion he was rooting out decadence in Germany. The barbarian has talked of the German need for *Lebensraum* (living space): perhaps he could find it during his crusade against Bolshevism. Hitler could be used and then dropped: monsters had their uses.

Labor now had a formidable enemy. In its dying phases, as they saw it, capitalism was employing hoodlums to protect itself against the challenge from the workers. Capitalist governments, both in Australia and overseas, were demonstrating their inability to find answers to the problems of poverty and unemployment. Their inability to do so, their impotence before the great problems of the day and their moral bankruptcy drove the worst elements in the capitalist class, and their political lackeys, to support Fascism, Nazism, and New Guardism. Labor needed all the strength it could muster to meet the new challenge. Labor must stop faction fighting, must regain its soul. The communists were already responding to the challenge. They had the right sense of urgency. The *Workers' Weekly* said not a moment must be lost. The masses must be won over to revolutionary activity to save society from Fascism and Nazism.[77]

The communists expected the coming of the revolution any day. They were messianic men and women. Their leaders have taken with them into the Party the Christian idea of salvation, but in their case salvation not by God, but by man. Christians had believed there was hope for God, but not for man. But now the Communist Party, as the vanguard of the proletariat,

[76] *Argus*, 10 April 1933; *S.M.H.*, 12, 28 April, 19 May 1933; A. H. Charteris, 'The Month in Foreign Affairs', *Today*, 1 May 1933; S. H. Roberts, 'The Rise of Hitlerism', *Australian Quarterly*, 14 June 1933; *Australian Worker*, 1, 8, 15 March, 5, 19 April 1933.

[77] *Australian Worker*, 31 May 1933; *Workers' Weekly*, 24, 31 March 1933.

was the saviour. Salvation was not in some future time and place, but here and now. John Normington Rawling had been a preacher in the Church of Latter Day Saints, a soldier of Christ, and then a soldier for God, King and Empire. The horrors of the war destroyed his faith in God and the Empire. He filled the void with rationalism, but found that was a creed for dry souls. He turned to Marxism, finding there the promise of the Apocalypse he had lost when the war made shipwreck of his Christian faith. Communism, he now believed, would lead humanity from the capitalist hell to the communist heaven. Pat Troy turned to the communist heaven when the heaven promised to him by the priests slipped away. Lance Sharkey, too, has substituted a heaven on earth for the inventions of the priests. Ralph Gibson, the son of the Professor of Philosophy at the University of Melbourne, abandoned the cheerfulness of the Student Christian Movement to become an advocate for communist piety. They were waiting for the tocsin to sound in the streets of Australia. But the cleansing fire of revolution did not sweep the country. The revolution never started. The communist intellectuals went on chanting the slogans they had borrowed from abroad, just as the conservatives went on chanting the litany of a country thirteen thousand miles away.[78]

That left the Australian Labor Party. Visionaries were already working for a recovery after the débâcle of December 1931. The bitterness against Jack Lang and Jack Beasley has not died away. The opponents of the Premiers' Plan behaved as though the most important thing in life was to punish the Labor Ministers who had supported that plan. But John Curtin's eye was single. He told his colleagues in the Party they must strip their platform of the phraseology of the past, and write in planks that were immediately called for. They must not cripple their revival by 'insensate turmoil'. He believed his destiny lay ahead. He must use his talents to 'mobilise the masses'. The key to the success of Labor at the ballot box lay in an alliance between the workers and the producers. There was much to do. The workers wanted better wages, employment, and houses to live in. They wanted bread and must be taught how they could get their bread. They must be taught how they could be liberated from the 'vampire exploitation'. For him agitation was the 'breath of life'. He was getting ready again to 'ride a storm'.[79]

The *Australian Worker* agreed. The situation was perilous. The conservatives now had behind them 'a semi-military force, infused with all the fanatical insolence of Hitler's hoodlums'. In the face of such a situation it was a crime for Labor to remain divided. Australia was now a battlefield. The

[78] Stephen Holt, J. N. Rawling, typescript in possession of the author; Stuart Macintyre, *Militant, The Life and Times of Paddy Troy* (Sydney, 1984).

[79] J. Curtin to E. G. Theodore, 30 September 1932, Theodore Papers, N.L.A., Canberra.

workers were not so strong, nor their enemies so weak, that Labor could afford to 'indulge in a family squabble'. Vain words. The squabble went on. At the Interstate Labor Conference in Sydney on 27 June, summoned to restore unity, Jimmy Scullin threw a bombshell into the proceedings by launching a virulent attack on Lang. The eyes of Jimmy Scullin were on the past: he was now squandering his vast talents as an orator in defence of his Government. Conference was bitterly divided between the Langites and those in favour of the old socialization objective. Unity was not achieved.[80]

The electorate was still volatile and unpredictable. In South Australia on 8 May 1933 the Labor Party was crushingly defeated in a State election. On the same day Labor defeated the Nationalists and the Country Party decisively in Western Australia, and in a referendum an overwhelming majority voted 'Yes' in favour of the secession of Western Australia from the Commonwealth of Australia. In New South Wales, Stevens decided to hold a referendum to win the approval of the people for his proposal to reform the State's Legislative Council. Conservatives were taking no chances. Lang has declared that his Labor Party had no need to attempt to secure their aims by revolutionary effort or force because they could get all they needed by consitutional means. There was nothing in the Constitution of New South Wales to stop a government—either revolutionary or fascist—getting all it wanted by constitutional means, because New South Wales had a Legislative Council which could be 'bent and twisted according to the caprice and whim of any unscrupulous Government'. The public changed its fickle mind from day to day. Stevens believed the only safe thing was to have a 'sheet anchor' in the second Chamber. Stevens proposed to remove the power of a government to swamp the Legislative Council. The power of nomination, he proposed, would be taken away from the Governor. (Even Sir Philip Game had bowed to Lang.) The members of the Legislative Assembly would elect the members of the Legislative Council. As de Tocqueville had pointed out in his work on Democracy in America, indirect election was an effective protection against the tyranny of the majority. Lang asked the people to reject the formation of an Upper House which would be a 'permanent constitutional oligarchy'. On 13 May the 'Yes' vote had a slender majority of 21–22 thousand in a poll of just over one and a quarter million votes.[81]

Conservatism had the constitutional means, and the control of opinion with which to usher in the great calm-down after the stormy years of 1929–31. Unemployment has begun to decline. In 1930, 19.3 per cent of trade union members were unemployed, in 1931 28 per cent, in 1932, 29.6 per cent, and by the third quarter of 1933, 25.1 per cent. Eviction riots still

[80] *Australian Worker*, 24 May 1933; *S.M.H.*, 28 June, 1 July 1933.
[81] *S.M.H.*, 10 April, 5 May, 7 April, 3 March, 15 May 1933.

occurred in the working-class suburbs. In Sydney the members of the New Guard protected the police against assaults by the members of the Labor Defence Army during an eviction riot. The police in Sydney, Melbourne and other cities broke up working-class meetings. In Melbourne the Chief Commissioner of Police, Major-General T. A. Blamey, instructed the police to break up meetings addressed by communists. In Sydney Road, Brunswick, mounted troopers drove men, women and children off the footpath, and into the path of the oncoming traffic on Friday nights. Citizens were being knocked down and injured. Blamey has boasted to his cronies in clubland that when there was a workers' demonstration he put his telescope to his blind eye.[82]

Joe Lyons told the people to be of good cheer. Australia was no longer 'sliding to financial ruin'. The pastoral industry was out of the woods: wool prices were 50 per cent above those in 1932. The architects of the plan to invite Joe Lyons to 'come over and help us' were now full of gratitude to Lyons. 'What a generous person you are Joe', Staniforth Ricketson told him in a letter on 16 August, 'and how attractive it is that you have preserved that early asset of yours—real genuine humility. Your friends are very proud of you'. Ricketson was concerned to see Lyons looking so tired: 'You are', he added, '. . . very essential to the continuance of well-being to this whole community'. Stanley Bruce was also full of praise: '. . . you have the satisfaction of knowing that you have done for Australia what no other man could have done'.

Others were not faring well. Jocka Burns and his unemployed mate used half their dole coupons at Yarraville (Sydney) to pay the rent. They relied on their persuasive powers to bite the butcher and the grocer for some meat and bread during their weekly attack of the 'shorts'. Stan Moran sang songs about the unemployed to audiences in the Sydney Domain on Sunday afternoons:

> Oh those beans, bacon and gravy, they nearly drive me crazy,
> I eat them till I see them in my dreams, in my dreams,
> But I wake up in the morning, another day is dawning,
> And I know I'll have another plate of beans.

The sons and daughters of the comfortable classes went to balls to raise money for the relief of the poor. Mungo MacCallum, the gifted grandson of the Mungo MacCallum who had wept when the Senate of the University of Sydney asked Chris. Brennan to resign, danced with his friends in the elegant ballroom on the top floor of David Jones in Sydney, or in the shoddy grandeur of the Sydney Town Hall, or in the homes of his friends from Hunters

[82] *Labour Report of C'wealth Bureau of Census and Statistics*, 1933, No. 24 (Canberra, 1933), p. 102; *Argus*, 9 June 1933.

Hill, the North Shore or the Eastern Suburbs. He observed the lore of his tribe: white tie for a ball, black tie for a dance. He learned the code: a man could be drunk, but he must not fall over, he must not vomit in public, or use four-letter words in the presence of ladies. A man could 'canoodle but display no passion'. The down-and-out slept on park benches. The sons of the patricians of Sydney and the sons of the squatters boasted to each other, 'Haven't had a night at home for a week'. The sons of the patricians wore cream trousers and shirts on the cricket field, and put on buckskin boots: the others wore 'whites' and sandshoes. The 'upper crusters' licked a Peters ice-cream, the 'lower crusters' a Swallow and Ariel ice-cream: even the colour was different.

While these 'unexercised stallions' looked at themselves in bathroom mirrors on mornings after and wondered whether this was the time for an 'amendment of life', Stan Moran was speaking to those who had marched to the Botanical Gardens behind the banner of the Unemployed Workers' Union. He climbed on to the statue of Shakespeare, just as Jack Kidd had addressed the poor and hungry in Shakespeare's *Henry VI*. A policeman dragged him off the statue and bashed him with his baton. At the same time in the Northern Territory, north Queensland and the north of Western Australia police were driving Aborigines in chains over hundreds of miles on foot, to police stations where they were charged under laws they had never made and never accepted.[83]

'Inky' Stephensen started the Endeavour Press and asked Australian writers to join him in a crusade against the domination of British and American culture in Australia. Norman Lindsay painted a picture of Apollo rising out of the cleansing waters of Sydney Harbour to confront the respresentatives of British philistinism in Australia—British Governors, wool men, gold diggers, bushrangers, drunkards, lechers, politicians and policemen, parsons, priests and gaolers. Stephensen asked Miles Franklin for a manuscript. He asked Eleanor Dark for a manuscript, sensing rightly she had something to say to Australians. William Baylebridge sent him the manuscript of *This Vital Flesh*. Xavier Herbert sent him the manuscript of *Capricornia*. Patrick White sent him a collection of poems, *The Ploughman and Other Poems*, Hal Porter a collection of stories. Like everything Stephensen touched, it all began in an orgy of enthusiasm. But by the second half of the year things have gone wrong. Norman Lindsay broke with the cultural chauvinists. Australians, he said, did not have 'the good conscience to help [their] own culture'. The literary establishment in Australia, the Palmers, Marjorie

[83] *S.M.H.*, 13 July, 29 August 1933; S. Ricketson to J. A. Lyons, 16 August 1933, Lyons Papers, Box 2, Folder 11; S. M. Bruce to J. A. Lyons, 11 April 1933, Lyons Papers, Box 2, Folder 11; Wendy Lowenstein, *Weevils in the Flour* (Melbourne, 1978), pp. 208–12; *Argus*, 9 June 1933; *S.M.H.*, 30 May 1933; Mungo MacCallum, *Plankton's Luck* (Hawthorn, 1986) p. 111.

Barnard, Katharine Prichard and others became suspicious of Stephensen. He attributed his financial troubles, the hole in his pocket, as he called it, to the indifference of Australians to things of the spirit, rather than to faults in his own clay. As D. H. Lawrence had put it, Australians had a 'rather fascinating indifference, a *physical* indifference to what we call soul or spirit', 'no inside life of any sort: just a long lapse and drift'. Eleanor Dark had her eye on the way forward: Australian writers must not look back to those 'awful monstrosities "Our Selection" [*sic*] and "The Squatter's Daughter" '. Australian writers must create a myth for the suburbs. But that seed, save in her own mind, has fallen on barren ground.[84]

The conservatives were not divided. They believed in the Empire: they believed in the 'Ottawa spirit'. Sir George Pearce, the Minister for Defence, has not allowed himself to be troubled by Bruce's warning from Ottawa that the British might not be willing or able to defend Australia if she were attacked. On 25 September he said again what conservatives had been saying ever since the 1880s and earlier, that Australia must rely on the power of the British navy to defend her against aggression. That was the stumbling-block to all those radicals and loud-mouthed advocates of independence: Australia depended on the British for survival, depended on the British for markets for her goods, and for loans. It was the old, old story, but conservatives believed with the hymn that the story should be told often because the people forgot so soon. On Wattle Day, 1 August 1933, for many the festival of the national flower of Australia, speakers instilled into the minds of the people a reverence both for their country and for the Empire. On that day volunteers, including Boy Scouts and Girl Guides, distributed sprays of wattle to passers-by in the streets. Honour boards and war memorials were decorated with wattle. The wattle represented Australian ideals: the combination of prosperity and material well-being with cheerfulness. Like Australians, the wattle thrived in adversity, like Australians, it grew best when uncontrolled. Australians could love both Australia and the Empire.[85]

Australia must cultivate good relations with the British. In a newspaper interview in England in May, Harold Larwood attacked Australian crowds, and accused Australian newspapers of running a campaign to wreck him as a bowler. He also accused Bill Woodfull of being too slow, and Don Bradman of being 'too frightened'. But the men in high places in England and Aus-

[84] Norman Lindsay, *Apollo's Vanguard*, painted Sydney, 1933; Craig Munro, op. cit., pp. 116–26; Patrick White, *The Ploughman and Other Poems* (Sydney, 1935); Norman Lindsay to Peter Hopegood, n.d., prob. 1933, R. G. Howarth and A. W. Barker (eds), *The Letters of Norman Lindsay* (Sydney, 1979), p. 324; D. H. Lawrence to Catherine Carswell, 22 June 1922, Aldous Huxley (ed.), *The Letters of D. H. Lawrence* (London, 1933), p. 549; Eleanor Dark to Nettie Palmer, 14 December 1933, Palmer Papers, Series 1, Box 6, Folder 57.

[85] *Age*, 21 July, 26 September 1933; *S.M.H.*, 1, 2 August 1933.

tralia could no longer afford a public slanging match between the heroes of the cricket field. Larwood and Jardine must be sacrificed on the altar of the Empire. The Australian Government has committed itself to strengthening the bonds of Empire. Taking a hint from their Governments, the Australian Board of Control and the Marylebone Cricket Club have exchanged cables to restore cordiality. On 22 September the Australian Board of Control asked the Marylebone Cricket Club whether the latter now conceded a direct attack by the bowler on the batsman was against the spirit of the game. They asked whether the English would take the field in 1934 against the Australians in England with that knowledge. They were most anxious that cordial relations between the English and the Australians should continue. The Marylebone Cricket Club was most conciliatory, though not contrite. The English governing classes had their motto: never apologize, never explain. They were not going to ask forgiveness, nor confess that it was all their own 'most grievous fault'. All men were sinners in thought, word and deed. They knew that: the Prayer Book told them so. But a form of bowling which was obviously an attack by the bowler on the batsman was, they agreed, an offence against the spirit of the game. The Australians could come to England knowing the game would be played in the same spirit as in years past. They added they were glad the Australians proposed to take the question of barracking into consideration. There would be a warm welcome for the Australians in 1934: every effort would be made to see that their visit was enjoyable.[86]

The text of these two cables was made public on 11 October 1933. On that day Sir Charles Kingsford Smith arrived in Darwin in his British made Percival Gull monoplane, after a flight of seven days, four hours and forty-seven minutes from Lympne in England. He had beaten the record of C. W. A. Scott by one day, fifteen hours and fifty-seven minutes. 'Smithy' was an Empire man, who shared the views of the members of the Old Guard on the need for eternal vigilance in Australia, their gospel of work, and their belief in purification by blood sacrifice. He was known to loathe all demagogues who inflamed the masses: he believed in the values of army and air force officers. He has saddened Labor leaders and the rank and file by saying in public that if the Labor crowd did not come to their senses then 'a bit of bombing might persuade them'. When he arrived at Mascot on 29 October he and the *Sydney Morning Herald* heralded the flight as a promise of future Anglo-Australian co-operation in the air mail service between England and Australia. 'Smithy' hoped the British and the Australians would remember him when the air mail contracts were placed. The aeroplane has brought England and Australia closer. England was now only a week away. Neither 'Smithy' nor the conservative politicians foresaw what the aeroplane would

[86] *S.M.H.*, 8 May, 11 October 1933.

do to the traditional defence of Australia. Members of the King and Empire Alliance and the Old Guard became the unwitting grave-diggers of the world in which they so passionately believed.[87]

All those who believed in the virtues of Old Australia, the virtues of the bushman, lately sanctified by the diggers with the sacrifice of their blood in war, were devoted passionately to the King and the Empire. Sir Harold Luxton had an idea for cementing that relationship to the great benefit of his own class. Sir Harold rowed in the first eight at Melbourne Grammar, and knew all about rowing the race of life: Sir Harold had been one of those who had searched for 'sterner foemen'. He had had a distinguished career in the war. He suffered grave injuries and was decorated by His Majesty for bravery. After the war he succeeded as a director of the firm of James McEwan and Company. There he worked with Alexander Mair, another hero from the war, who later became a U.A.P. Premier of New South Wales. Sir Harold has been three times Lord Mayor of Melbourne. Two of his sons have been prefects at Melbourne Grammar School where, like Sir Harold, they rowed in the first eight. Sir Harold sent them to Cambridge in England for their university education. During 1930 Sir Harold's wife achieved some fame by expressing sympathy with the fate of debutantes. They were having a hard time, she said: 'There are hardly any parties for them. People cannot afford it'.[88]

In April 1933 Sir Harold was in London to discuss with the British arrangements for celebrating the centenary in 1934 of British settlement in Victoria. He urged on Stanley Bruce the supreme importance of a visit from Royalty to Victoria that year. He and Bruce were both old boys of Melbourne Grammar School, both upholders of the values of 'Yarraside', exemplars of bourgeois affluence and success in Australia. Bruce liked the idea and took it a stage further. The presence of a Royalty, he told Lyons in a letter on 27 April 1933, at the Victorian Centenary celebrations might open the way for a Royalty as Governor-General of Australia. He knew this would mean a reversion from the previous practice of appointing an Australian, but he thought the needs of the times demanded it.[89]

Joe Lyons liked the idea. On 7 November he wrote to the British Prime Minister, J. Ramsay MacDonald, that the Victorian Centenary celebrations would stimulate in the minds of all participants an interest in Australian origins and the Imperial connection. He went on to claim that in loyalty to the Imperial connection and pride in membership of the British Com-

[87] Ibid., 12, 13, 30 October 1933.

[88] *Table Talk*, 29 November 1928; David Dunstan, 'Sir Harold Daniel Luxton', *A.D.B.*, vol. 10, pp. 170–1 (Melbourne, 1986); personal observations of Sir Harold Luxton and Alexander Mair.

[89] S. M. Bruce to J. A. Lyons, 27 April 1933, Lyons Papers, Box 2, Folder 11.

monwealth, Australia was equalled by few and excelled by none. But in present world conditions and tendencies, the encouragement of that pride and loyalty was 'a matter of considerable importance to the British Empire'. Nothing, he continued, was more 'certain to foster their loyalty and affection for the Motherland, than a visit from a member of the Royal Family'. It would help his Government and Party to improve the credit of Australia, and ensure the security of Australia's external creditors. It should be remembered, he added, that there was a disloyal element in Australia, associated politically with the section of the Labor Party led by Mr Lang. For Australia and the general interest of the Empire, send Royalty.[90]

The British Prime Minister agreed. 'Never', he wrote to Lyons on 14 December, 'was it so necessary as now for the Empire to stand indissolubly united'. Prince George would proceed direct from South Africa to Australia. The links that bound Australia to the Empire would be greatly strengthened. Australia and England shared a common history, a great literature and political traditions. The people would draw great inspiration from their Imperial connection. The mischief-makers and men of narrow vision in Australia would be confounded. They could not see that fellowship and co-operation were what was required to survive the storms that were to come. Royalty would be that outward and visible sign to Australians of the advantages to be enjoyed by those who followed the advice of the conservatives to 'Tune in with Britain'.[91]

While Ramsay MacDonald was telling Joe Lyons how a visit from Royalty would confound the mischief-makers of Australia, on 28 December Stan Moran was addressing a meeting of men and women on the dole outside the offices of the Mayor of Glebe. Stan Moran was a hero to the insulted and injured of Australia, a mob orator who could hold a crowd spellbound, or rouse them to outbursts of hysterical laughter as he exposed the follies and the foibles, the greed and the wickedness of those in high places. This day the Mayor has refused to receive a deputation from the unemployed. Stan was angry. Stan fumed and raved: the small crowd was with him. The police arrived. One policeman dragged Stan off his platform. The police 'got stuck into' these pitiable people with their batons. Many of the police were said to be intoxicated. Blood flowed. The wounded moaned and groaned. Stan Moran and his fellow communists wanted the people to draw political conclusions from such experiences. But to their dismay the victims of the Depression seemed interested only in the economic side: they wanted bread: they wanted work. To teach the Australian people 'a political approach', Stan Moran found, was 'not an easy job'.[92]

90 J. A. Lyons to J. Ramsay MacDonald, 7 November 1933, ibid.
91 J. Ramsay MacDonald to J. A. Lyons, 14 December 1933, ibid.
92 Lowenstein, op. cit., pp. 214–17; *S.M.H.*, 29 December 1933.

13

'THE OLD DEAD TREE' OR 'THE YOUNG TREE GREEN'?

FOR SIR HAROLD and Lady Luxton, for Bob Menzies, for all those who believed in 'Grammar and that sort of thing', and for all those who believed in the King and the Empire, the high summer of 1934 held out the promise of a good year. Unemployment figures published in January revealed that a steady progressive movement was taking place. Street scuffles, eviction riots, and confrontations between the police and the unemployed were diminishing in number. The roar of social protest was dropping to a whisper. A royal duke was coming to Australia to be the guest of honour at the Centenary celebrations in Victoria. A royal duke was to be there when the two shrines, sacred to all right-minded Australians, were dedicated—the Shrine of Remembrance in Melbourne, and the Anzac Memorial in Sydney.[1]

At the funeral of Sir Robert Gibson, Chairman of the Board of the Commonwealth Bank, on 3 January the heads of the banks, the finance companies, the pastoral companies, and the insurance firms acted as chief pall-bearers. Jimmy Scullin was in the forefront. Jimmy Scullin had a loving and forgiving heart. He could forgive his enemies in the banking world: he could not forgive his colleagues in the Labor Party such as Jack Beasley and Jack Lang who had stabbed him in the back. Messages of praise and thanksgiving for Sir Robert were sent from all over Australia. Stanley Bruce sent his words of appreciation from London. 'Australia', he said 'has suffered the irreparable loss of one of her greatest sons'. The parsons spoke of Sir Robert as a servant of God, a great man who had dedicated his vast talents to the service of his country. To Labor, Sir Robert Gibson was a walnut-hearted man who, in collaboration with the professors and Mr Money Bags, destroyed the Labor Government of Jimmy Scullin, put the financial squeeze on Jack Lang in Sydney, and helped to draft the odious Premiers' Plan.[2]

Labor was still divided. At the annual conference of the Victorian Labor Party on 28 January 1934 the militants did not forgive those who had supported the Premiers' Plan. The militants charged the moderates with timidity and lethargy. The 'frightened half-heartedness' of the moderates, the

[1] *S.M.H.*, 15 January 1934.
[2] Ibid., 4 January 1934; *Bulletin*, 10 January 1934.

militants said, was driving many of the visionaries and ideologues into the Communist Party. The moderates trembled timidly at the very idea of Labor adopting any advanced policy. *Without* the militants Labor was a political machine, a party without a conscience or a soul. *With* the militants Labor faced possible electoral disaster. Jimmy Scullin pleaded with the delegates not to throw to the wolves those who had been loyal to him, just for the sake of unity. But unity was now the 'great, good thing'. Without unity Labor was condemned to remain in opposition for a long time and possibly for ever. The question was: which faction would come out on top in the Party, and what would it stand for?[3]

That was what John Curtin was chewing over during those lonely walks on Cottesloe beach, when he asked himself what a socialist could now believe, and whether there was an alternative to the men of the King and Empire Alliance. He was waiting, as he had put it in a letter to Frank Anstey on 9 March 1934, for the 'great moment' to 'leap from the night of inertia'. He still had his faith that 'vibrant things' would 'emerge from the chaotic flux of the commonplace'. It was the task of a Labor leader to show the people the 'vibrant things', to give the people faith in their power to create something out of the 'chaotic flux of the commonplace'. No movement could 'rally without a personality in the front'. John Curtin might be Labor's man of destiny. John Curtin had something to say.[4]

From the lower depths there were still occasional upheavals. On 30 January 1934 there was a night of terror at Boulder on the Kalgoorlie goldfields of Western Australia. On 31 January there was another night of terror at Boulder. The miners of British descent met in the town to discuss what should be done about those 'bloody foreigners' who were easing them out of their jobs in the mines, and competing unfairly with British Australians in the business and shop-keeping world. While the meeting was in progress, and hotheads were swearing in the dinkum Aussie way of what they would do to the foreign elements on the fields, explosions were heard. The bloody foreigners were attacking Australians in their own country. Tempers flared: volunteers were called for. A mob armed with sticks, stones and rifles stormed over the railway bridge and advanced towards the camps where the foreigners were housed. Bullets flew. The police arrived. The Australians rushed forward to set fire to the camp of the foreigners, creating a flare which could be seen for miles. Two men, a Montenegrin and an Australian, were killed. Six Australians were wounded. As the Australian mob walked back to Kalgoorlie they set fire to every camp of foreigners they came across. The following day there were scenes of desolation at these camp sites. The

[3] *Age*, 29 January 1934; *S.M.H.*, 29 January 1934.

[4] John Curtin to Frank Anstey, 9 March 1934, Lloyd Ross Papers, Box 33; John Curtin to E. G. Theodore, 30 September 1932, Theodore Papers, N.L.A., Canberra.

summer air still reeked with the odour of burning tents, huts, furniture, clothing and other household goods. Foreigners huddled in groups, petrified. Some wandered into the surrounding bush for shelter from the bloodthirsty monsters who had robbed them of their livelihood. Some said it was all the work of young hotheads, who, happily for the believers in law and order, were without leaders and without any social or political ideology.[5]

The conservatives must prepare for the new political climate in Australia. Labor would not always be disunited. Labor was replacing those brains it had blown out of the Party during the conscription crisis. John Curtin has performed with distinction on a Government Commission: Ben Chifley was a man to watch. Australian politicians were arguing with each other, the *Bulletin* commented on 28 February, 'like small, angry boys throwing pebbles at an elephant'. Perhaps Joe Lyons had outlived his usefulness. The conservatives needed a man with backbone, a man with the courage to face the petty provincialism of the State politicians. There were two possibilities. One was Bertram Stevens, Premier of New South Wales, the other Robert Gordon Menzies, Attorney-General in the Victorian Government, but member-designate for Kooyong after John Latham announced his retirement from politics. They were both strong personalities. Their rivalry has been noted. They have clashed already at meetings of Commonwealth and State Ministers. Rivalry between Melbourne and Sydney was part of the struggle, as was the question of where power resided. Stevens was the man of iron discipline, the man who kept his cards close to his chest. The strengths and weaknesses of Menzies were now part of political gossip. Menzies was a shop-front man: Stevens was a man with a factory. The times called for a showman, and Menzies was a magnificent showman.[6]

The conservatives planned quite a few 'shows' that year. They were not interested in all this talk about fostering an Australian culture. As the *Sydney Morning Herald* put it on 7 April, 'all Australian cultural standards' were 'naturally and inevitably rather low'. Australia has not produced a poet of international standing. Australia was a province of British culture and Australians were that year putting on a show to demonstrate where their hearts lay. A royal prince was coming. In April it was announced it would not be Prince George, but Henry, Duke of Gloucester. Bob Menzies was delighted: 'We shall certainly welcome any son of the King', he said. Baron Culloden, Earl of Ulster and Duke of Gloucester, had much to commend him to Australians. He had all the qualities to make a good soldier: he was described as the best cricketer the royal family had ever possessed, chief proof of which being his boast that he could bowl the King out any time he liked. He took a

[5] *S.M.H.*, 31 January, 1 February 1932; *West Australian*, 30, 31 January, 1 February 1934.

[6] *Bulletin*, 28 February 1934; *S.M.H.*, 7 March 1934.

great interest in Rugby football. He had an eye for a pretty woman: according to report he was already well known for dancing not once but twice with the prettiest girl at a social ball.[7]

The Australian Test cricketers arrived in England in April 1934. They were there to obliterate 'the memory of a past misunderstanding', and to create a good atmosphere for relations between England and Australia. They were ambassadors for good will. The British race did not believe in winning at any cost: they believed in co-operation. The greatness of England was the theme at all the celebrations for St George's Day that April. While the Australian cricketers froze at the nets in the 'springtime, the merry, merry springtime' in Old England, Billy Hughes proposed the toast to 'St George, Old England and the Empire' at the Festival Dinner of the Royal Society of St George in Sydney. Australians, he said, should be grateful to the English: the English had given them all they possessed of liberty and free institutions. Australians were partners with England in the greatest Empire the world had ever known. The British flag was a reminder, another speaker said, that the British had known freedom when all other peoples were in chains.[8]

Not everyone on the Labor side felt such gratitude to and reverence and affection for the British. During the war Dr Mannix had declared he would never use the pulpit to perform the work of a recruiting sergeant, to persuade men to fight in wars overseas. Labor members of Parliament have denounced 'this accursed Empire'. Joe Lyons now said all the right things about the Empire, but there was a time when his love and loyalty had flowed first towards Erin, the land of his fathers. For socialists and communists the only flag they recognized was the Red Flag. The Union Jack and the Australian flag, with its two emblems of the Southern Cross and the Union Jack, were 'bosses' flags', which commanded neither their respect nor their loyalty. On 18 July the Workers' Industrial Union censured the Broken Hill Trades and Labor Council for flying the 'bosses' flag' over a working-class institution.[9]

But Australians were noted for their timidity. As Leslie Rees told Nettie Palmer, Angus and Robertson's would not publish a book if it had a line in it that would disturb anyone's complacency. Frank Dalby Davison also noticed another characteristic of Australians: to desecrate the countryside. 'We Australians', he told Vance Palmer, 'have plundered the delicate beauty of our continent and disfigured it with a careless tin-shanty semi-civilisation'. On a car journey up the coast of Queensland in 1932 he saw 'bare little farms without so much as a tree to hide their ugliness, frowsy little hamlets, and big

[7] *S.M.H.*, 30 April 1934.
[8] Ibid., 7, 24 April 1934.
[9] Ibid., 19 July 1934.

towns that could hardly have been more dreary than they were'. He saw 'a great deal of mutilated beauty', 'almost no created beauty', but 'a very great deal of created ugliness.'.[10]

Frank Dalby Davison was already well known as the author of *Man-Shy*, published in 1931, and *The Wells of Beersheba*, published in 1933. The latter was the story of how those 'resolute horsemen', the Australian Light Horse, knocked the Turks out of the war with their victories in Palestine and Syria. It was a story of how brave men contributed to the myth of Australia as a country which belonged to the strong. Davison was cradled in the bush. Born in Melbourne in 1893, he became a bush boy at the age of twelve, then migrated to America to learn his father's trade as a printer. He began to write at night, volunteered for the British army in the war, and saw action on the Western Front. He took up land as a soldier settler near Dalby in Queensland, an experience which cut so deep that he added Dalby to his name. He came to Sydney in 1923 where he worked in real estate, wrote stories and became friendly with Marjorie Barnard and the Palmers.

Davison already had doubts about the Labor Party. He was already shaping in his mind the story of a man from the bush discovering that the Australian dream of mateship and equality was not enough: there must be a social revolution. Davison was also a loner. His trouble, he told Vance Palmer, was that he had nerves. '*Don't discuss me with anyone and don't be sorry for me.*' But in Australia that was to ask the impossible. He was a bit of a prophet and chafed under the restrictions and taboos of Australian life. He wanted Australians to take the blinkers off their eyes and face the truth about themselves. He fought bravely against the unrelenting tyranny of opinion in Australia. He wanted Australians to liberate their minds from the teaching of the Christian Church and the assumptions of the law on homosexuality. He wanted Australians of European descent to change their attitudes to the Aborigines but found that to persuade European Australians to change their minds about politics, sex, or the Aborigine was no easy task.[11]

On 30 May 1934 'Tiger' and seven other Aborigines were found guilty in the Supreme Court of the Northern Territory, sitting in Darwin, of the murder of Albert Koch and Stephen Arinski, two white prospectors, at Fitz-

[10] Leslie Rees to Nettie Palmer, 7 February 1934, and Frank Dalby Davison to Vance Palmer, 12 August 1934, Palmer Papers, Series 1, Box 7, Folder 60; Frank Dalby Davison and Brooke Nicholls, *Blue Coast Caravan* (Sydney, 1935); Hume Dow, *Frank Dalby Davison* (Melbourne, 1971).

[11] Frank Dalby Davison, *Man Shy* (Sydney, 1931), *The Wells of Beersheba* (Sydney, 1933), and 'Further West', published in *The Women at the Mill* (Sydney, 1940); M. Barnard Eldershaw, *Essays in Australian Fiction* (Sydney, 1938), pp. 41–80; Frank Davison to Vance Palmer, 14 September 1934, Palmer Papers, Series 1, Box 7, Folder 60; personal conversations with F. D. Davison, Melbourne, 1946.

maurice River on or about 12 November 1932. The judge had the power under the amended ordinance to impose a less severe penalty than death. The lawyer for the accused urged him to do so, as seven of the accused knew nothing of civilization. Judge Wells explained to the Court why he did not propose to use that power. Retributive justice, he said, was all that a savage could understand. It was a treacherous and cold-blooded murder. If the courts permitted Aborigines to murder white men in any circumstances without fear of the extreme penalty, Aborigines would consider that white men placed a low value on life. The judge then asked whether there was anyone in the Court who had anything to say in favour of the Aborigines. There was no reply. The judge then sentenced them to death.[12]

The Australian Board of Missions, philanthropists and humanitarians asked that the lives of the eight Aborigines be spared. Vain hope. A meeting of citizens of every shade of political opinion in Sydney on 6 August urged the Federal Government to adopt a 'more humane, scientific, and civilised policy towards the original inhabitants of Australia'. They resolved to do their utmost to 'raise the standard of morality of the white Australians towards their fellow black Australians'. They asked the Government to proclaim more native reserves, to encourage assimilation for those Aborigines who could manage the white man's world, and segregation for those who could not. The white man has not started to talk of the right of the Aborigine to choose his own way of life—he still regarded Aborigines as little children, and white people as their guardians. The white man has not questioned his assumption that the Aborigines must accept the consequences of the white man's presence, or suffer all the rigours of the white man's law. He still believed he was dealing with 'stone-age savages'. The white man has not questioned his right to be there, nor heeded the words of the Psalmist: 'I am a sojourner here'. In the years of doubt about everything else, that doubt has not troubled the white man.[13]

God has disappeared. Australians showed little interest in replacing the Christian heaven with a heaven on earth. Their history, the spirit of the place, and the creeds to which they have attached themselves—the dream of getting on, the ideal of owning a home and a block of land, and the digger ideals of sacrifice, courage, resource and endurance—have made them wary of any promise about future harmony. Popular songs helped to fill the great emptiness and the sense of futility with the promise of love. Previous generations sang of their love of God:

> Naught be all else to me,
> Save that thou art.

[12] *S.M.H.*, 31 May 1934.
[13] Ibid., 3, 7 August 1934.

Now men and women were lavishing on each other the love they had once lavished on God: that year, 1934, people listened to:

> All I do, the whole night through,
> Is dream of you.

Men had hopes for women:

> Stay as sweet as you are
> Just as you are
> You're divine, dear.

A popular song put into memorable words that magical moment for a man when he first sees a woman who is more beautiful to him than anyone else is beautiful:

> You ought to be in pictures
> You're beautiful to see
> You ought to be in pictures
> Oh what a hit you would be.
>
> Your voice would thrill a nation
> Your face would be adored
> You ought to be in pictures
> My star of stars.

For those who wanted to hear some human reasons why they should belong to the Empire but had no interest in those public occasions when men wore a strange fancy dress costume, one song put it very nicely:

> All at once the girls got skittish
> Here come the British with a bang, bang.

There were words a girl might have to use if her suitor so far forgot himself, or was so carried away by passion that he offered her a fate worse than death:

> No! No! a thousand times No!
> I'd rather die than say Yes!

There were songs to comfort and relieve men who were 'a bit more on the tired side than usual', what with the office, all the worries about the children, and one thing and another. They could sing or, better still, have sung to them:

> Little man, you've had a busy day.

There were all those strange goings-on:

> On the good ship Lollipop.

Popular songs were a substitute for the lollipops of childhood. They gave everyone a good laugh. Like Luna Park in Melbourne they were 'Just for Fun'.[14]

Australian politics were like those things from eternity: they never changed. Australian Labor leaders wanted unity within the Party, and an end to faction fighting. On 23 April 1934 members of the Federal Executive of the Party met in Sydney to discuss how to bring about unity in New South Wales. After much discussion they decided it was useless to attempt to bring about unity with the present leader of the Lang Labor Party. The Lang men would not give an undertaking that they would accept the rules and constitution of the Australian Labor Party. John Curtin moved the resolution embodying the discussion of the delegates: the time has arrived when it must be recognized that the unity of Labor is not to be accomplished by the ignoble surrender of the Labor movement as a whole to the 'dictatorship of the Lang disruptionists'. Langites originated the division in March 1931, and had since accentuated it. The meeting therefore resolved that the terms for the Lang Party would be the same as for all loyal sections of the Labor movement, 'namely, the unreserved acceptance of the constitution and platform of the Australian Labor Party'. The resolution was carried, eight votes to two, with Arthur Augustus Calwell and Don Cameron, the two Victorian delegates, voting against it.[15]

The Commonwealth opposed the Western Australian request for secession. In a fit of provincial pique some Western Australians burned effigies of the Prime Minister, Joe Lyons, and the Minister for Defence, Sir George Pearce, a sand-groper himself from way back. The Western Australians decided to petition the British Parliament to pass an Act granting them secession. But all this was a cunning move to squeeze more out of the teats of the Canberra cow. The *Bulletin* cynically commented that the Premier of Western Australia could not resist the temptation of a free visit to Buckingham Palace, Madame Tussaud's, and Lords Cricket Ground. Joe Lyons had other plans to take the wind out of the sails of those State Governments who were forever grizzling about the effects of the federal system of government on their finances.

With federation the States lost their main source of revenue—customs duties. The States and the Commonwealth have made many attempts to find a formula for the distribution of the surplus revenue of the Commonwealth acceptable to all parties. The populous States argued for per capita payments, the less populous States for a distribution according to financial

[14] *Socialist*, 25 April 1919; Julius Mattfeld, *Variety Music Cavalcade* (New York, 1962), pp. 488–93.

[15] *S.M.H.*, 24 April 1934; *Australian Worker*, 25 April 1934; *Workers' Weekly*, 27 April 1934.

needs. Western Australia, with its huge area and sparse population, insisted from the beginning it was a special case.

In June 1933 Lyons decided to establish a Grants Commission to examine the problems of Commonwealth–State financial arrangements, and make recommendations. He made a shrewd choice of Commissioners. Freddie Eggleston, who had been making sour remarks about Australian politics ever since his own failure in the Victorian arena in the late 1920s, was made Chairman. By that appointment Lyons had lost a critic and gained a man of ability. L. F. Giblin ('Gibbie') was a second Commissioner—a maverick who always said the right thing, and J. W. Sandford, a South Australian businessman, educated at St Peter's College and in London, was the third. The sand-gropers howled that Lyons had passed them over, and favoured his own 'little Tassie'. But Lyons has made a shrewd decision. The first report of the Grants Commission on 21 July 1934 raised the level of the debate above all such petty squabbling. The federal system was essential to the preservation of bourgeois power. The members of the Grants Commission were showing how the 'lion in the path' could be overcome.

The survival of the Empire was also essential to bourgeois power, and more important than protecting the pride of individuals such as Jardine and Larwood. The forthcoming cricket Tests in England between England and Australia would show the value of the Empire. Press and radio gave the Australian team an 'overpowering reception' when their liner, the *Orford*, docked at Southampton in the spring of 1934. Bodyline was a thing of the past. Jardine would not be playing against them. Harold Larwood was sulking. Australians were 'welcome guests'. Larwood's reflections on Woodfull's courage were, to say the least, unfortunate. The English die-hards supported him. Why, they asked, give in to the Australians? Well, there were reasons, and they would learn of them in time. For the sake of Imperial unity, Harold Larwood and Douglas Jardine must be offered as sacrificial lambs. This sacrifice probably put the Australians on top again in the Tests. Bradman was far too skilled for Bill Bowes, who kept pounding them down short of a length in the first Test. All the fire has gone out of the combat between the two teams. Even Bradman was relaxed. After making 244 at Old Trafford in August 1934 he sipped champagne and puffed briefly at a cigarette with his team mates. He had had a great day. He had hit Bill Bowes all round the ground.[16]

From early in June the press ran stories about the imminent retirement from politics of the Attorney-General, John Latham. He was said to have had

[16] W. A. *P.D.*, 19 April 1934, vol. 92, p. 207 et. seq.; *S.M.H.*, 25 April, 29 May, 18 June, 23 July 1934; *Bulletin*, 2 May 1934; *Australasian*, 4 August 1934; *Equality in Diversity: Fifty Years of the Commonwealth Grants Commission* (Canberra, 1983); 'Tiger' Bill O'Reilly, *60 Years of Cricket* (Fontana books edn, Sydney, 1986), pp. 120–1.

enough. The rumour was revived that in 1931 during the negotiations between Latham, Lyons and the Committee of Six a bargain was made. If Latham resigned from the leadership of the Nationalist Party in favour of Lyons he would become Chief Justice of the High Court on the retirement of Sir Frank Gavan Duffy—a poet *manqué*, a hunter, a linguist, one of those polymaths and all-round men who graced the High Court in its first thirty years. The other part of the bargain was that Bob Menzies was to get Latham's safe seat of Kooyong. No written record of the discussion survived. All the parties denied there had been any such bargain. To their dismay Sir Frank seemed reluctant to retire, despite his age (in 1934 he turned eighty-two). So Latham did not wait for Sir Frank. He retired from politics.

Menzies announced he was a candidate for Kooyong. But doubts were expressed about him, as at every move he made on the great stage of life towards what he had always believed to be his destiny, to be Prime Minister of Australia. Bob Menzies has made political enemies. Every one knew he was clever. 'What a clever fellow Menzies is!', the *Bulletin* wrote. The trouble was his cleverness was often his downfall. He still could not suffer fools gladly: he still could not resist the temptation to use human beings as his 'whipping boys'. The satisfaction of the moment still led to the agony of counting the cost. He still could not resist the temptation to flick dandruff off the coat lapels of the mediocre, and say with a swift lift of the eyebrows: 'I'm surprised to see anything grows up there'. During his years in Victorian politics he has been constantly at loggerheads with the members of the Country Party. He was still much given to 'speaking his mind very definitely'. Nemesis would come, but not then. Lyons has decided to hang on. The time was not right for the 'stronger and more magnetic man' to take over the leadership and 'monopolise the limelight'.[17]

On 4 July Lyons announced in the House of Representatives that he proposed to wait on the Governor-General and advise him of the wish of the Government that the Governor-General should dissolve the House of Representatives in sufficient time to hold an election on 15 September. The following day Latham announced he was retiring from politics, as he put it, for 'private reasons'. Curtin announced he would stand for the seat of Fremantle. The two men who believed it was their destiny to be Prime Minister of Australia were soon at work in their electorates. Bob Menzies, with his gift for wit and repartee, told the electors he was 'British to the bootstraps'. John Curtin told the electors Labor would restore the Commonwealth Bank to the position it enjoyed before the establishment of the Commonwealth Bank Board and its subservience to Mr Money Man. Frank Anstey has decided to give up politics. Everything was sour in his mouth. He has decided the dif-

[17] H. A. Finlay, 'Sir Frank Gavan Duffy', *A.D.B.*, vol. 8; *S.M.H.*, 12, 14 June 1934, 6 July 1934; *Bulletin*, 7 March 1934.

ference between Labor and the conservatives was the difference between Tweedledum and Tweedledee. Both sides when out of power promised what they never meant to perform when in power. Nothing has changed. On 7 August, the day the House of Representatives was dissolved, Frank Anstey ceased to be a politician.[18]

The voice of Labor was now the voice of what Frank Anstey called 'the same servile men'. Labor leaders no longer stood up before the people. The radio speech was easing out the political meeting in a large hall. The age of the mob orators such as George Reid, Alfred Deakin, Jimmy Scullin, Jack Lang, Stan Moran and others was drawing to a close. The human voice was now the great persuader. Labor has become the 'big butter and egg man'. Ben Chifley opened the Labor election campaign for New South Wales in a speech broadcast by three commercial stations.

Joseph Benedict Chifley was a 'light on the hill man', a man who shared John Curtin's view that Labor was dedicated to a 'holy crusade'. Frank Anstey had once dreamed the same dream—but for him it had all turned to ashes. Chifley still had something of the crusader in him. He came from the working classes: he belonged to that same generation of self-taught Labor men who believed with John Curtin that the workers would form an army of liberation, that the workers had 'mighty work' to perform—they must set to it night and day. John Curtin in his youth had considered the lilies of the field: Ben Chifley was inclined by nature and upbringing to consider the human ant-heap. He had the same moral drive, the same conviction about the righteousness of the cause as John Curtin. 'We work for humanity', he said, 'when we fight for better conditions'.[19]

He was born in Bathurst, close to the railway yards, on 22 September 1885, the year in which John Curtin was born. His father and mother were Irish. His second name he owed to the Mother Superior of the Benedictine Convent at Queanbeyan. In childhood he lived the life of a farm-boy, who used what little leisure he had to read books on any subject. He subscribed to Dymock's Library in Sydney. He read Edward Bellamy's *Looking Backward* and *Equality*, Jack London and Bernard Shaw. They persuaded him to be a socialist. In his Church and associated societies he absorbed the teaching of Pope Leo XIII on the moral abominations of capitalist society. Like John Curtin he began to look on Labor as the vanguard in a 'holy crusade' for better conditions for the workers. He read Gibbon's *Decline and Fall* and Plutarch's *Lives*. They taught him wisdom on the field of the possible in human affairs: they put into words his own knowledge of what was in man.

[18] *C'wealth P.D.*, 4 July 1934, vol. 144, p. 173; *S.M.H.*, 5, 6 July 1934; *Bulletin*, 28 February 1934.

[19] *S.M.H.*, 5, 6 July 1934; *West Australian*, 30 August 1934; Frank Anstey, 'The Dead Tree', typescript in Lloyd Ross Papers, Box 33.

In childhood he had the innocence of the bush boy: in manhood he learned that the hearts of some men were filled with evil, that there was madness in men's hearts. Starting as a shop-boy in the locomotive shed of the New South Wales railways at Bathurst, he had such an abundance of natural ability that he quickly rose to be an engine driver.[20]

The war taught him much about the divisions in Australian society. The harsh and oppressive treatment of the railway strikers in 1917 planted in his mind the need to do something to protect the working man against the 'boss'. Years of experience in the trade union movement, the Labor Party and the Trades and Labor Council of New South Wales changed him from a utopian socialist to a pragmatist, just as the same years in the 'fiery furnace' of 1916–17 in Australia converted John Curtin from socialism to pragmatism. By the 1920s those who knew Ben Chifley found him a wondrous person, a Labor man with a mantle of tragic grandeur. Those who met him testified that they were in the presence of a remarkable human being. He had a sparkle in the eye: he dropped memorable remarks: he had no need of affectation or poses, or boasts. Those who met him were aware of the goodness of the man. Those who were with him thought about things that mattered, and dropped for a moment their own pettiness and small-mindedness. One of the great loves of his life was to listen to a brass band. He never discarded the puritanism in which he had been instructed in Irish Catholic circles. There was a Jansenist in him, but unlike St Paul he never assigned liars, fornicators and drunkards to Hell. He had a generosity and a magnanimity which suggested to those who knew him that if Ben Chifley were God he would forgive everyone. He had the charisma to draw all manner of men, women and children unto him. As with John Curtin, the hopes, the words, the phrases and the slogans of the utopian socialists never left him. He believed in the light on the hill until the day he died: life taught him the language of the pragmatist.[21]

When he spoke to the electors over the commercial broadcasting stations on the night of 9 August 1934 he spoke in part as a one-time utopian socialist. 'Scores of thousands of Australian men and women', he told the listeners in that unmistakable voice of his, the voice of a man who could and did attract disciples, followers, even worshippers, 'are hardly getting enough to keep body and soul together'. Something must be done, he said, because that would be an investment, as he put it, 'not only in material welfare but in the moral and physical well-being of the nation'. The time was past, he said, when a federal government could adopt a Micawber-like attitude and wait for something to turn up to waft away the Depression. He wanted Australians to face up to 'the afflictions of many thousands of our people'.

[20] *S.M.H.*, 10 August 1934; L. F. Crisp, *Ben Chifley* (London, 1961), pp. 1–3.
[21] Crisp, op. cit., pp. 6–10, 11–22.

But Ben Chifley, like John Curtin and many others of those fashioned by 1916–17, was a pragmatist—a vote-winner for the Australian Labor Party. The pragmatist spoke of what Labor would do. The light on the hill was both an inspiration and a source of sadness, the reason why he and John Curtin looked as though they were carrying some sorrow, some loss in their hearts about which they were not able to speak to anyone. It was the cross they had to bear.[22]

While Ben Chifley was campaigning in New South Wales John Curtin was saying the same sort of thing in Fremantle. Curtin the pragmatist has taken over from Curtin the crusader for better things for humanity. A valiant champion for Labor now displayed his solid grounding in economic knowledge. Joe Lyons, another man who had in the days of his youth and innocence in the wilds of north-western Tasmania drawn inspiration from the utopian socialists and the encyclical *Rerum Novarum* by Pope Leo XIII, spoke with pride on the night of 13 August of his role in cleaning up the mess left by two factions of the Labor Party—the Federal Labor Party under Scullin in Canberra, and the State Labor Party of New South Wales under Lang. A one-time Labor man spoke of how he had redeemed capitalist society in Australia, laid the foundations of recovery, and imposed an order on the chaos left by the Labor Governments. For the rest Lyons spoke like a plumber who had just plugged the leaks in the capitalist pipe the Labor plumbers had punctured. The *Workers' Weekly* snorted at all this tinkering and plumbing. The U.A.P., the Country Party and the Labor Party were all the same. They were all offering 'quack recipes'. And communists would draw the workers away from 'the treacherous policies of reformism': they would win over the masses to the struggle against capitalist society and the struggle against imperialist war and fascism.[23]

The workers of Australia displayed the same inertia as in the past. So firm was the indifference of the people, so strong their disinclination to attend meetings or party rallies that the press summed up the campaign as 'lifeless'. Lyons remained confident that the people wished to go in the direction he had indicated in 1931. On election eve—14 September 1934—Jimmy Scullin warned the electors that if there were a U.A.P./Country Party coalition after the election then the people would see a return of the class government they had known under the Bruce–Page Government. But Jimmy Scullin did not present any alternative. He spoke of a Labor tariff, of the protection of secondary industry, of a reform of the Constitution to give the Commonwealth Parliament sovereign powers. The audience sang 'For he's a jolly good fellow'. Labor leaders did not even arouse the people to sing a rebel chorus, let alone raise a rebel flag.[24]

[22] *S.M.H.*, 10 August 1934; *Westralian Worker*, 7 September 1934.
[23] *S.M.H.*, 14 August 1934; *Workers' Weekly*, 14 September 1934.
[24] *Age*, 15 September 1934.

By Monday 17 September it was clear that the U.A.P. and the Country Party had won a clear victory over Federal Labor and State Labor (i.e., Lang Labor). After the polls were all declared the U.A.P. had twenty-eight seats, the Country Party fourteen, the Liberal–Country Party five, Federal Labor eighteen and State Labor nine. The conservatives were delighted. The people have again rejected the 'wild cat' proposals of Labor: Australia's good name has been preserved in the eyes of the world. Labor has paid the just price for sacrificing its old ideals. The *Australian Worker* was not dismayed. The defeat, they said, was only 'a temporary repulse'. They took comfort from the fact that nearly one-half of the people of Australia 'cast their votes against the Money Power'. True, the people were still deluded by the lies of the capitalist press. But presently the people would wake up: they would 'rub their eyes and see things as they are with a stark vividness'. When it happened, it would be 'goodbye to Money Power and its political puppets in Australia'. The Communist Party remained incurably optimistic: a basis had been laid, they believed, for 'bigger things in the near future', for further strides towards proletarian dictatorship and socialism. They felt heartened.[25]

John Curtin won the seat of Fremantle by a majority of 1028 after the distribution of the preferences of an Independent. Bob Menzies won the seat of Kooyong by an overwhelming majority. The two men of destiny now faced each other across the table in the House of Representatives. Bob Menzies, it was said, would be a welcome change to a Party 'so ill-furnished with political brains', and, in the words of the *Bulletin*, so 'ordinary'. Bob Menzies would be the man to replace that 'tired, dull old man', Joe Lyons. They were all honourable men, all worthy men, but of a dullness so deep no one could fathom it. Australia now belonged, not to the brave and daring, but to the dull. That maverick from the lovely Brindabella valley, Miles Franklin, told Nettie Palmer Australia had urgent need of honest, courageous and wise men like Joseph Furphy, who stood out 'like an Eyre's [*sic*] Rock in an arid and featureless landscape'. Lyons' team was made up mainly of mediocrities, a coalition of the Mr Dry-As-Dusts from the suburbs and some 'cockies' from the bush.

On 10 October Lyons announced the names of the new Government. The same U.A.P. men were there to govern Australia, in the world after the Night of the Long Knives in Germany, the sabre-rattling of the new German Chancellor, Herr Hitler, the rise of Japan, and the awakening of Chinese peasants in millions to fight under the Red Flag. G. F. Pearce was Minister for External

[25] *Age*, 17 September 1934; *S.M.H.*, 17 September 1934; *Australasian*, 22 September 1934; Colin A. Hughes and B. D. Graham, *A Handbook of Australian Government and Politics 1890–1964* (Canberra, 1968), p. 351; *Australian Worker*, 19 September 1934; *Workers' Weekly*, 21 September 1934.

Affairs; the Party hack, Archdale Parkhill, was Minister for Defence; the elderly Billy Hughes was Vice-President of the Executive Council, and the worthy but ever so dull Senator A. J. McLachlan was Postmaster General. The Attorney-General was R. G. ('Bob') Menzies, a man who found it difficult to hold his tongue in the presence of mediocrities. T. W. ('Tommy') White, a man with an eye for communists and all seditious people, was Minister for Trade and Customs. The ambitious R. G. Casey was Assistant Treasurer, J. S. ('Josh') Francis and H. S. Gullett were Ministers without Portfolio. Australia, the *Bulletin* said, had a Government which threatened to shut out the ideas of the rest of the world, a Government which seemed determined to make Australia like its 'smuggest suburban constituency', a Government with no higher aim than to make Australia a country of people fashioned in the mental and social images of Kooyong.[26]

Australians were soon to learn what a glorious thing it was to be a royal duke. Prince Henry, Duke of Gloucester, was coming to preside over the celebrations organized to commemorate the founding of the first British settlement in Melbourne in 1834. The Duke, it was said, would teach Australians two truths. He would teach them what that wise man Stanley Bruce had said: 'The day the monarchy goes, the British Empire falls apart. Without a British Empire Australia was doomed'. He would teach them by example the 'ready adaptability of the British Crown to the democratic tendency of the times'. Australians would learn that the Duke, like other members of the Royal Family, was a people's man. The Fairy Prince of their dreams was approaching, bringing with him an air of gaiety and rejoicing. There were many excitements to come. There would be a Centenary Air Race from England to Australia, 'the greatest race in history'. Australians were brimful of gratitude. They were ready to yield to the Royal Duke 'Australia's heart'.[27]

The matrons of Toorak, South Yarra, Vaucluse, Wahroonga, and other parts of Australia where the inhabitants saw themselves as being a bit above the ordinary, were busy at their dressmakers. Wives extracted promises from their husbands to pay for new dresses for all the royal occasions. Daughters were measured for 'fetching fittings', the Duke being known in advance as a man who always asked the prettiest woman in the room for at least two dances. There would be a State Ball in Melbourne, a State Ball in King's Hall, Canberra, and a State Ball in Sydney. They would be the most brilliant functions ever to be held in Australia. Mothers who wished their

[26] *West Australian*, 27 September 1934; Miles Franklin to Nettie Palmer, 24 September 1934, Palmer Papers, Series 1, Box 7, Folder 60; *Bulletin*, 19 September 1934; *S.M.H.*, 11 October 1934; *C'wealth Gazette*, 12 October 1934; *Table Talk*, 26 July 1934; *To-day*, 1 September, 1 November 1934.

[27] *S.M.H.*, 4, 5 October 1934; *Table Talk*, 18 October 1934.

daughters to be introduced to Prince Charming were advised to communicate with his military and official secretary who would forward full instructions to them. Prince Charming would be protected against too much 'fervent hospitality'. Handshaking would be avoided. When guests met Prince Charming the Prince would bow. Prince Charming would also dedicate the Shrine of Remembrance in Melbourne and the Anzac Memorial in Sydney. There was to be gaiety: there was to be solemnity. There would be fun and games: there would also be moments when the people would worship at their shrine.

The communists and the Militant Minority men and women in the Australian Labor Party and the trade union movement were not impressed. As they saw it, the royal visit was a 'marvellous smoke screen for military preparations for yet another world war'. Look, they said, at the list of guests invited by the Victorian Centenary Committee: Lord Milne, mechanization expert of the British army, Sir Maurice Hankey, secretary of the Committee of Imperial Defence, and Sir John Cadman, a British army expert during the world war. The Duke and all the celebrations were a decoy to take the eyes of the people off the real business of the day. That was the discussion of imperial defence. Australia was to be tricked again by the cunning British into fighting in an imperialist war. The Poet Laureate, John Masefield, another apologist for the British Empire, would also be a guest of the Victorian Centenary Committee. He has likened the Anzacs at Gallipoli to the Greek heroes at the siege of Troy and to the English sea-dogs of the sixteenth century. Beware all that mystical nonsense. Beware, Australians, of what the British were up to. To counter the show to be put on by 'Yarraside' and their hangers-on, the communists and the Militant Minority proposed to hold an All-Australian Congress against War and Fascism, beginning in Melbourne on 10 November. One of their invited guests was Egon Kisch, a Czechoslovakian journalist and author, well known in Left-wing circles for his speeches and writings against war and fascism. Another was Gerald Griffin, a New Zealander. The Duke and the men in high places would glorify war at the Shrine in Melbourne but they would preach the gospel of peace. Theirs was the righteous cause.[28]

To the delight of the conservatives and those of like mind the Duke quickly endeared himself to the Australian people. The people of Perth experienced a wild ecstasy at the very sight of the Duke. On the trans-continental journey from Perth to Adelaide the Duke showed he had some of the qualities of the Australian bushman. At Ooldea he made a smart figure, dressed in riding breeches and a blue open-necked shirt, as he mounted an upstanding bay

[28] *S.M.H.*, 11 October 1934; *Table Talk*, 18 October 1934; Egon Erwin Kisch, *Australian Landfall* (Melbourne, 1969, first published 1937), pp. vii–viii; Joyce Manton, *The Centenary Prepares War* (Melbourne, 1934).

horse and cantered off into the bush. Aborigines, with painted bodies, sticks through their noses, and spectacular head-dresses of flowers sang hymns to him, after which they shouted their welcome to 'Big fella King's piccaninny'. The original tenants of the deserts of Australia have given proof of their loyalty and affection. The Duke was seen earnestly talking to Daisy Bates. Now it was Adelaide's turn, and then Melbourne's turn.[29]

Adelaide was dressed in a manner befitting the majesty of the occasion. There, too, the people went wild with excitement. Melbourne went in for an extravaganza for days. For weeks before boat-loads of people had been disembarking from ships, passengers arrived by train, men and women and children bumped over country roads in their cars to catch a sight of Prince Charming. On 18 October at Station Pier, and along the route from Station Pier to Government House, cheering crowds greeted him with spontaneous displays of loyalty and affection. The trees were decorated with flags, banners and shields: street poles were painted for the occasion. Gay bunting gave an impression of opulence and devotion. Hats and handkerchiefs went flying into the air in fervent demonstrations of good will. Men and women embraced as the Duke's cavalcade continued its triumphal progress. The royal presence was having the desired effect. Fraternization and a spirit of good will were obliterating class distinctions and differences of creed.

On the steps of Parliament House in Melbourne, dressed in military uniform, and surrounded by generals, admirals, members of the British aristocracy and knights of the Dominions, the Duke read out a special message from the King to the people of Victoria. The King was pleased to send his son to join them in commemorating the centenary of the settlement of Victoria. The occasion, the King said, would stir the hearts of all interested in Empire history. The Duke promised at another time to pay his tribute to the pioneers responsible for the settlement of Victoria and the foundation of the great city of Melbourne. 'I have much pleasure', he added, 'in declaring the Centenary celebrations open'. That night Melbourne was transformed into a fairyland by the illuminations and the fireworks.[30]

For days the people were reminded of all the benefits they received as British subjects. The Governor-General reminded Victorians of their good fortune in belonging to a 'world-wide Empire'. The British Government congratulated Melbourne on becoming one of the leading cities of the Empire only one hundred years after it began. On 23 October the House of Representatives agreed on the words of a loyal address to His Royal Highness, saying the people of Australia were proud of the compliment paid to them by the King in sending one of his sons to Australia, and expressing their 'deep affection for and loyalty to the Royal Family'. The Japanese Govern-

[29] *S.M.H.*, 11 October 1934.
[30] *Age*, 19 October 1934; *Argus*, 19 October 1934.

'DOWN IN THAT POOR COUNTRY
NO PAUPER WAS I'

John Shaw Neilson
Photograph in National Library, Canberra

THE PRIZES AND THE BLANKS IN THE HUMAN LOTTERY

Nettie Palmer: 'Why did all this happen to me?'

John Joseph Ambrose Curtin towards the end of life's fitful fevers

Robert Gordon Menzies with his own people

Photographs in National Library, Canberra

ment sent a message of good will to 'one of the principal members of the Empire' and a 'great nation in the Pacific.'[31]

The Empire was the great good thing: the King reigned over the Empire. So may God save the King, and let him reign over us, happy and glorious. The Centenary Air Race from England to Melbourne was further evidence of the advantages in being British. Sir Macpherson Robertson gave the prize money. Victoria was giving the British the chance to prove to the world their superiority in the air. Victoria was sponsoring 'the greatest race in history'. There has been the usual bitchiness between the aviators. 'Smithy' has been nasty about Amy Johnson (now Amy Mollison), saying a woman did not have 'the endurance of a man'. But the Royal Family was as usual gracious and supportive. The Prince of Wales was at the Mildenhall aerodrome to watch the planes take off in the first light of dawn on 20 October. But the militants of Labor did not share the prevailing enthusiasm. Australians, they said, were again the dupes of the British and lackeys of British imperialism.[32]

The British won the race in the air. On 22 October C. W. A. Scott and Captain Campbell Black landed at Darwin, at 8.45 a.m., after a journey of fifty-two hours, thirty-four minutes. The Dutch and the Germans have been defeated. On 23 October Scott and Black crossed the finishing line in Melbourne. The British have triumphed. The Fairy Prince told the two winners of the Centenary Air Race theirs was 'a wonderful achievement in a British machine'. England was now only three days away from Australia. Soon isolation and material backwardness, the products of geography and history, would be overcome. Man has triumphed over earthly limitations. The days of the mammoth luxurious passenger ships were drawing to a close. People would move from continent to continent in the air. The British, thanks to Victorian generosity and enterprise, have staked their claim to be the leaders in the intense international competition for traffic in the air. Australia had the 'sure shield of the British Crown' in an age of war and revolution. No one foresaw that the aeroplane might render obsolete the role of the British in the defence of Australia.[33]

Melbourne was having its moment of glory. It might have been one of the cities of the British Isles—Melbourne was just like England. The painted pomp and the showy splendours of a British aristocratic society were seen each day in the streets of the city. The city on the site chosen by that drunkard and Don Juan, John Batman, one hundred years before has become sodden with social snobbery. Captains and naval officers were seen walking the Block and 'hawking the bod', as the wits called it, in the la-di-da parts of

[31] *Age*, 18, 19 October 1934; *C'wealth P.D.*, 23 October 1934, vol. 145, p. 34.
[32] *Age*, 20 October 1934; *S.M.H.*, 20 October 1934.
[33] *Age*, 23 October 1934; *S.M.H.*, 23, 24 October 1934.

Melbourne. Dignitaries, speaking in natural English accents as distinct from the pseudo-English accents of aspirants to high social places, sat down in the shops and risked eating a meat pie, not knowing the local habit of dousing the pie in a bath of tomato sauce. Taxis were making a fortune. Verse-mongers rejoiced to find 'Prince Henry' rhymed happily with 'centenary'. The poet John Masefield lectured to young University students on English poetry. Gifted young men and women heard that to be English, unattainable though it was for an Australian, was the true goal of human aspirations.[34]

Prince Charming continued to say all the right things. At the State dinner in his honour in Canberra on 24 October, he told the assembled dignitaries he saw Australia as a country of vast possibilities, a country with a glorious climate, with a warm-hearted and sincere people, and a young generation which was being educated in the best ideals of loyalty and service. The Empire, he continued, was now 'a partnership of brothers', each directing the fortunes of his own house and all taking 'counsel together for the welfare of the family'. Joe Lyons was just as fulsome. He was glad the Duke had seen with his own eyes the 'expressions of fervent devotion to all the highest traditions of the human race'. The Duke, Joe Lyons added, had come to a continent where the people spoke 'one language—our mother tongue'; cherished 'the same ideals and traditions', took pride in 'a common ancestry', and rejoiced in 'the promise of a common destiny under the hand of Almighty God'. In Sydney, where the era of the British had begun, the expressions of loyalty and devotion and gratitude were just as fervent.[35]

The bishops and priests of the Catholic Church warned the members of their congregations that no festival, no ceremony, could overcome human evil. The sins of envy, hatred, malice, pride, covetousness and the lusts of the flesh would remain. Modern paganism taught the bleak doctrine that life led nowhere: modern paganism banished the superstitions of Easter Morn: it brought only 'the tidings of a great disaster'. Australians did not heed that warning. The people went on with the royal carnival. Bob Menzies bubbled over with confidence. On 2 November in the House of Representatives he wound up the debate on the Address in Reply. He was brilliant: he was witty: he was charming. The members were astounded at the ability of the man, the range of his mind, and the breadth of his knowledge. Bob Menzies was triumphant. Ted Holloway interjected: 'The honorable gentleman himself has been on a winner sometimes'. Bob Menzies: 'Very frequently, particularly when opposed to the honorable member for Melbourne Ports'. There was laughter. Bob Menzies joined in. Once again Bob Menzies has shown

[34] *Australasian*, 27 October 1934; personal memories of speeches by John Masefield at Trinity College, Melbourne, October 1934.

[35] *S.M.H.*, 25 October 1934.

what manner of man he was. Humpty Dumpty has sat on a high wall: Humpty Dumpty would have a great fall.[36]

The banquets and the balls for Prince Charming continued. British army officers saluted each other in the streets of Melbourne. The gaiety and the laughter went on. But not everyone was amused. The militants of Labor said again that the people were being deluded and cheated. The militants were about to start their counter-show. The people of Australia were being encouraged to sing 'God Save the King'. But on the P. & O. liner *Strathaird* in November there was a passenger who gave a different salute. He clenched his right fist, raised his right arm, and said: '*Rotfront*' (Red Front). He was Egon Kisch, the guest of the All-Australian Congress against War and Fascism. Gerald Griffin, having failed a dictation test in Dutch on 3 November, has been sent back to New Zealand. Now it was Kisch's turn. When the liner berthed at Fremantle on 6 November, Commonwealth officers went on board to tell Kisch his entry into Australia was forbidden. The Commonwealth Government had information from the British Government about Kisch. Bob Menzies advised Eric Harrison, Minister for the Interior since 12 October, to declare Kisch a 'prohibited immigrant', i.e., a person 'declared by the Minister to be in his opinion, from information received from the government of the United Kingdom or of any other part of the British Dominions or from any foreign government, through official or diplomatic channels, undesirable as an inhabitant of, or visitor to, the Commonwealth'. Journalists asked him if he was a communist. He replied: 'I come as an anti-Fascist, and as a militant opponent of war. There are members of all progressive parties in the movement against war and fascism, millions of communists, many scholars, and writers such as Henri Barbusse, Romain Rolland, and others'. At a time, he added, when British military chiefs were seeking support for their re-armament plans, and the British Prime Minister was making no secret of Britain's intention to re-arm, it was not seemly or wise to have all these banquets for a royal duke.

Kisch was Czech by birth, German by speech, and cosmopolitan by inclination. His newspaper articles and books have already won him the distinction of being known as 'a journalist of the highest order'. The titles of his books were a guide to his political convictions: *Zaren, Popen, Bolschewiken*, *Asien Gründlich Verändert* and *Paradies Amerika*. Kisch was an exuberant man, a man who would at one moment kiss a woman fair and square on the mouth, and the next clench the fist, and greet comrades with an enthusiastic 'Red Front'. The Congress against War and Fascism has made a brilliant choice for one of their guests. Kisch was the right man for the occasion. He was histrionic: he was a brilliant mass speaker: he liked to be lionized: he loved

[36] *Advocate*, 8 February, 5 April, 12 July 1934; *C'wealth P.D.*, 2 November 1934, vol. 145, pp. 164–8; *Argus*, 3 November 1934.

the applause of a crowd. He had a long experience in not telling people in power things they wanted to know.[37]

The men in power must be vigilant. There must be no wavering. On 7 November Joe Lyons announced he had reconstructed his Ministry. To ensure political stability he and Page agreed to form a coalition government on the same terms as the coalition between Bruce and Page. Page was to be Minister for Commerce and Deputy Prime Minister, Tom Paterson the Minister for the Interior, and H. V. C. Thorby and J. A. J. Hunter Ministers without Portfolio. A political party which polled 12½ per cent of the votes cast at the preceding election was to have a powerful voice in the government of Australia. The time has come for Bob Menzies to hold his tongue about members of the Country Party. The times were out of joint. The 'comfortable classes' must preserve their unity to have a chance to set them right. Each day there was a crisis.[38]

As the *Strathaird* pitched and rolled in the Great Australian Bight three hundred thousand people gathered in the Domain in Melbourne on 11 November to see the Duke dedicate the Shrine of Remembrance. It was the anniversary of Armistice Day. The Master of Ceremonies, Professor G. S. Browne, asked the people not to cheer when the Duke arrived. A mood of exaltation and devotion settled over the vast crowd, as the Duke and his party slowly made their way to the official dais. The sound of the trumpet broke the silence: drums rolled. The people sang the hymns, 'Nearer my God to Thee' and 'Lead kindly light'. For on all solemn occasions the minds of Australians still turned to acceptance and resignation. The Senior Chaplain of the Forces offered a prayer. The Premier of Victoria, Sir Stanley Argyle, made a spirited reading of an Ode specially written for the occasion by Rudyard Kipling:

> So long as Memory, Valor and Faith endure
> Let these Stones witness through the years to come,
> How once there was a People fenced secure
> Behind great waters girdling a far home

It was a tribute to brave men:

> Having revealed their Nation in earth's sight
> So long as Sacrifice and Honour stand,
> And their own sun at the hushed hour shall light
> The Shrine of these their Dead!

[37] *West Australian*, 7 November 1934; *Age*, 7 November 1934: Egon Erwin Kisch, *Landung In Australien* (Berlin, n.d.), pp. 1–20; Section 3 (gh) of the Immigration Act, 1901–1925, No. 7 of 1925, *C'wealth Acts*, vol. XXIII, 1925; Joyce Manton, op. cit., foreword by A. T. Yarwood in *Australian Landfall*, p. xiv; Kisch, *Australian Landfall*, p. 29.

[38] *S.M.H.*, 8 November 1934; *Age*, 8 November 1934; *C'wealth Gazette*, 9 November 1934.

It was a tribute from an outsider: it was a voice from abroad. The Australian hunger for approval from the British has not diminished. No Australian was invited to address the multitude on the tragic grandeur of human life in the ancient continent. Sir Stanley Argyle invited another voice from abroad to dedicate the Shrine. The Duke spoke of the Shrine as a token of the people's gratitude to those who had fought for them. Their sacrifice imposed a duty on those who came after them. Those who followed after these noble men and women should realize that it was only by giving such service that Australians could justify their enjoyment of the security, freedom and happiness made possible by such sacrifice. He then dedicated the Shrine 'To the Glory of God and in grateful memory of the men and women of this State who served in the Great War, and especially of those who fell'. There was another long roll on the drums, another fanfare of trumpets. Choirs and people then sang Kipling's 'Recessional', ending with the enigmatic words:

> Lord God of Hosts, be with us yet
> Lest we forget, lest we forget.

It was like the words from Psalm 137 which moved the listeners to tears during the American Civil War: 'If I forget thee, O Jerusalem'. But there was a difference. The Southerners knew what they meant by the word 'forget'. No Australian on that day tried to put into words what Australians should not forget. Perhaps it was not to forget they were British. Perhaps it was not to forget the qualities which had made them what they believed they were, those qualities of the bushman and the digger. But there was something more, something for which words were inadequate to convey 'what the heart doth say', something which made a lump in the throat. Dark clouds obscured the sun as the brass bands played Chopin's 'Funeral March'. All joined in singing 'God save the King'. Returned soldiers led the cheering as the Duke and his party departed. Victorians have erected their memorial to those brave men who heard 'the bugles of England blowing o'er the sea'.[39]

The day after the three hundred thousand sang those moving words: 'Lest we forget, lest we forget', the liner *Strathaird* with Kisch on board berthed at Station Pier, Port Melbourne. When Kisch appeared on one of the decks he raised his clenched fist and called out 'Red Front'. The small band of followers replied, 'Red Front'. They were like the grain of mustard seed which might one day grow into a great tree, and carried a banner bearing the words, 'Kisch Must Land'. Kisch called out: 'I want you'. Like the Duke, Kisch, too, was a voice from abroad. Lawyers for Kisch challenged in the Practice Court the power of the Commonwealth to refuse Kisch permission

[39] *Age*, 12 November 1934; *Australasian*, 17 November 1934.

to land. The Judge, Sir William Irvine, no friend to Labor, upheld the Commonwealth. But, said some, this law was not the people's law. The people must show their strength.

The following day, 13 November, a group of believers in the Red Front gathered on the wharf beside the *Strathaird.* Kisch appeared on the deck, to emotional scenes of waving, singing and shouting. His supporters sang the 'Internationale'. Impulsive as ever, Kisch jumped from the deck to the wharf. A policeman asked him if he had injured himself. Kisch said 'No', but he could not walk. He had broken his leg. He was carried back on board. Before the liner sailed for Sydney Kisch expressed great bitterness at having travelled 12 000 miles to be treated like this.[40]

On 14 November in the motion to adjourn the House of Representatives, Frank Brennan, Labor member for Batman, a lawyer and a well-known defender of civil liberties, said it was a mark of cowardice and weakness to exclude a man from Australia because one differed with his opinions. He accused Bob Menzies of 'sacrificing accuracy and a sense of responsibility' in his 'insatiable hunger for notoriety and the applause of the press claqueurs'. Bob Menzies had no difficulty in ignoring such abuse. Australia, he replied, like every civilized country, had a perfect right to indicate whether an alien would or would not be admitted to these shores. Parliament had already declared that any person who advocated the overthrow by violence of the established government of the Commonwealth or any State, or of any other civilized country, or of all forms of law, or who advocated the abolition of organized government, could be declared a prohibited immigrant. That, he declared with the confidence he always displayed when acting as an advocate for some higher power such as God or the law, was 'not an unfair way to describe the doctrines and attitudes of those . . . known to-day as communists'. The presence of this gentleman, he added, was not needed in a free self-governing country such as Australia, which had been able to achieve a very high degree of happiness and prosperity without the intervention of the 'subversive views' for which Kisch stood. He stood for parliamentary government. Raising his eyebrows in the gesture which always foreshadowed the crushing of opponents, he said he wanted to know whether the members of the Labor Party also stood for parliamentary government. He was not saying they did not, oh, dear me no, but he wanted to hear them say what they stood for. 'Can anyone pretend', he asked, as his eyes swept over the whole Chamber, 'that revolution involves anything else but force and bloodshed?'[41]

[40] Kisch, op. cit., pp. 53–5; *Age*, 13, 14 November 1934; *Argus*, 14 November 1934; *Australian Worker*, 14 November 1934.

[41] *C'wealth P.D.*, 14 November 1934, vol. 145, pp. 254–8; *Age*, 15 November 1934; *S.M.H.*, 15 November 1934.

Some Labor members of Parliament, some University professors, some writers and clergymen who believed Christ, if He were to come back to earth, would be on the side of the people, formed committees to protest against the exclusion of Kisch. The *Australian Worker* called on the workers to stop the imperialists 'yoking' our youth to the war chariots of Europe. 'Beware, Australians', they wrote, the British were about to blow the war bugles again. The communists called for a united front. Dear, kind Professor Walter Murdoch, friend and confidant of Mr Deakin and the Brookes family, biographer of Alfred Deakin, no spouter of revolutionary slogans he, said the exclusion of an author of international repute who was visiting Australia as a guest of the anti-militarists was a disgrace to Australia. His colleague, Professor R. Beasley, a lawyer, said the Government had paid a 'sorry compliment' to Australians by showing it did not consider they could think for themselves. Bishop E. H. Burgmann of Goulburn said a political system which feared public criticism had no healthy future. Public meetings were held. Rousing speeches were made. Australian democracy and the liberties of the people, speakers said, were under attack. Conservatives were threatening Australian ideals of mateship and equality. Communists fraternized with bourgeois intellectuals, artists and Labor back-benchers. The self-appointed spiritual popes of Australia advocated the liberties of the individual.[42]

A new hero of the people walked on to the stage of public life. He was Herbert Vere Evatt. When the *Strathaird* arrived in Sydney Harbour lawyers for Kisch asked the High Court whether Kisch was a prohibited immigrant within the meaning of the Immigration Act. The case was heard before Mr Justice Evatt on 15 November. The trade unions held a Kisch rally on the wharf. The *Workers' Weekly* called on all democratic Australians to demand entry into Australia for all those opposed to war. 'Down with those who would conscript the Australian toilers for new massacres overseas'. On that day Herbert Vere Evatt sat in judgement on Robert Gordon Menzies. A time would come when Bob Menzies would sit in judgement on Bert Evatt. For things would go hardly with Evatt: a time would come when the eye of pity would be more appropriate than the merciless words of a victorious politician. But not on 15 November. For on that day Evatt was moving into the flowering time of his life.[43]

Evatt and Menzies had much in common. They were born in the same year—Evatt on 30 April and Menzies on 20 December 1894. They were both country boys who went down to the city in search of fame and glory, Evatt from Maitland and Menzies from Jeparit. They were both scholarship boys

[42] *Workers' Weekly*, 16 November 1934.

[43] Foreword to *Australian Landfall*, pp. xii-xiii; *S.M.H.*, 15, 16 November 1934; *Workers' Weekly*, 9, 16 November 1934.

who performed brilliantly at school and at the University—Evatt at Sydney and Menzies at Melbourne. They were both interested in sport—Evatt in Rugby League and cricket and Menzies in Australian Rules football and cricket. They were both observers rather than players—Evatt on the Sydney Hill, and Menzies at Princes Park, Carlton, and the Melbourne Cricket Ground. They were alike, and yet worlds apart. Evatt was a left-hander with the bat—a 'molly dook'—and thereby, said the cruel, there surely hangs a tale. Menzies was a trier with bat and ball but what he lacked in those skills he more than compensated for by his witty talk and his passionate love for the romance, the glory and the magic moments when one half of a huge crowd shouts, 'Here comes Carlton'. Evatt saw Stan McCabe, the boy from Mosman, hook Larwood for four. Menzies saw Percy Chapman field in the covers, and Walter Hammond cover drive Jack Gregory for four.

There were differences. In 1916 Menzies saw the slaughter of Australian soldiers in France as 'valour for the right'. Evatt was a volunteer who had been rejected for military service. By 1916 Menzies had dedicated his life and his vast talents to the service of the King, Country and Empire, and the preservation of the established social order. Evatt has put his talents at the service of those who believed in the capacity of human beings for better things. He believed the Australian Labor movement could and would create the Kingdom of God on earth. Menzies also believed in the Kingdom of God, but that would be in the life of the world to come. Here we must make what we can of frail mortal flesh. Evatt wanted the whole of humanity to take a seat at the great banquet of life. Menzies believed only 'chaps' were worthy of a seat at that table.

Menzies had a great hunger to love and be loved. Evatt knew love. Evatt had an 'eternal mate'. During the war he fell in love with Mary Alice Sheffer, 'a little American girl', who had come to Australia during her childhood. They met outside a picture show. It was a case of 'elective affinities'. Their ardour for each other never waned. They were to love each other until that day of tragic grandeur in Canberra on 4 November 1965, when Bishop Clements preached the funeral sermon for Bert Evatt on the text, 'Judge not'. They wrote passionate love letters to each other when they were apart. 'Darling', he wrote to her in the early 1920s, 'I need you and want you . . . Dear sweet love, I send you my heart's love and devotion, & a thousand kisses for your heart'. And she to him, '. . . never a person could guess that you are a dear passionate lover, full of Romance and glory and tenderness . . . Darling mine, I love you, love you. Didi'. She gave him the glory.

He wanted all human beings to live in love and fellowship with each other. But nature had played tricks with him. Menzies had the Scots Presbyterian contempt for liars. The words of the *Book of Common Prayer* could be applied to Evatt: there were moments when the truth was not in him. There were also moments of rage when an evil spirit was upon him. When the evil spirit was upon him Mary Alice alone could do for him what David's playing on the harp did for Saul. The sight of her face would cause the evil spirit to depart from him, and he was comforted. He was a Joseph Furphy man: a believer in God, a believer in man, and a believer in Australia. He agreed with Furphy: '*Aut Australia Aut Nihil*'. He agreed with Henry Lawson, Australians must cultivate the 'Young Tree Green' to replace the 'Old Dead Tree' of British Imperialism in Australia. Menzies was a passionate believer in British civilization. Evatt believed that the history of Australia could teach Australians who they were and what they might be. Evatt was an internationalist: Menzies believed in a strong British Empire and a strong British navy. Evatt was drawn to the enlargers of life—the writers, the painters, some teachers, some parsons and some priests, who wanted all human beings to have life and have it more abundantly. He believed in the universal embrace: yet in moments of insecurity he talked and acted as though enemies were plotting his destruction.

He was the hope of all men and women of good will. Eleanor and Eric Dark thought he was a national treasure. Vance and Nettie Palmer expected great things from him. Men of promise such as Brian Fitzpatrick, Sam Atyeo and Geoffrey Sawer took their troubles to him. All those who looked to the day when Australia had overcome the giant of British philistinism, suburban smugness and grovelling to the English welcomed him as their leader. In such circles his name was mentioned with awe, a reverent hush or an extravagant gush. Yet at times he behaved like a little child. He had the talents and the ambition to take him to the high places he hungered after all his life: he also threw the tantrums and told the fibs of a little child. Menzies believed that in public life a man must tell the truth, the whole truth and nothing but the truth. Backsliders must be exposed. Circumstances would give Menzies his chance: Evatt, one of Australia's most gifted native sons, would become one of his whipping boys.[44]

But not on that day in Sydney on 15 November 1934. On that day Evatt and what he stood for were the victors. In his judgement on the declaration of Kisch as a prohibited immigrant he said that a declaration by a Minister in which he merely referred to 'another part of the British Dominions' as the source of his information, without specifying either the Dominion intended, or that the information was received by way of a Government declaration, was not a declaration within Section 5.3 (gh) of the Immigration Act, 1901–30. Evatt was the hero of the Labor movement, of all those who professed to

[44] Kylie Tennant, *Evatt: Politics and Justice* (Sydney, 1970), pp. 1–33; H. V. Evatt to Mary Alice Evatt, n.d., probably in early 1920s, and Mary Alice Evatt to H. V. Evatt, n.d., probably 1932, H. V. Evatt Papers, Family Correspondence, Flinders University Library, Bedford Park, Adelaide, S.A.; personal observations at funeral of H. V. Evatt, Canberra, 4 November 1965; personal talks with H. V. Evatt and A. A. Calwell, Canberra, 1954–58.

believe in democracy and the liberties of the individual, and all those who despised suburban smugness and conformism in Australia. Menzies was confirmed as the villain obstructing human progress in Australia. At the University parties, and in those places in Australia where the improvers of humanity seemed to need vast quantities of beer to make life bearable, a new song was heard—to the tune of 'Jesus loves me':

> Menzies loves us, this we know
> For the *Argus* tells us so
> The unemployed to him belong
> They are weak
> But Bob is strong
>
> Yes Menzies loves us
> Yes Menzies loves us
> Yes Menzies loves us
> The *Argus* tells us so.

At the University Menzies had been a figure of fun for his opponents. Now on that wider stage of public life in which he so desperately coveted admiration and respect, he has become a target for the mockers in the Labor movement. He saw himself as a man with a mission: his political opponents threatened to cut him down to the level of a joke. Evatt was like Sarastro in Mozart's *Magic Flute*: he was leading Australians away from ignorance and superstition, out of the darkness into the light. Menzies was like Wotan in Wagner's *Twilight of the Gods*, a man doomed to destruction for defending an anachronistic way of life. But in time Evatt would know the darkness, and Menzies the light. They would both be Time's fool.[45]

The anti-war fighters gave Kisch a tumultuous welcome when he came ashore at Sydney on 16 November. Kisch told them he detected the hand of Herr Hitler, the butcher of the Night of the Long Knives, behind the actions of the Federal Government. Labor supporters, democrats, civil liberties men, and all the improvers of humanity asked in shocked surprise how such a thing could happen in democratic Australia, the country where freedom was sacred. Menzies did not bow before the storm of public anger and indignation. Menzies said he was mystified by the report of the judgment of Mr Justice Evatt. Menzies was not a man to admit any error of his own. As he saw it, Kisch was a threat to the liberties of the people. Kisch was a threat to organized government as he understood it. Another reason must be found for his exclusion. Kisch would be given a dictation test of fifty words, a test he could not pass. This presented problems. Kisch was a linguist. The advisers

[45] The King against Carter *ex parte* Kisch, *C'wealth Law Reports*, vol. 52, pp. 221–33; *Workers' Weekly*, 23 November 1934.

had the answer: Kisch could not pass a test in Gaelic. The test was administered. An Australian police officer read the passage. Kisch failed. An order for his deportation was drafted.[46]

For weeks a legal battle was waged between the lawyers for Kisch and the lawyers for the Commonwealth. The battle was like the description of a professional wrestling match over Station 3DB, with the announcer shouting in mounting hysteria: 'He can't get out of it, he can't get out of it', and then in feigned surprise whispering hoarsely, 'He's out of it'. So it was in the wrestle between the lawyers. There were arguments in the police court, arguments in the High Court, arguments in Chambers. The lawyers had their satisfactions—their indulgence in their favourite sport. Outside the courts and the legal chambers another battle was raging—the battle for the minds of the people. On the Saturday morning of 17 November, Kisch appeared clad in pyjamas and overcoat in the Police Court where he was charged with having failed to write out a dictation test within the meaning of the Immigration Act 1901–1930. That day the lawyers split hairs over who should have the body of Egon Erwin Kisch.

The following day, Sunday 18 November, the anti-war fighters, led by the Communist Party, held a meeting in the Sydney Domain to mobilize the Australian people against war. Thousands gathered around the rostrum. Within minutes of the opening of the meeting the Chairman, Rev. A. Rivett, collapsed, and died soon afterwards. Some wanted the meeting to be cancelled. One comrade said: 'Lenin would have ordered the meeting to go on if he had collapsed'. So the speeches went on. Kisch arrived, and sat among the masses of people on the lorry. He waved a bundle of red poppies and clenched his fist and called out 'Red Front'. Later as the lorry drove him back to Macquarie Street he and the crowd sang with gusto the 'Internationale'. Kisch looked very happy. It was a flowering time for him: the people loved him: events have lifted him into the role of a hero of the people.[47]

On 20 November Kisch addressed his supporters in the Australian Hall in Sydney. He was in high spirits. 'My English is broken, my leg is broken', he told them, 'but my heart is not broken'. They loved it. They stood and sang of their determination to 'keep the Red Flag flying here'. An officer of the law arrived and handed Kisch a summons to appear in the Central Police Court to answer the charge that he was a prohibited immigrant. Amid much merriment the summons was offered for Dutch auction. Kisch has united briefly the Communist Party and the Federal Labor Party. Union leaders, A.L.P. officials and leading communists were sitting together on the same platform. But the Lang Labor Party has put a ban on the anti-war movement. Those present felt they were the forerunners of better things. They also felt

[46] *S.M.H.*, 19 November 1934; *Australian Worker*, 21 November 1934.
[47] *Workers' Weekly*, 16 November 1934; *S.M.H.*, 19 November 1934.

embattled. The Chairman warned them there were *agents-provocateurs* in the hall, yes and police officers, too, who were too cowardly to wear their uniforms. Kisch told them how Germany was a great armed camp, that German children were being taught to use hand-grenades and gas-masks, and how from the age of fifteen German boys wore military uniforms and carried swords. Germany was rebuilding her military might. Don't let Sir Maurice Hankey make a bargain with the Australian militarists for your bodies. Don't be fooled by the honour and praise the ruling class now bestowed on the bodies of dead Anzacs or the chauvinism generated by the Duke. Join the movement against War and Fascism. They cheered and stamped and hugged each other, and pledged themselves to the cause.[48]

Meanwhile Prince Charming was delighting the citizens of Tasmania. Everyone loved the Duke. When his special train left Hobart for Launceston on 16 November sustenance workers fired sticks of gelignite as a tribute. The Duke sent them a message of thanks for their novel tribute. On 16 November, when the Duke entered the hall of the High School in Launceston, the children cheered him with a will. Later that day, with the rain pouring down in torrents, the people of Launceston marched four abreast past the Duke. Every man took off his hat as he passed the Duke. The rain was too much for the women. They did not lower their umbrellas. That night the local gentry and others entertained Prince Charming at a ball. The Prince was a bit of a sport. He took the Lady Mayoress (Mrs Holingsworth) in to supper, and had two dances with Miss Isabel Boatwright, daughter of a former Lord Mayor of Launceston.[49]

In Sydney, the welcome was just as fervent. Membership of the New Guard had dwindled when the law and an English Governor and the flight of capital combined, rather than armed force, got rid of the Lang menace. But four hundred surviving members signed a petition to the King asking him to appoint one of his sons as successor to the Governor-General Sir Isaac Isaacs. On 22 November, the day of the Duke's arrival, there was all the usual pageantry, the gala festival by day and the Ball by night. Sydney struck the same note of loyalty to an illustrious Royal House as the other cities and the great Australian outback. But in Sydney, as in Melbourne, there was also solemn work for the Duke: he was there to dedicate the Anzac Memorial in Hyde Park. The Shrine of Remembrance was a secular temple of war, not a temple of peace. The sculptor of the Anzac Memorial, Rayner Hoff, sculpted a stone monument which was neutral. It conveyed to its beholders neither a clear message that war was 'useless travail' and 'the destruction of the flower of the nation's manhood for trivial and selfish ends', nor that war was a

[48] *S.M.H.*, 21, 29 November 1934; *Workers' Weekly*, 16, 23, 30 November, 7 December 1934; *Australian Worker*, 21, 28 November, 5 December 1934.

[49] *S.M.H.*, 17 November 1934; *Examiner* (Launceston), 17 November 1934.

means of glory for those endowed with the manly virtues. The Anzac Memorial in Hyde Park was a strange presence in a great city. It was not a hall for heroes, or evocative of heroic sentiments.[50]

At the unveiling and dedication of the Anzac Memorial on 24 November the principals in the ceremony spoke as though they were there to honour all those loyal sons and daughters of the Empire who had been prepared to make the supreme sacrifice. One hundred thousand people, including twenty to twenty-five thousand troops, stood there in brilliant sunshine to hear speaker after speaker tell the story of a 'great brotherhood and sisterhood of gallant men who proved worthy of the best traditions of the British race in the supreme test of nationhood', those who had given 'the great example of faithfulness and endurance even unto death'. It was a 'corporate fellowship of remembrance'. No words about the 'wide brown land', no words about the 'sunburnt country' and the visions of its people were uttered on that day. No words were carved on the walls of the memorial. Only the stone statues of the soldier, the airman, the sailor and the nurse with their expressionless faces looked down on the passers-by—dumb reminders of something too deep for words. They sang the hymns: 'O God our help in ages past', and 'God of our fathers known of old'. The Duke spoke calmly, deliberately and briefly. At the conclusion of his speech he unveiled the Memorial:

> To the glory of God, and in honoured memory of the men and women of New South Wales who gave their lives, and in gratitude to all who left this State to serve the Empire in the Great War.

The Last Post was sounded, followed by a minute's silence, and then a rousing rendition of the National Anthem.[51]

At the Sydney Domain on the following day, Sunday 25 November 1934, fifteen thousand people heard passionate men call on them to form a united front against the conservatives and the militarists. Supporters of the universal embrace and Schilleresque sentiments about the brotherhood of mankind, clergymen who believed Christ was a Labor man, and writers who thought excesses with the bottle were evidence of their love for life, joined together in cries of horror and outrage at the small-mindedness, stupidity and wickedness of Australian conservatives. It was a day of high comedy. Gerald Griffin, who had been smuggled back into Australia under another name and had been eluding the police by wearing a disguise, gave himself up to the police to shouts of laughter. The communists were making fools of the people in high places. The communists would lead the people on to victory.

[50] *Table Talk*, 22 November 1934; *S.M.H.*, 23 November 1934; *To-day*, 1 August 1934.

[51] *S.M.H.*, 26 November 1934.

These were heady times for those who believed there would be a New Jerusalem in Australia. The communists had the confidence of men who believed they were performing the historic role of speeding up 'the inevitable end of capitalist exploitation'.

In the afterglow of the enthusiasm, a magistrate considered the legal question of whether Kisch had failed in the dictation test, and was therefore an illegal immigrant. The Kisch supporters had another sort of satisfaction in a law court. The policeman who administered the test broke down under cross-examination and admitted he did not know Gaelic. But the law was not made to help a Kisch or a Griffin. The magistrate sentenced them both to six months' imprisonment on 28 November. Once again the Commonwealth has 'got out of it'. But wait and see. The lawyers have not ended their sport with Kisch and Griffin.[52]

Kisch offered to leave Australia, but the conservatives wanted more than a legal victory. They wanted Kisch to be punished. Kisch must serve at least part of his sentence of six months' imprisonment imposed by the police magistrate in gaol. The supporters of Kisch and Griffin were equally determined not to give the conservatives their victory. The Fellowship of Australian Writers insisted that Kisch be a distinguished guest at their luncheon in honour of John Masefield, the Poet Laureate. They were not going to give in to his 'ridiculously small-minded persecutors'. Norman Lindsay cracked jokes with Kisch. They were both, he said, victims of Australian 'suburban complacency'. The meetings of protest continued. Writers, artists, professors and communists again shook hands warmly at the Melbourne Stadium in front of seven to ten thousand people, and applauded with great enthusiasm the recitation of the litany against war and fascism.

The lawyers for Kisch did not give in. On 17 December A. B. Piddington, acting for Kisch, asked the judges of the High Court to decide whether the words in Gaelic read to the defendant were a European language within the meaning of Section 3a of the Immigration Act 1901–1930. The lawyers and the judges had a high old time putting each other right about what was and what was not a language, in particular, whether Scottish Gaelic was a language at all (ha! ha! ha!), and how many people could speak it. The argument went on for two days, as visitors to the Court heard 'great argument about it and about'. On 19 December four of the learned judges—Rich, Dixon, Evatt and McTiernan, with Starke dissenting—handed down their judgment. The expression 'a European language' in Section 3a of the Immigration Act 1901–1930 meant 'a standard form of speech recognised as the received and ordinary means of communication among the inhabitants of an European community for all purposes of the social body'. The four judges held that Scottish Gaelic was not such a language. Kisch was free. Kisch could

[52] *Workers' Weekly*, 23 November 1934; *S.M.H.*, 26 November 1934.

stay in Australia. Bert Evatt played a role in another victory over Bob Menzies.[53]

The militant minority within the Labor Party, the communists and the defenders of civil liberties celebrated their victory. Now was the time for them to maintain their rage, to preserve the united front formed for the defence of Kisch and Griffin. Now they must make sure that the 'hellish forces of the war lords' fall to pieces. The men and women of Australia could save Australia from the 'criminal tragedy' of war. Vain dream. The conservatives have not exhausted the resources of the law, which was their creation. Kisch must be deported as an 'undesirable immigrant'. The militant minority joined with the communists in calling for further protests. Demand, they shouted, that Kisch and Griffin leave the country as free men. Don't let Bob Menzies send Kisch back to a Fascist country where his life would be in danger. But by then much of the ardour and the enthusiasm have drained away. The gossips have done their work. Kisch, it has been whispered, like Isaac Isaacs, could never be a member of the Melbourne Club. Members of the Labor Party became more and more apprehensive of the electoral consequences of being associated with the communists. Labor must win the election of 1937. Lang Labor would have nothing to do with Kisch or his sympathizers. Lang might be greater than Lenin, but he had all the prejudices of the Australian petty bourgeois.[54]

Australians had other things on their minds. In Victoria the Yarra burst its banks, leaving six thousand people homeless. Charles Ulm, the companion of 'Smithy', the silent hero of aviation, had crashed in his plane somewhere in Italy, but searchers gave up hope of finding him alive. Henry Handel Richardson was telling Nettie Palmer it was to her a terrible thing that the human body, which was of itself such a lovely thing, should be allowed (especially in women) to grow obese, shapeless, deformed. It ought to be cherished, cared for, kept in order, just as human beings cared for their minds and their souls. Prince Charming has given his farewell message. He has told Australians all was well with the Empire: all was well with the world. The optimism of Australians was now fully justified. On 10 December 1934 the Duke inaugurated the first air mail service to Great Britain. Australia was making material progress as a member of the British race.

In Melbourne in December, a papal legate, cardinals, the members of the Australian hierarchy, priests and lay persons gathered for a Eucharistic Congress. The conservatives had their kingdom—the kingdom of the British Empire. Labor and the communists had their kingdom: they both promised

[53] *S.M.H.*, 18 December 1934; The King against Wilson and another, *ex parte* Kisch, 17, 18, 19 December 1934, *C'wealth Law Reports*, vol. 52, 1934–35.

[54] *To-day*, 1 November 1934; *Australian Worker*, 12 December 1934; *Workers' Weekly*, 14 December 1934.

happiness to human beings through the achievement of material well-being for all. The conservatives offered the kingdom of Mammon, Labor a Millennial Eden, and the Catholic Church offered another kingdom. They acclaimed the Galilean fisherman as the answer to the age of ruins and the idols worshipped by corrupt human hearts. Just as Prince Charming and what he stood for departed, Catholics professed their loyalty not to an earthly king, but to Christ. On 9 December a crowd estimated at fifty thousand persons watched in awe and wonder as the Host was borne in triumph through the streets of Melbourne. For them Australia was still the land of the Holy Spirit, and Mary the Holy Mother of God and patroness of Australia. Christ, not Prince Charming, was their King.[55]

The legal wrangle over Kisch rumbled on. The lawyers for Kisch asked the Commonwealth Government to return his passport and his ticket so that he could leave the country. The Government did not answer the letter, but once again prosecuted Kisch. They wanted a conviction so that Kisch could be kept under scrutiny wherever he went. Again the lawyers squabbled about the minutiae while outside the Court the public uproar continued. On 22 January 1935 a magistrate sentenced Kisch to three months' imprisonment, but released him on bail pending an appeal. Again the Communists accused the Commonwealth Government of persecuting a man who had come to Australia to expose a plot to involve Australia in another imperialist war. The law court has brought in a class verdict against a man who was fighting against the war aims of the ruling class and their sympathy with fascist barbarism. On 24 January the incurably optimistic Kisch told the Sydney Labor Council only a policy of militant class struggle and united action could defeat fascism and bring the workers to power. On 5 February lawyers for Kisch appealed to the High Court against his conviction for being undesirable as an inhabitant of or a visitor to the Commonwealth of Australia. The case came before Mr Justice Evatt, who gave Mr Piddington, lawyer for Kisch, leave to argue some questions before the Full Court. Application was made to the High Court to punish the editor and proprietor of the *Sydney Morning Herald* for publishing articles and letters purporting to criticize the decision of the High Court in declaring Scottish Gaelic not to be an European language within the meaning of the Immigration Act.[56]

By then high drama had degenerated into broad farce, as lawyers and others argued about who had a ticket and who had a certain passport. Kisch

[55] *Age*, 3, 8 December 1934, *S.M.H.*, 11, 13 December 1934; *Australasian*, 15 December 1934; *Advocate*, 29 November, 6 December 1934; *Argus*, 2, 7, 10 December 1934; Henry Handel Richardson to Nettie Palmer, 26 December 1934, Palmer Papers, Series 1, Box 7, Folder 61.

[56] *S.M.H.*, 15, 23 January 1935; *Workers' Weekly*, 25 January, 8 February 1935; *S.M.H.*, 6 February 1935; The King against Fletcher and another, *ex parte*, Kisch, 29, 30, 31 January, 1, 6 February 1935, *C'wealth Law Reports*, vol. 52, 1934–35.

had a message: the imperialists were preparing for war. The signs were ominous. The Chancellor of Germany, Adolf Hitler, was using bellicose language. The Japanese were talking about spheres of influence in the Pacific, but no one knew what that meant. Some Australians were already asking what would Japan's ninety millions think of Australia's seven millions. Neither side could agree with the other about Kisch. To the militant minority and the communists Kisch had come to Australia from the hell camps of Hitler's Germany to 'fight against Fascism, barbarism and war'. To Bob Menzies and those of like mind Kisch was 'not one of their kind' but a propagandist for the overthrow by violence of the established order of society. Bob Menzies believed in the Empire. On 21 January he told those attending a conference of the Associated Chambers of Commerce that the security of the Empire depended upon the distribution of the Empire's population. Australia could be a real source of strength within the Empire: Australia could contribute to the security of Great Britain herself. They gave their prolonged applause. Mr Menzies' world was their world. He was about to depart for England, about to embark on the great love affair of his life.[57]

But Australia was changing. In January 1935 the Lyons Government decided that for the first time the States would celebrate Australia Day in unison. On 26 January 1935 the whole of Australia would provide evidence of what the *Age* called Australia's 'increasing sense of nationhood'. Those in high places have not shifted their ground. At all the functions to commemorate the 147th anniversary of the ceremony under the gum tree on 26 January 1788 at Sydney Cove, prominent men still spoke of Australia and the Empire. The first Australian-born Governor-General, Sir Isaac Isaacs, told Australians their common thought on that day was 'of loyalty . . . to the King . . . [as] a symbol and guarantee of the stability of the Empire as a sound, solid and reliable political structure'. The Solicitor-General for Victoria, Ian MacFarlan, said the 'nation was determined that the great continent should remain a white continent. It was just as well the world knew it'. Australia, he added, was in the Empire because London was a good market for Australian wool, wheat, butter, eggs and meat. He wanted every Australian to arm for defence, adding that there was no need for Australians to be either fascists or communists. That was something for nations in decline. 'We could build up Australia in our own way and become a leading nation of the world'. It was like the argument for federation forty years earlier. Create a federal constitution, and meat will be cheaper. Now the argument ran: remain within the Empire, become a butcher-boy, or a dairy-maid, or a wool-gatherer for the British, and never be invaded.[58]

[57] *Australian Statesman*, 1 January 1935; A. F. Howells, *A Collection of the Facts of the Kisch Case* (Sydney, 1934); *Age*, 22 January 1935.

[58] *Age*, 26, 28 January 1935; *C'wealth Gazette*, 24 January 1935; Brian Fitzpatrick, *Australian Natives' Association 1871–1961* (Melbourne, 1961), p. 34.

Times were changing. On 23 January 1935 a Qantas Empire Airways plane landed at Darwin after a flight of fourteen days from Paris. It carried six hundred pounds of air mail on board. The Aborigines were also on the move. On 6 November 1931 the freak Aboriginal fast bowler Eddie Gilbert had knocked Don Bradman's bat out of his hand with his first ball, made him drop to the pitch with his second ball, and had him caught behind off the third. When his own people heard the news on the radio all the inhabitants of the dormitory on Barambah reserve near Murgon in Queensland cheered wildly. The Aborigines had a hero of their own. But he lost pace. White men questioned his bowling action. By the late summer of 1935 Eddie Gilbert was a spent force. Some white men said he lacked stamina, lacked that determination characteristic of British people. Aborigines said he was yet another victim of white discrimination. He ended his days in a mental asylum.

The Aborigines wanted more than the opportunity to applaud the sporting heroes of their people. As Eddie Gilbert slowed, as he dropped in pace from an express bowler to just above medium pace, representatives of the Aborigines League from all over Australia, together with white sympathizers, joined in a deputation to the Minister for the Interior, Tom Paterson, in Melbourne on 23 January 1935. William Cooper requested the Government to take urgent steps to preserve their race from extinction. He asked for the right of the Aborigines to select a member for every Federal and State House of Parliament. He asked the Commonwealth Government to establish a department of Native Affairs, and appoint a sympathetic administrator. Government must act quickly, because white people were driving Aborigines into barren wastes. Douglas Nicholls, the Aboriginal footballer, fleet of foot and a man with the graceful movements of a ballet dancer, also spoke. Tom Paterson, known to Australian farmers for his schemes to sell Australian butter overseas, told the Aborigines and their sympathizers the Government was doing the best it could. They were not the only ones, he said, without a Member of Parliament. The points the Aborigines made would be carefully considered. But William Cooper wanted more than tea and sympathy. He wanted the white man to allow the Aborigines to decide for themselves.

D. H. Lawrence had noticed in Australian suburbs the ugliness, the fly-blown shops with corrugated iron roofs, the endless stretches of 'cottages' with corrugated iron roofs, and the house-agents' booths plastered with 'For Sale' and 'To Let' signs. The inhabitants of suburbia had told him: 'You feel free in Australia'. Here, they said, there was a relief from tension. But by the mid-1930s the inhabitants of suburbia have become slaves to their own respectability, to their own rites. There was the rite of cleaning the car on a Saturday morning, hoping the neighbours were looking. There was the rite of the Sunday drive into the hills to get a breath of fresh air. There was the rite of the tea-time cake-stand: by the number of tiers it boasted, and the 'goodies' with which it was laden the standing of the host and hostess could be measured. There was the ritual console wireless cabinet, the rite of the pianola around which young people gathered to sing, some with hope, some with mockery, some with despair about that 'one alone' who had known their 'caresses'. There was the rite of winding the gramophone, any sign of it running down being a hint to Mum and Dad in their den that the youngsters were at it again. There were the rites of display, and some there were who took the number and size of the ebony elephants on their drawing room mantelpiece as indicators of their worth as human beings. Display and conspicuous consumption were the answers to emptiness and despair. The egalitarians of the suburbs enforced rigidly the grades of respectability.[59]

Many ideas were put forward as to how Australians should live in the 'Kingdom of Nothingness'. Norman Lindsay saw life in the suburbs as 'a cloud of midges in a frenzied love dance above the manure heap'. But that was not a faith by which men and women could be content to live. Hardy Wilson, the architect, wrote of Australia as a country where East and West would be finally reconciled. Australians would disprove the pessimism which maintained that 'East is East and West is West and never the twain shall meet'. Miles Franklin asked for something more for women than 'animal mechanics'. Frank Dalby Davison wanted Australians to stop building houses and townscapes which were a blot on the scene. The debate was part of the 'twentieth century din'. Many voices were heard singing their favourite arias. The parsons and the priests went on lecturing the people for preferring pleasure to obeying the laws of God. Freudians, Jungians, Marxists, advocates of yoga, and every -ology and -ism concerned with the needs of the human body, feverishly peddled their wares. At the Link Theatre in Sydney in February 1935 Florence Austral was singing the passionate words in Wagner's *Tristan and Isolde*: death in love was the answer.

Vance Palmer was still saying what he had first said during the Great War: Australians must create a culture of their own: Australians must give their own answers to questions about life. In an article on the 'Future of Australian Literature', published in the *Age* on 9 February 1935 he told Australians: 'We have to discover ourselves—our character, the character of our country, the particular kind of society that has developed here'. This, he believed, could be done only 'through the searching explorations of literature'. Australians, he believed, had begun 'the spiritual adjustment' to their surroundings. They had even learned to live with 'our bonny earth in a spirit of affection'. Over a hundred years ago Barron Field had thought God's punishment to Australians was to curse the land. Early observers had recoiled in horror on first seeing the plains of desolation. Charles Darwin had found the bush

[59] *S.M.H.*, 24 January 1935; *Cricketer*, November 1972; personal memories.

'desolate and untidy'. He had left the shores of Australia 'without sorrow or regret'. Marcus Clarke had written of the 'weird scribblings of nature' in the Australian bush. But this was an exile's view of Australia. A new generation of Australians has ceased to look on 'the haggard land . . . with loathing'. Palmer was hopeful. 'There has been', he wrote, 'a bubbling in our drought-sealed springs'.[60]

The crusaders for things Australian were delighted. Kate Baker told Vance Palmer: 'You have lighted a torch for Australian Literature'. C. H. Souter told Nettie Palmer her husband was 'the Australian Kipling without the flashness'. Ernest Scott, Professor of History at the University of Melbourne, made one of those 'Scotty' remarks which endeared him to generations of students. 'Are not the poems of Henry Lawson', he asked in his most engaging manner, 'as important nationally as dried apples?' Scott was a historian: he had no answers. He had a question: 'What can we do about it?' Only the bores and the supercilious believe they know the answers. Another English exile in Australia, George Cowling, the Professor of English at the University of Melbourne, answered that question as all exiles, natural or spiritual, had been answering it for years. The answer was: 'Nothing'. Nothing could help because there could not be an Australian Literature. In his article, 'The Future of Australian Literature', published in the *Age* on 16 February, Cowling repeated all the arguments the British had used for years to keep the Australians in their place. 'It seems to me', he wrote, 'that an Australian is a Briton resident in Australia'. Australia was not yet in the centre of the globe, and it had no London. He also repeated the exile's lament about the appearance of Australia. 'In spite of what the native-born say about gum trees, I cannot help thinking that our countryside is "thin" and lacking in tradition'. Do not misunderstand me, he pleaded. He was not attacking Australia. He was only saying how things were. 'What I mean', he said, 'is that there are no ancient churches, castles, ruins—the memorials of generations departed'. Besides, he added, 'Australia lacks the richness of age and tradition, lacks 'past glories', lacks 'a striking personality'. Literary culture in Australia must be 'from a European source'.[61]

Australian writers were incensed. Miles Franklin spluttered and spat as only she could splutter and spit that there must be an end of these exiled Europeans in Australia. 'Inky' Stephensen took up his pen, and began to

[60] Frank Davison to Nettie Palmer, early 1935, Palmer Papers, Series 1, Box 7, Folder 62, and Marjorie Barnard to Vance Palmer, 4 March 1935, ibid., Folder 63; *S.M.H.*, 1, 25 January 1935; D. H. Lawrence, *Kangaroo* (London, 1923), pp. 23–4; George Johnston, *My Brother Jack* (Fontana Books edn, London, 1967), pp. 258–9; Vance Palmer, 'The Future of Australian Literature', *Age*, 9 February 1935.

[61] Kate Baker to Vance Palmer, 11 February 1935, Palmer Papers, Series 1, Box 7, Folder 62; C. H. Souter to Nettie Palmer, 17 February 1935, ibid.; *Age*, 11, 16, 19, 23 February, 2 March 1935.

write a long reply. Australia, he wrote, was not a community of British exiles. Australia, he said, 'is a unique country . . . A new nation, a new human type is being formed in Australia'. Australian culture would evolve instinctively—and become quite different from British culture. He finished his first instalment in June, and published it in the *Australian Mercury* in July 1935. He published the whole work in a book, *The Foundations of Culture in Australia*, in 1936. Australians, he argued, were not British, Australians were not Americans: they were Australians.[62]

While 'Inky' Stephensen, Miles Franklin and others were proclaiming the Australia that was to be, Bob Menzies and his wife, Joe Lyons and others were preparing to attend the celebrations for the silver jubilee of George V in London, and an Imperial Conference. There were the usual heart-burns about who should be a member of the delegation. George Pearce, who had expected to go, has been left out. He was deeply hurt. At Outer Harbour, Adelaide, on 21 February a journalist entered Menzies' cabin while he was shaving. On the same morning another enterprising journalist chased Henry Gullett into the bathroom in search of an interview. Bob Menzies took the two incidents as examples of the decline of manners in a democratic society. Why, he asked himself in his diary on 21 February, were Australian newspaper reporters 'so frequently crude, illiterate and lazy'? Why did they have 'neither training, scholarship, real intelligence or independence?' *Today*, in its waspish way, has noticed a change in Bob Menzies. The boy from Jeparit, the barracker for Carlton in Australian Rules football, has developed into 'the darling of those prosperous financiers and business men who see in the Labour movement only an uncouth manifestation of a force that threatens the comforts and luxuries of the nicest people!' He was looking forward to the journey to England: there, he believed, he would be understood.[63]

While Bob Menzies was settling in on the *Otranto*, the coal miners on the northern fields gave Kisch and Griffin a rousing reception. Kisch gave the Red Front salute. Farewell dinners were held in Melbourne, for Kisch and the Australian Government have at last made a bargain with each other. If he agreed to leave, there would be no more prosecutions of Kisch as a prohibited immigrant. For him the real battlefield was Europe, not Australia. Torchlight processions were held: more speeches were made professing the determination of the supporters to fight against war and fascism. But the numbers attending the rallies dropped sharply. Even admirers have found

[62] P. R. Stephensen, 'The Foundations of Culture in Australia', *Australian Mercury*, July 1935; P. R. Stephensen, *The Foundations of Culture in Australia* (Gordon, N.S.W., 1936), pp. 1–15.

[63] Diary of R. G. Menzies, 21 February 1935, Menzies Papers, N.L.A., Canberra; *Today*, 1 September 1934; telegram of G. F. Pearce to J. A. Lyons, 5 January 1935, Pearce Papers, N.L.A. Canberra.

Kisch just as passionate about 'blatant lion-hunting' as he was about the movement against war and fascism. When one Australian girl failed to recognize him, Kisch was most indignant: '. . . this girl', he said, 'does not know who I am and I'm famous'. The Victorian Labor Party was becoming more and more wary, finally issuing a directive on 1 March that Kisch was not to speak on any Labor platform. On 11 March Kisch boarded the *Orford* at Fremantle. When he saw Katharine Prichard on the wharf, he rushed down the gang-plank and kissed her, as Henry Lawson used to say with understandable nostalgia, 'fair and square on the mouth'. Then he rushed back on to the ship, stood on the deck and gave the Red Front salute, and sang the song of hope:

Die Strasse frei
Rot Front!
Die Reihen fest geschlossen
Rot Front!
Der Tag für Freiheit
Rot Front!
Und für Brot bricht an
Rot Front![64]

Kisch was returning to the struggle for the liberation of humanity.

On the same ocean, Bob Menzies was being strengthened in convictions he had held ever since his student days. He was about to begin the great love affair of his life. On the ship he loved everything that was British. He still could not resist the temptation to make the witty remark even knowing it might wound. Listeners laughed—and that was very pleasing to him. On deck one day a woman asked him: '"What do you think of my shorts?" I (offensively leaning over the chair and peering at her), "Sorry, but I hadn't noticed them". (Sensation!)' He knew he should stop, that one day he would pay a heavy price. But, just now, he was enjoying mixing with young Englishmen. They had the 'usual attributes of cleanness, good manners, interest in Test Matches and the championship at Wimbledon'. 'Westward Ho!' for Bob Menzies. He was going to meet the loved one, while back in Australia the press was announcing that Australia would soon export pig iron to Japan, and John Curtin was still wondering about the future of Australia.[65]

On 21 March he saw the white cliffs of Dover. For him the 'journey to Mecca has ended'. England was one delight after another—the green fields,

[64] *S.M.H.*, 28 February 1935; *Workers' Weekly*, 22 February, 1 March 1935; Esmonde Higgins to Nettie Palmer, 27 January 1935, Palmer Papers, Series 1, Box 7, Folder 62; Egon Kisch, op. cit., pp. 131–47.

[65] Menzies Diary, 16, 17, 18, 19 March 1935.

leafless hedges and quietly grazing sheep, and the 'grey bulk of Buckingham Palace', the Mall and the Strand, followed by the Savoy. He was so excited that while his wife unpacked, 'I sneak out and look at Trafalgar Square and one of the Wren churches by starlight, and so to bed'. For him, this was possibly the only way he could savour and enjoy what meant so much to him. That was the trouble: he could only tell it to his diary. He was so happy, he could almost cry for joy. Englishmen in high places listened to him with respect. He sat in the Cabinet Room at Number 10 Downing Street, and pondered over the portrait of Robert Walpole, England's longest serving Prime Minister. Perhaps it was his destiny to hold the equivalent record in Australia. He travelled around the countryside, always seeking out the places associated with the two great passions of his life—literature and politics.[66]

He saw John Gielgud as Hamlet and Jessica Tandy as Ophelia. They were both 'wonderful'. Bob Menzies always knew what he liked. 'Will Bernard Shaw', he asked in his diary, 'last as long?' And he answered: 'Oh Yeah!' For he was still beneath it all unmistakably Australian. He was troubled by the behaviour of Hitler who has just torn up one of the clauses of the Treaty of Versailles. Bob Menzies was not certain whether Hitler was a patriot who had found his country suffering from a feeling of 'inferiority and servitude and was determined to restore her self-respect, and recapture political power as a means to that end'; or was he a 'swashbuckler who [was] preparing actually for an aggressive war?' Much, he noted in his diary on 8 April, turned 'on the faith of this one man'.[67]

England in the spring soon banished such dark thoughts from his mind. On 14 April he had a wonderful day passing through Windsor and Eton and on to Chequers—the sight of which led him to note with approval the regard the English had for their parliamentary institutions. He also liked Cromwell's remark, 'God made them as stubble to our swords'. He was moving around, he believed, 'in the very heart of English history'. How different things were in Australia. He walked reverently, bare-headed, despite the chill April wind, along the drive where the dead body of John Hampden, a hero in the history of British liberty, was carried by his Roundheads to the chant of the 90th Psalm. The great house and the church were still as they were in Hampden's day. The sight of them, Bob Menzies noted, 'would stir the soul of an Australian Trade Union Secretary!' He saw there a confirmation of his own faith. He was no political ideologue, no spouter of revolutionary slogans such as the Rights of Man. He was not interested in theories of politics, or constitutions based on abstractions. Like the English he was a political pragmatist. In the John Hampden country he realized that

[66] Ibid., 21, 23, 24 March 1935.
[67] Ibid., 25 March, 8 April 1935.

'a Parliament for England' was 'no mere result or adoption of a political theory (as it was on the Continent) but something growing from the very roots of the British life'.[68]

The beauty of the English countryside led him to make comparisons with Australia. 'Here [i.e., in Gloucestershire] are no wide roads as in Australia with muddy earth formations on either side, but narrow winding lanes with close grassy banks and hedges with now and then the straight stretch of an old Roman road travelling as straight as an arrow over hill and dale'. Here were 'green and flowering things—a beauty no new country town in Victoria could ever possess'. But England would have to be on guard. The canker of commercialism has already 'violently despoiled' Stratford-on-Avon, the birthplace of William Shakespeare. But England would not be besmirched by the money-grubbers. In England there was still 'a sort of civilised beauty . . . a wonderful stimulus to mind and spirit', something Australia so obviously lacked.[69]

The riches and the insights seemed without end. On 27 April he was at Wembley for the Cup Final. He stood with ninety-three thousand soccer fans to sing the hymn, 'Abide with me', the men bare-headed, all reverent. He was deeply moved. He wondered why a seemingly 'emotionless people' could be so carried away. 'An irreligious communism', he wrote in his diary that night, 'has no chance with these people'. England had the answer to the 'Reds'. But what of Australia? What were our traditions, our ceremonies, our attachment to the past which would guard us against foreign interlopers, disrupters and stirrers?[70]

At the Imperial Conference on 30 April he observed the statesmen of the Empire. James Barry Munnig Hertzog of South Africa was impressive, and very wise on the German question—'a proud and vigorous and high-spirited people cannot be kept in a state of subjection'. In the House of Commons on 2 May he heard the leaders of the conservatives speak. Ramsay MacDonald's voice, he found, was superb. He heard Winston Churchill speak. Bob Menzies was not impressed. 'I hear Winston Churchill', he wrote in his diary that night, 'and perceive that the idol has feet of clay'. As an orator Churchill indulged too much in repetition, and over-confident 'I told you sos'. 'If a first rater has once said an important thing he doesn't need to remind people that he's said it.' Churchill was 'an entertainer rather than a leader'. Bob Menzies was at his favourite exercise of grading men in public life. Most Labor men, all communists, most trade union leaders in Australia were 'yahoos'. Rivals on his own side in politics were 'squirts': mediocrities on his own side were 'little squirts'.[71]

[68] Ibid., 14 April 1935.
[69] Ibid., 19, 20 April 1935.
[70] Ibid., 27 April 1935.
[71] Ibid., 30 April, 2 May 1935.

Some of the things he heard worried him. He was shocked to find that Australians were lower in esteem in the corridors of power in London than New Zealanders. The reason was clear. New Zealand had no secondary industry and was 'therefore the good boy'. He found that to be an Australian butcher-boy in London was no easy task. Some men in high places such as Joe Thomas and Lord Runciman were quite 'unaware of the Empire'. That was disturbing. But he took comfort from the words of Edmund Burke: 'A great Empire and little minds go ill together'. He showed no sign then that he might one day pay a terrible price for not asking himself the question: if Australian and British interests collided, what then for Australia? He was not disturbed by any doubting fear that the British might be on the way down, or that he was meeting the principal characters who would preside over the break-up of the British Empire. He believed England was showing him the way to glory. He showed no sign that he was being enticed to his own destruction. He did not foresee that he would one day pay a high price for this year of fame and glory.[72]

The English flattered him. After a meeting with the senior men in the Foreign Office he wrote in his diary that he had been congratulated on his contribution. There was better to come. The English and the Scots gave him what was the most exquisite satisfaction of all. They made him feel, in his words, that he was a 'person of consequence'. Love has not blinded him nor flattery made him giddy. He met the Prince of Wales and summed him up: a 'small, weary, jumpy as to the nerves' man, he found him. He met the Duke of Gloucester, and thought he had improved since the days of the fruity centenary speeches, and the tedia experienced by those placed next to him at dreary official banquets. But there was more to the Royal Family than that. On 9 May he saw the King in Westminster Hall, and noted with pleasure 'a real bond of affection between the monarch and his people', a bond which defied 'all the academic arguments of the so-called revolutionaries'. That was the whole point: the Monarchy, the symbol of British tradition, was a bulwark against what he dreaded most in life, apart from death and damnation, namely, a revolution which would bring everything to ruin. The next day he had a talk with a barber in the Strand—one of the old school of English forelock-pullers to the nobility and the gentry. The barber asked him, 'Did you notice the weather . . . Sir? You can't tell me God didn't have a hand in that'. Menzies was not a superstitious or a credulous man. But at that moment he did in part believe that God was kind with the weather because, as the barber put it: 'He's [the King] one of us'.[73]

Doubts about the British attitude to Australia were soon buried. They

[72] R. G. Menzies to R. G. Casey, 18 April 1935, G. F. Pearce Papers, N.L.A.; Menzies Diary, 5 May 1935.

[73] Menzies Diary, 7, 9, 30 May, 22 July 1935.

would surface again in 1941, but by then it was too late. Cambridge and Grantchester kindled again the ecstasy and the rapture. Grantchester was a place of holy quiet, and the chapel of King's College reminded him of Wordsworth's remark that its creators were 'born for immortality'. Once again he was enjoying the 'revelation of all that is lovely'. Once again he was savouring 'peace and holy quiet', far, as it were, from the madding crowd in Australia, far from the 'yahoos' and the 'squirts'. Here in the 'shire for men who understand' he was at peace. He was not unaware of the fate of a man. He knew Rupert Brooke: he also knew his Alfred Housman. He knew the words of acceptance and resignation:

> There, like the wind through woods in riot,
> Through him the gale of life blew high;
> The tree of man was never quiet:
> Then 'twas the Roman, now 'tis I.[74]

The English had quiet minds: the Australians had vacant or turbulent minds. The English were attached to the belief that there was a moral order in the universe. The English had a tolerance for other people's views and conduct, a tolerance which was more than good manners and indicated their 'profound allegiance to the tradition of freedom of thought'. That made him ashamed, he said, of the 'Australian vice of censoriousness' and the uncontrollable Australian itch to 'regulate the lives and thought of others'. There were many magical moments. But that shadow from his past would not go away. On 29 May at a dinner in London Stanley Bruce threw discretion to the winds and told the diners, 'R.G.M. should be the next P.M.'. There were many hear, hears, many 'I couldn't agree more, old boy'. But the shadow was there: 'Shortly to be ex-Senator R. D. Elliott, who had got in somehow, registers a silent dissent!' What Bob Menzies wanted could never be: there was a man within who stood between him and the universal love and praise he coveted.[75]

In June, that magical month in England, he noticed again one of the sources of what he found pleasing. On 3 June he was in esctasies over the guardsmen on parade for the King's Birthday—the brass bands, the uniforms and the well-groomed horses. There was none of the Australian slovenliness, or that maddening 'Who cares?' The English were again displaying intense feeling for the Royal Family. That was the secret. 'These are poor days in England for the reds!' The world outside the British Isles was in uproar. Japan was gobbling up China: Mussolini was 'sabre-rattling' in Italy about Abyssinia: Germany was on the march. It was a 'queer, mad world'. But here there were 'hearts at peace under an English heaven'. He went to a

[74] Ibid., 11 May 1935; A. E. Housman, *A Shropshire Lad*, No. XXXI (London, 1896).
[75] Menzies Diary, 18, 29 May 1935.

performance of a Gilbert and Sullivan opera, 'the embodiment of everything that is excellent in the English humorous tradition'. They gave a man a 'good chuckle'. He liked a good chuckle. That was the trouble with Douglas Jardine: you never saw or heard him chuckle.[76]

The secret of what he loved in England was about to be revealed to him. On the evening of 13 June he and his wife Pattie went to the Buckingham Palace Ball. He was not dressed in gold braid, as what Moss Bros had to offer for hire would not accommodate his ample frame. (That, too, was always a struggle, like finding someone who would understand and forgive everything.) So he went dressed in 'sober black knee breeches and silk stockings' and what he called 'an enveloping mantle of consciousness'. He loved watching the 'Royal family dancing industriously at the Throne end of the Ballroom, and a vast concourse of the elect packed tightly into the rest of the room'. He gaped at the gold plate. The champagne was good and the guests very friendly, 'and we enjoy ourselves'.[77]

July 4 was a 'red letter day'. With Stanley Baldwin he made a speech in Westminster Hall, possibly, he believed, 'the first Dominion Minister ever to speak in this spot'. He was on trial. 'I think of Mother and Father listening in 12 000 miles away and trust not to dishonour them and get to my feet, and *mirabile dictu*, get away with it'. The magnificent audience (Dukes, Prime Ministers, Stanley Bruce, John Simon &c. &c.) gave him an ovation at the finish and he was deluged with congratulations. The following day his speech was the talk of the town. Scores of people wrote to him or spoke to him. *The Times*, 'to my joy', honoured him with a verbatim report and a leading article. Baldwin was more than kind to him. Even the Duchess of York had heard of it. She invited him and Pattie to come to tea to meet the children. 'Pattie is naturally thrilled and so am I.'[78]

He and Pattie went to tea with the Duke and Duchess of York and the little Princesses Elizabeth and Margaret Rose on 11 July. The Duchess had a 'fresh and simple charm' which he found 'irresistible'. The Duke had developed amazingly. There was hardly a trace of the stammer and the voice was resonant and pleasant. He and Pattie watched Princess Elizabeth and Princess Margaret having a dancing lesson. He distinctly heard Princess Margaret bullying Princess Elizabeth who, he noted with his usual flair for such things, had 'a perfectly comical capacity for acting'. He was delighted. 'This is a real family', he decided. 'We leave walking on air.' That night he went to dinner in the Merchant Taylors' Hall, where, according to tradition, the first rendering of the National Anthem was given in 1607. The great passion of his life has begun—a veneration for and worship of the Royal Family. Bob

[76] Ibid., 3, 10 June 1935.
[77] Ibid., 13 June 1935.
[78] Ibid., 4, 5 July 1935.

Menzies, the boy from Jeparit, has found something which he could bow down to and worship.[79]

He was moving away from the people. He has dined with the wealthy and the great. He has spent a weekend with Clive Baillieu in a country gentleman's house. There, thank God, there were servants who 'do you well without being seen or heard'. 'The women of England', he has decided, 'may have big feet but they understand training servants'. How different in Australia, the country where the 'yahoos' expected to be treated as the equals of the 'gens supérieurs'. Here in England and Scotland 'I am made to feel that an Australian Robert Menzies who is Attorney-General is a person of consequence'. In London he felt ashamed of Australians, of their coarseness, their lack of reading, their ignorance, their lack of interest in old civilization, and their lack of graciousness. 'It is about time', he wrote in his diary on 17 July, 'we woke up and grew up and realised that brains count!' He would be an apologist for the civilized values of the British, an apologist for monarchy, and old civilization. Every experience he had strengthened his resolve. On 22 July he went to the National Gallery. He looked at typical works of Van Gogh, Degas and Gauguin. There he saw the proof of what he stood for: '. . . your real modern', he wrote in his diary, 'is independent of drawing, composition, meaning and form'. He belonged to old civilization, to the melancholy and the gaiety of Housman's 'Bredon Hill':

> In summertime on Bredon
> The bells they sound so clear;
> Round both the shires they ring them
> In steeples far and near,
> A happy noise to hear.[80]

Everything he saw and heard in Canada and the United States of America confirmed his prejudices. He went to a cabaret in Montreal. He found the Canadians there a 'badly dressed crowd'. They reminded him of the 'crowd of yesteryear at Warracknabeal or Horsham. Jews predominate among the men'. It was all so incredibly coarse, loud-mouthed and vulgar after the grace and elegance of high society in London. In the New World the men were distinguished by a 'fat face, protruding paunch, and the strident nasality of the "big executive"'. He was disgusted. When dancing the men pressed 'their chin against the lady's forehead (as is the custom of the country)', or, worse still, seemed to find it nice to indulge on the dance floor 'in the collision of posterior against posterior'. In New York it was much the same: he found himself a stranger in tube railways 'with their freight of Jews and wops and the mixed races of the world'. He wanted to go home. He wanted to

[79] Ibid., 11 July 1935.
[80] Ibid., 30, 31 March, 17, 22 July 1935.

teach Australians about old civilization, civilized values, the Royal Family, yes, and teach his own people how English pomp, pageantry and ceremony would ensure that 'irreligious communism' had no chance in his own country just as it had no chance with the British. Australians must not be like Americans—materialist, coarse and vulgar. They must be like the British governing classes—refined and spiritual. The Americans had no grasp of the human situation: 'Vanity of vanities, all is vanity' meant nothing to an American. The Americans knew nothing of 'ordered justice', or tolerance: they knew racketeering, corruption, violence, intolerance, materialism, and selfishness. Bob Menzies has dedicated his life to the service of the 'Old Dead Tree'. The boy from Jeparit became the apologist for 'Englishmanism' in Australia.[81]

When his speeches were reported in Australia, Labor men and women were partly amused and partly angered, just as they had been tickled and shocked by the antics of Billy Hughes at Buckingham Palace in 1916. Labor was still in ferment, still faction-ridden. All attempts to heal the rift between Federal Labor and the Langites have failed. The communists wanted unity with the Australian Labor Party, but their proposal has been spurned. Labor was not prepared to commit electoral suicide. Labor was too cunning to be dominated and bullied by the spiritual popes of the twentieth century. Labor was groping its way towards a statement of what it stood for. The flowery speeches by Bob Menzies about the King and the Empire, and Bob's pose as tutor to the Australians on the manners, deportment and behaviour of the English, have at last stirred Labor to say something about itself, about the Australia they stood for.

The *Australian Worker* on 24 July was not amused to read the English praise for Bob Menzies. The *Sunday Times* in London had written that Menzies 'although Australian born . . . speaks precisely in the manner of a cultivated Englishman'. Well, the *Australian Worker* said,

> That sort of culture is no good to us. We want our representatives to speak not like cultivated Englishmen but like cultivated Australians. We want them to look at the world through Australian eyes. We want them to ponder on the problems of our times with Australian brains. [We want] a nation unfettered by traditions, capable of enthusiasm for the unconventional, and eager for a future ethically and in spirit different from anything that lies behind it in the past. Australian legislators [like Bob Menzies] moulded to the forms of English "culshaw" may tickle the ears of London's snobbocracy . . . We are creating a new nation, not duplicating an old one.[82]

[81] Ibid., 2, 3, 5, 7, 8, 14, 15 August 1935; *Age*, 11 April 1935.
[82] *Australian Worker*, 24 July 1935.

The times were ominous. The Japanese have sent a strong delegation to Australia in return for the Australian mission to Japan in the previous year. No one knew what the Japanese intentions were, or whether Australia was on their list. Mussolini was still sabre-rattling about Abyssinia. The British signed a naval agreement with Germany hoping to replace the state of tension with 'solidity and permanence'. The communists were calling on the workers to stand firm against war and fascism. Radicals were asking: Whither Britain? Labor was still striving for working-class solidarity to triumph over factional interests and personal ambition. Nettie Palmer thought there never had been a worse period for intellectual adventure in Australia. 'There is', she told Alice Henry that year, 'a terrible loneliness for a writer here: to publish a book, as my husband says, is to drop it into soft, soundless mud'.

She has gone to London, to live abroad for a while with her husband. While Bob Menzies was savouring his moment of glory in London she visited Ethel Robertson (Henry Handel Richardson) at Green Ridges in Sussex, and found that she (H.H.R.) looked very wise, and was still intensely Australian despite all those years abroad. Henry Handel Richardson told her she found P. R. Stephensen to be a 'violent and impulsive creature'. Nettie Palmer was still hoping for that word from her husband, that word which he either could not or would not say. She planned to go to Spain the following year. She was troubled, too, by what she called 'the world's general uncertainty'. She heard much speculation in London as to whether they were all witnessing the beginning of disintegration, and a relapse into barbarism. She heard Hitler speak on the German wireless of cleansing the German race which had been weakened at all points by the Jewish mixture. She heard Leipzig boys shouting war songs, and wondered again whether they were on the eve of a great catastrophe.[83]

Fear of another war strengthened the conservative belief in the old imperial tie. Early in August the press announced the appointment of an Englishman, Sir Alexander Hore-Ruthven, to replace the Australian-born Isaac Isaacs as Governor-General of Australia. The conservatives were delighted. Sir Alexander was such a nice man, and his wife such a popular social worker—altogether a 'peculiarly happy choice'. Labor did not think it was a 'peculiarly happy choice'. When Lyons announced the appointment in the House of Representatives on 23 September 1935, Labor members greeted the statement with cries of 'Shame', and Jack Beasley shouted: 'What about an

[83] *Age*, 24 April 1935; *Australian Statesman*, 1 May 1935; Nettie Palmer to Alice Henry, 13 November 1935, Palmer Papers, Series 1, Box 7, Folder 63; Nettie Palmer to her mother, 5 July 1935, ibid., Folder 64; H. H. R. (Henry Handel Richardson) to Nettie Palmer, 22 August 1935, ibid., Folder 65; M. Aurousseau to Nettie Palmer, 25 September 1935, ibid., Nettie Palmer to her mother, 15 November 1935, ibid., Folder 66.

Australian?' Once more, Labor said, the conservatives have belittled Australians by reviving the tradition of 'imported Governors' and all the drooling over the 'sentimental link'. Mr Lyons was, as Randolph Bedford put it in the *Australian Worker*, 'the butcher-boy sent to get orders for meat'. Lyons had returned with an order to pay the Governor-General's salary to somebody appointed by a power that pays nothing. Australians should grow up, and drop all this drivel about a sentimental link. The crimson thread of kinship has become a farce: the British have now got it running quite nicely through an Argentinian bull.[84]

On 6 September 1935 Bob Menzies returned to Sydney. He had a message for the Australian people, but before he delivered it he must warn them not to expect the British to buy any more Australian beef. Prospects, however, for Australian mutton and lamb were brighter. But that was not what he was interested in. Bob Menzies was no butcher-boy. The Empire was something more than a closed shop for commercial travellers. The English had much to teach Australians—much about freedom, tolerance and good nature in controversy. The Labor press treated him as a figure of fun. In Australia things were the same as ever, the same as when he was an undergraduate and S. C. Lazarus had held him up to derision for all his heady talk about democracy and the Empire. 'Chuck it, Bob'. But Bob never could and never would. He had the strength to endure. The *Labor Daily* fastened on him the label 'Bully Bob' and accused him of 'high flights of ambition'. But Bob Menzies must bide his time. He was the 'white hope' of the Victorians for the Prime Ministership. Labor pinned abusive labels on him, calling him 'Bob Super Ming' and 'Ming the Merciless'. Part of his anatomy became the subject of ribald student bar-room and party songs. The only attention he paid to such vulgar abuse was to cast doubts on the intelligence of his opponents. He dismissed them as 'yahoos' and 'squirts' and persons beneath his contempt. He had a noble vision. He knew what he believed. The aim of the State, he told the Constitutional Association of New South Wales on 30 September, was not to magnify its power but to ensure the liberty of the individual. He was quietly confident. In England the flower of British intelligence was still serving the Empire. All was well.[85]

The following day, 1 October, Caucus met in Canberra to elect a new leader of the Australian Labor Party. Early in August Jimmy Scullin had collapsed at Mass in a church in North Richmond. Doctors were summoned. They shook their heads gravely and counselled a long rest. The boy from Trawalla has lost the strength to go on. Jimmy Scullin must resign the leader-

[84] *S.M.H.*, 16 August 1935; *Argus*, 16 August 1935; *Australian Worker*, 4 September 1935; *C'wealth P.D.*, 23 September 1935, vol. 147, p. 29; *Labor Daily*, 24 September 1935.
[85] *S.M.H.*, 7 September, 1 October 1935; *Labor Daily*, 16, 25 September 1935.

ship of the Australian Labor Party. At a special meeting of the Labor members of Parliament in Canberra on 23 September Jimmy Scullin announced his resignation. His colleagues had the grace to thank him for his years of service. The movement, said the *Australian Worker*, had never had a 'more faithful and honorable worker'. Jimmy Scullin was turning his eyes towards heaven, hoping God would be more merciful than men. Labor must choose a new leader. Most thought Frank Forde would win the ballot. He was such a nice man, never forgot a name, one of the first but not the last of the glad-handers among Australian Labor leaders. Others had quite different ideas. Labor needed a man with something to say, a man who had an alternative to 'Yarraside'. and the Bob Menzies idea of Australia as a New Britannia in another world.[86]

Ted Holloway believed there was such a man. Labor, he believed, needed a man of vision, a man who had not supported the anti-working-class Premiers' Plan. Labor needed a man who could heal the divisions within the Party. Ted Holloway believed John Curtin was that man, and approached him. 'The chaps want me', he said to him 'to guarantee that you would remain sober'. John Curtin replied: 'Of course, I would. Each Labor leader during his term of office has been a total abstainer, and I will not break that wonderful record'. He was to keep his word. In the fulfilment of what he had always believed to be his destiny he found the strength to succeed where previously all else had failed.

On 1 October 1935 the Labor Caucus in Canberra elected John Joseph Ambrose Curtin leader of the Australian Labor Party by one vote. Jimmy Scullin was astonished. 'It can't be right', he said when told the result. The *Age* called the decision 'one of the greatest surprises in Federal political circles during recent years'. Curtin spoke with the dignity befitting the solemn occasion. 'My aim', he said, 'is to revive the spiritual unity of the Labor movement, to renew and vitalize its sobriety and commonsense so that it may once more serve the needs of Australia in an era in which the portents of evil are grave and ominous'.

The fruits of those walks on the beach at Cottlesloe were about to be given to Australians. He would teach Labor that it was possible to be pragmatic without being opportunist, that the inspired idealism of their founders need not disappear in the pursuit of political power. He would teach Labor to work for a 'new social order', and stop fighting about whether the carter of bread should be in the bread carters' union or in the carters' and drivers' union. Labor must not degenerate into a band of machine men and women.

[86] *Australian Worker*, 14 August, 4 September 1935; *S.M.H.*, 24 August 1935; *Labor Daily*, 28 August 1935; *Australian Statesman*, 1 September 1935.

The Henry Lawson vision lived on in him. Australians should and could banish from under their 'bonny skies'

> Those old-world errors and wrongs and lies
> Making a Hell in a Paradise
> That belongs to your sons and you.

Australians must make the choice:

> Sons of the South, make choice between
> (Sons of the South, choose true)
> The Land of Morn and the Land of E'en,
> The Old Dead Tree and the Young Tree Green,
> The Land that belongs to the lord and Queen,
> And the Land that belongs to you.

He would teach Australians that it was possible to have equality of opportunity without infringing individual liberty and without mediocrity, conformism or spiritual popery. He would teach Australians that the days of relying on the British navy for defence were over. The aeroplane has superseded the battleship.[87]

It was a bleak time for a man who believed in the capacity of human beings for better things. Mussolini's pilots were bombing Abyssinian towns and villages, murdering men, women and children. The communists were urging the workers not to let the war in Abyssinia spread to other parts of the world, and become the prelude to a new world slaughter. Prophets were talking of a relapse into barbarism. The consequences of nihilism were spreading to the masses. Political principles and faiths were now nothing but play-acting. There was an aura of the mediocrity and meanness of spirit Nietzsche had predicted would come in the century after human beings had killed their God.

The voice of Louis Armstrong, jazz singer and trumpeter, was heard more and more in the land. It was a voice of many moods, of gaiety, of gusto, of cheer, of bravado, and running through it all the melancholy of a man aware of a great darkness, aware of the vanity of all human hopes and desires. His was a voice from abroad.

The time was coming when an Australian voice would be heard in the age when men and women lived without faith either in God or in the capacity of human beings for better things. The time was coming when an Australian

[87] *S.M.H.*, 2 October 1935; *Age*, 2 October 1935; *Labor Daily*, 2, 3 October 1935; *Australian Worker*, 2 October 1935; Lloyd Ross, *John Curtin* (Melbourne, 1977), pp. 146–51; John Curtin to Lloyd Ross, 30 July 1935, Lloyd Ross Papers, Box 30; Henry Lawson, 'A Song of the Republic', *Bulletin*, 1 October 1887.

voice would be heard in the great debate on what it has all been for. The time was coming when an Australian voice would be heard telling the story of who Australians were and what they might be. A new discovery of Australia was about to begin. Australians must decide for themselves whether this was the land of the dreaming, the land of the Holy Spirit, the New Britannia, the Millennial Eden, or the new demesne for Mammon to infest.[88]

[88] *Workers' Weekly*, 8 October, 22 November 1935; *Advocate*, 10 May 1934; for the songs of 1934–35 see Julius Mattfeld, *Variety Music Cavalcade* (New York, 1962); James Lincoln Collier, *Louis Armstrong* (Pan Books edn, London, 1985), pp. 277–9; F. Nietzsche, *Der Wille Zur Macht, Erstes Buch: Der Europäische Nihilismis*, F. Nietzsche, *Gesammelte Werke* (Leipzig, 1911), Band XV, pp. 142–3; F. M. Dostoevsky, *A Raw Youth* (Constance Garnett translation, London, 1916), pp. 466–7; Thomas Hardy, 'The Oxen', James Gibson (ed.), *The Complete Poems of Thomas Hardy* (London, 1976), p. 468.

EPILOGUE

IN THE YEARS AFTER 1935 some of the persons in this history drew prizes, and some drew blanks in the human lottery. Bob Menzies drew the prize he had coveted so passionately. In April 1939 he succeeded Joe Lyons as Prime Minister of Australia. He told the people of Australia not to believe what his enemies said of him. He was neither aloof nor supercilious. 'I am', he said, 'a singularly plain Australian'. But two years later he paid a terrible price for his arrogance and his allegiance to the 'Old Dead Tree'. On the night of 28 August 1941 his colleagues suggested he should resign. He walked from the Cabinet room to the Prime Minister's room in Parliament House, Canberra, fell into the arms of his secretary, Cecil Looker, and cried out in anguish: 'Looker, I'm all in'. The tragic hero of Australian conservatism in the twentieth century paid a terrible price for his fatal flaws.

In the summer of 1941–42 the world Bob Menzies believed in threatened to collapse in ruins. The Japanese sank two British battleships off the east coast of Malaya on 10 December 1941. On 15 February 1942 the Japanese occupied the naval base of Singapore. John Curtin turned to America as the keystone of the defence of Australia. As ever, life was not as tidy as art. In art, Bob Menzies should have been destroyed. In life, Bob Menzies had the strength and the courage to rise from the politically dead. In 1943 he delivered his message to middle-class Australia. He professed again his passionate belief in free enterprise, the liberty of the individual, justice, toleration, and being 'dyed in the wool British'. He no longer spoke with disdain of the common people as 'yahoos'. Over a chat and a chuckle with friends and admirers his eyes still lit up when he dismissed his critics as 'squirts'.

Bob Menzies was about to enjoy the flowering time of his life. Prime Minister of Australia from 1949 to 1966, he retired full of honours and unvanquished. Almost two decades of Australian history were known as the Menzies era. It was the era of University expansion in Australia, the era of the growth of Canberra into a city worthy of being the nation's capital. He repeated at the age of eighty what he had said about Australia in the turbulent days of 1916. In return for his devoted services to the British in Australia and to the Royal Family, the cities and Universities of the United Kingdom showered him with honours and gifts. The boy from Jeparit became the darling of the British governing classes and the Royal Family.

The first time he exercised power men judged him harshly. Now he was haunted by the fear that history might punish him as cruelly as had his colleagues on 28 August 1941. He knew his *Hamlet*: 'Use every man after his desert, and who shall 'scape whipping?' The historians of Australia might wield the whip with the same relish as his political colleagues had done on that night of 28 August. His life was the tragedy writ large of the scholarship boy in Australia. It was not so much the tragedy of a man of vast gifts who yet lacked the one precious gift of reading the direction of the river of life. He knew the direction of that river: he knew what was inside him. But so clamorous were his passions for good food, good wine, the approval of the high and mighty and the honours the British conferred on their gifted loyal subjects in Australia, that his judgement was warped and his conscience stifled. To follow the path of reason and conscience meant shedding all the pleasure which was the stuff of life for him. So the boy from Jeparit, the 'singularly plain Australian', one of Australia's most gifted sons, served alien gods, and may have tasted deep damnation as the fruit of all his disquiet. History, he hoped, would view him with the eye of pity, and extend to him the love which had eluded him in life. He died on 15 May 1978 at the age of eighty-three.

John Curtin also drew the prize he coveted. He became a Labor Prime Minister of Australia on 3 October 1941. He was greatly loved. His political opponents praised him as the 'best and fairest' man in Australian public life, the charismatic leader, with an abundance of wisdom and understanding. Just over a month after he became Prime Minister the national song, 'Advance Australia Fair', was sung at the official opening of the War Memorial in Canberra on Armistice Day, 1941. He had had a great dream. He had dreamed that here in the South Pacific Australians would rear a nation that would be an example to all others. He never gave up that dream. But he believed Australians should postpone the fulfilment of the dream until after victory in the war. Death cheated him of the glory of teaching Australians how to cultivate 'The Young Tree Green'. He died in Canberra on 5 July 1945, at the age of sixty. He had always been an enigma. No one knew then or later why a man with such a lofty vision of Australia always wore a sad look on his face. Other human beings, what came up from inside him, and the spirit of the place have ravaged the face of the young man who had dedicated his life to a 'holy crusade' for Labor.

Ben Chifley drew two great prizes. He was loved. He was Prime Minister of a Government which put on the statute book much of what Labor had preached, but had never been able to practise. He gave capitalism a human face, he encouraged excellence in things Australian by creating the Australian National University, and he promoted material well-being for all, being faithful to the Labor belief that creature comforts are the *sine qua non* of human well-being and happiness. But the Australian past was even stronger than the mighty spirit of Joseph Benedict Chifley. On 10 December 1949 his Labor Government was swept out of office in an electoral landslide to the conservatives. As on 5 May 1917 and 19 December 1931, a society of immigrants and their descendants, a society with a working class entranced by petty-bourgeois ideas of private ownership of property, and a society distinguished by the wide extent of middle-class affluence, uncovered the strength of conservatism in Australia. Electors were to do the same in December 1975 when they feared that another man of vision, Edward Gough Whitlam, was enticing Labor to liberate Australians from the dead hand of the past. Australia was still evidence for the prophecy by Alexander Herzen that petty-bourgeoisiedom is the final word of any civilization based on the unconditional rule of property. Australia has not been liberated from its past. So Chifley died on 13 June 1951 with the light on the hill as far off as ever. He was then sixty-five.

Bert Evatt drew the prize of being elected, in October 1947, President of the General Assembly of the United Nations for 1948. But the office of Prime Minister of Australia eluded him. Under his leadership there was a split in the Labor Party which contributed to those twenty-three years in the political wilderness. The man who had the image of Christ in his heart and the teaching of the Enlightenment in his mind had to endure as best he could the humiliation of being the whipping boy of Bob Menzies for his frailties. The man who believed Labor was the Magic Flute leading Australians from ignorance and superstition up into the light, walked into a very dark night. He died on 2 November 1965, at the age of seventy-one.

The intimations of Enid Lyons on the fate of her husband proved to be correct. The man who persuaded her beloved Joe to abandon the Labor Party and rescue bourgeois Australia cast a shadow over the last years of his life. Labor colleagues had warned him: 'Don't do it, Joe don't do it'. But he did, and they never forgave him, and they never forgot. He died on 7 April 1939 at the age of fifty-nine.

Labor men and women never forgave Billy Hughes for the treachery of 1916. For thirty-six years he hoped for the gesture of forgiveness and reconciliation. But the gesture was never made. In March 1951 he attended the ceremony on Capitol Hill in Canberra to commemorate the choice of Canberra as the site for the capital city. It was forty years since he and his Labor brothers had dreamed of the day when the gross inequalities between the rich and the poor would disappear, and Australians learn to spurn the luxuries coveted by the worshippers of Mammon. Life had robbed Hughes of all these visions. Ever since those decisive days in 1916 he had dismissed all such hopes as 'empty vapourings', just as Bob Menzies had ridiculed all the improvers of humanity as spouters of 'twaddle'. Australia, he said on that day, was not a place for weaklings. On that day in Canberra Hughes stood alone under the vast sky, still the man with the indomitable spirit encased in the tiny frame. For him there was always the one: there could not be a second. He died on 28 October 1952 at the age of ninety.

During his years of retirement Jimmy Scullin enjoyed the prize that human beings award to those endowed with goodness. Men on both sides of politics looked on him with reverence and awe. But he was haunted by the ghosts of 1929–31, the never-ending pain of knowing that it had all gone wrong. He died on 28 January 1953, at the age of seventy-six. At the Requiem Mass in St Patrick's Cathedral, Melbourne, on 30 January, many wept, for Jimmy Scullin had been much loved. He had been the champion of the poor. For him Christ and Labor were one.

When his political career ended Ted Theodore pursued the other love of his life, the quest for the 'spangles of gold'. He had that satisfaction. But about his role in Mungana he spoke to no one. On one lovely day in autumn not long before he died, when the sun was painting golden fire balls on the waters of Sydney Harbour, an old friend, Alec Chisholm, a naturalist and editor, asked him: 'Tell me, Ted, what was the truth about Mungana?' Ted Theodore replied: 'Alec, of all the lovely things in life there is nothing more lovely than Sydney Harbour on a day in autumn'. He walked away. He died in 1950 at the age of sixty-five.

The Big Fella, Jack Lang, outlived them all—except Menzies. His quarrel was not with God or the conservatives. His quarrel was with the Australian Labor Party. The two passions of his life never left him—money and domination. Time did not soften him. But time conferred a mantle of majesty on Labor's great trouble-maker. He wanted to be remembered as the champion of the people. He died on 27 September 1975 at the age of ninety-nine. The huge crowd lining the streets of Sydney along which his funeral procession passed showed the people remembered that the Big Fella, the demagogue of Sydney Town, also had a capacious heart.

Stanley Bruce accepted with dignity the verdict of the Australian people that he could never again be the leader of a political party. In the autumn of his life he became the loyal and distinguished servant of both conservative and Labor governments. The man who spoke with passion about the birth of an Australian nation at the ceremony to inaugurate the Australian War Memorial on Anzac Day 1929 accepted a British viscountcy in 1947. But he chose to be known as Viscount Bruce of Melbourne, and before he died he directed that his ashes be scattered over Canberra. He was the noblest Australian-Briton of them all. He died on 25 August 1967 at the age of eighty-four.

Billy Cooper, the Aboriginal leader, did not win for Aborigines the right to elect their own members of Parliament, or land rights, or equality of opportunity. He died on 29 March 1941 at the age of eighty. David Unaipon's question to the white man: 'Is it nothing to you, all ye that pass by?' was still largely ignored. In his old age he had to endure the humiliation of being branded as the Uncle Tom of the Australian Aborigines. He died in 1967 at the age of ninety-four.

Nettie Palmer fought to the end for the development of an Australian culture. But what mattered most to her in life was never to be. She never heard or read the words she wanted to hear or read. She died on 19 October 1964 at the age of seventy-nine. Annie West on Phillip Island lost her second son Charlie to the Japanese near Johore Baru in 1941. Tormented by guilt and the shame of Charlie's death, her elder son, Gordon, went 'peculiar'. Katharine Prichard drew the prize of literary fame, but had the mortification of seeing her hopes for a communist Australia vanish into the great Australian silence. She was the 'child of the hurricane', but no social hurricane ever blew in Australia during her lifetime. She died on 2 October 1969 at the age of eighty-five. Things went hardly for all of them: for all of them things were not 'lastly as firstly well'. They deserve our pity: they deserve our love.

In the second half of the twentieth century Australians lived in a country where neither the historians, the prophets, the poets nor the priests had drawn the maps. Revolutions in transport and communications finally ended the material backwardness and the isolation. Immigrants from Europe and Asia helped to deliver a mortal wound to the Giant of British philistinism. Grovelling to the British almost disappeared. Intellectuals and artists no longer agonized over whether to be second-rate Europeans in their own country, or live abroad. Australians no longer apologized for the way they talked, the way they walked, or the way they behaved. They no longer confessed they had erred and strayed from British canons of behaviour, and that they would try not to err again. The domination of class over class, of white man over Aborigine, of man over woman, of teacher over student, and parent over child was challenged. Women wanted both equality and the right to control their own lives, especially the life of their bodies. Aborigines wanted to decide for themselves their way of life. Students wanted to decide how and what they should be taught. Women wrote their own history. Aborigines wrote their history, maintaining that their ancestors were not immigrants, but were always here, and that white man's history was a catalogue of 'white lies'. The New Left wrote their history. Accounts of the past became part of the struggle for power in Australia. In an age of doubt about everything, even the past lost its authority. There was no final court of appeal on the human questions.

Australians gradually ceased to look to Europe as 'the land of holy wonders', but rather as a museum of past glories, a 'precious graveyard' of the origins of the Europeans and their descendants in the haggard continent of Australia. Painters such as Arthur Boyd, novelists such as Patrick White, Eleanor Dark and David Malouf, poets such as Judith Wright, Kenneth Slessor, Alec Hope, David Campbell and James McAuley provided food for the hungers of the human heart, and ministered to the desire of the human mind to be there when everyone suddenly understands what it has all been for.

Restraints on human behaviour were thrown aside. Nothing was sacred, nothing escaped examination. Men and women walked naked on the beaches, the stage and the screen and they were not ashamed. Men and women no longer conceded to politicians, priests, parsons, professors, or presidents of the Returned Services' League the right to draw up codes of behaviour, or prescribe what could or could not be read. The people broke the Tablets of the Law. The people killed their gods. The people turned to the worship of the Golden Calf.

The survivors from earlier generations were bewildered and dismayed. In an age distinguished by an abundance of consumer goods, gadgets and creature comforts, an age which confounded greed and titillation with pleasure and well-being, Colin Cartwright, a fictional character created by Barry Humphries, but very representative of the mood of the new age said: 'I've come to the conclusion you can give kids too much'. An age which put a man into space, and saw a man walk on the moon was, paradoxically, characterized by doubt about everything. The two wars, the atomic bomb, the holocaust of the Jewish people, the mass murders for political purposes, shook humanity's belief in a benevolent, loving God, and in their own capacity for better things. It was forty thousand years and possibly more since the Aborigines composed their stories of creation. On 13 May 1987 it was two hundred years since the First Fleet left the abode of a civilized people and sailed to a land they believed to be inhabited by savages. Of all the dreams of those Europeans of what Australia might be—the south land of the Holy Spirit, or the land where the great dream of the Enlightenment would be fulfilled, or the land where blood would never stain the wattle, or a New Britannia in another world—all that seemed to survive was the idea of Australia as a place of 'uncommonly large profit'. History has blurred the vision of Eden, allowing Mammon to infest the land. A turbulent emptiness seized the people as they moved into a post-Christian, post-Enlightenment era. No one any longer knew the direction of the river of life. No one had anything to say.

This generation has a chance to be wiser than previous generations. They can make their own history. With the end of the domination by the straiteners, the enlargers of life now have their chance. They have the chance to lavish on each other the love the previous generations had given to God, and to bestow on the here and now the hopes and dreams they had once entertained for some future human harmony. It is the task of the historian and the myth-maker to tell the story of how the world came to be as it is. It is the task of the prophet to tell the story of what might be. The historian presents the choice: history is a book of wisdom for those making that choice.

INDEX

compiled by Elmar Zalums